German Immigrants

Lists of Passengers Bound from Bremen to New York, 1847–1854

German Immigrants

Lists of Passengers Bound from Bremen to New York, 1847–1854

With Places of Origin

Compiled by

Gary J. Zimmerman &
Marion Wolfert

Baltimore
Genealogical Publishing Co., Inc.
1985

Library of Congress Catalogue Card Number 85-80181
International Standard Book Number 0-8063-1128-2
Made in the United States of America

Contents

TO BRUCE

INTRODUCTION

The destruction of the original Bremen passenger lists has been a great hindrance to the historical and demographic study of German immigration to America. In many cases, the Bremen lists were the sole source of information concerning the place of origin of an immigrant family. The importance of Bremen as a port of departure makes this loss even more lamentable. Bremen had almost three times as many departures as Hamburg during the years 1847 to 1854, the period which this volume covers.

As far as can be ascertained by German archivists, lists of emigrants sailing from Bremen were kept beginning in 1832. These lists were used to compile statistical reports for the government and port authorities. Owing to a lack of space, the lists from 1832 to 1872 were destroyed in 1874. Thereafter the lists were shredded every two years. From 1907 the original lists were again maintained on a permanent basis, but with the destruction of the Statistical Land Office on October 6, 1944, all remaining lists perished. Transcripts of some twentieth-century lists (1907, 1908, 1913, 1914) were recently discovered at the German State Archives in Koblenz — the product of a college study — but no nineteenth-century transcripts have as yet been uncovered.

This partial reconstruction of Bremen passenger lists is based on American sources, specifically, *Passenger Lists of Vessels Arriving at New York* (National Archives Microfilm Publication M 237), wherein the passengers arriving from Bremen can be found. Not all Bremen passengers of the 1847–1854 period are included in this work, however; only those for whom a specific place of origin in Germany is given. Of the total number of passenger arrival records, only 21% provide such information; the other 79% give only "Germany" as the place of origin.

The benefit of having these 35,000 passenger arrivals indexed is that it provides immediate access to place of origin information, which the voluminous nature of the New York arrival lists has heretofore prevented. Future volumes in this series will cover later years of arrival, and eventually Bremen arrivals at other major U.S. ports.

ACKNOWLEDGEMENTS

We would like to express our appreciation to David C. Ottesen, Bruce D. Despain, Kip Sperry, Lyman De Platt, Wade C. Starks, and Steven R. Parkes for their help in compiling this book and readying the manuscript for publication.

Gary J. Zimmerman
Marion Wolfert

Explanation of the Text

This partial reconstruction of the Bremen passenger lists is a guide to the National Archives' microfilm edition of *Passenger Lists of Vessels Arriving at New York* (M237). Imperfections and peculiarities in the originals, as well as difficulties encountered in the computerization process, make it imperative that all entries found herein be compared against the originals.

It is apparent from the passenger lists that the information had been supplied verbally by the passengers, since obvious name and place-name misspellings occur frequently. All possible spelling variations must be searched for. A good example is the surname MEYER, which is found in these lists under eight different spellings: Meyer, Meier, Mayer, Meir, Mayr, Myar, Myer and even Mjar. With the majority of names the spellings may vary only slightly, but by virtue of the alphabetical arrangement of the work these variants are often separated.

In the original passenger lists many given names and surnames were partially or completely anglicized. More often than not given names were carried over into their English equivalents; and on rare occasions a surname had been translated. The name SCHMIDT, for example, might be listed as SMITH; BRAUN as BROWN, etc. When this occurs, as with other questionable spellings, an entry is added under what is assumed to be the original German spelling, to facilitate the researcher.

Misspelled place names have been corrected on a limited basis. Place names with spellings grossly in error were examined, and an accurate spelling sought. Sometimes a correct spelling could not be established, and the spelling as found in the original was retained. The corrected spellings sometimes represent the compilers' opinion of the way the original should read; but since there is the risk that an incorrect judgment was made, all entries should be compared with the original.

Some names may be difficult to locate because of peculiarities in the German language. German surnames that carry an "umlaut," i.e. a modified vowel (Ä, Ö, Ü), have been changed to their English equivalents; thus Ä = AE, Ö = OE, and Ü = UE, and are so indexed. Some surnames that should have modified vowels were left unmodified in the originals. The name MÜLLER is found as both MUELLER and MULLER in the text, as well as the anglicized form MILLER. Surnames composed of two or more distinct words have been alphabetized under the final word. Thus von WEGNER is found as WEGNER, v.; De GREVE as GREVE, de; and AUF DEM KAMP as KAMP, Auf Dem. French names like D'ARTENAY are not separated.

The majority of the records contain abbreviations which vary from list to list. Many are standard German abbreviations, but some given-name abbreviations are odd, and are therefore difficult to recognize. A table of the most frequently used abbreviations is included in this work. Names that have been abbreviated often make it difficult to tell the sex of the passenger. In many cases, therefore, the sex is noted in parenthesis. The German given name "Male" has several times been converted to "(m)," indicating a male passenger for whom no given name was legible. This error was discovered too late to be corrected in this edition.

When more than one person of a particular surname travelled together (as in a family), they have been grouped under the name of the first family member appearing in the list. Thus the wife and children of a passenger may follow on a line just below that of the head of household. The integrity of the families was in this way retained, but it is necessary to scan all entries of a surname in case the individual sought for is listed under another family member.

The reference numbers are composed of two parts. The first part is the year of arrival, the second the number of the passenger list for that year. Within each year all the lists are numbered. The table of references included in this volume provides the name of the arriving vessel, the date of its arrival in New York, and the call number of the National Archives' microfilm (series 237). A typical entry follows:

BEIERLEIB, Johann 60 Lustberg 51-1640

This entry states that the 60-year-old Johann Beierleib arrived in New York in 1851 (51=1851) and appears on list 1640 for that year. The table of references, under 51-1640, gives

Norma 10 Nov 1851 107

This indicates that Mr. Beierleib was on the ship *Norma* which arrived in New York on November 10, 1851. The original list can be found on microfilm roll 107.

A note regarding list 737 for the year 1849 must be made. In this list nearly all the passengers were recorded as from Mittelruesselbach, Germany. Undoubtedly many did come from that place, but some might not have, since a large number of the surnames given are not indigenous to that area. As it was not possible to identify exactly which of the immigrants were from Mittelruesselbach and which were not, it was thought best to retain the list as found.

Questions regarding the transcription of the names and places which appear in this volume can be directed to the German Immigration Archive, P.O. Box 11391, Salt Lake City, Utah 84147. This archive maintains the original transcriptions and will attempt to identify places for which correct spellings were not available.

TABLE OF ABBREVIATIONS

Places

A., Aus.	Austria
B., Ba.	Baden, Bavaria
Bad., Bd	Baden
Bav., Bv.	Bavaria
Br.	Braunschweig
C.H., Curh.	Kurhessen
H.	Hessen, Hannover
Ha., Hann.	Hannover
He., Hess.	Hessen
KH., KHe., Kurh.	Kurhessen
Na., Nass.	Nassau
N.Y.	New York
O., Old.	Oldenburg
Oest.	Austria
P., Pr., Prss.	Prussia
S., Sa., Sachs., Sax.	Saxony
W.	Wuerttemberg, Waldeck
Wa., Wald.	Waldeck
Wu., Wue., Wuert., Wrt.	Wuerttemberg

Ages (infants)

bob	born on board ship
by	baby
d	days old
m	months old
w	weeks old

Given Names

A.	Anna
Ad.	Adam, Adolph, Adalbert
Alb.	Albert, Albin, Albrecht
Andr.	Andreas

Ant.	Anton
Aug.	August, Augusta
Balt.	Balthasar
Bar., Barb.	Barbara
Bern., Bernh.	Bernhard
Carol., Carole.	Caroline
Cas., Casp.	Caspar
Cat., Cath.	Catharine
Charl.	Charles, Charlotte
Chr., Christ.	Christian, Christoph
Chr'tne	Christine, Christiane
Clem.	Clement, Clementine
Con., Conr.	Conrad
Dan.	Daniel
Diedr.	Diedrich
Dom.	Dominicus
Dor.	Dorothea, Dorette, Doris
Eberh.	Eberhard
Ed., Edw.	Eduard
El., Els.	Elisabeth
Em.	Emil, Emanuel, Emma, Emilie
Eman.	Emanuel
Eng.	Engel
Ern.	Ernst, Ernestine
Ferd.	Ferdinand
Fr.	Friedrich, Franz
Fr'd, Friedr.	Friedrich
Fr'ke	Friederike
Fr'z	Franz
Geo.	Georg
Gert.	Gertrude
Gottfr.	Gottfried
Gotth.	Gotthard
Gottl.	Gottlieb
Gust.	Gustav
Heinr., Hr., Hch.	Heinrich
Hen., Henr., Hen'tte	Henriette
Her., Herm.	Hermann, Hermine
Ign.	Ignatz
J.	Johann
Jac.	Jacob
Jas.	James
Joh., Johs.	Johannes
Jos.	Joseph
Jul., Juls.	Julius, Julie
Kath.	Katharine

Lor., Lor'z	Lorenz
Lud., Ludw.	Ludwig, Ludolph
M., Mar.	Maria
Magd.	Magdalena
Marg.	Margaretha
Mart.	Martin
Matth.	Matthias, Mathilde
Max.	Maximilian
Mic., Mich.	Michael
Nic., Nicol.	Nicolaus
Pet.	Peter
Ph., Phil.	Philipp
Reg.	Regina
Rob.	Robert
Ros.	Rosine, Rosalie
Rud.	Rudolph
Sal., Sol.	Salomon
Seb.	Sebastian
Sim.	Simon
Soph.	Sophia
Th.	Theodor, Thomas, Theophilus
Theo., Theod.	Theodor, Theophilus
Ther.	Therese
Traug.	Traugott
Val., Valen.	Valentine
Vic., Vict.	Victor, Victoria
Vin., Vinc.	Vincent
Wilh., Wm.	Wilhelm, Wilhelmine
Wilh'mne	Wilhelmine
Wolfg.	Wolfgang

Table of References

YR-LIST	SHIP	DATE OF ARRIVAL			FILM #
47-104	Hudson	15	Mar	1847	65
47-158	Atlantic	14	Apr	1847	66
47-672	Goethe	8	Sep	1847	69
47-762	Jas. Perlins	28	Sep	1847	69
47-868	Jas. W. Shepherd	2	Nov	1847	70
47-872	Alfred	4	Nov	1847	70
47-918	Harward	18	Nov	1847	70
47-987	Heinrich	15	Dec	1847	70
48-53	Diana	22	Jan	1848	70
48-78	Luise	29	Jan	1848	70
48-101	Eberhard	6	Feb	1848	70
48-112	Jason	17	Feb	1848	70
48-260	Arion	20	Apr	1848	71
48-269	Minna	22	Apr	1848	71
48-284	Alfred	24	Apr	1848	71
48-406	Atlantic	21	May	1848	72
48-445	Marianne	27	May	1848	72
48-447	Argonaut	27	May	1848	72
48-453	Elise & Charlotte	29	May	1848	72
48-565	Geo. Washington	14	Jun	1848	73
48-887	Napier	9	Aug	1848	74
48-951	Francis	24	Aug	1848	74
48-1015	Washington	7	Sep	1848	75
48-1114	Queen Victoria	28	Sep	1848	75
48-1131	Lion	30	Sep	1848	75
48-1179	Minna	15	Oct	1848	75
48-1184	Jason	17	Oct	1848	76
48-1209	Adam	30	Oct	1848	76
48-1243	Washington	6	Nov	1848	76
48-1355	Ann Welsh	11	Dec	1848	76
49-324	Minna	27	Apr	1849	78

YR-LIST	SHIP	DATE OF ARRIVAL			FILM #
49-329	Frederick	28	Apr	1849	78
49-345	Lessing	30	Apr	1849	78
49-352	Bessel	1	May	1849	78
49-365	Gil Blas	1	May	1849	78
49-383	Caroline	3	May	1849	78
49-413	Mary	3	May	1849	78
49-416	Diedrich	4	May	1849	79
49-574	Argyle	28	May	1849	79
49-737	Edmond	15	Jun	1849	80
49-742	Balticus	16	Jun	1849	80
49-781	Harriet	20	Jun	1849	80
49-912	Columbia	6	Jul	1849	81
49-1106	Napier	13	Aug	1849	81
49-1358	Ella	1	Oct	1849	84
49-1517	Freihandler	14	Nov	1849	85
50-21	Elise	11	Jan	1850	85
50-119	Erie	6	Mar	1850	86
50-292	Columbus	6	May	1850	87
50-311	Caroline	9	May	1850	87
50-323	Alexander	13	May	1850	87
50-366	Joh. Friedrich	17	May	1850	88
50-379	F. J. Wichelhausen	18	May	1850	88
50-439	Elizabeth	22	May	1850	88
50-472	Hermann Theodor	25	May	1850	88
50-746	Columbia	13	Jul	1850	90
50-840	America	30	Jul	1850	91
50-944	Francis & Louisa	20	Aug	1850	91
50-1067	Hudson	18	Sep	1850	92
50-1071	Catherine Auguste	19	Sep	1850	92
50-1132	Adler	2	Oct	1850	93
50-1236	Elise	30	Oct	1850	94
50-1317	Hermine	19	Nov	1850	94
51-48	Edmund	15	Jan	1851	95
51-326	Hudson	12	Apr	1851	97
51-352	Bessel	18	Apr	1851	97
51-384	Schiller	22	Apr	1851	97
51-405	Elise	25	Apr	1851	97
51-460	Minna	2	May	1851	98
51-500	Jason	8	May	1851	98
51-517	Carl & Emma	14	May	1851	98
51-652	Columbia	4	Jun	1851	99
51-654	Gazelle	4	Jun	1851	99

YR-LIST	SHIP	DATE OF ARRIVAL			FILM #
51-756	Copernicus	19	Jun	1851	100
51-757	Sanser	19	Jun	1851	100
51-1035	Livonia	31	Jul	1851	102
51-1062	Kunigunde	1	Aug	1851	102
51-1084	Magdaline	5	Aug	1851	103
51-1101	Adelheid	5	Aug	1851	103
51-1160	Itzstein & Welcker	14	Aug	1851	103
51-1245	Elise	29	Aug	1851	104
51-1438	Leontine	27	Sep	1851	105
51-1455	Charlotte Read	30	Sep	1851	105
51-1532	India	16	Oct	1851	106
51-1588	G. F. Patten	30	Oct	1851	106
51-1639	Josephine	10	Nov	1851	107
51-1640	Norma	10	Nov	1851	107
51-1686	Columbia	17	Nov	1851	107
51-1725	Humboldt	28	Nov	1851	108
51-1739	Magdalene	4	Dec	1851	108
51-1796	Wieland	23	Dec	1851	108
52-48	Hudson	14	Jan	1852	109
52-95	Admiral	3	Feb	1852	109
52-117	Albert	10	Feb	1852	109
52-279	Minna	2	Apr	1852	111
52-351	Constitution	16	Apr	1852	111
52-370	Favorite	20	Apr	1852	111
52-515	Alexander	11	May	1852	112
52-558	Wassily Schukoff	17	May	1852	113
52-563	Bessell	19	May	1852	113
52-652	Don Quixote	1	Jun	1852	114
52-693	Anna	10	Jun	1852	114
52-699	Copernicus	10	Jun	1852	114
52-775	Henriette	22	Jun	1852	115
52-807	Wieland	24	Jun	1852	115
52-895	Elizabeth	8	Jul	1852	116
52-960	Graf v. Schieflin	16	Jul	1852	116
52-1101	Luna	7	Aug	1852	117
52-1105	Schiller	7	Aug	1852	117
52-1129	F. W. Buddecke	11	Aug	1852	118
52-1148	Adelheid	13	Aug	1852	118
52-1200	Augustus	20	Aug	1852	118
52-1304	Zaretan	16	Sep	1852	119
52-1321	Espindola	17	Sep	1852	119
52-1332	Kosmos	20	Sep	1852	119
52-1362	America	25	Sep	1852	119

YR-LIST	SHIP	DATE OF ARRIVAL			FILM #
52-1410	Kunigunde	4	Oct	1852	120
52-1423	Peter	6	Oct	1852	120
52-1432	Elsfleth	8	Oct	1852	120
52-1452	Minna	18	Oct	1852	120
52-1464	Gil Blas	20	Oct	1852	120
52-1512	Admiral Broning	1	Nov	1852	121
52-1580	Magdalene	29	Nov	1852	121
52-1620	Patria	8	Dec	1852	122
52-1625	Hansa	9	Dec	1852	122
52-1661	Ella	23	Dec	1852	122
53-161	Schiller	8	Mar	1853	123
53-267	Philadelphia	19	Apr	1853	124
53-320	Louis	27	Apr	1853	125
53-324	Columbia	28	Apr	1853	125
53-435	Figaro	28	May	1853	126
53-473	Julia	1	Jun	1853	126
53-475	Solon	1	Jun	1853	126
53-492	Ella	3	Jun	1853	126
53-557	Ocean	13	Jun	1853	127
53-582	Kunigunde	20	Jun	1853	128
53-585	Luna	20	Jun	1853	128
53-590	Republic	22	Jun	1853	128
53-628	Wheland	30	Jun	1853	128
53-637	Heinrich	2	Jul	1853	128
53-652	Henrietta	8	Jul	1853	128
53-825	Pres. Smidt	15	Aug	1853	130
53-838	Orion	15	Aug	1853	130
53-888	Germania	26	Aug	1853	130
53-905	Itzstein & Welker	30	Aug	1853	130
53-914	Rome	1	Sep	1853	131
53-928	Elizabeth	7	Sep	1853	131
53-942	Humphrey	10	Sep	1853	131
53-991	Hansa	20	Sep	1853	132
53-1000	M. C. Day	26	Sep	1853	132
53-1013	Columbia	30	Sep	1853	132
53-1016	Jos. Holmes	30	Sep	1853	132
53-1023	Gilbert	1	Oct	1853	132
53-1062	Matilda	19	Oct	1853	132
53-1070	Herder	20	Oct	1853	132
53-1086	Julia	24	Oct	1853	133
53-1164	Hansa	17	Nov	1853	133
53-1170	Julie	18	Nov	1853	134
53-1174	Germania	19	Nov	1853	134

YR-LIST	SHIP	DATE OF ARRIVAL			FILM #
53-1226	Neptune	3	Dec	1853	134
54-53	Pres. Smidt	14	Jan	1854	135
54-131	Vesta	12	Feb	1854	136
54-305	Johann	14	Apr	1854	137
54-361	Rebecca	24	Apr	1854	138
54-362	Republic	24	Apr	1854	138
54-406	Gen. Jacobi	3	May	1854	138
54-559	Oahu	22	May	1854	139
54-600	Catherine	25	May	1854	140
54-688	Luna	12	Jun	1854	141
54-736	Suwa	19	Jun	1854	141
54-789	Juno	28	Jun	1854	141
54-790	Europa	28	Jun	1854	141
54-792	Hermine	28	Jun	1854	141
54-814	Metis	30	Jun	1854	141
54-830	Oceanus	1	Jul	1854	142
54-850	Texas	5	Jul	1854	142
54-872	Germania	10	Jul	1854	142
54-882	Bridget	12	Jul	1854	142
54-903	Bertha	21	Jul	1854	142
54-918	Rogule	24	Jul	1854	142
54-922	Henriette	23	Jul	1854	143
54-930	Pres. Smidt	26	Jul	1854	143
54-965	George	4	Aug	1854	143
54-980	Erb. Fried. August	7	Aug	1854	143
54-987	Hansa	7	Aug	1854	143
54-1011	Von Stein	11	Aug	1854	143
54-1078	Republic	16	Aug	1854	144
54-1092	Lina	17	Aug	1854	144
54-1094	Heinrich	17	Aug	1854	144
54-1158	Leontine	28	Aug	1854	144
54-1168	F. W. Brune	30	Aug	1854	145
54-1282	Clemens	19	Sep	1854	145
54-1283	Anna	19	Sep	1854	145
54-1297	Germania	22	Sep	1854	146
54-1341	Bernard	3	Oct	1854	146
54-1371	Hansa	9	Oct	1854	146
54-1419	Hump. Purinton	17	Oct	1854	147
54-1443	Audubon	23	Oct	1854	147
54-1452	Kunigunde	23	Oct	1854	147
54-1470	Ann Johnson	24	Oct	1854	147
54-1554	Coosawattee	14	Nov	1854	148
54-1566	Julia	17	Nov	1854	148

YR-LIST	SHIP	DATE OF ARRIVAL			FILM
54-1575	Art Union	20	Nov	1854	148
54-1591	Souter Johnny	24	Nov	1854	148
54-1601	Union	25	Nov	1854	148
54-1647	Agen & Heinrich	14	Dec	1854	148
54-1649	Rebecca	14	Dec	1854	148
54-1676	Gros. v. Oldenburg	19	Dec	1854	149
54-1716	Hermine	26	Dec	1854	149
54-1717	Alfred	26	Dec	1854	149
54-1724	Clio	26	Dec	1854	149

German Immigrants

Lists of Passengers Bound from Bremen to New York, 1847–1854

NAME	AGE	RESIDENCE	YR-LIST
AAB, Carl	28	Elpenrode	54-0053
AAL, Catharine	24	Gemuenden	51-0500
AARGEYER, Catharin	22	Deimingen	50-0840
AATHALB, Herrmann	24	Dresden	51-1101
ABASFELLER, Casper	29	Pappenhausen	52-0563
Josephine 29, Anna 5, Caroline 9m			
ABBES, Joh.		Drathum	54-1575
ABE, Georg	37	Fridelshausen	53-0905
Cunigunde 31			
ABE, Wilhelm	44	Berka a Werra	52-0370
Christine 42, Anton 16, Elisa 9m			
ABEL, A.	50	Wien	53-1086
Christiane 36, Mathilde 17, Alwine 14			
Josepha 15			
ABEL, A.M. (f)	22	Ellersroth	54-1094
ABEL, Christian	25	Bruchheim	52-0563
ABEL, Conr.	35	Hersfeld	51-0405
ABEL, John	17	Cassel	54-1724
ABEL, Jos.	18	Geyer	49-1106
ABEL, Marie A.	30	Huden	49-0324
ABEL, Valentin	26	Ober Geis	52-1321
ABELE, J.G. (m)	21	Wangen	54-0918
ABELER, Dina	21	Emsdetten	49-0416
ABELMANN, Engel	30	Winzlar	53-1164
Henry 16, Friederike 15			
ABELN, Caroline	17	Vahren	54-1371
ABELS, Martin Diet		Wayens	54-1297
ABENSCHEIN, J Geo.	18	Eichwiesen	53-1062
ABERLE, Marianne	19	Ommersheim	52-1625
ABHAU, Georg	32	Bufen	53-1062
ABLER, Lorenz	33	Unterwackerst	52-1200
Theresia 33, Michael 9, Joseph 7			
Florenz 1			
ABOOG, Christian	47	Hessen	53-0590
Elisabeth 47, Martha 22, Georg 18			
Catharina 14, Anna 9			
ABRAHAM, Berta	22	Strassburg	49-1358
ABRAMSKY, Dora	21	Rogasen	52-1105
Jette 18			
ABT, Carl	36	Schwetzingen	51-0384
ABT, Catharina	12	Noerdlingen	54-0872
Babette 10, Johann 5			
ABT, Loeb	17	Angenrod	53-1062
ABT, Michael	38	Kulcag	53-1062
Agnes 38, Maria 6, Michael 3			
ABT, Michael	3	Rakelwitz	53-1062
ACHELPOHL, Doris	24	Bremen	52-1432
ACHER, Wm.	22	Stuttgart	48-0269
ACHILLES, Charlott	30	Boernsen	51-1438
Friedrich 1			
ACHILLES, Louise	22	Wolfenbuettel	53-0928
ACHION, Marie	21	Grenzen	51-1035
ACHLE, Mad.	50	Gera	49-1358
Paul 25			
ACHSTELLER, M. (m)	25	Trienz	50-0746
J. (f) 2			
ACKER, Carl	40	Leichlingen	52-1580
Anna 44, Minna 20, Alvina 18, Julius 7			
ACKER, Johan	30	Gmuend	54-1283
ACKERMANN, Conr. F	30	Tringhausen	52-0563
Johann 28			
ACKERMANN, Jacob	22	Struempfelbac	49-0352
ACKERMANN, Lorenz	26	Veckerhagen	50-0323
Arnold 27			
ACKERMANN, Philipp	22	Struempfelbac	49-0352
ACKERSMANN, Georg	27	Bayern	53-0652
ACKMANN, Ludwig	51	Hattendorf	49-0413
Wilhelmine 48, Conrad 16, Wilhelmine 14			
Friedrich 11			
ADAM, David	34	Krotoschin	53-1023
ADAM, E.J.H.	22	Ratzlau	51-1160
ADAM, Fr.	55	Westerbrook	53-1016
Caroline 56, Carl 26, Caroline 22, Fr. 25			
ADAM, Matth.	21	Bonlanden	49-0352
ADAMETZ, Jos.	32	Kunitz	54-1575
Maria 41, G. (m) 12, daughter 9			
Franziska 15			
ADAMI, Anton	23	Bremen	48-1015
ADAMS, Carl	46	Schofen	51-1084
ADAMS, Chas. A.	26	Mittelruessel	49-0737
ADAMS, Robert	23	Solingen	48-0406
ADELMANN, Joh.	54	Koettmannsdor	54-1078
Marg. 52, Peter 32, Anna 33, Barbara 11			
Christoph 8, Michel 3, Johann 9m			
ADELSDOERFER, Sigm	17	Fuerth	50-0439
ADG, Ferdinand	31	Stargard	54-1168
ADICKS, Eibe	15	Cappeln	50-0366
ADIX, Diedrich	26	Bremerhaven	54-0053
ADLER, Ad.	14	Rothenberg	49-1358
ADLER, Fritz	26	Becke	49-0345
ADLER, Marie	25	Muenden	53-0590
ADLER, Sara	28	Londorf	54-1168
ADLER, Simon	17	Oberstein/Bav	53-0628
ADLER, Theresa	32	Milren	49-1517
Maria 8			
ADLER, Valt.	44	Sorga	51-1160
ADOLPH, Anton	19	Eichelsachsen	52-1321
ADRIAN, Christ.	58	Oberleis	52-1321
ADRIAN, Elise	49	Oberleis	54-0053
Caroline 15, Friedrich 14			
ADRIAN, Henr.	23	Rainrod	52-1321
Elise 25, Christian 21			
ADVENT, Paul Wilh.	22	Munster	49-0413
AEHMANN, Eduard	18	Goslar	53-1070
AEUSTADT, Zacharia	32	Walsrode	54-1371
AFF, Mathilda	21	Loden	53-1062
AGSTEN, Carl	22	Niederlichten	54-1168
Wilhelmine 25			
AHL, Christian	19	Hof/Baiern	53-0475
AHLBORN, Lina	20	Adeldsen	53-0991
AHLER, Caroline	32	Paderborn	51-1588
AHLERS, Christina	17	Hannover	51-1725
AHLERS, Elisabeth	19	Bohmte	52-1200
Heinrich 18			
AHLERS, Henry	26	New York	51-0326
AHLERS, Joh.	32	Hoya	54-0600
AHLERS, Joh. H.	17	Achim	51-1245
AHLHORN, Heinr.	30	Bovenden	54-1078
Wilhelmine 33			
AHLHORN, Wilh.	25	Wunstorf	50-0439
AHLINGER, Paul	20	Carlsruhe	54-0987
AHLWADE, F. (m)	40	Muehlendorf	48-0453
AHRBERG, Friedrich	20	Einbeck/Hann.	52-1620
AHREND, Christian	28	Neuenkirchen	53-0905
Friederika 31			
AHRENS, Aug.	22	Bruegge	50-1071
AHRENS, Catharine	20	Wahlhoefe	53-1086
AHRENS, David	56	Warfleth	53-0991
Friederike 48, Aron 27, Eliza 16			
Maurice 14			
AHRENS, Doris	22	Muenden	53-0991
Friederike 20			
AHRENS, F. Wilh.	52	Potsdam	52-0563
Caroline 48, Emilie 26, Mathilde 19			
AHRENS, Friedr Wm.	26	Braunschweig	53-0888
AHRENS, Hanna	20	Padingbuettel	54-1647
AHRENS, Heinrich	19	Beverstedt/Ha	51-1725
AHRENS, Heinrich	17	Altwistedt	51-0756
AHRENS, Heinrich	24	Potsdam	52-0563
Clara 16, Agnes 44			
AHRENS, Joh. Alb.	58	Jever	54-0872
Tina 55, Stina 12			
AHRENS, Joh. H.	38	Evern	47-0872
AHRENS, Julius	18	Dorum	50-0021
AHRENS, Martin	21	Hahneknop	54-1716
AHRENS, Metta	20	Wallhoefer	54-1575
AHRENSMEYER, Carl	30	Prussia	53-0628
AHTEN, Jantje	17	Ostermasch	53-0991
Henrietta 19, Gerd. 24			
AICHBICHLER, Anton	27	Vienburg	54-1443
AICHER, Simon	30	Ballenberg	54-1371
AIGNER, Ludwig	11	Eichendorf	52-1452
AIKENBRECHER, Hein	28	Dietendorf	53-0838
AKERMANN, Maria	30	Offenbach/Bav	54-1452
ALBAS, H. (m)	27	Solingen/Pr.	48-0447
ALBER, Georg	24	Aust Moddinge	51-1640

NAME	AGE	RESIDENCE	YR-LIST
ALBERS, Austine	22	Bremen	48-1209
ALBERS, Friedrich	36	Sulingen	53-1000
Sophie 30, Heinr. 7, Margarethe 5			
Wilh. 3, Adelh. 56, Heinr. 21			
Dorothea 21			
ALBERS, Henriette	24	Bederkesa	52-0699
ALBERS, Hermann	27	Sandharten	53-0905
ALBERS, Peter	27	Frankenbostel	53-0492
ALBERS, Wilhelm	17	Bremen	50-0379
ALBERS, William	23	Huettlingen	50-0840
ALBERT, Christine	25	Tossmannsreut	53-0825
ALBERT, Fideli	30	Irendorf	49-0912
Emilie 26, Maria 2, Christina 6m			
ALBERT, J.F.	27	New Orleans	48-1015
ALBERTI, Herm.	31	Koestritz	53-1000
ALBERTUS, Peter	25	Leer	50-1067
Anys 22			
ALBOHN, Maria	24	Hattenrod	52-1105
ALBRACHT, Fr'drike	25	Roden/Waldeck	54-1092
ALBRAND, Elisabeth	27	Lauterbach/He	52-0960
ALBRECHT, B. (f)	59	Hohengandern	54-1566
Sophie 47			
ALBRECHT, Caesar	27	Halberstadt	53-1164
ALBRECHT, Carl	42	Steinburg	52-1148
Charlotte 33, Carl 11, Wilhelm 10			
Theodor 8, Emilie 6, Pauline 4			
Charlotte 9m			
ALBRECHT, Cath.	17	Ebenmerken	49-0574
ALBRECHT, Charlott	29	Sachs.-Mein.	51-1686
ALBRECHT, Chr.	40	Hille	54-1283
ALBRECHT, Friedr.	40	Woldegk	53-0905
Caroline 36, Otto 12, Carl 8, Friedrich 3			
ALBRECHT, Giles	25	Hassum	48-1209
Charles 17, Henry 14, Marianne 60			
Minna 22, Christian 9m			
ALBRECHT, J. (m)	20	Leipzig/Sax.	48-0447
ALBRECHT, Joh.	46	Gr. Almerode	54-0930
Magdalena 47, Gustav 12, Louis 10			
ALBRECHT, Ludwig	24	Battgendorf	51-1062
ALBRECHT, Matth.	25	Mittelruessel	49-0737
ALBRECHT, Meta	27	Kassebruch	52-0048
ALBRECHT, St. (m)	40	Muenden	54-1575
ALBRECHT, W.	48	Stegelitz	50-1071
Christian 26, Carl 18, Johanna L. 16			
ALBRECHT, Wilh.	22	Weinsholz	51-1640
ALDAG, Ernestine	18	Obernkirchen	52-1321
ALDAG, Louis	23	Obernkirchen	52-1321
ALDEFELD, Friedr.	23	Letzlingen	53-0324
ALERS, Herm.	23	New York	49-1358
ALERT, F. Gerhard	23	Emsdetten	49-0416
ALEXANDER, Eduard	19	Bremen	52-0693
Jacob 17			
ALEXANDER, Eduard	25	Hemslingen/Ha	51-1532
ALEXIS, Philipp	17	Orlen/Nass.	48-0447
ALFENIUS, Friedr.	23	Wiesbaden	52-1105
ALLBACH, Wilhelm	31	Frubingen	52-1105
Christine 33, Heinr. 5			
ALLENBACHER, Carl	22	Memmingen	53-1062
Caroline 28			
ALLERS, Carsten	32	New York	48-1015
Eliza 25			
ALLERS, Maria Dor.	21	Misselwarden	52-1148
ALLERT, E. (m)	18	Gerabronn	54-1341
ALLES, Georg W.	25	Wettesingen	51-1245
ALLMANN, Lewis	38	Darmstadt	53-1164
ALMEROTH, Carl	17	Hilgershausen	51-1062
ALPERS, Claus	20	Bederkesa	50-1236
ALSES,	22	Hannover	50-0021
ALT, Ehrenfried	25	Hennig	53-0825
ALT, Joseph	54	Drackenstein	52-0279
ALT, Margarethe	23	Oberehrenbach	52-0693
ALTEL, Heinrich	15	Dorum	53-0905
ALTEMEYER, Philipp	43	Schwalenberg	51-1062
Caroline 40, August 10, Wilhelm 7			
Caroline 3			
ALTEMEYER, Simon	17	Leopoldsthal	52-0775
ALTEMUELLER, H.(m)	29	Westercappeln	49-0416
ALTENBOCKEN, Ann M	32	D-----nier	50-0944

NAME	AGE	RESIDENCE	YR-LIST
ALTENBRECHER, Hein	28	Dietendorf	53-0838
ALTENBURG, Lebrect	59	Luedendorf	54-0872
Marie 44, Melusina 13, Bertha 9, Emma 2			
Carl 11			
ALTENBURG, Otto	21	Bueckeburg	49-1358
ALTENBURG, Wilhelm	25	Hersfeld	47-0828
Sophie 21, Caroline 20			
ALTENEDER, Theodor	28	Bavaria	50-0311
ALTENHEIN, C. (m)	28	Waldeck	54-0918
ALTENSHER, Heinr.	87	Wohnfeld	51-1101
ALTER, Johann	54	Broda	52-0279
Caroline 52, Johann 23, Theodor 19			
Friedrich 13, Dorothea 16			
ALTERMANN, Fritz	26	Geestendorf	50-0366
ALTFUTBISCH, Marg.	21	Bruckenau	51-1455
ALTHAGE, Ernst	18	Rheme	54-1297
Charlotte 20			
ALTHANS, C. (m)	19	Vockerode	48-0453
ALTHANS, Ch. (f)	20	Warenfeld	48-0453
ALTHAUS, Carl Fr.	28	Cassel	53-1023
ALTHENE, Anton	34	Langoens/Hess	54-0965
Elisabeth 28, Elisabeth 4, Catharine 2			
ALTHENE, Cathrine	20	Langoens/Hess	54-0965
Conrad 27			
ALTHENE, Johannes	37	Langoens/Hess	54-0965
Anna 34, Catharina 59, Johannes 6			
ALTHOFF, H.	47	Olfen	54-1566
Catharine 49, Elisabeth 17, Joseph 14			
Franz 9, Wilhelm 5			
ALTMANN, Anna	19	Barmen	53-0914
ALTMANN, Johann	40	Hirschfeld	54-1168
Johanna 36, Rachel 19, Julie 15			
ALTMEIER, Conrad	22	Bundenbach	53-0991
ALTMEYER, Adolph	18	Schmuteten	54-1591
Wilhelmine 54, Helene 16, Charlotte 12			
ALTMUELLER, Moritz	51	Emsdetten	54-0903
Marianne 46, August 13			
ALTMUELLER, Theres	20	Emsdetten	53-1062
ALTSTADT, Jac.	40	Burgbaum	54-0600
ALTSTAEDT, Carl C.	18	Arnstaedt	51-0352
ALWES, Heinrich	27	Winfel	51-0352
AMBRONN, Gotth.	22	Baerungen	53-1164
Amelia 18			
AMBROS, Herm.	26	Karlsruhe	54-1078
Louise 30			
AMBROSIUS, Friedr.	19	Stockhausen	54-0882
AMEN, Johann	17	Reichenhausen	52-1661
AMENDT, Math.	18	Giessen	53-0590
AMMANN, Anton	41	Dorfen	52-1410
AMMANN, C.G. (m)	37	Memmingen	50-0439
Helene 34, Peter 94, Auguste 6, Carl by			
AMMANN, Jacob	22	Kastellaun	52-0563
AMMON, Cath.	20	Hammerbach	51-1160
AMMON, Friedrich	22	Neukirchen	50-0840
AMMON, Johann	34	Niedermarsber	52-0095
AMON, Gottfried	23	Roetha	53-0267
AMON, Joseph	25	Almen	52-1580
Johann 33			
AMREIN, Conrad	44	Cassel	54-1717
AMREIN, Heinrich	14	Momberg	54-1717
AMRHEIN, Anna Elis	22	Manberg	53-1062
AMTAG, Heinr.	49	Breslau	54-1419
Rosine 39, Emma 18			
AMTER, Elise	22	Egershausen	48-1131
AMTHAUER, Conrad	19	Cassel	52-1620
AMTHAUER, Maria	45	Koepern	53-1023
Carl 19, Heinrich 9			
AMTHOR, Gustav	20	Dresden	54-1168
Julius 18			
ANCOL, Alexander	28	Niewke	54-1168
ANDE, Adam	32	Albenberg	51-1639
ANDELMANN, August	28	Danzig	49-1106
ANDEMANN, S. (f)	33	Uhlstedt	50-0746
C. (m) 5			
ANDEREICH, Tillman	33	Vluyn	54-1371
Henriette 57			
ANDERITH, Gertrude	28	Bodelstadt/Bv	48-0053
Nicolaus 3			

NAME	AGE	RESIDENCE	YR-LIST
ANDERLE, Franz	17	Lusche/Austr.	52-0807
ANDERMANN, Johann	45	Hassbergen	54-1443
Dorothea 40, Johann A. 12, Sophia 18			
ANDERS, Carl Fried	40	Langnetz	54-0850
Joh. Elis. 35, Ernst Fried. 14			
Aug. Fran'ka 10			
ANDERSON, Chr'tine	26	Langschaden	49-0383
ANDING, Johann	36	Herrenbreidun	52-1410
Marie 36, Wilhelm 10, Eduard 8			
Bernhard 6, Casper 3, Wilhelmine by			
ANDRA, Julius	24	Meissen	54-0872
ANDRE, Carl	32	Bourgscheidt	54-1371
ANDREAE, F.A.	29	Esens	52-1148
Betty 35			
ANDREAS, Charles	15	Karlsruhe	53-0991
Friedrich 24			
ANDRECHT, Dorette	26	Herrenhausen	52-1105
ANDREE, Carl	26	Lanzenberg	50-1132
ANDREE, Joh.	34	Leer	51-0757
ANDREE, Johanne	31	Oberoelsbach	51-0757
ANDREE, Therese	24	Herrenhausen	50-0439
ANDREWS, Ant.	23	Baiern	54-1724
ANGEMUELLER, Elise	22	Coburg	50-0439
ANGER, Auguste	28	St. Andreasbe	52-0807
ANGER, Lewis	16	Erfurt	53-0914
ANGERMANN, Ludwig	37	Woelpe	54-1443
ANGERMUELLER, Eva	16	Gemuenden	52-1105
ANGERMUELLER, Ludw	38	Gmuenden/Bav.	52-1620
ANGERMULLER, G. Fr	27	Bodelstadt/Bv	48-0053
ANGSTMANN, Dina	29	Lippstadt	51-1160
Pauline 6m, August 4			
ANIMOS, Mathias	31	Linz	54-1371
ANNAKER, Anna	18	Glattbach	54-1575
ANNEGARN, Henry	25	Warendorf	54-1724
ANNIESER, Georg	31	Baden	52-0370
ANSBACHER, Adolph	18	Sulzburg	50-1071
Fanny 24			
ANSCHUETZ, Christ.	44	Humpfershause	53-1023
Sophie 44, Catharine 16, Eva 11, George 8			
Philipp 5			
ANSCHUETZ, Wilh.	23	Weimar	52-0895
ANSKE, Joh. Heinr.	28	Weimar	52-0895
ANSLER, Margaret	26	Klein--sbach	50-0439
ANTE, Heinrich	23	Hallenberg	53-0585
ANTE, Jacob	24	Hallenberg	53-0585
Peter 17			
ANTE, Philipp	33	Hallenberg	53-0585
ANTELMANN, August	28	Haugsdorf	53-0888
ANTENBRINK, G.(m)	30	Grebenstein	52-0652
APEL, Christian	20	Gerberthausen	54-0850
Catharina 19			
APEL, Christoph	20	Eiterfeld/Hes	51-1532
Mariana Barb 17			
APEL, Francis P.	26	Mittelruessel	49-0737
APEL, Jacob	43	Giesen	53-1000
Cath. 36, Marg. 6			
APEL, Joh Benedikt	31	Eiterfeld/Hes	51-1532
Elisab. Cath 23			
APEL, Johannes	33	Moellenfelde	54-1168
APEL, John	38	Botenburg/Hes	50-0323
APEL, L.	51	St. Andreasbe	54-1566
Johanna 38, Gustav 13			
APEL, Maria	58	Wolf	52-1661
APEL, Michael	36	Gilfershausen	48-0887
Anna 27			
APEL, Mina	23	Lemgo	54-1297
APEL, Sophie	19	Grund	54-1297
APENDORF, Joh.	31	Luenen	51-1084
APFEL, Abraham	31	Beberah	51-1686
APFELBACH, Fr.	36	Neunstadt	54-1575
APFELBAUM, Gottl.	25	Danzig	54-1001
APFELD, Cath.	24	Leer	51-0757
APFELD, Eduard		Rosenberg	51-0757
APITSCH, Charles	29	Seehausen	48-1209
APPEL, Egidius	27	Burggub	53-0324
Margrete 26, Margrete 9m			
APPEL, Elisabeth	20	Mainek	54-1168
APPEL, Franz	41	Ellensen	52-0563
APPEL, Georg	49	Lindewerra	51-1438
Julia 45, Friedrich 3m			
APPEL, Herrmann	34	Sachsen	52-0699
APPEL, Jac.	40	Hanau	51-1160
APPEL, Johann	48	Baiern	53-0324
Magreta 30, Edward 16, Nicolaus 13			
Friedrich 12, Sophia 7m			
APPEL, Johann	23	Weisenbrun/Bv	53-0628
APPEL, Moritz	25	Bremen	52-1105
Charlotte 30			
APPELHAUS, H.	30	Boebber	53-1086
Louise 30, Wilhelm 5, Clara 50			
APPELL, Catharina	22	Vendershausen	53-1086
APPELT, Wenzel	40	Althartzdorf	53-0928
Caroline 34, Carl 8, Amalie 10, Anna 6			
Eduard 2m			
APPEN, Anna	22	Gerstetten	50-0366
APRATH, Joh. Heinr	28	Wesel	51-1101
Maria Elisa 34			
ARBEITER, Jul.	33	Breslau	54-1283
ARBOGAST, Joh Geo.	30	Carlsdorf	52-0370
ARDING, Heinrich	32	Beverstedt/Ha	51-1725
ARENBERG, Wilhelm	46	Kohlenfeldt	53-0492
Dor. 42, M. 18, W. 16, H. 12, S. 10, L. 8			
D. 4			
AREND, Conr. Diedr	26	Laemershagen	54-1371
AREND, Otto	18	Moedrath	53-1070
Heinrich 13			
AREND, Wilhelm	21	Cassel	53-1013
ARENHEITER, Marg.	29	Darmstadt	54-1566
ARENS, August	33	Preussen	53-0590
Christine 26, Antony 9, Oscar 2, baby			
ARENS, C. (m)	23	Affenwarden	52-1625
ARENS, Christian	16	Oldenburg	49-0329
ARENS, Heinr.	32	Nienburg	53-1013
ARENS, Joh. Gottfr	23	Bremen	53-1013
ARENS, Margaretha	23	Hannover	50-1317
ARENS, Maria	23	Brake	52-0807
ARENSBERG, J. Conr	38	Martinhagen	48-0053
Cath. Elisab 38, John 11, Henry 8			
Ann Elisa 5			
ARFMANN, Heinr.	17	Meyenburg	53-1070
ARFTMANN, Meta	21	Meyenberg/Han	54-1092
ARHELGES, Margaret	27	Barmen	48-0565
ARIAANS, J. (m)	28	Heumuehlen	49-0329
ARING, E.W. (m)	18	Amt Grueneber	50-0746
ARLANT, Chr. F.	30	Quasnitz	52-1321
ARMBRICHT, Wilhelm	27	Aerzen/Pr.	51-1796
ARMING, Carl	58	Meinsen	52-1321
ARMSTRUP, Carolina	20	Muehlberg	53-0473
ARNDT, Albert	33	New York	50-0311
ARNDT, Heinr.	33	Kirchbaum	54-1078
Anna Elis. 31, Marg. 10, Christoph 6			
Jacob 4, Cath. Elise 9m			
ARNECK, E.(m)	24	Geier	54-0918
ARNHOEBEL, Anton	42	Issenberg	53-0435
ARNHOLZ, Albrecht	18	Bremen	53-0161
ARNINGS, Leonore	56	Dankersen	52-1321
Philippine 24, Engel 2			
ARNKEN, Joh. H.	25	Wupeloh	54-1371
ARNOLD, Ad. (m)	26	Peterweil	51-1640
ARNOLD, Andreas	37	Gleina	54-1371
Caroline 35, Louis 9, Gustav 3			
Henriette 8, Minna 5m			
ARNOLD, Bernard	18	Jebenhausen	53-0991
ARNOLD, Casp	21	Meiningsen	54-0918
ARNOLD, Christian	41	Moersingen	52-0370
ARNOLD, Elisabeth	21	Lengsfeld	53-0942
ARNOLD, Georg	33	Muehlbach	50-0439
ARNOLD, Henry	28	Croelpa	53-0914
ARNOLD, Jacob	3	Giessen	54-1470
ARNOLD, Magdalena	16	Poppenhof	52-0693
ARNOLD, Marie	23	Frankfurt/M.	53-1000
ARNOLT, Chr.		Gross Kelle	47-0868
ARNSTEIN, Caecilie	22	Turnau	49-0574
AROCHA, Franziska	19	New Orleans	53-1062
AROLD, Joh.	29	Bayern	53-0590
Margret 28, Friedrich 7, Margret 4			

NAME	AGE	RESIDENCE	YR-LIST
ARPS, Hermann	22	Steltge	48-0284
ARSHAUER, Wilhelm	24	Mengeringhaus	54-1092
Christian 19			
ARSMANN, Christel	22	Scharmbeck	52-0048
ARTEL, Edmund	23	Olduschin	53-0905
ARTES, Casp.	33	Meiningen	51-1739
Catherine 30, Emma 9, Christine 7, Carl 5			
Therese 2			
ARTIGS, Regine	18	Misselwarden	53-0838
ARZBERGER, Christ.	18	Wunsiedel	53-0888
ARZBERGER, Fr.	47	Thiersheim	52-1129
Marg. 48, Anna B. 25, Johanna B. 22			
Joh. Peter 20, Georg Adam 16, Margar. 14			
Sophia 12, baby			
ARZBERGER, Marg.	48	Winterreit	52-1129
ARZBERGER, Rosalie	22	Wunsiedel	54-1282
ASAM, Johann	33	Spalt	50-0311
ASCHEBERG, B. (m)	22	Emsdetten	49-0416
ASCHEBERG, Herman	20	Emsdetten	53-1062
ASCHENBACH, Carl	28	Hessen	50-0021
Luise 20			
ASCHENBACH, Fr.	40	Ringleben	49-1358
ASCHENBRENNER, Cat	24	Vockerode	52-0558
ASCHENBRENNER, Luk	26	Hilgershausen	52-0807
Friedrich 32			
ASCHENMOOR, Louise	15	Wagenfeld	51-0500
ASCHERMANN, Eduard	20	Eberschuetze	54-0930
ASCHMANN, Carl	27	Mittelruessel	49-0737
ATTSCHEL, Heinr.	25	Prag	49-0383
AU, v. Philipp	55	Hugenfeld	51-1245
Christine 50, Margar.(m) 18, Juliana 9			
AUBEL, Jenne	21	Alstette	48-0269
AUCH, Fr.	20	Esslingen	54-1283
AUCKENBRAND, Ed.	26	Linz	53-1164
AUE, Doris	23	Grogenweiben	53-0652
Carl 1			
AUENSE, Auguste	26	Gittelde	49-0324
AUER, Anton	27	Neustadt	53-1062
AUER, Henriette	27	Mittelruessel	49-0737
Friedrich 2			
AUERBACH, Magdalen	35	Eisenach	54-1371
AUERSWALD, Joseph	41	Raudnitz	47-0672
Theresia 35, Elisabeth 15, Frantz 12			
Joseph 2, Wentzel 6m			
AUGUST, E.	26	Froburg	54-1283
AUGUSTIN, Bernhard	40	Wachstadt/Hng	51-1532
AUGUSTIN, Johann	26	Meinsheim	52-0370
AUMANN, Wilhelm	19	Londorf	54-0965
AUMILLER, Andres	30	Bamberg	54-1717
AUMUELLER, Christ.	25	Coburg	52-0895
Berbel 24			
AUMUELLER, Simon	23	Bavaria	53-0628
AUMUND, H. (m)	20	Arsten	49-0383
AUPURT, Gottlieb	38	Salzungen	53-1000
AURAN, Xaver	28	Helba	54-1341
AURICH, Gottlieb	43	Altmiche/Sax.	50-0323
AUSMANN, Winnie	26	Sachsenberg	53-0838
AUSSAN, Christ. Fr	30	Steinweisen	53-0914
AUSSFILE, Friedr A	27	Bayreuth	48-1131
AUST, Gottlieb	21	Dresden	53-1070
AUSTEN, Julius	40	Berlin	53-1000
Charlotte 32, Charlotte 4			
AUSTERMANN, Friedr	17	Telgte	54-1283
AUSTIN, Samuel H.	29	America	47-0987
AUSTMANN, Fanny	24	Breslau	54-0053
AUSTRUP, Bernh. H.	29	Roxel/Pr.	51-1532
AUTH, Johann	24	Neuhof	48-1184
Nicol. 18			
AVERBECK, Friedr.	19	Muenster	49-0912
AWERQUELT, Ferd. W	31	Bielefeld	52-0117
AXEN, v. Ludwig	17	Hagen	51-0326
AXT, Charles	29	Wehrstadt	49-0416
AXT, Nicolaus	29	Marbach	51-0352
BAABE, Auguste	25	Klosterstein	52-1101
BAACK, Heinrich	22	Holn	51-1639
BAACKE, Christian	25	Mettesingen	52-0370
BAADER, Fabian	30	Zinsheim	51-1796
Franciska 25			

NAME	AGE	RESIDENCE	YR-LIST
BABBELTHAL, Gestud	28	Wedellack	48-1131
BABE, Cath.	25	Osnabrueck	52-1512
BABE, Heinrich	26	Milisch	53-0905
BABEL, Paul		Grafenkirchen	53-0942
(f)			
BABMEIER, L.W. (m)	28	O.Cappeln/Han	52-0960
BABO, Anna Cath	21	Fichtelberg	54-0903
BACH, Catharina	19	Mehmels	52-1321
BACH, Ludwig	15	Heidingfeld	53-1000
BACH, Margr.	57	Langenberg	54-0872
BACHARACH, Aron	23	Neukirchen	53-0590
Moses 22			
BACHARACH, Wolf.	16	Hansbach	54-0930
BACHART, Wilhelm	16	Struemphelbru	51-0384
BACHELLE, v. Rosa	28	Hannover	51-1160
BACHEM, Mathias	28	Coblenz	53-0825
Maria 36			
BACHENHEIMER, Hanc	20	Holzhausen	53-1062
BACHIN, Eva	20	Bayern	53-0590
BACHMANN, Adam	40	Wehren	50-0472
BACHMANN, Auguste	27	Erfurt	50-1067
Ernstine 4			
BACHMANN, Christ.	21	Lauchroeden	53-1013
BACHMANN, Conrad	33	Ostheim	51-0352
Anna Elis. 32, Conrad 8, Wilhelm 6			
George 1			
BACHMANN, Elise	20	Duesseldorf	48-1243
BACHMANN, Fr. (m)	25	Habenshausen	54-0918
C. (m) 20			
BACHMANN, Hermann	26	Ronneburg	53-0590
BACHMANN, Johann	17	Rengshausen	54-0930
Cath. Elisab 17			
BACHMANN, Marianne	25	Schwanfeld	52-0807
BACHMANN, Simon	18	Korbach	51-1160
BACHMANN, widow	43	Sooden/Hess.	52-1423
Wilhelmine 9, Ernestine 8			
Georg Christ 9m			
BACHMEYER, Agathe	26	Au	54-1168
BACHRACH, Maria	25	Angenrod	53-1062
BACHSCHMIDT, Chr.	31	Kempten	53-0492
BACHTEL, H.	19	Reburg	50-1067
BACK, Christine	24	Frankenberg	50-0379
BACK, Maria	27	Staphorst	49-0912
BACKARD, John	17	Lichtenfels	51-0405
BACKE, Wilhelm	47	Heisebeck	47-0840
Adolph 19, Minna 9, Dorothea 1			
BACKERT, Carl	20	Waldkatzenbac	51-0384
BACKERT, Catharina	16	Bavaria	53-0628
BACKERT, Johann	21	Kuebs	52-1362
BACKFREDE, Ld.	16	Ottersberg	49-1358
BACKHAHN, Hirsch	28	Lengsfeld	49-0413
Jette 56, Roschen 24			
BACKHAUS, Carl	25	Selbach	48-1179
BACKHAUS, Elis.	56	Netze	54-1575
BACKHAUS, Louisa	24	Hoya	53-1164
Minna 21			
BACKMANN, Hermann	26	Ronneburg	53-0590
BACKMEISTER, Otto	20	Esslingen	54-1371
BACKRISS, Theo	30	Steinfeld	54-1724
Anne 31, John 8, Marg. 5			
BACURLE, Johannes	20	Gebhausen	54-1717
BADE, Carl	36	Erfurt	54-1371
BADE, Conrad	40	Paligreif/Bav	52-0351
Rosina 40, Catharina 18, Kunigunde 16			
Johann 9, Maria 4, Tomme (died) 10m			
BADE, J. (m)	24	Wunstorf	50-0439
BADE, Joseph	22	Paderborn	50-0021
BADER, Conrad	40	Kalifrat/Bav.	52-0351
BADER, Joseph	25	Pfaffenschwen	52-1625
BADER, Math.	22	Preussen	52-0370
Joh. 20			
BADER, Matthias	24	Drumpelking	54-1092
BADERDORFER, Anne	20	Harrote	49-0912
BADUM, Johann	29	Hemhofe	51-1640
BAEBE, Amana	25	Neuoltmannsdo	53-0914
Caroline 24			
BAEBENROTH, August	31	Hannover	53-0991
BAECH, Eduard	42	Liebenau	52-1410

NAME	AGE	RESIDENCE	YR-LIST
BAECHER, Sophie	22	Wuestenselbit	53-0637
baby			
BAECHERT, Johann	25	Behrenkirch	49-0345
BAECKER, Georg	25	Hanau	52-1101
Maria 28			
BAECKER, Gertrude	24	Darmstadt	48-1184
BAECKER, Heinrich	37	Alingenrode	51-1796
Christine , Louise 6			
BAEHR, August	24	Heustaedt	53-0905
BAEHR, Catharina	21	Homberg	51-1101
BAEHR, Friedrich	28	Landau	52-0279
Christian 23			
BAEHR, Heinr.	22	Neuenheim	52-1321
BAEHR, Heinrich	23	Eishausen	53-0320
BAEHR, Joh Friedr.	40	Bremen	50-0323
BAEHR, Johann	39	Sachsen	53-0590
Elise 34, Mathilde 9, Leonhard 5, Elisa 3			
BAEHR, Johannes	24	Bayern	53-0590
BAEHR, Louise	21	Schuetzingen	54-1168
BAEHR, Ludwig	24	Albshausen	52-0279
BAEHRE, Carl	18	Hannover	51-0048
BAEHRJE, Henry	18	Lesumstotel	51-0048
BAEHRWOLF, Carl	28	Erfurt/Pr.	53-0475
Bertha 26			
BAEKER, Anton	27	Lichtenau/Pr.	51-1532
BAEKER, Heinr.	17	Peine	51-0405
BAELLEKE, Heinr.	18	Stadtlohe	50-1236
BAENDER, Heinr.	23	Rauscholdhaus	50-0323
BAER, Chr.	19	Kuebs	51-1160
BAER, Eduard	21	Schleiz	49-0352
BAER, G. (m)	24	Wuerzburg	50-0439
Louise 25			
BAER, Heinrich	36	Muhlhausen/Pr	53-0628
Joh. Elisa. 34			
BAER, Henriette	28	Worms	53-1023
BAER, Hermann	58	Robenhausen	54-0836
Betha 57, Betha 26, Rebecca 18, Hanna 16			
BAER, Leopold	23	Hainsfahrt/Bv	52-1423
BAERENREUTH, Alb.	43	Floritzdorf	51-0352
BAERENSTIEL, Elise	18	Bremen	53-0590
BAERER, Heinr.	17	Kirchheim	54-1566
Adam 15			
BAERGER, Charlotte	40	Frestorf	48-1355
Heinrich 20			
BAERINGER, Georg	24	Neuburg	54-1443
BAERMANN, Jette	18	Einartshausen	53-0991
BAERMANN, Lene	23	Brueckenau	54-1282
Jette 50			
BAERTHLEIN, Albr.	25	Cincinnati	54-1371
BAESEL, Melchior	52	Grosselfingen	52-1423
Barbara 54			
BAESLER, Ernst	30	Leer	51-0757
Meta 29, Maria 4			
BAETJEMANN, Beta	22	Wallhoerde	51-1101
BAETJER, Herrm.	18	Bremen	51-1245
BAETJERMANN, Herm.	23	Bockeln	51-1101
BAETZ, Anna Barb.	30	Obern Jossa	51-0352
Catharine 29			
BAEUERLEIN, Niklas	47	Sperhoefen	54-1371
Barbara 48, Barbara 18, Michael 15			
Conrad 12, Maria 9, Erwin 5			
BAEUHOY, Magdal.	26	Trobelsdorf	54-1078
BAEUMER, Fr. Hein.	18	Riemsloh	54-1443
BAHLE, Jos.	38	Boerthe/Wuert	53-0435
BAHLER, August	36	Zeitz	53-0320
BAHLS, (m)	28	Berlin	48-1243
BAHMKAMP, Henry	30	Schledehausen	51-1588
Maria 30, Catharine 2			
BAHN, Johann	28	Bruch/Aschwar	47-0672
BAHN, Margarethe	58	Ansbach	54-1566
BAHR, George	30	Heldritt	51-1588
BAHR, Heinr.	32	Gamsen	51-1455
Henrietta 26			
BAHR, William	19	Hochheim	53-1164
BAHRLEIN, Barbara	20	Gips/Bav.	53-0628
BAIER, Friedrike	27	Koenigstein	53-0888
BAIER, George	21	Weinheim	49-1106
BAIER, H.	26	Grossmansdorf	54-1419
BAIER, Jette	23	Hirschberg	53-0928
BAIER, Johann	20	Baiersdorf	52-0693
BAIER, Kunigunde	27	Grasmundsdorf	53-0928
BAIERLEIN, E. (m)	37	Hohenfecten	51-0517
BAIERSDORF, Johann	17	Gmuenden/Bav.	52-1620
Johann 28			
BAINN, Salomon	20	Lahr	49-0912
BAIR, Anton	24	Pfaffenschwen	52-1625
BAIRER, S.G. (m)	48	Cannstadt	49-0329
Cath. 42, C.D. 6, R.F. 4			
BAITMANN, Joh Jac.	18	Reichenberg	49-0352
BAITZ, Joh.	28	Berchnig	49-0352
BAKRITZ, Margr.	21	St. Churg	52-0804
BALEER, Carl	25	Geldorf	52-0279
BALEMEIER, L.W.(m)	28	O.Cappeln/Han	52-0960
BALEWIG, Johann	44	Rippenberg	52-1101
Barbara 46, Johann 17, Friedrich 15			
Carl 9, Louise 7			
BALEY, Sara	22	Ungedanken	53-0838
BALIN, Levi	26	Heiligenstedt	53-0838
Simon 24, Mayer 20			
BALLAUF, Adolf	14	Muenden	53-0590
BALLAUF, Christian	58	Goettingen	53-0991
BALLHAUSEN, Carl	25	Nordhausen	49-0737
Caroliona 18			
BALLIN, Kallm	32	Frankenhausen	53-0320
Petite 30, Moritz 6m, Jacob 22			
BALLIN, Levi	26	Heiligenstedt	53-0838
Simon 24, Mayer 20			
BALLMUELLER, Barb.	28	Schauerheim	49-1106
BALLOF, Andreas	19	Berka	54-1554
BALMTAG, Johann	38	Schweiningen	52-0895
BALS, Caspar	48	Lippstadt	51-1245
BALSMEYER, Henry	40	Holstein	51-1588
Gesche 18, Joseph 16			
BALSS, C.	28	Benrode	54-1283
BALTHASAR, Conr.	38	Lengsfeld	52-1321
BALTHASAR, Meta	39	Elsfleth	48-0887
BALTHAUSER, Joh.	27	Steinbach	52-1661
Franziska 31, Thekla 7			
BALTJER, Johann	21	Bremen	53-0628
BALZ, Caspar	47	Frankenberg	53-1016
Eliese 12			
BALZER, Georg	35	Engelhelms	53-0320
BALZER, Heinrich	44	Pirmasens	52-1148
Maria 27			
BALZER, Johann	29	Cassel	52-1321
BALZER, Laura	48	Naumburg	54-0872
BAMBERG, Franz	16	Mettwitz/Bav.	53-0628
BAMBERGER, Georg	30	Damshausen	53-1000
BAMBERGER, Jacob	16	Bueckeburg	54-0850
BAMM, Heinrich	39	Dettum	52-0775
Sophie 39, Hermann 12, Minna 10, Anna 4			
BAMSBERGER, Wilh.	23	Benzingen	50-0292
BANDIFS, Friedr.	28	Schweinitz	54-1282
BANDY, David	21	Boehmen	54-1724
BANGER, Hermann	25	Leherten	49-0324
BANGERT, Anna	25	Wirthheim	50-1071
BANGERT, Heinrich	21	Darlitter	54-1717
BANK, Caroline	22	Stebin	48-1184
BANK, v. Carl	21	Obergimpern	49-0912
BANKWIRTH, Joseph	23	Rinzel	50-1236
BANLE, Christian	24	Hildesheim	53-1070
BANSAF, Jacob	20	Heidenheim	52-1580
Michel 17			
BANSBACH, Joseph A	40	Friedrichsdor	51-0384
Mariana 33, Rosa 10, Elisabeth 8			
Johanna 6, Joseph 3, Sophia 2m			
BANZEL, Maria	21	Kirschhaut	52-0515
BARANDON, Augustus	25	Verden	53-1164
BARBEL, Joh.	19	Bergzabern	54-0053
BARBER, Theodor	41	Goslar	54-1591
BARGEN, Friedr.	23	Frankenhausen	53-0492
BARGEN, v. Gesche	22	Ottersberg	52-0048
BARGFELD, Georg	41	Hundelshausen	52-0563
Cathar. M. 38, Anna C. 18, Wilhelm 14			
Sophie 10, Georg 8, Carl 6, Rosine 3			
BARGMANN, Gustav	27	Egele	54-1282

NAME	AGE	RESIDENCE	YR-LIST
BARKEWITZ, Thomas	46	Gulden	52-0095
Ludowike 26, Mehaline 10m			
BARKHAUS, Ottoline	25	Varel/Old.	51-1725
BARLAGE, Anton	20	Oldenburg	50-0311
Caroline 16, Lisette 19			
BARLAGE, Herm.	24	Forde	49-1106
BARLEPSCH, Chr. Fr	28	Weidenhagen	51-1062
Caroline 26			
BARMENFOER, Cath.M	15	Nord Wohle	52-0563
BARMEYER, Gesina	26	Mittelruessel	49-0737
BARNING, Herm.	17	Hannover	50-1317
BARNSCHEIER, Heinr	18	Altenhain	50-0379
Elisabeth 23			
BARNSCHEIN, Doroth	55	Loessnitz	54-1371
Mathilde 20			
BARRE, M. (f)	33	Ellwaenden	48-0453
BARTA, John	42	Boehmen	54-1724
Cath. 40, John 17, Wenzel 14, Cath. 12			
Anne 2			
BARTEK, Wenzel	29	Buda	54-1676
Marie 21, Elisabeth 4			
BARTEL, Helene	10	Erlangen	52-1200
BARTEL, W. (m)	30	Hildburghause	49-1358
BARTELS, Carl	28	Alberdiesen	52-0048
Friederike 24			
BARTELS, Friedrich	24	Graben	53-0825
BARTELS, Henry	16	Dudensen	53-0914
Dorothea 19			
BARTELS, Johanne	18	Mehrbach	51-1438
BARTELS, Maria	21	Buehne	50-0379
BARTELS, Sophie	23	Isernhagen	54-1078
Dorette 19			
BARTH, Adam	19	Sersheim	52-1580
BARTH, G.W.O. (m)	21	Leipzig	50-0311
Heinr. 27			
BARTH, Johann	35	Steinfeld	51-1639
BARTHEIL, Heinr.	50	Gehrden	51-1640
Soph. 32, Soph. 10, Heinr. 6, Charlotte 4			
Georg 9m			
BARTHEL, Georg	43	Dehlau	52-1129
Anna 36, Adam 15, Marie 13			
BARTHEL, Paulus	35	Allesheim	51-1455
BARTHELHEIM, Ernst	30	Boerninghause	54-0965
BARTHELMES, Anna	25	Gerschfeld	52-1362
Catharina 20			
BARTHELMES, Thuisc	20	Zella/Sachsen	54-0965
BARTHFELDT, Engelh	20	Rotenburg	53-1070
BARTHOLDT, S.M.(m)	23	Leese	49-0329
BARTHOLMA, Emilie	25	Gillhaus	54-1371
BARTHOLNESS, Math.	34	Batsberg	49-0737
BARTHOLOMAE, Wilh.	28	Gildehaus	53-0991
BARTHOLOMAEUS, Con	27	Rasdorf	48-0284
BARTLING, Henry	20	Manausloh	53-0914
BARTMANN, Carl	56	Lintig	49-0329
L. (f) 26			
BARTOLD, Rudolf	36	Hellern/Pr.	52-1432
Amalie 30, Christian 6, Friederike 3			
Caroline 11m			
BARTOLOMAUS, Anna	24	Reichenbach	52-0558
BARTRAM, Hermann	22	Dettum	52-0775
BARTSCH, Hermann	32	Wiesenberg/Pr	54-1092
BARTSCH, Johann	24	Leobschuetz	52-1625
BARULER, Joseph	22	Herrenwies	54-0928
BARUTH, Isidor	32	Linkov/Pr.	54-1092
Caecilie 19, J. by			
BARZMANN, (m)	25	Ascheberg	49-0324
BASCH, Wilhelm	18	Berlin	53-0267
BASE, Conrad	28	Stolzenau	52-1362
Friederike 26			
BASEL, Martin	44	Hissenbrunn	48-0951
Kunigunde 33, George 12, Anne 5, John 3			
BASINSKI, Eva	33	Ploeschen	53-0991
Maurice 9, Bertha 8, Hermann 6			
Theophila 3			
BASSELMANN, Friedr	21	Steltge	48-0284
BASSELMANN, Marta	30	Homberg/Hess.	51-1796
BASSENDORF, Carl	31	Daspich	54-1168
BASSLER, Franz	35	Iglan	53-1070

NAME	AGE	RESIDENCE	YR-LIST
Barbara 36, Maria 11, Franz 9, Mathilde 7			
Johann 3, Emanuel 1			
BASSONHORST, Luise	21	Seggen	54-1470
BASTHAGEN, Constan	26	Emden	53-0324
Catrina Fr. 24			
BATHIANI, Maria	32	Freyburg	51-1640
BATTERMANN, H.W.	55	Kohlenfeldt	53-0492
D. 55, L. 11, W. 9, D. 5, Heinrich 6m			
BATTERMANN, Heinr.	37	Kohlenfeldt	53-0492
W. 35			
BATTIST, Anna Mar.	28	Moeresheim	54-1443
BATWESEN, Chr.	26	Kohlenfeldt	53-0492
W. 23, W. 1			
BATZ, Carl	17	Ringshausen	54-0930
BATZ, Joseph	40	Berginn/Bav.	49-0365
Maryanne 41			
BAU, Peter	52	Fischbach/Nas	53-0628
Elisabeth 51, Peter 14			
BAUBERGER, Mathaus	41	Geislingen	48-1184
BAUCH, Ed.	16	Urberach	53-1023
Catharine 51, Kunigunde 8			
BAUCH, J.C.	42	Altenburg/Sax	48-0053
BAUCH, Joh. F.	43	Chemnitz	50-1071
BAUCH, Niclaus	32	Schweppenhaus	54-0987
Catharine 28, Catharine 6, Niclaus 3			
Jacob 16			
BAUCH, Wal.	41	Wuertt.	54-1724
Math. 39, Marg. 14, Math. 5			
BAUEN, Anna Barb.	23	Fichtelberg	54-0903
BAUER, Adolph	21	Breslau	54-1092
BAUER, Ana Matilde	23	Eiterhagen	54-1566
BAUER, Anna	30	Untermoessrin	54-1554
BAUER, Aug.	30	Hauptmannsgru	54-1282
BAUER, Baptist	28	Bayern	53-0557
BAUER, Baptist	25	Bayern	53-0557
BAUER, Barbara	19	Neustadt	52-1512
BAUER, Barbara	24	Bamberg	49-0345
BAUER, Carl	30	Hallstadet	48-1131
BAUER, Carl	25	Treysa	51-1160
BAUER, Caroline	29	Sachsen	53-0590
BAUER, Catharine	66	Lauterbach	51-0352
BAUER, Conr.	24	Hohenschwarz	52-0693
BAUER, D. (m)	20	Bremen	51-1796
BAUER, Elisabeth	18	Wuertenberg	53-0557
BAUER, Elisabeth	19	Auerbach	54-1371
BAUER, Ephraim	35	Fuerth	53-0267
BAUER, F.	52	Ahorn	53-0582
H. 12, Caroline 51, Ludovica 18, Mary 16			
Eliza 14			
BAUER, F.	26	Eisenberg	54-1470
BAUER, Fr. (m)	18	Steppenhausen	54-0918
BAUER, Franziska	22	Mistelfeld/Bv	51-1532
BAUER, Friedr.	30	Ansbach	50-1317
Wilhelmine 28			
BAUER, Fritz	34	Roda	52-1105
Maria 40			
BAUER, Geo.	37	Lennep	48-0565
Joh. 38, M. 6, A. 3			
BAUER, Georg	26	Sachsen	53-0585
BAUER, George	29	Hafenpreppach	51-0048
BAUER, Gottfried	49	Langenroda	53-0267
BAUER, H. (m)	20	Obertrippach	54-1078
BAUER, Heinrich	23	Oberlangersta	52-1200
Magdalena 19			
BAUER, Heinrich	21	Baiern	54-1554
BAUER, Heinrich	36	Humendorf	51-1588
BAUER, Henriette	35	Gillershausen	53-0320
BAUER, Isaac	18	Alsfeld	54-1341
BAUER, J.B. (m)	50	Luppensdorf	50-0379
BAUER, Jacob	21	Terstenhof	49-0352
BAUER, Joh Friedr.	58	Muenden/Hann.	50-0323
Margarethe 54, Ernst 15, Louise 31			
BAUER, Joh.	24	Fernabrunst	54-1282
BAUER, Johann	25	Hasberg/Bav.	53-0628
BAUER, Johann	16	Arzberg	53-0557
BAUER, Johann	27	Michingen	54-0903
BAUER, Johann	32	Ingolstadt	52-1105
Anna 25, Maria 7, Joseph 4, Max 2			

NAME	AGE	RESIDENCE	YR-LIST
BAUER, Johann	27	Kemmen	48-1179
BAUER, Johann	25	Schwetzingen	51-0384
BAUER, Johann	23	Bernstein/Bav	53-0475
Margarethe 26, child 8m			
BAUER, Johannes	25	Irreloh/Bav.	51-1725
Barbara 25			
BAUER, John	17	Baden	50-0021
BAUER, John A.	31	Meiningen	50-0021
BAUER, John Martin	26	Schleidorf	53-0628
BAUER, Johs.	29	Mittelruessel	49-0737
BAUER, Joseph	18	Geistesletz	52-1512
BAUER, Lissette	17	Alsfeld	54-1341
BAUER, Maria	23	Ebnath/Bav.	52-1423
BAUER, Marie	33	Bessenlingen	54-0053
BAUER, Martin	28	Degingen	52-1512
BAUER, Michael	52	Gungolding	54-1371
Anna 33, Michael 19, Mathias 9, Johann 7			
Joseph 5			
BAUER, Michel	39	Heidenheim	48-0887
BAUER, N. (f)	bob		50-0746
BAUER, Philipp	29	Dudeldorf	50-0439
BAUER, R.	23	Goettingen	48-1355
BAUER, St. (f)	21	Trienz	50-0746
F. (m) 19			
BAUER, Wm.	21	Schwab-Gmuend	48-0447
BAUER, Wolff.	46	Irreloh/Bav.	51-1725
Margareth 45, Elisabeth 19, Christoph 16			
Joseph 12, Margaret 9, Anna 6, Wilhelm 3			
Anne Elise 6w			
BAUERNSCHMIDT, M.	22	Settenreuth	53-0825
BAUERNSCHMIDT, Pet	34	Steinach	53-0652
BAUERS, Carl	28	Friedrichssta	50-0379
BAUERSACHS, M Barb	22	Effelden	51-1160
BAUERSFELD, Carl	33	Emden	53-0324
Dirtje 32, Ludwig 4, Richard 9m			
BAUERSFELD, H Fr'd	45	Haickstaedt	52-0279
Anna Maria 42, Christine F. 8			
BAUERSHAEFER, Wilh	29	Salzheim/Pr.	48-0053
BAUERWEIN, Fran'ka	23	Degendorf	52-0515
BAUKNECHT, Maria	58	Huntsbach	53-0928
BAUM, (m)	25	Unteressen	54-1419
BAUM, Anna	23	Hellersberg	52-1580
BAUM, Carl	53	Vienna/Baden	54-1092
BAUM, Carl	25	Iburg	50-1067
BAUM, Helene	23	Ebelsbach	53-0320
Lazarus 19			
BAUM, Isaak	23	Nordheim/Bav.	53-0628
Hanna 20			
BAUM, James	52	Schwerzenz	53-0991
BAUM, Joh. S.	40	Cadolzburg	50-0439
Elise 39, Carl 11, Gust. 7, Soph. 4			
Therese by			
BAUM, Johanna	18	Empfingen	52-0279
BAUM, Johannes	20	Rigelsdorf	54-1649
Martha 19			
BAUM, John	17	Welkendorf/Bv	48-0053
BAUM, Jos.	23	Prettbraun	54-1283
BAUM, Kosman	15	Nordheim/Bav.	53-0628
BAUM, Levi	23	Gehaus	53-0942
BAUM, Meier	20	Mittelberg/KH	53-0628
BAUM, Rosa	30	Ebelsbach	52-0807
BAUMAN, Christian	49	Waldmichelsba	51-1532
BAUMANN, Adolph	18	Terstenhof	49-0352
BAUMANN, Barbara	32	Pappenheim	54-0850
BAUMANN, Christine	17	Langenberg	54-0872
BAUMANN, G. (m)	27	Selb	52-0652
BAUMANN, Georg	25	Lichtenfels	52-1661
BAUMANN, Georg Mic	33	Birkenfeld	53-0324
BAUMANN, Jacob	22	Pappenheim	53-0905
BAUMANN, Johann	18	Buehne	50-0379
BAUMANN, Johann	26	Gelb	50-0379
BAUMANN, Johann	20	Villingen	51-1438
BAUMANN, John	30	Windelheim	53-0492
BAUMANN, Mathilde	15	Wuertt.	54-1724
BAUMANN, Michel	52	Gries	48-0887
Margareth 68, Adam 25, Margareth 21			
Margaretha 18			
BAUMANN, Nic.	27	Oberkietz	49-0781
BAUMANN, Stephan	19	Ferlage	52-0563
BAUMANN, Thomas	46	Wildenholz	52-0515
Rosina Barb. 41, Maria Barb. 18			
Johann Andr. 14, Johann Wilh. 10			
Anna Maria 7			
BAUMANN, Victoria	20	Winterofingen	54-0903
BAUMBACH, Nicolaus	50	Cabarz/Bav.	52-0351
Anna Maria 52, Carl 24			
BAUMBUSCH, Peter	41	Ferdinandsdor	51-0384
Christine 47, Peter 20			
BAUMEISTER, Elis.	32	Wardefeld/Lip	53-0628
BAUMEISTER, Friedr	20	Prichsinstad	48-1131
BAUMGAERTEL, Georg	46	Storkheim	52-0095
Margaretha 36, Kunigunde 17, Mathilde 12			
Maria 8, Georg 10, Barbara 5, Johanne 1			
BAUMGAERTNER, Chr.	18	Koenigsbrunn	52-1332
BAUMGAERTNER, Joh.	34	Tiefenort	52-1410
Margarethe 31, Andreas 9, Heinrich 5			
BAUMGAERTNER, Joh.	22	Wollitz/Bav.	52-0351
Maria Eva 27, Barbara 4			
BAUMGARDT, Carolin	24	Gehaus	53-0942
Bluemchen 17			
BAUMGARDT, S. (m)	24	Gehaus	54-1341
Jette 28, Willie 50, Joseph 16			
BAUMGART, Anna M.	25	Marlas/Hessen	49-0365
BAUMGART, Aug.	26	Minden	51-1455
BAUMGART, C. (f)	28	Creba-k	50-0439
H. (f) by			
BAUMGART, Johann	28	Kirchheim	52-1661
Anna 28, Anna bob			
BAUMGARTEN, Georg	26	Moller	47-0828
BAUMGARTEN, Jules	26	Eissberg/Sax.	48-0053
BAUMGARTEN, Louise	19	Eisenberg	52-1661
BAUMGARTER, Maria	25	Landwursten	50-1067
BAUMGARTH, Joh.	39	Mittelruessel	49-0737
BAUMGARTH, Maria	21	Heilbronn	52-1580
Pauline 17			
BAUMGARTNER, C.	24	Aufhausen	54-1419
BAUMGARTNER, Casp.	27	Ansbach	54-0987
BAUMGARTNER, Jacob	36	Dachgrube/Sac	53-0628
Anna Marg. 27, Anna Barbara 7			
Sebastian 5, Herodica 3, Heinrich 27			
Anna 29			
BAUMHARD, Martha	16	Asbach	54-0053
BAUMLER, Ed.	26	Oschatz	51-1084
BAUREISS, J. Georg	33	Buergel	54-1283
BAUSCHENBERGER, J.	25	Mittelruessel	49-0737
BAUSEWEIN, John	27	Ermeshausen	53-0582
BAUSEWEIN, Valent.	35	Elertshausen	48-1131
R. (m) 16			
BAUTHER, Eva	18	Rotenhof	54-1282
BAVENSBERG, Wilh.	24	Glinde	49-0345
BAYER, Bathaus	38	Langenhagen	49-0345
BAYER, Berthold	17	Muensterberg	54-1443
BAYER, C.J.	24	Fulda	51-0405
BAYER, Cath.	24	Lenabach	51-1739
BAYER, Catharine	23	Ampferbach	54-1575
BAYER, Christian	40	Basdorf	48-1184
Maria 39, Anton 12, Jacob 11, Lina 7			
Caecilia 6			
BAYER, Georg	24	Baiern	54-1724
BAYER, Georg	35	Letten	52-0693
Georg 27, Kunig. 6, Johann 4			
BAYER, H.L.	30	Zwickau	53-0161
BAYER, Johann	36	Spermuehle	53-0628
BAYER, Johann	29	Hizles	52-0693
BAYER, Joseph	21	Neuses	53-0914
BAYERL, Johann	28	Flohr	48-1184
BAYERLEIN, Lorenz	42	Blittelschenb	50-0366
BAYERS, Anna	19	Appeln	52-1625
BAYERSDORF, Johann	17	Gmuenden/Bav.	52-1620
Johann 28			
BAYRHOFF, Gotlieb	50	Stoetten	52-1200
Francisca 46, Therese 18, Georg 17			
BEAR, Georg	24	Melsungen	52-0804
BEAUPRET, P.F.	34	U.S.	48-1243
BEBER, Elisabeth	24	Reichelsrode	54-1282
BEBLER, Lisette	26	Wetzlar	51-1455

NAME	AGE	RESIDENCE	YR-LIST
BECH, Sophia	26	Gengenbach	52-1101
BECHELMEIER, Ant.	29	Obersteinach	49-1358
BECHER, Carl	29	Elberfeld	48-0565
BECHER, John	34	Lesering	53-0914
BECHER, Mendel	21	Schrimm/Pr.	52-0807
BECHMANN, August	18	Buerkhausen	54-1297
BECHSTEIN, Carl	37	Ziegenhain	52-1580
Anna 35, Lorenz 8, Johannes 9m, Anna 6			
BECHSTEIN, Georg	40	Rossstadt	54-1554
BECHSTEIN, Heinr.	23	Friedberg	52-0895
BECHTEL, Georg	18	Hessen	53-1013
BECHTHOLD, Johann	43	Ferdinandsdor	51-0384
BECHTHOLT, Anna M.	38	Rainrod	48-1131
(f) 12, (m) 8, (m) 2			
BECHTOLD, John	35	Schneckenlohe	51-1588
Margaret 18			
BECHTOLD, Margaret	18	Neuses	51-1588
BECK, Anna Cath.	3	Waldcappel	49-0352
BECK, Auf Der Joh.	25	Osnabruck	49-0413
BECK, Camillo	15	Schondra	51-1796
BECK, Christian	31	Bavaria	53-0628
BECK, Christine	18	Rockenhof	52-1105
BECK, D. (m)	25	Bremerhafen	48-1114
BECK, Dorothea	20	Neumarkt/Bav.	52-0807
BECK, Eleonore	15	Anspach	54-1283
BECK, Elisabeth	21	Hermending	52-1580
BECK, Ernest W.	20	Redwitz	53-0888
BECK, Eva M.	16	Woernitz	54-1094
BECK, Franz	24	Freudschaft	53-0628
Ernstine 27, Albina 1			
BECK, Fried.	20	Hannover	49-0383
BECK, Georg	25	Muenster-Schw	54-1283
BECK, George	32	Hohenberg	53-0888
Jane 29, Friederike 6, Wilhelmine 4			
Christina 1			
BECK, Gottlieb	33	Raudvannen	54-0053
BECK, J.G. (m)	23	Prettheim	50-0746
BECK, Jacob	42	Moshain	54-1419
Barbara 42, Wilhelmine 11			
BECK, Jean	4-	Ravensburg/Wu	49-0365
Marianne 44, Marianne 17, Auguste 9			
BECK, Joh.	26	Kalteneures	54-1575
BECK, Joh.	30	Dormitz	49-1358
BECK, Joh.	26	Kalteneures	54-1575
BECK, Marie	23	Feuchtwange	52-1332
BECK, Valentin	30	Erlangen/Bav.	52-0117
BECK, Wilhelm	29	Allwaldenberg	52-0370
BECKEL, Johs.	57	Naunheim	49-0574
BECKEMAYER, Carl	30	Luebbecke	54-0872
Henriette 22			
BECKENDORF, Heinr.	39	Bodenfelde/Ha	50-0323
BECKENDORF, Hen'tt	34	Borenfelde	54-0882
BECKER, (m)	27	Gmuenden	54-1283
BECKER, A.	22	Oelde	51-0517
BECKER, A. (m)	21	Hillegossen	54-1575
BECKER, A. (m)	21	Hillegrossen	54-1575
BECKER, Albertine	27	Lennep	52-1580
Martha 15			
BECKER, Alois	19	Prussia	50-1317
BECKER, Anna	21	Fuerstenreuth	54-1554
BECKER, Anna M.	23	Niederklein	52-1321
BECKER, Anton	27	Hildesheim	53-1000
BECKER, Anton	25	Boettinghause	50-1236
BECKER, August	23	Brunswick	50-0311
BECKER, August	25	Osnabrueck	54-1297
BECKER, Auguste	24	Hessen	50-0021
BECKER, Barbara	45	Soemmern	54-1554
Johann 16, Nicolaus 18			
BECKER, Bertha	32	Dresden	49-0742
BECKER, Carl	30	Hofgeismar	54-1566
BECKER, Carl	21	Holzhausen	51-1160
BECKER, Carl	21	Prussia	50-0311
BECKER, Catharina	26	Cassel	47-0828
BECKER, Catharine	24	Tocksbach	52-1452
BECKER, Catherine	22	Cassel	51-1588
BECKER, Cathr.	22	Hessen	50-0021
BECKER, Christ.	25	Fuerstenau	49-0324
BECKER, Conr. Mar.	63	Giessen	47-0918

NAME	AGE	RESIDENCE	YR-LIST
Phillip 21			
BECKER, Dina	13	Ebersberg	48-1114
BECKER, Dorothea	37	Vendershausen	53-1086
BECKER, Dorothy	24	Magdeburg/Pr.	49-0365
BECKER, Elisabeth	25	Lauterbach/He	52-0960
BECKER, Ernst	35	Neustadt	54-0850
Linna 33, Guido 10, Ernst 7			
BECKER, Ferdinand	22	Elzenfeld	54-0987
BECKER, Fr. Em.	19	Huettensteinb	53-1164
BECKER, Friedrich	26	Dillenburg	52-1101
BECKER, Friedrich	26	Wiesbaden/Nas	52-0807
BECKER, Heinrich	18	Wettingerrode	53-0320
BECKER, Heinrich	33	Preussen	53-0590
Marie 29, Christine 6, Eduard 3, baby 3m			
BECKER, Heinrich	24	Heiligenstadt	52-0699
BECKER, J.C. (m)	43	Wunstorf	50-0439
Otto 16, Mad. 40, Helene 11, Adolphine 9			
Ottilie 7, Wilhelmine 4			
BECKER, Joh.	26	Nieste	52-0563
Charlotte 22, Heinr. L. 29			
BECKER, Joh.	24	Treffurt	54-1297
BECKER, Joh. Heinr	15	Grosshegersdo	54-1168
Sophie 19			
BECKER, Johann	36	Bleidenrode	54-0830
Anna Cath. 29, Wilhelm 4, Conrad 9m			
BECKER, Johann	14	Waldshut	51-1686
BECKER, Johannes	59	Nauheim	54-0830
Jacob 28, Catharina E. 58, Elise 24			
BECKER, Justine	23	Wehnde/Hann.	54-0965
BECKER, Lina	19	Giessen	54-0987
BECKER, Louisa	30	Wendhoe	53-0991
BECKER, Maria	25	Lohr	52-1512
BECKER, Max	28	Petermain	51-0326
BECKER, Meta	23	Wehden	47-0872
Christine 19			
BECKER, Philipp	26	Reiskirchen	54-0965
Anna 22			
BECKER, Swene	31	Hankoerten	51-0500
BECKER, Theodor	21	Wildeshausen	54-1554
BECKER, W.	25	Niederklein	51-0460
BECKER, Wilh.	52	Osterode	47-0918
Louise 22, Emilie 17, Wilh. 20			
BECKER, Wilhelm	16	Manrode	52-1410
BECKER, Wilhelm	28	Londorf	54-0965
Margarethe 22			
BECKER, Wilhelm	25	Bartholfeld	54-0987
BECKER, Wilhelmine	37	Neucherschen	49-0781
Christ. Fr. 15			
BECKEWEG, Heinrich	25	Ofenstedt	51-1438
BECKMANN, Aug. H.	26	Nordleda	51-1160
BECKMANN, Diedrich	17	Kuehrstedt	50-0366
BECKMANN, Doris	25	Braunschweig	47-0158
BECKMANN, Fr'drka	59	Wehe	51-1639
BECKMANN, Heinr.	57	Drakenburg	54-1371
Marie 56			
BECKMANN, J. Heinr	53	Gemen	48-0887
Anna Margart 42, John 21, Elisabeth 18			
John Hermann 14, Catharine 10, Joseph 8			
William 3			
BECKMANN, Joh.	24	Voerden	51-1640
BECKOLT, Richard	27	Halle	53-0267
BEDDIGER, Christ.	34	Lichtenfels	53-0652
BEDDIGES, William	24	Hildesheim	53-0991
Wilhelmina 21			
BEEK, Heinr.	24	Ebingen	51-1640
Friederike 31, Friederike 9			
BEEK, Heinrich	29	Gunzenhausen	53-0905
BEEK, Johann Georg	38	Bakenau	49-0345
Gottlieb 31			
BEER, Carl		Elm	53-0942
Caroline			
BEER, Ernst	23	Baake	49-1358
BEERBACH, Geo. Aug	19	Salzungen	52-1321
BEERHOLD, Eduard	33	Frankenhausen	49-1358
BEERMANN, G. (m)	23	Gotha	48-0445
BEGEMANN, Wilhelm	8	Baiern	53-0585
BEGNER, Friedricke	18	Schrylok	51-1639
BEGSTEIN, Johann	23	Baiern	52-0370

NAME	AGE	RESIDENCE	YR-LIST
BEHA, L. (m)	26	Rehberingen	48-0447
BEHLING, August	19	Voerde	54-1647
BEHLING, Heinrich	29	Hannover	53-0590
BEHLMER, Peter	30	Fardinghausen	52-0563
Rebecca 30, Hermann 8, Johann H. 4			
Joh. Peter 1			
BEHM, Joh.	20	Darmitz	49-1358
BEHNE, H.	14	Kohlenfeld	53-0492
BEHNKE, Hermann	50	Braunschweig	54-1649
Hermann 17, Rebecca 19			
BEHNKE, Johanna	30	Stettin	54-0053
BEHNKEN, Anna	23	Padingbuettel	54-1647
BEHNKEN, Christ.	17	Langwedel	53-1000
Gesche 20			
BEHR, Anton	22	Pesth	53-0914
BEHR, August	29	Dresden	48-0565
BEHR, Cath.	24	Coburg	54-1282
BEHR, Conrad	23	Ingeln	54-1554
BEHR, Georg	25	Oberegers	52-0095
BEHR, Gustav	40	Kreuznach/Pr.	52-1332
BEHR, Ludw.	28	Meinessen	51-1084
BEHR, Sebast.	29	Absdorf	48-1355
Magdalina 24, Andreas 3			
BEHREND, Cusel	55	Rothenberg	49-1358
Ulricke 45, Johanne 10, Leopold 8			
Mathilde 3			
BEHREND, Jacob	16	Rodenberg	53-0492
BEHREND, John	36	Breslau	51-0048
BEHRENDES, Marg.	31	Ottendorf	52-1129
Bertha 8, Wilh. 4			
BEHRENDS, Heinr.	32	Ostendorf	51-1686
BEHRENDT, Andreas	36	Breidenberg	50-0292
BEHRENS, Adelheid	24	Brochhusen	50-0292
BEHRENS, Carolina	22	Sutheim	53-0825
BEHRENS, Chr.	20	Kohlenfeldt	53-0492
D. 18			
BEHRENS, Chr.	17	Vacha	51-0405
BEHRENS, Christian	24	Beverstedt/Ha	51-1725
BEHRENS, Claus	27	Zelle	53-1000
BEHRENS, Heinrich	39	Hannover	54-0987
Marie 26, August 9			
BEHRENS, Herm.	60	Prussia	50-1317
Peter 23, Marie 18, Wilhelm 16			
BEHRENS, Jac.	27	New York	47-0158
BEHRENS, Joh Heinr	20	Hannover	53-0557
Johann 26			
BEHRENS, Joh. Chr.	35	Lusen	54-1168
BEHRENS, Joh. Hein	20	Hannover	53-0557
Johann 26			
BEHRENS, Johann	20	Arensberg	52-0699
Louise 22			
BEHRENS, Johann	20	Basdahl	51-1035
BEHRENS, Marie Cat	23	Huenteln	49-0324
BEHRENS, Meta	22	Fischerhude	52-1362
BEHRENS, Moritz	28	Maedebach	53-0585
BEHRENS, Nicolaus	23	Bremen	48-0101
BEHRENS, Sophia	15	Bremen	50-1317
BEHRENS, Wilh'mine	23	Lemfoerde	52-1512
BEHRINGER, J. Mich	32	Plettenhofen	53-0637
Marianne 25			
BEHRINGER, Wolfg.	20	Lissberg	52-1321
BEHRMANN, Elise	20	Hasbergen	53-1000
BEHRMANN, John	24	Bremen	53-1164
BEHRMANN, Minna	20	Detmold	52-1580
BEHRNHARDT, Conrad	10	Dornbach	54-1554
BEHRS, Margrethe	24	Giersdorf/Han	52-1332
BEICKE, Elisabeth	22	Emsdetten	48-0260
BEIDEKE, Carl	54	Roden/Waldeck	54-1092
Caroline 27			
BEIDERLIEB, Joh.	60	Lustberg	51-1640
BEIDLER, Franz	30	Eilenburg	49-1358
Johanna 33, Fr. (f) by			
BEIER, Anna Marg.	31	Unterweisenba	53-0637
BEIER, Carl	24	Querfurt	53-1164
BEIER, Gottfried	20	Farmbach	51-1455
Marg. 20			
BEIER, Jacob	19	Meiningen	52-0895
BEIER, Johann	31	Curhessen	52-1432

NAME	AGE	RESIDENCE	YR-LIST
Heinrich 27, Johann 22			
BEIERLEIN, J. Jac.	40	Neustadt	52-1105
Catharina 46, Friedrich 17, Georg 15			
Marg. 9			
BEIERLIEB, Johann	60	Lustberg	51-1640
BEIERSDORF, Johann	17	Gmuenden/Bav.	52-1620
BEILFUSS, Wilhelm	29	Berlin	54-0903
BEIMBR, Anton	26	Bremerhaven	53-1023
BEIMER, A.F.	21	Braunschweig	54-0872
BEINE, Carl	14	Hannover	50-1317
BEINE, Carl	59	Meinberg	52-0775
BEINHORN, Friedr.	30	Braunschweig	52-1423
BEINICKE, August	19	Rembeck	52-0515
BEINLE, Joh. G.	31	Neustadt	51-1245
BEISEN, Christine	28	Dankersen	52-1321
BEISLE, Christine	28	Kirchen Tell.	52-0351
BEISNER, Fr.	20	Oldendorf	51-0460
BEISSER, Paul	42	Evending	53-0905
Anna 28, Therese 6, Johann 2			
BEISSHEIM, Theodor	21	Cassel	51-0352
BEISSINGER, Eduard	23	Schwab-Gmuend	48-0447
BEISSLER, Michael	29	Hegesack	54-1168
BEISSNER, August	23	Bensen	49-0413
BEISSNER, Justine	30	Welsede	48-0445
Amalie 9m			
BEISSNER, L. (m)	45	Welsede	48-0445
W. (f) 40, H. (m) 18, L. (m) 12			
F. (m) 10, A. (m) 7, G. (m) 4, W. (f) 2			
BEISSNER, Louise	17	Hannover	51-1160
BEISSWENGER, Marie	19	Sulzbach	51-1796
BEITH, Victoria	24	Deiningen	54-0903
BEITZ, Anton	24	Langhaim	53-0324
BEJONES, E. (m)	22	Bremen	48-0453
BEKER, August	20	Usfeld	54-1717
BEKNAGEL, Albert	25	Kunzenhausen	51-1084
BELERSON, Henry	52	Furstenau	52-0804
Elisa 50, Garbin 28, Henry 13			
Wilhelmina 16			
BELING, Meta	22	Wolmerhausen	50-1071
BELLENBICK, James	19	Mittelruessel	49-0737
BELLINGER, Herrman	17	Alsfeld	53-0905
Elisabeth 28			
BELLINGRATH, L.(m)	39	Lennep	48-0565
BELLMER, Joh.	26	Emtinghausen	48-0053
BELMER, Christ. H	17	Stadel/Hann.	51-1796
BELNICKE, August	19	Rembeck	52-0515
BELOW, Elise	18	Kassel	52-1580
BELSCHNER, G. (m)	27	Rodenburg	49-0416
BELSKE, John	55	Holitz	54-1591
Anna 36, Franz 11, Joseph 3, Desert 10			
BELTE, Johann	35	Petershausen	53-1023
BELTE, Wilhelm	33	Petershausen	53-1023
BELZNER, Joh.	32	Rueckersdorf	52-1129
BEMM, Bruno	27	Mittweida	52-1321
BEMM, Ernst Eduard	32	Mittweida	53-1070
BENCKE, Carl	21	Hannover	48-1184
BENCKE, Charles H.	42	Philadelphia	53-0991
BENCKERT, Joh.	50	Stadtilm	48-1179
Elisabeth 54			
BENDER, Bazili	33	Ottersweier	53-1164
BENDER, Bernhard	29	Obergimpern	49-0912
BENDER, Carl	30	Hesse-Darmst.	51-1725
BENDER, Christ.	32	Cassel	54-0053
BENDER, Georg	20	Neuenheim	52-1625
Catharine 27, Jacob 4, Catharine 2			
BENDER, Heinrich	30	Homberg	54-1676
Elisabeth			
BENDER, Joh.	41	Neuwied	54-0987
Justine 38			
BENDER, Peter	30	Niederschelde	49-0781
Wilhelmine 21			
BENDL, Louise	48	Neuenkirchen	52-0558
BENECKENSTEIN, Chr	60	Nordhausen	54-0987
Christiane 24			
BENEDIKT, Henriett	17	Lichtenstadt	54-1297
BENEKE, Carl	52	Hartwigshof	53-0905
Friederika 51, Caroline 19, Hanni 13			
Auguste 11, Maria 7, Friedrich 21			

NAME	AGE	RESIDENCE	YR-LIST
BENETT, Edmund	22	Hamburg	53-0590
BENGES, Johannes		Frischborn	54-1575
BENHOLD, J. (m)	33	Niedergossa	52-0652
BENHOLZNE, Frank	26	Mittelruessel	49-0737
BENINJA, Hermann	29	Olden	51-1101
Ricka 24			
BENINJA, Ricka	24	Emden	51-1101
BENKER, Joh. Adam	28	Kirchenlainit	54-0930
BENNDORF, August	31	Altenburg	53-0942
BENNER, Georg	42	Nassau	53-0652
Sophie 24			
BENNER, Georg	37	Dillenburg	52-1105
Helene 37			
BENNIGSEN, George	27	Verden	53-1164
BENNING, D. (f)	58	Nenndorf	49-0416
BENNKEN, Hermann	48	Oldenburg	53-1164
BENS, Maria	24	Elberfeld	48-0565
Ferdinand 2, Maria 6m			
BENSCHNER, Cacilie	19	Neustadt	51-0756
Isidor 17			
BENSEN, L.	22	Bueckeburg	53-0492
BENTELS, Cacilie	26	Ravensberg	49-0574
BENTIEL, L. (m)	29	Altona	48-0453
BENTLER, Friedrich	40	Alsdorf	52-1410
Friedrike 37, Wilhelm 9, illegible			
BENTZ, Babette	21	Castell	54-1371
BENZ, Michael	25	Enkenbach	52-1661
BENZNEDER, Louise	24	Loewenstein/W	54-1092
BERBEG, Albertine	26	Coburg	53-1013
BERCKERT, Johann	26	Marztburg	51-1639
Wilhelmina 26, Carl 3			
BEREL, Mary	21	Breslau/Pr.	48-0053
Cis. 1			
BERER, Matthias	34	Illiconete	54-0918
Catharine 31, Franz 9, Mathias 6			
Albert 4, Johannes 3			
BERG, Bernh.	48	Hirschfeld	52-1661
Anna 48, Cath. 24, Ernst 16, Maria 6			
BERG, Catharina	23	Torgau	52-1661
BERG, G. Ludwig	35	Alsfeld	53-0905
Susanna 34, Amalie 9, Carolina 8, Georg 5			
BERG, Phil.	21	Germany	50-0472
BERG, v. Andr.	22	Schernek	50-1071
Eva 21			
BERGE, Chr.	27	Lispenhausen	52-1661
Anna 4			
BERGEN, v. Chr.	19	Hannover	50-0311
BERGER, Albert	34	Berlin	48-1184
BERGER, Anna	23	Nentershausen	53-0942
BERGER, Carl	52	Carlsruhe	53-0905
BERGER, Carl Ernst	12	Lauterberg	48-1131
BERGER, Emil	17	Giesen	53-1000
BERGER, Emilie	25	Bueckeburg	51-1245
Eduard 22, Bertha 32			
BERGER, F. Benj.	38	Burgstadt	53-1016
BERGER, Friedrich	52	Roringen	52-0563
Charlotte 54, Carl 30, Charlotte 25			
Lisette 24, Emilie 10, Wilhelm 5, Carl 15			
BERGER, Georg	30	Oberschnat/Bv	53-0628
BERGER, Joseph	26	Pest/Hungary	54-1092
BERGER, Marg.	29	Wiesenbach	52-0515
BERGER, Philipp	43	Wiesbaden/Nas	48-0447
Elizabeth 43, Wm. 19, Philippine 13			
Chr. 8, Sophia 5, Paul 11m			
BERGER, Pius	26	Kirchheim	54-0053
BERGFELDT, (m)	21	Hamburg	48-1243
BERGFELDT, Edward	34	Vienna	50-0944
BERGHAUS, Wilhelm	23	Prussia	54-1724
Wilhelmine 24, Juliane 6m			
BERGHORN, Wilh.	21	Henndorf	50-1317
BERGK, Martha	49	Gotha	54-0872
BERGK, Wilhelm	64	Gotha	54-0872
BERGLER, Therese	25	Carlsbach	53-0905
Agnes 20			
BERGMANN, Cath.	26	Coburg	54-0600
Gesine 28			
BERGMANN, Deric	30	Wachtendorf	53-1164
BERGMANN, E. (f)	22	Oelde	51-0517

NAME	AGE	RESIDENCE	YR-LIST
BERGMANN, Fr.	17	Duderstadt	51-1084
BERGMANN, Friedr.	26	Berka	54-1554
Karl 31, Heinrich 2, Karoline 25			
BERGMANN, Friedr.	16	Preussen	53-1086
BERGMANN, Gottfr.	19	Salzungen	52-0960
BERGMANN, H. (m)	21	Mariendorf	48-0453
BERGMANN, Hch Herm	24	Strange	48-1179
Caroline 20			
BERGMANN, Heinrich	30	Haste	51-1639
Maria 31, Mieche 3, Maria 9m			
BERGMANN, Heinrich	27	Meinberg	52-0775
Wilhelmine 48, Wilhelmine 24, Elisbeth 18			
Wilhelm 21, August 16, Conradine 14			
Sophie 12			
BERGMANN, Hermann	58	Hespehausen	54-1092
Johannetta 36, Caroline 12, Friedrike 4			
H. by			
BERGMANN, Joh. Ch.	61	Barmen	48-0565
Casp. 33, Carolina 31, Emilie 23			
BERGMANN, Johann	22	Strallendorf	54-1554
BERGMANN, Jos.	24	Brehlohn	51-1686
BERGMANN, Louise	19	Hagen	54-1443
BERGMANN, M.E. (f)	24	Engter	48-0445
J.D. (m) 22			
BERGMANN, Peter	38	Schiredorf	52-0775
Agnes 36, Margareth 14, Anna 8, Conrad 5			
Margarethe 9m			
BERGNER, Franz	18	Gr. Walbur	52-0370
BERGNER, J.	30	Schney	47-0868
Els. 34, F. 5			
BERGNER, Johanne	25	Kattenborn	50-0379
BERGS, Anton	43	Waldshut	51-1686
BERGSCHMIDT, W.(m)	24	Leiden	49-0416
BERK, Pauline	26	Tuebingen	54-1575
BERKENBUSCH, Carl	20	Einbeck	50-1317
BERKENKAMP, Henry	28	Schledehausen	51-1588
BERKENSTOCK, Maria	30	Strebensdorf	54-0600
Anna E. 27			
BERKER, Conrad	26	Offenbach	53-0991
Barbara 20, Anna Marg. 3m			
BERKER, Martin	30	Waldshut	51-1686
Gregor 29			
BERKERDON, Leanore	47	Peppinghausen	51-1588
Christine 15, Louise 17			
BERKES, Johann	21	Waldshut	51-1686
Caroline 21, Catharine 39, Jacob 7			
Anton 4			
BERKHAUSEN, Carl F	23	Pommern	53-0557
BERKHOLZ, H.	17	Kallenberg	52-1512
BERKING, August	26	Osterlinde	54-1371
BERKMANN, Engel	28	Linne	51-1588
BERKMEYER, Marie	68	Goettingen	52-1362
Marie 28			
BERKOWITZ, David	31	Erfurt	54-1649
Auguste 28, Carl 3, Linda 9m			
BERL, Francisca	23	Pelchau	48-1179
BERLEIN, Adam	42	Schippach/Bav	51-1532
Theresia 43, Martin 9			
BERMANN, Christian	47	Steinebkiel	53-1023
Dorothea 52, Heinrich 25			
BERMANN, T. (m)	21	Kirchbil	49-1517
BERMANT, Hermann	30	Wangen	49-0345
BERNAYS, Friedr. M	41	Frankenthal	54-1371
Franz Jocob 35, Amalie 28, Clementine 8			
BERNDT, Ernst	43	Berlin	48-1243
BERNDT, Gust. Jos.	18	Cassel	51-1160
BERNDT, H.G.	48	Koenigsberg	50-0439
BERNDT, Joh. Mich.	40	Scheuerbach	54-1094
Anna Barbara 37, Joh. Mich. 14, Johann 13			
BERNDT, Johannes	20	Lixfeld	52-1105
BERNDT, Martin	25	Kamenz	54-1078
BERNEMANNS, Marie	25	Bielefeld/Pr.	51-0048
BERNER, Chr.	19	Lengenfeld/We	52-0960
BERNER, Christine	19	Fredilslohe	51-0405
BERNERUNGEN, Wilh.	25	Altendorf	54-1716
BERNHARD, Elisabet	33	Ober Langerst	52-1200
BERNHARD, Franz	31	Steinfels/Bav	48-0053
Eva 25			

NAME	AGE	RESIDENCE	YR-LIST
BERNHARD, Gottlieb	50	Treben	54-0600
BERNHARD, Hannes	48	Steinau	53-0473
Maria 46, Louise 19, Elisabeth 16			
BERNHARD, Leopold	17	Gniewkowo	53-0888
BERNHARD, Wilh.	26	Bahlhorn	51-1160
BERNHARD, William	3-	Merseburg/Pr.	49-0365
BERNHARDT, Gottfr.	39	Sara	50-1132
Christine 37, Sophie 17, Johann 13			
Hermann 10, Ernestine 8			
BERNHARDT, Heinr.	17	Hirschberg	53-1062
BERNHARDT, Peter	28	Albertshausen	52-0563
BERNHEIMER, Minna	22	Baiersdorf	51-1245
BERNHOLD, J. (m)	33	Niedergossa	52-0652
BERNING, Marianne	22	Hoerstel	48-0269
BERNING, Wilhelm	41	Eikhorst	51-0352
BERNSCHLEGEL, Math	19	Wohnfels	48-1355
BERNSTEIN, August	22	Bieber	47-0828
BERREIS, Johann	30	Hessdorf	53-1016
Catharina 32			
BERRING, Hermann	21	Minden	54-1566
BERRING, Rudolph	20	Minden	52-1580
BERS, Heinr.	31	Wisloch	51-1686
BERSCHNEIDER, Conr	28	Eisentshafen	50-0379
BERSELE, Johann	18	Mroch	49-0345
BERT, David	17	Rohrbach	51-0352
BERTHAUS, August	40	Calbsried	50-0379
Judite 40, August 20, Christoph 18			
Fritz 12, Johanne 9, Minna 7, Edward 5			
BERTHOLD, Michael	31	Rossbach	51-1639
Pankratz 27, Margrethe 19			
BERTHOLD, Philipin	25	Bruck	53-0991
BERTLEIN, J. Mart.	23	Castell/Bav.	52-1332
Johann 27			
BERTOLD, Walburga	17	Richertswiese	52-1200
Therese 14			
BERTRAM, August	22	Gennersheim	54-1717
BERTRAM, Joh.	30	Osnabrueck	53-0590
BERTRAM, Joh. Pet.	39	Elberfeld	48-0565
BERTRAM, Therese	40	Buehren/Pr.	49-0365
Carolina 12, Carl 10, Fritz 8, Therese 7			
BERWALD, Joseph	58	Posen	51-1245
BERWALD, Wilh'mine	31	Rawitsch	51-1062
Cacilie 9, Gustav 8, child 5			
BESE, Andreas	26	Sperode	49-1106
BESEMANN, August	42	Illinois	51-1725
BESICH, Julie	35	Vienna	50-1236
BESKO, Charles	25	Berlin	48-1243
BESKO, Wilhelm	26	Berlin	48-1243
BESOLD, Georg	24	Nuernberg	50-1071
BESSLING, Heinrich	23	Rehburg	53-1070
BEST, Aug. Wilh.	50	Sachs.-Gotha	50-1236
BEST, Auguste	24	Muenden	52-1200
BEST, Margrethe	22	Holzappel	54-1371
BESTE, F. Arnold	24	Heepen	51-1160
BESTGEN, Carl	28	Gummersbach	50-0292
BETHEL, Cath.	21	Lageloh	49-0742
BETHGE, Emilie	27	Berlin	53-1164
BETHGE, Gustav	21	Bernburg	54-0987
BETHMANN, Auguste	22	Braunschweig	51-1245
Antonia 18			
BETTENHAUSEN, Meta	24	Nesselreden	48-0284
BETTER, Francisca	23	Vienna	48-1243
BETTER, Joseph	25	Geislingen	49-0345
BETTERMANN, Ern'tn	20	Freiburg	53-1062
BETTICH, Arwis	27	Schweinfurt	50-1317
BETTIN, Engel Mar.	20	Grosshegersdo	54-1168
BETZ, Adelheid	23	Eiterfeld/Hes	51-1532
BETZ, Johann	54	Burkersreuth	53-0637
Elis. Marg. 53			
BETZ, Valentin	41	Treysa	49-0345
BETZART, Johanna	31	Gera	53-0838
BETZINGER, Eberh.	28	Treuenberg	51-0352
BETZNER, Sophia		Fruchtwangen	54-1443
BETZOLD, Gunther	27	Breslau	49-1106
Karoline 24, Johann 23, Friedrich 21			
Johanna 19, Louise 17, Franz 15			
Karoline 11, Herrmann 9, Gottfried 7			
Henriette 5, Auguste 6m, Johanna 43			

NAME	AGE	RESIDENCE	YR-LIST
BEUCHER, J.F. (m)	21	Muhlhausen	49-1517
BEUER, Heinrich	36	Lobenstein	54-0987
Johanne 48, Louise 21, Carl 16, Anton 4			
Emma 9, Christian 8			
BEUERMANN, Ludwig	35	Imsen	48-1184
BEUGMANN, A.M. (f)	20	Fecku	51-0517
BEUKE, J.H.	38	Holte	52-1512
Maria 39, G.H.(m) 15, J.C.(m) 13			
J.F.(m) 10, T.M.(m) 8, J.H.L.(m) 6			
J.H. 6m			
BEULER, H.	44	Oberschmith	54-1716
BEULSHAUSEN, Hch A	20	Brunswick	51-1532
BEUMEL, Johann	36	Kernat/Bav.	52-1332
BEUNER, Margrethe	59	Humrechtshaus	54-1283
BEUNLEIN, Joh.	28	Humrechtshaus	54-1283
Dorothea 28, Catharina 3, Bernhard by			
BEUSCHLAG, J Fried	22	Noerdlingen	54-1297
BEUTEL, George A.	22	Mittelruessel	49-0737
BEUTEL, Gottfried	30	Gramzow	53-0585
Marie 28, Friedrich 4, Auguste 2			
Ernestine 1			
BEUTEL, Wilhelmine	23	Grabzow	54-0872
BEUTLER, Franz	30	Eilenburg	49-1358
Johanna 33, Fr. (f) by			
BEUTLER, Helene	23	Groppel/Pr.	53-0628
BEUTLER, Joh Georg	31	Untergoetting	49-0352
BEVER, Heinrich	36	Lobenstein	54-0987
Johanne 48, Louise 21, Carl 16, Anton 4			
Emma 9, Christian 8			
BEVERSEN, Charles	22	Bueckeburg	52-1304
BEVERUNG, Henry	49	Milwaukee	53-0991
BEWANDEWSKY, Aug.	21	Elbing	54-0850
BEY, Friedericke	27	Heyn/Hannover	51-1725
BEYEL, Christian	32	Fischbach/Nas	53-0628
Catharina 27, Johannes 5			
BEYER, Adolph	16	Soden	53-0838
BEYER, Anna	24	Berkheim	49-0329
BEYER, August	40	Gebstedt	52-1148
Christ. Mar. 34, Carl 12, Pauline 11			
Robert 3, Ernst 9m			
BEYER, Bernh.	31	Lesering	53-0914
BEYER, Caspar	20	Farmbach	51-1455
BEYER, Cath. Anna	15	Frankenberg	53-1016
Cath. Maria 22, Andreas 14, Werner 15			
BEYER, Chr. Frdr.	44	Berlin	51-0352
BEYER, Christ Gott	53	Kodritzsch	52-1148
Eva Maria 42, Christ. Teod 23			
Augustine F. 15, Ida Albertin 9			
BEYER, Christ.	44	Wiedelah	54-0987
BEYER, Christoph	27	Moenchhosbach	53-0320
Catharine 26, Heinrich 6m			
BEYER, Conrad	35	Rengshausen	54-0930
BEYER, Elisabeth	18	Freirittenbac	48-1179
BEYER, Elisabeth	19	Frankenberg	47-0828
BEYER, Heinrich	16	Beverstedt/Ha	51-1725
BEYER, Joh. Georg	18	Lichelau	54-0987
BEYER, Johann	33	Hagenspitz	52-1148
Wilhelmine 34, Johann G.H. 6			
BEYER, Josepha	31	Straf/Bav.	49-0365
BEYER, Louis	30	Lichtenstein	48-1131
BEYER, Magdalene	35	Hettenhausen	50-0840
Mathias 8			
BEYER, Mathias	8	Culmbach	50-0840
BEYER, Oswald	21	Schuerzingen	52-1148
BEYERN, Auguste	18	Frankenhausen	54-0918
BEYERSDORF, Fanny	27	Frankfurt/M.	53-0991
BEYFUSS, Kunigunde	25	Kalterbrunn	48-1131
BEYHL, Joh. George	33	Sunzenhausen	52-1304
Friederike 40			
BEYRER, Jacob	24	Frauenberg	53-0652
BEYSCHLAG, Carl	34	Noerdlingen	51-1532
Catharina 30, Carl 5, Emma by			
BFEUSS, Kunigunde	25	Kalterbrunn	48-1131
BHOME, Carl	50	Greifendorf	53-0590
Caroline 48, Emil 19			
BIBELMANN, August	27	Brisenenhaus	53-0825
BICKEL, Anna Marg.	3m	Laufe	54-1647
BICKEL, Carl	22	Schweigau	52-0370

NAME	AGE	RESIDENCE	YR-LIST
BICKERS, Margareth	18	Wittlage	49-0413
BICKING, Friedrich	29	Immenrode	54-0903
Friederike 25, Carl 3, Gunther by			
Christoph 58, Fritz 12			
BICKMANN, Justine	16	Ikenhausen	53-1070
BICKNAESE, H. (m)	47	Windheim	54-1566
S. (m) 20			
BIDER, J. (m)	18	Russern	50-0746
BIEBER, Heinr.	19	Homburg	49-0383
BIEBERBACH, Christ	24	Weilsdorf	53-0324
Elisabeth 23, Moritz 1			
BIEDENBENDER, J. H	40	Salchendorf	52-1512
Maria 36, Georg 17, Philipp 14			
Christina 12, Adam 9, Heinrich 5			
Johannes 1			
BIEDERKEB, Wilhelm	28	Goddelheim	50-1067
BIEDERMANN, J. Chr	29	Lichtendanna	48-0887
Margarethe 33, Christoph 61, Richard 7			
Ernestine 4			
BIEDEROFF, Friedr.	19	Leugast	52-1512
BIEG, Valentin	36	Fussach	53-1164
BIEGERT, Friedrich	32	Moringen/Hann	51-1532
BIEHENBERG, Marie	18	Bremerhaven	54-0987
BIEHL, Carl	27	Fritzlar	47-0828
BIEHL, Christine	26	Huenfeld	52-0563
BIEHL, Ludw.	20	Homburg	54-1575
Nicolaus 17			
BIEHL, Philipp	24	Holzhausen	52-1304
BIEHLER, Carl	23	Altenburg	50-0311
Anna 19			
BIEHLMUELLER, Andr	20	Mittelsinn	52-0563
BIEKER, Wilhelm Fr	20	Tharnbach	53-0838
BIEL, Heinrich	37	Churhessen	52-1620
Helene 28, Anna 2			
BIELER, Gottlieb	49	Crimmitschau	54-0987
Christine 49			
BIEMANN, Heinrich	30	Hannover	49-0329
BIENFANG, Joh.	18	Seufsen	51-1640
BIENLEIN, Georg	33	Weissmein	53-0267
BIER, E.	16	Bremerhaven	53-0914
J.P. 18			
BIER, Philipp	30	Altenmarschen	52-1661
Catharina 31, Martha 24, Johannes 8			
Heinrich 3			
BIERHAGEN, J.H.	24	Essen	53-1086
Marie 23			
BIERMANN, C.F.	22	Hoplingen	54-0918
BIERMANN, Carl	25	Herford	53-1000
BIERMANN, Charles	27	Saffenhausen	50-0840
BIERMANN, Christ.	50	Uslar	54-1283
W. 49, Dietr. 15			
BIERMANN, Heinrich	31	Olbersleben	54-1283
BIERMANN, Johann	52	Frankenberg	54-0918
Conrad 20, Heinrich 14			
BIERMEIER, Leonh.	30	Doeckingen	54-0903
Mar. Cath. 32, Wilhelm 4, Marie by			
BIERSACK, Anton	23	Irreloh/Bay.	51-1725
Anna 25, Joseph 11m			
BIERSACK, Therese	28	Panholz	54-1078
BIERWIRTH, Anna	21	Grossmansgroe	52-1661
BIESENBRUCH, (m)		Harmen	54-0987
Catharina 37, Marie 10, Emilie by			
BIESSEN, A.M.	28	Unteressen	54-1419
BIGGE, M. (f)	30	New York	40-1015
BILEKE, Martin	50	Katzmad	54-1676
Katharina 63			
BILK, Andreas	21	Trossingen/Wu	52-0351
BILKER, Cassen	19	Luneberg	54-1716
BILLER, Elisabeth	22	Kohlgrund/Wal	53-0628
BILLET, Joh Friedr	21	Ruppern	52-0370
BILLIARD, Madame	27	Baltimore	48-1015
BILLING, Gottlieb	29	Geuzeldorf	53-0942
BILLMANN, Henrica	21	Burwangen/Bad	52-0117
BILSE, Dorothea	13	Bringhausen	54-0600
Gertrud 16			
BILZ, Franz	33	Limbach	49-0742
BIMBACH, Rosalie	42	Halle	54-0987
BINDER, August	28	Mergenheim	53-0905

NAME	AGE	RESIDENCE	YR-LIST
Johanna 28, Gottlieb 7			
BINDER, Conrad	27	Soetern	54-0918
BINDER, Gottlieb	18	Mittelruessel	49-0737
Carth. 23, Wilhelmine 21			
BINDER, Isaac	19	Mohringen	54-1341
BINDER, Joh. Fried	26	Dorf Riedinge	49-0352
BINDER, Michael	42	Altenstadt	54-1341
Ursula 28, daughter 10m			
BING, Loise		Salzing	53-0324
BINGBACH, Johann	45	Dietz	53-0825
BINGEN, Diedr.	19	Marburg	53-1013
Juliane 25			
BINKE, George	52	Elsching	53-0914
Sophie 56			
BINNER, Joh. Georg	50	Bettwar	53-0590
BINNING, Wilhelm	19	Kleinern	50-0840
BIRBAUM, Maria	56	Richmond	52-1512
BIRCHOFF, Meta	21	Hannover/Hann	51-0048
BIRK, Andreas	23	Lauffen/Wuert	51-1725
BIRK, J. (m)	40	Mannheim	48-0445
BIRKENHAUER, Heinr	33	Helminghausen	54-1092
BIRKENSTOCK, Gust.	24	Breslau	54-0053
BIRKLE, Christiane	31	Kirchberg	49-0352
BIRKMANN, Heinrich	28	Holzhausen	49-0352
BIRNER, Wolf	32	Arzberg	50-1236
BIRNEWEISS, Ludw.	28	Sibecksen	54-1078
Heinr. 28			
BISCHGER, J. F.(m)	22	Osnabrueck	52-1512
BISCHOF, Heinr.	28	Frankenau	54-1554
Philipp 24			
BISCHOF, Johannes	24	Ornshausen	53-0585
BISCHOF, Nicolaus	16	Oldenburg	49-0329
BISCHOFF, Adolph	19	Achim	52-1512
BISCHOFF, Carl	19	Schlossheltru	49-0781
BISCHOFF, Christ.	26	Wartmannsroth	54-1168
Ehrhardt 22			
BISCHOFF, Elis.	33	Rormebeck	53-1164
Catharina 8, James 6, Eliza 4, Theodor by			
BISCHOFF, Ferd.	28	Gruenberg	52-1512
BISCHOFF, Friedr.	20	Levern	53-1000
BISCHOFF, Friedr.	20	Ornshausen	53-0585
Paulus 17			
BISCHOFF, Heinrich	24	Bremen	54-1717
BISCHOFF, Henry	26	New York	53-0991
Amalia 21, Amelia 2, Henry by			
BISCHOFF, Hermann	29	Heuten/Pr.	51-1532
Theresia 28, Franz Jos. 1			
BISCHOFF, Joh.	24	Leeste	50-0439
BISCHOFF, Meta	20	Ressnen	52-1362
BISCHOP, Victor	43	New York	48-1015
BISIG, Caspar	30	Einsiedeln	53-0991
Thomas 21			
BISINGER, Georg	38	Osterberg	53-0324
BISMANN, F. Carl	28	Oberkreisstad	49-0365
BISSLER, Maton	35	Albany	48-1131
BISWANGEN, Joh.	25	Wilhelmsburg	54-1168
BITSCH, Johann	22	Reitelsbach	54-0872
Anna 21			
BITSFELD, Joseph	37	Bayern	54-1716
BITTEL, Barbara	33	Nidda	52-1321
Carl 10, Caroline 8, Marg. 9m			
BITTEL, Peter	40	Nidda	52-1321
BITTER, Berh.	28	Muenster	54-1724
BITTER, Heinrich	14	Altendorf	54-0987
BITTER, Ludwig	28	Braunschweig	52-1423
Henriette 24			
BITTER, Wilhelm	23	Warburg	50-0292
BITTLINGMAIER, Chr	30	Waldhausen	53-0320
BITTMANN, Hermann	18	Ikenhausen	50-0292
BITTNER, Ferdinand	36	Schlesien	52-1620
Caroline 22			
BIVOUR, August	27	Quedlinburg	52-1580
Louise 28			
BLACK, C.	21	Arnsheim	51-0517
BLACOTTA, Joh.	18	Kleinwalfersd	49-1358
BLAM, Joh.	20	Eichelsachsen	52-1321
BLANK, Heinrich	16	Beverstedt	51-1725
BLANK, Lisette	35	Isny	54-1371

NAME	AGE	RESIDENCE	YR-LIST
BLANK, Marg.	20	Suzburg	51-1455
BLANK, Marie	24	Aschbach	52-1464
BLANKE, August	23	Palermo	54-1371
BLANKE, Cath.	26	Bederkesa	49-0574
BLANKE, Engelbert	44	Muenster	52-0563
BLANKE, Fr. Wilh.	34	Elberfeld	48-0565
BLANKE, Johann	29	Lehe	52-1580
BLANKEMEYER, Henry	60	Holstein	51-1588
Louisa 59, Charles 35, Catherine 33 Anna 16, Louisa 9			
BLANKEN, Joh.	21	Hepstedt	54-0987
BLANKEN, Nicolaus	19	Kuhstedt/Hann	50-0323
BLANKENMEIER, J.M.	33	Osnabrueck	52-1512
Cath. 38, Christina 12, G.H.(m) 8 E.H.(m) 6			
BLANKENSEE, Nanny	23	Warburg	53-1023
BLANKMEIER, Clara	48	Halle	54-1554
Anna 12, Hermann 54, Hermann 18			
BLASCHKE, F. (m)	36	Schildberg	52-0652
Cath. A. 34			
BLASS, Mathilde	16	Noerdlingen	54-1297
BLASSER, Joseph	25	Amerbach	51-1739
BLAU, Meier	24	Gehaus	53-0942
Moses 24			
BLAUME, Philippine	18	Meinsen	52-1321
BLAUROCK, Elis.	23	Tiefenort	49-0413
BLECHMANN, Lisette	35	Essen	53-1086
Adolphine 8, Emil 7, Herrmann 2			
BLECHSCHMIDT, H.	30	Limburg	49-0416
BLECKE, Louisa	20	Iloese	54-1470
Diedr. 29			
BLECKENSCHMIDT, M.	21	Bayern	53-0557
BLEECK, Friedrich	23	Reburg	50-1067
BLEESINE, Helene	34	Aurich	54-0987
Marianne 30			
BLEIBTREU, Adam	22	Babenhausen	54-0987
Caethchen 25, Amalie by			
BLEILE, Rosina	17	Welzheim	53-0320
BLEISENSTEINER, V.	32	Schmatzhausen	54-1443
BLESSMANN, Wilhelm	30	Wehnde/Hannov	54-0965
BLETTNER, Heinr.	23	Konradsreuth	47-0868
BLEXENTORF, Cath.	22	Landhausen/Ha	51-1796
BLIBOLD, Margrete	20	Hintersteinen	52-0370
Andr. 15			
BLIEMER, Julius	19	Altheinrichau	54-1443
Franz 23			
BLIND, Beta	24	Coburg	53-1013
Franciska 3			
BLIND, Chr.	25	Wuertt.	54-1724
BLISANE, Gerhard	39	Bremen	54-0987
Marie 39			
BLISS, Friedrich	20	Stargard	53-1000
BLOCH, Juditha	18	Swihan	54-1078
BLOCK, Adolph	16	Molutzka	54-1078
BLOCK, Jane	36	Hannover	48-1209
BLOEMEKE, Franz	31	Welda	52-1304
BLOEMER, Elisabeth	50	Dinklage	49-1358
Elisabeth 73, Bernhard 24, Andreas 26 Dom. 24, Clem. 15, Fina 18, Elisabeth 22			
BLOEMKER, Wilhelm	18	Leinen	51-1438
BLOENIEKE, Franz	31	Welda	52-1304
BLOETNER, Christ.	27	Schleusingen	52-1512
BLOHM, Gottl.	20	New York	52-0895
BLOHM, Johann	25	Geestendorf	48-1355
Wilhelm 23			
BLOHM, Margareta	25	Varel	51-0652
BLOHM, Wilhelm N.	19	Langenhausen	53-0905
BLOHME, Fr.	20	Kirchbuetzen	51-0460
BLOICHER, M.	39	Itelhofen	47-0868
A. 37, Joh. 8, Ba. 7, A. 5			
BLOMS, An. Kat.	37	Rostuek/Olden	51-1796
BLUECHER, Peter	28	Oberhoerle/He	52-0807
BLUECKER, J Traug.	23	Tappshoedel	51-1101
BLUEGGE, Louis	39	Gnoeren/Meckl	52-0807
Maria 36			
BLUEHR, J. Gesine	26	Bornitz	51-1686
BLUM, Bernh.	20	Aufhausen	54-0872
BLUM, Christ.	24	Jlagfeld	53-0582
BLUM, Christoph	19	Baden	52-1512
BLUM, Conrad	31	Werda	54-0930
Catharina 31, Anna Doro. 56, Catharina 7 Elisabeth 5, Conrad 3, Margaretha by Catharina 28, Anna Doro. 5			
BLUM, Daniel	16	Keittenau	54-1419
BLUM, Friedrich	26	Liebenstein	51-1588
BLUM, Heinr.	37	Petersberg/He	52-0960
Cath. 37, Emil 8, Eleanore 6, Mathilde 5			
BLUM, Heinr.	21	Arolsen	52-1321
BLUM, Heinrich	18	Hessen	52-0699
BLUM, Joseph	22	Tierkheim	53-0888
BLUM, Xaver	53	Herrischried	54-0850
Marie 53, Magdalena 22, Max 11			
BLUMANN, Barbara	19	Neuhof/Bav.	53-0628
BLUMBERG, Joseph	53	Lauban	53-0888
Charlotte 51, Agnes by			
BLUME, Carl	58	Greifendorf	53-0590
Caroline 48, Emil 19			
BLUME, Ernest	35	Coppenbruegge	53-0991
Christina 31, Lina 9, Friedrich 7 Henry 5, Adolphus 2			
BLUMENFELD, Gerh.	17	Momberg	53-0590
BLUMENFELD, Mos.	16	Westheim	53-0928
BLUMENFELDT, Rosa	21	Bayreuth	48-0887
BLUMENSTEIN, Cath.	18	Bonshausen	53-1023
BLUMENSTEIN, H.	18	Schmalkalden	54-1716
BLUMENTHAL, Moses	27	Hessen	52-0895
BLUMER, Herm.	30	Bausdorf	52-1512
Friedr. 26			
BLUMFELD, Marie	24	Waldstetten	53-0320
Simon 30			
BLUMFELD, Simon	30	Wolferstadt	53-0320
BLUMGART, Moses	33	Muenchen/Bav.	52-1423
BLUTH, Martha	46	Prussia	54-1724
BLUTIAN, John	16	Waechtersbach	53-0825
BLYN, Ludwig		Zwesten	53-0942
BOBEL, Conrad	25	Maden	52-0095
Johann 23			
BOBEL, Robert	32	Bitterfeld	53-0473
BOCHHOF, Heinrich	17	Aschen	53-1062
BOCHMANN, Theodor	26	Schneeberg	53-1164
BOCHME, Carl	21	Biberach	47-0672
BOCK, Bernh.		Telligt	54-1575
BOCK, Bernh.		Telgte	54-1575
BOCK, Carl	38	Bederkesa	51-1084
Anna 30, Johann 9, Trina 5, Anna 7 Marie 3, Mathias 40			
BOCK, Elise	20	Gudensberg	52-0370
BOCK, Ernst	48	Baiern	51-1245
BOCK, Friederike	56	Wahrendahl	54-1575
August 27, Otto 18, Ferdinand 15			
BOCK, Friedrich	21	Lausnitz	54-1283
BOCK, Gottlieb	53	Sachsen	53-0590
BOCK, H.F.	30	Bodenwerder	54-1470
Catharine 30, son 7m			
BOCK, Heinr.	33	Brunswick	50-1317
Wilhelmine 21, Friederike 19, Adolphine 8 Anna 4, Otto 8m, Dorothea 40			
BOCK, Henry	19	Darmstadt	53-0991
BOCK, Joh. Andr.	25	Gibese	52-0563
BOCKELMANN, Aug'te	48	Herford	48-1179
Marie 12			
BOCKER, Carl	43	Meinbrixen	49-0781
Friederike 35, Auguste 15, Heinrich 13 Louise 11, Caroline 4, Doretta 3, baby			
BOCKER, Carl Fried	30	Stanau	54-1297
Rosina 28, Therese 6, Hermann 4			
BOCKER, Christ. Fr	40	Grosspuerschu	54-1297
Marie 45, Charlotte 14, Rosine 7, Carl 4			
BOCKER, Christian	20	Gellenhausen	53-1023
BOCKHAUS, Marie	16	Lindewerra	51-1438
BOCKMANN, Heinr.	18	Hannover	50-1317
BOCKMANN, Joh.	25	Lehe	49-0329
BODANI, Louisa	33	Sinzheim	53-1164
BODANI, Marie	9	Sinsheim	54-1371
BODDENBURGER, Jul.	16	Leidsmansdorf	53-1062
BODE, Franz	22	Gieboldshause	51-1640

NAME	AGE	RESIDENCE	YR-LIST
BODE, Henry	21	Barrien	53-1164
BODE, Johann	25	Hilscheid	53-1023
BODE, Julius	40	Gebhardshagen	54-1443
Dorothea 36, Hermann 6			
BODE, Wilhelm	24	Berka	54-1554
BODEFELD, Fr. Wm.	18	Hille	51-1455
BODEKER, Wilh'mine	38	Ottenhausen	48-0565
BODEMEYER, Ludw.	19	Landsbergen	50-1071
BODEN, Sabine	34	Wehnde/Hann.	54-0965
BODENBERG, Peter	20	Ebersdorf	49-0345
BODENER, Elisabeth	19	Fichtelberg	54-0903
BODENSCHATZ, Joh.	26	Selwitz	53-1023
BODENSTAB, Amalie	29	Nordheim	53-0492
BODENSTEIN, Bertha	18	Gotha	54-0987
BODENSTEIN, Georg	34	Liebenstein	54-0987
Ernestine 24, Carl 2			
BODENSTEIN, Julia	22	Sontra	52-1304
BODESHEIM, Therese	26	Grossenbach	52-0515
M. (f) 20			
BODETZ, Friedr.	36	Calbe	48-1131
BODI, Diedr.	55	Hehlen	48-1114
Johanna 49, Diedr. 24, Carl 18, W. Grs 15			
Anna 12			
BOEBER, Heinrich	55	Freudschaft	53-0628
Martha Elisa 57			
BOECK, Georg	35	Augsburg	54-1001
Caroline 27, son 3			
BOECKER, Arnold	20	Bremen	53-0991
BOECKER, Friedrike	18	Bofzen	49-0574
BOECKLER, Christof	35	Heiligenstadt	52-0699
BOECKNER, Julius	17	Dissen	54-1371
BOEDEKER, E. (f)	26	Altona	48-0453
BOEDING, Friedr.	26	Grotsch	49-1106
Ernst. 28, Therese 2, Friedrich 9m			
BOEDJER, Heinr.	26	Ritterhude	51-1686
Catharine 22			
BOEDKER, Wilhelm	21	Lewertia/Prus	53-0628
BOEGELEIN, Marie	21	Weinberg	52-1661
BOEGER, Friedr.	18	Erckeln	54-0600
BOEHACK, E.C.	24	Osterwranna	51-1160
BOEHLING, Claus	27	Rhade/Hann.	53-0475
BOEHLING, Joh.	21	Wihldorf	49-0574
BOEHM, Conrad	36	Oberzell	53-0435
Catharine 42, Anna 15, Andreas 25			
Wilhelm 23			
BOEHM, Georg	36	Massenhausen	52-1423
BOEHM, Gerson	15	Hoeringhausen	54-0987
BOEHM, Heinr.	29	Oberfranken	50-1236
BOEHM, Joh.	52	Burgham	50-0472
BOEHM, John	22	Selbitz	49-1106
BOEHM, John	27	Lutter/Bav.	50-0323
BOEHM, John	47	Wurstenselbit	49-1106
BOEHM, Valentin	26	Wittgen	47-0828
Peter 27			
BOEHME, Bertha	15	Celle	53-1164
BOEHME, C.G.	58	Stelzendorf	53-1070
Appolonia 57			
BOEHME, Carl	31	Crimmitschau	53-0928
Wilh. 28, Hermann 9, Richard 6			
Friedrich 5, Hermann 3, Paul 3m			
BOEHME, Carl	23	Laxes	54-1443
BOEHME, Fritz	45	Freiburg	50-1067
BOEHME, Heinr Aug.	32	Osterfeld	53-1000
BOEHME, John	28	Reumintz	50-0840
Christiane 34, Augustus 1			
BOEHMER, Friedr.	29	Boelhorst	49-0329
W. (m) 26			
BOEHMER, Heinrich	29	Bohnhorst	52-1661
Anna 24, Chr. 20, Emilie 18, Aug. 15			
Carl 13, Maria 9, Caroline 4, Ernst by			
BOEHMER, Heinrich	27	Gieboldshause	52-0563
BOEHMER, Herrmann	22	Magdeburg/Pr.	52-1332
Hermine 18			
BOEHMER, Wilhelm	50	Bohnhorst	52-1661
Christine 47, Char. 7, Sophia 59			
BOEHNE, Friedr.	20	Hannover/Hann	51-0048
BOEHNER, Regina	23	Roth	52-0279
BOEHNLEIN, John	20	Steinweisen	53-0914

NAME	AGE	RESIDENCE	YR-LIST
BOEKE, W. (m)	22	Oke	54-1341
BOEKEL, Johann	27	Holte/Hann.	51-1725
BOEKELMANN, Johann	31	Bennreuth	54-1554
BOEKER, Johann	46	Lennep	54-1371
Julie 23			
BOELE, Wilhelm	22	Sudeck	52-1661
BOELER, Carl	45	Bayern	53-0590
Sophie 43			
BOELKEN, H.	28	Wulsdorf	51-0460
BOEMER, Wilh.	21	Bollhorst	52-1661
BOEMERS, Gustav	17	Dresden	48-0406
BOEMKE, Fritz	19	Dortmund	53-0552
BOENERT, Marie A.	22	Altenburg	50-0311
BOENING, Christian	42	Wuertenberg	53-0557
BOENNIGER, Friedr.	29	Noerdlingen	51-1438
BOENNINGER, Friedr	29	Noerdlingen	51-1438
BOERGES, Elise	21	Osnabrueck	52-1512
BOERGHAUSEN, Juls.	20	Brudershausen	54-0882
BOERMANN, Friedr W	30	Nordholz/Lipp	51-1725
BOERMANN, Heinrich	42	Nordholz/Lipp	51-1725
Caroline 37, John Henry 9, Friedr. Wm. 5			
Christine 10m			
BOERNER, Ernestine	18	Ditschenbora	54-0987
BOERNER, Heinrich	18	Lengsfeld	49-0413
Catharina 14			
BOERNER, Henry	25	Wiesbaden/Nas	48-0447
BOERNER, W. (m)	27	Wiesbaden/Nas	48-0447
BOERRIKE, Anton	36	Lauga	52-1105
BOES, Carl	33	Visselhoevede	47-0872
Maria 31, Carl 12			
BOESCHE, Theod.	25	Freren/Hann.	51-0048
BOESCHEN, Johann	20	Walling	54-1168
BOESCHLE, Jacob	18	Leonberg/Wuer	52-0351
BOESE, Carl M.	20	Buttel/Old.	54-1092
BOESE, Friedrich	25	Ovelgoenne	49-0324
BOESE, Georg	30	Gotha	53-0473
BOESE, Heinr.	19	Wunsdorf	50-0439
BOESENBERG, Adolph	26	Neustadt	48-0887
BOETCHER, Friedr.	18	Weihe/Hann.	54-1092
BOETN, Johann	23	Hunelsmoder	48-0101
BOETTCHER, Clothar	29	Leipzig	51-0460
BOETTCHER, Ed.	21	Frankenberg	49-1358
BOETTCHER, Joh Got	32	Schoenbonn	53-1000
Auguste 25			
BOETTCHER, Valent.	22	Mengsdorf/Hes	52-0960
A.M. (f) 20			
BOETTER, Walpurga	33	Pfoerring	54-1078
BOETTGER, Auguste	45	Crimmitschau	54-0600
BOETTGER, John	48	St. Annen	53-0991
Louisa 20			
BOETTIGER, Melch.	24	Niederstolzin	54-0600
BOETTNER, Anna	23	Zelle	51-1160
Johanna H. 6m			
BOETTNER, Christ.	37	Hersfeld	53-1164
BOETZEL, Carl	20	Heina	53-0585
BOGEN, Conrad	19	Riepen	50-1132
BOGNER, Steph.	28	Badenhofen	52-1129
Anna M. 19, Anna 17, baby (f) bob			
BOHDE, Caroline	28	Angerstein	54-1371
BOHL, Anna	17	Lehe	51-0756
Claus 14			
BOHL, Mathias	31	Mittelruessel	49-0737
BOHLE, R.	35	Auma	54-1566
Johann 28, Carl 4, K. 6m			
BOHLE, Wilhelmine	19	Melle	54-1297
BOHLEN, Heinrich	18	Hannover	53-0628
BOHLEN, Herm.	25	Sittling	54-1078
BOHLKEN, Johann	27	New York	54-0987
BOHLS, Becka	21	Lehe	54-1371
BOHLSEN, B.	34	Hannover	54-1724
BOHLSEN, Meta	24	Marx/Deckhaus	53-0435
BOHLZ, Friedrich	49	Hannover	53-0825
Eleonore 26, August 16, Charlotte 7			
BOHM, Carl	28	Treusin	54-1371
BOHM, Conrad	18	Kalchreuth	52-0515
Conrad 27			
BOHM, Eva	25	Haag	48-0951
BOHM, Joh.	26	Gerafeld	52-0558

NAME	AGE	RESIDENCE	YR-LIST
H. (f) 20			
BOHME, Fr. Louis	17	Schilbach	48-1114
BOHME, Lud.	30	Badenburg	49-0781
Adalgunde 18, Wilhelm 14			
BOHME, Traugott	24	Berlin	48-1243
BOHMER, Wm.	30	Helden	51-1588
BOHMKORF, A. (f)	27	Leer	48-0453
BOHN, August	26	Wunstorf	53-0585
BOHN, C. (m)	18	Lengsfeld	54-1341
Catherine 16			
BOHN, Franz	36	Waldmichelbac	52-0117
BOHN, Henriette	15	Lengsfeld	49-0413
BOHN, John	25	Mittelruessel	49-0737
BOHN, Lorenz	30	Gerschfeld	52-1362
BOHN, Maria	44	Langensalza	54-0987
Ernst 14, Hermann 9, Marie 5, Albert 2			
BOHNE, Christina	28	Armsfeld	51-0405
BOHNE, Ferd.	29	Elberfeld	54-1168
BOHNE, Fr. (m)	36	Zerbst	49-0324
Auguste 29			
BOHNE, Georg	49	Gleichen	52-1661
BOHNE, Hein.	24	Laden	52-1321
BOHNE, Henry	28	Coesfeld	53-0991
Josephine 25			
BOHNE, Wilh.	15	Dankersen	52-1321
BOHNER, John	26	Weingarten	52-0279
Regina 28, Carl 5			
BOHNEWALD, Wilhelm	25	Spanbeck	54-1168
BOHRBACH, Anna Cat	22	Meckburg/Hess	52-0351
BOHRER, Johann	26	Ansbach	54-1566
Anna 26			
BOHRES, Adolph	33	Kohlenbeck	53-0825
Theresia 34, Adolph 4, Joseph 2			
BOIK, Conrad	22	Hilpoldstein	50-0840
BOIKEN, Betty	23	Jewer	53-0590
Sophie 22, Emil 17			
BOLEG, Sophie	24	Wuerttemberg	53-0557
Theckla 24			
BOLEG, Sophie	24	Wuertenberg	53-0557
Theckla 24			
BOLEY, Mendel	14	Ungedanken	54-0053
BOLKE, Friedrich	37	Siegen	53-0324
BOLKENIUS, Albert	27	Coeln	48-0887
BOLL, Gottlieb	20	Reutlingen	49-0329
BOLL, Melchior	23	Besse	54-1566
BOLLAND, Marie	21	Bremen	54-1168
BOLLE, Carl Fr.	25	Estedt	54-1371
BOLLE, Christian	24	Spanbeck	54-1168
Friedrich 22			
BOLLE, Franz	17	Schleusingen	54-0903
BOLLE, Gertrud	24	Senden	54-1554
BOLLE, W.	33	Eberschuetz	54-1168
Ludwig 24, Martha 59			
BOLLMANN, Anna	20	Arsten	53-1070
BOLLMANN, Heinrich	16	Bremen	51-1245
BOLLMANN, Lima (m)	54	Schorst	48-1131
Georg 23, Minna 19, Doris (m) 16			
Louise 13			
BOLLMEYER, Dietr.	30	Dorum	49-0329
BOLLWAGEN, Louis	25	Hohm	51-1640
BOLLWINKEL, Johann	21	Hannover	49-0329
BOLOOGT, W. (m)	35	Bielefeld	52-0652
BOLSEN, Andreas	41	Roringen	52-0563
Caroline 37, Louis 13, Heinrich 10			
Eduard 8, Caroline 6, Carl 8m			
BOLT, Elisabeth	27	Baiern	54-1554
BOLTE, Christian	20	Hoexter	53-0991
BOLTE, Wilhelm	19	Verden	52-1452
BOLTEN, Sophie	22	Brockhausen	52-1512
BOLTZ, Marie	48	Leimersheim	54-1168
Anna 20			
BOLZ, Heinrich	53	Erdmannsroth	52-1661
Heinr. 23, Joh. 17			
BOMM, Fr. (m)	21	Nentershausen	48-0269
BOMMERSBERGER, J.	30	Munster	52-0558
BOMMERSHEIM, Peter	53	Obernhofen	52-1105
BONAKER, August	18	Frankenberg	53-1016
BONDET, Pauline	22	U.S.	48-1243
BONER, Louis	33	Muenster/Pr.	51-1532
BONERT, Jacob	18	Ostheim	51-0500
BONGARDS, G. (m)	33	Schwafheim/Pr	48-0447
Jacob 23			
BONIKEL, Jakob	30	Bayern	52-1620
Margareth 30, Adam 9m			
BONING, Charlotte	41	Holdorf	48-0887
Henry 13			
BONKE, Herm. Bernh	43	Hannover	51-1725
BONNE, Caroline	19	Ironheim	53-0905
BONNE, Ester	24	Cronheim	52-0895
BONNET, H.S.	24	Wolfshagen	54-1566
BONORELEN, Carl	18	Weirlen	52-1321
BONSCH, Henriette	25	Gnadenfeldt	53-0914
BONTZE, Heinrich	15	Grundt	51-0756
Wilhelm 10			
BOOKEN, Marie	15	Hannover	49-0329
BOOMATH, George	25	Mittelruessel	49-0737
BORCHARD, Eduard	38	Duben	51-1739
Herman 15			
BORCHARD, Herman	15	Amerbach	51-1739
BORCHEN, Dorothea	20	Vatterode	54-0850
BORCHEN, Wilhelm	24	Buffalo	54-0850
BORCHERDING, H.	21	Hegendorf	54-1716
BORCHERDT, Friedr.	42	Wisconsin	53-0991
Albrecht 35			
BORCHERDT, Friedr.	27	Eilenburg	54-1554
BORCHERS, Chr.	32	Windesen	49-0742
BORCHERS, Engeline	19	Diele	53-0888
Henry 18, John 16, Gebhardine 15			
BORCHERS, Harm	32	Schortens	53-0942
Elise 22			
BORCHERS, Heinr.	22	Rodenburg	52-0370
BORCHERS, Sophie	18	Kohlenfeldt	53-0492
BORCHERS, Udo Sand	32	Diele	53-0888
Devertje 36, Friedrich 11, Anna 8			
William 9			
BORCHERT, Ed.	15	Dieben	53-1000
BORCHERT, Ferd.	26	Eilenburg	53-1000
BORGER, Carl	20	Naila	54-1371
BORGFELD, Diedr.	18	Basdalen	51-1084
BORGMEYER, Wil'mne	15	Ottenhausen	48-0565
BORGS, Anna Maria	27	Ballhausen	52-0279
Maria 29			
BORIUM, Cath Heide	20	Wehlmansel	53-0590
BORKHARDT, Chr.	36	Stroit	54-1554
Ernst 33, Ludwig 28, Wilhelm 7			
Caroline 33, Dorothea 4, Caroline 1			
BORMAN, Wilh.	43	Etzendorf	48-0112
BORN, August	18	Frankenhausen	54-0918
BORN, Christ.	26	Muehlhausen	52-1625
BORN, Ferdinand	42	Egeln/Prussia	53-0628
Charlotte 32			
BORN, Friederike	55	Nassau	53-0652
Ottilie 27			
BORN, Johannes	27	Netphen	53-1062
BORNACK, Joh Fried	29	Schwotsch	54-1168
BORNEMANN, Conrad	25	Pattersen	54-0930
BORNEMANN, Friedr.	21	Bueckeburg	50-0366
BORNEMANN, Hein. F	34	Labelin	53-0825
Johanna 36, Henriette 4			
BORNEMANN, Henry	45	Hackshorst	51-1588
Caroline 40			
BORNEMANN, Joh. H.	19	Braunschweig	49-0324
BORNEMANN, Johann	22	Darmstadt	52-0699
BORNEMANN, Luis	21	Braunschweig	47-0672
BORNEMANN, Regine		Herringbostel	50-0366
BORNEMANN, Susanne	39	Muenden	53-0590
BORNER, F.C.L.	18	Stadtilm	48-0269
BORNHAUSEN, Balt.	36	Waldshut	51-1686
BORNKESSEL, Carl	31	Coburg	53-1013
BORNSDORF, Heinr.	24	Plaunitz	52-0563
BORNSTEIN, D. (m)	38	Herstgen/Pr.	48-0447
BORSCHERS, Engel M	28	Axdorf	47-0672
BORST, Caroline	22	Koenigshofen	53-0590
BORST, Cath.	22	Roetterbach	51-1160
BORTMANN, B.F.	23	Schirchnitz	51-1160
BOSCH, Andreas	29	Fruchtelfinge	51-1640

NAME	AGE	RESIDENCE	YR-LIST
Joh. Georg 59, Barbara 21, Friedr. 34w			
BOSCH, Georg	28	Notzingen	54-1283
BOSCH, Matth.	24	Unterschmedin	51-1640
BOSCH, Wilhelm	27	Soest	52-1625
BOSCHEL, Martin	58	Weideroda	54-0600
Anna E. 14			
BOSCHEN, Diedrich	15	Hassendorf	51-1101
BOSCHING, H.	43	Lageloh	49-0742
BOSE, Hans	22	Meckelstedt	51-1055
BOSENGER, Maria	22	Gerstungen	52-1410
BOSER, Joseph	34	Ommersheim	52-1625
BOSHARD, J.H.	29	Zuerich	52-1661
BOSNER, Johanne	17	Unterfarnbach	53-1062
BOSSE, Christoph	25	Nenndorf	52-0563
BOSSE, Joh. Georg	29	Sachsen	54-1566
BOSSE, Joh. Heinr.	26	Linne	51-0352
BOSSER, Johanna	19	Gehaus	54-1341
BOSSLER, Johann	19	Urach	52-1580
Michel 22			
BOSSNER, Margareth	20	Mohrlach	54-1716
BOST, Heinrich	24	Ostfriesland	50-1067
BOSTELMANN, Henry	44	Gemen	52-0804
Margreth 36, Henry 14			
BOTE, Anna Martha	54	Koeppel	53-1070
BOTE, Matilda	23	France	48-1015
Victor 2			
BOTLAND, Friedrich	19	Hagen	52-0095
BOTT, Christian	22	Elmshausen	52-0095
BOTTCHER, Gottfr.	39	Kahlenberg	54-1283
Carl 32, D.H. 15			
BOTTE, Ludwig	16	Achim	52-1512
BOTTGER, H. (m)	21	Hohenauerberg	49-0383
BOTTHEIMER, Georg	23	Stuttgart	54-1078
BOTTMANN, Caroline	23	Engenstein	52-0807
Mathilde 24			
BOTTWALS, Carol.	17	Ramrod	52-1321
BOURDOUSE, J.G.(m)	27	Alsfeld	54-1341
Mary 58			
BOURGUIGNON, Ferd.	24	Hannover	54-1371
Clara 24			
BOURGY, Joseph	43	Baltimore	48-1015
Mrs. 38			
BOURTCHUZKY, Rob.	35	Erfurt	49-1106
Martha 26, Emelia 2			
BOUTON, H.J.	45	Gt. Britian	48-1015
BOUXEM, Anna	20	Herdinghausen	52-1464
BOVE, Drevis	21	St. Bassen	50-1236
BOVER, Wendelin	24	Kunzendorf	54-1452
BOWACH, F. (m)	18	Arnstadt	49-0416
BOWE, Eva	56	Dresden	52-1321
BOWE, Fr. W.	26	Dresden	52-1321
BOXHEIM, Christ.	20	Gemuenden	54-1282
BOYER, Albert	24	Braunschweig	54-0987
BOYER, Carl Jos.	27	Brakel	51-1796
Theresa 34, Heinr. 8m			
BRABAND, H.	31	Vickerhagen	51-0517
BRABERT, Heinrich	21	Bockhorst	49-0352
BRACHET, Carl	29	Holzappel	54-1371
Catharine 26, Ludwig 9m, Philipp 26			
BRACHT, Theodor	36	Volkmarem	53-0914
B. 46, August 9, Friedrich 7, Victor 4			
Bernhard 9m			
BRACK, Anne	30	Canton Argau	51-0048
Jacob 9m			
BRACKEMANN, E.	44	Semien	53-1086
A. Marie 43, Maria 18, Ernst Fr. 15			
Leonore 11, Heinrich 9, Anna Marie 3			
BRAENTGAM, Mar.	28	Eisfeld	54-1282
BRAEUER, Heinr.	55	Gera	54-0600
Friedr. 34			
BRAEUNIG, Michael	46	Ferdinandsdor	51-0384
Anna Maria 46, Franz Joseph 19, Jacob 17			
Franz Vinc. 14, Maria Anna 11, Sophia 8			
BRAEUNLICH, Fr. G.	50	Dresden/Sach.	51-1725
Henriette Fr 44, Gustav Hugo 20			
Emil Albert 17, Adolph Wilh. 15			
Adelh'd Paul 12, Ernst Carl 10			
Conrad Herr. 8, Emilie Helen 3			

NAME	AGE	RESIDENCE	YR-LIST
Robert Conr. 2			
BRAEUTIGAM, Elise	24	Cassel	49-0413
BRAEUTIGAM, Johann	36	Dankenfeld	52-1321
BRAEUTIGAM, Mar.	28	Eisfeld	54-1282
BRAEUTIGAM, Mich.	30	Zermitsch	54-0872
Christine 21			
BRAEUTIGAM, Michel	30	Hessen	50-1236
BRAEUTIGAM, Rosale	25	Altenburg	52-1661
BRAEVE, Jacob	28	Lengerich/Pr.	52-1432
Friedrich 24			
BRAGER, Louise	20	Wiedersheim	52-1321
BRAGG, Isaac F.	42	New York	48-1015
BRAHM, Catharine	21	Ramrod	51-0352
BRAHMEIER, Heinr.	40	Salmenhausen	53-0628
Carolina 34, Carolina 4, Hanna 2			
BRAHMSTETTEN, B(m)	22	Borgau	49-0324
BRAIER, Heinrich	19	Oldendorf	52-1512
BRAMICKL, Christ.	20	Mittelruessel	49-0737
BRAMSTEDT, Heinr.	53	Armsen	53-0838
Christian 13, Hermann 9, Fritz 6			
Heinrich 2			
BRANCH, M. (m)	52	Trienz	50-0746
M. (f) 56, M. (f) 21, H. (f) 21			
Ch. (f) 16, M. (f) 12			
BRAND, Babela	24	Wertheim	49-0912
BRAND, Elise	27	Hellburg	54-1282
BRAND, Johann	26	Faven/Hann.	53-0475
Peter 17			
BRAND, Jos.	23	Wuerzburg	51-1796
BRAND, Ludwig	25	Meinberg	52-0775
BRAND, William	43	Lothe	53-1164
Elisabeth 45, Carolina 25, Sophia 23			
William 20, Henry 13, Friederike 9			
Friedrich 8, Charles 2, Louisa 2			
BRAND, William	24	Rothenburg	50-0021
Kathrine 21			
BRANDAU, Gustav	27	Harmuthsachse	47-0828
BRANDAU, Heinrich	38	Raunsbach	54-1371
BRANDAU, Marie	28	Eisenach	54-1649
BRANDEL, Johann	36	Neumark	53-0905
Barbara 40, Margareth 12, Rosa 10			
BRANDENBURGER, Hch	45	Altena/Pr.	48-0053
BRANDENSTEIN, Eli	41	Grabenstein	51-0352
Zerline 36, Jettchen 19			
BRANDER, Conrad	26	Wettorf	48-0284
BRANDES, August	31	Hildesheim	53-1016
Dorthea 29			
BRANDES, Christian	36	Braunschweig	54-1717
BRANDES, Friedrich	21	Eichshagen	53-1164
BRANDES, Friedrich	17	Hannover	54-1371
BRANDES, Gesine	21	Eimbeck	53-1070
BRANDES, Gott.	42	Hornburg	49-0383
Charl. 47, Emma 7, Emilie 4			
BRANDES, H.	21	Ahorn	53-0492
BRANDES, Heinr.	28	Wien	49-0383
Minna 24			
BRANDES, Heinrich	48	Leiferte	52-1512
Wilh. 16			
BRANDES, Wilhelm	23	Alvesse	54-1297
BRANDES, Wilhelm	19	Wolkhausen	54-1371
BRANDFAS, Caroline	27	Lindau	54-0882
BRANDHORST, Jette	12	Minden	53-1023
BRANDHORST, Louise	25	Hille	53-1023
Jette 12, Ferdinand 9			
BRANDIES, Adolph	26	Prague	48-1015
BRANDIN, E.	25	Heldrungen	53-0492
BRANDING, Dorothea	34	Bueckeburg	53-0492
BRANDIS, Aug.	31	Erfurt	54-1647
BRANDMEIER, Andr.	23	Hausen/Bav.	52-0960
Marg. 27, Andre 2			
BRANDNER, Cathrine	47	Maria Culm	54-0987
Anna 16, Therese 2			
BRANDT, F. (f)	26	Bremen	48-0453
J. (f) 6m			
BRANDT, August	35	Naumburg	54-0987
BRANDT, C. (m)	17	Seedorf	54-0918
BRANDT, C. (m)	27	Herford	47-0762
BRANDT, C.F. (m)	19	Braunschweig	49-0324

NAME	AGE	RESIDENCE	YR-LIST
BRANDT, Carl	57	Duesseldorf	53-1000
BRANDT, Carl	25	Hesse Wendorf	51-1084
BRANDT, Cath(died)	by	Rothenburg	50-0021
BRANDT, Clau(died)	25	Kutenholz	52-0095
BRANDT, Claus	51	Brestedt	54-0918
C. Margareth 45, Marie 18, Sophie 11			
Margarethe 5			
BRANDT, Elisabeth	22	Arnstein	54-0053
BRANDT, F.H. (m)	25	Wandersloh	54-0918
BRANDT, Heinr.	26	Gehrden	51-1640
Louise 50, Henriette 25, Sophie 22			
Friederike 20, Anna 32w			
BRANDT, Herm.	27	Magdeburg	53-1013
BRANDT, Johann	21	Hof/Baiern	53-0475
BRANDT, Luise	25	Bensen	49-0413
BRANDT, M. (f)	34	Bremen	48-0453
BRANDT, Maria	48	Kirchheim	54-1716
Gottfr. 18, Catharine 20			
BRANDT, Meta	24	Verden	50-0021
BRANDT, Michael	19	Steinach	52-1304
BRANDT, Minna	35	Vollbrechshau	50-0439
Johanne 6			
BRANDT, Robert	20	Naumburg	54-0987
BRANDT, Wilhelm	22	Hannover	52-0699
BRANDT, Wm.	50	Feldheim	54-1078
Regine 47, Dorothea 17, Regina 10			
BRANESBERGER, Anna	24	Neiderhof	54-0930
BRANNING, Conrad	50	Heinsen	48-1179
August 16			
BRANNWALD, Fr.	34	Hildesheim	52-1625
BRASCH, Michael	32	Pelsien	52-1304
BRASCHER, Jud.	22	Ulmbach	54-1419
BRASE, Cord	19	Scheeszel/Han	52-0351
BRASE, Heinrich	24	Wolpe	48-0887
BRASE, J.G.	27	Oberneissen	54-1566
BRASISCH, Elis.	19	Mittelruessel	49-0737
BRASMANN, Carl	31	Lebeschitz	49-0383
Louise 27, Friedr. 5			
BRASS, Edward	23	Lennep	48-0406
BRASSE, Gesche	21	Friedrichsdor	53-0905
BRATFISCH, Traugot	27	Scheifreisen	52-1512
BRATSCH, August	44	Pasewalk	53-1023
Wilhelmine 32, Rosamunde 19, Emanuel 2			
BRATZ, Gottl.	23	Lichtenberg	50-1071
BRAUCH, Sophia	21	Doemitz	53-0991
BRAUCHLE, Aloys	34	Geissbaiern	49-0352
BRAUER, A. (m)	40	Supplingen	48-0453
BRAUER, Francis	56	Robitzau	53-0914
Anna 37, Therese 30			
BRAUER, Kath.	23	Thiesendorf	49-1106
BRAUER, Wilhelmine	22	Stadt Ilm	52-1464
BRAUKMEYER, Wil'ne	23	Derental	54-1443
BRAUMLER, (m)	40	Weremberg	48-1243
Mrs. 34, (m) 9, (m) 6, (f) 5, (f) 3			
(f) 21			
BRAUN, Adam	30	Oberpriesheim	48-0053
BRAUN, Albert	29	Berlin	54-1371
BRAUN, Anton	34	Vollkirchen	51-1245
Elisabeth 38, Peter 9, Marie 6			
BRAUN, Carl Chr.	19	Dreissigaker	52-1321
BRAUN, Christian	29	Dillingen	54-0053
BRAUN, Eleonore	57	Chodziesen	54-0987
Emilie 22			
BRAUN, Elisabeth	23	Wiedberg	54-1341
BRAUN, Fr.	32	Ditterswind	54-1078
Sybilla 32, Marg. 2			
BRAUN, Franz	40	Hamberg	52-0515
BRAUN, Franziska	18	Neubau/Bav.	52-1423
BRAUN, Georg	36	Freiensteinau	53-1000
Sybilla 35, Elisab. 8			
BRAUN, Gottlieb Fr	28	Oberessling	53-0914
Louise 27, Charles 3, Louise 9m			
BRAUN, Hermann	20	Berlin	48-1243
BRAUN, J. (m)	29	Wiedehaulhaus	52-0652
BRAUN, Jacob	17	Sulzbach	53-0888
BRAUN, Jane	25	Gerline	53-0991
BRAUN, Joh.	29	Goegging	54-1078
Marianne 32, Marianne 5			
BRAUN, Joh.	21	Markuhl	52-0558
BRAUN, Joh. C.	26	Magdeburg	53-0914
BRAUN, Johann	23	Wuertenberg	53-0557
BRAUN, Johann	27	Seuversholz	54-1443
BRAUN, Johannes	18	Weilheim/Wuer	52-0351
BRAUN, Jos.	27	Goegging	54-1078
BRAUN, Kunigunde	23	Hallendorf	54-1554
BRAUN, Leonhard	16	Alsfeld	51-0352
BRAUN, Martha	22	Cassel	52-1620
BRAUN, Max	26	Reckendorf	48-0887
Hannchen 19, Jane 17			
BRAUN, Philipp	21	New York	52-0563
BRAUN, Thomas	24	Mittelruessel	49-0737
BRAUNBACH, Sebast.	17	Offenbach/Hes	54-1092
BRAUNE, Anna	52	Aslerschwang	52-1464
BRAUNFELD, Carl	30	New York	51-1245
BRAUNHOLD, Fritz	20	Hannover	53-1070
BRAUNIGGER, Ignatz	42	Herrenwies	53-0928
Christine 56, Constance 17, Caroline 14			
BRAUNS, August	20	Eisenberg	53-0942
BRAUNSCHEIDT, Fr'd	19	Poppelsdorf	53-0991
BRAUNSCHEIDT, J.H.	45	Duesseldorf	53-0991
John Wm. 35, Fred. Theoph 19			
BRAUNSCHEIDT, J.W.	35	Koeln	53-0991
BRAUNSPAN, Julius	28	C. Ulm	54-1591
Fanny 28			
BRAUNWALDE, Adam	33	St. Gallen	51-1686
BRAUSE, Franz	23	Dresden	50-0472
BRAUSEN, H.	54	Porstel	54-1341
Mary 59, Mena 26, Sophia 21, Caroline 6			
BRAYER, Christ.	24	Pr. Minden	51-0405
BRECHER, Philip	21	Illerreichen	48-0447
BRECKE, Friedrich	25	Hille	54-1168
BRECKEN, Therese	32	Paderborn	50-0021
Bernhard 12, Heinr. 9, Josephine 3			
BREDE, Andreas	26	Engeln	54-1554
BREDE, G. (m)	24	Lackstadt	48-0453
BREDE, Nicl.	22	Simmershausen	51-1640
BREDEMEYER, Heinr.	22	Rheren	53-1086
BREDEMEYER, Henry	40	Uchte	53-0991
BREDEMEYER, Wilh.	33	Loecum	50-1067
Doris 23, Charlotte 40, Heinrich 18			
Sophie 16, Fritz 12, Wilhelm 8			
Wilhilmine 6, Caroline 9m			
BREDEN, Jacob	24	Wittstedt	52-0699
BREDHORST, Meta	20	Osterholz	53-0991
BREEMER, Wilhelm	31	Weissenburg	50-0439
BREEST, Ferdinand	28	Brasdorf	53-0905
Hanna 20			
BREETEMEYER, Aug	17	Minden	53-0905
BREHE, Franz	35	Langenleube	54-1168
BREHER, Caroline	19	Gottingen	51-1739
BREHM, Barbara	24	Schweinbach	54-1078
BREHM, Christine	27	Ettinghausen	51-0352
BREHM, Conrad	33	Ellingshausen	48-0951
Mary E. 24, William 3, William 33			
Francis 3w			
BREHM, widow	64	Darmstadt	49-0324
BREHN, A. (f)	26	Seitmannsdorf	47-0868
BREIDENBACH, Lud.	56	Dudenbach	51-1084
Ernestine 48			
BREIDING, W. (m)	56	Munden	49-1106
BREIER, Heinr.	21	Minden	50-1236
BREIER, Heinrich	50	Muenden	52-0699
Marie 55, Ferdinand 14			
BREIT, (f)	41	Wien	53-1086
BREIT, Georg	28	Grossenlueder	54-1554
BREITENBACH, Clem.	13	Linden	52-1625
Rosalie 53, Marie 18			
BREITENBACH, Mart.	42	Oberdzilsen	49-0742
BREITENBERGER, Ant	24	Mernis	52-0563
BREITENBUECHER, C.	19	Bietigheim	53-0838
BREITENSTEIN, Fr.	34	Almerode	54-1452
Anna Marta 32, Heinrich 10, Wilhelm 1			
Louise 4			
BREITENSTEIN, Joh.	23	Kassel	51-1062
BREITENSTEIN, Leon	21	Gelnhausen	54-1297
BREITENSTEIN, Ludw	27	Werda	54-1717

NAME	AGE	RESIDENCE	YR-LIST
BREITHOF, Aug.	20	Klausthal	54-1283
BREITSTADT, Ernst	36	Marburg	54-1717
BREITSTEIN, Conr.	17	Germany	50-0472
BREM, Margaretha	19	Rodach	53-0637
BREMER, Andreas	30	Koenighafen	54-1717
Elisabetha 30, Nicolaus 2			
BREMER, August	23	Braunschweig	54-1717
BREMER, Daniel	21	Wichtringham	47-0672
BREMER, Elisabeth	24	Clappenberg	52-0095
BREMER, Friedrich	51	Wunstorf	52-0095
BREMER, Georg	56	Ferninghausen	47-0872
BREMER, N. (m)	18	Schiffdorf	48-0447
BRENDECKE, Friedr.	41	Gittelde	52-0699
Louise 50, Louise 10, Marie 7			
BRENDEL, Joh Heinr	51	Blindendorf	52-1200
Anna Maria 44, Eva 21, Sophia 18			
Christian 10, Friedrich 5			
BRENDEL, Joh. Geo.	26	Seibes	48-1184
BRENDEL, Johann	35	Druegendorf	52-0095
Kunigunde 26, Maria 11m, Anna 21			
BRENDEL, Margareth	20	Rabenshof	52-0693
BRENGEL, Martha	23	Neidernhof	54-0882
BRENN, Heinr.	17	Salzungen	52-0960
BRENNEMANN, Joseph	44	Radenhausen	52-0699
Elisabeth 34, Elise 5, Bertha 4, Oskar 2			
Julius 6m			
BRENNEMANN, Mich.	54	Wohra	52-0699
Elise 47, Marie 24, Joseph 22			
Christian 18			
BRENNER, Anton	18	Schweningen	49-1106
BRENNER, F.G.	43	Erfurt/Pr.	48-0053
BRENSE, Therese	34	Oetdorf	51-1035
BRENZEL, Wilhelm	21	Niederndorf	54-1168
BRENZELL, Gebh.	39	Rotenburg	51-0405
Cath. 36, Caroline 9			
BRER, Heinrich	36	Muhlhausen/Pr	53-0628
Johanna Elis 34			
BRESSEL, Pauline	28	Zuelke	54-1371
BRESSELI, Elis.	16	Lindenau	53-0320
BRETHAUER, William	25	Veckerhagen	50-0323
BRETSCHNEIDER, Gus	20	Breslau	54-1575
BRETTER, Friedrich	42	Crimmitschau	54-0987
BRETTHAUER, Friedr	20	Mainzholzen	51-1438
BRETTHAUER, Marie	9m	Marburg	51-1796
BRETTHAUER, Marie	9m	Marburg/Hesse	51-1796
BRETTING, Georg	16	Boxdorf	52-0693
Margar. 18			
BREUER, Charles	20	Dresden	50-0840
BREUN, John	37	Doerndorf	53-0928
BREUNE, de As (m)	34	Schower	49-0912
Joh. 35			
BREUNIG, Cantal.	28	Altenbach	53-1164
BREUNING, Georg	53	Flensungen	53-1000
Marie 42, Johs. 20, Georg 13			
BREUNSBACH, Wilh.	23	Schiffarth	54-1371
Daniel 20, Anna 23			
BREUSCHER, Georg	26	Kirchhoedenha	48-1355
BREUSEL, Carl Wilh	28	Benhausen	51-0352
BREUSSCHER, Heinr.	41	Klein Geldern	47-0672
Eleanor 38, Sophia 17, Minna 8			
Heinrich 6, Helena 18m, Wilhelm bob			
BREUSTAET, Con.	19	Westerrode/Br	51-1796
BREVES, Sophie	50	Loecum	50-1067
BREY, Georg	50	Neukirchen	54-0882
BREYMANN, Mathilde	20	Bockenem	48-1179
BRICHLE, Georg	37	Reichholzren	52-1512
BRICK, Fr. (m)	28	Hamberg	52-0515
BRICKWEDE, A. H.	34	Luchting	49-0324
BRIEBSCHWERT, Eva	18	Bernau	52-0515
BRIEDE, Heinrich	14	Sachsen	53-0590
BRIEHL, Friedrich	21	Tringhausen	52-0563
BRIEL, Lisette	17	Marburg	54-0987
BRIESE, Friedr. Wm	42	Batz/Pr.	51-1532
BRIESS, William	24	Bischofsheim	50-0840
BRIETRUCK, Carl Wm	27	Mittelruessel	49-0737
Wilhelmina 27, Frank A. 25			
BRILL, Andreas	27	Grossensee	48-0284
BRILL, Anna Marie	29	Geroch	51-1062

NAME	AGE	RESIDENCE	YR-LIST
BRILL, G. (m)	26	Bosserode	52-0558
BRILL, Johannes	46	Kleinensee	48-0284
Anna Cath. 36, Anna Cath. 14			
Eva Elisa 12, Anna Marg. 4			
BRINCKHOFF, Fr.(m)	19	Binden/Hann.	52-0960
BRINCKMANN, F.	26	Lemgo	52-1148
Anna 21			
BRINGMA, Charlotte	19	Loecum	50-1067
BRINGMANN, Doroth.	23	Hahler	54-1282
BRINK, H. (m)	25	Heberstedt	49-0329
BRINKER, Christoph	58	Radsick	53-0825
Maria 47, Dorothea 28, Heinrich 22			
Wilhelmine 18, Louise 16, Christian 15			
Caroline 9			
BRINKER, Heinr.	18	Zitter	51-0326
BRINKHOFF, Heinr.	30	Werder	53-1070
Lotte 32			
BRINKMAN,	23	Windheim	50-0944
BRINKMANN, Anna M	31	Alstaette	48-0269
BRINKMANN, Bernh.	34	Beelen/Pr.	53-0628
BRINKMANN, Chr.	31	Glasenbach	54-1470
And. 29			
BRINKMANN, Christ.	38	Ilscheid	49-1106
Friederike 29, Friederike 5			
BRINKMANN, Fried.	16	Windheim	47-0762
BRINKMANN, Friedr.	31	Behrensen	50-1236
BRINKMANN, Wilhelm	32	Hartdorff	54-1591
Mary 26, Hermann 9m			
BRINKMEIER, Friedr	24	Osnabruck	52-1512
Joergen 17			
BRINKMEIER, J.H.	58	Osnabrueck	52-1512
Anna 55			
BRISTEL, C.G. (m)	28	Glauchau	49-0383
BRITTING, BM(died)	-1	Frankendorf	50-0021
BRITTING, Georg	35	Frankendorf	50-0021
Margar. 30			
BROCK, Ana Gertrud	56	Hofgeismar/He	51-1532
August 29, Elisabeth 16, Sabina 14			
BROCK, Fanny	16	Frankenstein	53-0991
BROCK, Julius	28	Minnesota	53-0991
BROCKHAGE, Wm.	28	Moellenbeck	51-1160
BROCKHUS, Diedrich	20	Brockhus	53-0888
BROCKLAGE, Wil'mne	23	Versmold	49-0352
BROCKMANN, Cath.	25	Armsen	53-0838
Peter 23			
BROCKMANN, Georg	33	Gilten	50-1132
Sophie 28, Friedrich 8, Sophie 4			
Heinrich 28			
BROCKMANN, Heinr.	16	Bremen	54-0053
BROCKMANN, Julius	24	Obernkirchen	51-1035
BROCKMANN, W.			51-1455
wife , child			
BROCKMANN, Wilhelm	34	Muenster	54-1371
BROCKMEIER, Cath.	54	Muenchen	52-1512
BROCKMEYER, A. Mar	26	Bernnien	54-1443
BROCKMEYER, Theod.	30	Paderborn	53-0473
BROD, Gottlieb	18	Grossaspach	49-0352
BROD, Jacob	29	Grossaspach	49-0352
Barbara 25, Gottlieb 11m			
BRODECK, Aron	19	Krotoschin	54-1078
BRODER, Johannes	30	Sargans/Sw.	51-1725
BRODRECHT, Joh.	49	Grebenau	47-0868
Cath. 48, H. (m) 25, Fr. (m) 78, Joh. 14			
Cath. 12, Jul. 9, H. 9			
BRODT, Jacob	20	Cassel	54-1168
BRODTE, August	42	Haugsdorf	53-0888
Caroline 35, Laura 15, Charles 13			
Bertha 8, Robert 4			
BROECKELMANN, Herm	20	Bremen	50-0439
BROEHM, Andreas	59	Guttenberg	53-1062
Elisabetha 23, Andreas 15			
BROEHM, Anton	26	Chicago	53-1062
Sophie 54			
BROEHM, Sophie	54	Guttenberg	53-1062
BROEKAMP, Henry	27	Osterweg/Pr.	51-0048
BROEKEL, F.W.	25	Leer	49-0574
BROEKEL, Gottlieb	30	Augsburg	54-1092
BROEKER, Mariane	28	Nordwalde	49-0324

NAME	AGE	RESIDENCE	YR-LIST
BROEMLAGE, Elis.	19	Aukum	54-1554
BROEREN, Behrend	29	Wissfels	54-1371
BROETE, Sophia	24	New York	53-0991
Henry 1			
BROGLI, Martha	30	Canton Aargau	51-1245
Mar. Rosine 5, Thomas 4			
BROHASKE, Regina	46	Naila	48-0565
Gustav 21, Sophie 29, Johanne 18			
BROKE, Catharine	22	Veckerhagen/H	50-0323
BROKING, Hermann	31	Logsen	51-0352
Margareth 20			
BROMBACH, Louise	24	Bremen	50-0292
Johanne 27			
BROMLEY, Girard	33	Riesenbeck	53-0991
BROMM, Mich.	34	Staulbach	50-0472
BROMM, Reinh.	20	Rausheuebg	50-0472
BROMSEN, Adam	27	Fischbach/Nas	53-0628
Philippine 28, Carl 2, Philip Heinr 28			
BROMSEN, Catharine	24	Fischbach/Nas	53-0628
BROOKER, Benjamin	29	Philadelphia	48-1015
BROSCHE, Joseph	26	Langenbrueck	53-1164
Ferd. 22			
BROSI, Erhard	30	Grossaspach	49-0352
Christiane 27, Carl 3, Marie 11m			
BROSI, Erhard	67	Grossaspach	49-0352
Doroth. 64			
BROSI, Marie	20	Grossaspach	49-0352
BROSS, A. (f)	26	Grosscharnsta	47-0868
BROSSIG, John	26	Rohrbach	49-1106
BROTZMANN, Eduard	19	Fritzlar	54-1566
BROWN, Friedrich	23	Philadelphia	53-1164
Rosalie 23			
BROWN, Jacob	17	Sulzbach	53-0888
BROWN, Max	26	Reckendorf	48-0887
Hannchen 19, Jane 17			
BRUCH, Ferd.	43	Solingen	48-0406
Marie 43, Henriette 19, Lisette 14			
Ferdinand 12, Ida 8, Albert 3, Emma 9m			
BRUCK, Joseph	47	Schweidnitz	53-1086
BRUCKER, Amalie	21	Koenigsberg	50-0840
BRUCKMANN, Moritz	37	Coeln	49-0912
Elisabeth 31, Capetan (m) 11m			
BRUCKMANN, Theodor	21	Cassel	48-1184
BRUCKMEYER, Anna	24	Triftern	54-1078
BRUCKNER, Joh.	25	Schwarzenbach	52-1129
BRUCKNER, Kunig.	42	Hilmannsberg	52-1129
Anna 9, Barbara 7, Paul 1, Joh. 25			
BRUCKNER, Peter	36	Gottfriedgrun	47-0672
Magdalena 30, Barbara 17, Georg 11			
Cathrina 9, Sabina 3			
BRUDER, Joh.	26	Eisenach	50-0021
BRUDER, John	24	Ottersmeyer	53-0991
BRUECKENER, Ern'tn	26	Muenchenberns	47-0828
BRUECKER, P. (m)	24	Capellen/Pr.	48-0447
BRUECKMANN, A. (m)	30	Wisbaden/Nass	52-1423
BRUECKNER, Carl H.	23	Rossweil	52-0563
BRUECKNER, Georg	34	Roetha	53-0267
Catharina 28, Eduard 10m			
BRUECKNER, Heinr.	23	Feierheits/Pr	52-1332
BRUECKNER, Kunig.	20	Donnern	48-1179
BRUECKNER, Marg.	29	Oschwitz	51-1640
Anna Cath. 19, Marg. Barb. 22			
BRUEGEMANN, Louise	17	Wagenfeld	51-0500
BRUEGGEMANN, Edw.	18	Braunschweig	52-0279
BRUEGGEMANN, Fr. W	21	Wueffelringen	52-1332
BRUEGGENKOCH, Aug.	21	Hoerste	50-0366
BRUEL, Agnes	28	Koeln	54-0987
Therese 6, Clemens 4			
BRUEMANN, Wilh.	21	Daspe	50-1132
BRUEMER, H. (m)	24	Brunk	49-0742
H. (m) 20, Caroline 19			
BRUEMMER, Wilhelm	22	Schwarzburg	53-0473
BRUENING, Christ.		Dohlberg	54-0987
BRUENING, Joach.	34	Menninghausen	52-0563
Johann 36, G. Margar. 30			
BRUENING, Joseph	27	Ahrhaus	54-0600
BRUENNER, C.G.	44	Auma	54-1566
Gertrude 44, Allwine 23, August 21			
Julia 17, Hermine 15, Minna 11, Carl 9			
Anna 6, Thekla 6			
BRUENNINGS, Herrm.	12	Holzen	51-0756
BRUENS, Johann	25	Osterholz	49-0345
BRUENS, John	20	Achim	53-0991
BRUENS, Meta	20	Sievern	50-0366
BRUENSTRUP, Louise	18	Vinsbeck	54-1078
BRUESKE, Elise	25	Ostbevern	50-0292
BRUETT, H. (m)	17	Zeven	54-0918
BRUETTE, Otto	17	Zeven	54-0918
BRUETTIN, Margaret	42	Niedermirsber	52-0095
BRUETTING, Johann	27	Obersaumbach	54-0850
Anna Rosine 26, Margarethe by			
BRUETTING, Kunig.	33	Bamberg	54-1649
BRUJA, Catharina	14	Boehmen	53-1000
BRUKLACHER, Joseph	20	Wolferstadt	53-0320
BRUMM, Gottlob Her	27	Lunznau	53-0825
BRUMM, Sabine	25	Castle	53-0914
BRUMMER, Joh.	36	Oberheimbach	54-0053
BRUMWIEDE, Friedr.	27	Wendelbottel	53-1023
Dorothea 24, Maria 48, August 19			
BRUNE, Cath.	25	Oelfeten	54-1554
BRUNE, Jacob	42	Wolften	52-1625
Louise 42, Daniel 9			
BRUNGIE, Mart.	17	Osterhold	51-1796
BRUNHOEFER, Johann	40	Vorbach	53-0320
BRUNIN, Carl	21	Rodenwedel	50-0472
Heinr. 20			
BRUNING, Anna	20	WesterBeverst	54-1716
BRUNJES, Meta	21	Hambergen	51-1101
BRUNKHORST, Margr.	21	Westerwann	50-0366
BRUNLEWE, Diedr.	40	Wiener	54-0987
Clasine 27, Swantje 6, Johann 4, Clara 3			
Diedrich by			
BRUNN, Gottlieb	47		54-1419
Carl 11			
BRUNN, Jos.	40	Saaz	49-1106
BRUNNER, Christina	19	Feuchtwangen	52-0515
BRUNNER, Friedrich	19	Wien	52-1410
BRUNNER, Isidor	26	Warmsteinach	52-1423
BRUNNER, Joh. Wilh	36	Sunzenhausen	52-1304
Babetta 35, Johanna 9, Marie 7, Charles 5			
Henry 3			
BRUNNER, Marg.	21	Feuchtwangen	52-0515
BRUNO, Caspar	24	Anruechte	51-1686
BRUNO, Hermann	25	Minden	52-1580
BRUNO, Joh. Georg	35	Kleinwichberg	49-0574
BRUNOTTE, Carl	26	Rheden	52-1410
Caroline 28			
BRUNOW, Franz	28	Borgholz	54-1282
BRUNS, Anna	24	Hagen	54-1094
BRUNS, Ernst	31	Diepholz/Hann	52-0807
Friederike 29			
BRUNS, Franz	22	Beverstedt	52-1661
BRUNS, Fritz	26	Wollings	52-1625
BRUNS, Hanna	1d		53-0991
BRUNS, Heinr.	18	Gramberg	52-1512
Wilhelm 18			
BRUNS, Herm.	27	Halte	49-0324
Marie Gesine 30			
BRUNS, Johann	32	Metzendorf	52-0095
BRUNS, Lewis	22	Quackenbrueck	54-1470
G. 25			
BRUNS, Ludwig	20	Sielen	54-1676
BRUNS, Margarethe	20	Ochtmeyer	53-0928
BRUNS, Oltmann	54	Neuenkruge	54-1470
Jean 52, Mette 22, Ann 15			
Alert H. Erh 10			
BRUNSEN, Wilhelm	20	Bremen	48-1184
Herm. 32, Anna 31, Mita 18m			
BRUSCHWITZ, Wilh.	33	Glogau	51-1245
BRUSE, Louis	30	Olfen	54-1566
BUBERT, Juerg	45	Badbergen	50-1132
Cath. Adelh. 40, Cath. Marie 19			
Cath. Adelh. 16, Heinrich 13, Gerhardt 10			
Hermann 4, Diedrich 1			
BUCH, Christ	45	Oker	51-1686
Anna 32, Heinr. 22, Richard 17, August 7			

NAME	AGE	RESIDENCE	YR-LIST
Wilhelm 7			
BUCH, Diedr.	31	Leese	51-1455
BUCH, Rud.	18	Bamberg	48-1114
BUCHBINDER, Adolph	25	Sommerda	53-0888
Elisabeth 23, Charles by			
BUCHEL, Fr. Ed.	20	Eisenberg	48-1114
BUCHER, Johann	28	Hammerbach	51-1160
Appolonia 25, Kunigunde 3, Georg 9m			
BUCHFEIT, Jacob	17	Solzberg	53-0652
BUCHHEIT, Carl	22	Sulzburg	51-1455
BUCHHOLTZ, Fr.	31	Kolzharn	50-0439
BUCHHOLZ, Carl	24	Celle	52-1410
BUCHHOLZ, Frantz	25	Vechta	47-0672
BUCHHOLZ, Friedr.	8	Zina	53-0652
BUCHHOLZ, Friedr.	31	Steimke	47-0762
Christian 23			
BUCHHOLZ, Fritz	17	Hannover	53-0590
BUCHLE, Albertine	19	Herrenwies	53-0928
BUCHLER, Heinrich	32	Honost	54-1717
Anna 44, Sophia 14, Dorothea 10			
BUCHMANN, Catrine	15	Holzhausen	52-0370
BUCHMANN, H. (m)	32	Gr. Schwulpen	52-0559
BUCHMANN, J.	20	Adelsdorf	50-0439
BUCHMANN, Sophie	17	Weselow	47-0872
BUCHMANN, Theresa	32	Wien	53-0991
BUCHMUELLER, Mich.	30	Burksinn	52-0563
BUCHNER, Asmus	23	Ackerhausen	50-0472
BUCHOLZ, Friedrich	8	Zina	53-0652
BUCHS, Sebastian	30	Niederlauer/B	53-0628
BUCHSBAUM, Babette	22	Trabelsdorf	54-1554
BUCHTKAUN, Heinr.	24	Sachsenburg	53-0492
baby bob			
BUCK, Friedr.	26	Essen/Hann.	52-0960
Christine 27			
BUCK, Fritz	25	Winterbach/Wu	49-0365
BUCK, Heinrich	17	Ostenbrueck	53-1062
BUCK, Jacob	22	Oppenweiler	49-0352
BUCK, Mathias	58	Bederkesa	52-0699
Anna 46, Heinrich 15			
BUCK, Wilhelm	16	Schledehausen	53-1086
BUCKDORFER, Baltia	33	Aholening	54-1443
BUCKER, Henry	28	Frille	51-1588
BUCKERT, Caspar	28	Humrechtshaus	54-1283
BUCKGAEBER, Moritz	30	Rottenburg	53-0825
BUCKGARBER, Johann	25	Feldorf	53-0825
BUCKLER, Joseph	28	Ferlage	52-0563
BUCKREUS, Johann	27	Steinberg	48-1355
BUCKY, Friedr.	34	Luechow	54-1297
Doris 27, Anna 6m			
BUDDE, Anton	29	Emsdetten	48-0260
BUDDE, Cath.	29	Brockbultting	51-1160
BUDDE, Wilhelm	20	Prackel	53-0267
BUDDEHORN, C.	15	Fockenroth	51-0517
BUDDEL, Rosine	23	Schweigan	52-1661
Johann 14			
BUDDEMEIER, Herm L	17	Hespe	54-0987
BUDELMANN, Herm.	20	Brinkuem	49-0324
BUDKE, Friedricke	23	Leiden	50-0292
BUECHENAU, Elis.	19	Storndorf	49-0742
BUECHENAU, Mar.(f)	63	Storndorf	47-0868
BUECHL, G. (m)	21	Schoenlind	54-1566
BUECHLER, Bertha	19	Osterode	52-0895
BUECHLER, Friedr.	39	Huelse	54-1443
BUECHNER, Adam	-1	Kaltensundhei	50-0323
BUECHSMANN, F.L.	26	Windelheim	53-0492
BUECHTMANN, Heinr.	19	Barnstorf	54-0903
Doris 25			
BUECKER, A.M. (f)	23	Holte/Hann.	52-0960
BUECKER, Chr. H.	26	W. Ottendorf	52-0960
A.M. (f) 23			
BUECKER, L. (f)	14	Recke	48-0445
M. (f) 13			
BUECKER, Mary	24	Osnabrueck	54-1470
BUECKLER, Magareth	24	Dellbach	51-0384
BUECKMANN, Friedr.	17	Bornhagen	51-1438
Christine 24			
BUECKMANN, Heinr.	18	Wetschen	53-1062
BUECKNER, John	36	Baiern	54-1724

NAME	AGE	RESIDENCE	YR-LIST
Ottilie 30, Marg. 64, Barbara 28, July 26			
Barbara 6			
BUEHL, Nick.	36	Ansbach	53-0320
BUEHLER, Eduard	42	Berlin	49-0324
Richard 11			
BUEHLER, Georg	20	Semertfeld	51-1739
Regina 24			
BUEHLER, Joh. Ch.	27	Aalen	52-1625
BUEHLER, Joseph	37	St.Gallen	53-0888
BUEHLER, Rosine	22	Noerdlingen	52-1625
BUEHM, Gottfried	45	Elbendorf	48-0887
Margarethe 34, Friederika 6			
BUEHNER, Adam	29	Gefaell/Bav.	51-1725
Barbara 29			
BUEHR, Heinr.	17	Riepen	50-1132
BUEHRE, Engel	31	Riepen	50-1132
Conrad 7			
BUEHRMANN, Friedr.	18	Sattenhausen	51-0352
BUEK, Diedrich	26	Basdahl	51-1035
BUELLING, Georg	33	Gmuenden/Bav.	52-1620
Barbara 29, Magdalena 9, Valines (f) 3			
BUENGER, Maria	30	Hannover	52-0699
BUENTHE, Wilhelm	25	Haeverstaedt	52-1410
BUERGEL, Friedr. W	20	Bergerhoehe	54-0930
BUERGER, Bernhard	18	Pappenheim	54-0850
BUERGER, Franz	31	Twischringen	54-1282
BUERGER, Georg	54	Aslebach/Bav.	53-0628
Johann 27, Margaretha 25, Catharina 20			
Elisabeth 19, Georg 15, Sebastian 10			
Joseph 29			
BUERGER, Georg	25	Bamberg	48-1355
BUERHAUS, Heinrich	28	Hagen	51-0352
BUERK, Jacob	28	Chandorf	52-1580
Leonh. 30			
BUERKLEIN, Elis.	19	Fuerth	54-0850
BUERKLER, Franz	28	Baden	52-1148
BUERMANN, Fr'drike	16	Winzlar	53-1164
BUERNER, Gottfried	31	Weimar/Sachs.	51-1725
BUERSTEL, H.E. (m)	11	Dettan/Bav.	52-0960
H. (f) 9			
BUESCHEL, Chr.	27	Ottstedt	48-1179
BUESENER, Louis	18	Pyrmont	54-1566
Hermann 40			
BUETECKE, Heinrich	27	Otterndorf	52-0699
Anna 26, Marie 1, Margareth 6m			
BUETER, Ernst	33	Minden	50-1071
BUETLER, F. (f)	23	Leiden	49-0416
BUETTIG, W. (m)	21	Zelle	49-0416
BUETTNER, Babetta	34	Meiningen	53-0991
BUETTNER, Carl	66	Gotha	47-0828
BUETTNER, Cath.	35	Schwarzberg	48-0887
Christian 12			
BUETTNER, Ch.	19	Einhausen	53-0582
BUETTNER, Charles	37	Teupen	54-1649
BUETTNER, Dorothea	40	Gmuenden/Bav.	52-1620
BUETTNER, Heinrich	18	Lobenstein	53-1070
BUETTNER, J Adolph	40	Zilgendorf/Bv	48-0053
BUETTNER, Joh.	34	Osterwicke	54-1078
BUETTNER, Johann	22	Weigenburg	53-0557
BUETTNER, Leon.	29	Huchelheim	53-0435
BUETZ, J.J.	46	Elberfeld	47-0868
Soph. 49, Ana. 15, Rop. 10, Jul. 8			
BUFF, Joh.	36	Carlsbad	50-1317
Anna 32			
BUFFLER, Joseph	19	Braggen	54-1371
BUHL, Joh. Simon	24	Coburg	52-1625
Elis. Barb. 31, Joh. Georg 54, Barbara 42			
Heinrich 15, Catharine 9, Elisabeth 7			
BUHL, Mathias	50	Bavaria	53-0628
BUHL, Seifert	26	Damshausen	53-1000
BUHLERT, Georg F.	26	Achim	48-0406
BUHLMANN, B. (m)	30	Hildrub	49-1358
BUHMANN, Bernh'din	24	Coburg	53-0888
BUKER, H. Wilh.	29	Tringhausen	52-0563
Anna G. 28, Anna G. 1			
BULACHER, Emma	22	Basel	54-0872
Amalie 18			
BULLE, Catharine	27	-ietelsheim	48-0101

NAME	AGE	RESIDENCE	YR-LIST
Lina 4, Friedr. 2			
BULLERMANN, F. (m)	30	Porstel	54-1341
Louise 23, Henry 4, William 16			
Friedrich 3			
BULLHILLER, Joseph	28	Bayern	53-0590
BULLING, Rosina	22	Bargau/Wuertt	54-1092
BULLINGER, Raimann	19	Baden	51-1245
BULLMANN, Friedr.	20	Glissen	53-0267
BULLMANN, Wilhelm	47	Lienen/Pr.	52-1432
Elisabeth 44, Friedrich 24, Charlotte 21			
Elisabeth 18, Heinrich 17, Wilhelm 10			
BULLWINKEL, Juerg.	25	Achstaedt	52-0095
BULLWINKEL, Meta		Hambargen	50-0366
BULTMANN, Aug Wilh	21	Bremen	53-1070
BUMANN, Christian	27	Nienburg	48-1209
BUMMEL, Carl	28	Wehlmansel	53-0590
Georg 24, Marie 26			
BUMMEL, Friederike	17	Demar/Sax	54-1092
BUNGER, Henry	17	Salzwedel	54-1591
BUNKE, Maria	22	Baden	52-1362
Dorothea 20			
BUNTE, August	25	Alhorst	52-0775
BUNTE, Barthold	16	Eichholz	49-0352
BURBACH, Andreas	31	Hoechheim	51-1438
Elisabeth 29, Elisabeth 5, Maria 6m			
BURCHARD, Bernhard	26	Springe	54-1554
BURCHARD, Jacob	21	Gerlingen	49-1106
BURCHARDT, G.F.(m)	56	Marolterode	52-1321
BURCHARDT, Joh. H.	38	Neugarmsiel	54-1371
Wilhelmine 34, Maria 9, Mathilde 4			
BURCHARDT, John	49	Magdeburg	48-1209
Sophia 38, Austin 9m			
BURCHER, Friedrich	43	Guethersloh	52-1410
BURCHHARD, Carl	23	Kamstadt	52-1580
Rosine 16			
BURCKHARDT, Chr'ne	27	Wuertt.	54-1724
BURDORF, Lewis	32	Heisfeld	53-0914
Elise 22, Sophie 7, Anna 5			
BURENHAGEN, Christ	22	Richmold	52-1512
BURG, Conrad	19	Maden	50-1067
BURG, Peter	29	Kueppentendro	51-1084
Catharina 19			
BURGALLER, Emma	26	Koenigsberg	54-1282
BURGARD, Susanne	54	Alderode	52-1321
Christian 46, Christian 21, August 18			
Friedrich 16, Carl 15, Ernestine 13			
BURGEL, Nicolaus	22	Bayern	52-1620
BURGER, J.A. (m)	20	Altendorf	49-0416
BURGER, Leon	31	Baiern	49-0912
BURGER, Philipp	24	Stebin	48-1184
BURGERT, Eberh.	30	Meiningen	51-0405
BURGES, Philipp	20	Hohenroth	49-1358
BURGHARD, Heinr.	16	Frankenberg	54-0600
BURGHARD, P. (m)	26	Wichmannhaus	52-0652
BURGHARDT, F.	23	Hanstadt	53-0435
BURGHOFF, F.	20	Polle	51-0460
Aug. 15			
BURGHOFF, Friedr.	39	Stendal	54-1371
BURGHOFF, Sophie	18	Hameln	53-1000
BURHAM, Cathrina	23	Huentelshause	51-1639
BURHOP, Anna	19	Brinkum	50-0292
BURK, Jos.	25	Wagendorf	49-1106
BURK, Wilhelmine	22	Ammerhausen	54-1443
BURKARDT, Johana C	20	Feuchtwangen	52-0515
BURKE, Josepha	29	Rothenfels	51-1455
BURKEL, Ernst	24	Coburg	52-0095
BURKHARD, Augustus	22	Giessen	53-0991
BURKHARD, Marianne	20	Hessen	51-0405
BURKHART, Barbara	25	Rhinau	54-0882
BURLAGE, Anna	29	West Bevern	52-1464
BURLEIN, Christoph	27	Bimbach/Bav.	52-0807
BURMANN, Eduard	25	Roemisch Eich	54-1371
BURMER, Susanna	22	Steinbach	54-1647
BURMESTER, Heinr.	33	Linwiedel	47-0762
Caroline 32, Sophie 11, Georg 8			
Caroline 6, Fried. Ferd. 3, Dorette 3m			
BURMESTER, Wilh.	23	Uelzen	51-0460
BUROW, Wilhelm	39	Fahrwald	54-1297

NAME	AGE	RESIDENCE	YR-LIST
BURRG, Christiane	23	Geisburg	53-0435
BURROKE, Wilh'mine	28	Zeitz/Pr.	52-1332
Auguste 9, Emma 8, Pauline 5, Franz 9m			
BURSKEN, Adam	19	Weiderode/Hes	51-1532
Johannes 9			
BUSCH, Adolph	20	Oldenburg	53-0628
BUSCH, Anna	34	Ruettenau	53-0585
Anna 4			
BUSCH, Carl	9	Milz	54-1716
Johannes 6, Robert 3			
BUSCH, Christoph	23	Rosenthal	50-0292
BUSCH, Claus	16	Ebersdorf	49-0345
BUSCH, Friedrich	30	Burg	53-1023
BUSCH, Friedrich	16	Silberbach	54-0987
BUSCH, Maria	23	Aber	54-1283
BUSCH, Rosa	25	Noerdlingen	54-1282
BUSCH, Simon	37	Prag	48-1131
BUSCH, Wilh.	27	Otterndorf	51-0460
Christine 24, Heinrich 2			
BUSCH, William		Horn	53-1164
BUSCHE, Anna Marg.	28	Harpstedt	54-0872
Johann by			
BUSCHER, William	21	Mittelruessel	49-0737
BUSCHMANN, Alb.	25	Helmstedt	51-1160
Ernst 30			
BUSCHMANN, Carl	40	Dorf Burg	54-1647
Amalie 41, Mathilde 16, Louise 15			
Amalie 11, Gustav 10, Sophie 8, Ernst 6			
Rudolph 3			
BUSCHMANN, F. Hein	43	Barmen	48-0565
BUSCHMANN, Ferd.	19	Erfurt	54-1078
BUSCHMANN, Fr'drke	26	Heilbronn	49-0329
BUSCHMANN, John	19	Bremen	53-1164
BUSCHMANN, Julian	24	Haugsdorf	53-0888
BUSCHMANN, Louise	24	Boebber	53-1086
BUSCHMEYER, Marie	23	Diebingen	52-1362
BUSENLANGE, August	16	Clappenburg	50-0379
BUSS, August	17	Kohlenfeldt	53-0492
BUSS, Caecilie	44	Krotoschin	54-1078
BUSS, Elisabeth	28	Marburg	47-0762
BUSS, Henry	35	Mannheim	53-0991
BUSSE, Charlotte	11	Neuenkirchen	53-0905
Christian 24			
BUSSE, Dorothea	28	Eldegson	51-1588
BUSSE, Fried.	37	Peine	51-0405
Sophie 32, Rieke 8, Carl 5, Louis 3m			
BUSSE, Heinrich	46	Daterberg	47-0672
Sophia 41, Louise 15, Heinrich 11			
Dorethe 6, Sophia 3			
BUSSE, Sophie	21	Barsinghausen	52-1410
BUSSEMAKER, Clara	24	Altenluenne	53-0991
BUSSENMEIER, Fried	33	Lengerich/Pr.	52-1432
BUSSIAN, Aug. Sieg	28	Steinweisen	53-0914
BUSSMAN, H.C.	22	Denmark	47-0987
BUSSMANN, Carl	27	Altena	54-1371
BUSSMANN, Joh Hein	28	Wetter	54-1168
BUSSMANN, Joh. Wm.	29	Altona	54-1371
BUTH, Jacob	19	Bergen/Hessia	52-0807
BUTHE, Carl	27	Pyrmont	54-0882
Carl 3, Mine 6m			
BUTKE, Gerhard	27	Luesche	52-0563
BUTLER, Max	27	Stuttgart	54-1341
BUTOLD, A. (f)	27	Vockerode	48-0453
BUTSCHE, Carl	38	Unferstadt	52-1148
BUTT, Egid.	26	Steinhaus	51-0352
Theresa 19			
BUTT, W. (m)	26	Haste	54-0918
BUTTER, Juliane	51	Hungen	54-1282
Margareth 16			
BUTTERBROD, C. (m)	30	Bielefeld/Pr.	52-1332
BUTTERBRODT, Fried	21	Obedissen/Pr.	50-0323
BUTTERBRODT, Hanna	55	Frodisen	54-1168
BUTTERHOF, Anna	25	Grasmundsdorf	53-0928
BUTTERHOF, Johann	27	Burchgebreuh	53-0928
Anna 25			
BUTTMANN, Conr.	36	Gemen	52-0804
Elise 35, Friedr. 8, Henry 6, Mary 2			
BUTTNER, Friedr.	28	Grossheisa	51-1455

NAME	AGE	RESIDENCE	YR-LIST
BUTZ, Doroth.	26	Kuebs	51-1160
BUTZE, Ed.	39	Wunstorf	50-0439
Mad. 34, H. (m) 7, A. (m) 6, L. (m) by			
CACKERSON, Martin	31	Christiania	54-1297
CAESAR, August	30	Calbsried	50-0379
Christine 28			
CAESAR, Julius	37	Soellichan	54-1168
CALDEMEIER, Johana	22	Lengerich/Pr.	52-1432
CALLOTT, Friedr.	23	Kirchen Telli	52-0351
CAMEHL, Friedr.	33	Gansen	51-1455
CAMPBELL, John	33	Scotland	51-1532
Auguste 30, Charlotte 3			
CAMPEN, Joh Friedr	40	Carolinensiel	53-0991
Clara Mary 45, Louisa 18, Eliza 15			
Ernst 12			
CANNOT, Jean	18	Hanau	53-1164
CANTUS, George	16	Frankenberg	53-1016
CAPELLE, Anna	47		54-0872
Julius 15, Pauline 13, Julie 9			
Ernestine 8, Anna 6, Auguste 5			
CAPELLE, Julius	27	Hannover	54-1716
Carl 30			
CAPPES, Maria	22	Oberkessbach	53-1062
Chatarina 24			
CARBY, Albertine	23	Halberstadt	50-0840
CARCAU, Jonas	22	Zempelburg	53-1062
CARL,			52-1200
CARL, Christian	26	Wiedebach	54-1716
CARL, Jacob	19	Walldorf	54-1470
CARLE, Gottfried	35	Heilbronn	54-0987
CARLIPP, A.	34	Brandenburg	53-0492
Gustav 30			
CARO, Minna	33	Berlin	54-1371
Heinrich 6, Flora 2			
CARRELS, Friedrich	21	Dufmark	54-0987
CARSK, Heinr.	32	Breslau/Pr.	51-0048
Caroline 28			
CARSTANIEN, Jul Th	21	Koeln	53-0991
CARSTENS, Elise	20	Burhafe/Old.	51-1725
CARSTENS, Heinr.	27	Lahde	50-1317
CARSTENS, Peter	35	Otterndorf	52-0699
CARSTENSEN, Peter	34	Lauterberg	51-1101
CARSTINS, Henry	27	Mittelruessel	49-0737
CARTHAEUSER, Isac	27	Wernigerode	53-1062
CASCH, Ferdinand	23	Nejdorf	47-0672
CASIOL, Carl	46	Rosenberg	51-0757
Emilie 34, Ignaz 3			
CASPARI, Elisabeth	26	Bergmuende	52-1452
CASPARI, Hermann	22	Bueggenmuende	50-0323
CASPER, Joh. Carl	30	Freudenstadt	51-1532
Catharina 28			
CASPERS, Helene	24	Grabstede	53-0928
CASSEL, Julius	56	Salzgitter	53-1164
CASSENS, H.	25	Boebber	53-1086
Maria 24, Johann 22			
CASTENS, Friedrich	18	Hannover	49-0329
CASTENS, J.H.		Graue	54-1575
Carl , H. , A. , Louise , daughter			
CATTMANN, Soph.	21	Dueddenhausen	51-0048
CAUFLER, Hulda	23	Neustadt	53-1164
CECANDI, Paul	32	Gardelegen	53-0652
CECHTA, Joseph	30	Rokitzau	53-1164
Rosalie 23			
CELERI, Math.	26	Boehmen	51-1084
Therese 24			
CHALLIOL, David	29	Udenhausen	54-1554
Jacob 4, Elisabeth 22, Christine 55			
CHAN, Herrmann	21	Geldern	49-0912
CHARLES, C. (m)	33	Elschwege	48-0951
CHARLES, John	37	New York	53-1164
CHRENBERGER, Gotth	19	Lintersdorf	52-1321
CHRIST, Andreas	38	Wuertenberg	53-0557
Cathrine 40, Friedrich 11, Andreas 9			
Georg 6, Cathrine 2			
CHRIST, Auguste	40	Deimsen	51-1639
Louise 22, Fritz 18, Auguste 13, Emma 1			
CHRIST, Bernhard	25	Schweinfurt	54-1554
Catharina 21			

NAME	AGE	RESIDENCE	YR-LIST
CHRIST, Franz	29	Elbingsroth	52-1661
CHRIST, Georg	36	Wuertenberg	53-0557
Johanne 28, Jacob 8, Gottl. Seib. 7			
Carl August 4, Johanne 11m			
CHRISTEL, Babette	29	Uttenreuth	52-1200
CHRISTGAU, Joh.	25	Bremen	54-1078
Marie 20			
CHRISTIAN, Wilhelm	23	Ansbach	52-1661
CHRISTIANI, Wm.	20	Steinbild	54-1078
CHRISTINE, Dorothe	24	Mecklenburg	53-0628
CHRISTL, Walburga	27	Bischofsreith	54-1283
CHRISTMANN, Herm.	24	Dresden	50-1071
CHRISTOF, G.	21	Marbach	54-1283
CHRISTOPH, Dorothe	38	Kissingen	51-1455
Dorothea 17, Augustus 8			
CHRISTOPH, Lorenz	30	Tauernfeld	54-0930
Anna 21			
CHYRANSKY, Gottfr.	31	Inowratzlaw	53-1016
CHYTRIE, Joseph	26	Stab	54-0053
Magdalena 23			
CLAAS, Friedrich	20	Eichholz	49-0352
CLARMANN, Nicolaus	27	Knetzgau	52-1661
Anna 28			
CLAUS, Anna Marie	22	Leimbach	48-0284
CLAUS, Balthasar	27	Merseburg	50-0311
Therese 31			
CLAUS, Christian	39	Unterschmitte	54-0965
CLAUS, F.H. (m)	23	Lambersdorf/S	48-0447
CLAUS, Louisa	20	Gottsbueren	53-0991
CLAUS, Wilh.	19	Apelern	54-1168
Dorothe 54			
CLAUS, Wilhelmine	18	Eisenberg	53-0942
CLAUSENIUS, Elise	20	Neukirchen	54-1078
CLAUSS, Heinr.	30	Kohlenfeldt	53-0492
W. 28, H. 2, William 6m			
CLAUSS, Wilhelm	23	Braunschweig	53-0590
CLAUSS, Wilhelm	40	Berlin	54-1647
Albertine 40, Emilie 8, Albertine 4			
CLAUSSEN, Fritz	16	Itzehoe	54-1297
CLAUSSEN, Heinrich	16	N.Y.	53-1013
CLAUSSEN, Wilh'mne	22	Sachsen	53-0585
CLEMEN, Soph. Marg	21	Erbach	54-1566
CLEMMEL, Jakob	29	Hirschheim	54-1283
CLEVE, Gerhard	29	Heinstetten	54-0903
CLOESNER, Johann	42	Stockhausen	54-0882
Philippine 18, Magdalene 14, Jacob 16			
Heinrich 12			
CLUDIUS, Marie	20	Braunschweig	54-0830
COBELLI, Carl	32	Kolsharn	50-0439
Franz 25, Wilh. 2, H. by			
COBERG, J.H. (m)	48	Quackenbrueck	52-1512
COERNEFFER, Carol	21	Metzgels	53-0582
COERS, Hermann	24	Lippe	54-0882
COHEN, James J.	40	Hamburg	53-0991
COHN, Betty	20	Neuhaus	53-0838
COHN, Henriette	20	Tatschi	54-0987
COHN, Joseph	19	Manslau/Pr.	53-0628
COHN, Max	19	Schwarzburg/R	53-0628
COLEDO, M.F. (m)	23	Iborg	52-1512
COLLISDON, Mathias	28	Weiher	52-1200
Cunnigunde 37, Friedrich 7			
COLLITZ, Mary	20	Oldenburg	53-1164
Amanda 18			
COLLMEYER, Heinr.	25	Alhausen	53-0267
COLONEL, Conrad	26	Ebrach	52-1200
Joseph 18			
COMPER, Augustus	29	Schneeberg	53-1164
CONRAD, Carl Fried	29	Berlin	49-0324
CONRAD, David	29	Mittelruessel	49-0737
CONRAD, Ferdinand	27	Berlin	54-1371
CONRAD, Fritz	22	Eisfeldt	53-1062
CONRAD, Heinrich	56	Brinkum	50-0292
Anna 57, Elise 30, Marie 26			
Margaretha 21			
CONRAD, Lorenz	25	Neukirchen	54-1371
Josepha 19			
CONRADAN, Ferd.		Leere	51-1455
CONRADI, Elisabeth	28	Lauter	52-1452

NAME	AGE	RESIDENCE	YR-LIST
CONRAED, Johann	28	Ramrod	48-1131
Anna Marie 34, Jacob 36			
CONSTANTINI, Carl	33	Thamsbruck	54-1371
Adelheid 32, Ernst 7, Carl 4			
COOK, Joseph	26	Grosseneder	52-0095
CORDENS, Dietrich	24	Etelsfeden	53-0838
CORDER, Heinr. Wm.	20	Altenbruch/Ha	51-1532
CORDES, Diedrich	16	Marskamp	50-0366
CORDES, Gerhard	21	Klinkendorf	50-0292
CORDES, Heinrich	25	New York	52-0048
CORDES, Herm. Chr.	20	Driftsethe	53-0991
Lucca Cath. 24			
CORDES, Joh. H.	16	Tarmstedt	54-0987
CORDES, Meta	28	Bramstedt	50-0366
CORDREY, Johann	32	Bassum/Hann.	52-0807
CORDS, Anna	15	Hannover	49-0329
CORNEHLSEN, Mich.	27	Lehmstedt	54-0053
Anna 32			
CORNET, Helene	21	Bederkesa	50-1317
COROETZ, Stephen	34	Prussia	54-1724
CORS, Nicolaus	32	Stotel	54-0053
CORSEPIUS, Otto	24	Koenigsberg	50-0840
CORTES, Gerhard	21	Klinkendorf	50-0292
CORTHES, Maria	22	Bothel	52-1625
COUDRES, Des Louis	25	Cassel/Hessen	51-1725
COURTS, Francois	46	Pohlhausen	48-0406
Wilhelmine 48, Friedrich 22, August 18			
Alwine 16, Mathilde 14, Wilhelmine 10			
Hermann 7			
CRAMER, Chr.	25	Leer	51-0757
CRAMER, Herrm.	12	Frauenberg	47-0828
CRAMER, Jenny	23	Oldenburg	48-0101
CRAMER, John	30	Aschendorf	51-1588
CRAMER, Marie	25	Biedenkoph/He	51-1725
CRASZ, Anna Cath.	22	Meckburg/Hess	52-0351
CRAUEL, Hermann	38	Foersle	53-0161
CRAUSE, Julius	36	Waldenburg	53-1062
CREMER, Bd.	42	Neukirchen	48-0447
CREMER, Joh. Wilh.	33	Barmen	48-0565
CREMER, Peter C.	52	Rensdorf	48-0565
Margar. 40, Christiane 16, Alwine 14			
Laura 11, Robert 9, August 6, Juliane 2			
CREVECVEUVE, H.	40	Voerde	54-1168
CRONAUER, John	26	Baiern	54-1724
CROON, Clara	17	Bremen	54-1647
CROSA, Gustav	27	Berlin	54-1168
CRUSIUS, Oscar	26	Glaz	53-0473
CUEK, M. (f)	74	Baltimore/Md.	48-1015
CUERS, Hermann	24	Lippe	54-0882
CUMPRECHT, Gustav	16	Stargard/Pr.	54-1092
CUPER, Anton	30	Arnsberg	53-1016
CYBELL, Heinrich	28	Hessen	48-0284
CZAPETZ, Joseph	41	Lichau	54-0600
CZECH, Vinzenz	30	Marienbad/Boe	54-1092
Anna 26			
D'ARTENAY, Adolph	32	Marysville	53-0991
Minna 20			
DABBERICH, Thomas	24	Niester/Nass.	53-0475
DACHENHAUSEN, Fr'z	55	Ostenholze	50-0944
Madeline 55, Dorothy 17, Mary 14			
DACHS, Xaver	17	Leinen	52-1362
DACKMAN, Henry U.	22	Mittelruessel	49-0737
DACKOEL, J. (m)	29	Bergdorf	52-0652
DAEBEL, Johann	32	Treptow	54-0872
Minna 26, Friederike 5, Hermann 3			
Bertha by			
DAEDERLEIN, August	32	Dinkelsbuehl	47-0828
DAEHN, Friedr.	26	Woldegk	53-0905
Friederika 25			
DAEHNERT, Friedr.	32	Blankenburg	54-1371
Dorette 32, Dorette 9, Marie 6, Louise 5			
Friedrich 3			
DAENICK, Johann	21	Strzitech	52-0699
Franz 26			
DAENNIGES, Heinr.	22	Gutensberg	50-0379
DAER, Peter	21	Bleidenrode	54-0830
DAETTENHAUSEN, H.F	28	Ostenholz	47-0872
DAEUBLER, Lorenz	28	Adelsdorf	51-1245

NAME	AGE	RESIDENCE	YR-LIST
DAHIN, Mich.	35	Hildburg	49-1358
DAHL, Edward	23	Wekskotten	48-0406
DAHL, Ludwig	19	Rotenburg	54-1649
DAHL, v. Christine	27	Noerten	53-1164
DAHLMANN, Henry	25	Leer	54-1591
DAHLMANN, J.J.	47	Elberfeld	48-0565
Anna 38, Helene 18, Jacob 17, Otto 2			
August(died) 1			
DAHLMANN, Wilh.	26	Harpenfeld	49-0352
DAHM, Joh. Gottfr.	33	Lennep	48-0565
Maria 29, Lidia 3, Friedr(died) 1			
DAHME, Caroline	24	Muenster	50-0840
DAHNE, Wilhelm	25	Braunschweig	47-0672
DAHNIEL, Julius		Germany	50-0472
DAHNKEN, M. Cath.	25	Delmenhorst	50-0021
DAIMAN, Friedrich	34	Schwetzingen	51-0384
Regina 27, Lorentz 9, Adam 8, Teresia 4			
Appolonia 6m			
DAIMANN, Wilhelm	30	Duesseldorf	54-1371
Franziska 28			
DALLER, J.G.	20	Cadolzburg	50-0439
DALLMEYER, H. (m)	23	Boellhorst	49-0329
DAMBER, Louise	23	Fredilslohe	51-0405
DAMER, Johannes		Willofs/Hess.	54-1575
wife			
DAMES, Franz	26	Irlich	49-0912
DAMES, Wilh.	31	Preussen	51-1160
Pauline 28, Lise 3			
DAMM, Anna Cathr.	21	Geismar	50-1236
DAMME, F. (m)	24	Berkenhain/Sa	48-0447
DAMMEIER, Friedr.	32	Lundesbergen	51-1062
DAMMEIER, Louis	34	Rinteln	53-0324
Ernestine 49			
DAMMER, A.M. (m)	20	Menninghausen	52-1625
DAMMERMANN, Johs.	18	Badbergen	50-0292
DAMMEYER, Chr'tine	22	Heimsen	48-1131
DAMMSMANN, A. (m)	25	Wallsrode	47-0868
D. 4, F. 2			
DANAI, Hianari (f)	20	Sachsen	50-1067
Antonia 18, Pauline 14			
DANGEL, Michel	27	Baldringen	49-1358
DANIEL, Enoch	26	Klattau	54-1575
DANIEL, Julius	25	Frankfurt/M.	51-1245
DANIEL, P. (m)	16	St.Thomas	49-0413
B. (m) 14			
DANKELMANN, H. (m)	41	Muenster	49-0324
DANKERS, Paul	22	Mulsum	54-1647
DANKMEIER, Heinr.	29	Braunschweig	52-1423
DANKMEIER, Johann	27	Buer	53-0652
DANKMEYER, J.J.(m)	24	New York	50-1236
DANMELMEIER, Jos.	40	Arnsing	54-1371
Walburga 40, Anna 10m			
DANNEBAUM, Abraham	56	Leeste	50-0366
DANNEBERG, William	26	Windheim	50-0944
DANNEMANN, A. Aug.	19	Dinklage	54-1371
DANNENBERG, Arnold	27	Wolgast	54-1371
DANNER, Barbara	34	Kemmathen	53-1070
Heinrich 12, Christina 10			
DANNER, Caroline	24	Lahr	49-0912
DANNER, Ludwig	32	Geisbach	52-0095
DANNEWITZ, Herrman	24	Frankfurt	52-1625
DANZ, Carl	19	Rossdorf	48-1131
DANZBERGER, Friedr	33	Herper	52-1200
DANZIGER, Hirsch	42	Rietberg/Pr.	48-0053
DARBAUM, Anna	30	Wiesbaden	54-1716
Marie 10m			
DARMSTADT, Barbara	28	Bodenheim/Hes	48-0447
DARMSTAEDTER, Marg	39	Bollstein	53-0991
DARMSTAEDTER, Wilh	25	Eberstadt	53-0991
DARSTEIN, Margaret	16	Gleissterbach	53-1070
Margaretha 43, Barbara 13, Amalia 6			
DASCHNER, M. (f)	26	Nordstaetten	47-0868
DASS, A. Marg.	29	Tauperlitz	52-1129
DASSAU, Emil	24	Bernburg	54-0987
DASSMANN, Minna	20	Waldsachsen	51-0405
DATOW, Wilhelm	25	Berlin	48-1243
DATTERBEI, Marg.	19	Hallendorf	54-1554
DAUB, Johann	24	Schwetzingen	51-0384

NAME	AGE	RESIDENCE	YR-LIST
DAUB, Rosina	21	Baiern	54-1724
DAUBLEIN, Johannes	29	Bavaria	53-0628
DAUBLER, Franziska	35	Hausen	51-1160
Therese 33, Johannes 5			
DAUBLER, Joh Georg	26	Wehnmansel	53-0590
DAUD, Wilhelm	32	Mainz	53-1062
DAUE, Heinr.	35	Zaekerick/Pr.	52-0351
DAUM, John	45	Ernsthofen	54-1470
Elisabeth 45, Elisab. 15, Elisabeth 9			
Lewis 20, John 18, Adam 12, Ernst 6			
DAUM, Marie	34	Anspach	54-1283
DAUNER, Jacob	20	Goering	49-1106
DAUSOLD, Mich.	23	Bavaria	50-0311
DAUT, Anna	25	Kalkersbrunn	53-0320
DAUWALD, Wilhelm	23	Baiersgruen	54-1554
DAVID, Anton	29	Rorup	48-0951
DAVIDER, J. Heinr.	19	Bieren	54-1452
DAVIDSOHN, Elise	27	Hamm	53-1023
DAVIS, Henry	23	Porkholz	52-0515
DEBIAAL, L.F.	34	Oberod	53-0914
Marie 30			
DEBIDAL, L.F.	34	Oberod	53-0914
Marie 30			
DEBUS, Johann	22	Dillbrecht/Na	52-1620
DECHANT, Andreas	21	Bamberg	51-1304
Margarethe 20			
DECHER, Conr.	27	Vadenroth	49-0742
DECHER, Peter	49	Bulfenrode	54-0830
Anna Elis. 46, Dorothea 15, Maria 13			
DECHTA, Joseph	30	Rokitzau	53-1164
Rosalie 23			
DECKE, Friedrich	21	Sonnebostel	53-1023
DECKER, Caspar	52	Angenrod	51-0757
Heinrich 27, Johanne 20, Conrad 17			
Elisabeth 51, Elisabeth 14, Marie 24			
Elisabeth 18			
DECKER, Claus	20	Bockeln	50-0366
DECKER, Friedrich	18	Koenigsberg	53-0590
DECKER, Peter	29	Cassel	54-1724
DECKER, William	17	Burhave	48-0887
DECKERT, Andreas	35	Maar	54-0053
Marie Elis. 39, Elisabeth 10, Heinrich 6			
Conrad 3			
DECKS, Carl	16	Quakenbrueck	54-0987
DEDEKIND, Eduard	47	Lauchsted	49-0345
Henriette 33			
DEDEMEIER, Charlot	32	Schlehausen/H	52-0960
DEDERT, Wilhelmine	60	Eger	54-0872
DEDMAR, J. H. (m)	18	Quackenbrueck	52-1512
DEDOLPH, Marie	32	Cassel	53-1086
DEDON, Friedrich	22	Uenzen/Hann.	51-1725
Gesche Marie 22, Bertha 6			
DEECKE, Carl	36	Celle	50-1132
DEEG, Theodor	42	Galdorf	51-1639
Rosine 35			
DEEMAR, Franz	18	Zelle	52-0895
Valentin 16			
DEETERS, Henry	22	Gemen	52-0804
DEETJE, Jacob	30	Bremervoerde	51-1725
DEETJEN, Georg Chr	34	Bremen	51-1101
Johanna Ant. 32, Nicolaus 20, Adelheid 5			
Friedrich 2			
DEGEDORF, Elis.	30	Oetdorf	51-1035
DEGEN, Johann	27	Wolmedingen	54-1443
DEGEN, Wilhelm	28	Stelle/Pr.	52-1620
DEGENER, Daniel	25	Rheda	53-1164
Friederika 24			
DEGENER, Friedrich	19	Braunschweig	54-1554
DEGENHARDT, Anna	19	Sand	54-1566
DEGENHARDT, M. (m)	29	Vockerode	48-0453
C. (f) 23, L.D. (m) 2			
DEGENHARDT, Martin	25	Marburg	53-0991
DEGLOW, Philipp	33	Rosenheim	53-0585
DEHLE, Jacob	24	Baden	52-1512
DEHLER, G. Carl	28	Steppack	52-0279
DEHM, Conrad	28	Neuenschmied	51-1588
DEHMANN, Wilhelm	22	Armelsen	53-0492
DEHMERT, Christian	50	Salefeld	52-0699
Susanna 48, John 25, Andreas 23			
Martha 20, Friedrich 17, Caroline 13			
Dorothea 10, Wilhelmine 8			
DEHNE, Georg	51	Ohrenbach	51-1438
Eva Margaret 50, Johann 25, Anna Marg. 19			
Joh. Michael 19, Georg Mich. 16			
Joh Leonhard 16, Joh. Georg 14			
Eva Margaret 13, Joh. Friedr. 4			
DEHNERT, Andreas	47	Frankenberg	53-1016
Maria 46, Catharina 17, Elisabeth 15			
Leontine 13, Heinrich 12, Auguste 9			
Helene 7, Friedrich 6, Conrad 4			
DEHRENKAMP, Friedr	25	Osnabrueck/Ha	52-1332
DEICHMAN, Wilhelm	22	Hofgeismar	52-0515
DEICHMANN, Geo Chr	16	Hof Geismar	53-0888
DEICHMANN, Georg	36	Hermannsgruen	54-0600
DEICHMANN, Heinr	58	Hofgeismar	54-1566
DEICHMANN, Wilhelm	46	Osnabrueck	54-0903
DEICHMANN, Wilhelm	27	Cassel	49-0413
DEICKMANN, Joh.	32	Lippe	49-0329
Henriette 26, Fritz 3			
DEIME, Magdalena	36	Carlsbad/Boh.	51-1532
DEINHARDT, Ulrich	30	Osterberg	54-1554
DEININGA, Lorenz	23	Hessia	50-1317
DEININGER, Maria A	19	Noerdlingen	54-0903
DEINLEIN, Phil.	18	Hippolstein	52-1129
DEINNER, Carl	15	Schotlow/Bav.	52-1332
DEISCHMANN, E.	50	Froburg	54-1283
Fr. 11			
DEISINGER, Jac. Fr	25	Heidenheim	49-0352
DEISSEL, Pankraz	28	Neustadt	53-0914
DEISSLER, Maria	15	Ballenberg	54-1371
Amalie 19			
DEISSLER, Therese	25	Solothurn	50-0439
DEIST, Elisa	23	Hezewye	51-1455
DEISTER, Edward	14	Bundenbach	53-0991
DEISTLER, Johann	23	Baiern	53-0585
DEITERMAN, Casper	40	Schledehausen	51-1588
Catherine 38, Mary 18, Anna 3			
DEITRICH, Chr. Fr.	18	Zich	51-1455
Ludw. 28			
DELCH, Nicolaus	36	Winterstein	53-0825
Martha Elis. 30			
DELGMANN, Conr.	41	Altenburg	53-1013
Jacobine 40, Elise 16, Wilhelm 10			
Martha 7, Catharine 4			
DELIKAT, Joh Heinr	36	Sulingen	53-1000
Margarethe 32, Heinr. 9, Anna 4			
DELINGER, Joseph	47	Boxdorf/Hann.	53-0475
Eva 37, Gregor 13, Franz 11, Johannes 7			
dau (died) 6m			
DELKESKAMP, H.	34	Boebber	53-1086
Leonore 32, Ilsabe 11, Heinrich 7			
Johanna 3, Louise 2, August 6m			
DELKESKAMP, Marie	19	Boebber	53-1086
DELLER, Friedrich	16	Sondershausen	53-0473
DELLER, Henry	26	Memelsdorf/Bv	48-0053
DELOTNER, Joh Hein	26	Wieza	51-0352
DEMAR, Auguste	21	Zelle	52-0895
DEMELING, Sebast.	32	Neustadt	54-0882
DEMM, Friederike	20	Arzberg	47-0672
DEMME, Hermine	23	Hersfeld	54-0053
DEMME, Julie	34	Muehlhausen	54-0872
Hermann 8			
DEMPKE, Carl	27	Storchau	54-0600
DEMPS, Heinr.	25	Springe	54-1554
Conrad 23, Christ 15			
DEMUTH, Lorenz	52	Hamburg	52-0515
Kunigunde D. 48, Anna 18			
DENECKE, Conrad	19	Nuernberg	48-1355
DENECKE, Heinrich	18	Oerlinghausen	54-1297
DENHARDT, Chas.	20	Mittelruessel	49-0737
DENICKE, Anna	26	Bassum/Hann.	52-1332
DENIGEN, Anna	23	Greisbach	52-1452
DENK, Eva Maria	27	Pheilenhofen	52-1304
DENK, John	21	Veltendorf/Br	50-0323
DENKER, Carl	30	Ferninghausen	47-0872
Lisette 26, Christel 12			

NAME AGE RESIDENCE YR-LIST

DENNELEIN, Adam 28 Putterheim 48-0887
DENNER, Friedr. 34 Trendel/Bav. 52-1332
DENNERLEIN, Conr. 28 Hohenschwarz 52-0693
Friedr. 18
DENNINGER, Christ. 29 Maroldsweisac 54-0872
DENNSTEDT, A. 57 Frankenhausen 53-0492
Marie 46, Ida 23, (m) 21, Herm 18
Therese 16, Julius 9, Louise 12, Minna 3
Rudolph 5
DENTLER, Joh. Hein 22 Michelbach 54-1443
DEPKEN, Fritz 17 Bremen 52-1105
DEPPE, Christine 23 Oerlinghausen 54-1297
DEPPE, Hermann 18 Wehnde 54-0872
DEPPE, Louise 17 Berka 54-1554
DEPPEL, Carl 14 Cronbach 54-0930
DEPPENDAL, J.H.(m) 27 Osnabrueck 52-1512
DEPPER, Casp. H. 34 Muenster 49-1358
DERENKAMP, Gertrud 18 Luesche 52-0563
DERGMANN, Friedr. 30 Beringen 52-1304
Theresia 23, Emma by
DERING, Adam 53 Rumpspringe 52-0563
Elisabeth 56, Minna 25
DERSCH, Bar. 17 Grenzenhausen 53-0928
Minna 6
DESBAND, W. (m) 29 Lennep 50-1317
DESBOROUGH, R.A. 29 Great Britian 48-1015
DESCH, Joseph 20 Frommersbach 53-1062
DESENISS, Chr. 28 Auhagen 53-0492
Dor. 24
DESILUSE, Maths. 35 Mittelruessel 49-0737
DESS, Johann 26 Schleising 54-1282
DESS, Sebastian 23 Rudershofen 54-1554
DESSAUER, Adolf 16 Bruch 52-1105
DESSAUER, Ludw. 18 Kleinsteinach 54-0872
DETELS, J. (m) 20 Wabswede 49-1517
DETERD, Friedr. 18 Luebbecke 50-1236
DETERT, Catharine 46 Versmold 49-0352
DETHMAR, Wm. 42 Deisel 50-0472
Wilhelmine 40, Argus 14, Carl 11
Amalia 9, Julius 4, Aug. 7m
DETJE, Christian 36 Lueneburg 54-1168
DETJEN, H. 22 Selringen 51-1084
DETMERING, Carl W. 30 Milwaukee 48-1179
DETTELS, Heinrich 17 Osterholz 50-1067
DETTJEN, Albert 36 Brinkum 50-1067
DETTLING, Johann 25 Basel 51-1438
DETTMANN, Wilhelm 22 Armelsen 53-0492
DETTMAR, Aug. 7m Langenthal 50-0472
DETTMAR, Franz 2- Fulda/Hessen 49-0365
DETTMAR, Matilde 25 Hannover 52-1148
DETTMER, F. 28 Oldenburg 53-0492
H. 21
DETTNER, Elisa 22 Goering 49-1106
DEUBEL, Casper 32 Gumbelstadt 52-0563
Margarethe 16
DEUBERT, Margareth 16 Gumbelstadt 52-0563
Casper 32
DEUBERTS, Magdalen 28 Gelhausen 50-0292
Johannes 9, Jacob 7, Marie 4, Heinrich 2
Johannes 35
DEUBLER, Caspar 50 Hausen/Bav. 52-1332
Regina 49, Marie 12, Margrethe 9
Josepha 6, Caspar 14
DEUBNER, Christ. 18 Marksuhl 51-1640
DEUKER, Wm. 27 Schwarzenfels 52-1625
DEULING, Catharine -7 Nagel 52-1464
DEUSCH, Julius 30 Urach 53-1164
DEUSING, Therese 21 Gumbelstadt 52-0563
DEUTCH, Bernhard 39 Vienna 48-1015
DEUTCHER, Eva 23 Albertsfeld 48-0260
DEUTSCHER, Charles 26 Rebnitz/Sax. 51-0048
DEVENDER, Wilhelm 19 Buehne 50-0379
DEWITZ, Georg 46 Rendel 52-0515
DEZEL, Friedr. 21 Ebermannstadt 54-0600
DICHMER, Conrad 28 Billerthausen 51-0460
DICHTEL, C. (m) 15 Wackenroth 52-0558
DICK, Theodor 17 Giessen 54-1443
DICKEL, J. 55 Freiensehn 51-0517

NAME AGE RESIDENCE YR-LIST

DICKENBERGER, G. 22 Ilbenstedt 49-0383
DICKHAUT, H. 30 Schrecksbach 51-1160
A. Maria 31, Peter 8, Elise 4, Ludwig 6m
Catharine 24, Elise 26
DICKHOFF, Joh. Fr. 18 Ottersberg 49-1358
DICKMANN, Albrecht 27 Flohe 54-0882
DICKMANN, Diedrich 16 Lene 54-0918
DICKMANN, Hein. 20 Walhorst 49-1106
DIDELIUS, Andreas 47 Grosswalbur 54-1282
DIDRICHS, Henry 37 Hannover 54-1724
DIDRICHS, Herm. 30 Lippstadt 54-1724
DIEBOLT, Joh. 27 Rothenberg 50-1071
DIECHMANN, Sophie 31 Bremen 49-1358
DIECKMANN, Ferd. 30 Seffenbergen 53-0838
DIECKMANN, Johanne 20 Spaden 52-0699
DIECKS, Clement 24 Quakenbrueck 54-0987
DIECKS, Gustav 19 Quackenbrueck 53-0825
DIEDERICH, Ernst 52 Muenden 53-0590
Wilhelmine 50, Carl 14, Johannes 15
Wilhelmine 20, Carl 13, Luye 10
DIEDERICHS, Johann 30 Wulfsdorf 50-0366
DIEDRICH, A.J. 30 New York 51-1160
DIEDRICH, Adam 24 Pretzfeld 54-1554
Margaretha 20
DIEDRICH, Fr. Carl 36 Coburg 53-1013
DIEDRICH, George 40 Nat-op 50-0944
Conrad 21
DIEDRICH, Ivan 28 Nuernberg 50-0439
DIEDRICHS, C. (m) 26 Vockerode 48-0453
DIEFENBACH, Peter 46 Fischbach/Nas 53-0628
Maria Cath. 42, Elisabeth 18
Philipp Hein 16, Carl 13, Peter 11
Wilhelm 7, Catharina 1
DIEGEL, Johann 51 Nuernberg 51-1739
DIEGEL, Maria Cath 26 Ehringshausen 54-0830
DIEGEL, Martin 27 Goeningen 53-1070
Maria 57
DIEGELE, Catharina 23 Gutlingen 53-1164
DIEGELMANN, John Niederbiber 49-0365
DIEHL, Caroline 24 Wittgenborn 51-0460
DIEHL, Catharina 54 Seckbach/Hess 52-0807
Dorothea 24, Catharina 20
DIEHL, Conrad 21 Holzheim 54-0830
DIEHM, Friedrich 24 Bamberg 49-0345
DIEHMER, Conrad 28 Billerthausen 51-0460
DIEK, Bernh. H. 30 Twiess 49-0324
Jan H. 28
DIEKHARDT, Georg 18 Niedereschbac 52-0095
DIEKMANN, Heinrich 16 Spaden 50-0366
DIEKMANN, Marg.Adl 52 Bevensen 53-0991
DIEKRUEGER, Sophie 25 Ehrenberg 51-1160
DIEKWELT, Manwelt 27 Neuaschenkenb 52-0563
DIELEN, Dorothea 26 Dransfeld 48-0887
DIELER, Margaret 42 Kirchlanitz 48-1209
Catharine 18, Sabine 7, Jane 2
Margaret 5
DIELIUS, Wilhelm 37 Scherneck 53-0590
Barbara 35, Margareth 35, Barbara 9
Martin 5, Bernhard 3
DIELMANN, Adam 23 Unterschmitte 54-0965
DIEM, A. (m) 20 Bassauer 50-0746
DIEMER, K. 51 Niederbessing 47-0868
DIEMER, Max 30 Muenchen 54-0850
Catharina 27, Maria 3
DIEMPFEL, Josephus 22 Fromberg 53-0582
Marie 19
DIENER, Fr., Sr. 54 Anhalt 51-1160
Marie 29, Fr. Junior 24
DIENER, Georg 22 Wildenbosten 53-0585
DIENSTLAKE, Marg. 30 Brenke 53-0991
DIEPOLD, Josephine 17 Rotenburg 51-0352
DIERBAUM, Anna Cat 26 Hofgeismar 53-1062
DIERING, Anna Elis 19 Fatenrode 51-0352
DIERKER, Anna 25 Boebber 53-1086
DIERKES, Joh. 28 Loewen 51-0405
DIERKING, Dorette 20 Wienhagen 47-0762
DIERKING, Friedr. 59 Rodewald 47-0762
Eleonore 52, Dorothea 28

NAME	AGE	RESIDENCE	YR-LIST
DIERKING, Wilh.	45	Essel	50-1132
Marie 45, Doris 17, Heinrich 15			
Sophie 12, Caroline 9, Emma 6			
DIERKS, Eleonora	19	Woelpe	54-1443
Dorothea 21			
DIERKS, Friedr.	28	Borstel	48-1131
Friedr. 27, H. (f) 22			
DIERKS, W. (m)	35	Schessinghaus	54-1341
Marie 30, Friedrich 7, Wilhelmine 1			
DIERKSEN, Johannes		Emden	48-1131
DIERKSEN, Siefke	60	E------	50-0021
Martin 16			
DIERMANN, Ferd.	48	Gellmarn	51-1245
Christine 49			
DIERS, Meta	22	Wersabe	50-1067
DIERS, Peter N.	23	Steinau	51-0500
DIERSEN, Heinrich	21	Warsapeck	51-0756
DIESENISS, Chr.	28	Auhagen	53-0492
Dor. 24			
DIESTELHORST, J.L.	22	Diepholz	53-1062
DIETEL, Georg	24	Bayern	53-0557
Helene Cath. 45, Anna 22, Nicolaus 20			
Maria 17, Margrethe 13			
DIETENMANN, F. (m)	36	Leipzig	54-1341
DIETRICH, Andreas	25	Bavaria	53-0628
DIETRICH, B. (m)	23	Unterkatz	52-1661
DIETRICH, Cath.	22	Coburg	50-1071
DIETRICH, Friedr.	31	Eisenach	53-0652
Margarethe 28, Georg 1			
DIETRICH, Friedr.	29	Laufingen	54-1591
DIETRICH, Joh Hein	56	Tennstedt	48-1355
Marie 56			
DIETRICH, John	17	Umstadt	53-0991
DIETRICH, Lina	20	Lich	53-0590
DIETRICH, Marie	30	Bavaria	50-0311
Caroline 31, Amalie 4			
DIETRICH, Nicolaus	18	Kitzingen/Bav	52-0807
DIETRICH, Therese	26	Schwarzburg	50-0311
DIETRICH, Wilhelm	35	Obergornsberg	53-0492
DIETRICHS, Lorenz	35	Neustadt a/S.	52-1580
Elisabeth 32, Paulus 6			
DIETSCH, Heinr.	24	Kirchgottendo	53-0825
Johann 56, Elisabeth 21			
DIETSCH, Louise	18	Batschel	53-0914
DIETSCH, Marie	18	Buerthen	51-0500
DIETTRICH, A.	16	Sachsenburg	53-0492
DIETTRICH, A.	48	Frankenhausen	53-0492
Friedr. 45, Louise 17, Caroline 14			
Albert 9, Amalie 7, Ernst 4			
DIETZ, A.J. (m)	19	Achenbach	53-1086
DIETZ, Anna Maria	27	Ermenroth	51-1101
DIETZ, Gustav Ferd	22	Coburg	52-0895
DIETZ, Joh. Just	18	Wahlen	54-0830
DIETZ, Johannes	29	Angernrode	51-0352
Valentin 20			
DIETZ, Philipp	30	Karlsmuhl	52-0095
DIETZ, V.	20	Angenrod	51-0517
DIETZE, J.	25	Nordheim	54-1470
DIETZEL, Elise	25	Hessen	50-1236
DIETZEL, L. (m)	25	Bielefeld	52-0652
L. (m) 30			
DIETZEL, L. (m)	30	Leitz	52-0652
DIGELMANN, Therese	31	Mabergell	53-0320
DILBMAR, Christian	53	Aldesleben	51-1035
Elisabeth 37, Friederike 23, Friedrich 18			
Albert 15, Marie 13, Laura 11, Auguste 9			
Alexander 3			
DILK, David	24	Sethen	53-0652
Sophie 21			
DILKEN, Georg	48	Beinbaum	49-1106
DILLENBERGER, J.W.	59	Elberfeld	53-0557
Anna 59, Charlotte 26			
DILLER, Margarethe	49	Wedelbach/Hes	52-1620
DILLMANN, G. H.	19	Luesche	52-0563
DILLNER, John	28	Luebeck	50-0021
DILMERS, H.	44	Georgia	54-1716
DIMA, Emma	20	Curhessen	52-1620
DIMMERLING, Joseph	22	Blankenau	52-1200

NAME	AGE	RESIDENCE	YR-LIST
DINEMANN, Gustav	28	Gutmanshausen	52-1512
DINGELMANN, Carl	25	Beitingen	49-0345
DINGELSTEDT, Juls.	20	Rinteln	49-0324
DINGFELDER, Grida	34	Bremen	49-1106
DINGFELDER, Peter	41	Gerdeshofen	49-1106
Grida 34			
DINGLER, Barb.	28	Gr. Dechsendo	49-0574
DINGMEYER, H.	27	Dorum	51-0460
DINN, Heinr.	6m	Germany	51-0460
DIPPEL, Auguste	18	Dresden	53-0888
DIPPEL, Chr.	18	Cassel	54-1470
DIPPEL, Martin	51	Bargen	54-1566
Amalie 45, Julie 23, Caroline 20			
Moritz 19, Friedrich 18, Henriette 16			
Wilhelm 13, Wilhelmine 11, Marie 8			
Carl 5, Amalie 2			
DIPPEL, Wilhelm	22	Melsungen	52-0563
DIPPENSTEDT, Minna	20	Geestendorf	50-0366
DIPPMANN, Friedr.	52	Sachsen	53-0590
Christiane 48, Friedrich 22, Amalia 16			
Emilie 14, Marie 12, Ernst 8, August 7			
DIPPOLD, Georg	32	Burk/Bav.	52-0960
DIRKER, W.	40	Schelenburg	54-1566
Caroline 43, Lotte 5			
DIRKMANN, Franz	23	Ascheberg	49-0324
DIRKS, Marg.	36	Wueppel	54-0872
DIRR, Jos.	33	Niederklein	51-0460
Margaretha 34, Marianne 6			
DIRRLAM, Franz	28	Pilsen	52-1200
Theresia 23			
DIRTER, Carl Alb.	26	Irendorf	49-0912
DIRTSCH, And.	20	Aber	54-1283
DISCH, Wilh.	30	Roess	49-0912
DISCHEL, Martha	21	Steindorf	54-0930
DISKE, Joh. Heinr.	46	Frossen	54-1297
Johanne 29, Johann 26, Marie 12, Adam 17			
Gottlieb 7, Christian 4			
DISSELHER, Maria	35	Anem	49-0912
Christiane 10, Weinant 8, Dora 6, Mina 3			
Albertine 10m			
DISTEL, Agatha	25	Villingen	52-1101
DITMAR, Carl	52	Artern	50-0439
DITRICH, Fr.	32	Hasserode	54-1283
Henriette 32, Henriette 2, Diedrich by			
DITTES, Bernhard	19	Dresden	52-0370
DITTIG, Georg Ad.	56	Schweina	54-0987
Friedrich 29			
DITTMAR, Anton	30	Fulda	53-0473
Margaretha 29			
DITTMAR, August	18	Braak	54-1575
DITTMAR, Gottfried	58	Pfiffelbach	52-1148
Charlotte 64			
DITTMAR, Johannes	23	Massfeld	53-0585
Friederike 26			
DITTMAR, Wilh.	21	Gerstungen	52-1304
DITTMER, Georg	22	Oberstetten	47-0672
DITTMER, Johann	31	Siemerswald	51-0460
DITTMER, P. (m)	18	Bullstadt	49-0416
DITTMERS, William		Hohenauerberg	50-0323
DITTRICH, Abraham	28	Langenlaube	54-0930
Gottfried 24			
DITTRICH, Joseph	24	Bremen	49-0383
Philipp 19			
DITZ, Heinr.	30	Hessen	50-0021
DITZ, Jos.	30	Minden	48-1114
DITZ, Leonard	32	Northeim	52-1101
DITZEL, Barbara	23	Gelnhausen	53-0914
DITZEL, Conrad	30	Neuwart	53-0942
DIX, John James	20	Steinach	52-1304
DOBELT, Mich	26	Strassburg/Po	51-1796
DOBMEYER, Magdal.	24	Hanneried	54-1078
DOCKERN, Charl.	22	Boelhorst	49-0329
Wilhelmine 19			
DOCKHORN, Henry	18	Bueckeburg	53-0888
DODE, Heinrich	15	Albertshausen	52-0563
DOEBEREINER, Georg	29	Bayern	53-0557
DOEBERITSCH, Chr.	37	Kahla	54-1297
DOEBL, Aloys	28	Mandelstadt	54-0850

NAME	AGE	RESIDENCE	YR-LIST
Rosina 35, Walpurga 7			
DOEBLING, Hein Chr	43	Salzungen	54-0987
Marie Christ 33, Cath. Doroth 9			
DOEHLER, And. Paul	30	Hohenbuch	52-1200
DOEHLER, Fr. Aug.	19	Leipzig	49-0574
DOEHLING, G. (m)	34	Messelhausen	51-1796
DOEHRER, Wm. Fr.	15	Beldstedt	51-0756
DOEHRING, Gabriel	39	Salzoden/Hess	51-1725
DOEHRSCHAEDEL, Ph.	38	Baden	53-0590
Elisabeth 38, Joseph 13, Franciska 10			
Mathias 8, Andreas 5			
DOELITZ, Georg	24	Magdeburg	48-0284
DOELL, Adam	19	Wippersheim	53-0942
Heinrich 14			
DOELL, Barbara	51	Prichsenstadt	52-0807
DOELL, Caspar	49	Bersroth/Hess	52-0807
Philipp 21			
DOELL, Ernst	18	Wippersheim	50-0311
DOELL, Nicolaus	45	Bornhagen	54-0053
Christine 26			
DOELLE, Heinr.	29	Heiligenstadt	49-1106
DOELLE, Joh. Adam	45	Dieterode	54-0903
Anna Marg. 38, Joseph 14, Anna Cath. 22			
Christoph 10, Herb 7, Peter 4, Maria 2			
DOELLER, Carl	32	Hofgeismar/He	51-1532
Anna Gertrud 24, Christoph 9m, Elise 2			
DOELLFELDT, Meyer	19	Rotenburg	54-1649
DOEMER, Catharina	29	Sparwissen	52-0095
DOEMERL, Joseph	19	Nordwalde	49-0324
DOENCH, V.	27	Holzhausen	51-0517
DOEPPLER, Therese	22	Erfurt	54-1649
DOEPPNER, Caroline	26	Altenstein	48-1179
DOEREN, Joseph	17	Memmingen	54-1566
DOERFER, Christina	24	Wolfersdorf	54-0930
DOERFER, Wilh'mine	19	Vogelsang	54-0872
DOERFFULT, C. (m)	38	Geyer	49-0416
DOERFLER, Georg	53	Egelsheim	53-0905
DOERFLER, Johann	19	Wasserkurt/Bv	52-1332
DOERFUSS, J.	28	Lauf	53-0582
DOERGE, Robert	19	Berlin	54-1371
DOERGEL, Joh.	41	Eggeten	53-0825
Anna Barbara 34, Anna Cath. 14			
Anna Christ. 11, Johann 6, Anna Maria 9m			
DOERGES, Christian	36	Meinersen	52-1410
Christiane 28, Heinrich 7, Christian 4			
Ferdinand			
DOERING, Christine	25	Atens	53-1070
DOERING, Elisabeth	19	Feidenroth	51-0352
DOERING, Friedrich	26	Schmiedeberg	49-0345
DOERING, Josepha	23	Gieboldshause	51-1640
DOERING, Sebastian	26	Muehlhausen	51-0326
DOERINGER, Heinr.	33	Bersrod	52-1105
Dorothea 31, Catharina 6, Jacob 4			
Caspar 2, Philipp 21, Louise 60			
Caspar 26, Dora 22			
DOERINGSFELD, Aug	42	Leustrup	54-0987
Friedrich 32			
DOERNBERG, Feist	59	Vacha	54-1371
Meyer 29, Bertha 25, Susanne 23			
DOERNTE, Wilhelm	25	Suelbecke	53-0585
Caroline 23			
DOERNZ, Kunigunde	23	Nuisberg	49-1106
DOERR, Joh.	35	Holzborn	51-1160
Adam 32, Marie 25, Johannes 9m			
DOERR, Joh.	16	Wielinghausen	51-1160
DOERR, Sophie	23	Elberfeld	48-0269
DOERRES, Barbara	25	Handhof/Bav.	53-0628
DOERRJES, Heinr.	39	Holzminden	53-1013
Haennchen 2, Friedr. 35			
DOERSCH, Elise	22	Hessen	53-0590
DOERSCH, Friedrich	20	Neuenburg	52-0351
DOERSCHER, Carsten	27	Wilmington	52-1620
Louise 27			
DOERSCHNER, Angel.	32	Cur-Hessen	53-0557
Anna Margret 4			
DOERSCHNER, Angel.	32	Kur-Hessen	53-0557
Anna Margret 4			
DOERSEN, Margrethe	28	Duessenheim	52-0351

NAME	AGE	RESIDENCE	YR-LIST
DOESCHER, Anna	19	Ohrstaedt	52-1625
DOESCHER, Cath.	25	Hannover	52-0699
DOESCHER, Claus	15	Lintig	50-0366
DOESCHER, Heinr.	16	Bederkesa	50-1317
DOESCHER, Margaret	18	Lintig	51-1084
DOEST, Hugo	17	Len-ldt	50-0944
DOETSCH, Marg.	28	Gerolshafen	51-0405
DOETSCHER, Elis.	26	Voelkershause	53-0942
DOETTER, Anna	18	Lohr	54-1297
DOEVERS, H.	31		54-1716
DOHLEN, v. Anna	20	Drangstedt	50-0366
DOHLING, Doroth.	34	Hinstadt	47-0918
DOHLMANN, Mary	24	Eimelrode	53-1164
DOHM, Conrad	20	Ehger	49-0345
DOHM, Georg Ludwig	28	Schopfloch	53-1070
DOHN, Elisabeth	32	Eisenach	53-1013
Wilhelm 7, Georgine 3			
DOHN, W. (m)	16	Crefeld	49-0416
M. (f) 21, J. (m) 3			
DOHREN, M. (f)	13	Schopfloch	50-0746
A. (m) 20			
DOHRMANN, Diedrich	19	Buecken	54-0987
DOHRMANN, John	37	Asendorf	48-1209
Christina 30, William 7, Dorette 2			
DOLCH, Nicolaus	36	Winterstein	53-0825
Martha Elis. 30			
DOLL, Adelheid	25	Rheinbreitbac	51-1035
DOLLE, Wilh.	28	Hameln	51-1084
DOLLINGER, Conrad	31	Klausaurach	54-1371
Elisabeth 31, Anna 2, Michael 3m			
DOMERBERG, Heinz	32	Engter	54-0987
DOMEYER, Anna	24	Norden	50-1236
DOMEYER, Johann	43	Wildungen	53-1023
Susanne 33, Friedrich 14, Benjamin 10			
Catharine 7, Carl 4, Daniel 2			
DOMEYER, Trine	25	Hohenhorst	54-1716
DOMHAHN, Johann	29	Itzlingen	52-1625
DOMHOF, Joh. Heinr	25	Gretisch	54-0930
Marie Elis. 24, Cath. Maria 3			
DOMHOFS, Maria	18	Osnabrueck	52-1512
DOMMEYER, Carl	45	Veldrau	54-1078
Sophie 50, Heinrich 29, Marie 18, Carl 14			
Adolph 11			
DONAI, Caroline	44	Dresden	51-0352
Ernst 10, Robert 8			
DONAI, Ernst	10	Altenburg	51-0352
DONEISKE, Wilhelm	50	Nitzwalde	54-1371
Justine 40, Adeline 20, Bertha 16, Ida 8			
Wilhelm 6			
DONNERLEIN, Georg	20	Hohenschaerz	52-1129
DOOBER, August	23	Bromskirchen	53-0492
DOPKE, Wilhelmine	29	Grossenrode	54-0987
DORBAUM, Diedrich	33	Westtoffeln	51-1639
Anna 38			
DORBERT, Franz	17	Frensdorf	52-0370
DORCH, Lorenz	18	Friesen/Bav.	53-0628
DORER, August	23	Waldkirch	54-1371
DORESCHLER, Wilh.	37	Solingen	48-0406
Wilhelmine 34, Reinhold 13, Hugo 11			
Auguste 1, Hulda 8, Ida 6, Berta 2			
Emilie 46			
DORFLER, Ernst	21	Brieg	53-0161
DORFLER, J. (m)	20	Wasserknoden	54-1341
DORFUSS, Joh.	35	Muehlburg	51-1796
DORFUSS, Joh. Geo.	20	Herzogenaurad	51-1532
DORFZAUN, S. (m)	31	Rodelmeyer	53-0942
DORING, Mary	22	Alsfeld	54-1341
DORMANN, Christ	42	Hartzberg	54-1575
Louise 20, Friedr. 12, Heinrich 9			
August 4			
DORMANN, Christian	15	Hartzburg	54-1575
DORMANN, Christian	42	Hartzberg	54-1575
Louise 20, Friedrich 12, Heinrich 9			
August 4			
DORMANN, Marie	28	Poicken	53-0652
DORMEYER, Conr.	23	Ahlden	49-0742
B. (f) 20, T. (f) 19, J. (f) 4			
DORN, Anna	24	Gasseldorf	54-1283

NAME	AGE	RESIDENCE	YR-LIST
DORN, Elisabeth	19	Oberzell	53-0435
DORN, Johann	29	Altdorf	51-1035
DORN, John	23	Utrictshausen	52-0515
DORN, Rosa	36	Ermreuth	53-0320
DORN, Wilhelm	48	Zeitz	53-0652
DORNBERGER, Johann	28	Rehburg	54-0930
DORNBUSCH, Wilhelm	26	Passon/Hann.	51-1796
DORNENBURG, Fr.	47	Mettmann	48-0565
DORNER, Joh. Georg	40	Ditterheim	49-0574
Marg. 32			
DORNER, John	49	Wessennoter	49-0737
Cathrina 50, George 27, John G. 14			
Barbara 12, Margaretha 8			
DORNER, Leopold	30	Wien/Oest.	52-1620
DORNHEBER, Joseph	30	Wiseck	54-1554
DORNHOSEN, C. (f)	19	Weydenberg	52-0804
DORNPACH, Engel	27	Salchendorf	54-1092
Clara 25			
DORNUTZER, Hein. J	21	Prague	48-1015
DORNWELL, Fred. Wm	23	Appenrode	53-0991
DORR, Christ.	16	Weisenohr	52-0693
DORRING, Paul	27	Lispenhausen	52-1661
Anna 21			
DORSCH, Carl F.	27	Hoff/Bav.	54-1092
DORSCH, Joh.	28	Konradsreuth	47-0868
Wilh. 34			
DORSCHEL, Leonhard	25	Wuertenberg	51-0405
DORSCHEL, Margaret	25	Aalen	48-1355
DORSCHEL, Rohmann	20	Blankenau	52-1200
DORTLANG, Marie	20	Prussia	50-1317
DORWITH, (m)	21	Batschel	53-0914
DOSTAL, John	56	Boehmen	54-1724
Rud. (f) 40, Chr. 17, John 16, Mary 12			
Helena 9, Chr. 7, Rosalie 3			
DOTSCHEL, P. (m)	29	Oberweisingen	50-0379
DOTTERVICH, James	30	Prag	49-0737
Anna 26, Gertraut 4, Mary by			
DOTTERWEILER, Conr	24	Steindorf	53-0590
DOVEEN, Arndt	27	Borsum	53-0652
DRACKE, Friedrich	27	Radsick	53-0825
DRAEGER, Conrad	25	Poxdorf	53-1062
DRALLE, August	32	Reborg	54-1282
Caroline 30, Wilhelm 3, August by			
DRALLE, Hermann	14	Bremervoerde	51-1035
DRAMING, Friedr.	17	Einbeck/Hann.	51-1532
DRANDORFF, Julius	45	Schneeberg	52-0699
DRAPP, Franz	35	Roehlbach/Bav	50-0323
DRASKOVITCH, Mich.	31	Italy	51-1245
DRATZ, Mrs.	39	New York	48-1243
Carl 8, Francis 6, Emma 4, (f) 25			
DRAWIEL, August	28	Preutzlitz	53-0324
DREBERT, John	42	Meerholz	53-0888
DRECHSEL, Caroline	18	Lobenstein	54-0987
DRECHSEL, Dorothea	28	Hof	49-1106
DRECHSLER, Conrad	25	Hannover	51-1245
Carl 32			
DRECHSLER, Jane Ch	56	Crimmitschau	53-0991
DRECHSLER, Joh.	19	Longstein	53-1013
DRECHSLER, Theodor	31	Goerlitz	54-1554
DRECHSLER, Valent.	27	Wittgen	47-0828
DRECK, Heinrich	42	Buer	52-1625
DREES, Gesine	21	Altenhagen	49-0324
DREFES, Anna	22	Leiste	54-0872
DREHMANN, Ernst H.	22	Ottersberg	52-1362
DREIER, Caral	24	Hameln	48-1114
DREIER, Christ.	25	Wenzhagen	52-1661
Wilhelmine 18, Wilhelm 22			
DREIER, Fr.	16	Ottersberg	49-1358
DREISMANN, J Fried	29	Verel/Pr.	50-0323
DREISSIGACKER, Hel	37	Tolheim	53-1164
DREIWER, Gottlieb	22	Singe	53-0928
DREIZ, Phil.	40	Holstein	51-1160
DREKER, Clemens	20	Mittelruessel	49-0737
DREMMING, Caspar	27	Odenhausen	53-0492
Phil. 30			
DREPS, Philipp	22	Heerdorf	51-1084
DRES, Clamor Heinr	24	Bohnde	49-0352
DRESCHEL, El. Marg	42	Dessau/Bav.	51-1796
DRESING, Georg	15	Essen	53-1086
Louis 17			
DRESLER, Jos.	41	Harrburg	54-1283
DRESSEL, D. (m)	33	Altona	48-0453
DRESSEL, Georg	18	Eisshausen	53-0320
DRESSEL, Georg	21	Rodach	53-0590
DRESSEL, Joh Heinr	28	Hohendorf	53-0825
DRESSING, Georg	15	Essen	53-1086
Louis 17			
DRESSING, Wilhelm	35	Essen	53-1086
Marie 38, Christine 11, Louise 9			
Minna (died) 2, Marie (died) 7			
Henriette 12, Joh. 9m			
DRESSLER, Adam Hr.	18	Erbenhausen	48-1114
August 14			
DRESSLER, Carl	25	Gunzenhausen	54-1371
DRESSLER, G. (m)	24	Saxony	50-0311
DRESSLER, Wilh'mne	52	Coelln	52-1332
Adolphine 18			
DREULER, Jos.	41	Harrburg	54-1283
DREUMANN, Lorenz	19	Muehlhausen	53-0928
Rosa 10			
DREWES, Fr.	36	Waldeck	53-0942
Cath. 44, Elise 15			
DREWES, Herman	17	Bessern	52-1362
DREWES, Joh. Fried	18	Reessum	51-1101
DREWES, Louise	28	Bremervoerde	52-0807
DREYER, Alida	18	Ottersberg	49-0574
DREYER, Catharine	17	Nathbergen	54-1371
DREYER, Doris	26	Uthlede	47-0872
Johanne 3			
DREYER, Eivert	28	Beverstedt	51-1084
DREYER, H.	18	Spieka	54-1716
DREYER, Henry	28	New York	53-0991
DREYER, Herrmann	16	Hannover	52-0699
DREYER, Joh.	28	Bruchhausen	47-0918
DREYER, W. (m)	23	Detmold	54-0918
DREYER, Wilhelm	19	Wittlage	53-0628
DREYER, William	19	Altena/Pr.	48-0053
DREYFUSS, Minna	17	Dransfeld	54-1297
Doris 20			
DRIES, Franz	20	Osnabruck	49-1106
DRIFFMEYER, Friedr	39	Boebber	53-1086
Clara 47, Wilhelm 14			
DRILLING, Franz	50	Arensberg	52-0699
Sophie 52, Johann 30, Margarethe 26			
Anna 22, Heinrich 13			
DRISCOLL, John	33	Gt. Britian	48-1015
Elisabeth 29			
DROEGE, Friedrich	44	Oesede	54-0872
Anna 43, Franz 20, Joseph 14, Goswin 9			
Friedrich 7, Catharina by			
DROEGE, H.C. (m)	27	Brunswick	50-0311
DROEGEMEIER, Fried	21	Bremen	50-0021
DROELLINGER, W'mne	23	Tiembach/Bav.	52-1332
Anna Barbara 20			
DROENERT, Friedr.	51	Warendorf	54-0872
DROESCHER, Georg	39	Hirschbrun	53-1062
Johann 30, Barbara 27, Georg 4			
DROESTEN, M. Elis.	21	Ellingerholz	49-0352
DROMM, Wilh.	30	Lenkirch	49-0574
DROSSLER, Gottlieb	26	Muhlhausen/Pr	53-0628
Maria Johane 24, Gottlieb by			
Heinr Albert 2			
DROSTE, Louise	18	Buchen	54-0987
DROTH, Margaretha	18	Roth	52-0515
DROWATZKY, Johann	31	Treptow	54-0872
DRUCKER, Heinr Geo	32	Ahden	47-0918
DRUCKER, Johann	25	Guethersloh	52-1410
Johanne 3			
DRUCKER, Johann	22	Lehste	51-0352
DRUCKER, Meyer	20	Rennertehause	54-1371
DRUESELDOW, Albert	38	Seehausen	54-0987
Wilhelmine 33, Albert 14, Rudi 9			
Louise 8, Gustav 6, Waldemar 5, Emilie 2			
August by			
DRUGE, John	31	New York	53-0888
DRUKE, H.	9m	Bayedorf	54-1716

NAME	AGE	RESIDENCE	YR-LIST
DRULLMANN, Theodor	46	Wetzlar	53-0590
DRUMMER, Georg	35	Baiern	53-0585
Walburga 28, Martin 3			
DRUPE, Johann	29	Bayedorf	54-1716
DUBBERS, J.H.	20	Farven	54-0918
DUBBERT, Minna	24	Blomberg	54-1168
Elise 20			
DUBENHORST, F.	25	Freidorf	47-0872
Maria 24, Johann 4, Heinrich 9m			
DUCKWITZ, August	22	Stettin	53-1023
Louise 19, Therese 3m			
DUDLINGER, Joh. G.	22	Blumigs	49-0912
DUEBER, Johannes	45	Obernetphen	53-1070
Catharina 38, Johannes 12, Pauline 9			
DUEFFEL, Rud. Aug.	34	Essens/Hann.	51-1725
DUEHME, Jacob	41	Dettau/Sax.	54-1092
DUEHNINGER, Jacob	23	Hagelbach	50-0366
DUEHRS, Joh.	21	Zeven	54-0918
DUEKER, Catharine	18	Beverstedt	53-0991
DUELFER, Balthasar	15	Ziegenhein	54-1566
DUEMEN, Claus	30	Armstorf/Hann	51-1725
DUEMLER, Aug.	19	Dresden	50-1071
DUEMLER, Conrad	24	Bremen	51-1438
DUEMLER, Elisabeth	26	Sigenz	54-1443
DUEMMING, Joh.	27	Halbersdorf	52-1321
DUENKEL, Herrmann	27	Stargard	51-0652
DUERGELOH, G.H.(m)	20	Vlotho	49-0329
DUERHOLZ, August	27	Melsungen	54-0053
DUERING, Meta	28	Neulandermoor	50-0366
DUERING, Otto	25	New York	52-0048
DUERING, Wilhelm	49	Lutter	53-1016
DUERR, Caspar	22	Markelsheim	54-1371
DUERR, Emelius	38	Zwickau	53-0991
DUERR, Franz	25	Suelzfeld/Bav	52-0807
DUERR, Georg	37	Pommern	52-0693
DUERR, Joh. Friedr	40	Rochingen	48-1355
DUERR, Peter	41	Gerschfeld	52-1362
DUERRFUSS, J Peter	30	Kleinseebach	48-1355
DUESSLING, A. Mar.	25	Gletchheim	52-0279
DUESTER, Ann Mary	22	Solingen	48-0406
DUESTERDIEK, Fr'ke	26	Bolensen	51-0500
DUETHORN, Conrad	43	Steinfeld	51-1639
Maria 31, Mariane 17, Cathrina 11			
Barbara 5, Michael 4, Kunigunde 2			
DUEWEL, Heinrich	8	Polle/Hann.	54-1092
DUFENDACHS, Mar. E	21	Osnabrueck	52-1512
DUFFREUT, Wilhelm	32	Neckarsweinme	52-0117
DUFFRIAN, Nicolaus	49	Struemphlbrun	51-0384
Catharina 52, Catharina 27, Christian 22			
Friederike 22, Joseph 14, Franz 3			
DUHNSING, Marie	63	Steimke	47-0762
Sophie 23			
DUHRMANN, Johann	34	Reienberg	54-0872
Minna 30, Carl 5, Maria by			
DUISSEL, William	45	Sulzfeld	51-1588
Maria 40, Elizabeth 18, Anna 10, George 7			
John 3			
DULL, Barbara	26	Ostheim	53-0825
DUMBROF, Anton	13	Oberkuebs/Bav	52-0351
Johann 17			
DUMMLEIN, Joseph	19	Cronach	53-0914
DUNGER, Marie	19	Hamburg	47-0158
DUNKAKE, F.H.	26	Deedendorf	53-0492
DUNKAKE, Joh. Herm	21	Dedendorf	54-0987
Friedrich 18			
DUNKE, August	20	Braunschweig	50-0379
DUNKEL, Wilhelm	22	Vippbach	51-1062
DUNKELBERG, August	26	Prussia	54-1724
DUNKER, Heinrich	22	Schneeren	54-0882
DUNKER, Wilhelm	35	Engter	54-0987
Louise 23			
DUNTEMANN, Heinr.	26	Ferlingehause	47-0872
DUNTZE, Eduard	29	Fritzlar	54-0053
DURBAUM, Friedr.	36	Wittingshause	54-1716
Marie 33, Anna 8, Burkhard 6, Alwina 5			
Ote 2, Amalia 11m			
DURELS, Eibe Hinr.	21	Kappeln	47-0872
August Fried 17, Anna Rebecka 20			

NAME	AGE	RESIDENCE	YR-LIST
Helene Wilh. 13, Aug. Doroth. 11			
Anna Margret 49			
DURMANN, Nic.	30	Eger	54-1575
DURNBERGER, Jos.	20	Hamberg	52-0515
DURR, Henry	18	Queck	48-0284
DURRHAMMER, N. (m)	26	Baden	52-1512
DURSCHMANN, Gott.	24	Rothenbach	47-0868
DUSCHANECK, Joseph	29	Freiburg	52-0699
Marie 24			
DUSCHEN, H.J. (m)	29	Moelle/Hann.	52-0960
DUSS, Ed.	27	Heinigen	53-1000
DUSSEL, Georg	52	Goettingen	49-1106
DUTSCH, John	30	Rostadt	48-0887
DUTSCHER, Ernest	18	Dumgdorf	51-1588
DUTSCHLER, Caspar	31	Heidelbach	51-1084
EADENBERGER, Ferd.	24	Gehstedt	54-1094
EBBECKE, August	14	Bremke	54-1443
EBBECKE, Wilhelm	29	Blankenburg	54-1575
EBBEL, Joh. Lorenz	18	Arzberg	51-1640
EBBINGHAUSE, Fried	20	Iserlohn	54-1452
EBEL, Andreas	25	Ferdinandsdor	51-0384
EBEL, Everhard	27	Algermissen	51-0048
EBEL, J. (m)	25	Landsberg	49-0416
EBEL, Just. Fred.	26	Duermenz	53-1164
EBELE, J.G. (m)	21	Wangen	54-0918
EBELE, Theresia	21	Nuernberg	53-0473
EBELING, Anna	18	Hagen/Hann.	47-0987
EBELING, Ludw.	46	Goslar	50-1317
EBELING, Theodor	22	Hameln	51-1640
Minna 18			
EBELL, Wolf	20	Arzberg	50-1236
EBEN, Eugen	23	Weilendorf	48-0887
EBEN, Isidor	24	Berlin	48-1243
EBENHACK, Joh Albr	29	Obersambach	54-0850
Barbara 33, Johann by			
EBENHACK, Johann	31	Ermreuth/Bav.	52-0351
Margarethe 26, Johann(died) 9m			
EBER, Maria	22	Eisenach	53-1013
EBERBECK, A. (m)	28	Steineck	52-1661
EBERDING, H. (m)	21	Bueckeburg	52-1321
EBERELING, H. (m)	21	Bueckeburg	52-1321
EBERHAGEN, Harry	25	Moringen	53-0582
EBERHAND, Friedr.	30	Stade	53-0652
EBERHARD, Anna	24	Dorumul	50-1317
EBERHARD, Friedr.	20	Gotha	54-1649
EBERHARD, Georg	40	Edelschutz	52-1101
EBERHARD, J. (m)	24	Deizling	52-0652
EBERHARD, Johann	28	Dessingen	54-1419
EBERHARDT, Cath.	30	Waldcappel	49-0352
EBERHARDT, Diedr.	34	Bernsdorf	52-1512
Anna 33, J.D. (m) 9, Dorothea 7			
Anna Sophia 3, Caroline 1			
EBERHARDT, G. (m)	32	Weitroth	52-0652
EBERHARDT, G. (m)	33	Waldkappeln	52-0652
M. (f) 31, F. (m) 10			
EBERL, Christina	23	Mettwitz	53-0324
EBERLE, Aphra	28	Fulda	54-1554
EBERLE, Georg	32	Bissingen	52-1200
EBERLE, Georg	26	Terstenhof	49-0352
EBERLEIN, Christ.	33	Erlangen	52-1200
EBERLEIN, Joh.	40	Oberlenden	52-0558
M. (f) 33			
EBERLEIN, William	29	Steinbach	53-0914
Barbara 40			
EBERLING, Clara	19	Dillenburg	53-1023
Catharine 14			
EBERS, Andreas	42	Hagen	52-0048
Arnold 13			
EBERSBERGER, Balth	34	Birkach	52-1304
EBERT, Alexander	24	Pillan	50-0840
EBERT, Augustus	30	Fondulac, Wis	53-0991
EBERT, Caroline	22	Kaunstein/Pr.	50-0323
EBERT, Caspar	22	Wuertemberg	51-0405
EBERT, Catharine	20	Heilbronn	53-0590
EBERT, Ernst Heinr	23	Hohenalten	54-0987
EBERT, Ferdinand	24	Rothholz	50-0840
EBERT, Ferdinand	36	Schwarzberg	52-0117
Chr. Michela 39, Caroline 17			

NAME	AGE	RESIDENCE	YR-LIST
Wilhelmine 13, Gottliebe 11, Carl 8			
Theodore 5, Emil 1			
EBERT, Henriette	39	Cohnberg	54-1168
EBERT, J.H.	26	Niederschelds	53-1016
Louisa 24			
EBERT, Joh Andreas	51	Schwarzberg	52-0117
Maria 56, August 20, Louise 27, Minna 16			
EBERT, M.M. (m)	32	Trienz	50-0746
EBERT, Peter	25	Ferdinandsdor	51-0384
EBERT, Rudolph	19	Beage	48-1184
EBERTIN, Barbara	19	Oberstetten	53-0914
EBERTS, Henn.	43	Crefeld	52-1321
EBERTSBACH, Carl G	38	Lichtenstein	48-1131
EBLING, August	33	Krimmensen	54-1717
EBNER, Marg.	28	Grafenheinsfe	54-1575
ECK, Andreas	26	Steinbach	52-1105
Christine 19, Maria 3			
ECK, Georg	18	Flohe	54-0882
ECKARDT, Chr.	45	Neustadt	53-0914
ECKARDT, Elisabeth	17	Niederorschel	53-0267
ECKARDT, Elisabeth	19	Neustadt	53-0320
ECKARDT, Heinrich	25	Berlin	52-0563
ECKARIUS, Andreas	46	Gotha	53-0473
Ernst 14			
ECKART, Michael	48	Lollar	54-0965
Ludwig 15, Margretha 43, Margretha 24			
Elisabeth 17, Friedrich 10, Heinrich 8			
Magnus 5, baby			
ECKARTE, Joh. Fr.	48	Schleiz	49-0352
Marie 46, Louise 20, Gustav 19			
ECKEL, H.E.	23	Darmstadt	54-1566
Marie Philip 21			
ECKEL, Herm.	21	New York	52-0895
ECKEL, Joh.	18	Bringhausen	54-0600
ECKERMANN, L. (m)	42	Bassinghausen	48-0445
R. (f) 40, J. (f) 17, H. (m) 10, D. (f) 8			
L. (m) 6, C. (m) 2, J. (f) 6m			
ECKERT, Georg Hein	27	Arendorf	53-1000
Cath. 27, Christ. 3			
ECKERT, Gottlieb	17	Kittethal	50-0379
ECKERT, Heinrich	23	Gotha	53-0473
ECKHARD, Adolph	3	Coburg	51-0405
ECKHARD, N.	18	Lohne/Hess.	51-0048
ECKHARDT, Adam	26	Kirchoff	53-1000
ECKHARDT, Heinr.	57	Braunhausen	48-0101
Elisab. 55, George 26, Peter 24, Anna 22			
Elisab. 20, Heinr. 18, Ernst 16			
Catharine 14, Mariane 11, Martha Elis. 11			
Johannes 9, Elisabeth 28			
ECKHARDT, Louise	22	Laufen	48-0565
ECKHOFF, A.H.	28	Mojenhopt	54-0918
ECKHOFF, Christ.	22	Pyrmont	47-0918
Sophie 25, Helene 20, Lisette 7			
ECKMANN, Fr.	42	Omdorf	54-1470
Rosa 38, William 10, John 6, daughter 9m			
ECKMANN, Sara	17	Altenmuhr	51-1160
ECKOFF, Jacob	15	Setdorf/Hann.	53-0475
ECKSTEIN, Anton	27	Boxdorf/Bav.	53-0475
ECKSTEIN, Conr.	31	Vadenroth	49-0742
ECKSTEIN, Elise	26	Storndorf	52-0652
ECKSTEIN, Erhard	21	Coburg	53-1013
ECKSTEIN, Hermann	24	Gr Engersheim	53-0838
ECKTENDUCK, Wilh.	43	Schoetmar	50-0944
Wilhelminna 45, Wilhelminna 12			
William 11, Friedrich 9, Louisa 7			
Henrietta 4			
ECKUEN, Franz	30	Luebbecke/Pr.	51-1725
Eva 44, Friedrich 5			
EDDEL, Christoph	30	Peppinghausen	51-1588
EDE, Cathrine	28	Germersheim	49-0912
EDELBROCK, Anton	35	Duelmen	50-0944
Ann Mary 35, Ann Mary 8, Anton Jr. 7			
Bernhard 5, Anton Joseph 3, Anna by			
EDELBROCK, Bernh.	35	Duelme	50-0021
EDELER, Heinrich	52	Ostermunsel	51-1588
Louisa 50, Henrietta 18, Wilhelmina 9			
Caroline 7			
EDELING, Aug.	31	Elze	54-1168
EDELMANN, Edward	30	Wingershausen	48-1209
EDER, Herm. Johann	40	Gunzenhausen	53-0905
EDER, Jacob	46	Seckenheim	52-1625
Eva 32, Jacob 18, Susanne 10, Mathias 8			
Johann 7, Philipp 4, Peter 2			
EDER, Math.	26	Thalenmais	53-0435
Gerth. 31			
EDER, Michael	37	Breitenloh	54-0872
Mathias 38, Peter 26, Franz 32			
EDING, Catharine	20	Rotenburg	54-1649
EDING, Johann	29	Badbergen	54-0987
EDKE, Calr. (m)	21	Rebbra	49-0737
EDLER, Heinr.	25	Ostermunzel	50-0439
EFFINGER, Eh. (m)	22	Oberkirk	51-1796
EGEL, Herman	18	Mittelruessel	49-0737
EGER, Gustav	15	Eisenberg	52-1661
EGER, Heinrich	33	Werdau	53-0637
Wilhelmine 32, Franz 7, August 5, Anna 2			
Pauline 11m			
EGER, Johann	36	Empfingen	52-0279
EGERT, Carl	29	Stralsund	54-0882
EGGEMEYER, Friedr.	25	Feldrup	54-0872
Louise 27			
EGGER, Johann	35	Koetzing	53-0905
Anna 37, Anna 9, Elisabeth 5, Rosina 3			
Maria by			
EGGERMEIER, John	20	Holstein	51-1588
EGGERS, Fr.	26	Sibecksen	54-1078
EGGERS, Helene	22	Dorum	53-0905
EGGERS, Joh Ludolf	21	Bremen	51-0352
EGGERS, Johann	16	Buchholz	54-0903
EGGERS, Leonhardin	19	Hossenassel	50-0323
EGGERS, Minna	60	Creba-k	50-0439
EGGERS, Minna	62	Gald-----	50-0439
Marie 17			
EGGERT, Conrad	38	Neustadt	48-1209
Barbara 49			
EGGERT, John	23	Bremen	48-1015
EGGERT, Louisa	16	Wassenborn	54-1470
Friederike 24			
EGGERT, Wilhelm	27	Berlin	53-0161
EGLAUCH, Conrad	28	Hofheim	53-1086
EGLER, Fritz	32	Schwedt	53-0585
Friederike 30, Auguste 4, Fritz 6			
Marie 2, Georg 9m			
EGLOFFSTEIN, Fr.	37	Greussen	54-0600
EHARDI, Georg	37	Spalt	54-0850
Christine 35, Victoria 8, Joseph 7			
Anton 5, Georg 3			
EHEBRECHT, Aug.	23	Wasserborn	54-1470
EHEIDE, Gottfr.	22	Lohmach	54-1282
EHEMAN, Christ.	20	Bielefeld	51-1739
EHEMANN, Joh. G.	48	Seerstetten	50-1071
Dorothea 48, Anna Maria 15			
Anna Barbara 13, Dorothea 7, Balthaser 3			
EHLEN, Claus	33	Neu Bullstedt	49-0574
Anna 42, Diedrich 16, Gesche 5			
EHLERS, Adelheid	3	Westerwich	52-0515
EHLERS, Adelheid	29	Thedinghausen	49-0574
EHLERS, Amalie	22	Barfeld	53-0652
EHLERS, D. Heinr.	16	Uentzen	52-0563
EHLERS, Friedr.	24	Neuenkirchen	50-0472
EHLERS, Joh. Diedr	52	Oetzen	52-0515
Rebecca 46, Rebecca 16, Diedreth 14			
Johann 9, Henry 6, Adelaide 3			
EHLERS, Wichmann	22	Leste	49-0324
EHLERS, Wilhelm	20	Harsefeld	52-0895
EHLERT, Carl	19	Bohnde	49-0352
Anna Marie 18			
EHLERT, Wilhelm	50	Goettingen	54-1717
EHLGEN, Margaretha	19	Ruesselsheim	52-0807
EHM, Cath.	22	Treysa	51-1160
EHM, Conrad	26	Baiern	52-1362
EHMAN, George	27	Mittelruessel	49-0737
EHNBORM, Dina		Schwarz	54-1575
EHNERT, Gottlieb	35	Eisenberg	53-0942
Henriette 24, Hermann 2, baby			
EHNES, Georg	32	Munnigberg	51-1739

NAME	AGE	RESIDENCE	YR-LIST
Anna 50, Rosine 25, Friedr. 2			
EHNINGER, Rosine	19	Hirschheim	54-1283
EHRENBECK, Therese	34	Godheim	48-0260
EHRENBERG, A.W.	36	Salzwedel	51-1160
EHRENBERGER, Gotth	19	Lintersdorf	52-1321
EHRENBRINK, Herm R	25	Osnabrueck	51-0352
EHRENGRONER, A.(f)	28	Lichtenbrg	50-0746
EHRENPFORTEN, Joh.	37	Osterode/Hann	54-0965
EHRHARD, Felicitas	30	Neuhaus/Baden	53-0475
EHRHARDT, Gottf.	54	Breitenbach/T	52-0960
EHRHARDT, Heinrich	60	Bassum	54-0987
Heinrich 30, Maria 32			
EHRHARDT, Johann	30	Nuernberg	54-0053
EHRLICHER, Heinr.	18	Darmstadt	48-0887
EHRMANN, Anna	32	Unterschwanin	54-1566
Andreas 2			
EHRMANN, Jacob	33	Oberhinterhof	52-0515
EHRSAM, Michael	38	Birkath	51-1588
EHRTZMANN, Heinr.	19	Hetteroth	52-1101
EIBEL, Jacob	15	Altendorf	52-1105
EICHBAUER, Georg	29	Feuchtwangen	52-0515
Simon 56, Anna M. 58, Friedr. 31			
Anna M. 30, George 9, Joh. Mich. 2			
EICHE, Carl	16	Rosenthal/Hes	52-0807
EICHE, Georg	14	Rosenthal	53-0928
EICHEL, Carl Otto	30	Schmalkalden	50-1236
EICHEL, Chr.	15	Lengsfeld	48-1114
Louise 22			
EICHEL, Joh.	50	Heiningen	54-1001
Cath. 38, Caspar 18, Marg. 14, Caspar 4			
EICHELBERGER, Carl	50	Zwoda	52-0095
EICHENAUER, Conrad	23	Lauterbach	52-0960
EICHENBERG, Fulm	29	Neuses	52-1464
EICHENBERG, W.	21	Hasberg	54-1470
EICHENGRUEN, Moses	37	Tilch/Hess.	51-1532
EICHER, Francisca	24	Breitenloh	54-0872
EICHHAMMER, Margr.	26	Hohenfels	53-0825
EICHHAUER, M.	bob		52-0515
EICHHOFF, Josephin	14	Marientrepper	53-1062
EICHHOLZ, Fr. Ed.	30	Zurich	51-1686
EICHHORN, Babette	24	Regensburg	54-0987
EICHHORN, C.H.(m)	18	Schneeberg	54-1341
EICHHORN, Carl	38	Marburg/Hess.	51-1725
Maria Luzia 40, Joh. Georg 14			
Carl Friedr. 13, Joh. Christ. 10			
Joh. August 8, Susanne 5			
EICHHORN, Friedr.	21	Meiningen	49-0383
EICHHORN, Johann	23	Siebeldingen	48-0284
EICHHORN, Maria	22	Schernberg	54-1554
EICHLER, August	28	Roben/Prss.	54-1092
EICHLER, Hermann	23	Trebtitz	54-0872
Agnes 25			
EICHLER, Reinhardt	23	Driesen	54-1554
EICHMANN, Bertha	22	Herford/Lippe	54-1092
EICHMULLER, M. (f)	19	Volla	48-0445
E. (f) 6m			
EICHNER, Math.	40	Biche	53-1164
EICHWALD, Callmann	20	Wruemenberg	53-1062
EICHWALD, Caroline	21	Erdmanrede	52-1321
EICKE, Julius	21	Salzgitter/Ha	52-1332
EICKEL, Peter	19	Dreisach	53-1013
EICKHAMMER, Margr.	26	Hohenfels	53-0825
EICKHOFF, Anna	17	Bederkesa	51-1084
EICKHOFF, Mathias	29	Iburg	51-1101
EICKMEIER, Johanne	35	Reitren	48-1179
Marie Theres 27			
EICKS, B. H.	31	N.Y.	53-1070
EIDAM, Alex	23	Weimar	50-0021
EIDENWEIL, Joseph	28	Schwetzingen	51-0384
EIDLER, Margaretha	26	Noerdlingen	54-0903
EIDNER, Heinr. Ad.	26	Leipzig	51-1455
Heinr. Ed. 21			
EIERMANN, Joh Nic.	46	Heldburg	49-0781
Eva Margaret 37, Margarethe 15, baby			
EIERMANN, Margaret	19	Coburg	54-1282
EIFERT, Elisabeth		Frischborn	54-1575
EIFERT, H. V. (m)	24	Warenrode	52-0652
EIFFNER, Nicol.	25	Birkenfeld	50-1236

NAME	AGE	RESIDENCE	YR-LIST
EIGEN, Joh. Franz	50	Vilseck	54-1078
Cath. 17, Marg. 48, Anna 19			
EIGENBROD, Elis.	18	Viermunden	50-0379
EIGENBROD, F. (m)	26	Boedes	52-0652
Philipp 28			
EIGENRAUCH, Fr'd W	24	Rhaden	53-1164
EIGNER, George	37	Plainfeld	53-1164
EIKHOFF, Wilhelm	17	Hannover	50-1317
Louise 59			
EIKOF, Hannchen	23	Springen	53-0652
EILERMANN, Marg.	21	Aukum	54-1554
EILERS, Clara	21	Bohnde	49-0352
EILERS, Diedrich	33	Langwarden	54-1371
Conradine 38, Minna 3, Herm. 9m			
EILERS, Friedrich	38	Landlust	54-0872
Christine 39, Christine 9, Mathilde 7			
Johanne 4, Hermine by			
EILERS, Gottfried	16	Wehe	54-0987
EILERS, Herm.	29	Stockdorf	48-1179
Friedr. 25			
EILERS, Joh. Hein.	50	Bochhold/Pr.	51-1796
Eberhard 18			
EILERT, Ernst	48	Suedstade	53-1016
Louise 46, Hermann 18, Ernestine 16			
Ernst 8, Louis 3, Ferdinand 1			
EILEST, Anna Marg.	17	Wittlage	49-0413
EILTZ, Herrm.	19	Breslau	49-1106
EIMER, Charles	30	Darmstadt	53-1164
EIMER, Philipp	20	Friedberg	52-0279
Valentin 28			
EINECKE, Eduard	22	Guetersloh	51-0460
EINFALT, John	37	Heidenheim	53-0928
EINSIEDLER, Carl	34	Gratz	51-0352
Caroline 26			
EIPSEN, Henry	38	Dorum/Hann.	50-0323
EISEK, Elisabeth	30	Treuchtlingen	53-0905
EISEL, Conrad	41	Dankmarshause	48-0284
EISELE, Barbara	22	Soehnstetten	54-0600
EISELT, Constant	25	Tischstedt	54-0987
EISEMANN, Cath.	22	Unterbruender	49-0352
EISEN, August	28	Dillenburg	53-1023
EISEN, Elisabeth	30	Treuchtlingen	53-0905
EISEN, Joh.	33	Ostheim	51-1245
Christine 27			
EISENACH, Kaetchen	19	Carlsruhe	54-0987
EISENACHER, Joh.	35	Christes	51-0405
EISENBACH, Fr. Wm.	28	Wels	53-0991
Rosa 22, Gustavus 9m			
EISENBEIL, Joseph	20	Neuenburg/Hes	52-0351
EISENBRAND, Ant.	25	Wolfersdorf	47-0918
Barbara 20			
EISENHAUD, Elias	19	Eishausen	53-0320
EISENHOEFER, Monik	23	Muenchen	53-0267
EISENHUT, Friedr.	17	Ebergoetzen	54-0882
EISENHUT, Kunig.	19	Neuhof/Bavari	53-0628
EISENHUTH, Christ.	24	Hungen	53-0557
Cathrine 25			
EISENKOLB, Barb.	24	Sissbach	52-1321
EISENLOHE, Heths.	17	Mittelruessel	49-0737
EISENMENGER, Lis.	32	Bieberich/Nas	48-0053
EISENTRAUD, Elias	19	Eishausen	53-0320
EISENTROUT, John	27	M---ch	50-0944
Augusta R. 31, Augusta A. 4			
Friederike A 3, Charles F. 18m			
Carl Franz 3m			
EISERT, Adam	48	Churhessen	52-1620
Anna 47, Adam 15			
EISFELD, Amelia	28	Nordhausen	49-0737
EISFELD, Theodor	37	Ballenstedt	54-0987
Theodor 19			
EISFELDER, Hep.	34	Bamberg	51-1084
EISFELDT, Wilhelm	32	Magdeburg	54-1591
Matilde 32, Auguste 4, William 3			
Henriette 56			
EISMANN, August	31	Annaberg	54-1371
EISMANN, Et. (m)	23	Weiseln	50-0746
EISMANN, Robert	34	Waldenburg	54-1168
EISNER, Marie	22	Ramrod	51-0352

NAME	AGE	RESIDENCE	YR-LIST
EITEL, Johann	23	Bersenbrueck	49-0345
EITLER, A. (m)	22	Dietmannsried	50-0311
EITZEL, Johann	28	Schoellkrippe	54-0903
EITZEN, v. Heinr.	18	Wehldorf	51-0756
EKARD, Johann	38	Schwarzenbach	53-0475
EKARDT, George	34	Lintorff	54-1470
Mary 25, Christian 3, Lewis 3m			
EKEN, Martin	45	Popens	52-1304
EKERT, Amalie	36	Gross Strelit	54-1717
EKETIN, Els.	35	Pastheim	47-0868
EKHARD, John	25	Hessen	51-0405
EKOLT, Friedrich	16	Schney/Bav.	52-1620
Christine 19			
ELBELL, Friedrich	55	Bayern	53-0557
Susanne 52, Erhard 29, Christian 27			
Heinrich 16, Caroline 12			
ELBERG, Bernhard	27	Lingen/Hann.	51-1532
ELBERS, William	27	Barmen	53-0914
ELBERT, Amalie	19	Trennfurt	51-1455
ELBRECHT, Hein. Fr	29	Ottersberg	52-1362
Clara 30, Clara 25, Johann 10m			
ELFERS, Clemens	58	Muenster	50-0292
ELFIEN, Heinrich	16	Clappenburg	50-0379
ELFRINGER, Conrad	42	Waldshut	51-1686
ELIAS, Hirsch	37	Krotoschin	53-1023
ELIEL, Falk	27	Iburg	52-0895
Lambert 33			
ELING, Heinrich	28	Hirschfeld	52-1661
Maria 23, Johann 2			
ELL, Babetta	28	Fuerth	53-0991
ELLBRECHT, Friedr.	21	Goettingen	50-0021
ELLER, Clasimir	32	Winterthur	51-1725
ELLER, Harry	19	Ermeshausen	53-0582
ELLERBROOK, Heinr.	29	Lingen/Hann	51-1725
Sophie 26			
ELLERMANN, E.H.(m)	26	Gotha	48-0445
ELLERT, Cathr.	18	Goettingen	51-0326
ELLERY, J.G.	26	American	53-1000
ELLGES, Wilhelm	28	Bevertshausen	53-1016
ELLINGER, Jette	21	Fischbach/Bav	53-0628
ELLINGER, M. Marg.	22	Ramsreuth	48-0951
ELLINGER, Magd.	43	Sultzberg	48-0951
ELLINGHAUSS, Heinr	27	Eistruff	54-1554
ELLINGHUYZEN, J.P.	26	Tava	51-1160
ELLIS, Sophia	53	Minden	51-1455
Charlotte 15			
ELLWANGER, Johann	31	Mekarens	54-1443
ELM, Charles	24	Reinsdorf/Hes	50-0323
ELM, Heinr. Chr.	29	Hannover	50-0311
ELM, v. Wilhelm	26	Speicker/Neuf	47-0872
ELMERICH, Chr.	33	Ballstedt	54-1575
ELMS, Nicolaus	26	Bederkesa	52-1625
ELSASSER, John	33	Volmerz	50-0840
Margarethe 34, Georg 12, Louis 9, John 5			
Louis 69, Elizabeth 69			
ELSBACH, Caroline	23	Waldorf	48-0887
ELSER, Johann	58	Friedrichsdor	51-0384
Marianna 48, Johann Mich. 17			
ELSINGER, Anna	15	Poppenhof	52-0693
Magdal. 27, Kunig. 9m			
ELSINGER, Magdal.	27	Herbersdorf	52-0693
ELSNER, Heinrich	19	Luchtenhugel	54-0987
ELSOHN, Emilie	18	Wurzburg	52-0807
ELSTRAE, John H.	17	Schinkel	54-1470
ELTESTE, Henriette	23	Bayern	53-0590
EMDE, Gustav	37	Schmitlinghau	54-1554
Friedrich 39			
EMDER, Catharina	6m	Berlingerode	47-0828
EMDER, Heinr.	64	Berlingerode	47-0828
Catharina 21, Maria 19, Georg 31			
Helene 28, Heinr. 8, Christine 5			
Christoph 3			
EMER, Joseph	22	Horn	52-1580
EMERLING, August	34	Polle	52-1362
EMERT, Margaretha	25	Gehrenberg	52-0515
EMICH, Martha	26	Weisenburg	54-1724
EMMEN, Heinr.	25	Dorum	53-1000
EMMENDORF, Franz	28	Fuenfstaedt	52-0279

NAME	AGE	RESIDENCE	YR-LIST
Michael 26, Anton 22			
EMMERICH, Kitty	30	New York	54-1371
Margarethe 6			
EMMERT, Wilhelm	24	Bayern	53-0590
EMMRICH, Christine	18	Dossel	54-1168
EMSHOFF, Anna Mar.	20	Bohmte	52-1200
Christian 17			
ENBOHM, Heinrich	33	Memphis	54-1371
ENDE, Emanuel	52	Deitz	53-1164
Pauline 18, Theodor 9			
ENDER, Nicolaus	22	Salzungen	53-1000
ENDERLE, Carl	49	Obersekingen	52-0279
ENDERLIN, Nicolaus	32	Turgau	53-0888
ENDERS, Conrad	18	Unter-Seibert	54-0830
ENDERS, Georg	27	Voelkershause	53-0942
ENDERS, Traugott	36	Herrmannsgrun	49-1106
ENDERS, Wilhelm	21	Heiligenstadt	53-0473
ENDESLEIN, Adam	15	Luer	51-1455
Anna 25			
ENDRES, Adam	33	Lohfeldt	51-1062
ENDRES, August	21	Osnabrueck	51-1796
ENDRES, Johann	31	Baiern	52-0895
ENDRISS, Nicolaus	28	Niederwerren	48-0260
ENDTER, Adam	20	Naeherstiller	54-1575
Therese 28			
ENGEL, A. (m)	21	Bremen	48-1114
ENGEL, Chr.	26	Ostheim	49-0574
Casp. 21			
ENGEL, Christine	25	Ostheim/Bav.	52-1620
ENGEL, Dorothea	26	Gipfendorf	52-0279
Margaretha 21, Georg 15, Anna Maria 17			
Johann Nikol 13			
ENGEL, Elisabeth	26	Wirlsdorf	50-0840
Christine 15			
ENGEL, Franz	35	Hirschberg	50-0292
Franzisca 36			
ENGEL, Heinr.	30	Arp	49-0324
ENGEL, Jacob	27	Euwinberge	52-1101
ENGEL, Joh.	23	Ernsthausen	48-0565
ENGEL, Johann	24	Berka	54-1554
ENGEL, Johann	31	Mettwitz	53-0324
ENGEL, Juliana	55	Holzheim	54-0830
ENGEL, Julie	18	Raudnitz	54-1647
ENGEL, M. (f)	22	Engter	48-0445
A.M. (f) 19			
ENGEL, Marg.	58	Wellingen	54-1470
ENGEL, Maria	23	Osnabrueck	52-1512
ENGEL, Maria	24	Schleckhausen	52-1304
ENGEL, Maria M.	18	Heilbronn	52-0515
ENGEL, Mary	21	Harpenfeld	54-1470
ENGEL, Minna	24	Magdeburg	53-0991
ENGEL, Nicolaus	9	Wirlsdorf	50-0840
William 2, Elizabeth 9m			
ENGEL, Theres	19	Landau	54-1283
ENGELBERG, Gertrud	63	Schower	49-0912
ENGELBERTH, Wilh.	30	Bensen	53-0928
Maria 30, Maria 19, Margarethe 58			
ENGELBRECHT, Anna	30	Lauf	54-1371
ENGELBRECHT, Fr.	24	Wenzhagen	52-1661
ENGELBRECHT, V.(m)	40	Rothenditmold	52-0652
G. (m) 32, J. (m) 26			
ENGELBRECHT, Val.	28	Rothenditmar	52-1625
Friedrich 26, Joseph 30, Carl 6			
ENGELER, Gustav	30	Neudiedendorf	51-1725
ENGELHARD, Anton	26	Bilshausen	52-1625
Elise 26, Carl 9m			
ENGELHARD, Conrad	24	Halzeld	51-1035
ENGELHARD, Georg	24	Coburg	50-1071
ENGELHARD, Heinr.	25	Sachsenberg	53-0838
ENGELHARD, Henry	31	Tiegenhagen	51-1588
ENGELHARD, Joh.	32	Baeldingen	54-1282
ENGELHARD, Justus	42	Blankenbach	48-0269
Bernhard 52, Marie 22, Louise 23			
ENGELHARDT, Adam	20	Marburg/Hess.	52-1620
ENGELHARDT, Elis.	40	Gansbergen	54-1443
ENGELHARDT, Elise	24	Eschenau	52-1105
Marg. 17			
ENGELHARDT, F. (m)	29	Prussia	50-0311

NAME	AGE	RESIDENCE	YR-LIST
ENGELHARDT, Friedr	32	Holtdorf	54-1443
Dorothea 28, Maria 5, Friedrich 3			
ENGELHARDT, Georg	20	Fuerth	52-1200
ENGELHARDT, Joh.	21	Hoenebach	48-0284
ENGELHARDT, Wilh.	29	Wemding/Bav.	52-1423
ENGELHART, Niel	22	Cronach	52-0515
ENGELHART, Otto	27	Wolfenbuettel	51-1796
ENGELHARTH, Edward	23	Remscheid	48-0406
ENGELHAUPT, Marie	22	Mittelsinn	52-0563
ENGELHRDT, Chr. Fr	27	Neuendorf	54-0930
ENGELKE, Friedrich	28		50-0944
ENGELKING, F. (m)	22	Wenzhagen	52-1661
ENGELKING, Heinr.	47	Glessen	54-0930
ENGELKING, Sophia	27	Meinsen	52-1321
Engel 25, Wilhelmine 9m			
ENGELKING, Sophie	25	Bueckeburg	51-1725
ENGELKING, Wilh.	27	Meinsen	52-1321
ENGELMALL, Sophie	25	Fuerth	54-0987
C. 26			
ENGELMANN, C.	26	New York	54-0987
Sophie 25			
ENGELMANN, Franz	30	Wertheim	53-0492
ENGELMANN, Heinr.	26	Langenschaden	49-0383
ENGELMANN, Julius	22	Leipzig	48-0053
ENGELS, Ludw.	34	Remscheid	48-0565
ENGELS, Sophie	25	Quakenbrueck	54-0872
ENGERMANN, Franz	26	Loewen	51-0405
Joseph 17			
ENGERT, Friedr.	25	Mittelruessel	49-0737
ENGERT, Sebastian	29	Ritzingen	49-0912
ENGHAUSEN, Sophie	27	Gilten	50-1132
ENGLAENDER, Vannet	24	Hainfate	54-0930
ENGLE, Julius Theo	24		52-1362
ENGLER, Louise	23	St. Gallen	54-1297
ENK, Herrm. Georg	19	Schleiz	49-0352
ENKE, Joh. Wilhelm	30	Volkmannsdorf	54-0872
ENKEL, Georg	19	Schonstadt	52-0515
ENKLER, Lorenz	38	Goettingen	52-1661
ENSLIN, Leopold	21	Hornberg/Bad.	52-0807
ENTEL, Barbara	25	Pillenhofen	52-1101
ENTELMANN, Friedr.	20	Bergedorf/Han	51-1725
ENTEMANN, J. (m)	25	Delmenhorst	49-0324
ENTORF, Amalie	24	Uchtdorf	53-1164
ENTZENBACHER, Jos.	50	Rudolphshoffe	49-0781
Anna Maria 56, Andreas 20, Anna Maria 22			
Marianna 20			
ENZ, Otto	18	Mausebrunn	49-0345
ENZELMANN, Johann	22	Klinkendorf	53-0905
ENZENBERGER, Jos.	32	Dattenried	53-0492
EPHAF, Wilh.	24	Brecherfeld	51-1796
EPPENAU, Johann	26	Fuerth	52-1661
Georg 29, Elisabeth 32, Margaretha 13			
EPPING, Peter	35	Charleston	54-1371
EPPLER, Friedr.	30	Brunershausen	52-0370
EPSTEIN, Benjamin	15	Gehaus	53-0942
Sara 28			
EPSTEIN, Sussmann	67	Gehaus	48-1179
Caroline 60, Barbara 18			
ERASMI, Joh.	22	Kirchlinde	50-0439
Christ. 18			
ERATH, Anton	56	Rothenburg/Wu	51-1532
Antonia 58, Ana 27, Dorothea 25, Beata 20			
Max 19, Paul 2			
ERATH, Wilh.	28	Rothenberg/Wu	50-1071
ERB, Johanna	23	N.Y.	52-1512
ERB, Otto	39	Geibshausen	54-0850
Margaretha 38, Elisabetha 14, Christina 8			
Balthasar 5			
ERB, Titus	25	Rosenfeld	52-1661
ERB, W. (m)	24	Marksuhl	52-0558
V. (f) 22, E. (f) 4			
ERB, Wilh. Ferd.	25	Arnhausen	49-0352
ERBACHER, Joh Ant.	37	Buchen	52-0370
ERBE, Adam	35	Rothensee	49-0329
ERBE, Christiane	30	Salzungen	53-1000
ERBE, Johannes	24	Kleinensee	48-0284
ERBER, Bartel	23	Barchfeld	48-0284
ERCK, Franz	19	Miltenberg	51-1639

NAME	AGE	RESIDENCE	YR-LIST
ERCKHARDT, Wilh.	28	Magdeburg	54-0600
ERDEL, Franz	45	Grottau	54-1717
Mathilde 22, Franz 19, Pauline 18			
Robert 15, Louise 13, Wilhelm 10			
Julius 4			
ERDMANN, Carl	18	Obergrenzbach	51-1035
ERDMANN, Caroline	26	Katzhuette	53-0585
ERDMANN, Friedr.	49	Prussia	50-1317
ERDMANN, Heinr.	25	Orbicke	50-1132
Bernh. 22			
ERDMANN, Henriette	17	Niedenstein	52-1105
ERDMANN, Isaac	22	Bueckenbach	53-0888
ERDMANN, Ricke	18	Haarke	54-1283
ERDMANN, Robert	24	Schkeuditz	50-0840
ERDMANN, Walther	28	Niedenstein	52-1105
Cath. 32, Anna 1, Heinr. 52, Magd. 49			
Elisab. 25, Heinr. 17, Georg 12			
ERDMEYER, Heinrich	32	Radsick	53-0825
Caroline 28, Caroline 18m			
ERFURT, Henriette	28	Ronneburg	52-1580
ERGERS, Adelheid	16	Brinkum	51-0405
ERHARD, August	35	Bloda	53-0652
ERHARD, Carl	15	Ringleben	49-1358
ERHARD, Johann	30	Oed	53-0905
Margaretha 23, Therese 9m			
ERHARD, Paul	20	Tuebingen	50-0021
ERHARDT, Christina	25	Uslar	48-1015
ERHARDT, Conrad	18	Weiderode/Hes	51-1532
ERHARDT, Daniel	2	Grossassbach	49-0352
ERHARDT, Joh.	26	Theinfeld	49-0781
ERHARDT, Johann	26	Bernreuth/Bav	52-0807
Maria 26			
ERHARDT, Theodor	25	Eisenberg	54-1283
ERICHS, Friederika	23	Dorum	49-0329
ERICHS, Luehr	29	New York	50-0366
ERICHS, Marie	22	Hambargen	50-0366
ERICHSON, Klaus	22	Christiania	51-1084
ERL, Carl	22	Schoenlind	54-1566
ERLACH, Johannes	33	Hohengandern	54-1566
Marie 28, Bertha 4, Joh. 6m			
ERLE, Marie	17	Roderoth	54-1168
ERLE, Marie Elis.	24	Harzfeld	53-1000
ERLEBACH, Max.	22	Bayreuth	54-1297
Caroline 23			
ERLWEIN, Georg	42	Guttenberg	52-0693
Cathar. 36, Margar. 17, Cathar. 15			
Elisabeth 13, Margar. 9, Kunig. 6			
Elisabeth 2, Barbara 6m			
ERMANN, Alex	28	Senden	54-1078
ERMER, Magdelen	32	Kaltenbrunn	48-0951
ERNE, Joh.	23	Muehlberg	51-0460
ERNEL, Heinrich	20	Angenrod	51-0460
ERNEST, Geo.	28	Schwimmbad	47-0918
ERNLE, Joh. Ant.	29	Aussnang	49-0352
ERNST, Aug. Albert	30	Eissberg/Sax.	48-0053
ERNST, Barbara	26	Wiesbaden/Nas	48-0447
ERNST, Catharina	23	Rhina	52-1661
ERNST, Eduard	24	Paderborn	51-0405
ERNST, F. (f)	32	Brunk	49-0742
ERNST, Franz	21	Baden	52-1625
ERNST, Franz	28	Beinbach	52-1625
ERNST, Friedrich	26	Corbach	52-0095
ERNST, Georg	25	Iber	54-1168
ERNST, Heinrich	18	Friedewalde	50-0311
Elisabeth 21			
ERNST, Joh.	27	Goettingen	52-0370
ERNST, Johann	45	Lengsfeld	53-0942
Christel 17, Friedrich 12, August 18			
ERNST, Johann	52	Friedewald/He	51-1532
ERNST, Joseph	26	Holzingen	48-0887
ERNST, Leonhard	20	Dallmessing	53-1062
ERNST, Marg.	18	Bechreuth	54-1371
ERNST, Martin	30	Mistefeld/Bav	51-1532
ERNSTHAUSEN, Fried	50	Win----	53-0825
Clara Ilsebe 48, Marie Elis. 20			
Joh. Friedr. 18, Maria Clara 16			
Maria Eleon. 13, Maria Elis. 9			
ERNSTING, Friedr.	25	Langendamm	52-1512

NAME	AGE	RESIDENCE	YR-LIST
Adelheid 20			
ERNSTING, Theophil	27	Nienburg	53-1164
ERNTE, Wilh.	37	Elberfeld	48-0565
ERP, Georg	25	Lenbach	49-0781
ERPENBECK, Clemens	20	Lengerich/Pr.	52-1432
ERPENBECK, Friedr.	29	Hannoverschen	52-1432
ERSTPANIER, H.H.	32	Wesuwe	49-0324
ERZGRAEBER, Sophie	18	Barsinghausen	52-1410
ESBERG, Mendel	21	Dankelshausen	53-0991
ESCHELBACH, Theres	28	Eggenfelden	48-0887
ESCHENBACH, G. (m)	30	Weitroth	52-0652
ESCHERICH, Maria	27	Hohenschwarz	52-0693
ESCHLER, J. (m)	24	Limbach	50-0746
ESCHMEYER, J Heinr	29	Ladbergen	48-0260
Elisabeth 60, Sophie 23, Elisabeth 6m			
Wilhelm 26			
ESDORN, Heinrich	16	Bremen	48-1184
ESSENDORF, John E.	33	Coesfeld/Pr.	48-0053
ESSENHAVEN, A. (m)	27	Annberg	50-0746
ESSIG, Heinr.	24	Ballern	53-0585
ESSLINGER, Ferd.	37	Tinglingen	51-1796
ESSMANN, Fr.	27	Rodenberg	52-1580
ESSROGER, Bernard	20	Prag	53-0991
ESTERE, Maria	28	Regen	54-1341
ESTERMANN, Cath.	29	Leer	52-1304
ESWEIM, Cresenza	28	Almen	52-1580
ETZEL, Gabriel	13	Curhessen	52-1432
ETZEL, Joh.	28	Schellkrueppe	47-0868
ETZEL, Johann	28	Schoellkrippe	54-0903
EUBEL, Georg	16	Cassel	51-1101
Elisa 23			
EUGGASS, H. (m)	26	Rodelmeier	53-0942
EULBERG, Johann	24	Sainerholz	54-1297
EULER, C. (f)	27	Warenrode	52-0652
EULER, Elisabeth	17	Maar	54-0053
EULER, Heinrich	25	Storndorf	51-1455
EULER, J. (m)	25	Niedergossa	52-0652
EULER, Joseph	26	Wetzhusen	47-0762
EUSLIN, Rosine Cat	20	Barmen	53-0914
EVER, Casp.	40	Motten	51-1796
Kath. 29			
EVERHARD, Chr.	24	Wilburg/Nass.	48-0447
EVERING, Bernhard	31	Emsdetten	53-1062
EVERS, Bernhard	25	Bremen	51-1245
EVERS, Carl Conr.	24	Bremen	51-1725
EVERS, Christian	29	Rittahude	53-1164
EVERS, Derie	19	Ritterhude	53-0991
EVERS, Harm	46	Staphorst	49-0912
Margia 36, Wilhelm 15, Harm 11, Evert 8			
Heinrich 6, John 3, Classin 15, Niche			
EVERS, Helmuth	25	Luebeck	50-1132
EVERS, J.H. (m)	25	Versen	49-0324
EVERS, Joh. Alb.	26	Wilsen	47-0918
EVERS, Maria Luise	20	Eimbeck/Hann.	51-1725
EVERSBERG, Aug.	25	Ankum	54-1371
EVERT, Louise	26	Gross Fiden	53-0905
Sophie 21, Christiane 55, Caroline 18			
EWABEL, Severin	35	Oberbernhard	48-1184
EWALD, Franz	29	Hallenberg	53-0585
Catharine 30, Franz 1			
EWALD, Heinr.	32	Hallenberg	53-0585
Elisabeth 32, Daniel 2, Franz 1			
EWALD, Heinr.	32	Senden	54-1554
Bernh. 18, Jenny 22			
EWALD, Henry	23	Saxony	54-1724
Mary 24			
EWALD, Louise	25	Hallenberg	53-0585
EWALD, Wilhelmine	54	Frankfurt	54-1371
Hedwig 6, Anna 4			
EWE, Carl	31	Wernigerode	54-1078
EWIG, Maria	21	Breitenborn/H	52-1620
EXTER, D. (m)		Bremen	53-0942
EYLERS, Juergen	32	Zetel	54-0872
wife 26, Johanne 2			
EYMANN, Carl	19	Osnabrueck	48-0951
EYMANN, Jacob	22	Gaildorf	52-1105
Catharine 27			
EYSEL, Louis	22	Berlin	53-0590

NAME	AGE	RESIDENCE	YR-LIST
EYTH, Th.	28	Wuertenberg	54-1724
Luise 21			
FAAS, Ernst	22	Culm	54-1470
FABARIUS, Ferd.	32	Muehlheim	52-1200
Wilhelmine 27			
FABER, Alwin	21	Eisshausen	53-0320
FABER, Gustav	19	Greutzschen	52-1200
FABER, Gustavus	30	Tuttlingen/Wu	49-0365
FABER, Hermann	15	Heuchelheim	52-1105
Caroline 19			
FABER, Joh. Berend	34	Tenninghausen	51-0352
FACHS, C.G. (m)	41	Oberkunersdor	48-0447
FADT, Leonhard	40	Geildorf/Wuer	52-0351
FAECHER, Andreas	29	Mondfeld	52-1661
Margaretha 25, Catharina 3			
FAEGER, Theodor	20	Hauswurz	53-0320
FAERBER, Joh Georg	28	Frauendorf	52-0095
FAERBER, Tobias	22	Blasbach	54-0830
FAETKE, Amalia	32	Bromberg	51-0756
Leonhard 6, Herrmann 3, Rudolph 11m			
FAHENER, Simon	28	Thirschenreit	54-1283
Rosine 28, Georg 3			
FAHLBUSCH, Gottfr.	16	Linteln	51-1101
FAHN, Marg.	25	Griesel	53-0320
FAHR, Christine	27	Naundorf	54-0872
FAHRMANN, John	22	Wittlage	54-1341
FAICK, Cath.	60	Weissenbrunn	51-1160
FAJEN, Claus	19	Reesum	50-0366
FALBAUSCH, Aug.	38	Erhardshausen	52-0370
Andrea Cath. 26, Ignatz 9m, Anton 32			
Arnold 29, Elisabeth 25, Cathrine 3			
Carl 6m			
FALEN, Simon	27	Muehingen	54-0903
FALK, Aloys	22	Ottersmeyer	53-0991
FALK, Johannes	50	Hessen	53-1086
Margaretha 51, Elisabeth 12			
FALK, Tewes	22	Bremervoerde	51-1725
FALKE, Heinrich	68	Istrup/Pr.	54-0965
Maria 29			
FALKENAU, Ad.	54	Prague	48-1015
Henriette 49, Theresa 21, Sophie 15			
Treak (m) 11, Ignatz 9, Ludw. 8			
FALKENSTEIN, Adam	23	Grossendorf	54-1566
FALKENSTEIN, Gust.	19	Bruchhausen	48-0269
FALKIN, Eva M.	28	Dentlein	52-0515
FALKNER, George	30	Hegendorf	53-0888
FALKNER, Joh.	25	Ballhof	48-1179
FALLIER, John Matt	43	Langenzenn	53-0991
Barbara 48			
FALLNER, Carl	33	Burg	53-0267
Johanne 32			
FALMON, Wilh.	29	Frankenheim	51-1245
Elisab. 24, Anna 2			
FALTEN, Johann	29	Bayern	52-0699
FALTER, Anna Mar.	32	Neckarhausen	48-1355
FAMBACH, Andreas	29	Erlach	52-1200
FANEZKY, Wilhelm	40	Strehlen	54-1717
Caroline 31, Reinhard 6, Pauline 3			
Caroline 11m			
FANKE, Joh. Gottfr	24	Muehlhausen	52-1304
FAPRIE, Heinrich	22	Bamberg	53-1062
FARBER, Carl	26	Boeblingen	53-0825
FARENHOLZ, Ferd.	35	Loewendorf	48-1355
Wilhelmine 28, Wilhelm 4, Therese 2			
FARENHOLZ, W. (m)		Alboxen	50-0746
K. (f) 29, H. (m) 9m			
FARMY, Christian	26	Massenbachhau	48-0053
FARNBACHER, Carol.	18	Fuerth	53-0585
FARNUNG, Damian	25	Gais	52-0320
FARRELMANN, Lina	26	Oldenburg	50-0311
FARTSCH, Andrew	45	Burgitz/Bav.	48-0053
Margaret 42, Margaret 16, Georg 6			
FARWELL, L.J.	33	U.S.	48-1243
FASSBINDER, Peter	46	Wirkelthausen	48-0406
Marie 27, William 12, Rosette 7			
FASSHAUER, Christ.	25	Ruedershausen	48-1209
FASSHAUER, Leonard	38	Frohengardern	54-1282
Catharina 46, Elisabeth 9, Anna 4			

NAME	AGE	RESIDENCE	YR-LIST
Berthold 15, Christoph 7, Leonore by			
FASSNACHT, Jacob	38	Auffenau	54-1168
Anna 23			
FAULSTICH, Johann	37	Lipharz	51-0500
FAULSTICH, Magnus	23	Fulda	53-0585
FAUSER, H. (m)	29	Dueben	52-0652
FAUST, Barbara Catharina		Hutzdorf	54-1575
FAUST, Cathr.	22	Weimar	50-1317
FAUST, Christian	27	Goddelsheim	50-0379
FAUST, Conrad	32	Hannover	50-1317
FAUST, Ferd.	23	Grosseneichen	51-1101
FAUST, Franz	34	Wiedelah	54-0987
FAUST, Hugh	27	Mittelruessel	49-0737
FAUST, Thomas	15	Hauswurz	53-0320
FAUST, Wilhelm	33	Erfurt	54-1371
Johanne 25			
FAUT, Louisa	24	Ortenberg	53-1164
FECHANT, Valentin	29	Oberflachinge	53-1062
FECHMEYER, Carl	26	Hannover	51-1725
FECKE, Fritz		Osnabrueck	54-1575
FEDDERMANN, Joh.	16	Brinkum	49-0324
FEDDERWITZ, Peter	27	Wallhuefers	54-1575
FEDER, Rudolph	25	Nusel	49-1106
Julie 34			
FEDER, Samuel	39	Breslau	54-1092
Hannchen 39, Salus 13, Moritz 10			
Amalia 12, Minna 10, Georg 2, Isidor 26			
FEDERLEIN, Mar.(f)	30	Graefenberg	49-1358
FEDERWITZ, Gesche	20	Wollhoefen	51-0326
FEGGE, Carl	27	Goddelsheim	50-0379
Henriette 23			
FEHN, Franz J.	17	Kehlbach	52-0515
FEHRENKAMP, Heinr.	21	Hannover	53-0590
FEIERTAG, Lorentz	32	Pfaffenschwen	52-1625
FEIGEL, Richard	24	Saatz	52-1580
FEIGELER, Franz	32	Schweinfurt	50-1317
FEIGLE, Joh.	31	Bitz	51-1640
FEIK, Elisabeth		Rimbach	54-1575
FEIK, Valte	46	Telbershausen	54-1575
Christ. , Andreas 22, Johannes 17			
Julius 14, daughter 12, Margarethe 20			
daughter 9, daughter 9			
FEIL, Gabriel	24	Bilenz	48-0951
FEILER, Caroline	20	Wunsiedel	51-1035
FEILER, Joh Samuel	18	Duermenz	53-1164
FEILER, Johann	24	Birkenfeld	52-1580
FEILHUBER, Thomas	49	Niederhofen	52-1452
FEINKING, Louise	27	Wagenfeld	51-0500
Friederike 17			
FEIST, August	39	Boberrohrsdor	54-1452
Agnes 40, Marie 15, Friederike 14			
Anna 12, Christine 11, Paul 8, August 7			
Ernestine 4, Robert 2			
FEIST, Lenny	19	Schermbeck	54-1297
FEISTER, Meta Adel	33	Gekersdorf	53-0637
Joh. Hinrich 2			
FEITE, C.		Rimbach	54-1575
FEITZINGER, Anna	35	Wien	54-1297
Carl 8, Anna 2, Rosalie 12			
FELBINGER, Stephan	50	Fettendorff	49-0413
Margarethe 40, Anna 14			
FELD, Carl	37	Kreuznach	53-1086
FELD, Elizabeth	40	Gerbershausen	51-1588
Louisa 14			
FELD, Friedrich	27	Frankenstein	52-1148
Marie 22			
FELD, VOR DEM J.H	37	Ottersberg	52-1362
Clara 40, Friedrich 17, Florentine 15			
FELDERS, B. Nennen	33	Leer	50-1067
Christine 27			
FELDHAN, Fanette	25	Muenchen	53-1070
FELDHAUSEN, Friedr	22	Ritterhude	51-0326
FELDHAUSEN, H. (m)	28	Herford	47-0762
FELDHAUSEN, J.F.	35	Ritzbuettel	47-0987
Anna K. 34			
FELDMANN, Abraham	37	Bruel	52-1580
Doretta 35, Eva 11, Georg 7, Christoph 3			

NAME	AGE	RESIDENCE	YR-LIST
Elisabeth 9m			
FELDMANN, Berend	19	Spaden	52-0699
FELDMANN, Casper H	22	Hamersen/Hann	52-0351
FELDMANN, Friedr.	18	Oefingen/Bad.	51-1725
FELDMANN, Heinrich	28	Hersmold	53-1023
FELDMANN, Henry	36	Neuenkirchen	53-1164
FELDMANN, Herman H	36	U.S.	47-0987
FELDMANN, Joh. Fr.	36	Moerendorf	51-0352
FELDMANN, Johann	39	Hilchenbach	52-1512
FELDMANN, Johann	20	Badbergen	50-1132
Cath. Adelh. 60, Herman Gerh. 22			
FELDMANN, Ludwig	22	Apenrode	49-1106
Henriette 30, Henriette 6, Sophia 36			
Johanna 15, Christiana 10, Elisabeth 5			
Heinrich 2			
FELDMANN, Theod.	21	Bautzen	49-0574
FELDMANN, V. (m)	23	Altenmuhr	50-0439
FELDMEIER,	38	Sanderhan	54-1283
FELDPAUSCH, Ludw.	18	Germany	50-0472
FELDSTEIN, Leop.	50	Boehmen	54-1724
FELIX, Friedrich	32	Emmeln	49-0324
FELK, Joh Gottlieb	31	Steinweisen	53-0914
FELKEL, Anton	33	Maehren	53-1000
Anna 31, Aloys 6, Marie 2			
FELKMANN, Anton	36	Wandersloh	54-0918
FELL, Ant. R.	24	Gera	54-1575
FELLER, Gottfried	35	Dillenburg	53-1023
Charlotte 37, Caroline 8, Carl 5			
FELLERMANN, Joh Fr	55	Unzen	54-0872
Joh. Friedr. 17, Friedrich 17			
Adelheid 22			
FELLINGER, Conrad	32	Schwetzingen	51-0384
FELLMETH, Friedr.	23	Sulzbach/Wuer	53-0435
Loise 27			
FELS, Aug.	21	Haeverstedt	52-1661
FELT, August	19	Luhra	51-1686
FELTEN, v. A. (m)	32	Un. Glogau	50-0746
FELTHAUS, Friedr.	37	Mohrhausen	52-0370
Anna 41, Anna 8, Elise 5			
FELTMACHER, Aron	21	Prag	48-1131
FENNEL, Anna	17	Grossenglis	52-0775
FENNEL, Conrad	40	Grossenglis	52-0775
Elisabeth 19, Anna Martha 14			
Joh. Heinr. 12, Nicolaus 10			
FENNER, Cathrine	18	Seissen	52-0370
FERBEL, Casp.	31	Blasbach	49-0574
G.F. 20, Conr. 61			
FERBER, Heinrich	30	Maden	50-1067
Maria 30, Anna 58, Anna Caths 2			
FERBER, Joh Herman	41	Budesheim	54-0987
FERBER, Oswald	40	Greitz	52-1580
FERDECKBERG, Jacob	23	Ungarn	49-0352
FERDINAND, Joseph	36	Podelwitz	52-1512
Elisab. 34, Anton 15, Anna 13, Pauline 8			
Jos. 6, Emilie 6m			
FERG, Arfra	20	Germheim	54-1297
FERG, Wilhelm	19	Meiningen	53-1000
FERGE, Christian	42	Unteralten	50-0944
Anna 34, Catherine 11, Elizabeth 8			
Heinrich 4			
FERLAGE, Joh. G.	22	Luesche	52-0563
FERNBACH, Isaac	52	Breslau	54-1371
FERNE, Friedrich	28	Lippe-Detmold	54-1717
FERNHABER, Johanne	22	Stotel	53-1023
FERNHOEFER, Joseph	40	Bonland	47-0872
Catharine 6			
FERTEN, Joh. Fried	25	Honenknopf	51-1796
FERTIG, G. (m)	18	Reichenbach	49-0416
FESSENFELD, Joh.	23	Achim	52-1512
FEST, Ernst	40	Muenden	54-1647
FEST, Joh Gottfr.	41	Freiburg	53-1062
Helene 40, Hermann 14, Amalie 9, Hugo 7			
Oscar 10m			
FETTE, Antoinette	24	Hildesheim	53-0928
FETTE, Christian	22	Loeningen	53-1062
FETTE, Ernst	25	Hannover	53-0928
FETTE, Friedrich	22	Blomberg	54-1168
Conrad 20, Arnold 15, Dorothea 17			

NAME	AGE	RESIDENCE	YR-LIST
Georg 27, Wilhelmine 27, Henriette 11			
FETTE, Georg	25	Stolzenau	51-1035
FETTER, Crescenza	38	Schweinfurt	50-1317
FETTGEMEYER, J. Fr	35	Ottersberg	52-1362
Margaretha 34, Clara 9, Johann 7			
FETZER, Joh.	31	Niederstolzin	54-0600
Barbara 32			
FEUERHAKEN, Doro.	22	Cassel	52-0095
FEUERLEIM, Christ.	27	Horchstadt/Bv	53-0628
FEUERLEIN, J. (m)	30	Mergentheim	48-0447
FEULBACH, Anton	33	Fischbach/Nas	53-0628
Johannette 23, Georg Heinr. by			
FEULER, Michael	28	Baunach/Bav.	52-0351
FEURIEGEL, August	22	Osterode	48-1355
FEUSNER, Conrad	25	Fulda/K.-Hess	53-0628
FEUSNER, Heinr.	38	Goettingen	52-0370
FEUSNER, Philip	16	Fulda	53-0628
FEUSS, G.W.	26	Herzberg	48-1015
Caroline 21, Beth 58			
FEUSSNER, Stephan	38	Marburg	50-1236
FEUST, Adam	16	Gemuenden	54-1282
FHEMEYER, Carl	20	Bunde	54-0882
Herman 29			
FICHI, Josepha	69	Luetzen	52-0699
FICHT, Carl	26	Greene/Brauns	52-0117
FICHTELN, W. (m)	29	Boellhorst	49-0329
FICK, Georg	17	Wuerbens	53-1016
FICK, Johann	29	Siegen	53-0324
FICK, John	22	Worbitz/Bav.	52-0960
FICK, Margareth	50	Bayern	52-1620
Margareth 21			
FICKE, Catharina	40	Bayern	53-0590
FICKE, Heinrich	17	Eggestedt	47-0872
FICKEN, Casper	19	Hagen	52-0699
Martin 25			
FICKEN, Heinrich	20	Barthen	52-1362
FICKENDE, Louise	20	Muenchberg	54-1282
FICKENWIRTH, Chr.	19	Greussene	53-1164
FICKERT, Carl Aug.	27	Weissenfels	49-0324
FICKERT, Louis	28	Baiern	54-1724
FIDDELKE, Joh. H.	29	Hoya/Hann.	52-0117
FIDEL, Adam	24	Landberg	54-1283
FIDLER, Anton	25	Schlettau/Sac	52-1620
Edmund 3			
FIDLER, Karl		Sara	54-1283
FIEBES, Anna		Oberod	53-0914
FIEBIG, August	26	Breslau	54-1283
Auguste 26, Pauline 2, Auguste by			
FIEBINGER, Thadeus	31	Rathsdorf	54-1297
FIEDEL, Jacob	24	Leckenheim	51-0460
FIEDEL, Johann	26	Ochsentrarot	54-1443
FIEDELER, Franz	16	Tretterode	53-0838
FIEDELER, Gottfr.	39	Wolfersdorf	51-0500
FIEDELER, Moritz	31	Heiligenstadt	52-0699
FIEDEMANN, Karsten	24	Bremervoerde	52-1580
FIEDLER, A.C. (f)	23	Landenhausen	51-0517
FIEDLER, Anton	29	Trappstadt	51-1640
FIEDLER, Carl	39	Gelnau	53-1070
Johanna Ros. 35, Anna Selma 11			
Heinr Moritz 9, Anna Clara 8			
Friedrich Em 3, Louise Hedw. 11m			
FIEDLER, Carl	22	Fretterode	51-1245
FIEDLER, Christian	27	Laufe am Holz	52-0279
Elise 24			
FIEDLER, Friedr.	22	Moedlareuth	47-0872
FIEDLER, Friedr.	25	Wolfersdorf	50-0439
FIEDLER, Heinr.	24	Prussia	50-0311
FIEDLER, Margareth	23	Mainek	54-1168
FIEGE, Johannes	19	Orlinghausen	51-1035
FIELEN, Dorothea	44	Braunschweig	47-0672
Dorothea 21			
FIELLGRAFF, Ludolf	17	Berlin	48-0269
FIENKEN, Diedr.	19	Osterholz	54-1094
Anna 24, Meta 22, Adelheid 16			
FIERING, Heinr.	26	Hannover	50-0311
FIERNSTAN, Johann	29	Hollfeldt	53-1062
FIERSTER, Gottfr.	20	Grosshirschen	49-0365
FIESCHLER, Joseph	33	Warburg	51-0352
Therese 19			
FIESS, Henry	28	Duermenz	53-1164
FIESTNER, Joh Wolf	29	Etzelheim	53-1062
FIKE, Henriette	36	Dieren/Pr.	52-1620
Franciska 5			
FIKEN, Joh. Friedr	23	Sepen	52-0279
FILLING, John C.	30	Schmiedemeise	53-0914
FILS DE CHAUMON, F	42	Prag	51-1796
FIMCKE, Jas. M.	21	Mittelruessel	49-0737
FIMMER, Marg.	35	Pofferthausen	51-1455
FINCK, John	40	Oelsnitz	53-0928
FINDEN, v. J.Wm.Ad	19	Norden	48-1114
FINDLING, Philip	25	Fischbach/Nas	53-0628
FINGER, Adolph	24	Bernsosten/Pr	50-0323
FINGER, Reinh.	23	Frankenberg	53-1016
FINGERHUT, Franz	18	Neucherschen	49-0781
FINGERHUT, Joh.	35	Berlin	48-0269
FINK, Anton	39	Fischbach/Nas	53-0628
Dorothea 36, Philippine 6, Elisabeth by			
FINK, Beta	18	Ringstedt	47-0872
FINK, C. (m)	20	Ringstaedt	49-0329
FINK, Casimir	23	Doeringstadt	54-0053
FINK, Conrad	53	Strebendorf	54-0053
Juliana 42, Elise Cath. 10, August 10			
FINK, Eugenia	26	Rohrbach	51-0352
FINK, Friedr. C.	40	Haus	49-0737
FINK, Hans	48	Seckbach/Hess	52-0807
Catharina 51, Peter 23, Jacob 21			
Conrad 19, Margaretha 12, Philipp 9			
FINK, Liborius	28	Prussia	54-1724
FINK, Martin	50	Homberg/Hess.	51-1796
Marta 30, Louise 3, Carl 6m			
FINK, Wilhelm	41	Fischbach/Nas	53-0628
Christine 40, Philipp 13, Johannette 9			
Christine 6, Heinrich 3, Elisabeth 2			
FINKE, Becka	20	Lohe	50-0366
FINKE, Cath.	32	Verden	54-1297
FINKE, Georg	17	Osnabrueck	54-0987
FINKE, Heinrich	28	Dornberg	54-1554
FINKE, Heinrich	24	Munster	54-1717
FINKE, J.	17	Lohe	54-1716
FINKE, Johanne	29	Verden	54-1297
FINKE, Theodor	29	Clausthal	54-1371
FINKEL, Betti	24	Zeven	50-1132
FINKELDEG, Chr	30	Hameln	52-1129
Doroth. Fr. 20			
FINKELDEG, Dor. Fr	20	Holtensen	52-1129
FINKEMEYER, Heinr.	22	Bielefeld	54-0600
FINKEN, Diedrich	19	Osterholz	54-1094
Anna 24, Meta 22, Adelheid 16			
FINKEN, Minna	18	Meinertshagen	54-1575
FINKENSTEDT, Wm.	33	Wagenfeld	49-0742
FINKENZELLER, Jos.	41	Langenmoor	54-1371
Walburga 14, Ottilie 9, Elisabeth 8			
FINKER, Marie	26	Neustadt	54-1168
FINKERNAGEL, Elise	23	Altenstedt	54-1282
son by			
FINNIG, Minne	64	Borgenteich	50-0840
FINSTERWALD, Sarah	53	Vacha	54-1371
Henriette 26			
FINZEL, Georg	19	Hoellburg	54-1717
FIPP, Joh. Mathias	19	Doehren	54-1443
FIPS, Peter	58	Coeln	53-0914
FIRECKER, J.A. (m)	28	Wasserknoden	54-1341
FISCH, Jeanette	37	Burgebrach	48-0887
Rebecke 16			
FISCHBACH, Heinr.	29	Hanau	53-1062
FISCHBECK, Herm.	17	Bremervoerde	52-1512
FISCHBECK, Johann	17	Langenhausen	50-0292
FISCHE, Friedr.	24	Lunin	47-0918
FISCHEL, Gustav	36	Prague	48-1015
Rosalie 27, Ludo (f) 6, Victor 5			
Ottilie 3, Caroline 1			
FISCHEL, Henry	36	Wallsrode	48-1015
FISCHEL, Michel	20	Grevenstein	51-0048
FISCHENDORF, Aug.	22	Ahldorf	52-1101
FISCHER, A. (m)	27	Uhrbach	52-0558
U. (f) 20, C. 3			

NAME	AGE	RESIDENCE	YR-LIST
FISCHER, Adam	43	Hameln	53-1013
Catharine 33, Anton 15, Anna 10			
Barbara 5, Catharine 2			
FISCHER, Anna E.	18	Vallach	51-0405
FISCHER, Anna Marg	20	Kornbach	51-1101
FISCHER, Annette	21	Bavaria	50-0311
FISCHER, Anton	23	Ummerstadt	52-0370
FISCHER, Anton	19	Herzogenaurac	52-0693
FISCHER, Asmus	36	Ronsbach	51-1062
FISCHER, August	27	Aerzen	52-1200
FISCHER, Balthasar	25	Wasmuthausen	53-1062
FISCHER, C.	23	Bittershausen	51-0517
FISCHER, Carl Jul.	25	Crimmitschau	53-0991
Augusta 28, Jane 59			
FISCHER, Caspar	25	Traeuan	54-1566
Kunigunde 22, Barbara 2, Apollonia 4			
FISCHER, Cath. (m)	28	Gauerstadt	50-0439
FISCHER, Catharine	19	Melle	54-1297
FISCHER, Chr.	23	Baiern	54-1724
FISCHER, Chr.	29	Cassel	50-0021
FISCHER, Chr.	25	Gotha	50-1071
FISCHER, Chr.	30	Frisau	49-0383
Herm. 5, Dorothea 27, Caroline 7			
FISCHER, Chr. Phil	40	Offershausen	51-1455
FISCHER, Christian	28	Amoeneburg	54-1566
Elisabeth 25			
FISCHER, Christine	18	Reichenbach	53-1070
FISCHER, Conrad	29	Netphen	53-1062
FISCHER, Doris	29	Hambro	50-1317
FISCHER, Eber.	40	Baiern	54-1724
Cath. 39, Magd. 15, Mich. 13, Rosina 12			
Christoph 9, Christian 5, Christoph 3			
John 1			
FISCHER, Elisabeth	55	Berka	54-1554
FISCHER, Elisabeth	18	Ramrod	50-0292
FISCHER, Elizabeth	18	Alstadt	51-1588
FISCHER, Ernst	24	Rerschdorf	49-1517
FISCHER, Ernst Chr	27	Tennstaedt	48-1355
FISCHER, F.M.	21	Fexen	53-0492
FISCHER, Ferd.	24	Heideck	49-0329
FISCHER, Fr Gottfr	29	Liebau	51-0460
FISCHER, Fr. Carl	29	Donaueschinge	51-1686
FISCHER, Friedr.	21	Preussen	52-0895
FISCHER, Friedrich	21	Dresden	50-0840
FISCHER, Friedrika	24	Nordhausen	48-1209
FISCHER, Georg	46	Badenhausen	52-1423
FISCHER, Georg	28	Schmidtmuehle	54-0965
Cathrine 28			
FISCHER, Georg	28	Baiern	53-0324
FISCHER, George	28	Huettensteinb	53-1164
FISCHER, H. (m)	24	Galla	54-0918
M. (m) 22			
FISCHER, H.G. (m)	29	Scharmbeck	50-0311
FISCHER, Heinr.	15	Hischberg	52-1200
FISCHER, Heinr.	23	Zeitz	53-1013
Sophie 30, Herm. 4			
FISCHER, Heinr.	42	Riskirchen	54-1078
FISCHER, Heinr.	20	Scharmbeck	51-1796
FISCHER, Heinrich	43	Ankum	53-1070
Catharina 41, Gerhard 16, Catharina 12			
Hermann 9, Diedrich 6, Fritz 4, Dina 4m			
FISCHER, Heinrich	52	Schoenau	54-1554
FISCHER, Helene	50	Altenburg	50-0311
FISCHER, Henry	31	Kleinensee	48-0284
Anna 30, Elisabeth 3			
FISCHER, J.	29	Wahrberg	51-0517
FISCHER, J. (m)	25	Kingsheim	50-0746
B. (f) 28, Th. (f) 4			
FISCHER, Jacob	39	Bashoff	54-0053
Anna Cath. 35, Elisabeth 13, Liowa (m) 11			
Theresia 8, Joseph 6, Zacharias 3			
Johanna 9m			
FISCHER, Jacob	26	Schoenthal	49-0352
FISCHER, Jacob	20	Eichelsachsen	52-1321
FISCHER, Joh Carl	24	Mettwitz	53-0324
FISCHER, Joh.	34	Geisingen	52-0370
Sophie 28			
FISCHER, Joh. Wilh	23	Roetha	53-0267

NAME	AGE	RESIDENCE	YR-LIST
FISCHER, Johann	15	Wuertenberg	53-0557
FISCHER, Johann	32	Seiderdorf	49-1106
Friederike 23, Robert 3, Gustav 9m			
FISCHER, Johann	23	Nixdorf	54-1371
FISCHER, Joseph		Arnschwaing	53-0942
Georg			
FISCHER, Joseph	44	Meidt	47-0672
Anna 47, Gabriel 19, Carolina 17			
Joseph 13, Frantz 6, Teresa 4			
FISCHER, Lothar	20	Blankenau	52-1200
FISCHER, Lotte	19	Lichtenstadt	48-1179
FISCHER, Louis	18	Arnstadt	49-0416
FISCHER, Marg.	21	Frainau	54-0053
FISCHER, Marie	22	Grossbottwar	53-0161
FISCHER, Mathias	23	Baden	52-0699
FISCHER, Matthias	44	Hablowitz/Boe	54-1092
Maria 40, Wenzel 16, Catharina 14			
Carl 10, Franz 8, Anna 6			
FISCHER, Peter	25	Neustadt	52-1512
Ernst 19			
FISCHER, Peter	19	Sachsen	51-1686
FISCHER, R. (f)	20	Boehmen	54-1724
C. (f) 24			
FISCHER, Robert	22	Ostruff/Gotha	50-0323
FISCHER, Sophie	24	Ofenstaedt	51-0500
FISCHER, Valt.	18	Rodach	52-0370
FISCHER, Wilhelm	37	Pfaffenreith	53-0475
FISCHER, Wilhelm	42	Stelzendorf	53-1070
Maria Appol. 36, Maria Louise 15, Clara 7			
Ernestine 5, Bertha 3, Gustav Adolf 10m			
FISCHER, Wilhelm	29	Pforzheim	48-1015
FISCHER, Wilhelm	42	Sulzbach	52-1304
FISCHER, Wolfgang	24	Hofdorf	52-1452
FISCHHABER, Elis.	25	Rosstall	47-0828
Sophie 23			
FISCHNER, Martin	28	Kreiselbach	54-0930
Barbara 37			
FISHER, R. (f)	20	Boehmen	54-1724
C. (f) 24			
FISSEL, Friedrich	25	Humbressen/He	51-1532
FISTE, Victor		New Orleans	48-1015
FITTEL, Herm.	31	Bauen	54-1283
Louise 23			
FITZ, Adam	25	Gethles	54-0903
FITZENBERG, Marie	20	Gellenheim	51-1686
FLACH, Adam	37	Fischbach/Nas	53-0628
Elisabeth 42, Caroline 10, Heinrich 8			
Christiane 6, Louise 35			
FLACH, Charles	27	Berlin	53-0888
FLACH, Henry	26	Ippinghausen	48-0053
FLACH, Philipp	18	Kettenschwalb	48-0447
FLAD, Joseph	19	Boettingen	54-0872
FLAFF, Andr.	31	Utrictshausen	52-0515
FLAGGE, Franz	29	Mark Oldendor	52-1200
Amalie 27			
FLAKE, August	30	Schwalenberg	51-1588
FLAKE, Sophia	18	Schledehausen	51-1588
FLAMBACH, Michael	28	Cronstadt/Bav	48-0053
FLAMMENKAMP, Luise	20	Leopoldsthal	52-0775
FLAMMER, William	21	Jebenhausen	50-0840
Sophie 24, Robert 2m			
FLASCHNER, Midard.	33	Magdeburg	48-1015
Caroline 25, Julius 1			
FLATUNG, Valentine	28	Siegen/Hessen	49-0365
FLAUDERER, W.	33	Emmetzheim	47-0868
FLAUSNICK, Franz	28	Koenigsberg	54-1443
Margarethe 24			
FLECK, Joseph	39	Hilders	52-1625
FLECKENSTEIN, Lew.	36	Wuerzburg	53-0991
Amalia 40, Sophia 6m			
FLECKENSTEIN, W.	19	Obernkirchen	52-1321
FLEER, Carl	24	Herford	52-1452
Christine 27			
FLEETZ, Peter	27	Hilberheim	54-0987
FLEIDERN, Ludw.	20	Hall	49-0352
FLEISCHER, David	17	Kliestow	49-0352
FLEISCHER, Ernst	38	Ostrieff/Sax.	50-0323
FLEISCHER, Ferd.	26	New York	53-1164

NAME	AGE	RESIDENCE	YR-LIST
Antoinette 21			
FLEISCHER, Moses	16	Aufsees	53-0991
FLEISCHHAUER, Crln	20	Frankenhain	54-0600
FLEISCHHAUER, Hein	21	Wiera	51-0500
Anna 21			
FLEISCHHAUER, Joh.	25	Wiera	49-0345
FLEISCHHAUER, Jost	23	Glattbach	54-1575
Casp. 21, Casp. 18			
FLEISCHHAUER, Leo.	28	Buchenau	52-1661
FLEISCHHEIT, Alex.	35	Suhl	51-1639
FLEISCHMANN, Alb.	22	Koenigsberg	50-0840
FLEISCHMANN, Berm.	18	Oberlangstadt	48-0887
FLEISCHMANN, Conr.	33	Mosheim	53-1016
Anna 22, George 4m			
FLEISCHMANN, Doro.	18	Oberlangensta	53-0628
FLEISCHMANN, Elias	31	Suschon/Boehm	52-1332
Abagail 31, Elisabeth 9m, Leopold 2			
FLEISCHMANN, Georg	29	Lettenreuth	52-1661
FLEISCHMANN, John	27	Weidenau	50-0840
FLEISCHMANN, Phil.	25	Kueps	53-0888
Simon 13, Pauline 22			
FLEISCHMANN, Seb.	23	Eisnach	52-0370
FLEISENER, Jacob	23	Walddorf	53-0914
FLEMMING, Chr.	19	Naumburg	53-1164
FLENTGE, Friedr.	18	Cathrinhagen	52-0563
FLENTJE, Christ.	21	Katrinhagen	53-1086
Carl 17			
FLERLAGE, Johann G	22	Luesche	52-0563
FLERSHEIM, Betty	10	Gehaus	53-0942
FLESCHUTZ, B.	26	Buchloh	53-0492
FLICK, Christiane	24	Wahlbach	53-0590
FLIEDEL, John	24	Blaustaedt/Bv	49-0365
Therese 32			
FLOEL, Carl	19	Tiefenort	51-1739
FLOERCKEN, Friedr.	19	Bremen	53-1013
FLOERKE, Christian	32	Huelsede	48-1209
FLOERKE, H.	36	Hesse Wendorf	51-1084
FLOHR, Gerh.	31	Linns	51-1588
FLOR, Adam	19	Osnabrueck	52-1512
FLORSCHUTZ, Diedr.	58	Oeslau	54-1282
Anna 58, Carl 22, Georg 20			
FLUEDEL, Christ.	22	Sulzbach	49-1106
FLUEGEL, Carl	37	Oefingen/Bad.	51-1725
FLUEGEL, Wilhelm	24	Ehrigshagen	48-0887
FLUEGER, Anna M.	25	Hundelshausen	52-0563
FLUEGGE, Simon	30	Blomberg	54-1168
FLUES, Eberhard	29	Barmen	53-0991
Bernard 23			
FLUGE, Joh Heinr.	36	Altenrod	53-1062
FLUGEL, Christian	18	Pottigo	54-0987
FLUTNEL, Catherine	58	Alsfeld	54-1341
FOCH, Herm.	25	Langenstadt	48-1179
FOCKE, D.H. (m)	16	Bremen	50-1317
FOCKE, H.W. Carl	28	Bockenim	52-0563
FOCKENTAENZERIN, E	28	Ebersbruenn	51-1245
FOCKEROTH, Margret	24	Dambrock	48-0951
FOCKHAUSEN, Jos. C	40	Bremerlehe	50-0840
FOEHLING, Johannes	15	Fraurombach	54-1575
Margarethe 13			
FOERSTEL, Georg	22	Schweintal	52-0693
FOERSTER, Anna El.	15	Maebenberg	53-0905
FOERSTER, Anna El.	15		53-0905
FOERSTER, August	19	Geibsdorf	53-0888
FOERSTER, Dorothea	30	Schleusingen	54-1649
FOERSTER, Friedr.	23	Hildesheim	54-1283
FOERSTER, Julius	38	Dresden	50-1067
Caroline 34			
FOERSTER, Leonh.	28	Amerndorf	54-1282
FOERSTER, Leonhard	33	Schmalenbuehl	54-1566
Barbara 31, J.C. 3, A. Margareth 25			
FOERSTER, Magdalen	23	Curhessen	52-1432
FOERSTER, Margar.	38	Muenchsteinac	54-1282
FOERSTER, Wilhelm	30	Waldsleben	52-0279
FOERSTNER, Alois	38	Wien	54-1554
FOERTSCH, Robert	19	Schleusingen	53-0991
FOGGTE, Georg	30	Stilte	50-0439
FOLGER, Sebastian	37	Tatschenbrunn	48-0101
Mariane 59, Stephen 28, Magdalene 25			
Kunigunde 21, A. Maria 17, Friedr. 14			
FOLKE, William	36	Mittelruessel	49-0737
Friederike 35			
FOLLHARDT, Johann	21	Einsheim/Hess	52-0117
FOLMER, Johann	16	Steinau	51-0500
FOLTMANN, H. (f)	21	Wecherheid	54-1341
FONTANA, John B.	40	New York	48-1015
FORBRIGER, Arthur	21	Hamburg	53-0161
FORCHT, Ludwig	15	Sattenhausen	51-0352
FORDEMFELDT, J.H.	37	Ottersberg	52-1362
Clara 40, Friedrich 17, Florentine 15			
FORESTI, E. Felix	36	New York	48-1015
FORK, Carl Friedr.	18	Heidenheim	49-0352
FORKE, W. (m)	21	Olenbutt	49-0416
FORKEL, Wilhelm	54	Coburg	54-1297
Anna 18			
FORMANN, August	23	Bielefeld/Pr.	52-0117
FORMHALS, Th.	20	Londorff	51-1160
FORSBERG, Carl W.	47	Koenigsberg	50-0840
Albertine 42, Emmy 21, Clara 5, illeg. 18			
Alexander 16, Gustav 12			
FORSTER, Joh.	38	Bavaria	50-1236
Joh. 22			
FORSTER, Joseph	24	Bernau	52-0095
FORSTER, Sebastian	30	Bavaria	53-0628
Barbara 35, Anna Maria 10, Elisabeth 10			
FORTMANN, Elis.	58	Muenster/Pr.	52-1432
Gertrude 23			
FOSTER, Hans Adam	50	Heinefeld/Hes	50-0117
FOSTY, Georg	27	Chea	50-0840
Cathinka 24, Charles 3			
FOTENBACHER, Carol	37	Calm	53-1164
FOTH, Lina	28	Neu-Brandenbu	52-1423
FOUTZ, Joh. Georg	33	Pfunzenhausen	53-1062
FRAEHRS, Johann	6m	Landwursten	50-1067
FRAGE, Friedr.	24	Mittelruessel	49-0737
Henry 19			
FRAGER, Charles	18	Melsungen	54-1341
FRANCK, C. (f)	35	Forkendorff	51-0517
F. 13, G. 9, M. 7			
FRANCK, Heinr. Chr	60	Tennstaedt	48-1355
Friederike 54			
FRANCKE, A.	23	Frankenhausen	53-0492
Friedrich 20, Jette 17			
FRANCL, Anton	23	Prag	51-1084
FRANER, Wenzel	41	Wobora	54-1647
Anna 35, Wenzel 10, Anna 12, Josepha 6			
Valentina 4, Franz Jos. 1			
FRANK, Andreas	27	Gerholzhofen	54-1443
Johanne 28, Rosalie 10m			
FRANK, Barthel	26	Friedrichsdor	51-0384
Valentin 39, Eva 22			
FRANK, Bernhard	17	Roedelsee/Bav	52-0807
FRANK, Caroline	17	Schopfloch	52-0515
FRANK, Caroline	25	Coburg	52-0563
FRANK, Charles	3-	Kirberg/Nas.	48-0447
FRANK, Christian	52	Branderode	54-0850
Maria Rosina 42, Wilhelmine 16			
Friedr. Alb. 14, Carl 3, Friedr. Aug. by			
FRANK, Christian	26	Rodendorf	54-0872
FRANK, David	24	Lengsfeld	49-0413
FRANK, Fr. Louis	27	Udestedt	54-1078
Magdalena 27			
FRANK, Gottfried	24	Wuertenberg	53-0557
Friedericke 26			
FRANK, Josepha	49	Friedrichsdor	51-0384
Peter 30, Maria 21, Amor 13			
FRANK, Kaufmann		Hebenhausen	51-0048
FRANK, Lorenz	34	Bug	54-1078
FRANK, Maria	22	Schwaigheim	53-0320
Catharina 20			
FRANK, Philipp	15	Lengsfeld	53-0942
FRANK, Regina	36	Grossassbach	49-0352
Daniel Erh. 2			
FRANK, Rosine	24	Weiler	53-0435
FRANK, Sarah	51	Schotten	53-0991
Amelia 14			
FRANKE, A.	27	Breuna	54-1078

NAME	AGE	RESIDENCE	YR-LIST
FRANKE, Andreas	59	Weimar/Sach.	51-1725
Friederike 57, Wilhelm 18, Emilie 26			
FRANKE, Carl	8	Schwelm	54-0930
FRANKE, Ch. Wilh.	35	Groben	52-0279
FRANKE, Fr.	28	Bruecken	49-1358
Leda (m) 22			
FRANKE, George	28	Grillheim	53-0928
FRANKE, Greschen	20	Bremen	54-0987
FRANKE, Gustav	24	Goslar	50-1236
FRANKE, Heinrich	57	Bremervoerde	54-1371
Anna 57, Anna 18			
FRANKE, Jacob	40	Meue/Sax.	54-1092
FRANKE, Johann	44	Niederhalslum	52-1332
Friederike 45, Ernestine 16, Caroline 14			
Joh. Heinr. 12, Joh. Ernst 8			
FRANKE, Margarethe	20	New York	54-1371
Wilhelm 2			
FRANKE, Maria Fr.	25	Langensalza	51-1796
FRANKE, Moritz	20	Koppenbruegge	54-1168
Gustav 18			
FRANKE, Philipp	24	Dessau	52-0895
FRANKE, Theodor	37	Pittburg	54-1371
FRANKE, Wilh.	19	Bremke	51-1640
FRANKEL, Jakob	20	Diesfuck	50-0840
Sarah 15			
FRANKENBERG, E.C.	63	Gera/Gotha	52-0960
FRANKENBERG, Jos.	24	Voerden	54-1443
Gunipert 24, Jette 22			
FRANKENBERG, Jos.	24	Berkel/Bav.	54-1443
Gunipert 24			
FRANKENBERG, v. Am	35	Goettingen	53-0991
FRANKENBERG, v. Em	19	Goettingen	53-0991
E. Theod. 26			
FRANKENBERGER, Ros	27	Wildenberg	51-1160
Cathar. 6m			
FRANKENFELDER, Abr	17	Heu-ngfeld	53-1000
FRANKENHEIM, Moses	30	Neustadt	54-1371
FRANKENHEIMER, Mos	32	Bruck	53-0991
FRANKENSTEIN, Bert	30	Detmold	51-1160
FRANKENSTEIN, Hein	32	Boeringfeld	51-1796
Joh. Sabels. 26, Caroline 3, Waldemar 9m			
Marie 24			
FRANKENSTEIN, Mar.	24	Hoechster	51-1796
FRANKENSTEIN, Mose	26	Roesingfeld	48-0260
FRANKLE, M.	44	Schtlesthal	51-1455
FRANKTURTA, Veit	14	Obendorf	54-0872
FRANZ, Georg	20	Hof/Baiern	53-0475
FRANZ, Joh. Theoph	36	Paris	53-0991
FRANZ, Marie	18	Hof/Baiern	53-0475
FRANZ, Simon	33	Derschitz	53-1000
FRANZEN, Adelheid	21	Schale	52-0279
Catharina 19			
FRAS, Christian	50	Groschlatengr	53-0928
Eva 34, Johann 22, Heinrich 9, Erhard 4			
FRASS, Philipp	36	Spielberg	48-1209
FRAUENDOERFER, Jos	31	Greisbach	54-1078
Catharina 28			
FRAUENKNECHT, Geo.	28	Ermenreuth	54-1647
Kunigunde 34, Magdalena 8			
FRAUENSCHU, Clara	56	Ferdinandsdor	51-0384
FRAUNDFELDE, C.(m)	36	Duisburg/Pr.	48-0447
FRAUSNICK, Marg.	26	Koenigsberg	54-1443
FRAUTSCH, Henriett	26	Ronis/Prussia	53-0628
FRECH, Magdalene	21	Ibenhausen	51-0757
FREDE, Conrad	20	Homberg	54-0053
FREDE, Friedrich	53	Semien	53-1086
Marie F. 60, Christoph 20, Bernhard 22			
FREDEN, v. John	24	Richmond	53-0161
FREDENSTEIN, Jos.	21	Niederwald	54-1676
FREDERIK, Louis	19	Hannover	50-1067
FREENER, Gottlieb	28	Chemnitz	53-1070
FREESE, Albert	50	Torpien	54-0872
Catharine 41, Friedrich 18, Waldemar 15			
Otto 9, Julius 8, Jette 6, Bertha 3			
Anna by			
FREESE, Anton Hein	21	Luesche	52-0563
FREESE, Doris	24	Bederkesa	50-1317
FREESE, Wilh.	20	Schussebburg	51-1455

NAME	AGE	RESIDENCE	YR-LIST
FREHRKING, Chr.	30	Rodewald	47-0762
FREHRS, Johann	31	Hildesheim/Ha	51-1532
Johanna 29, Franz 28			
FREI, Aug.	22	Bavaria	50-0311
FREI, Carl	21	Baden	50-1317
FREIBOUT, Gottf.	23	Altesleben	49-1358
FREIER, Julius	23	Freiberg	53-0473
Amalia 25			
FREIS, Jacob	30	Rauschenbg	50-0472
FREISCHE, M.	51	Schlingen	53-0492
Agathe 50, Marianne 22, Genovefa 15			
Polo 21, Marie 14, Xaver 9			
FREISLEBEN, Gustav	36	Magdeburg	54-0987
Ludwig 26, Louis by			
FREISLOH, Eva	56	Helbra	54-1341
Florina 18, W. (f) 15			
FREISSLEICH, Ant't	18	Meiningen	51-1588
FREISTUELER, Heinr	27		51-0352
Elisabeth 27, Bessel (m)			
FREITAG, Anna	23	Felsberg	50-0292
FREITAG, David	18	Baiersdorf	53-1164
FREITAG, H.	24	Altenbuettel	50-1071
FREITAG, Johanne	26	Wurzburg	54-1716
FREITAG, Luise	19	Schoningen	47-0872
FREITAG, Therese	18	Markelsheim	54-1371
FREMBES, Andrae	36	Grossheirath	52-0279
FRENKEL, Christoph	21	Hof	50-1071
FRENKEL, Israel	34	Rudolstadt	54-1647
FRENKLING, Carl	26	Braunschweig	47-0672
FRENZEL, Carl Gott	43	Litz	51-1455
Carl 15			
FRERICHS, Elise	28	New York	54-0053
FRERKS, Arian	27	Rissum	54-0987
Heike 23, Hilke 20			
FRESE, Anna	17	WesterBeverst	54-1716
FRESE, Doris	24	Bremen	51-1084
FRESE, E.	22	Babber	53-1086
FRESE, Georg	26	Arensberg	52-0699
FRESELER, Heinrich	37	Oldendorf/Pr.	54-1092
FRESELMANN, Maria	22	Holte	52-1512
FREUDENBERG, C.(m)	30	Camenz	49-1358
FREUDENBERG, P.(m)	25	Teplitz	47-0762
FREUDENBERGER, Mar	19	Hoechstadt/Bv	51-1796
FREUDENTHAL, Aug.	24	Hannover	52-0699
FREUDHAFER, Math.	30	Fraggenstalle	54-1283
FREUND, Catharine	18	Umstadt	53-0991
FREUND, Charles	30	Hannover	53-0582
FREUND, Franz	16	Rodach	53-0585
FREUND, Friedr.	19	Schneckengrue	48-0053
FREUND, Henry	24	Neustadt	53-0991
FREUND, Henry	31	Neu.Sagen/Sax	48-0053
FREUND, Louise	17	Rodach	53-0585
FREUND, Louise	24	Ost Friesland	54-0903
FREUND, M. (m)	32	Prague	48-1015
FREUND, Michael	17	Audenhausen	48-1179
Eva 19			
FREUZ, Marg.	27	Ohrenbach	54-1078
FREY, Andreas	45	Huningen	53-1000
FREY, August	20	Erfurt	54-1649
FREY, Babtist	22	Bayern	52-1620
FREY, Dav.	19	Unsleben	48-1179
FREY, Herod	45	Emsdetten	51-1455
FREY, Theophil	22	Heilbronn	49-0912
Albert 21			
FREY, Valentin	17	Treysa	49-0345
FREYDER, Wilh'mine	26	Taisnig	54-1649
FREYER, Joh. Th.	21	Arnstadt	48-0269
FREYSCHLAG, Ant.	30	Lauda/Baden	51-1796
FREYTAG, Wilhelm	27	Rosendahl	54-1649
FRICK, Carl Louis	26	Wuerzen/Sach.	51-1725
FRICK, Christian	49	Leiberstadt	51-0384
FRICKE, Auguste	28	Cassel	51-0352
Theodor 20			
FRICKE, Carl	24	Cincinnate/Oh	52-1332
August 28			
FRICKE, Conrad	28	Polle	50-0292
Fritz 18, Wilhelm 25			
FRICKE, Dor.	21	Meinessen	51-1084

NAME	AGE	RESIDENCE	YR-LIST
FRICKE, Gottfried	22	Wernigerode	53-0557
FRICKE, Joh.	30	Guetersloh	51-1686
FRICKMANN, Albert	19	Hastedt	48-0887
FRIDAG, Barbara	20	Baiern	54-1724
FRIEBACH, Georg	15	Breitenbach	52-1512
FRIEDEL, Barb.	21	Baiern	54-1724
FRIEDEMANN, Heinr.	37	Heiningen	54-1001
FRIEDEMANN, J Gott	30	Coestritz	53-0838
FRIEDEMANN, Joh.	27	Widdershausen	48-0284
Eva Barb. 22			
FRIEDENBERG, Moses	34	Buren	51-1455
Hannah 34			
FRIEDERICH, Herman	19	Langerich	52-1362
FRIEDERICH, Wilh.	22	Mooringen	48-0260
FRIEDERICHS, Aug.	23	Stadthagen/Br	50-0323
FRIEDERICHS, v. M.	32	New York	53-0991
FRIEDGEN, Cornel.	15	Bieberach	52-1512
FRIEDGEN, Elise	17	Osnabrueck	52-1512
Cornelius 15			
FRIEDHOFF, Louis	27	Warendorf	54-1724
FRIEDLANDER, J Sol	20	Czarnikau	52-1304
FRIEDLER, Ignatz	18	Bodlem	54-1647
FRIEDLICH, Hermann	55	Wireschen	54-1297
Cacilie 21			
FRIEDMANN, Heinr.	18	Kulmbach	51-1640
FRIEDMANN, Jette	42	Ackerhausen	50-0472
Nathan 19, Hermann 17			
FRIEDMANN, Joh. Fr	29	Lucka	54-0872
FRIEDMANN, Lotte	17	Burgkundstadt	48-0269
FRIEDMANN, Mar.	13	Reckendorf	53-0888
FRIEDMANN, Wolfg.	20	Limmersdorff	49-0413
FRIEDMANN, Xaver	28	Reuwosch	51-1639
FRIEDRICH, Caspar	54	Zell	54-0830
Caspar 26, Peter 21, Christine 18			
FRIEDRICH, Caspar	17	Dormitz	51-1245
FRIEDRICH, Conrad	25	Wacha	50-0292
FRIEDRICH, Daniel	29	Hildesheim	52-0095
FRIEDRICH, Georg	34	Ermreuth	53-0320
FRIEDRICH, Jacob	23	Hohenberg	48-0565
FRIEDRICH, Juliane	30	Diedeldorf	54-0965
FRIEDRICH, Wil'mne	21	Lobenstein	53-0557
FRIEDRICHS, Christ	33	Buetgow	54-1371
Henriette 22, Johanne 4, Ferdinand 23			
FRIEDRICHS, Claud	32	Wuerttemberg	53-0557
FRIEDRICHS, Claud.	32	Wuertenberg	53-0557
FRIEDRICHS, Franz	37	Hannover	50-0021
Dorette 10, Heinr. 4			
FRIEDRICHS, Joseph	21	Meschede	51-0460
FRIEMANN, Friedr.	22	Groenberg	49-0345
FRIES, Andreas	17	Dormitz	53-1023
FRIES, Charles	36	Goldscha	53-0928
FRIES, Henry	24	Segeberg	53-0888
Mary 20			
FRIES, Ludwig	27	Terschen	52-0807
FRIES, Pet. Lorenz	32	Fuerth	54-0850
FRIES, Rud.	29	Schlingen	54-1001
FRIES, de W.	35	Groningen	49-1517
Mrs. 40, Heinrich 10, Bernhard 6			
Gaiob 3m			
FRIESCHE, Engel	27	Altenbruch/Ha	51-1532
FRIESE, Wilh.	24	Quackenbrueck	52-1512
FRIESENECKER, Mar.	24	Baiern	50-1067
FRIESNER, Isaac	16	Ermershausen	48-1179
FRIETZSCHES, Joh.	23	Petzenrodig	53-0267
FRIKE, H.	27	Hesse Wendorf	51-1084
FRIKE, Wilhelm	30	Hessen	54-1716
FRILSS, Wilhelmina	23	Coburg	53-1164
FRINKEN, Heinrich	20	Loeningen	53-1062
FRISCH, Cath. Barb	24	Schweinengen	51-1455
FRISCH, James G.	18	Mittelruessel	49-0737
FRISCHMANN, Joh.	34	Kleinensee	48-0284
Elisabeth 30, Conrad 10, Johannes 8			
Nicolaus 4			
FRITSCH, Andreas	36	Gossengruen	53-1070
Dorothea 21, Carl 13, Joseph 8			
Franz Joseph 5			
FRITSCH, Carl	27	Lobenstein	48-0951
FRITSCH, Carl	29	Treussen	54-1649

NAME	AGE	RESIDENCE	YR-LIST
FRITSCH, Christian	20	Treysa	49-0345
Johannes 19			
FRITSCH, Claus	16	Bese	49-0345
FRITSCH, Julia	24	Nieheim	51-1101
FRITSCH, Wilhelm	22	Alle	49-0345
FRITSCHE, Ferd.	25	Lobeda	53-0942
FRITSCHE, Godfrey	38	Blankenhain	53-1164
FRITSCHE, Gottfr.	52	Reichstaedt	50-1071
Gustina 23, Friedr. Wm. 24, Michael 18			
FRITSCHEL, Gottf.	19	Lichtenfels	51-0405
FRITSCHLER, Matias	33	Wuestenfels	54-1419
Charlotte 55			
FRITZ, Adolph	22	Fesbach	50-1132
FRITZ, Andreas	30	Eberbach	47-0828
FRITZ, August	21	Suhl	53-0928
FRITZ, August	28	Schleisingen	50-1132
FRITZ, Caroline	24	Henneberg	51-1686
FRITZ, Chr.	24	Pudenz	52-1464
FRITZ, Eva	25	Sulzfeld	51-1588
Maria 4, Friederike 11m			
FRITZ, Georg	25	Batschel	53-0914
FRITZ, Gottlieb	18	Mechsteidt	51-1640
FRITZ, Herm.	23	Prussia	50-1317
FRITZ, Jacob	27	Lauffen/Wuert	51-1725
FRITZ, Maria	20	Irendorf	49-0912
FRITZ, Paul	36	Ulmbach	52-1625
Georg 24, Heinrich 17			
FRITZ, Wenzel	27	Boehmen	53-1000
Marie 27			
FRITZ, Wilhelmine	22	Umstadt	53-0991
FRITZE, Constantin	22	Bremen	47-0158
FRITZEL, Catharina	20	Bergen/Hess.	52-0807
FRITZMANN, E. (f)	21	Gotha	48-0445
FRITZSCH, Caroline	59	Lobenstein	54-1371
FRITZSCHE, Eduard	18	Ronneburg	53-0590
FROBST, John F.	28	Heilbronn	52-0515
FROEBEL, Catharina	22	Oberhellingen	53-0637
FROEBER, Heinr.	18	Keise	53-0914
FROEDEL, Johann	39	Bayern	53-1013
Anna 34, Christian 13, Sabine 9, Georg 8			
Michel 5, Ferdinand 5, Monika 6m			
FROEDER, Elise	49	Pollensen/Han	51-1532
Georgine 22, Wilhelm 7m			
FROEHLICH, Carl	35	Aschersleben	53-1023
FROEHLICH, Fidel	31	Wahlries	49-0574
FROEHLICH, Ludwig	22	Erbach	54-0930
FROEHLICH, Max	15	Aufhausen	54-0872
FROEHLICH, Michael	22	Peink-Punk	53-0914
FROEHLICH, Michael	29	Iphofen	54-1371
FROEHLICH, Victria	34	Steinau	53-0320
FROEHLING, Conrad	30	Frankfurt/M	54-0830
FROEHLKE, Wilhelm	30	Rheme	54-1297
Dolores 31, Eduard 12, Dolores 3			
FROEHLUKE, Fr. Wm.	25	Heepen	51-1160
FROEHNLEIN, Cath.	18	Ohrenbach	51-1438
FROELICH, Balthas.	21	Aubnach/Sachs	53-0628
FROELICH, Friedr.	18	Stargard/Pr.	54-1092
Auguste 21			
FROELICH, Victoria	19	Brakel	52-1661
FROESE, Rudolph	18	Koenigsberg	50-0840
FROETER, Pius	24	Empfingen	52-0279
FROH, Louise	39	Zierow	54-1297
FROHBARTH, Heinr.	32	Hemmrotha	53-0267
FROHBERG, Christ H	27	Bremen	51-0500
Sophie 27, Carl F. 9m			
FROHBOESE, Heinr.	17	Bieren	54-1452
FROHLICH, Johannes	22	Heeringen	48-0284
FROHMANN, Johann	44	Filsbiburg	54-1717
FROHN, Peter	22	Bonn	54-1371
FROHSINN, Bienchen		Voerden	54-1443
FROHWEIN, Theobald	18	Pfuhlborn	54-0872
Richard 23			
FROHWITTER, Wilh.	22	Luebbecke/Pr.	51-1725
August 18			
FROLICH, Aug.	24	Kleinfena/Pr.	52-0117
Emilie 21			
FROLICK, William	27	Mittelruessel	49-0737
Rosina 29			

NAME	AGE	RESIDENCE	YR-LIST
FROLLINEL,	28	Prag	48-1131
FROMM, Hermann	28	Berlin	51-1062
FROMM, Johann	32	Rheinhausen	52-0117
Veronica 34, Elisabeth 5, Christine 3			
Maria 1			
FROMM, Johannes	30	Istrup/Pr.	54-0965
FROMME, Sophia	38	Braunschweig	53-0991
FROMMER, Henry	26	Bielefeld	54-1649
FROMMEYER, Chr. C.	27	Bramsche	51-0500
FROMMHOLD, Amalie	16	Lunzenau	53-1023
FROST, Jos.	34	Mittelruessel	49-0737
FROSTZ, Jos. G.	25	Mittelruessel	49-0737
FRUEHAUF, August	24	Rappelsdorf	52-0807
FRUEHLING, Hemmen	32	Leer	50-1067
Aske 38, Gretje 34, Ida 35, Hermine 28			
FRUEHSANG, Heinr.	27	New York	54-1647
FRUESANG, August	25	Sterbehausen	52-0563
FRUTTIGER, Jacob	23	Blumensteig	49-0912
FRY, Elis.	45	Wismar	54-1724
Henry 23, Leo. 16			
FUCH, Friedrich	35	Buberschlag	53-0914
FUCHS, Alouise	34	Wien	52-0699
Joseph 11, Franz 6			
FUCHS, Anna	24	Lageloh	49-0742
FUCHS, Barbara	25	Schwarzenau	53-1023
FUCHS, Bernh.	47	Arzberg	50-1236
Joh. Regina 43, Joh. 21, Carol. 18			
Heinr. 12, Carl 8, Catharina 3			
FUCHS, Emma	30	Koenigsberg	50-1236
Johanne 7, Agnes 4			
FUCHS, Ernst	35	Gera	52-0095
FUCHS, Franz	25	Wettringen	54-1554
FUCHS, Friedr. Aug	18	Saninwitz	53-0825
FUCHS, Georg	47	Zochenreuth	52-1200
Johann 16, Margaretha 12, Anna 11			
Johann 8, Johann 6, Peter 38			
Margaretha 33, Gertrud 6			
FUCHS, Georg	23	Oberhausen	49-0352
FUCHS, Henry	23	Affelde	53-0914
FUCHS, Jacob	23	Hottenbach	51-1062
FUCHS, Joh. Mich.	32	Sondernohe	52-1304
Maria 27, Anna Marie 2			
FUCHS, Johann	29	Weiher	54-1443
FUCHS, Joseph	27	Roth	48-0951
Anne E. 24, John A. 30, John bob			
FUCHS, Maria	44	Kraftshof	52-0693
Regine 12			
FUCHS, Michael	30	Winterhausen	54-0600
FUCHS, Peter	38	Langenlohe	52-1200
FUCHS, Philipp	21	Baiern	52-0895
FUCHS, Therese	24	Niederleiss	53-0942
FUCHSBERGER, Thom.	35	Oberheking	52-1452
Johanne 32, Ursula 52, Maria 6, Alois 5			
Sophie 3, Jacob 9m			
FUEHRER, Franz	24	Hindelang	53-0492
FUEHRER, Johann	27	Neustadt	54-0872
FUEHRER, Seb.	33	Warmbingen	54-0918
FUELLEN, Hanna	30	Culmitzsch	54-1371
Rosine 28			
FUELLER, August	17	Ober-Schoenau	53-1000
FUELLER, Sabina	24	Blankenau	51-0405
Beatrix 21			
FUELLGRABE, Wm.	23	Lauterberg	48-1131
FUELLING, Anna	24	Essen	53-1086
Friederike 21			
FUELLMANN, August	24	Kehlbach	49-0352
FUERBRINGER, Lor.	30	Arzberg	50-1236
FUERST, A. (f)	28		52-1321
FUERST, Carl	35	Wallis	52-1321
FUERST, Dorothea		Paffeldorf	54-1283
FUERST, Johann	28	Reifenberg	52-1321
FUERST, Josephus	27	Landau	48-0053
FUERST, Kunigunde	24	Druegendorf	52-0095
FUERST, Marg.	28	Klatteneggols	54-1575
FUERST, Marg.	28	Klatteneggals	54-1575
FUERST, Maria	22	Theisau	52-1321
FUERSTENBERG, Joh.	46	Krenzeler	54-0850
Margaretha 24, Elisabetha 44, Lorentz 16			

NAME	AGE	RESIDENCE	YR-LIST
Joseph 13, Catharina 9			
FUESHAUS, Bernh.	54	Muenster	54-1724
FUHLROTH, Louis	21	Leinefelde	52-0279
FUHRMAN, Wilh.	31	Braunsschweig	51-1796
FUHRMANN, August	46	Kittethal	50-0379
Caroline 43, Heinrich 19			
FUHRMANN, Christ.	21	Zillbach	52-1200
FUHRMANN, Henry	35	Gera/Prussia	49-0365
FUKAR, Johann	49	Oberingelheim	49-0912
FULD, Samuel	17	Willmers/Bav.	53-0628
FULDA, Conr.	49	Grosseneichen	52-1200
Marie 45, Friedrich 20, Anna Maria 14			
Maria 10			
FULDA, Matthias	25	Offenbach	53-0991
FULDNER, Louis	19	Kleinern	53-1023
FULLE, Gottfr.	19	Krechtschutz	50-1071
FULLER, Diedrich	20	Schweringen	53-1000
FULS, John	53	Diele	53-0888
Feutje 52, Steffentje 26, Dierk 24			
Tjake 21, Albert 18, Schwantje 16			
FULSCHE, Christian	50	Gorsleben	54-1371
Johanna 36, Hermann 14, Carl 12			
Wilhelm 9, Ferdinand 7, August 4			
FULTE, Eliza	25	Hartborn	48-1209
FUNCK, Friedr.	28	Memphis	54-1566
FUNCK, G.C.	49	Berlin	48-1243
FUNCK, Johannes	30	Tollenroth	51-1101
FUNCKE, Christian	14	Bornhagen	51-1438
FUNK, Adam	21	Grossendorf	51-1532
FUNK, Christian	27		49-1106
Ludwig 19			
FUNK, Jacob	21	Frankfurt/M.	49-0345
FUNK, Jacob	26	St. Goarshaus	49-0345
FUNK, Johann	28	Cur Hessen	53-0557
FUNK, Johann	28	Kur-Hessen	53-0557
FUNK, L.	31	Wieseth	54-1283
FUNKE, Carl	24	Wagenfeld	51-0500
FUNKE, Christian	25	Rimbach	54-0850
Henriette 18			
FUNKE, Christian	26	Thonhausen	54-1168
FUNKE, Friedr.	38	Erzberg	53-0590
FUNKE, Gottlieb	42	Mitschwitz	50-1132
FUNKE, Heinrich	23	Neustadt	53-0590
FUNKE, Heinrich	48	Frankenberg	54-1168
FUNKE, Henry	30	Algermissen/H	51-0048
Fritz 19			
FUNKENSTEIN, Berta	26	Esch	53-1070
FUPPERT, Peter	28	Coburg	50-0021
FURSTMEIER, A.	31	Bluckenbleck	51-0517
FUSEL, Johann	15	Gestensted	49-0345
FUSELER, Pusta	25	Rombeck	52-0515
Christine 18			
FUSELER, Heinr.	25	Rombeck	52-0515
FUSS, Elise	26	Schlizenhause	53-0942
FUSS, Hermine	36	Zeitz	53-1164
Emma 3			
FUSS, Joseph	16	Steinach	52-1304
FUSS, Margaretha	27	Neuwart	53-0942
FUTTOR, Conr.	43	Memelsdorf	52-0515
FUTTOR, Conr.	40	Memelsdorf	52-0515
GABAIN, v. Eduard	27	Koenigsberg	51-0652
GABEL, Casp.	23	Hessendorf	50-1071
GABEL, Christiane	26	Mittelruessel	49-0737
GABLER, Gottfried	23	Crimmitschau	53-0914
Sophie 20			
GABOT, Wilhelm	19	Hamm	50-0379
GABS, Heinrich	24	Markeldorf	53-1023
GABSCH, Friedrich	22	Sachsen	53-0590
GADE, Louise	17	Bahnssen	54-0850
Elise 15			
GADERMANN, P. (m)	33	Ruhrort/Pr.	48-0447
GADJOHANN, F. (m)	28	Osterkappel	48-0453
GAEBEL, J.C. (m)	36	Dresden	50-0379
Johanne 34, Auguste 4, Franz 1			
GAEBLER, Wilh'mine	17	Freyburg	54-0872
GAEHLE, Henry	42	Baltimore	53-0991
GAEPZE, Johann	30	Wildesheim	53-1023
GAERSTENER, Gottl.	41	Altenburg	52-1321

NAME	AGE	RESIDENCE	YR-LIST
GAERTNER, Anton	52	Kirchgoens	54-0965
Johannes 18, Elisabeth 16			
GAERTNER, August	18	Oberhaslum/Sa	52-1332
GAERTNER, Friedr.	49	Treptow	54-0872
Caroline 50, Marie 25, Hermann 17			
Fritz 14, Carl 9			
GAERTNER, Heinrich	22	Diepholz	53-0557
GAERTNER, J. (m)	17	Stuttgart	49-0329
GAESTEL, Franz	27	Marienstein	52-0279
GAFFRON, A.H. (m)	19	Bielefeld	47-0672
GAGE, Gottfd.	20	Wiesbaden/Nas	48-0447
GAGE, Heinr.	20	Oberhaslum/Sa	52-1332
GAHL, Wilhelm	34	Demmin	51-0326
GAHR. Elise	49	Neustadt	52-1105
Matthias 30, Magdalene 12, Elise 17			
GAIL, Johann	21	Nassau	53-0590
GAIL, Mar.	18	Giessen	47-0918
GAILING, Hermann	24	Bremerhafen	48-1184
GAKENHOLZ, Carl	21	Wienhausen	54-1168
GALBEM, Conrad	40	Lautenthal	54-1168
Carl 13			
GALLEKER, Alois	24	Muehlhausen	49-0352
GALLEM, Conrad	40	Lautenthal	54-1168
Carl 13			
GALLIARD, Leopold	31	Eppingen	53-1164
GALLMEYER, Charles	45	Windheim	50-0944
Mary 48, Christian 16, Conrad 10			
Wilhelmine 9, Sophia 8, Lisetta 6			
Louisa 4, Ernst 8m			
GALLO, Ferdinand	29	Camberg/Nass.	52-1332
GALOPKOFSKY, C.A.	25	Erfurt	49-1358
GALSTER, Andreas	28	Defersdorf	47-0828
Gertrude 28			
GAMDRUM, Justus	32	Alsfeld	51-1455
GAMPERT, Jeanette	21	Neuses	53-0914
GAMSTETTER, Ferd.	30	Breitenloh	54-0872
Francisca 29, Maria 4			
GANDOR, Franz	22	Lichtenfels	51-0405
GANEKE, J.F.	65	Nd. Stade	47-0672
GANGENMEYER, Andr.	30	Mittelruessel	49-0737
GANS, Alexander	23	Weimar	52-0895
GANS, Joachim	26	Jungbunzlau	48-1184
GANS, Lorenz	25	Hagenbach/Bav	50-0323
GANS, Maeuchen	50	Hebenshasen	53-0838
Rachel 52, David 14, Abraham 12			
GANSS, Agathe	25	Canton Aargau	51-1245
GANSS, Maria	40	Lanzenheim	52-1304
Henry 15, Philipp 13			
GANZ, Barb.	25	Seebach	48-1355
GANZEMUELLER, L.C.	29	Ansbach	53-1016
GAR, Lorenz	23	Kalkershofen	52-0515
GARAUS, Sebastian	28	Schweinfurt	54-1554
GARBADE, Friedr.	20	Bloklande	51-0326
GARDELN, Joh.	22	Gottland/Swed	50-1071
GARDES, Heinrich	16	Rechtenfleth	51-0756
GARKE, Caroline	37	Zehdenick	52-0699
Franz 9, Anna 7			
GARMS, Claus	22	Stade/Hann.	53-0475
GARMS, Wilhelm	28	Gilten	50-1132
Catharine 28, Marie 9m			
GARNIER, Gustav	26	Remirmonte/Fr	51-1796
GARREIS, Johann	30	Grafengehug	53-0825
GARRELMANN, Claus	17	Waterhorst	50-1067
GARRELMANN, Heinr.	14	Hagen	50-1067
GARRELS, Gesche M.	18	Prussia	51-1725
GARRELT, Christian	26	Holland	50-0311
GARSTENER, Chr'tne	40	Meinsen	52-1321
Henriette 19, Julius 7			
GARTELMANN, Heinr.	56	Hagen	52-0699
Rebecca 50, Diedrich 14, Anna 7, Carl 3			
GARTENHOF, Casper	28	Bruekenau	53-1062
GARTHE, Ida	22	Marburg/Hesse	54-1001
GARTNER, Christoph	25	Mittelruessel	49-0737
Maria 22, Paulina 20			
GASH, Ernst Julius	25	Ziegra	51-1101
Gustav 23, Fuerchtegott 27			
GASSENHEIMER, Lob.	17	Bibra	49-1358
GASSINGER, Franz	29	Muenster	49-1358

NAME	AGE	RESIDENCE	YR-LIST
GASSNER, Franziska	24	Hagenhille	54-1078
GASTEIER, F. Lewis	28	Braunschweig	52-0563
GATHMANN, Johs.	23	Rothenburg	51-0757
GATHO, Wilhelm	25	Cassel	48-1184
GATTEN, August	20	Dresden	48-1184
GATZEROFSKY, Joh.	47	Millewetsch	53-0905
Barbara 45, Maria 18, August 17			
Elisabeth 15, Barbara 10, Joseph 9, W. 6			
Marg. 3			
GATZERT, Anton	53	Kirchgoens	54-0965
Johannes 56, Johannes 23, Anton 16			
Catharina 44, Elisabeth 14, Catharina 2			
Cathrine 20			
GAUCKLER, Ann Marg	56	Sommersdorf	48-0260
Conrad 29, Michael 22			
GAUDIER, Conr.	15	Rauschenbg	50-0472
GAUER, Georg	18	Baden	54-1724
GAUGHUNT, Barbara	48	Solzberg	53-0652
GAUL, Christian	54	Elpenrod	54-0053
Elisabeth 50, Amalie 17, Anna Marie 15			
Heinrich 5, Georg 13			
GAUL, Johanette		Maulbach	54-1443
GAUL, Peter	29	Albshausen	54-0830
Louise 25			
GAUL, Wilhelm	18	Maulbach	54-1443
GAUM, Mathaeus	48	Augsburg	53-1023
Waldburga 44, Allevis (m) 21, Vincent 19			
Joseph Anton 18, Kilian 13			
GAUMER, Matth.	33	Isny	49-0352
GAUNITZ, A.Therese	28	Lambersdorf	51-1084
GAUNITZ, Fr. W.	28	Oschatz	51-1084
Therese 28, Fr. Herm. 2			
GAUS, Caroline	24	Carlshafen	54-1566
GAUS, Conrad	25	Roth	54-1566
GAUS, Georg	22	Eisenach/Weim	54-1092
GAUS, Rudolph	32	Canton Aargau	51-0048
Elisab. 35, Louise 7, Ursula 5, Rosina 2			
Joseph 6m			
GAUSMANN, F. (m)	26	Wever	52-1661
GAUSS, Jos.	25	Kreuz	54-1078
Josepha 33			
GAUTIER, Catharine	16	Rauschenberg	52-1464
GAUTIER, Franz	41	Rauschenberg	47-0918
Peter 16			
GEBAUER, Georg	41	Heringen	52-0370
Elisabeth 35			
GEBEL, Margrethe	15	Giesen	52-0699
GEBHARD, Anna	22	Steinbach/Bav	53-0628
GEBHARD, Barbara	33	Birolzheim	50-0439
GEBHARD, Carl	26	Hof/Baiern	53-0475
GEBHARD, Carl	38	Braunbach	53-0905
Maria 36, Dorothe 11, Herrmann 8, Mina 3			
Henriette 26			
GEBHARD, Friedr.	17	Graefenberg	49-0574
GEBHARD, Johann	19	Hetzeldorf	54-1452
GEBHARD, Laura	33	Prussia	51-1160
Alma 4			
GEBHARD, Mich.	58	Dachstadt	52-0693
Magd. 51, Kunig. 17, Georg 58			
Cath. Kunig. 38, Johann 26, Georg 23			
Cath. 13, Heinr. 8, Johann 6, Cath. 3			
GEBHARDT, Carl Gus	37	Marienfeld	54-1168
GEBHARDT, Christ.	16	Wunsiedel	53-0888
GEBHARDT, Christne	22	Weydenberg	52-0804
Margr. 20			
GEBHARDT, Friedr.	24	Sangerhausen	49-1106
GEBHARDT, George	25	Mittelruessel	49-0737
GEBHARDT, Joh.	27	Freirittenbac	48-1179
GEBHARDT, Joh.	27	Gumbelstadt	52-0563
Joh. Georg 7, Barbara E. 31, Christine 5			
Joh. Friedr. 6m			
GEBHARDT, Jos.	22	Knollgraben	49-0574
GEBHARDT, Maria	20	Nentershausen	53-0942
GEBHARDT, Michel	25	Suess	48-0887
GEBHARDT, Nicol.	22	Ballhof	48-1179
GEBIAN, Albert	19	Wesselotz	54-1647
GEBRINGER, Joh.	20	Vauheim	54-0987
GEBSER, Eduard	42	Langensalza	48-0887

NAME	AGE	RESIDENCE	YR-LIST
GECHTER, Conr.	39	Bruck	53-0320
GECK, Heinrich	27	Ofenbach	53-0928
Maria 40, Carl 7			
GECK, Heinrich	27	Oehringen	53-0928
GECKEL, H.	28	Rommerad	51-0517
B. (f) 28, H. 3, G. 9m			
GECKENT, Friedrich	16	Dedendorf	53-0492
GECMEN, Joseph	33	Rokitzau	53-1164
Anna 25, Rosina 3, Anna 2			
GEDOECKE, Heinrich	30	Hulitz/Meckl.	51-1796
GEELDERT, David	25	Niedwitz	53-0905
GEERDES, Georg	17	Stoodtel	50-0366
GEERKE, Friedrich	33	Hamersen	53-1000
Wilhelmine 30, Friedr. 8, Wilhelmine 5			
GEERKEN, Adelheid	26	Hagen	52-0699
GEERKEN, Charles	19	Hagen	53-0991
GEERKEN, Heinrich	15	Hagen	50-1067
GEERKEN, Johann	20	Weyerberg	50-1067
GEERTKE, John J.	22	Gemen	52-0804
GEFFERT, Friedrich	58	Rennau	54-1297
Dorothea 58			
GEFFKEN, A.	27	N.Y.	53-0991
C.M. (f) 25			
GEFKEN, Heinr.	20	Scharmbek	51-0326
GEFKEN, J.H.	18	Drofset	50-1067
GEFKEN, Wilhelm	22	Scharmbeck	50-1067
GEGELEIN, J. (m)	51	Schopfloch	50-0746
B. (f) 16			
GEGENWART, Wilhelm	22	Vertheim	54-0987
GEGER, Israel		Storndorf	54-1575
GEGNER, Albr.	32	Baiern	53-0585
GEGNER, Barbara	23	Obersachs	50-0840
GEHAGEN, Ludwig	29	Frankfurt	52-0804
Ottilie 21, Amanda 10m			
GEHAUT, Chr.	18	Minden	53-0905
GEHLE, Peter Heinr	34	Ottersberg	52-1362
Elisabeth 44			
GEHR, Melchior	30	Zollichen Por	52-1464
Cath. 30, Marg. 4, Cath. 3			
GEHRING, Anton	26	Dreyerwalde	51-0405
Adolph 20			
GEHRING, Dorothea	24	Stellingen	51-1640
GEHRING, John H.	22	Bremen	54-1724
GEHRKE, Friedr.	28	Waldeck	51-0352
GEHRKE, Martin	18	Friedrichsdor	50-0323
GEHRKENSMEIER, A.M	23	Wittlage/Hann	52-0960
GEHRKENSMEIER, Cat	30	Wittlage/Hann	52-0960
GEHRMANN, Fritz	24	Cassel	48-1355
GEHRT, Michael	26	Thonhaim	53-0914
GEHSE, Friederike	18	Ehrdriessen	53-0888
GEIDEL, Michael	58	Kuschuetz	53-0492
Eva 56			
GEIER, Adam	28	Grub	54-0965
Margaretha 22, Jakob 2, baby			
GEIER, Joh. Jac.	33	Schaback	53-1013
Anna 33, George 2			
GEIFFUSS, Friedr.	34	Sachsen-Weim.	51-1739
Margaretha 21, Albert 4, Adelheid 2			
GEIGENMAYER, Carol	17	Backnang	54-1717
GEIGER, Anton	31	Roetha	53-0267
Christiane 32, Marie Elise 10m			
GEIGER, Anton	22	Beeswangen/Wr	54-1092
GEIGER, Chr Friedr	22	Wardau	52-0370
GEIGER, Georg	19	Duedenhofen	51-0757
GEIGER, Hermann	22	Uberlingen	49-0912
GEIGER, Joh.	19	Augsfeld	54-0053
GEIGER, John	22	Selbitz	49-1106
GEIGER, Louisa	27	Stuttgart	53-0991
GEIGERMANN, Adelh.	19	Gratz	54-0987
GEIGMUELLER, John	37	Selb	53-0991
Henrietta 34, Martin 4, John 2			
Christina 4m			
GEIL, Paul	17	Kirtorf	54-0830
GEILFUSS, Adolph	17	Gr.Breitenbch	53-0585
GEILHAAR, Joh.	27	Prussia	50-0311
GEILS, Christian	54	Hohenaverberg	53-0838
Catharine 29, Marie 21, Elisabeth 14			
Margarethe 10, Diedrich 7, Margarethe 51			

NAME	AGE	RESIDENCE	YR-LIST
Elise 17			
GEILS, H. (m)	19	Hohenaverberg	49-0383
GEILS, Heinrich	21	Mattfeld	53-0838
GEISE, Therese	24	Arensberg	52-0699
GEISEL, H. (m)	30	Dahl	54-0918
Amalia 26, Martha Elisa by			
GEISER, Chr. Folke	25	Geroldsgruen	54-1371
GEISER, Ernst	26	Brokelde	52-1625
Maria 24, Carl 9m			
GEISFEL, Eduard	30	Minden	52-1101
Luise 30, Auguste 8, Clara 6, Laura 4			
GEISHARD, Julianne	25	Coburg	51-0405
GEISING, Joseph	32	Emsdetten	48-0260
GEISLEL, H.(m)	30	Pahl	54-0918
Amalia 26, Martha Elis. by			
GEISLER, Julius	4	Bremen	48-1243
GEISLER, Marie		Lollar	54-0987
GEISMAR, Chr. Aug	14	Stockum	53-0991
GEISMAR, Franziska	24	Doessel	52-1304
GEISREITER, Jacob	43	Pfaffenhofen	54-1078
Eva 45, Jacob 16, Sophie 15, Sebastian 14			
GEISS, A.M.	37	Obernbreit	51-1796
GEISSEL, Caroline	24	Steinau	52-1200
GEISSEL, Peter	30	Montabaur	52-1580
GEISSLER, Matt.	40	Zell	53-0942
GEIST, P. (f)	24	Bernbach	48-0445
GEISTER, Babette	28	Wetzlar	53-0590
GEISTHARDT, Barb.	18	Coburg	52-1332
GEIT, Johanne	29	Genzeldorf	53-0942
GEITDORFER, Christ	21	Murchau/Wuert	52-0117
GEITERLING, Mich.	30	Molverstadt	51-1796
Dorotha 30, Anna Luise 6, Georg Christ 4			
Marie Christ 9m			
GEITZ, Catharine	22	Wohra	54-1575
GEITZENAUER, Matth	31	Wien	53-0991
GEIZ, Leonhard	27	Bayern	51-1686
GEIZ, Simon	33	Bayern	51-1686
Sophia 29, Carl 3			
GEIZMANN, Valentin	53	Wilmars	51-1455
Friederike 59, Margaretha 17			
Friederike 11, Julianna 6			
GELBACH, Margareth	26	Elsoff	52-0563
GELBTA, Carl	22	Wubrode	54-0987
GELDMANN, Julius	29	Waechtersbach	52-1625
GELEIDER, Georg	21	Ingenheim	52-0370
GELFIUS, Augustus	17	Darmstadt	53-0991
GELHARDT, George	25	Mittelruessel	49-0737
GELLER, Carl Chr.	19	Zich	51-1455
GELLERT, Elise	23	Grabenstein	54-0882
GELLERT, Friedr.	29	Sizke	50-0021
Anna Marg. 32, Heinr. 5			
GELLHARD, August	51	Gotha	49-1106
GELLHAUSEN, Friedr	28	Bergkirchen	51-0352
GELRIKE, Herm.	27	Leipzig	48-1131
GELTNER, Moritz	15	Werdau/Sax.	52-1332
GEMANHARDT, John	27	Baiern	54-1724
GEMOEHLING, Friedr	22	Eichau	53-0590
Elmert 18			
GENAU, Daniel	24	Doepel	50-0472
GENEGER, Ignaz	22	Eche	52-1580
Catharina 49, Eledia 25			
GENERICH, August	27	Windheim	50-0944
GENNERT, Gottl.	27	Neupel	54-0987
GENSLER, Carl	43	Hessen	51-0405
Julianne 38, Marianne 13			
GENTELE, Johann	27	Grossorham	54-1168
GENTEN, A. Lena	20	Alsum	51-0756
GENTER, Carl	23	Dreischwitz	49-1517
GENTER, Conr.	21	Urach	54-0600
GENTH, D. (m)	23	Marburg	48-1131
A. (m) 19			
GENTNER, Christine	18	Ludwigsburg	51-1640
GENTSCH, Christ. W	20	Wiesenmuehle	54-0872
GENTSECH, Jane F.	25	Mittelruessel	49-0737
GENTZSCH, Heinrich	25	Maltiz	53-0320
GENZ, Henning	18	Hannover	53-0628
GENZLER, Cath.	20	Grossenbach	52-0515
GEORG, Carl Heinr.	40	Stadtilm	48-1179

NAME	AGE	RESIDENCE	YR-LIST
GEORG, Georg	32	Niederwesselb	53-0320
GEORGE, John	19	Rotekirchen	54-1716
GEPHARDT, Philipp	41	Heilbronn	52-1580
Johanna 46, Auguste 23			
GEPPEL, Johann	21	Nuernberg	53-0473
GERAI, F.T. (m)	27	Baden	52-1512
GERARD, Georg	24	Carlshaven	47-0672
GERATEN, A. Lena	20	Alsum	51-0756
GERB, Christian	17	Altenschlief	54-1716
GERBER, Florian	20	Reichenthal	52-0351
GERBER, Friederike	54	Zwickau	54-0882
GERBER, Friedr.	21	Werdau/Sax.	52-1332
GERBER, Lorentz	22	Mistelfeld	48-0284
GERBER, Mor.	23	Tissa	54-1575
GERBER, Peter	26	Hottenbach	51-1062
Elisabeth 22			
GERBLER, An. (f)	59	Nonnenroth	47-0868
GERCKE, Bernhard	21	Salzwedel	54-1591
GERCKE, Carl	24	Goettingen	54-0965
GERDE, Jacob	21	Christianseck	52-0563
GERDES, Adelheid	26	Apeldorn	49-0324
GERDES, Friedrich	18	Siedenburg	54-0987
GERDES, Heinr.	24	Jever	54-0987
wife 20			
GERDES, Hermann	15	Siedenburg	54-0987
GERDES, Robert Ant	20	Seer	53-1023
GERDES, Valentin	25	Abenheim	54-1716
GERDING, John	30	Nordhausen	51-1588
Maria 30, John 2, Anna 11m			
GERDING, Wilh'mine	39	Hille	51-1101
Luise 13, Friedrich 9, Heinrich 7			
GERDTS, Catharine	18	Bremervoerde	54-1297
GERECHTE, Maria	47	Alsfeld	54-0600
GERECKE, Ludwig	23	Hordorf	52-1625
Heinrich 21			
GERGEN, Karl H.	36	Dettmolt/Pr.	51-1796
GERHARD, A. (m)	28	Leipzig/Sax.	48-0447
B. (f) 20, J. (f) 21			
GERHARD, Caspar	1-	Grossenbach/H	49-0365
GERHARD, Cathr.	22	Marburg	51-0048
GERHARD, J.H.	27	Frohenhausen	51-0048
Cathr. 22			
GERHARD, Joh Georg	23	Schopfheim	51-1686
Barbara 23			
GERHARD, Jos.	27	Neustadt	54-1283
Dorothea 36			
GERHARD, Joseph	39	Fischborn	51-1588
GERHARD, Reinhard	23	Frankfort	48-1184
GERHARDT, Carl	35	Hudenmuehlen	52-1625
GERHARDT, Gottlieb	33	Doehlen	50-0379
GERHARDY, Philip	15	Norten	53-1164
GERING, Friedr. W.	17	Wittlage	49-0413
GERING, Wilhelm	37	Gold	54-1443
wife 38, Friedrich 6, Luderine 2			
Ernst 2m			
GERINGER, Alois	33	Lippach/Wuert	53-0435
GERINGER, Cresc.	9	Schwabsberg/D	53-0435
Vict. 4			
GERKEN, Catharina	36	Rothenburg	51-0756
GERKEN, H. (m)	18	Ritt	47-0104
GERKEN, Johann	28	Bockel	50-0366
GERKEN, Julianne	30	Achim	48-0406
Henriette 18			
GERLACH, Casp.	32	Kaltennordhei	48-1114
Christine 28, Chr. 1			
GERLACH, Fr.	30	Eschwege	48-0269
Johanne 24			
GERLACH, Franz	27	Rhumspring	53-0905
Wilhelmine 24			
GERLACH, Friedr.	25	Dambrock	48-0951
GERLACH, G. (m)	23	Weitroth	52-0652
GERLACH, Herm.	16	Prussia	50-0311
GERLACH, Marie	20	Erfurt	54-1649
Caroline 18			
GERLACH, Martha	19	Frauensee	53-0942
GERLEIN, Joh.	25	Langenstadt	47-0918
GERMAN, Johann	59	Meyberg	52-1101
Karl			
GERMAN, Mathias	23	Friedrichsdor	51-0384
GERMANN, Hermann	26	Braunschweig	52-1580
GERMANN, S.	20	Thueringen	51-0517
GERMEROSCH, Gebh.	21	Rotenburg	54-1649
GERMESHAUSE, Ant.	35	Dudenbach	51-1084
GERN, Robert	43	Breslau	54-1078
GERNER, Joseph	23	Leipstadt	53-1023
GERNER, Phil.	17	Siebenstadt	51-1640
Christ. 21			
GERNERT, Regina	18	Wuerzburg	53-0991
GERNGROS, Nathan	19	Forth	50-0439
GERNGROSS, Fr.	52	Soltengreesba	49-0781
Anne Maria 23			
GERNHARDT, Anton	30	Hoenebach	48-0284
GEROLD, Chas. M.	39	Mittelruessel	49-0737
Augusta 40, Anna 5			
GERS, Carten	15	Ritterhude	51-0326
GERSCHMANN, August	25	Koenigsberg	50-0840
GERSDORFF, v. Ern.	28	Bremen	48-0078
GERST, Heinrich	26	Ansbach	54-1575
GERSTACKER, G. (m)	23	Volla	48-0445
GERSTEMAYER, Georg	29	Berghuelen	52-1200
GERSTENBERG, Alwin	22	Sachsen	53-0590
GERSTENBERG, J.H.	22	Langenau	54-1419
GERSTENDOERFER, C.	31	Nuernberg	54-1371
Babette 34, Henriette 3, Johann 9m			
GERTANNE, Wilhelm	29	Helsa	53-0838
GERTH, Gottfried	25	Polzig	54-0872
Ernst 15			
GERTH, Phil.	20	Asslar	49-0574
GERTH, Sophie	39	Darmstadt	53-0590
GERTZWAGE, Ludwig	16	Rheme	54-1297
GERWIN, Friederike	25	Bohnde	49-0352
Franz 24, Heinrich 19			
GESCHWINNER, Jos.	25	Pillenhofen	52-1101
GESELE, Catharina	22	Arzberg	47-0672
GESELLER, John	28	Urach	53-0582
GESSLER, Johann	30	Grebenau	54-0930
Catharine El 42, Catharine El 13			
Engelhard H. 9			
GETZLER, Ludwig	24	Ruehrchen	54-1168
GEUS, Georg	31	Heiligendorf	51-1640
Dorothea 35, Joh. Georg 10			
GEUSS, Andrew	51	Zilgendorf/Bv	48-0053
Barbara 47, Henry 20, Ann. Marg. 8			
Margaret 3m			
GEUTNER, Christine	18	Ludwigsburg	51-1640
GEVENSLEBEN, Fr.	41	Wennigstadt	54-1078
Marie 43, Friedr. 16, Christ 12, Marie 10			
Friederike 4			
GEWINNER, Adam	28	Arzberg	53-0557
GEYER, Agnes	27	Steinberg	48-0887
GEYER, Christian	17	Wunsiedel	53-0888
GEYER, Christian	47	Asch	48-1209
Catharine 48, John 25, Giles 21			
Laurence 20, Christian 18, Margaret 16			
Barbara 14, Catharine 13, Mary 11			
Elizabeth 6, Eliza Bertha 5, Michael 2			
Elisabeth 23			
GEYER, Elise		Reichhardshof	49-1106
GEYER, Friederike	25	Hildesheim	52-0807
GEYER, Heinr.	47	Hannover	50-0311
GEYER, John	24	Possek	48-1209
Martin 31, Agnes 27			
GEYER, John	24	Posseck	48-0887
GEYER, Martin	31	Posseck	48-0887
Agnes 27			
GICKEL, Joseph	24	Paritz	54-1297
GIDEON, August	24	Elberfeld/Pr.	51-1725
GIEBEL, Charles	29	Bollenstedt	53-0991
GIEBEL, Felicita	22	Leimbeck/Hess	51-1532
GIEBEL, Simon	29	Kernbach	52-0515
Bertha 21			
GIEBELER, Eberd.	25	Treisbach	48-0269
GIEBELER, Ludwig	33	Preussen	53-0590
GIEBELHAUS, Conrad	29	Frankenberg	53-1016
Georg 18, Phil. 32			
GIEBELHAUS, Phil.	32	Savannah	53-1016

NAME	AGE	RESIDENCE	YR-LIST
GIEBENER, Johanna	29	Lauterbach	51-1101
GIEBNER, Heinrich	21	Muenchdorf	54-1297
GIEPEL, Chr.	48	Friedenmanns	54-1371
GIERER, John F.	31	Kitschendorf	48-0951
Mary 21			
GIERING, Fr.	20	Bettensiedel	49-1358
GIERING, J.F.	21	Kuelte	51-1160
GIERS, Louis	25	Carlshafen	54-1566
GIERSCH, Friedr. W	30	Lammadsch	53-1023
GIES, Ido (m)	20	Bemhols	52-0370
GIESCHEN, John	30	New York	53-0991
Mary 29			
GIESE, Friedrich	41	Altena/Pr.	48-0053
GIESE, Wilh. Heinr	21	Ottersberg	52-1362
Elise 25			
GIESEKE, Fritz	25	Aerzen	52-0515
GIESEKE, Heinrich	27	Gittelde/Brns	51-1725
Alwine 27, Johanne 3			
GIESERING, Fr.	32	Lahde	50-1317
Louise 31, Wilhelm 5, Heinr. 9m			
GIESKE, J.	37	Brockhausen/H	51-0048
GIESSBACHER, Marg.	32	Beckendorf	54-1554
Babette 13			
GIESSE, Conrad	15	Ottersburg/Ha	52-0117
GIESSELMANN, Carol	18	Neunkirchen	54-1470
GIESSELMANN, Edw.	27	Wildeshausen	52-0895
GIESSER, Joh Heinr	27	Reutlingen	48-1355
GIESSHOFF, Albert	40	Rebersen	52-0515
Anna 32, Diedrich 5, Adelheid 1			
GIESSLER, Gustav	18	Frankenhausen	54-0918
GIETJE, Regina	50	Bremen	51-1084
Anna 8, Bernhard 5, Amalie 5			
GILBERT, Maria	33	Mudau	51-0460
GILBERT, Valentin	28	Finkler	52-0370
Anna 26			
GILBERT, Wilhelm	21	Saxony	54-1724
GILDEHAUS, Heinr.	30	Wetschen	53-1062
Heinr. Wilh. 27, Bernh. Fried 25			
Heinr. Fried 19, Elisabeth 58			
GILFERT, Henry	24	Widdershausen	48-0284
GILFERT, Wilhelm	21	Wittershausen	51-1455
GILGEN, Johann	28	Rheinbreitbac	51-1035
Anna 3m			
GILLE, Carl	30	Burg	52-1362
GILLER, Sebastian	43	Buch/ Bav.	52-1620
Catharine 45, Andreas 21, Anna 19			
Marie 13, Dorothea 9, Johanne 7			
GILLING, Johann	40	Markseid	52-1661
Kunigunde 34, Michael 11, Matthias 10			
Anna 4			
GILLJOHANN, F. (m)	34	Elberfeld	48-0565
Caroline 24, Friedr. 1			
GILSEMANN, Friedr.	25	Wallenfels	54-0903
GIMMERN, Hugut	33	Mittelruessel	49-0737
GIMPEL, Elise	25	Marburg	52-0370
GIMPEL, Heinrich	56	Gemuenden	51-0500
Elisabeth 49, Maria 14, Conrad 8			
GINAND, Adolph	21	Luebeck	54-1078
GINKER, J. M. (m)	25	Osnabrueck	52-1512
GINZ, Anna Sabina	24	Hersfeld	51-0405
GISCHEN, G.	23	Willar	54-1168
GISKING, Heinrich	27	Minden	54-0850
Pauline 26, Heinrich by			
GIVERS, Mary	28	Peppinghausen	51-1588
Mary 2			
GLADE, Chr.	18	Kohlenfeldt	53-0492
(m) 16			
GLAESER, Carl Hein	36	Lichtenstein	50-0292
GLAESER, Catharina	24	Wels	53-0991
GLAHM, Heinrich	24	Wollings	52-1625
GLAHN, Caroline	18	Wehnde/Hannov	54-0965
GLAHN, v. Christ.	18	Dracheln	50-0366
GLAHN, v. Friedr.	18	Beverstedt	49-0345
GLAHN, v. Regina	20	Wiemen	50-0021
GLAHR, v. F.	19	Dursing	54-1716
GLAIBER, Philipp	42	Memmingen	54-1717
Clementine 32, Maximilian 6, Maria 4			
Amalia 2			

NAME	AGE	RESIDENCE	YR-LIST
GLANDER, Joh.	23	Verden	48-1179
Anna 19			
GLANZ, Jos. Joh.	29	Schmichten	51-1245
GLANZ, Peter	26	Steller	52-0563
Cletus 24			
GLASEMEYER, Joseph	20	Hagen	50-0292
GLASER, Adam	18	Gronenberg	49-0912
GLASER, Dorothea	28	Coburg	49-0352
GLASER, Eduard	25	Weimar	52-0895
GLASER, Goths,	21	Mittelruessel	49-0737
GLASER, Heinrich	45	Wildenberg	51-1160
Marg. 19, Georg 16, Peter 12			
GLASSAUER, Georg		Geesweinstein	50-0323
GLATZ, Henry	27	Koenigsberg	50-0840
Pauline 25, Anna Sophie 4, Emmy Clara 3			
GLAUBITZ, Franz	40	Tscherna	53-0888
GLAUSER, Caroline	40	Berstein	51-1588
GLEICH, Gottlieb	16	Mondelsheim	52-1580
GLEICHMANN, Bertha	25	Leipzig	48-0887
Theodor 18, Mary 10			
GLEICHMANN, Franz	15	Mockrehna/Pr.	52-1620
GLEICHMANN, Gottfr	26	Gemeinda	48-0951
GLEIMANN, Bernhard	26	Emsdetten/Pr.	50-0323
GLEISCHMANN, Adam	19	Cronach	53-0825
GLEISSNER, Barbara	27	Erlach	54-1078
GLEISTMANN, Adam	19	Cronach	53-0825
GLEITZMANN, Joh G.	44	Fronsdorf/Sax	54-1092
Sophia 42, J. Ernst J. 16, Eduard 12			
Amalia 9, Hugo 3, J. 3m			
GLESSING, John G.	30	Ipshof	54-1341
GLIESMANN, Wilh.	28	Reburg	50-1067
GLIETSCH, Franz	28	Neuenhirschen	52-0117
GLINDMEYER, Louis	20	Nordhemman	51-0500
GLITSCH, Catrine	24	Seidelsdorf	52-0370
GLITSCH, H.	27	Landenhausen	51-0517
GLITSCH, Michael	22	Seidelsdorf	51-0460
GLITSCHKA, Wilhelm	37	Gifhorn	53-1164
GLOCKE, Hermann	32	Geritzheim/Sa	54-1092
Maria 28			
GLOCKMER, Fr. Ludw	18	Zich	51-1455
GLOECKNER, Emil	30	Annaberg	53-0267
GLOECKNER, Friedr.		Neustadt	53-0914
GLOEGA, August	24	Pommern	52-1362
GLOM, v. Christ.	28	Wremen/Hann.	51-1796
GLORIGOW, James	25	London	54-0987
Marianne 20			
GLOSS, Ewald	39	Stolberg/Harz	48-0269
GLOTH, Johann	48	New York	48-1184
Mathilde 8			
GLOTH, Mathilde	8	Cuxhafen	48-0484
GLUECK, Johann	20	Neustadt	52-1580
GLUECK, Marie	27	Wartmannsroth	54-1168
GLUECKERT, M. Cath	42	Darmstadt	53-0838
Franz 17, Anna 14			
GLUKER, G.H. (m)	25	Osnabrueck	52-1512
GLUSING, Behrend		Lahmstedt	53-0838
GNADE, Carl	36	Rischenau	54-1371
GNAU, August	44	Emsdorf/Hesse	52-0960
Elisabeth 47, Peter 8, Johannes 6			
GNAU, Margret	18	Hessen	53-0590
GNIBE, G.H. (m)	25	Barmen	48-1114
GNUESLEBEN, J. (m)	19	Olfen	54-1566
GOB, Carl	25	Bergeheim/Bav	47-0987
GOBEL, Maria	20	Mengeringhaus	54-0882
GOBERT, Therese	54	Breslau	54-1716
August 26			
GOCKE, Wilhelm	21	Pyrmont	54-0872
GODFEL, Christian	38	Schneeberg	51-0500
GODPHEL, Christian	38	Schneeberg	51-0500
GOEBBNER, Johann	30	Durchendorf	51-1062
GOEBEL, Anna Elis.	22	Elnrode	47-0828
GOEBEL, Catharine	26	Blankenburg	54-1371
GOEBEL, Cornelius	20	Grossalmerode	52-1200
GOEBEL, Friederike	25	Goettingen	50-0021
GOEBEL, H.	27	Nepsen	48-0269
GOEBEL, Johann	25	Hersfeld	47-0828
GOEBEL, Johann	60	Schmuteten	54-1591
Josephine 45, Theodor 17, Friedrich 15			

NAME	AGE	RESIDENCE	YR-LIST
Anton 11			
GOEBEL, John	26	Veckerhagen/H	50-0323
GOEBEL, Martin	26	Motzfeld	50-0292
GOEBEL, P. (m)	59	Ellenrode	49-0416
H.E. (f) 17			
GOEBELER, Ernst	21	Steinbrexen	52-0279
GOEBLING, Heinr. C	43	Salzungen	54-0987
Marie Christ 33, Cath. Doro. 9			
GOECKE, Heinrich	30	Schoeningen	54-1283
GOEDEKE, Daniel	24	Barendtrup	52-1148
GOEDEKE, Ernst	33	Marburg	53-0888
GOEDEN, Anna	17	Minden	53-0991
GOEGE, Johann	23	Darmstadt	52-0699
GOEHL, Fr'dr. Fied	26	Bavaria	50-0311
GOEHRING, Marie	24	Reust	54-0872
GOEHRUNG, Charles	20	Brackenheim	52-1304
GOEKE, Wilhelm	21	Pyrmont	54-0872
GOELCHEL, Albert	40	Altenburg/Sax	54-1092
GOELLER, Joseph	20	Einsiedel/Boh	54-1092
GOELLNER, John	23	Rappoldshause	53-0991
GOELLNER, Joseph	38	Istrup/Pr.	54-0965
Justine 28, Johanne 2, Wilhelm 32, baby			
GOELZENLEUCHTER, E	27	Gr. Altenstad	49-0574
GOENNEL, Gottfried	44	Schonrhyden	54-1283
GOEPFERT, Alb.	19	Fuechsen	52-1321
GOEPFERT, Chr.	29	Nentershausen	48-0269
Wm. 16, Jacob 4, Susanne 30			
GOEPFERT, Fr.	37	Meiningen	51-0405
Barbara 29, Anna M. 7			
GOERGES, Christ.	27	Pattzehne/Pr.	51-0048
Soph. 23, Friedr. 9m			
GOERING, Henriette	36	Wien	54-1591
GOERING, Peter	49	Roetha	53-0267
GOERLE, Heinrich	24	Waltersdorf	54-1371
GOERLING, Friedr.	21	Pyrmont	49-0345
GOERNER, Johann	24	Plattendorf	53-1070
GOESCH, Joh.	29	Brodhagen/Mec	51-1796
GOESCHEL, Fried Wm	50	Hirschberg	54-1168
Hermann 17, Eduard 16			
GOESER, Wilhelmine	26	New York	47-0840
GOESMANN, Johann	28	Wasserlosen	48-0887
Barbara 24			
GOETEL, Gottfr.	28	Barnsbach	54-1282
GOETHE, H.	27	Salzwedel	51-0517
GOETHERT, E.	24	Haugsdorf	53-0888
GOETTE, Bernh.	24	Bruchhausen	54-1078
GOETTE, Chr.	28	Rasten	54-0600
GOETTER, Joh Jacob	25	Schweinfurt	51-1532
GOETTERT, Caroline	22	Haugsdorf	53-0888
GOETTGEN, Johannes	26	Bremervoerde	51-1725
GOETTING, Carl	21	Braunschweig	50-1132
GOETTLICH, Christ.	34	Raunsbach	54-1371
GOETZ, Christian	36	Darmstadt	48-1184
Maria 26, Elise 6m			
GOETZ, Christoph F	24	Rodach	53-0914
GOETZ, Ferdinand	23	Laub	50-0840
GOETZ, Georg	22	Rodach	54-0872
GOETZ, Herm. Alb.	29	Neuenkirchen	48-1355
GOETZ, Johann	32	Wallerstein	54-0850
Rosalia 29, Joh. Anton 6, Joh. Evang. 5			
Maria Rosal. by			
GOETZ, John	24	Lauterbach/Bv	49-0365
GOETZ, Margaretha	19	Coburg	52-0895
GOETZ, Moses	15	Schnaidach	53-0320
GOETZ, Ursula	16	Buskenstadt	50-0439
GOETZ, Wilhelm	20	Obersinn	52-0563
GOETZE, Heinr.	28	Quedlinburg	54-1078
Rosalie 19			
GOETZE, Heinrich L	40	Berlin	54-1092
GOETZE, Theobald	25	Nienburg	53-0991
GOETZE, Wilhelm	32	Immenrode	52-1410
Marie 36, Heinrich 9, August 6, Johanne 3			
GOETZINGER, Georg	23	Reichenbach	54-0872
GOETZINGER, Philip	14	Reitelsbach	54-0872
GOGARN, Julius	19	Neukirchen	53-1164
GOHRING, Ellen	26	Mittelruessel	49-0737
Amelia 21			
GOHS, Jos. Henry	44	Cincinnati	53-0991

NAME	AGE	RESIDENCE	YR-LIST
GOHSEN, Gertrude	20	Kroppe	50-1132
GOLD, Christina Fr	25	Peusen	53-1062
GOLDBACH, Anna	54	Glattbach	54-1575
GOLDBACH, Carl	27	Frankenhausen	49-1358
GOLDBACH, H.	25	Utrictshausen	52-0515
GOLDBACH, Joh Adam	26	Kips	53-0324
GOLDBACH, Peter	33	Hollenbrun	51-1035
Johann 1			
GOLDBECK, Sabine	18	Hofgeismar	54-1078
GOLDBERGER, Lazar.	28	Neumittel	54-1078
Joseph 20			
GOLDENBERG, Daniel	18	Kestrig	54-0830
Debel 16			
GOLDENSTEIN, Elean	27	Nienburg	54-1647
GOLDFOIT, Johann	29	Martinlausmet	53-0914
GOLDMANN, Barbara	19	Burgebrach	48-0887
GOLDMANN, Carl Aug	9	Leipzig	48-1131
GOLDMANN, Joseph	17	Manslau/Pr.	53-0628
GOLDMANN, Wilh.	53	Bavaria	50-1317
Ann. Doroth. 46, Aug. Diedr. 9			
GOLDSCHMIDT, Berta	28	Altona	54-1297
GOLDSCHMIDT, Isaac	23	Werda	52-1625
Jeanette 20			
GOLDSCHMIDT, Joh'a	19	Fuerth	52-1105
GOLDSCHMIDT, Leo.	17	Ewersbach	54-1566
GOLDSCHMIDT, Levy	28	Oberlistingen	53-0991
GOLDSCHMIDT, Meier	17	Oberschlichti	52-0895
GOLDSCHMIDT, Moses	29	Lemfoerde	53-1086
GOLDSCHMIDT, Reb.	33	Osterode	52-0895
Gustav 13, Bernhard 10, Minna 7, Emilie 6			
Meta 3, Anna 9m			
GOLDSCHMIDT, Sams.	41	Springe	51-0352
GOLDSCHMIDT, Sieg.	32	Frankfurt	53-0267
GOLDSCHMIDT, Soph.	28	Willebardesse	50-0472
GOLDSTEIN, Aron	19	Neustadt	51-0756
GOLDSTEIN, Meyer	40	Hildesheim	53-1070
Betty 36, Lina 14, Henriette 9, Carl 5			
Selig 3, Leopold 11m			
GOLDSTERN, Louis	52	Breslau	54-0987
GOLDSTROM, Conrad	42	Nied	54-1717
Conrad 20, Heinrich 18, Maria 11			
GOLINGHORST, J Hch	19	Badbergen	50-0292
GOLL, Casper	36	Hanau	49-1106
GOLLER, Ewi	20	Muenchbergen	53-0838
GOLLER, Joh.	27	Lageloh	49-0742
GOLLIZ, Louis	32	Breslau	54-0987
Louise 34, Elisabeth 2, baby			
GOLLNER, Christine	18	Hoeschstedt	53-0825
GOLTA, Johann	16	Schoetlas	53-0628
GOLTERMANN, Heinr.	17	Ehrigshagen	48-0887
GOMMEL, J.G. (m)	23	Hartmannshof	49-0574
GONDER, Anton	20	Neuberg	49-1106
GONTHE, F.	17	Dedendorf	53-0492
GONZE, August	42	Hanau	53-1164
Emelius 15			
GOOS, Jacob	43	Frankenberg	53-0838
Catharine 36, Johst 13, Catharine 15			
Elisabeth 4			
GORSTENHOFER, Jac.	17	Reichhardshof	49-1106
GOSCHENHOFER, Joh.	27	Noerdlingen	54-0903
Sophie 20, Barbara 18			
GOSDORFER, Jette	20	Feueth	54-0872
GOSEN, Joh. Gerh.	35	Suedlohn/Neth	48-0053
Henrika 35, Joh. Gerh. 2			
GOSLINER, Juda	25	Rogasen	52-1105
Minna 23			
GOSMANN, Nicolaus	24	Evelter	50-1067
GOSSTROECK, Libor.	24	Lindewerra	51-1438
GOSTEL, Elisabeth	18	Bremerlehe	51-0500
GOTCHER, H.	18	WesterBeverst	54-1716
GOTFEL, Christian	38	Schneeberg	51-0500
GOTH, Catharina	31	Herriden	54-1282
GOTH, Margarethe	21	Markseid	52-1661
GOTSCH, Emilie L.	25	Gieba	52-0807
GOTSCH, Moritz	56	Ziegelheim	52-0807
Amalie Luise 44, Julius Herm. 24			
Emil Oscar 21, Clemens Iren 16			
Benjamin 14, Paul Justus 5, Edmund Tim. 2			

NAME	AGE	RESIDENCE	YR-LIST
Agnes Theod. 16, Clara Paul. 9			
GOTTBERG, Wilhelm	32	Cincinatti	48-1184
GOTTE, H. (m)	26	Braunschweig	49-1517
GOTTESBUEHUN, Jac.	37	Borgenstreich	50-0323
GOTTLIEB, Christ.	20	Stelzendorf	53-1070
GOTTLIEB, Herrmann	16	Grebenau	51-1101
Rebecca 21			
GOTTMANN, J.H.	18	Kuelte	51-1160
GOTTSCHALK, Elis.	26	Speckwinkel	54-1716
GOTTSCHALK, Johane	22	Kleinballhaus	54-0053
GOTTSCHALK, Ludwig	40	Koenighafen	54-1717
GOTTSCHALK, Marian	29	Sellingerbusc	52-1464
GOTTSCHALK, W'mine	20	Poling	54-0053
GOTTSTEIN, Wilhelm	25	Breslau	54-0930
GOTZ, Marg.	28	Schwarzad	47-0918
GOUBEAUD, Carl	21	Staubhausen	52-1410
GOUZE, August	42	Hanau	53-1164
Emelius 15			
GOYERT, Friedr. H.	58	Semfoerde	52-1304
Caroline 28			
GRAB, J.A. (m)	32	Hassel	49-0781
GRABAU, J.H.	27	Rothenburg	49-1358
Minna 18			
GRABE, August	24	Bielefeld	54-1575
GRABE, Ludwig	25	Wake	54-1283
Auguste 25, Caroline by			
GRABEN, J.W. (m)	39	Dahlen	52-1512
GRABS, Friedrich	34	Mosheim	53-1016
GRADE, August	18	Braunschweig	52-0279
GRAEB, Michael	40	Ottendorf	48-0260
GRAEBER, Adam	42	Bonsweier/Hes	52-0807
GRAEBNER, Andreas	20	Wallenfels	53-1023
GRAEF, Edmund	16	Stadt Ilm	52-1464
Johanne 65			
GRAEF, Friedrich	50	Ilmenau	53-1023
Dorothea 50, Adolph 16, Wilhelmine 17			
GRAEFFE, David H.	37	France	48-1015
GRAENE, F. (m)	33	Estrup	48-0453
GRAESER, Carl	32	Weidau	49-1358
Chr. , F.			
GRAESER, Heinr.	20	Weidau	51-1640
Wilhelmine 18			
GRAETZ, Friedrich	24	Canstein	50-0840
GRAETZ, Ludwig	28	Salzungen	49-0413
GRAEVER, Bernhard	15	Geestendorf	52-0699
GRAF, Adam	36	Langenbrandt	54-1078
GRAF, Amalia	31	Nabburg	54-0872
GRAF, Cath.		Pfordt	54-1575
GRAF, Crescentia	22	Luhmannshause	48-0951
GRAF, Ernst	16	St. Annen	54-0850
GRAF, Franz	22	Mannheim	48-1184
GRAF, Louise	26	Muenden/Hann.	50-0323
GRAF, Maria	25	Wurtenberg	49-0912
GRAF, Wilhelm	24	Erdorf	53-0320
GRAFE, Johann Adam	53	Langenlaube	54-0930
Christine 52, Christine 48, Abraham 25			
GRAFELMANN, Friedr	19	Clueversboste	51-1101
GRAFEN, Carlton	41	Essen	48-1131
GRAFF, Albert	25	Coburg	53-1013
GRAFF, Aug.	33	Halle	50-1071
GRAFF, B. (m)	22	Bremen	48-1114
GRAFF, Johann C.	32	Lindersheim	53-1023
Anna Marg. 28, Johann 4, Anna Marg. 2			
Johann Georg 9m			
GRAFT, Georg	30	New York	50-1071
GRAFT, Heinr.	26	Hausburchert	54-0600
GRAGE, Friedrich	17	Winzlar	53-1164
GRAHER, Johann	21	Baden	52-1148
GRAHL, Michael	26	Bayreuth	54-1591
GRAHLO, Pauline	24	Soldin	54-1168
GRAHLS, Margaretha	29	Guetersdorf	53-1164
GRAMAN, C. (m)	18	Amtgehren	49-0416
GRAMBART, J Conr F	66	Strange	48-1179
GRAMBORST, Joh.	16	Geestendorf	49-0329
GRAMP, Bernhard	18	Marburg	54-0987
GRAMUELLER, Engelb	38	Coburg	54-1283
GRANCHAU, Nicol.	27	Rinzenberg	50-0439
GRANDY, Johanna	26	Grossbuchen	52-0515

NAME	AGE	RESIDENCE	YR-LIST
GRANER, Heinrich	22	Badbergen	54-0987
GRANIER, Querin	42	Du---d	50-0944
Eva 50, Anna , Catherine 7, Mat. by			
GRANNEMANN, Friedr	34	Brockhusen/Ha	51-0048
GRANTNER, Otto	25	Griesbach	54-1283
Johanna 21			
GRAPPE, Johannes	25	Otbergen	49-0574
GRASER, Eduard	25	Weimar	52-0895
GRASER, Franz	33	Koenigsberg	54-1443
Marg. Barb. 25, Franz 11m			
GRASMUD, Jos.	48	Carlsbad	51-1160
Sabine 50, Andr. 22, Barbara 17			
GRASS, G. (m)	31	Unterbergstet	52-0652
GRASSE, Alexander	28	Wohnau	52-1200
GRASSEL, Aug. Wilh	38	Altflemming	54-1297
Anna 35, Johann 9, Heinrich 7, Anna 5			
GRASSEL, Marianne	19	Nietheim	52-0515
GRASSMAK, Lisette	24	Steppack	52-0279
GRASSOLD, Johann	31	Bayern	53-0557
GRATTER, Joh Georg	35	Conreuth/Bav.	52-0351
Magarethe 27			
GRAU, Friedr.	36	Zella	49-0383
Dorothea 37, Fr. August 6, Chr. M. 3			
GRAU, Georg	52	Wuertemberg	49-0912
GRAU, Georg	22	Hessen	50-0021
GRAU, H.W.E. (m)	25	Erfurt	50-1067
Anna Maria 30			
GRAUCH, Leopold	27	Wollitz	50-0292
GRAUE, Catharina	36	Visselhoevede	47-0872
Wilhelm 6			
GRAUE, Gottlieb Fr	34	Silbingsdorf	54-0930
GRAUE, Helena	22	Threiss	53-0991
GRAUE, M. Barbara	28	Korbussen	52-1625
GRAUEL, Charles	23	Rudolstadt	48-0053
GRAUER, Maria	30	Maehring	47-0828
GRAUMANN, K.	48	Iserlohn	47-0868
GRAUREGEL, Simbert	29	Baiern	54-0903
GRAUSEN, August	20	Ikenhausen	50-0292
GRAVE, Josephine	35	Neustadt	54-1297
GRAVE, de Gerhard	21	Seer	53-1023
GRAVE, de Gesine	25	Leer	48-0887
Wimma 22, Hendrina 2, Cornelia 17			
GRAWE, Joh.	47	Werden	54-0600
GRAWINKLE, Agnes	24	Munster	49-0781
GREBE, Adam	19	Hammershausen	53-0320
GREBE, Augusta	20	Ihringhausen	53-0991
Gertruda 25			
GREBE, Heinrich	28	Kennersdorf	49-0345
GREBE, W.	28	Wrexen	54-1575
Louisa 23, Emilie 7m			
GREBNER, Alexander	26	Greiz/Reuss	50-0323
GREBNER, Charles	19	Greitz/Greitz	50-0323
GREBNER, Friedrich	21	Bairied	54-1554
GREBNER, Herrmann	21	Weissenfels	52-0095
GREEN, Anna	40	Herzstein	52-0095
GREEN, Peter Allon	26	N.Y.	52-1452
GREENING, Christ.	25	Seebach	52-1304
GREESE, Joh. Georg	34	Schreufen	51-1084
GREESEMEYER, Heinr	25	Bielefeld	47-0672
GREFFEL, Henry	22	Nienburg/Hann	50-0323
GREGER, Margrethe	21	Bayern	53-0557
GREGER, Maria	24	Bayern	53-0557
Margrethe 21			
GREIBE, Catharine	26	Deisel	50-0472
GREIER, Fr.	2-	Koenigsberg	49-1358
GREIM, Heinrich	32	Neudorf	51-1438
GREIM, Julie	57	Heidelberg	54-1341
GREIMERT, Margaret	25	Arensberg	53-0991
GREIN, Ernestine	17	Heidelbach	51-1084
GREINER, Anton	30	Wallendorf	54-1419
Bertha 24, Matilda 4			
GREINER, Bernhard	28	Leipzig	48-1131
GREINER, Carl	25	Baunach	54-0053
GREINER, Friedrich	28	Stetten	52-0095
Catharina 24			
GREINER, Gertrude	40	Wesel	54-1297
GREINER, Gotts.	25	Mittelruessel	49-0737
GREINER, Moritz	32	Stuetzelbach	52-1105

NAME	AGE	RESIDENCE	YR-LIST
Antonette 26, Herm. 7			
GREIS, Anna Marie	32	Obergensburg	49-0324
GREIS, F. (m)	45	Trienz	50-0746
A. (f) 46, V. (m) 23, A. (m) 17, A. (f) 9			
GREMEN, Heinrich	19	Warpswede	54-0053
GREMPEL, Marie	25	Neustadt	53-0320
GRENE, Rebecca	22	Berne	51-1101
GRENEL, Ernst	25	Hagenburg	53-0492
GRENKEL, Ad.	40	Frankenhausen	53-0492
GRENZEL, Johanna	54	Muhlhausen/Pr	53-0628
GRENZER, Wilhelm	18	Dondhein/Weim	53-0628
GREPE, Ludwig	21	Offenbach/Hes	54-1092
Moritz 20			
GRESE, Wilhelm	40	Barmen	48-0565
Cath. Elise 39			
GRET, A. (f)	22	Aschenbach	50-0746
GRETE, Louise	21	Moelle	50-1067
GRETEN, Ferdinand	27	Bremen	53-1164
Bertha 27, Wilhelmine by			
GRETEN, Georg	18	Bremen	51-1640
GRETHEN, Aug.	22	Hannover	51-1160
GRETSCHMANN, Fr'ke	38	Milzen/Sax.	52-1332
GREUEL, Ernst	25	Hagenburg	53-0492
GREUL, Mich	22	Hermannsberg	54-1575
GREUL, Michael	22	Herrmannsberg	54-1575
GREVE, Anna	30	Ottinghausen	54-1716
Johann 3, Anna 6m			
GREVE, Friedrich	18	Brunswick	53-1164
GREVE, Heinrich	19	Bieren	54-1452
GREVE, Hermann	20	Emsdetten	54-0903
GREVE, Rosina	33	Weifenbach	53-0838
GREVEN, Elisabeth	25	Hoerstel	48-0269
GREVEN, Heinrich	57	Frankenhausen	53-0492
GREVEN, T. (m)	23	Camp/Prussia	48-0447
GREVENKAMPEN, J.T.	57	Boushave	50-0746
C. (f) 52, F.W. (m) 26, E.H. (m) 24			
J.H. (m) 20, J.F. (m) 16, C.F. (m) 13			
M.E. (f) 19			
GREWE, C.L.T. (m)	36	Aminghausen	49-0329
GREWE, Christoph	34	Ottenhausen	48-0565
Elisabeth 30, Agnes 7, Joseph 5			
Johannes 2, Elisabeth 22			
GRIBNER, Lorenz	20	Rossdorf	49-0574
GRIEB, Wilhelm	29	Lauffen/Wuert	51-1725
Fanny 22, Carl 21			
GRIEBES, Anna	29	Bamberg	49-0345
GRIEF, Christian	18	Preussen	53-0590
GRIEF, Justin	23	Lenbach	49-0781
GRIEGLING, Gottl.	23	Springstilla	51-1455
GRIES, Fr. Wilh.	27	Ruenderath	48-0565
GRIESBACH, Joh. H.	23	Schwarzenbach	54-1371
Johanne 22, Christian 11m			
GRIESBACH, Johann	23	Goehren	54-1371
GRIESING, AM(died)	4	Blankenbach	50-0021
GRIESING, Conrad	45	Blankenbach	52-1148
Anna E. 38, Agnesa 16, Heinrich 14			
Anna Chat. 9, Elisabeth 7, Anna M. 9m			
GRIESING, Dorothea	36	Blankenbach	50-0021
Elisabeth 12, Anna Cathr. 4			
Maria Elis. 1			
GRIESMANN, Carl	19	Mettwowoerth	53-1062
Gerhard 16			
GRIESMANN, Christ.	20	Budingen	49-1106
Christine 24			
GRIESMANN, Georg	54	Brunnersthaus	52-0370
GRIESMANN, Mary	-1	Wildeshausen	50-0323
GRIESS, Margaretha	32	Hessia	50-0311
GRIESS, Maria	27	Danz	53-1062
GRIESSLER, Niclaus	29	Wellingerrode	53-0320
GRIESSMER, Georg	30	Nieder Rossba	54-0830
GRILL, Christian	31	Boeblingen	53-0320
GRILLENBERG, Eva	26	Duerenungen	52-0693
Maria 22			
GRILNOV, Margaret	21	Remschlitz	51-1588
GRIM, Rosina	28	Gelingen	51-1796
GRIMBACHER, Xaver	24	Trochtelfinge	52-0515
GRIMM, Catharine	20	Ritterbude	51-0352
GRIMM, Christine	25	Hirschberg	54-1649
GRIMM, Joh.	22	Grosslossnitz	48-0565
GRIMM, Johann	36	Hohlenbrun	47-0672
GRIMM, Johann	19	Schopback	51-1639
Heinrich 18			
GRIMM, Peter Heinr	17	Schopfloch	53-1070
GRIMM, Salomon	30	Hirschberg	53-1062
GRIMM, Wilhelm	28	Czyste	54-1168
GRIMME, Louis	17	Adelebsen	52-1464
Lina 17			
GRIMMEL, Elisabeth	27	Herborn	54-1554
GRINDLINGER, Ignaz	26	Oberndorf/Aus	52-0807
Barbara 24, Ignaz 9m			
GRINE, Elisabeth	20	Felme	49-1517
GRINNEKE, Jakob	36	Aahausen	47-0672
GRINSSFELD, S. (m)	16	Schopfloch	50-0746
GRIP, Magdalena	58	Heidenbergen	54-0987
Elisabeth 28			
GRIS, Magdalena	58	Heidenbergen	54-0987
Elisabeth 28			
GRISINGER, Philipp	40	Wuertt	53-0557
Margrethe 28, Friederike 10m			
GRISINGERE, Philip	40	Wuertenberg	53-0557
Margrethe 28, Friederike 10m			
GROB, Caspar	34	Schlizenhause	53-0942
Elise 31, Johann 27			
GROBE, Conrad	26	Osnabrueck/Ha	52-1332
Adelgunde 24			
GROBE, Joh. D. Lud	23	Dedendorf	54-0987
GROBELEN, Marie	48	Mielinghausen	54-1092
GRODE, Heinrich	21	Darferden	53-0838
GROEBEL, Joh Mart.	35	Grossdabartz	52-0351
Cath. Louise 42			
GROEBER, Caroline	29	Loebenstein	54-1575
GROEGER, Gottl.	31	Tilsit	54-1168
GROEGER, Leopold	34	Walsrode	53-0991
GROEGER, Otto	25	Karlsruhe	54-1078
GROEGER, Robert	24	Prussia	50-0311
GROEHLING, Heinr.	28	Freiburg/Pr.	53-0475
GROELING, Georg	50	Hundelshausen	52-0563
Cath. M. 36, Georg 37			
GROELING, Wilhelm	29	Hundshausen	54-1554
GROELL, Catharine	16	Schwarzenbach	53-0475
GROELL, Christoph	58	Immenrode	52-1410
Johanne 58			
GROENERT, Andreas	36	Eltmann	54-0053
GROENEWALD, G.W.			51-1455
GROENLEIN, Matilde	21	Rotenburg	51-0352
GROER, Adolf Fried	40	Sprebeck	51-1796
GROESCHEL, Eleonor	22	Hannover	53-1164
GROESCHEL, Friedr.	16	Hannover	52-1304
GROESCHEL, J. Andr	59	Hannover	54-1371
Dorothea 54, Anna 9			
GROESCHEL, Martin	29	Melsungen	52-1200
GROETHAUSEN, Heinr	18	Rachereissted	53-0475
GROETZINGER, Kath.	19	Lautern	54-0872
GROH, Michael	17	Urberach	53-1023
Carl 17			
GROHMANN, J.G. (m)	38	Dresden	50-0379
GROJANS, Gerhard	21	Fulhoern	50-0366
GROLL, Joh Wilhelm		Stotternheim	50-0323
GROLL, Peter	20	Wuestenbuchau	53-0320
GROLLE, Bernhard	32	Riesenbeck	54-0987
GROLLE, H.W. (m)	18	Bonn	50-0746
GROMANN, August	48	Schleising	54-1282
Eva 16, Carl 19, Eduard 16			
GRON, Nicolaus	19	Gaettendorf	53-0825
GRONAU, Anna Gert.	19	Ernsthausen	48-0565
GRONEMEYER, Heinr.	57	Osnabrueck	52-1101
Friedrich 18			
GRONHOLZ, Sophie	31	Willehn	53-0838
GRONHOLZ, Wilhelm	58	Mehringen	52-1452
Lowoese 25, Heinrich 40, Doris 37			
Elisabeth 12			
GROOTE, de W. (f)	38	Prussia	50-1317
Albert 6, Julia 4			
GROPENGIESSEN, Wm.	17	Barnstorf	54-0903
GROPP, Marie	40	Burgelhausen	50-0292
GROPPE, Franz	18	Erckeln	54-0600

NAME	AGE	RESIDENCE	YR-LIST
GROPPE, Friederike	15	Oerlinghausen	54-1297
GROPPE, Jakob	26	Fihtelbach	51-1084
GROSARDT, Ludwig	21	Osnabrueck	50-0366
GROSCH, Georg	37	Zella/Sachsen	54-0965
Wilhelmine 36, Gustav 9, Maria 1			
GROSCHNER, Johann	29	Grossenritt	54-0965
Anna 24			
GROSS, Carl	19	Oldenburg/Old	52-0117
GROSS, Casp.	26	Einhausen	52-1321
GROSS, Christian	39	Weitramsdorf	53-0267
GROSS, Eliese	39	Oeslau	54-1282
Carl 16			
GROSS, Friedrich	32	Schwab	53-0942
GROSS, Georg C.	40	England	50-0366
Emma 24, Fanny 22, Caroline 11, Clara 7			
GROSS, Joh.	39	Buchbach	54-1078
Elisabeth 24			
GROSS, Johann	27	Marburg	51-0352
GROSS, Joseph	28	Geiselwind/Bv	52-0807
Jacob 25, Dorothea 20			
GROSS, Leopold	25	Hessen	51-0405
GROSS, Magdalena	19	Balingen	54-1717
GROSS, Marg.	22	Ilbenstedt	49-0383
GROSS, Math.	30	Meiningen	51-0405
GROSS, Nicolaus	27	Eisen	51-1640
Franziska 28			
GROSS, P. (m)	24	Limburg	49-0416
GROSS, Paulus	16	Momberg	54-1078
GROSS, Simon	12	Schweinfurt	50-1317
GROSS, Simon	36	Fisselbach	54-1470
Beta 30, Jane 6, Beta 4			
GROSS, Wolfgang	69	Bremerhafen	53-0825
GROSSE, Carl Gottl	27	Lohma	54-0987
GROSSE, Christine	36	Altstadt	50-0292
Ricke 15			
GROSSE, Franz	36	Oberndorf	49-0912
GROSSE, Heinrich	16	Bremen	52-1580
GROSSE, Heinrich	36	Hazberg	52-0699
GROSSE, Paulus	27	Dingelstedt	48-0887
GROSSE, Rudolph	17	Prenzlau	54-1168
GROSSENSACHER, Ulr	50		52-0279
GROSSGEBAUER, Cath	20	Sellstedt	48-1179
GROSSKOPF, Wilhelm	23	Dachgrube/Sax	53-0628
Ernst 15			
GROSSKURTH, Joh.	25	Waldcappel	47-0918
GROSSLICHT, Carl	20	Mitzkowitz	53-1062
GROSSMANN, Carl	34	Hayda	48-1355
GROSSMANN, Johann	26	Hassenberg	52-1661
GROTE, C. (m)	48	Hiddessen	48-0453
J. (f) 44, H. (m) 22, C. (m) 18			
C. (m) 14, August 12, H. (m) 3			
GROTE, Caroline	34	Minden	54-1168
GROTE, Caroline	20	Peine	51-0405
GROTE, Conrad	24	Kolstadt	52-0775
Louise 21			
GROTE, Justine	28	Edewissen	54-1078
GROTE, Wilhelm	24	Lasbrock	49-0345
GROTE, Wilhelm	28	Hagenburg	49-0324
Sophie 26, Dorothe 6			
GROTE, Wilhelm	32	Stolzenau	50-0021
GROTHEIM, Ernst	47	Scheppehausen	52-0563
Wilhelmine 46, Heinrich 13, August 10			
GROTHEIM, Keh. (m)	50	Thedinghausen	52-0515
H. (m) 17			
GROTHEIM, Marg. El	52	Herbehausen	54-1647
GROTHOFF, John	23	Allendorf	53-0991
GROTNER, J. (f)	56	Trienz	50-0746
A. (m) 46, J. (m) 22, S. (m) 20			
GROTRIAN, Aug.	30	Cramme/Bruns	51-0048
GROTRIAN, Dorothea	12	Augsburg	54-1092
GROTSCHMANN, P'lne	18	Eisenberg	54-1283
GROTTHER, Hermann	15	Burgdom	53-1164
GRUB, Andreas	21	Torgau	52-1661
GRUB, Jos.	26	Reichenbach	49-1106
GRUBE, Carl	20	Wende	54-1094
GRUBE, Claus	23	Brelet	50-0292
GRUBE, Joh. Alb.	23	Sicke	52-1512
Anna 17			
GRUBE, Johann Carl	29	Bremen	54-0872
GRUBE, Stina	20	Bederkesa	54-1716
GRUBEN, Dorothee	22	Grusen-Heinse	53-0492
GRUBER, Anton	50	Weilheim	52-1200
Catharina 47, Marianne 24, Johann 18			
Walburga 20, Thomas 10			
GRUBER, Dionis	41	Aurolfingen	54-1371
GRUBER, Friedrich	29	Illingen	52-1580
GRUBER, Georg	34	Giesing	54-0850
Magdalena 31, Ludwig 3, Georg 2, Anton by			
GRUBER, Joh.	27	Wieseth	54-1283
GRUBER, Johann	22	Kitzingen/Bav	52-0807
GRUBER, Theodor	24	Breitenloh	54-0872
GRUBER, Xaver	34	Mittelruessel	49-0737
GRUEGEL, Andr.	30	Dachstadt	52-0693
GRUEMMER, Wilhelm	20	Harste/Hann.	54-0965
GRUENAST, Anna	50	Breslau	53-0637
Dorothea 30			
GRUENBAUM, Vogel	18	Raboldshausen	52-0279
GRUENBECK, Johann	19	Burgstall	52-1661
GRUENBLATT, Ernstn	21	Geisa	54-1168
GRUENDEL, Wilh.	20	Leiben	48-1179
GRUENE, Friedrich	25	Stolzenau/Han	51-1725
Dorothea 26, Wilhelm 10m			
GRUENEKLE, Louis	21	Wehnde/Hann.	54-0965
GRUENEKLEE, A. (f)	24	Wende	54-1094
L. (f) 22			
GRUENER, Franz	38	Reichenberg	53-0905
Carolina 40, Anna 4, Marie 4, Caroline by			
Ferdinand 15			
GRUENER, Friedrike	27	Lobenstein	53-1070
GRUENEWAELDER, Am.	32	Friedrichsdor	53-0905
GRUENEWALD, Anna	18	Grebenau	54-1566
Catharina 15			
GRUENFELD, David	22	Libochswitz	48-1184
GRUENFELD, Leopold	18	Libochowitz	53-1070
Lotte 20			
GRUENHOLD, Franz	44	Wien	54-1297
GRUENTHAL, Heinr.	17	Wunstorf	50-0439
GRUENWALD, Wilhelm	19	Buethgow	54-1371
GRUENZWEIG, Ant'ia	36	Vienna	53-1164
Anna by			
GRUETTMEYER, Chr H	29	Jever	52-1452
Anna Maria 24, Maria 2, Hanche(died) 1			
Joh. Heinr. 6m, Wilhelm 24			
Marie Elis. 56, Elise 23, Wilhelmine 21			
GRUHL, Carl Ed.	34	Klein Wolka	54-1371
GRULGER, Chr.	36	Raden	51-1796
Louise 38			
GRUMER, Gabr.	50	Oedern	49-0574
Ernst 18			
GRUNBURG, Caroline	28	Prague	48-1243
GRUND, A.	38	Berlin	50-1071
GRUNDENBERG, Fried	25	Heideck	49-0329
Heinr. 16			
GRUNDLACH, H.	22	Erlachstruth	54-1575
Elis. Cath. 53			
GRUNDMANN, Carolin	15	Bielefeld	52-1512
GRUNDMANN, Engel	17	Essen	53-1086
GRUNDMANN, Heinr.	27	Bielefeld/Pr.	51-0048
GRUNDNER, Anton	29	Insbruck	53-0888
GRUNER, Alois	23	Dingolfing	52-1200
GRUNER, Anna	30	Bergdorf	51-0757
GRUNER, Aug.	30	Altenburg	50-1071
Ferdinand 10			
GRUNER, Aug.	37	Bergdorf	51-0757
Heinr. 8			
GRUNER, Franz	54	Reichenberg	54-0987
Catharine 55, Anna 12, Philipp 10			
Anna 20			
GRUNER, Mary	20	Darmstadt	53-1164
GRUNER, Philip	21	Darmstadt	53-1164
GRUNKEMAYER, Carl	30	Melle	52-1410
Christiane 25, Eduard 4			
GRUNSFELD, Rachel	52	Hebenshasen	53-0838
GRUPE, Ferdinand	24	Heyn/Hannover	51-1725
August 21			
GRUPE, Henry	38	Duingen	54-1716

NAME	AGE	RESIDENCE	YR-LIST
Justine 36, Christine 12, Gottfried 7			
Emma 3			
GRUPP, Anna	21	Behmenkahle	49-0345
GRUPP, Benedict	30	Neustaedtles	52-1620
GRUSS, Nicolaus	29	Holstadt/Bav.	52-1620
GRUTTEN, William	30	Wulwade	53-1164
Doris 26			
GUBER, John	38	Walddorf	53-0914
GUDE, August	20	Grebenstein	52-0515
GUEBER, Gesche	28	Bremervoerde	51-1725
GUELDNER, F Christ	51	Waldsleben	52-0279
Christine 36, Christian 16, Wilhelmine 26			
GUELLICH, J.A.(m)	33	Lattenbuch	54-1094
GUELLIS, Louis	28	Mariendorf	52-1464
Elisabeth 28, Anna 3, baby 8w			
GUELZER, Charlotte	31	Flemmingen	54-1297
GUENTER, Andreas	21	Ziegenhain	52-1580
GUENTER, Johann	20	Versmold	50-0366
GUENTER, Josepha		Wodemann	53-0942
GUENTHER, Adolph	19	Saalfeldt	54-1078
GUENTHER, August	24	Wernigerode	48-1179
GUENTHER, Carl	42	Plauen	53-1016
Wilhelmine 30, Anna 7			
GUENTHER, Carl F.	26	Leipzig	48-0406
GUENTHER, Edmund	24	Schwersberg	54-1371
GUENTHER, Elise		Marburg	48-1355
GUENTHER, Fr.	25	Zwoenitz	48-1179
GUENTHER, Fr. R.	27	Detmold	54-0918
GUENTHER, Franz		Wodman	53-0942
wife , child			
GUENTHER, Friedr.	15	Pollwitz	53-0991
William 21			
GUENTHER, Georg	40	Oerlinghausen	54-1297
Friedrich 35, Caroline 24			
GUENTHER, Gottlob	26	Brembach	54-0872
Friederike 23, Carl by			
GUENTHER, Herm. H.	18	Brukum	54-1443
GUENTHER, Johanne	25	Luetzenau	52-1661
Christiane 28			
GUENTHER, Louise	22	Hildesheim	51-1101
GUENTHER, Margreth	26	Kirchlein/Bav	51-1532
Catharina 6			
GUENTIUS, Christ.	22	Eisenach/Sax.	52-1620
GUENZBURG, Juda	59	Eperies	53-0991
Miriam 57, Leonora 19			
GUERTELMEYER, Elis	32	Cassel	52-0699
GUERTELMEYER, Hein	34	Muenden	52-0699
Elise 32, Anna 7, Friedrich 4, Anton 2			
GUERTLER, Johann	49	Alschwil	52-0095
Anna 49, Peter 23, Maria 20, Rosalia 14			
Philomena 6, Anton 4, Johann 26			
Catharina 22, Albert 8m			
GUERTNER, Christ.	20	Prussia	52-0699
GUESBACHER, Maria	22	Bayern	53-0590
GUETHER, Hanna	16	Mosen	54-1371
GUETHER, Joh. Aug.	14	Mosen	54-1371
GUETHLEIN, Franz	38	Bamberg	52-1304
Ottilie 37, John 12			
GUETHLEIN, Georg	24	Igelsdorf	52-1625
GUETLE, Jacob	24	Ruedersberg	54-1168
GUETLEIN, John	26	Bamberg	50-0021
GUETTINGER, Joh.	27	Wemding	52-0279
GUFLER, Anton	22	Leitershofen	54-1168
GUGLER, Anna Maria	26	Gailshaim	53-1062
GULDMANN, Therese	27	Donauwoerth	54-0872
Mina 26			
GULHOLDT, Julius	28	Berlin	54-1297
Caroline 25			
GULL, Joh. Otto	20	Aurich	50-0379
GULNER, Therese	30	Tapolza	53-1164
GUMBERT, Carl	19	Grieselbach	47-0828
Aug. 18			
GUMMER, Margaretha	34	Norkheim	52-0279
GUMPEL, Bertha	24	Mahl	53-1062
Ernestine 22			
GUNDEL, M. (m)	38	Tauberschonba	52-0558
M. (f) 38, J. (m) 6			
GUNDELACH, Louis	25	Coburg	50-0439

NAME	AGE	RESIDENCE	YR-LIST
GUNDELACH, Wm.	30	Braunschweig	50-1071
GUNDELFINGER, Dan.	17	Grafenberg/Bv	53-0628
GUNDERBERGER, S.	18	Alsfeld	54-1341
GUNDERMANN, Ferd.	19	Nordhausen	53-0582
GUNDINA, Lewis	23	Goettingen	53-0991
GUNDLACH, Adolph F	24	Hofgeismar/He	51-1532
GUNDLACH, Eduard	26	Gross Almerod	54-1297
Marie 21, Julius 3			
GUNDLACH, Johannes	23	Lautenbach	51-1101
GUNDLACH, Mar. Cat	16	Bremervoerde	54-0987
GUNGL, Joseph	35	Berlin	48-1243
Cajetana 27, Maria 7			
GUNKLE, Conrad	26	Gerbershausen	51-1588
Henry 24			
GUNSCH, Augustus	15	Neuburg	50-0944
Wilhelm 13, Ernst 9			
GUNTERLEB, J. (f)	23	Huvslieb	51-0517
GUNTERMANN, A. (m)	27	Heborn	52-0652
GUNTEROTH, Fritz	23	Dambrock	48-0951
GUNTHER, John D.	20	Moringen	54-1341
Joseph 18			
GUNTLACH, Johann	24	Lauffenbach	54-1566
GURTH, Christian	28	Heiligenstadt	53-0905
Maria 27, Maria by			
GUSDORF, Jette	22	Chugde	54-1443
GUSHERP, Carl M.	24	Dresden	52-1321
GUSKING, Heinrich	27	Minden	54-0850
Pauline 26, Heinrich by			
GUSMANN, Adam	20	Rotenburg	54-1649
GUSSMANN, Carl	22	Hirzenhain/He	52-1423
GUSSMANN, Wilhelm	21	Neuschmiden	53-0928
Heinrich 16			
GUSSREGEN, Georg	25	Hallstadt	54-1297
Margarethe 25, Margarethe 11m			
GUTABER, J.A. (m)	25	Altendorf	49-0416
GUTBERLET, M. (f)	22	Mengsdorf/Hes	52-0960
GUTEKUNST, Daniel	26	Waldorf	48-1355
GUTEKUNST, Rosine	42	Goeppingen/Wu	51-1532
GUTGESELL, Valent.	39	Ostheiten	53-0928
GUTH, Elisabeth	27	Salzungen	51-1739
Cath. 3			
GUTHARDT, Elias	21	Borken	52-1200
GUTHMANN, Heinrich	21	Gereuth	52-0370
GUTHMANN, Johann	17	Alwestedt	52-1580
Heinrich 14			
GUTMANN, Babette	20	Fuerth	52-1512
GUTMANN, Caroline	20	Ironheim	53-0905
GUTMANN, Caspar	20	Oberweida	54-1554
GUTMANN, Heinrich	32	Eisnach	52-0370
GUTMANN, Helene		Bederkesa	54-0987
GUTMANN, Joh. G.	32	Irmelshausen	51-1160
GUTMANN, Joseph	25	Hainsfahrt/Bv	52-1423
Moses 18			
GUTMANN, Julia	24	Tattenhausen	54-0930
GUTMANN, Metha	26	Alwestedt	52-1580
GUTMANN, Moriz	26	Neustadt	54-0930
Hirsch 18			
GUTMANN, Moses	18	Berolzheim/Bv	52-1423
GUTMANN, Nathan	24	Duisbeck/Bav.	50-0323
GUTMANN, Ruthcken		Bederkesa	54-0987
GUTMANN, Salamon	22	Bavaria	53-0628
GUTMANN, Victoria	21	Hainfate	54-0930
GUTSCHE, Friedr.	40	Niederherzogs	49-0352
GUTSMUTH, Ernst	28	Magdeburg	54-0850
GUTTE,	21	West Prussia	50-0021
GUTTMANN, Jul.	21	Mittelruessel	49-0737
GUTWILLIG, Albert	19	Weseritsch	51-1796
GUTZEL, W.	29	Sonnefeld	47-0868
GUYOT, Adolph	38	France	48-1015
HAACKE, Christ. Fr	28	Krauthum	50-0292
HAACKE, F.	26	Engelade	51-0517
HAAG, Jan Friedr.	21	Geldingen	47-0672
HAAG, Theodore	24	Berlin	48-1243
HAAG, William	38	Solingen	48-0406
HAAGEN, A.	20	Gotha	54-1716
HAAGEN, Carl	21	Stuttgart	54-1717
HAAGEN, Carl Ludw.	23	Oidersleben	54-1371
HAAKE, Heinrich	26	Hille	51-1455

NAME	AGE	RESIDENCE	YR-LIST
Chr. L. 22			
HAAKE, Joh. Heinr.	20	Holsen	54-1452
HAAKMANN, B.J.	21	Bichsten	48-0284
HAAMANN, Heinrich	28	West Bevern	52-1464
Bernh. 30, Anna 24			
HAAN, Friedrich	23	Beckersdorf	47-0672
HAAR, Anna	21	Worpswede	54-1647
Mette 18			
HAAR, Geerd	23	Bergedorf/Han	51-1725
HAAR, Helene	31	Doksbach	48-0887
HAARHAUS, Carl	22	Rehnsaal	51-0326
HAAS, Carl	22	Bietigheim	53-0838
HAAS, Caroline	20	Spiegelberg	52-1580
HAAS, Christoph	35	Baiern	53-0585
Johann 26			
HAAS, El. Doris	18	Bietigheim	53-0838
El. Cathrina 15			
HAAS, Engelbert	16	Lennep	54-1371
HAAS, Fanny	20	Storndorf	54-1341
HAAS, Georg	28	Darmstadt	54-1283
HAAS, Georg	30	Reitlingen	52-0095
David 38			
HAAS, Heinrich	34	Herborn	54-1575
Heinrich 36			
HAAS, Henrietta	10	Stuttgart	54-1341
HAAS, Henriette	34	Herborn	54-1575
Henriette 36			
HAAS, Jean Louis	23	Frankenthal	54-1371
HAAS, Joh. M.	26	Salzfeld	49-0781
Margarethe 21			
HAAS, Marie	25	Ilbenstedt	49-0383
HAAS, Reinhard	30	Darmstadt	53-0991
Lewis 17			
HAAS, Vinz.	19	Limbach	53-0928
HAASBENS, Heinrich	33	Jena	51-1639
HAASE, Georg	32	Cassel	52-1304
HAASE, Liberius	33	Krenzeler	54-0850
Dorothea 33, Catharina 6, Maria Elis. by			
Christina 4			
HAASLOP, Carl Fr'd	21	Scharmbeck/Ha	50-0323
HAASS, Catharina	23	Ladenburg	53-0267
HAASS, Wilhelm	23	Schriesheim	53-0267
Catharina 23			
HABBER, Anna E.	22	Borgholz	54-0600
HABENICHT, C.	16	Wunstorf	50-0439
HABENICHT, Emilie	30	Hanover	51-0500
HABENICHTS, August	34	Springe	54-1554
HABENICHTS, Carol.	31	Springe	54-1554
HABENSTRICKER, Th.	20	Nuernberg	50-0439
HABERBERGER, Georg	26	Muehldorf	54-1443
HABERDASCH, Marg.	26	Greisbach	52-0693
HABERKARN, Cath.	22	Ornshausen	53-0585
HABERKERN, Jacob	23	Eberswang	54-1443
HABERL, Jacob	27	Hanau	51-0500
HABERMAN, Seb.	24	Mittelruessel	49-0737
HABERMANN, Joh Aug	23	Lauerstadt	52-0279
HABERMANN, Leopold	36	Iglan	53-1070
Theresia 38, Johann 29			
HABERMANN, Marie	24	Hemmichshause	52-0807
HABERMANN, Philipp	51	New York	53-0914
Marie 34, Marg. 54, Philipp 9, Mag. 5			
Elise 9m			
HABERMANN, Regina	14	Uelhof	48-1179
HABERMAYER, James	32	Reichertshofe	52-1304
Marie 41			
HABERSITZER, N.(m)	36	Baiern	50-1067
Barbara 38, Leonhard 7, Maria 5			
HABERTSCH, J.G.	20	Doerfles	54-1575
HABICH, Heinrich	22	Bokenem	50-1132
HABICH, Theodor	26	Hessen	51-0500
HABICHT, Reinh.	28	Schmalkalden	49-0324
HABKE, Heinrich		Schnol	54-1371
HABLICH, Susan	28	Gollhausen	51-1796
HACHBERN, John		Herbach/Darms	50-0323
HACHE, Friedrich	25	Giefhorn	52-1512
HACHLEFELD, Herman	37	Altenburg	54-1282
Christine 36, Carl 7, Ricke by			
HACHTEL, Catharine	19	Michelbach	51-1686

NAME	AGE	RESIDENCE	YR-LIST
HACHTEL, Georg	25	Milbach	51-1686
HACHTEL, Magd.	22	Metzholz	51-1686
HACHTMEISTER, Carl	25	Hannover	54-0903
HACK, Bath	19	Utrictshausen	52-0515
HACK, John	24	Utrictshausen	52-0515
HACK, Ludwig	23	Reichenbach	53-1070
Christian Fr 14			
HACK, Margarethe	25	Eglofsteinhue	54-0850
HACKE, Georg	27	Beuthen	49-0781
Anna 24			
HACKEL, Barbara	48	Wien	53-1013
Paul 9, Martha 7, Joseph 3			
HACKENBERG, Dietr.	54	Unnei	52-1410
HACKENBERG, Georg	30	Waldeck	52-0804
HACKENFELD, Fr.	28	Berlin	54-1283
HACKER, Joh. Ad.	25	Redwitz	47-0918
HACKER, John	33	Wiesbaden/Nas	48-0447
HACKER, Martin	32	Knetzgau	54-0053
Anna Marie 30, Ignatz 3			
HACKNAGEL, John A.	17	Dentlein	52-0515
HADAM, Barbara A.	27	Aalen/Wuertt	54-1092
HADDENBRICH, E.(m)	27	Remscheid	49-0416
HADDENHORST, H.(m)	28	Laage	49-0329
HADELER, Johann	27	Cappel-Neufel	50-0366
HADEN, v.Christoph	15	Altwistedt	51-0756
HADERTHAUER, Henry	20	Steinweisen	53-0914
HADLER, Georg	28	Buch	54-1419
HADLER, Wilhelm	24	Bederkesa	47-0872
Jacob 27			
HADSKENESKEY, Carl	29	Geagua	54-1341
HAEBEL, Georg	22	Gr. Ameredo	53-0825
HAEBERLE, Anton	19	Unterupfingen	54-1717
Crescens 29			
HAEBERLE, Jacob	19	Preussen	52-0370
HAEBERLEIN, Marg.	18	Kuntzenhausen	53-1016
HAEBERLIN, Cath.	25	Schachheim	52-1512
HAECKEL, Chr.	53	Leitersdorf	49-1358
Chr. 18, Casp. 11, Chr. Ad. 9, Fr. 25			
Marie 22			
HAEDERICH, Joh.	23	Billingsdorf	47-0828
HAEFELE, Anton	45	Dalkingen	53-0435
Crescenzia 49, Crescenzia 16, Xaver 14			
Anton 11, Niklolaus 9, Victoria 6			
HAEFELE, Cres.	49	Schwabsberg	53-0435
HAEFELE, Joh.	36	Ammerdingen	54-1371
HAEFELE, Martin	47	Fezen	54-0053
Johanna 50, Beatha 20, Theodor 15			
Pius 12			
HAEFFLER, H.F.	20	Frankfurt/M.	51-0405
HAEFNER, Joachim	26	Schleifhausen	52-0095
HAEFNER, Maria	25	Hesselried	54-1554
HAEGER, Conr. H.	3m	Fulda	51-0405
HAEHLING, Friedr.	24	Gleisingen	54-0965
HAEKSTEIN, Friedr.	29	Frille	51-1588
Caroline 29, Mary 60			
HAEMMERING, Friedr	42	Cassel	54-1724
Mary 31, Carol. 4, Joseph 6m, Christ. 54			
Caroline 21, Sophie 17			
HAENCKEL, Heinr.	23	Regensberg	50-0439
HAENDEL, Carl	21	Plauen	54-1283
HAENE, Friedr.	18	Gotha	53-0473
HAENEL, Gotthilf	32	Eisenberg	52-1105
HAENEL, Joh. Georg	57	Chemnitz	52-1105
Gotthilf 32, Christine 29, Karl Herm. 9			
Joh. Louis 5			
HAENSELMANN, Luise	42	Stuttgart	53-1164
Lisette 9, Sophia 7			
HAENSKE, Eva Maria	53	Gebstedt	52-1148
Caroline 23, Ferdinand 20, Christiane 16			
Reinhold 14, Bertha(died) 3m			
HAEPNER, August	24	Pommern	50-1236
HAER, Mathew	30	Mittelruessel	49-0737
Joh. H. 24			
HAER, Peter	38	Mittelruessel	49-0737
Maria 39, Anna Maria 6, Johann M. 5			
Jacob 3, Allegunde 1			
HAERINGKLEE, Barb.	24	Tagmatz	48-1355
HAERTEL, Ferdinand	35	Untochen	54-0930

NAME	AGE	RESIDENCE	YR-LIST
Henriette 38			
HAERTEL, Henriette	22	Tischitz	54-0872
HAERTEL, Joseph	32	Bayern	53-0557
Josepha 24, Maria 7			
HAERTLE, Joh.	18	Bergenweiler	54-0600
Joh. Georg 23			
HAESCHE, Heinrich	16	Sievern	50-0366
HAESELER, Chr Theo	44	Hannover	53-1164
HAESLOP, Anna	24	Plauen	53-1016
HAETSCHOLD, C.M.	27	Wiesenfeld	50-1071
HAEUBLEIN, Lina	28	Suhl	54-1717
Lida 7, Gebhardt 5, Louis 10m			
HAEUSER, Charlotte	24	Idelsberg	51-1035
HAEUSLER, Cath.	19	Niederstolzin	54-0600
HAFEN, Emma	29	Mittelruessel	49-0737
HAFER, Gerhard	27	Aukum	51-0352
HAFER, Jacob	33	Lixfeld	52-1105
Elisabeth 47, Jacob 17, Johannes 14			
HAFER, Johannes	56	Strang/Hess.	51-1532
Ana Cathrina 56, Gertrud 9, Georg 25			
HAFERSIEK, Wilhelm	35	Herford	53-0928
HAFF, Ganding	22	Voellinghause	50-1236
HAFFER, Charles	33	Alsfeld	51-1455
Maria 32, George 6			
HAFMANN, H. (m)	34	Riefenbeck	48-0445
HAFNER, Elis.	26	Dessingen	54-1419
HAGE, Friedrich	37	Horsten	53-1164
Anna 39, Gerhard 14			
HAGE, Ida	46	Gotha	54-1566
HAGEDORN, Albert	35	Braunschweig	54-1282
HAGEDORN, Carl		Telbenstedt	54-1575
wife			
HAGEDORN, Georg	32	Hiddingsen	51-1160
Elisabeth 22, Heinr. 2			
HAGEDORN, Gerhard	23	Osnabrueck	52-1512
HAGEDORN, Heinrich	36	Wolfssage	54-1168
Friederike 36, Franz 9, Johanne 6			
HAGEMANN, Adam	31	Hersfeld	51-0352
HAGEMANN, Bernhard	24	Lingen	49-0912
HAGEMANN, Carl	28	Barmen	54-0600
HAGEMANN, Eduard	24	Corbach	53-0991
Catharina 24			
HAGEMANN, Eliza	19	Muenden	53-0991
HAGEMANN, Herm.	30	Lippe-Detmold	50-0311
Dorothea 31			
HAGEMANN, Hermann	20	Grapeln/Hann.	52-0117
HAGEMANN, Johann	12	Pueppen	53-1062
HAGEMANN, Josephin			48-0269
HAGEMANN, Wilh.	22	Wagenfeld	51-0326
HAGEMEIER, Fr.	24	Germany	50-0472
HAGEMEISTER, Simon	21	Heiersfeld	54-0987
HAGEN, A. (f)	27	Emsdetten	49-0416
J. (m) 20			
HAGEN, Aug.	16	Lobenstein	54-0053
HAGEN, Caroline	20	Hameln	51-1796
HAGEN, Conrad	45	Baunn	54-0903
HAGEN, Friedrich	30	Exbeck/Pr.	51-1796
HAGEN, Heinrich	22	Blankenburg	54-0987
HAGEN, Joseph	36	Baiern	52-1512
HAGEN, Sofie	43	Banensiker/Ha	51-1796
Caroline 20			
HAGENMUELLER, Ther	16	Bavaria	50-0311
HAGER, Aug.	35	Gotha	54-1470
July 30, William 12			
HAGER, Heinrich	26	Rodach	52-0370
HAGER, Joh.	21	Gochren	54-1283
HAGER, Johann	28	Foerbau	53-1062
HAGER, Joseph	50	Eisen	54-1282
Marie 20			
HAGER, Sophie	51	Unterkotzen	54-0053
HAGER, Theodor	19	Altenburg	51-1245
HAGERLEBEN, Sophia	18	Hassbergen	54-1443
HAGIMANN, Bernh. H	29	Neisenmaihors	48-1114
HAGMANN, Bernd	18	Beverungen	51-1455
HAHM, v. August	22	Richmond	53-0161
Heinrich 19			
HAHN, Albert	21	Warmsen	48-1184
HAHN, Andreas	29	Beikheim	53-0324
Kunigunde 41, Barbara 2			
HAHN, Anna	31	Kossmann	49-0324
HAHN, Anna Rosine	48	Freiburg	53-1062
Gottfried 28, Pauline 20			
HAHN, Caspar	51	Coburg	51-0405
Margareth 50, Paulus 15, Carl 10			
HAHN, Catharina	19	Heidelbach	53-0905
HAHN, Elisabeth	25	Atzelrode	53-1023
HAHN, Emma	19	Dingen	48-0951
HAHN, Ernst	22	Nordheim	51-1101
HAHN, Friedr.	30	Vacha	47-0828
Josephine 22			
HAHN, Heinrich	46	Langensalza	53-0324
August 14			
HAHN, Heinrich	42	Hochheim	54-1647
Friederike 33, Eva 8, Gustav 5, Sophie 9			
HAHN, Johann	26	Holzel	50-0366
HAHN, Julie	21	Sandhausen	52-1661
HAHN, L.	14	Neuserss	47-0868
E. 11, D. 7			
HAHN, Louisa	16	Alsfeld	54-1341
HAHN, Math.	17	Gemaringen	54-1283
HAHN, Michel	27	Steinsdorf	51-1245
HAHNIEN, Friedrich	23	Lilienthal	50-0292
HAHS, Guergen	26	Braunschweig	52-1580
HAI, August	19	Langenschwalb	53-1000
HAID, Barbara	20	Hohenschwarz	52-0693
HAID, Georg	31	Boxdorf	52-0693
Margareth 25, Margareth 8m			
HAID, Johann	21	Hohenschwarz	52-0693
HAIDT, Elisabetha	20	Eschennau	53-0320
HAIGUTH, Marg.	15	Kotha	51-1035
HAINS, Franz	25	Karlsbrunn	54-1724
Anne 28, Anne 6m, John 51, Cath. 48			
John 18, Thr. (f) 20			
HAINS, Johann	52	Nartau	51-0326
Catharina 55, Marg. 27, Gesche 13			
HAISLER, Magdalena	26	Breitenloh	54-0872
HAJECK, John	20	Pilsen	53-0914
HAKES, Jette	19	Burgkundstadt	48-0269
HAKEWESSEL, Alex.	22	New York	50-1067
HAKMANN, Friedr.	52	Sontra	52-1304
Charles 24			
HAKSPACHER, Joseph	17	Nordhausen	54-1575
HALBACH, Fr. Wilh.	27	Barmen	48-0565
Amalia 24, F.W. 1			
HALBANN, Christine	28	Seligenstadt	54-0930
HALBAUER, Nicolaus	26	Beitingen	49-0345
HALBBAUER, Sophie	24	Goetzdorf	54-1554
HALBE, Heinrich	56	Lamspring/Han	52-1423
HALBFOERSTER, Lou.	19	Wagenfeld	51-0500
HALBLEIB, Eva B.	21	Ried	53-0320
HALBLEIB, Marie	20	Ried	54-1168
HALBRICK, Anton	28	Wien	51-1035
HALBRUETTER, J Mic	27	Ohrenbach	54-1094
Anna Barbara 26, Michael 9m			
HALDE, K.F. (m)	20	Kabechald	49-0329
HALDENERE, Mag.	20	Urach	52-1580
HALL, John	40	Wahlen	54-1724
HALLBAUER, E.W.(m)	27	Reichenbach	52-1625
HALLE, Heinrich	37	Brembach	54-0872
Caroline 33, Friedrich 9, Bertha 8			
Lina 4, Emilie 2			
HALLE, Joh Wilhelm	25	Schloss Wieba	49-0365
HALLE, Joseph	26	Carlsruhe	54-0987
HALLE, Loeb	31	Willmars	53-0991
Regina 28, Samuel 9m			
HALLE, Teige (f)	59	Willmars	53-0991
Biele 26, Abraham 36			
HALLENLEB, R.	11	Nordhausen	47-0868
HALLER, Eliza	25	Schrezheim	53-0991
HALLER, W.	27	Schuetzingen	54-1168
Louise 29			
HALLIG, Joseph	44	Pommern	54-1591
Anna 30, Franz 18, Joseph 13, Emanuel 11			
Vincenz 2, Anna 5			
HALLINGS, Johann	22	Barchen	49-0345
Joh. Juergen 22			

NAME	AGE	RESIDENCE	YR-LIST
HALLMANN, Konrad	33	Sielen	54-1676
HALLWEG, Maria	15	Beverstedt	54-0903
HALMICH, Amand	50	Schoenheide/S	51-1725
Johanne 50, Caroline 19, Therese 22			
Johanne 16, August 12, Wilhelm 10			
HALTE, Christine	34	Veitsteinbach	52-1661
HALTEMEYER, John	37	Windelheim	53-0492
HALTER, Heinrich	30	Neuwied	54-0872
Regine 22			
HALTMANN, Franz	24	Grombach	49-0912
HAM, Barbara Jos.	49	Hunfeld	47-0672
Nurbad (f) 12			
HAM, Maria	26	Fuld	47-0672
HAMANN, Maria	50	Quackenbrueck	52-1512
HAMANN, William	20	Gera/Prussia	49-0365
HAMBERGER, Cath.	28	Maisheid	48-0887
Cathrine 24			
HAMBERGER, Johann	18	Baiern	53-0324
HAMBRACK, Franz	28	Gemen	52-0804
HAMBRECHT, Georg	22	Balleberg	49-0912
Cathrine 24			
HAMBURG, Abraham	24	Breunau	52-1321
Baruth (m) 24			
HAMDLIN, Anna Mar.	19	Georgenzell	49-0781
HAMEL, Heinrich	17	Goettingen	52-0370
HAMEL, Martin	49	Schalitz	54-1676
Franziska 49, Franz 19, Joseph 6			
HAMFELD, Heinr.	17	Achim	51-1640
HAMM, Justine	30	Gothharz	51-0500
HAMM, Wilhelm	31	Gossau	53-0320
HAMMEL, August	39	Soldin	54-1168
Wilhelmine 38, Louise 7, Carl 3			
Albert by			
HAMMEL, Joh. Fried	29	Niedernhall	53-0267
Louise 23			
HAMMER, Bernh.	18	Rudolstadt	54-1078
HAMMER, Caspar	23	Oberplechtfel	47-0872
HAMMER, F.R.	19	Hadersleben	52-1661
HAMMER, Fr. (m)	30	Frankenhausen	54-0918
Charlotte 28			
HAMMER, J.Fr.	26	Norway	51-0048
HAMMER, Louis	16	Wetzlar	54-1443
HAMMER, Michael	52	Seckenheim	52-1625
Elisabeth 45, Joseph 18, Barbara 16			
Catharine 11, Maria 2			
HAMMER, Michel	50	Oberkessbach	53-1062
Catharina 49, Mariana 21, Paulina 19			
HAMMERSCHLAG, Lud.	19	Bederkesa	54-0987
HAMMERSCHMIDT, Bab	22	Altrelle	54-0987
HAMMERSCHMIDT, C.	14	Eltwille	54-0987
HAMMERSTEIN, Hen't	34	Solingen	48-0406
HAMMET, Heinrich	29	Hoeringhausen	54-0987
HAMPE, Emma	17	Braunschweig	54-0987
HAMPE, Friederike	22	Geismar	54-0882
HAMPEL, Jost	34	Hasselfeld	50-0366
HAMROTH, Dorothea	35	Fuerstenreuth	54-1554
Sophie 7			
HAN, Kuno	16	Linkensoen/Bv	51-1796
HANAUER, Heinrich	20	Alsfeld	51-0352
HANDEL, Sophie	21	Kleinensee	48-0284
HANDELMANN, Wilh.	23	Neuenwalde	53-0928
HANDFELD, Mar.	19	Achim	51-0326
HANDSCHLEGEL, Seb.	20	Zwerchstrass	52-0279
HANDSHUG, Martin	17	Sachs.-Weimar	53-0628
HANDTMANN, Friedr.	28	Biberach/Wuer	52-1423
Henriette 35, Wilhelmine 15, Sophie 12			
Ernstine 10, Louise 8			
HANDWERKER, Fr.	28	Lennep	50-1317
HANENSCHWAGER, Lud	23	Cur Hessen	53-0557
HANENSCHWAGER, Lud	23	Kur-Hessen	53-0557
HANF, J. (m)	22	Hafenpreppach	52-0652
HANF, John Georg	33	Erfurt	53-0991
HANFELD, William	34	Solingen	48-0406
HANFF, J.G. (m)	30	Watzendorf	50-0379
HANFRING, Marianne	42	Sallenberg	54-0053
Elisabeth 7			
HANFT, Cath.	18	Arzberg	50-1236
HANFT, Gustav	17	Rodach	52-0370

NAME	AGE	RESIDENCE	YR-LIST
HANFT, Gustav	15	Sonneberg	53-0557
HANFT, Magdalene	24	Mohrlach	54-1716
HANGE, Fr. G.	30	Almenhausen	48-0269
HANIXMANN, Cath.	21	Osnabrueck	52-1512
HANK, Joh. Anton	22	Baiern	52-0370
HANKE, Anton	21	Stemme	49-0345
HANKE, F. (m)	18	Barkhausen	49-0329
HANKEN, Eliza	23	Minden	51-1455
HANNE, Henry	42	Gifhorn	53-1164
HANNEMANN, Mich. F	39	Welzin	54-1371
Friederike 34, Ludwig 14			
HANNER, Peter	26	Langenstadt	47-0918
HANNER, Ursula	21	Sigmaringen	52-1580
HANNY, August	19	Mittelruessel	49-0737
HANS, Adolph	18	Warftith	50-1071
HANSEL, Hans	40	Norn	54-1717
Renske 32, Ullrich 8, Ida 5, Lina 3			
HANSEN, Emilie	20	Allenbruch	54-1371
HANSEN, Heinrich	26	Husum	54-1676
Wilhelmine 25			
HANSEN, W. (m)	21	Marolterode	52-1321
C.M. (f) 24			
HANSMANN, Amalie	24	Haeversen/Han	52-1423
HANSMANN, Jos.	19	Lendorf	48-1179
HANSMANN, Sophie	28	Atens	54-1371
HANSTEDT, Maria	44	Krautheim	50-0472
Carl 20, Aug. 15, Wilhelm 9, Amalie 20			
HANSTEIN, Daniel	20	Friedberg	52-0279
HANTELMANN, Rud. C	30	Bromberg	54-1078
HANTHSEN, Friedr.	25	Gerden	49-0574
HAPEL, Conrad	30	Borgholz	54-0600
HAPKE, Aug.	35	Michelau	54-1371
HAPP, Dorothea	20	Wiesenthal/Sa	53-0475
HAPP, Henry	32	Flieden/Hess.	48-0053
HAPPE, Wilhelm	32	Corbach	52-0095
Caroline 32, Hermine 4, Auguste 9m			
HAPPEL, Franz	36	Grossenglis	52-0775
Anna Martha 31, Catharina 13			
Elisabeth 10, Martha Elis. 5			
George Adam 9m			
HAPPEL, Heinrich	23	Fussen Erfurt	53-0942
HARBEKE, Conrad	22	Soessborn	52-0563
HARBENSTEIN, Fr. W	21	Mittelruessel	49-0737
HARBERS, Ann Marie	19	Stapelfeld	54-1371
HARBERS, John	20	Oldenburg/Old	48-0053
HARBIG, Georg	30	Wien	53-1070
HARDEN, Wilhelm	22	Magdeburg	54-0882
HARDER, Gustav	24	Celle	53-1062
HARDTEN, Heinr.	25	Beversfleth	52-1512
HARDTMANN, Peter	33	Ebern	48-0887
HARFF, Johann D.	35	Emden/Hann.	54-1092
Lisette 32, Agatha 5			
HARFNER, Sevilla	31	Hannover	50-1317
HARGMANN, Joh.	22	Spika Neufeld	49-0329
HARJES, Friedr.	64	Sebaldsbrueck	54-0987
HARJES, Friedr.	19	Bloklande	51-0326
HARJES, Gesche C.	26	Basdahl	53-0905
HARJES, John	25	Schwaben/Hann	51-0048
HARKE, Ch. (m)	26	Eschede	54-0918
HARKHOF, Fr. (m)	21	Nordhummen	52-1321
HARLING, Friedrich	30	Leisnitz	54-0930
HARMENING, Ernest	30	Hespe	51-1588
Christine 28			
HARMS, Carl	29	Mustadt	54-1341
Henrietta 37, Sophia 6, Dorretha 4			
child 10m, Dor. (m) 57			
HARMS, Claus	37	Misselwarden	54-0987
Anna 40, Anna 9, Lena 5, Maria by			
HARMS, Claus	18	Hanstadt/Hann	53-0475
HARMS, Claus	18	Heustaedt	53-0905
HARMS, Elise	19	Wanden	50-1067
HARMS, G. (m)	20	Hanstadt	48-0453
HARMS, Gretchen	22	Hanstedt	54-1371
HARMS, J.W. (m)	20	Oldenburg	50-0311
HARMS, Rebecca	17	Hannover	50-0311
HARMSEN, Anna	25	Langen	51-0756
HARN, Jacob	21	Dueren/Pr.	49-0365
HARNING, J.C.	37	Salzburg	54-1716

NAME	AGE	RESIDENCE	YR-LIST
HARPE, Meta	20	Lohne	52-1625
HARREL, G. (f)	25	Emstetten	49-0416
HARRER, Joseph	36	Wissing	51-1639
HARRISON, Thos. B.	37	New York	48-1015
HARS, Gust.	31	Braunschweig	50-1071
HARSCH, Johann	21	Mende	52-1580
HARSCHER, Georg	38	Braunsbach	54-1647
HARSTEIN, Friedr.	1	Dankersen	52-1321
HART, Emilie	21	Sachsen	53-0652
HARTEL, Friedrich	30	Muenchen/Bav.	50-0323
HARTGE, Heinrich	32	N.Y.	52-0563
Marie 15			
HARTHAHN, Barbara	19	Weisenbrun/Bv	53-0628
HARTHAN, Catherine	38	Hoff	51-1588
Eliza 15, Wm. 14, Alfred 13, Lousia 4			
Friederike 11m			
HARTHRING, Anna	20	Obermoellrich	50-0472
HARTIG, Charlotte	23	Jesphale/Hann	50-0323
HARTIG, Philippine	18	Meinsen	52-1321
HARTING, Heinr.	19	Berk a.M.	54-1575
HARTING, Heinrich	53	Wende	52-1464
Anna 53, Amalia 23, baby 5m			
Wilhelmine 21, Zohrina 19, Carl 17			
Louis 6, Heinr. 2			
HARTING, Heinrich	19	Berk	54-1575
HARTING, Jacob	45	Dermbath	51-1588
Henry 23, Elizabeth 21, Eliza 15, Wm. 8			
Friedrich 12, Lisa 5			
HARTINGS, Engel	23	Meinsen	51-1588
HARTJE, F. (m)	26	Mommingen	54-1341
HARTJE, Friedrich	34	Mooringen	48-0260
Lotte 24			
HARTJE, Wilhelmine	6	Bremen	48-1243
HARTKE, Johann	28	Untzen	54-0872
Anna 28, Margarethe by			
HARTKEMEYER, Chr.	17	Waldenhorst	54-0987
HARTKOPF, Anna	25	Henndorf	50-1317
HARTLING, Elise	25	Uslar	54-1297
HARTMAN, Casp. Jos	21	Eiterfeld/Hes	51-1532
HARTMANN, Adam	24	Bockendorf	54-1716
HARTMANN, Anna	30	Heinhoff	51-1639
HARTMANN, August	26	Tauschem	54-0850
Emilie 21, Ludwig by			
HARTMANN, August	18	Westphalen	54-1554
HARTMANN, Balt.	39	Pfaffenhausen	52-0563
Catharine 28, daughter bob			
HARTMANN, Bernd	23	Balen	49-0324
HARTMANN, Carl	28	Riga	54-1649
HARTMANN, Charles	55	U.S.	51-1588
Chas. 23			
HARTMANN, Charles	23	Hemfurt	50-0840
Catharine 21, Friederike 18, Diana 17			
HARTMANN, Chr'tine	24	Melle	51-0500
HARTMANN, Claus	18	Brameln	50-0366
HARTMANN, Fr'drike	24	Eisenach	53-0942
HARTMANN, Friedr.	27	Makensen	50-0292
Caroline 22			
HARTMANN, Friedr.	55	Altenrode	48-1179
Christiane 54, Wilhelmine 24, Johanne 18			
Friedrich 14			
HARTMANN, Georg	26	Oberquembach	53-1000
HARTMANN, Heinrich	26	Lippe	52-1362
HARTMANN, Heinrich	23	Coburg	53-0267
HARTMANN, Heinrich	32	Neustadt	54-1297
HARTMANN, Heinrich	30	Altenrode	48-1179
Louise 27, Louise 5, Wilhelmine by			
HARTMANN, Joh Hein	31	Bielefeld	48-1355
HARTMANN, Joh.	42	Hohengandel	54-1282
Regina 36, Cath 11, Elisabeth 9, baby			
HARTMANN, Joh.	20	Rinzenberg	50-0439
HARTMANN, Joh.	38	Coburg	51-0405
Marg. 21, William 12m			
HARTMANN, Johann	37	Unterelldorf	50-0379
Margarethe 35			
HARTMANN, John	21	Dalheim	49-1106
Charlotte 28, Minna 2			
HARTMANN, Joseph	32	Hindelang	53-0492
HARTMANN, Jurgen	17	Brameln	50-0366

NAME	AGE	RESIDENCE	YR-LIST
HARTMANN, Justus	23	Wabhershausen	54-0930
HARTMANN, Ludwig	27	Muckefeld	51-1455
HARTMANN, Mahle	25	Manrode	54-1168
HARTMANN, Margaret	18	Lissmuehle	51-0517
HARTMANN, Michael	50	Erfurt/Pr.	53-0475
Marie 33, Wilhelmine 11, Carl 9, Louise 7			
Clementine 4, son 6m			
HARTMANN, Michael	23	Waldsachsen	51-0405
HARTMANN, Peter	18	Mannheim	53-0991
HARTMANN, Philip	18	Darmstadt	53-0991
HARTMANN, Philipp	19	Oberquembach	54-1078
HARTMANN, Regina	21	Geisdorf	48-1179
HARTMANN, Robert	23	Coburg	53-0928
HARTMANN, Thomas	30	Erlangen	53-1023
HARTMANN, Wilh.	25	Wiesbaden	54-1566
HARTMANN, William	44	Radegast	53-0914
HARTMEYER, Carolne	30	Gr. Cottmar	54-1575
HARTONG, Georg H.	30	Brake	51-1084
HARTUNG, Christ.	25	Lobenstein	49-0383
HARTUNG, Christoph	34	Gumbelstadt	52-0563
Martha 27, Adam 7, Elisab(died) 6m			
HARTUNG, Clara	18	Lengsfeld	51-1455
HARTUNG, Franz	-0	Lutter/Bav.	50-0323
HARTUNG, Friedrich	28	Lobenstein/Re	52-0960
HARTUNG, Peter	28	Rotenburg	54-1649
Christine 30			
HARTUNG, Zacharias	20	Aldershausen	52-1321
HARTUNG, Zacharias	25	Loden	53-1062
HARTWIG, Adolph	15	Ehrdriessen	53-0888
HARTWIG, E. (f)	23	Abeshausen	51-0517
HARTWIG, Franz	23	Potsdam/Pr.	53-0628
HARTWIG, Friedrich	18	Hornburg	53-0991
HARTWIG, Heinrich	17	Niedernebuch	54-0930
HARTWIG, Joh.	29	Niederaula	51-1084
HARTWIG, John	58	Ehrdrissen	53-0888
Blondine 53, daughter 18			
HARTWIG, John H.	43	Leipzig	48-0406
HARTWIG, Ludwig	21	Harste/Hann.	54-0965
HARTWIG, Ulrich	30	Lippe-Detmold	52-1512
Francisca 24			
HARTWIG, Victoria	27	Ellwangen	53-0991
HASE, Carl Christ.	28	Hopfgarten	54-0987
HASE, Heinr. Aug.	24	Luegde	50-0292
HASE, Heinrich	34	Hannoverschen	52-1432
Anna 36			
HASE, Heinrich	53	Hagen	54-1443
Sophie 55, Sophie 24, Eliese 18			
Wilhelmine 15, Caroline 13			
HASEITS, Eberhard	36	Eppach	47-0828
HASELBAUER, Johann	46	Ingolstadt	54-1649
Barbara 43			
HASEMOLEVEN, J.J.	40	Remscheid	53-0888
Eduard 20			
HASENBUSCH, Bened.	44	Bavaria	53-0628
HASENBUSCH, Lazar.	21	Kurhessen	53-0628
Jette 46			
HASENFRAZ, Maria	20	Grafenhausen	52-1105
HASENJEGER, Anna S	20	Beckersdorf	47-0672
HASENMEYER, Wilh.	18	Wolbrechtshau	50-0366
HASHAGEN, Johann	18	Hagen	52-0048
HASKAMP, Bernhard	57	Wippingen	54-1371
Anna 50, Gesine 20, Marie 17			
J. Heinrich 14, Thekla 9			
HASKO, M.P. (m)	32	Vienna	48-1243
Anna 30, Julius 6, Albert 3m			
HASLEVER, Heinrich	33	Osnabrueck	54-1717
HASS, August	24	Hochstedt	51-0756
Kunigunde 14, Maria 13			
HASS, Maria	13	Bromberg	51-0756
HASSEL, Conrad	20	Baiern	52-0895
HASSELBACH, Aug.	26	Caasen	54-0872
HASSELHUHN, Carl J	19	Altenburg	48-1355
HASSELKUS, Franz	19	Lennep	54-0930
Wilhelm 18			
HASSELMANN, Ehler	32	Hoya	50-1132
HASSELMANN, Heinr.	28	Baiern	52-1362
HASSENAU, Annanias	29	Mues/Hess.	50-0323
HASSENPFLUG, Diedr	25	Kirchheim	52-1661

NAME	AGE	RESIDENCE	YR-LIST
HASSENPFLUG, Joh.	19	Kirchheim	53-1070
HASSENPFLUG, John		Herbach/Darms	50-0323
HASSFELD, Sophia	18	Lenabach	51-1739
HASSFUDER, M.	29	Humrechtshaus	54-1283
HASSMANN, Wilh.	22	Holzminden	50-0439
HASSOLDT, Lewis	34	Gunzenhausen	53-1164
HASTEDT, Rebecca	23	Nartum	49-0574
HATN, J.C. (m)	21	Miehlhausen	54-1341
HATTENDORF, Friedr	19	Thedinghausen	47-0828
HATTENDORF, H. (m)	25	Weirlen	52-1321
HATTENDORF, Johann	20	Riepen	50-1132
HATTENDORF, Martin	20	Scheie	52-1321
HATTERSCHEIDT, Pet	67	Rambrucken	54-1371
Christine 63			
HATZMANN, Fritz	17	Holzappel	54-1371
HAU, Hermann	18	Ant Hagen	51-1686
HAU, Nicolaus	19	Culmbach	50-0840
Anna 25			
HAUBACH, Catharina	50	Giessen	53-1062
HAUBKE, Friedr. J.	21	Spieka/Hann.	51-1796
HAUCHMANN, Emil	14	Willmers/Bav.	53-0628
HAUCK, Carl	52	Erfurt	52-1200
Auguste 23, Christine 21, August 19			
Eduard 12			
HAUCK, Georg	22	Prichsenstadt	48-1131
HAUCK, Wenzel	24	Prag	54-1591
HAUEISEN, Chr.	25	Gelnhausen	52-1580
Barbara 28, Wilhelmine 9m			
HAUEISEN, Emilie	18	Bavaria	50-0311
HAUER, Christian	20	Ziegenhein	54-1566
HAUER, Dorothea	28	Maulbach	53-0905
HAUERKAMP, J. Hein	21	Riemsloh	54-1443
HAUF, Barbara	33	Schallhausen	48-0951
Leonard 12			
HAUF, John George	33	Erfurt	53-0991
HAUFE, Carl Gottfr	46	Adelsbach	53-1062
Maria 48, Johanne 26			
HAUFFE, F.	50	New York	53-0161
HAUG, Friedrich	30	Notzingen/Wue	52-0351
HAUG, Gottlieb	21	Ostdorf	54-1168
HAUGELS, Fina	18	Anhelo	49-0329
HAULE, Jacob	20	Goeningen	53-1070
HAULICK, Friedrich	21	Hanau	53-0991
HAUMBAUM, Elis.	16	Lichtenfels	54-0872
HAUNROTH, Christ.	24	Springe	54-1554
Ernst 9, Christian 3			
HAUPH, Magdalena	42	Endringen	52-1580
HAUPT, Christine		Tiefenort	53-0942
HAUPT, Joh. Georg	24	Heeritsch	49-0352
HAUPT, Johann	30	Itzing/Bav.	54-1092
HAUPT, Johanna	30	Hanover	53-0905
HAUPT, Sophie	48	Santztenhagen	48-1131
HAUS, Carl	29	Austria	53-0628
Charlotte 22			
HAUS, Charlotte	22	Kurhessen	53-0628
HAUS, Elisabeth	52	Neukirchen	52-1105
HAUS, Friedrich	22	Wunsiedel	54-1371
HAUSCH, Alfred	17	Kammersberg	53-0628
HAUSCH, Carolina	19	Bakenau	49-0345
HAUSCHILD, Carl F.	26	Gesau	48-0445
HAUSCHILD, Hermann	15	Zeven	54-0918
HAUSCHILD, Trine	20	Hoplingen	54-0918
HAUSCHILDT, Justne	53	Schmolln	53-0914
HAUSE, Wilhelm	33	Herzberg	52-1148
HAUSEN, v. Heinr.	23	Weilmuenster	54-0600
HAUSER, F. (m)	32	Berkheim	49-0329
Josephin 23			
HAUSER, Georg	28	Tyrol	47-0828
Franz 25			
HAUSER, Max	29	Sachsen	53-0585
HAUSHMANN, Emil	14	Willmers/Bav.	53-0628
HAUSING, Sophia	23	Letell	52-1321
HAUSKNECHT, Ursula	27	Bayern	48-1209
Elizabeth 60			
HAUSMANN, Edmund	9	Mitteleschenb	50-0840
Therese 2			
HAUSMANN, Fr'drike	28	Hachingen	54-1168
HAUSMANN, Georg	26	Freyerdorf	51-1639

NAME	AGE	RESIDENCE	YR-LIST
HAUSMANN, Joh.	18	Bayern	53-1013
HAUSMANN, Josephin	26	Grevenbroich	53-1013
Ed. 6			
HAUSMANN, Martin	32	Berka a Werra	52-0370
HAUSSEN, Ferdinand	21	Marolterode	52-1321
HAUSSLER, Eduard	22	Georgstadt	54-1297
HAUSTAEDTER, J.	25	Erltrug	49-0329
HAUTMANN, Maria	25	Fichtelberg	54-0903
Adam 33, Franzisca 31, Johann 6			
HAVENSTEIN, Casp.	44	Bettenhausen	54-0918
Anna Marg. 44, Susanna 33, Johannes 13			
Caspar Eman. 9			
HAVERGAU, Friedr.	25	Grupenhagen/H	53-0628
Louise 22			
HAVERKAMP, Fr.	30	Harne	54-1470
HAXELROTE, Lewis	26	Hannover	54-1168
HAY, Lt. Col. Chas	39	Gt.Britian	48-1015
Ella 35, Ella 5, Charles 3, Blanche 1			
HEBEG, Anna M.	23	Weideroda	54-0600
Anna Cath. 20			
HEBEL, Heinrich	28	Bebra	51-0352
HEBEL, Magdalene	30	Lochum	52-1580
Elisabeth 3			
HEBELER, Carl Hein	24	Schledehausen	50-0292
HEBELER, Johann	25	Heeringen	48-0284
HEBENER, Martin	60	Crumbach/Bav.	48-0053
Elisabeth 55, Joachim 15			
HEBERER, Christine	23	Bremen	54-1566
HEBERLE, Hugo	50	Oberndorf	53-0492
Rosine 46, Franziska 20, Caroline 17			
Genovefa 16, Josepha 11, Jos. 9			
HEBERLEIN, Johann	16	Ermreuth	52-0693
HEBERLEIN, Julius	16	Gunzenhausen	54-1092
HEBESTEIN, Madg.	19	Ermreuth	52-0693
HECHEL, Margaretha	22	Rockenhof	52-1105
HECHMANN, Gottfr.	50	Langenlaube	54-0930
Johanna Chr. 48, Ernestine 23			
Johanna Chr. 21, Auguste 19, Emilie 18			
Emma 7, Friedrich W. 1			
HECHT, Friedrich	29	Zerbst	54-1649
Amalie 24			
HECHT, Joseph	24	Giebram	49-0324
HECHT, Josephus	27	Fromberg	53-0582
Marie 23, Josephus 2			
HECHT, Mathilde	22	Nordheim/Bav.	53-0628
HECK, Catharine	24	Niederurf	53-0942
HECK, J. (m)	25	Gladenbach	49-0383
HECK, Joh.	17	Lauterbach	49-0742
HECK, Johannes	21	Lauterbach	51-0352
HECKEL, David	34	Memmingen	47-0828
Margaretha 28, Maria 9, David 6			
Elisabeth 4, Margaretha 1			
HECKEL, Joh. Georg	28	Weilersdorf	49-0352
HECKEL, Therese	36	Spalt	50-0311
HECKEMANN, Ch.	16	Fodtenhausen	48-0565
HECKER, Afra	22	Schweinfurt	50-1317
Caroline 20			
HECKER, Anton	22	Wesuwe	49-0324
HECKER, Friedrich	22	Breslau	52-1580
HECKER, W.	27	Sommerzell	51-0517
HECKERS, Marie	27	Schlehausen/H	52-0960
HECKMANN, H. (m)	19	Ostrop	52-1512
HECKMANN, Heinr.	26	Gasdorf	51-0405
HECKSCHEER, Jette	24	Wallerstein	50-1071
HECTOR, Cathrine	24	Jever	50-1067
HEDBAWNI, Caspar	24	Kallalalitz	47-0672
HEDDERICH, George	21	Wiesbaden/Nas	48-0447
HEDDERICH, Wm.	24	Wiesbaden/Nas	48-0447
HEDDRICH, Elise	24	Landenhausen	54-0053
HEDELIG, Flor.	31	Forbach	53-0928
Ros. 26, Hort. 3			
HEDEMEYER, J.C.	20	Bremen	53-0161
HEDENRICH, Friedr.	40	Neustadt/Sach	52-1620
Wilhelmine 31, Louis 9, Therese 7, Ida 5			
Hermann 2, Oscar 3m			
HEDIG, Johann	27	Lobenstein	53-1000
HEDLER, Ernst.	30	Gera	52-0095
HEDRICH, Wilhelm	25	Sickendorf	53-0435

NAME	AGE	RESIDENCE	YR-LIST
Carol 25			
HEEDER, F.H.	23	Bremen	48-0112
HEEGEN, Carl	23	Berlin	51-0326
HEER, Lewis	19	Cassel	53-0991
HEEREN, Heinrich	27	Heise	52-1410
HEERWAGEN, Fr. Wm.	18	Stadtilm	48-0269
HEESCH, Heinr.	31	Brumstedt	54-0987
HEESTER, Johann	29	Lindach	54-0930
HEGELE, Casper	30	Almen	52-1580
HEGELEIN, C. (m)	32	Restenburg	50-0746
HEGEMANN, Cath.	22	Pramke	51-1686
HEGENER, Sophie	21	Rothenoven	54-0987
HEGER, Carl	36	Rothenoven	54-0987
Christiane 22, Carl 4, Jette 1, August			
HEGER, Carl Fried.	21	Linsen	49-0345
HEGER, Gottfried	40	Rothenoven	54-0987
Christiane 40, Christiane 22			
Gottfried 19, Johann 14, Marie 9			
Caroline 3			
HEGER, Wilhelmine	19	Bremen	51-1438
HEGNER, Johannes	27	Sachs.-Coburg	53-0628
Margaretha 20			
HEGWEIN, Christoph	65	Kitzingen	52-0807
HEGWEIN, Henriette	28	Mainstockheim	52-0807
HEHLMANN, Diedr.	18	Binden/Hann	52-0960
HEHMANN, Wilhelm	22	Hagen	52-0095
HEHNKEN, Johanna	22	Germany	54-1591
HEIB, Nic.	19	Hintersteinen	52-0370
HEIBACH, Chr.	23	Obersteinach	49-1358
HEIBERTSHAUSEN, J.	20	Staufenberg	54-1470
D. 16			
HEIBNER, Caroline	20	Ertuck	54-1341
HEICHENBAN, George	40	H------l	50-0944
John 30			
HEID, Amann	19	Ulmbach	54-1419
HEID, Cajus	27	Irendorf	49-0912
Ursula 34, Christian 6, Melchior 2			
HEID, Elise	45	Bleidenrod	54-0053
Heinrich 18			
HEIDE, Catharine	20	Deuz/Pr.	53-0475
Marie 16			
HEIDE, Friedrich	27	Radsick	53-0825
HEIDE, H.	58	Rassen	51-1160
HEIDE, Heinrich	22	Brehlohn	51-1686
HEIDE, Heinrich	25	Frendelburg	48-1184
HEIDEL, Joseph	40	Fahreisfuerze	53-0928
Catharine 38, John 8, Joseph 9			
HEIDEL, Sophie	18	Lindenau	54-0882
HEIDELBERG, Heinr.	26	Mausbach	54-1554
HEIDELBERG, Mary	34	New York	47-0158
Elisabeth 15, Adelaine 11, Georg 9			
Clarence 4			
HEIDEMANN, August	23	Cherte	54-1443
George 15			
HEIDEMANN, F.W.	26	Oberfalkenbec	48-0269
HEIDEMANN, J. Fr.	34	Ostkilver	54-1452
Anna Kath. 34, Anna Maria 4, Katharina 20			
Joh. Heinr. by			
HEIDEMANN, Joh. Fr	26	Rodenberg	47-0672
HEIDEMEIER, Chr'ne	33	Lemfoerde	51-0405
HEIDEMULLER, Heinr	22	Lamstedt	51-1639
HEIDENREICH, A.	24	Ulmbach	54-1419
HEIDENREICH, H.	22	Jena	53-0492
HEIDENREICH, Heinr	21	Schnablwein/B	53-0628
HEIDENREICH, Joh.	18	Suess	48-0269
HEIDENREICH, W.	27	N.Y.	53-0492
H. 22			
HEIDER, Barbara	49	Pyrbaum	54-0053
HEIDERICH, Aug.	20	Frankenstadt	49-0383
HEIDKAMP, G.	30	Duesdorf	54-1001
HEIDMANN, Reinhard	47	Affinghausen	51-1062
Marie 50, Adelheid 19			
HEIDOLF, Joh. G.	35	Nienburg	53-1013
Catharina 28, Elisabeth 4			
HEIDORN, C. (m)	29	Mordorf	54-1341
HEIDRICH, Maria	24	Paritz	54-1297
HEIDT, St.	26	Genteskirchen	51-0517
HEIDTMANN, Heinr.	21	Hastedt	48-0887

NAME	AGE	RESIDENCE	YR-LIST
HEIEREIS, Joh.	26	Neundorf	52-0693
HEIERT, Lorenz	17	Untersteinach	53-1062
HEIERTH, Margareth	28	Stammbach	54-1554
HEIFANG, Georg	27	Sonderbach	53-0838
HEIFERT, Friedrich	26	Woelpe	54-0987
HEIFMANN, Sophia	22	Stolzenau	54-1647
HEIGELE, Jacob	50	Hoehringen	53-0838
Mattaeus 17, Jacob 10, Philip 2, Marie 18			
Barbara 13, Rosina 18, Margaretha 7			
HEIGER, John	28	Telgte	54-1724
HEIGERT, Charlotte	27	Curhessen	52-1432
HEIKERS, Friedrich	23	Anruechte	51-1686
HEIL, August	19	Waler	54-1341
HEIL, F. (m)	21	Stuttgart	54-1341
HEIL, Joh. Ant.	9	Brenig	54-1297
HEIL, Johann	36	Ramrod	48-1131
HEIL, Marg.	56	Utrictshausen	52-0515
HEIL, Margaretha	22	Creuzlichtes	52-1101
HEILAND, Albert	19	Gandersheim	54-1094
HEILAND, C.C.	36	Buenkhausen	48-0565
HEILAND, Caroline	23	Giessen	53-1086
HEILBRAUN, Clara	14	Oberwald	49-0742
HEILE, Benedikt	28	Foltlage	51-1686
HEILER, Joseph	29	Mendl	52-1580
HEILIGENTAG, Carl	32	Helmstadt	50-0292
HEILKAMP, Joh. Geo	28	Puesselbuehre	48-0269
HEILMANN, Carl	30	Sulzheim	52-1200
Johann 24			
HEILMANN, Friedr.	24	Rinzenberg	50-0439
HEIM, Anton	27	Landshut	54-0903
HEIM, Bruno	28	Bischofsheim	52-1620
Valentin 22			
HEIM, Johann	38	Birgenlach	52-1464
HEIM, Joseph	52	Aschbach	52-1464
Anna M. 52, Johann 23, Georg 19, Cath. 16			
Anna M. 9			
HEIM, Louise	32	Erfurt	52-0095
HEIM, Math.	20	Hessia	51-0048
HEIM, Susanna	27	Regensfeld	54-1554
HEIMANN, Adam	42	Niegelhuden	52-0558
M. (f) 11, W. (f) 42, J. (m) 10			
HEIMANN, Joh Georg	20	Coburg	53-1013
HEIMANN, Sophie	24	Barmen	48-0565
HEIMBRECK, Ferd.	39	Remscheid	48-0565
HEIMBUECHER, Thim	33	Sulzbach	54-1297
HEIMBURG, F. (f)	21	Gotha/Sax.	52-1423
HEIMER, August	16	Altenburg	53-0942
HEIMERS, Georg	26	Aerzen	53-1000
Dorothea 26			
HEIMLE, Fidel	16	Reichenbach	54-1283
HEIMSATZ, J.A.	50	Hofgeismar	54-1566
Marie 44, Sabine 21, Wilhelm 14, Louis 9			
Fritz 8, Heinrich 6, August 4			
HEIMUND, Adam	42	Niegelhuden	52-0558
M. (f) 11, W. (f) 42, J. (m) 10			
HEIN, Andreas	29	Reichenbach	53-0320
HEIN, Carl	41	Holzappel	54-1371
Christine 39, Carl 60, Philippina 60			
HEIN, Chr.	59	Gotha	52-1661
HEIN, Christian	24	Schleusingen	52-1362
HEIN, Ed.	28	Muensterberg	54-1078
HEIN, Gottlieb	53	Loppe	54-0882
HEIN, H.	47	Neurode	54-1575
wife 46, Otto 21, Maria 7, Hugo 8, Ida 3			
HEIN, Heinr.	26	Benningsen	49-0574
HEIN, Marg.	57	Mansbach	53-1086
Gustavine 18			
HEIN, Meta	16	Rechtenfleth	50-0366
HEINBOEKEL, John	16	Selsing/Hann.	51-0048
HEINCKE, Jacob	27	Gieba	52-0807
Emilie Louis 25, Marie 1			
HEINDEL, Andrew	31	Eschenbach	48-0951
HEINDEL, Anton	42	Boxdorf/Bav.	53-0475
Rosine 20			
HEINDEL, Christoph	25	Sachsen	53-0585
Margarethe 23, Barbara by			
HEINDEL, Franzisca	46	Boxdorf/Bav.	53-0475
HEINDL, Bonifax	37	Arnsberg	52-1200

NAME	AGE	RESIDENCE	YR-LIST
HEINDORF, W.	31	Zellerfeld	49-1358
HEINE, Carl	26	Elberfeld	54-1168
HEINE, Carl	21	Guentersdorf	51-1062
HEINE, Charles	18	Varmissen	52-1304
HEINE, Charles	50	Andreasberg	54-1575
HEINE, Ferd.	28	Krebeck	50-0439
HEINE, Friedrich	24	Northeim	53-0582
HEINE, Joh. Heinr.	48	Delmenhorst	50-0021
Wilhelmine 38, August 16			
HEINE, Louis	42	Schildau	50-1071
HEINE, Louis	30	Lindenau	54-1371
Friederike 31, Auguste 5, Johann 3			
HEINEBERG, Adolph	26	Warburg	48-0101
HEINECKE, Franz	20	Altenburg/Sax	51-1725
HEINEKE, George	16	Bremen	50-0366
HEINEL, Jacob	22	Minden	52-1105
HEINEMAN, Josephne	28	Hannover	52-1620
HEINEMANN, Adam	18	Cronach	53-0825
HEINEMANN, Bertha	21	Muenden	53-0991
HEINEMANN, Char.	66	Duderstadt	51-1084
Christian 43, Wilhelmine 33, Catharine 41			
Elisabeth 26, Louise 13, Therese 11			
Caroline 9, Marie 7, Johannes 5			
Nikolaus 3			
HEINEMANN, Friedr.	35	Beuna	52-1512
HEINEMANN, Friedr.	28	Wernigerode	53-0557
HEINEMANN, Friedr.	28	Werningerode	53-0557
HEINEMANN, G. (m)	26	Oldenburg	48-0453
HEINEMANN, Gertrud	19	Wattenbach	52-1105
HEINEMANN, Heinr.	42	Gangerkisse	51-1796
Anna Cath. 37			
HEINEMANN, J. Casp	58	Angelhausen	52-1304
Charles 33			
HEINEMANN, Joh.	18	Offenbach	53-0590
HEINEMANN, Johann	24	Duderstadt	51-0500
HEINEMANN, Johanne	21	Hannover	50-1317
HEINEMANN, Joseph	22	Hannover	54-1371
HEINEMANN, Louise	28	Duderstadt	51-0500
HEINEMANN, Michel	21	Quentil	54-1554
Christian 31			
HEINEMANN, Theo.	31	Telgte	54-1724
HEINEN, Joh.	44	Schiffarth	54-1371
Catharine 57			
HEINER, Elizabeth	20	Alsfeld	51-1455
HEINER, G.	26	Mehmels	53-0582
HEINESKE, Austin	28	Leipzig	48-1209
HEININGER, Chr.	22	Neussen	48-0269
HEINKE, Aug.	24	Altenburg	50-1132
HEINL, Jacob	60	Neubau/Bav.	52-1423
Joseph 22, Andreas 13, Michael 28			
Therese 4, Johann 24			
HEINL, Johann	24	Koeglitz/Bav.	52-1423
HEINLEIN, Andreas	18	Dettendorf	52-0693
HEINLEIN, Elisab.	20	Eschenau	52-1105
HEINMUELLER, Wilh.	27	Treysa	50-0379
Babette 24			
HEINRICH, Andreas	55	Querfurt	53-1000
Leonore 26, Edmund 18			
HEINRICH, Caroline	21	Cur Hessen	53-0557
HEINRICH, Caroline	21	Kur-Hessen	53-0557
HEINRICH, Gregor	36	Oberwalting	47-0918
Maria 45, Johann 10, Maria 9, Gregor 6			
Catharina 5			
HEINRICH, Heinr.	28	Dettan/Bav.	52-0560
E.M. (f) 36, C. (m) 2			
HEINRICH, Herm.	54	Schleusingen	52-1512
Anna 50, Anna Maria 18, F.W.(m) 16			
Wilhelmine 14, Angelica 12, Anna 9			
Friedr. 5m			
HEINRICH, John	19	Kirchheim	53-0888
HEINRICH, Louis	35	Waldbroel	48-0053
HEINRICH, Ludwig	50	Nordhausen	49-1106
Friederike 47, Christian 20, Johanna 18			
HEINRICH, Oscar	27	Schmiedeberg	53-0991
HEINRICH, Valentin	27	Rauschenberg	52-1200
HEINRICK, Theod.	27	Beuthen	49-0781
Amalie 24, Anna 2			
HEINS, An.	18	Hoehen	49-0329
HEINS, Carolina	19	Wetschen	53-1062
HEINS, Diedrich	16	Drangstedt	50-0366
HEINS, Dorothea	18	Hoya	54-0987
HEINS, Hermann	15	Beverstedt	49-0345
HEINS, John H.	22	Hoplingen	54-0918
HEINSAAT, Carl	20	Hessen	52-0895
HEINSAAT, J.H. (m)	40	Hohenaverberg	49-0383
HEINSCHKOL, B. Fr.		Triptis	53-0942
HEINSOHN, Augustus	34	Bremervoerde	53-0991
Clementine 33, Sophie 4, Dorothy 2			
HEINSON, Anna	26	Bremervoerde	52-1580
HEINTSCHEL, Nicl.	32	Neustadt	53-0914
HEINTZE, Js.	28	Rudolstadt	48-0269
HEINZ, C. (f)	24	Gorga	50-0746
HEINZ, Heinrich	24	Stockhausen	54-0882
HEINZ, Margaretha	19	Ruppertenroth	51-1101
HEINZ, Martin	22	Hugenfeld	51-1245
HEINZAWEG, E. (f)	16	Lengerke	48-0445
HEINZE, Christian	20	Erfurt/Pr.	51-1725
HEINZE, Gustav	22	Prussia	50-0311
HEINZE, Otto	21	Priessnitz	50-0439
HEINZE, Wilhelm	31	Ziegenhain	51-1245
Luise 29, Catharine 6m			
HEINZERLING, Anna	53	Ringshausen	54-0930
Anna Maria 24, Heinrich 20, Heinrich 11			
Susanna 17			
HEINZMANN, Genov.	19	Behrenkirch	49-0345
Barbara 20			
HEIPEL, Wilhelm	52	Ibra	52-1580
Anna 51			
HEIPSTREUM, Friedr	21	N.Y.	52-1452
HEISE, Albert	20	Noerten	53-0991
HEISE, Carl	34	Nordheim	50-0439
HEISE, Friedrika	22	Duderstadt	51-1084
Fr. 55, Louise 40			
HEISE, Herm.	19	Schleusingen	52-1512
HEISE, Wilhelm	28	Wernigerode	53-0557
Caroline 34, Johanne 32, Friedrich 24			
HEISE, Wilhelm	35	Cassel	50-1236
HEISE, William	32	Monra	53-1164
HEISEN, Heinr.	24	Grossen---	50-0439
HEISENBERG, Dorett	47	Detmold/Lippe	50-0323
HEISENBUETTEL, Her	20	Osterholz	50-1317
HEISERLING, Ph.	26	Stiedenkopf	54-1470
HEISINGER, Fran'ka	19	Coburg	53-1013
HEISLER, Paulina	21	Berlin	54-1724
HEISS, Anna Maria	22	Altenhuedinge	54-1371
HEISSEL, Martin	23	Kirch. Tellin	52-0351
HEISSENSCHUETTEL,H	35	Brunshusen	53-0825
HEISSRENGEN, F.(m)	24	Wasserknoden	54-1341
HEISTER, Heinrich	30	Bonn	54-1371
Catharine 40, Marie 5, Margar. 3			
Ludwig 2, Peter 10m			
HEITEMEYER, Alex	24	Paderborn	51-0460
HEITERICH, Mary	33	Notzingen/Pr.	50-0323
Aloisius 8, Mary 3			
HEITMANN, Anne	24	Bederkesa	52-0048
HEITMANN, Elis.	21	Wittingshause	54-1716
HEITMANN, Gerd.	57	Affinghausen	47-0872
Hermann 22			
HEITMANN, Heinrich	26	Verden	49-0413
HEITMANN, Val.	22	Wernsdorf	53-0492
HELBIG, Simon	29	Steinbach	52-1105
Barbara 23, Elise 1, Ottilie 56			
HELD, Elis.	8	Guttenberg	52-0693
Johann 4, Anna (died) 2m			
HELD, Ernst	25	Halle	48-1355
HELD, Friedrich	28	Hatendorf	47-0672
HELD, Johann	16	Grafenberg/Bv	53-0628
HELD, Johanne Soph	63	Mensdorf	48-0887
HELD, L.	37	Staedten	47-0868
HELD, Martin	27	Guttenberg	52-0693
Elisabeth 29, Anna 23			
HELD, Paul	25	Breslau	50-1236
HELDMANN, Charlott	23	Severns	53-0942
HELENCATO, Jacob	36	Gemen	52-0804
Cathr. 5			
HELENKAMP, John H.	17	Schinkel	54-1470

NAME	AGE	RESIDENCE	YR-LIST
HELFER, Georg	24	Ellerbach	50-0439
HELFER, Heinrich	35	Leubingen/Pr.	54-0965
HELFERICK, Fr.	17	Netze	54-1575
HELFRICH, Casper	35	Dreschhoff	51-1455
HELFRICH, Philipp	22	Deidershausen	51-1455
HELGANG, Cord	23	Hattendorf	52-0563
HELGEMEYER, Christ	21	Maislingen	54-0930
HELL, F.A.	33	Stetten	53-0492
HELLER, Carl	25	Massow	50-1071
HELLER, G.	33	Pflugfeld	53-0582
HELLER, Georg	16	Schwarzenbach	53-0475
HELLER, Hermann	32	Minden	54-0850
HELLER, Jacob	58	Wuertenberg	53-0557
Euphina 58			
HELLER, Joh Franz	26	Welle/Hann.	51-1725
HELLER, Joh.	38	Reulbach	47-0918
HELLER, Joseph	20	Grossendorf	54-1566
HELLER, M. (m)	42	Schoenlind	54-1566
HELLER, Mathaeus	27	Emmingen	54-1371
HELLER, Moses	18	Breitzfeld	49-0742
Babette 17			
HELLERS, Henry	21	Oberod	53-0914
HELLFAIER, Joseph	30	Nauenburg	54-1168
HELLIG, Albert	32	Halberstadt	53-1164
HELLMANN, Chr.	41	Sachs.-Gotha	50-1236
Wilhelmine 35, Carl 7, Theodor 4, Marie 2			
HELLMANN, Henry	24	Guetersloh/Pr	49-0365
HELLMANN, Joh Hein	29	Ottersberg	52-1362
HELLMANN, Johanne	21	Hof	54-1554
HELLMANN, Lazarus	16	Reckendorf	53-0888
HELLMANN, Wilhelm	16	Holtorf	48-1209
HELLMENSTEIN, Joh.	45	Barmen	48-0565
Wilhelmine 43, Joh. 20, Wm. 17			
Friedr. 15, Friedricke 13, Lisette 11			
August 8, Wilhelm 6, Emilie 2			
HELLMER, Fr.	25	Steinbergen	52-1321
HELLMER, Heinr.	28	Oldendorf	50-0472
HELLMER, Nicolaus	35	Hannover	53-0628
Sophia 32, Heinrich 9, Fritz 5			
HELLMERS, Bernhard	41	Emsdetten	54-0903
Christine 33, Bernhard 3			
HELLMERS, Heinrich	30	Hennstedt	54-0965
Elisabeth 29, Carl 4			
HELLMERS, Joseph	25	Emsdetten	48-0260
Christine 28			
HELLMERS, Marie	29	Seine	51-0405
HELLMICH, Charles	30	Scheibe/Schwb	48-0053
Jane 30, Pauline 4, Otto 2			
HELLMUTH, Emil	22	Burghaslach	53-1000
HELLMUTH, Wilhelm	43	Oppin/Pr.	51-1532
HELLNER, Moritz	48	Dresden	51-1686
HELLNIG, A.C. (f)	18	Cassel	54-1341
HELLNING, Heinrich	18	Emsdetten	54-0903
HELLSTERN, Michael	30	Empfingen	52-0279
Reinhard 9, Agatha 28			
HELLVOGT, Ernst	28	Lichtenfels	54-1283
HELLWEGEN, Heinr.	32	New York	54-1078
Marie 28, Heinr Adolph 2, son 3m			
HELLWIG, Anna	21	Grossenglis	52-0775
HELLWIG, Heinr. W.	20	Zirzow	53-0905
HELLWIG, Jacob	30	Bremervoerde	51-1725
HELM, Carl Gottl.	29	Weissenfeld	54-1297
Johanne 29			
HELM, Georg Adam	33	Salzingen	53-0324
HELMBOLDT, Fr.	18	Celle	51-1455
HELMBROLD, Georg S	30	Melbeck	49-0737
Moriden 27			
HELMCKE, Neoldus	18	Pechshofen	53-0590
HELMERS, Mary	24	Vilsen	53-1164
HELMKE, Joh.	22	Liebenthal	54-1716
HELMKEN, Heinrich	23	Padingbuettel	54-1647
HELMKEN, Peter	21	Otterndorf	52-0699
HELMKEN, Wilhelm	43	Armelsen	53-0492
Henriette 41, Ad. 16, Heinrich 6m			
HELMOLD, Adolph	20	Hannover	53-1164
HELMOLD, Bruno	27	Bremen	53-1013
HELMS, Anna	18	Rothenburg	49-1358
HELMS, Joh. Albert	25	Sieke/Hann	52-0117

NAME	AGE	RESIDENCE	YR-LIST
Sophie 23			
HELMSTEDT, Chr.	25	NY	51-1245
HELMSTEDT, Georg	15	Neuenkirch/Ha	54-1092
HELMSTEDT, J Heinr	16	Neuenkirchen	49-0352
HELPERT, Johanna	33	Stadthagen	54-1078
HELPERT, Joseph	23	Mehmels	53-0914
HELT, Jacob	28	Wefersdorf	50-1071
Barbara 30, Catharina 25, Elisabeth 5			
HELTERMANN, Anton	20	Veldrow	53-0492
Fr. 26			
HELTHALER, Ruprect	30	Elenden	50-0944
HELTJER, Gustav	35	Peine	50-1132
HELWIG, J (m)	30	Bosserode	52-0558
E. 28, C. (m) 3			
HELWIG, Joh.	24	Homberg	51-0405
Elise 18			
HEMART, Johann	23	Fladungen	50-0472
HEMART, Ottilia	27	Seebach	50-0472
HEMBOLDH, Georg	18	Oberweyd	49-0781
HEMCKEL, Elisab.	21	Speckswinkel	50-0439
HEMEL, Mich.	28	Taubersbach	50-0439
HEMEYER, Christ.	29	Diepenau	52-0148
HEMHAUSER, Mich.	41	Westheim	47-0918
Marg. 33, Barbara 10, Sophia 4			
Kunigunde 1, Margarethe 22			
HEMKING, Ch.	35	Salzwedel	54-1591
HEMLEBEN, Wilhelm	30	Koenigsee	48-1184
Pauline 20			
HEMMANN, C. (m)	25	Doeppeln/Reus	52-0960
HEMMANN, Carl	22	Schaaben	53-0267
HEMMER, Angela	26	Wupeloh	54-1371
HEMMERLING, Friedr	31	Markeldorf	53-1023
Sophie 35, Catharine 5, Heinrich 3			
Anna 9m			
HEMPE, A.M. (m)	27	Apelhorn	49-0324
Helene 30			
HEMPEL, Louis	24	Dorna	54-0872
HEMPELMANN, Adam	21	Pyrmont	50-1071
HEMPFLING, Adam	39	Stockheim	50-0439
HEMPFLING, Chr'tne	22	Burggrub	53-0324
HEMPFLING, Johanne	17	Lobenstein	50-0311
Lina 13			
HEMPSATH, Heinrich	42	Hohenauffenbe	53-0838
Marie Theres 39, Joh Heinrich 9, Marie 7			
Diedrich 5, Catharine 2			
HEMPSATH, Margaret	51	Hohenaverberg	53-0838
HEMPSATH, Margaret	51	Hohenauffenbe	53-0838
HEMSBACH, v. Theo.	28	Eichstaedt	54-1443
HENCKE, Christ.	18	Buloehe	48-0284
HENCKEL, Wilhelm	34	Allendorf	53-1016
Eva 36, Margaretha 8, Peter 8, Adolph 7			
Josephine 6, Stephan 4			
HENCKEL, Anna	32	Mengshausen	53-1013
Maria 3			
HENCKEL, E. (f)	20	Arnsheim	51-0517
HENDEL, Carl Georg	22	Crimmitschau	53-1070
HENDEL, Franz	3-	Forchheim/Bav	49-0365
Eva 25, John Henry 4			
HENDLER, Carl	24	Muehlberg	48-1184
HENDRICH, Amalie	31	Meiningen	49-0574
Rosalie 10, Antonia 7, Ludwig 4			
Gotthard 2			
HENDRICK, Friedr.	24	Sangerhausen	49-1106
HENEG, William	25	Lutterbeck	54-1470
HENERUTZKY, Heinr.	28	Schildesche	54-1554
Friederike 27, Heinrich 2			
HENF, Elisabeth	34	Heidelberg	51-1245
HENGER, Isidor	28	Empfingen	52-0279
HENGERER, Louise	19	Weinsberg	49-0324
HENIES, Christian	49	Bledeln	54-1371
Dorothea 46, Heinrich 18, August 11			
HENIES, Christian	40	Bledeln	54-1371
Christiane 38, Sophia 14, Hermann 9			
August 2			
HENIGSTLER, Alex.	25	Roschitz	48-1131
HENIKA, Fr. Chr.	19	Wunsiedel	53-0888
HENJSSEN, Norman	23	Essen	48-1015
Friedrich 31			

NAME	AGE	RESIDENCE	YR-LIST
HENKE, Heinr.	62	Brackelsick	49-0781
Fritz 19, Friedrich 17			
HENKE, Lina	25	Loge	51-1160
HENKE, M.H. (f)	19	Sinne	50-0746
HENKEL, Anna	23	Mittelruessel	49-0737
HENKEL, Asmus	52	Curhessen	52-1432
HENKEL, August	16	Rennershausen	53-0585
HENKEL, Balthasar	39	Homberg	54-0053
HENKEL, Beatrix	17	Schwarzbach	53-0928
HENKEL, Cathrine	25	Baiern	52-0370
HENKEL, Christian	25	Apfelbach	47-0158
HENKEL, Joh.	29	Baiern	52-0370
Heinrich 20			
HENKEL, Johann	21	Bernstadt	52-0095
HENKEL, Klara	39	Unterbernhard	53-0928
HENKEL, Ludw.	24	Marburg	49-0383
HENKEL, Wilhelm	16	Wenigentaft	48-1131
Carl 20, Franz 14			
HENKELMANN, Andr.	26	Milz	54-1716
HENKELMANN, Carl	25	Fredilslohe	51-0405
HENKEN, Heinrich	16	Misselwarden	54-0987
HENKEN, Luster	18	Dingen	48-0951
HENKEN, Margaretha	23	Lueneberg	53-0473
HENKEN, Martin	19	Bederkesa	50-1071
HENKER, Karsten	36	Bremerhafen	52-0279
HENLEIN, C. (f)	19	Schopfloch	50-0746
B. (f) 17, H. (m) 4			
HENN, William	26	Bubenschlag	53-0914
HENNE, Johann	19	Ottenbach	49-0345
HENNEBERGER, A Mar	22	Augsfeld	51-0352
HENNEBERGER, Jos.	27	Unterhohewied	51-0352
Anna Maria 22			
HENNEL, C.W. (m)	18	Tambach	52-0558
HENNEMANN, Anton	23	Putrasch	49-0574
HENNER, Anton	59	Warburg	54-1649
Johannes 22, Therese 18			
HENNERS, Heinrich	21	Landforsta	49-1517
HENNETTE, Gerth.	40	Luebbecke	52-1321
Carl 2			
HENNETTE, Heinrich	18	Bennau	52-1321
HENNIES, Heinr.	28	Bakede	54-1297
HENNIG, Moritz	27	Geringswalde	54-1371
Emilie 23, Anna 6m			
HENNIG, Wilhelm	34	Hundelshausen	51-1438
Christine 36, Maria 12, Dorothea 10			
Georg 8, Margaret 6, Friedrich 3			
Margaret 3m			
HENNING, Dorothea	32	Berlin	54-1297
HENNING, Friedrich	21	Berka/Werra	52-1410
HENNING, Heinrich	28	Lengerich/Pr.	52-1432
HENNING, Johann	27	Radewitz/Bav.	53-0628
HENNING, John	40	Grebenau	54-1341
Elisabeth 35, Sophia 13, daughter 6m			
Mary 58			
HENNING, Wilh.	44	Oels	50-1071
HENNINGE, Friedr.	25	Schoenau	54-1554
HENNINGE, Rosine	25	Schoenau	54-1554
Emilie 3			
HENNINGS, Friedr.	24	Ostrieff/Sax.	50-0323
HENNRICO, Wil'mine	21	Burgstadt	52-1321
HENRICH, Christian	47	U.S.A.	53-0557
HENRICH, Christian	47	United States	53-0557
HENRICH, Peter	30	Preussen	53-0590
Marie 24, baby 6m, Marie 50, Heinrich 26			
HENRICHS, Ludwig	19	Wensen	52-1512
HENRICI, Gotth.	23	Bingstaedt	52-1321
HENRICIE, Hermann	16	Lunzenau	53-0825
HENRICKS, Aug.	62	New York	54-1371
HENSCH, Charles	27	Solingen	48-0406
HENSCHEL, Andreas	15	Botenburg/Hes	50-0323
HENSCHEL, Carl	39	Sachsen	51-1725
Barbara 44, Georg 12			
HENSEL, Adolph	29	Beuthen	49-0781
HENSEN, Bernard	35	Cincinnati	53-0888
HENTZSCHELL, Wilh.	32	Fellendorf	53-1164
HENZ, Johannes	15	Metzingen	54-1168
HENZE, Joseph	24	Grosseneder	50-0292
HENZEL, Christian	40	Bledeln	54-1371

NAME	AGE	RESIDENCE	YR-LIST
Christiane 38, Sophie 14, Hermann 9			
August 2			
HENZEL, Christian	49	Bledeln	54-1371
Dorothea 46, Heinrich 18, August 11			
HENZEL, Georg	74	Boenstadt/Hes	51-1725
HENZELMANN, Johann	30	Freudenstadt	53-1023
HEPP, Casper	25	Hofheim	52-1321
HEPPACH, Joh Fried	28	Norden	53-0991
HEPPE, Georg	17	Niedernebuch	54-0930
HEPPE, J.	40	Altenburg	52-1661
Justine 36, Hermann 16, Anna 13			
Friedrich 10, Richard 6, Anna Bertha 4			
HEPPLING, B. (m)	23	Unterkremmach	48-0447
HERALD, Adam	20	Ober Rodenbac	51-0352
HERB, Ludwig	50	Langenalp	53-0928
HERBENER, Carl	21	Sachsen	53-0590
HERBENER, Heinr.	28	Kuelstadt	54-0600
HERBENER, Valentin	33	Eppsdorf/Kurh	53-0628
HERBER, Margrete	20	Klesberg	54-1419
HERBERGER, Ottomar	22	Georgstadt	54-1297
HERBERT, Adam	67	Muehlheim	54-0987
Johann 36, Friedrich 34, Charlotte 32			
HERBERT, Albert	39	Bayern	53-0590
HERBERT, Barbara	23	Wilmeborg	52-1101
HERBERT, Carl Aug.	30	Sachsen	51-1686
HERBERT, Ernst	32	Neu Haslau	54-1078
HERBERT, J.A.	28	Fulda	51-0405
HERBERT, J.A. (m)	22	Kirchschuette	48-0445
HERBERT, Johanna	53	Longstein	53-1013
HERBERT, Josepha	30	Fulda	51-0405
HERBERT, Michel	29	Niederkuentig	53-0324
Ludwig 22			
HERBIG, Rudolph	28	Berlin	48-1243
HERBST, Chr. Henry	32	Hoya	53-0991
Anna Marg. 24			
HERBST, Georg	19	Hohenstadt	49-0574
HERCHENRODER, Joh.	26	Storndorf	48-1131
HERCHT, Theodor	24	Hamburg	53-0628
HERD, Martin	35	Rinderbeck	53-0435
HERDAS, John	36	Ebersbach/Bav	49-0365
Barbara 29			
HERDEGEN, Anne Mar	28	Cinsmansdorf	53-0582
Margretha L. 2, Jos. 30			
HERDEN, Henriette	22	Wald	48-0406
HERDER, Martha	30	Thueringen	52-0095
HERDERICH, Andrew	27	Ampferbach/Bv	48-0053
Ann Mary 17, Margaretha 25, John 30			
HERDFELDER, G. (m)	33	Schopfloch	50-0746
HERDT, Johann	21	Humerchhausen	50-0292
HERDT, Ludwig	28	Gladenbach	52-1304
HEREMER, Jacob	50	Rhina	54-1647
Elise 50			
HERENT, Johann	22	Fleckenstedt	54-1283
HERFORD, J.G.	18	Oberkaufungen	54-1566
HERFT, Mich.	30	Holzhausen	48-0447
HERFURTH, Gustav	33	Crimmitschau	51-1640
HERGENROEDER, Casp	20	Cur Hessen	53-0557
HERGENROEDER, Casp	20	Kur-Hessen	53-0557
HERGEREDER, Georg	23	Mauswinkel	53-1062
HERGERT, Heinrich	31	Dietershausen	51-1640
HERING, Johann	34	Berka	50-0379
HERING, Wilh.	26	Kleinern	54-1566
HERITSCH, Friedr.	28	Altenburg	52-1512
HERKHEIM, Fr'drike	19	Goppingen	54-1371
HERLE, C.	27	Arnsheim	51-0517
HERLE, Christine	17	Megscheidt	50-0366
HERLE, Justus	24	Mercheid/Hess	52-1620
Johann 19			
HERLEIN, Maria	28	Bayern	53-1013
HERLETT, Eva	31	Heustreu/Bav.	53-0628
HERLING, Catharine	25	Siegen/Pr.	53-0475
HERLING, Conrad	28	Reinershofen	53-1023
HERLING, Constant.	32	Kitscher	53-0991
Herm. 31			
HERMAIN, Stephen	37	Insingen	52-0515
Anna Barb. 36, Joh. Leonh. 12			
HERMAN, Christ.	27	Eckardsweiler	52-0515
HERMAN, Maria F.	20	Feuchtwangen	52-0515

NAME	AGE	RESIDENCE	YR-LIST
HERMANN, Amalie	21	Martinrode	53-0942
HERMANN, Carl	26	Herrenwies	53-0928
HERMANN, Eduard	50	Berlin	49-0742
T. (f) 27, B. (f) 18, J. (m) 21, C. (m) 9			
F. (m) 7, C. (m) 6, B. (m) 5, J. (m) 6m			
HERMANN, Elisabeth	25	Grumbach	54-1717
HERMANN, Fidelius	28	Neustadt	50-0292
HERMANN, Friedr.	48	Giessen	52-0895
Emil 19			
HERMANN, Georg	29	Windheim	52-0515
HERMANN, Henriette	16	Hainfate	54-0930
HERMANN, Hirsch	28	Berlin	54-1371
Johanne 54			
HERMANN, J.	27	Heinsfarth	53-1164
HERMANN, Jacob	19	Weinsdorf	50-0379
Susanna 18			
HERMANN, Lina	18	Horchfeld	52-0279
HERMANN, Lorenz	29	Oberflacht/Wu	51-1725
Sophie 26			
HERMANN, Margareth	46	Weisenbrun/Bv	53-0628
Margaretha 16			
HERMANN, Mathilde	31	Feuerbach	54-1443
HERMANN, Rudolph	41	Marburg	51-1725
HERMANN, Valentin	27	Reisnau	51-1455
HERMANN, Wilhelmne	24	Pr. Eylau	50-0840
HERMANNS, Marie	52	Tueringen	52-1432
HERMENING, Heinr.	43	Riepen	50-1132
Catharine 42, Anna 15, Engel Maria 12			
Dora 9, Heinr. 7, Hans Heinr. 4			
HERMS, Heinr.	27	Emsdetten	51-1455
Catherine 28			
HERMSDORF, Carl	42	Neu Schoenfel	49-0574
HERNWECK, Gottlieb	20	Unterturkheim	53-0320
HEROLD, Andreas	48	Birkenfeld	53-0628
Michael 17, Elisabeth 15			
HEROLD, Carl	25	Coburg	50-0439
HEROLD, Caspar	16	Wildenberg	51-1160
HEROLD, Georg	27	Eschweh	54-1282
HERP, Johann	19	Buechiz	51-1686
HERR, Elisabeth	23	Stunds	51-0500
HERR, Gottfried	43	Grauenstadt	54-1647
Margr. 45, Valentin 12, Margr. 9			
HERR, Joh. August	21	Walling/Hess.	52-0960
HERRICH, Louise	33	Lauchstedt	52-0699
Marie 3			
HERRIG, Heinrich	31	Minden	53-1023
HERRLEIN, Fr.	26	Weistaden	47-0762
Doris 24			
HERRLEIN, Georg	60	Fuerth	48-1355
HERRLICH, Victoria	23	Langenbiber/H	49-0365
HERRMANN, Aquale	34	Bernbach	50-1067
HERRMANN, Charles	25	Gr. Zerbsdorf	54-1470
HERRMANN, Christ.		Ravensburg/Wu	49-0365
HERRMANN, E. (f)	23	Alsfeld	54-1341
HERRMANN, Philipne	28	Oberscheld	52-0807
HERRMANN, Philipp	24	Niemburg	52-1410
HERRMANN, Wilhelm	33	Cassel/Hessen	51-1725
HERRMANSDORFER, J.	36	Fesselsdorf	52-0775
Elisabeth 35, Johann 13			
HERRWIG, Heinr.	32	Salzgitter/Ha	52-1332
Elisabeth 25			
HERSCHEL, Heinrich	32	Feuchtwangen	52-1362
Caroline 22			
HERSCHER, Wilh'mne	26	Wetzbach	53-0590
HERSCHNER, Johann	23	Michelbach	51-1686
HERSE, Joh.	25	Rahmstadt	49-0383
HERSTEIN, Meyer	57	Rennertehause	54-1371
Friederike 57, Bertha 20			
HERSTEN, Heinr.	18	Cassel	54-0987
HERTEL, Anton	28	Kleineichen	48-1184
HERTEL, Joh. Georg	31	Oberehrenbach	52-0693
Margarethe 27, Elisabeth 1			
Georg. Joh. 25			
HERTEL, Johann	-2	Kirchyleden	52-1464
HERTEL, Juls. Carl	60	Ordruff	53-0905
Franziska 40, Wilhelm 23, Marta 21			
Friedrich 19, Emilie 16, Lena 11			
Eduard 9, Emma 9m			

NAME	AGE	RESIDENCE	YR-LIST
HERTIG, Ed.	21	Weimar	51-1245
HERTING, Ludwig	30	Marktatafft	50-0379
Dorothea 26			
HERTINGER, Jacob	49	Asselfingen	54-1566
Catharine 50, Louise 14, Justine 19			
Margarethe 21, Carl Jacob 2			
HERTLE, Johann	54	Koenigsbrunn	52-1332
Margrethe 47			
HERTLEIN, Andreas	41	Marktsteft	52-0807
HERTLEIN, Andreas	37	Neuburg	51-1084
Marie 33, Georg 3			
HERTZBERG, v. Herm	30	Kiel	51-0652
HERUPY, Simon	17	Hukstitz	49-1106
Simon 26, Anna 26, Maria 5, Katharina 3			
HERWALD, Gottlieb	19	Schleiz	54-0882
HERWICH, J.	36		54-0987
Maria 21			
HERWIG, Adam	25	Churhessen	52-1620
HERWIG, Charles	56	Helmstadt	49-1517
HERWIG, Eduard	30	Goettingen	52-1625
HERWIG, Franz	27	Berlin	48-1243
HERWIG, Gertrude	28	Hersfeld	49-1358
HERWIG, Johann	37	Niedernbrich	54-0930
HERWIG, Joseph	23	Langenbieber	51-0500
HERZ, August	28	Egele	54-1282
Doris 27			
HERZ, Elise	22	Cothen	53-1086
HERZ, Jette	23	Fuerth	50-0840
HERZBERG, Bluemche	38	Anklam	53-0991
Taeubchen 16, Louisa 9, Aron 8, Maurice 6			
HERZBERG, Heinr.	26	Liebau	51-0460
HERZBERG, Joseph	18	Anklam	53-0991
HERZBERG, Moritz	22	Aerzen	52-0515
HERZELD, Casimir	27	Hilders	51-1438
Catharine 33, Catharine 6			
HERZELEIN, Joh.	34	Oberehrenbach	52-0693
Georg 27			
HERZER, Guenther	19	Willingen	52-1304
HERZER, Joh Gottfr	54	Langensalza	53-0324
Elisabeth 48, Heinrich 17			
Gottfr. Aug. 24, Apollonia 34, Wilhelm 2			
HERZER, v. Emilie	30	Baden Baden	53-0161
Hugo 7			
HERZING, Carl	20	Bavaria	50-0311
HERZNER, Richard	30	Plainfeld	53-1164
HERZOG, A. (m)	22	Ebersdorf	49-0383
HERZOG, Bertha	58	Tennstedt	53-0991
HERZOG, Catharine	24	Oberzelt	48-0887
Conrad 2			
HERZOG, Franz	35	Canton Aargau	51-1245
Rosine 43, Marie 8			
HERZOG, Friedr.	36	Elberfeld	48-0565
Chr. 30			
HERZOG, Heinr.	30	Sachsen	52-1512
Henrietta 23			
HERZOG, Johann	26	Freiburg	54-1452
HERZOG, Joseph	18	Reichenberg	53-0905
HERZOG, Mad. (f)	29	Hamm	49-1358
Reg. 5, Jette 2			
HERZOG, Margarethe	28	Rothwinden	54-1566
HERZOG, Maria	17	Schwarzenbach	53-0928
HERZOG, Rudolph	27	Berlin	54-1371
HERZOID, Andreas	31	Sachsen	53-0590
HESELER, Lisette	40	Hannover	54-0987
Theda 24, August 18, Ernst 17			
Caroline 17, Amalie 9, Wilhelmine 7			
Eduard 5, Louis by			
HESLER, Gottliebe	22	Mittelruessel	49-0737
HESPE, A.	21	Bueckeburg	53-0492
O. 16			
HESPE, Carl	24	Bueckeburg	48-1355
HESPE, E. (m)	28	Bremen	52-1625
HESPING, Ludowina	25	Heinstetten	54-0903
HESS, Anna Maria	25	Friedrichsdor	51-0384
Theresia 44, Helene 18, Josephine 11			
Mathilde 8, Rosine 47, Maria 19			
HESS, Conrad	20	Wallenrod/Hes	50-0323
HESS, Eva	27	Herlheim	52-1200

NAME	AGE	RESIDENCE	YR-LIST
HESS, Friedrich	29	Rittling/Bad.	52-0960
HESS, Georg	53	Leigestern	53-1000
Cath. 50, Adam 24, Georg 20			
HESS, Georg	64	Gruenberg	47-0840
Elisabeth 54, Otto 13, Caroline 11			
HESS, Jac.	27	Harsfeld	52-1321
HESS, Justus	47	Rothhelmshaus	47-0918
Elisab. 43, Jacob 14, Anna 10			
Christina 6, Carl 6m			
HESS, Kar. (m)	20	Lohrhaupten	47-0868
HESS, Lebrecht	30	Fischborn	51-1588
Louisa 28, Caroline 2			
HESS, M. (f)	38	Rienach	50-0746
HESS, Mar. (f)	25	Vaiha	47-0868
Dor. (f) 24, Chr. 15			
HESS, Maria	64	Darmstadt	50-1067
HESS, Mich.	17	Bunshausen	53-0582
HESS, Michael	34	Boppard	54-0850
HESS, Otto	27	Cassel	53-1013
Caroline 21			
HESS, Wilhelmine	28	Hersfeld	52-1321
Calengo (f) 10, Carl 6, Sophia 5			
Herm. 18, Adolph 15, August 11			
HESSBERG, Isaac	21	Schleusingen	53-0991
HESSBERG, Magnus	15	Burgpreppach	54-1297
Heinrich 18			
HESSBERG, Theresa	20	Burgpreppach	53-1164
HESSBERG, Therese	32	Schleusingen	53-0905
Regina 13, Clara 12, Liebmann 10			
Amalie 7, Theodor 5, Fanni by			
HESSE, A.	21	Bueckeburg	53-0492
O. 16			
HESSE, Carl	22	Schwarzburg	53-0473
HESSE, Charles A.	34	Gerbstedt	54-1470
Caroline 34, Mary 9, daughter 5			
Charles 3			
HESSE, Christian	19	Grossenglis	52-0775
HESSE, Elisabeth	17	Rennertshause	52-1105
HESSE, Ferdinand	25	Dachwig	54-1297
HESSE, Friederica	29	Stade	53-1164
HESSE, Georgine	24	Rossdorf	53-0492
HESSE, Heinr.	-2	Renertshausen	48-0565
Cath. Elise			
HESSE, Heinrich	19	Carlshafen	52-1304
HESSE, Joh. D.	28	Frankenberg	53-1016
Friederike 26			
HESSEDING, Joseph	31	Oldenburg	54-1716
HESSELBACH, August	23	Aula	52-1321
HESSELBACHER, Elis	32	Diedelsheim	51-0352
HESSELBEIN, Herman	32	Marburg	53-0590
HESSELE, Jacob	32	Hochberg	54-1716
HESSELMEYER, Joh R		Osnabrueck	54-1575
Auguste			
HESSELS, Louise	38	Minden	51-1160
HESSEN, Ed. Johane	22	Frankenhausen	49-1358
HESSEN, Philippine	19	Bilshausen	52-1625
HESSEN, Wilhelmine	23	Buchholz	52-1321
HESSERT, Nicolaus	38	Hochdorf	54-1371
Jos. Franz. 38			
HESSLER, Charles	27	Roesden	48-0406
Alwine 24, David 15			
HESSLER, Heinrich	45	Helba	51-1588
Catherine 42, Godfried 20, Anna 18			
Maria 16			
HESSLI, John	19	Glaus/Switz	52-1304
HESSLING, George	38	Elbingerode	52-1304
Luise 31, Adolph 7, Charlotte 3			
Auguste by			
HESSMANN, Joh.	24	Osnabrueck	50-0021
HETTER, Rosine	15	Duerrmenz	54-1168
HETTINGER, Carl	19	Gotha	54-1283
Theodor 18			
HETTMANN, C. (m)	35	Westen	54-1566
M. (m) 30			
HETTMANN, Henriett	22	Schildesche	54-1554
HETZEL, Peter	13	Ebera	54-1078
HETZLER, Maria	20	Sachsenberg	52-1105
Friederike 15, Carl 18			

NAME	AGE	RESIDENCE	YR-LIST
HETZMER, Chr.	23	Rothenburg	54-1283
HEUBACHER, Erhard	19	Mainsck	51-1455
HEUBNER, Heinrich	31	Drogen	54-0987
HEUER, Carl	23	Herford	48-1355
HEUER, Dit.	27	Schnepke/Hann	51-1796
HEUER, Ernst	14	Suhlingen	54-0987
HEUER, Friedr.	26	Eickhorst	54-0600
HEUER, Heinr. Fr'd	51	Rannetze	48-1131
Marie 33, Heinr. Fried 9, Heinr. Aug. 7			
HEUER, Heinrich	22	Mahner/Hann.	52-1332
HEUER, Heinrich	24	Minden	50-0366
HEUER, Hermann	22	Lorrum	54-0987
HEUER, Johanne	25	Kohlenfeldt	53-0492
HEUER, Jurgen Hein	54	Bannetze	48-1131
Lette 58, Heinrich 32, Sophie 28			
Marie 26			
HEUER, Sophie	23	Sulingen	53-1000
HEUER, Wilhelm	17	Schweringen	53-1000
HEUER, William	27	Watertown	54-1297
HEUERMANN, J.	24	Wiesenstein	54-1283
HEUKE, Wilhelm	19	Bielefeld	52-1321
HEUMANN, J.	38	Erfurt	53-0914
Caroline 19			
HEUMANN, Maria Ann	20	Gips/Bav.	53-0628
HEUMANN, Sophie	20	Peppinghausen	51-1588
HEUMEISTER, Elis.	20	Bavaria	53-0628
HEUSCHKIL, Julius	20	Triptis/Weim.	52-1620
HEUSE, Friedrich	29	Arnsberg	48-0565
Georg 34			
HEUSEN, Carl	14	Beverstedt	54-0903
HEUSER, C.H. (m)	17	Neustadt	49-0329
HEUSER, Heinr.	19	Bavaria	50-1317
HEUSER, Monika	19	Kurhessen	53-1000
HEUSER, Wilhelm	37	Frankenberg	53-0825
Elise 28, Charlotte 6, Hieronimus 3			
Carl 11m			
HEUSLER, John	39	Wuertt.	54-1724
Louise 33, Fred. 7, Rosine 3m			
HEUSSNER, Bernhard	17	Zella/Sachsen	54-0965
HEUTZENROEDER, Wm.	24	Altenstadt/He	52-0807
HEUZE, E. (m)	18	Bayreuth	48-1015
HEY, August	15	Spika Neufeld	49-0329
HEY, Friedrich	26	Schleusingen	53-0991
HEY, Jacob Ludw.	46	Kappeln	47-0872
HEYDE, Georg Mart.	22	Cuhnbach	48-1131
HEYDE, v.d. Chr.	24	Hannover	50-1317
HEYDER, Chr.	18	Beverstedt	53-1164
HEYDER, Franzisca	37	Waltersberg	50-0840
Barbara 45			
HEYDER, John	24	Nienburg	53-1164
HEYDER, Louise	55	Nuernberg	52-1105
Lina 20			
HEYDT, Caroline		Pyrmont	53-1016
HEYE, August	17	Minden/Pr.	53-0628
HEYE, Carl	25	Goslar	54-1591
HEYER, Friedr. Chr	28	Gottern	51-1455
HEYER, Friedrich	54	Hoya	54-1297
Sophie 54, Julie 24, Doris 14			
HEYER, Joseph	33	Neuoltmannsdo	53-0914
Caroline 30, Joseph 7			
HEYMANN, Abraham	31	Glueckstadt	54-1452
HEYMANN, Basel (f)	17	Poland	54-1591
Ernestine 16			
HEYMANN, M. (m)	15	Conruden	54-1341
HEYMANN, Rosalie	29	Hamburg	54-1452
HEYNE, Adolph	19	Berlin	53-0473
HEYNE, C. Robert	27	Gosslau	48-1015
HEYNER, Carl Gottl	50	Chemnitz	53-1023
Wilhelmine 37, Anna Chr. 58, Heinrich 19			
Carl Gust. 16, Amalie 13, Friedrich 7			
Robert 5, Anton 10, Nathan 7, Otto 3			
Amalie Ernst 30			
HEYNOLD, William	26	Hemersdorf	53-0914
HEYROTH, Albert	26	Moltmerschwen	48-1179
Herm. 24			
HEYSE, Friedrich	21	Hildburghause	52-1620
HEYUM, Salomon	16	Hechingen	50-0292
Ernst 21			

NAME	AGE	RESIDENCE	YR-LIST
HICK, Simon	31	Seufert	52-0370
Margarete 28, Rosa 9m			
HICKE, Henry	23	Rausse	53-0991
HIDDELDORF, G.(m)	32	Emsdetten	49-0416
HIEBEL, Bernhard	25	Althartzdorf	53-0928
HIEBER, Barbara	28	Ebnat	52-0515
HIEBER, John	28	Elchingen	52-0515
HIEBER, Joseph	25	Elchingen	52-0515
HIEBER, Louise	27	Bopfingen	54-0872
Carl 3			
HIEL, Maria	24	Minden	49-1517
HIERONIMUS, Heinr.	48	Guentersleben	51-1438
Caroline 42, Mathilde 21, Louise 19			
Wilhelmine 17, Ernestine 10, Friedrich 8			
Emil 6, Ernst 9m			
HILBERT, Cathrina	22	Schopback	51-1639
Carolina 4			
HILBERT, Johannes	19	Eiterfeld/Hes	51-1532
HILBERT, John	2-	Grossenbach	49-0365
HILD, Chr.	23	Ortenburg	50-1071
HILD, Friedrich	21	Mittelruessel	49-0737
William 20			
HILDEBRAND, Anton	24	Arensberg	52-0699
HILDEBRAND, August	23	Grootheim	54-1716
HILDEBRAND, Barb.	30	Hersfeld	53-1023
HILDEBRAND, Carl	40	Haevensen/Han	52-1423
Friederike 34, Wilhelm 7, Karoline 4			
Sophie 9m			
HILDEBRAND, Caspar	24	Herford	52-0895
HILDEBRAND, Eva	20	Haard	51-1438
Margaret 18			
HILDEBRAND, Georg	19	Kleinensee	52-1148
HILDEBRAND, Heinr.	25	Dorum	49-0329
Anna 20			
HILDEBRAND, J Andr	25	Binsendorf	50-1236
HILDEBRAND, Joh.	26	N.Y.	52-0895
HILDEBRAND, Ludwig	42	Deisel	50-0472
Anna 38, Heinr. 18, Friedr. 17, Theod. 14			
Philipp 11, Gottl. 9, A. Maria 4, Carl 4m			
HILDEBRAND, Marie	33	Deissel	54-0053
Marie 10, Amalie 7, Ludwig 5, Theodor 2			
HILDEBRAND, Mich.	24	Belingshausen	54-0053
HILDEBRANDT, A Cat	60	Saxony	50-0021
HILDEBRANDT, Carl	29	Volpriehausen	48-0053
HILDEBRANDT, Joh'a	24	Schoningen	47-0872
HILDEBRANDT, Jos.	22	Boehmenskirch	50-0840
HILDEBRANDT, Mart.	31	Berlin	54-1168
HILDEBRECHT, Heinr	24	Wohlbrechthau	48-0260
HILDEL, M. Salome	22	Furth	49-0352
HILDENSTEIN, Marg.	27	Heilgeisdorf	50-0379
HILFMANN, Heinrich	21	Leese	54-0882
HILKEMEYER, Chr'ne	19	Hoya	54-1297
HILL, Charles	58	Alsfeld	54-1341
Catherine 50, Henry 26			
HILL, Joh Gottlieb	26	Geisberg	53-0435
HILL, Joseph	27	Homes	52-0370
HILLBERG, C. (m)	35	Rethen	54-1566
HILLE, Georg	20	Osnabrueck	54-0850
HILLE, W.	24	Wagenfeld	54-1470
HILLE, Wilhelm	27	Erfurt	53-0557
HILLEBRANDT, Georg	3-	Rotenburg/Hes	50-0323
HILLECKE, Carl	29	Aschersleben	54-1649
Wilhelmine 26, Ida 2			
HILLEMANN, August	30	Langholtensen	53-1164
HILLENGER, Marg.	26	Hemau	49-0324
HILLER, Bertha	32	Chemnitz	53-0991
Fernandina 4			
HILLER, Gustav	24	Wuerzburg	54-1168
HILLER, Johann	28	Naundorf	54-0987
HILLER, Johann	24	Mistelfeld	48-0284
HILLERS, Margaret	24	Schledhausen	51-1588
HILLES, John M.	42	Gt. Britian	48-1015
Mrs. 39, John 7, Richard 6			
HILLGAERTNER, Ludw	19	Londorff	51-1160
Cath. 17			
HILLMANN, J.H.	30	Uenzen	51-1160
HILLMANN, L.W.O.	17	Vegesak	49-0352
HILLMANN, William	19	Windheim	50-0944

NAME	AGE	RESIDENCE	YR-LIST
HILLMEYER, Martin		Schermede	54-1575
HILLS, Heinr.	61	Alsfeld	51-1455
Heinr. 30			
HILMER, Carl	26	Barentrup	53-0928
HILNIERS, Justus	17	Cassel	54-1716
HILPERT, Carl	18	Grossenbach	54-1647
HILS, Johanne	45	Giesen	53-1000
Maria 18, Heinr. 15			
HILSBRECHT, Wilh.	23	Vollbrechshau	50-0439
Ed. 26			
HILSEBECHER, Carol	25	Goldberg	53-0324
HILSMANN, Heinr W.	28	Neuenkirchen	54-0987
Friedrich 17			
HIMBEER, Christian	29	Lobenstein	52-0895
HIMEL, Simon	45	Rosenhaus	52-0515
HIMLER, Christian	45	Kirchleis/Bav	52-1620
HIMMELMANN, An Cat	23	Oberneissen	54-1566
HIMMELMANN, Friedr	21	Hofgeismar	54-1566
HIMMELMANN, Marie	23	Frankenberg	54-0918
HIMMELMANN, Marie	20	Hannover	54-1724
HIMMELREICH, Doris	25	Bodenwerder	51-0405
HIMMER, Joseph	34	Roebersdorf	54-1554
HIMRICH, Margareth	31	Unter Rode	54-1716
HINCKE, Heinrich		Bederkesa	54-0987
HINDEL, Carl	37	Schoenegg	54-1283
HINDELAM, Alex.	34	Obersdorf/Bav	54-1092
HINDELANG, Xaver	24	Hausen	53-0492
HINDS, Carl	28	Ilserhaide	51-1588
HINERICHS, P.C.(m)	23	Duesseldorf	49-0416
HINGES, Amalie	20	Larstedt/Sax.	50-0323
HINIKA, Fr. Chr.	19	Wunsiedel	53-0888
HINKE, Alfred	18	Ebersdorf	49-0345
HINKE, Franz	23	Bese	49-0345
Alfred 18			
HINKE, Joh.	28	Grimmen	49-0383
HINKE, Laurence	29	Cuxhaven	53-1164
HINKEL, Casp.	43	Teckach	47-0918
Eva 45, Friedr. 18, Louise 14			
Christian 12			
HINKEL, Christian	18	Meiningen	52-1423
Ottilie 22, Amande 1			
HINKEL, Margaret	21	Wenings	51-1588
HINNE, Christian	2-	Magdeburg	49-0365
Louise 24, Louis 3, Gustavus 6m			
HINRICH, Christ.	28	Giesen	53-1000
Kaetchen 20			
HINRICH, Margareth	31	Unter Rode	54-1716
HINRICHS, Carl Rud	28	New York	54-0850
HINRICHS, Eberh.	26	Jever	54-0987
HINRICHS, J. (m)	23	Scharmbeck	48-0453
HINRICHS, Margaret	23	Varel	48-0887
HINRICHS, Oscar	16	Braunschweig	51-1160
HINSSLER, Johannes	18	Altensteig	49-0574
HINTEMIT, Friedr.	42	Schlesien	52-1620
HINTERER, Friedr.	25	Oberndorf	51-1739
HINTERER, Rosine	18	Welzheim	54-1566
HINTSCH, Otto	21	Coethen	51-1245
HINTZ, Georg	44	Kaltenburg	54-1283
HINTZE, Doris	22	Axstedt	50-1067
August 15			
HINTZE, Maria	60	Lueneburg	50-1071
Theresa 19, Helena 23			
HINZE, F. (m)	45	Burgdam	47-0104
HINZE, Georg	17	Axstedt	49-0329
HINZE, Marie	17		54-1716
HINZER, Ferdinand	38	Erfurt	54-1649
HINZLER, Johannes	26	Altensteig/Wu	52-0351
HINZMANN, J.B.	28	Westbevern	54-1078
Maria Anna 30			
HIOB, Friedrich	27	Meiningen	52-1423
Sophie 26, Elise 9m			
HIPMANN, Eleonora	26	Arlsberg	54-1282
HIPPMANN, Elenore	24	Arzberg	53-0557
HIRCHE, Ernest	28	Paritz	54-1297
HIRPEL, Conr.	20	Eichelsachsen	52-1321
HIRSCH, Adam	26	Eimelrode	53-1164
HIRSCH, Benjamin	38	Triest	53-0838
Regine			

NAME	AGE	RESIDENCE	YR-LIST
HIRSCH, David	16	Inseratlon	54-1283
HIRSCH, Friedrich	31	Minden	53-1023
HIRSCH, Jacob	20	Kuttinglat/Bo	53-0628
HIRSCH, Jonas	17	Kaiserlindach	53-0320
HIRSCH, Lorenz	32	Oettingen	49-1106
HIRSCH, Peter	22	Bavaria	50-0311
HIRSCHFELD, Eduard	26	Nordhausen	52-0095
Louise 28			
HIRSCHFELD, Marth.	26	Gotha	49-0574
HIRSCHHOLTZ, J.(m)	23	Schopfloch	50-0746
HIRSCHLEIN, Georg	32	Schweinbach	54-1078
Cath. 33, Marg. 4			
HIRSCHMANN, Friedr	40	Stuttgart	54-1078
HIRSCHMANN, Georg	22	Treuchtlingen	53-0888
HIRSCHMANN, M.	18	Treuchtlingen	51-1160
HIRT, Casp.	37	Gegenheim/Bav	51-1796
A.M. 37, A. Mag. 8, A. Mag. 8			
Joh. Friedr. 6, Joh. 4, Joh. Mart. 2			
HIRT, Joh. Friedr.	6	Wessendorf	51-1796
HIRTEL, Martin	29	Frankenthal	54-1371
Eleonore 25			
HIRTENSTEIN, John	21	Wurtenberg	54-1724
Henriette 27, John 2			
HIRTH, John George	19	Greglingen	52-1304
HIRTZEL, Minna	29	Berlin	54-1371
HISBERT, Wolfg.	22	Bavaria	51-0405
HISSLEITNER, Eva R	28	Bernau	52-0515
HISSLER, Friedr.	31	Mittelruessel	49-0737
HISTIN, Luis	24	Haissingen	51-1084
HITTEL, Mary	30	Liegnitz	53-1164
HITZ, Friedrich	24	Silkeroda	49-1106
HOBEDITZEN, A. Cat	68	Eberschuetz	51-0460
HOBLICH, Marc.	35	Wesloch	54-1282
HOBURG, Gottlieb	22	Marienhuette	50-0292
HOCH, Andreas	19	Burgstall	52-1661
HOCH, Theresia	39	Rottweil/Wuer	52-1620
HOCHREIN, Johann	15	Aslebach/Bav.	53-0628
HOCHRHEIN, Marg.	23	Aidhausen	47-0872
HOCHSTETTEN, Joh.	28	Betteweis	54-1554
HOCKEMEYER, Henry	24	Belm	51-1588
HOCKEN, Elise	21	Doruml	50-1317
HODAMM, Rosine	58	Steinburg	52-1148
HOEBEL, Johann	33	Naufraunhof	54-1554
HOEBELER, Anton	28	Zeller	53-1070
HOECHSTAEDER, Jona	23	Dechingen/Bav	48-0447
HOECK, Justus	26	Mischeid/Hess	52-1620
Elisabeth 23			
HOECKER, Heinrich	19	Filingen	53-1062
HOECKER, Herm. Ph.	24	Osterwede	49-0352
HOECKER, Wilh'mine	23	Melle	54-1297
HOEFER, August	29	Buchholz	54-1566
Therese 29, Theodor by			
HOEFER, Bernh.	25	Wustenhorn	50-0439
HOEFER, Friedrich	22	Mengsdorf/Bav	52-0960
A. Marg. 21			
HOEFER, Georg	30	Roetha	53-0267
HOEFER, Henry	20	Geroldsgruen	53-1164
HOEFER, Jac.	19	Cassel	49-1358
HOEFFNER, Barbara	23	Mainz	52-0807
HOEFLICH, Heinrich	36	Uffenheim	54-0903
HOEFLING, August	68	Meiningen	52-0699
HOEFLING, Eberh.	45	Baiern	54-1724
Marg. 41, Leonh. 15, Elisa 4			
HOEFLING, G.(died)		Wuerzburg	49-0324
HOEFT, Martin	27	Hannover	53-0590
Anna 24			
HOEGEN, Gustav	25	Berlin	53-0590
HOEGER, Heinrich	23	Detmold	52-1580
HOEHL, Hermann	19	Frankenberg	53-1016
HOEHN, Albert	25	Coburg	53-0320
Barbara 25, Auguste 3			
HOEHN, Erhard	32	Bruenn	53-0905
Margareth 23			
HOEHN, Wilhelmine	25	Waldeck	53-0585
Johannes 40, August 5, Johanne 2			
HOEHNE, Chr.	25	Mehlen	53-0492
HOEHNE, Elisab.	29	Gosfeld	50-1236
HOEHNE, Fr.	25	Frankenhausen	49-1358

NAME	AGE	RESIDENCE	YR-LIST
Emilie 20			
HOEHNER, Heinr.	16	Schildesche	54-1554
HOEHSTER, Fanny	18	Angenrod	54-1341
HOEING, Elisabeth	60	Gosfeld	50-1236
Alexand. 22, Franziska 27, Georg 15			
HOELLANDER, Emil	24	Breslau	54-1092
HOELSCHER, David	27	Wellingholzha	51-0352
Anna Elise 25			
HOELTER, Carl	33	Eickhorst	54-0600
Caroline 33, Caroline 9, Chr. Friedr. 5			
Chr. Friedr. 9m			
HOELTER, Carl Hein	31	Eikhorst	51-0352
HOELTER, Caroline	22	Riesigheim	54-1566
HOELTER, Ferd.	24	New York	54-1566
HOELTING, Stephan	32	Paderborn/Pr.	51-0048
HOELTJE, William	25	Kl.Berkel	52-1304
Luise 23			
HOELTJER, Carl	26	Minden	53-0473
HOELTMANN, C. (m)	31	Remscheid	49-0416
HOELZ, Georg	27	Prussia	54-1724
HOELZINGEN, Wilh.	23	Budingen	49-1106
HOEMER, Barbara	40	Steinfeld	51-1639
HOENE, Wilhelm	19	Osnabrueck	54-0850
HOENECKE, Herm.	17	Woelpe	54-0987
HOENIG, Anna M.	42	Ferdinandsdor	51-0384
Johann 21, Maria 13, Otto 4			
HOENIG, Simon	26	Waldkatzenbac	51-0384
HOENLE, Afra	32	Geissling	54-0903
HOEPER, Heinrich	26	Borstel	54-1443
HOEPHEL, Christine	30	Obernrieth	47-0868
Els. 26, (m) 23			
HOEPKE, Friedrich	42	Qinten	50-0840
HOEPKEN, Joh Heinr	25	Rothenkirchen	53-0991
HOEPP, Maria	21	Weissenstadt	52-0279
HOERATH, John	30	Stein	54-1341
Catharine 22			
HOEREN, Heere	21	Otum	54-1078
HOERHARD, Wilhelm	20	Crimmitschau	54-0987
HOERIG, Magdalena	29	Eiterhagen	54-1554
HOERLESBERGER, Frz	35	Wien	53-0905
HOERMANN, Louise	20	Stuttgart	54-1078
HOERSEMANN, Jost	22	Buer	54-1371
HOERSTING, Bernh.	43	Emsdetten	53-1062
Gertrud 6, Franciska 3, Gerhard 11m			
HOERTER, Dorathea	32	Hamm	52-0279
HOERTING, Joh Gott	27	Naundorf	49-1358
HOESEL, Charles	30	Chemnitz	53-0991
HOESER, Ludwig	34	Kirchenlaibac	52-1332
Anna Marie 28, Barbara 6, Baptist 4			
HOESSELER, J.C.	26	Doebetschen	52-1321
HOESSLER, Chr. G.	36	Glauchau	49-0383
Therese 36			
HOEVE, Anna	20	Brinkum	51-1101
HOEVELMANN, Georg	39	Elberfeld	48-0565
Henriette 39			
HOF, August	26	Flammersbach	52-0807
HOF, Jacob	23	Hersfeld	51-0405
HOF, Landslien	36	Kippenheim/Bd	52-0351
Caroline 24			
HOFBAUER, Mathias	23	Falkenfels	54-0053
HOFEDANK, P.W.	27	Muehlhausen	54-1724
HOFELITZ, Maria	20	Sieler	54-1554
HOFER, Marg. Barb.	14	Gunzenhausen	54-1371
Lisette Dor. 21			
HOFER, William H.	20	Mittelruessel	49-0737
HOFF, Carl W.L.	26	Bremen	54-1092
HOFF, Caroline	22	Meinsen	52-1321
HOFFA, Mich.	30	Cassel	49-0742
HOFFA, Rebecca	17	Cassel	50-0840
HOFFELD, Johanna	48	Bunde	54-0930
Louise 15, Hermine 10, Auguste 6			
HOFFERSCHMIDT, Cl.	24	Zeil	52-1321
HOFFMAN, Andrew	23	Mittelruessel	49-0737
Henr. 32			
HOFFMAN, Carl		Lichtenfels	48-1131
Marie , August 4			
HOFFMAN, John G.	46	Breitenau	52-0515
Anna B. 43, Maria 18, Joh. G. 13			

NAME	AGE	RESIDENCE	YR-LIST
Joh. Friedr. 11, Joh. Adam 8			
Ann Margaret 3			
HOFFMAN, Julius	16	Bederkesa	48-1015
HOFFMANN, (m)	27	Hennersdorf	54-1371
HOFFMANN, Andreas	46	Niederschelds	53-1016
Catharina 42, Catharina 19, Elisabeth 15			
Louise 9, Heinrich 7, Henriette 9m			
HOFFMANN, Anna	24	Bayern	53-0590
HOFFMANN, August	14	Tueringen	52-1432
HOFFMANN, Auguste	26	Breslau	54-1168
HOFFMANN, Barbara	24	Folt/Bav.	52-0351
HOFFMANN, Barbara	16	Bavaria	50-1317
HOFFMANN, Bernhard	48	Follmersdorf	51-0384
Margaretha 50, Margaretha 23			
Catharina 21, Julianna 19, Heinrich 16			
Georg 16, Johann 14, Reinhard 11			
Babette 6			
HOFFMANN, Carl	30	Leipzig	48-0260
HOFFMANN, Caroline	20	Marisfeld	48-1131
Meyer Sam. 17			
HOFFMANN, Cathrine	40	Follmersdorf	51-0384
Jacob 17, Marianna 14, Julianne 21			
Philippine 3m, Catharina 19, Franz 11			
HOFFMANN, Christ.	32	Niederohmen	52-1452
Elise 34, Heinrich 8			
HOFFMANN, Christ.	22	Bramsche	47-0762
Grete 20			
HOFFMANN, Christne	31	Luederbach	51-1640
Andreas 7, Heinr. 23w			
HOFFMANN, Conrad	26	Willingshain	52-1580
HOFFMANN, Conrad	48	Oberquembach	54-1078
Catharine 40, Margaretha 16, Conrad 13			
Peter 9, Catharine 7			
HOFFMANN, Conrad	30	Feltkriken	51-1101
HOFFMANN, Crescent	20	Bruckenau	51-1455
HOFFMANN, Daniel	19	Staffelbach	52-1661
HOFFMANN, Daniel	19	Barntrup	54-0053
HOFFMANN, Diedr.	25	Norden	50-1071
HOFFMANN, Dorothea	26	Auringen/Nass	53-0628
HOFFMANN, Dorothea	30	Strelitz	54-0987
HOFFMANN, Elis.	31	Aslesshausen	54-1716
Catharine 6			
HOFFMANN, Elis.	18	Griesin	54-1282
HOFFMANN, Elisabet	60	Giessen	53-1086
HOFFMANN, Ewald	50	Dillenburg	52-0807
Wilhelmine 46, Philippine 21			
Wilhelmine 19, Elise 17, Gottfried 14			
Wilhelm 10, Caroline 7			
HOFFMANN, Franz	32	Lichtenberg	54-1717
Verona 30, Franz 9			
HOFFMANN, Friedr.	19	Neustadt	53-0914
HOFFMANN, Friedr.	26	Frankenhausen	54-0918
Amalie 26			
HOFFMANN, Friedr.	41	Waldenburg	54-1566
Juliane 44, Oscar 4, Clara 8			
HOFFMANN, Friedr.	29	Ortrof	50-1132
Theod. 24			
HOFFMANN, G.	24	Leipzig	52-1661
HOFFMANN, Georg	31	Mansbach	52-0563
Wilhelm 15, Mattias 11			
HOFFMANN, Georg	22	Bimbach/Bav.	52-0807
HOFFMANN, Georg	44	Roetha	53-0267
Susanna 48, Andreas 39, Margaretha 40			
Georg jr. 5, Emil jr. 4			
HOFFMANN, Georg	38	Viernau	54-0600
Michael 20, Margarethe 42, Georg 14			
HOFFMANN, Gustav	27	Fremstedt	53-0825
HOFFMANN, Heinr.	20	Rodach	53-0590
HOFFMANN, Heinr.	28	Bibra	49-1358
HOFFMANN, Heinrich	42	Erlenhausen	54-0830
Caroline 42, Elisabeth 58, Anna Maria 18			
Elisabeth 16			
HOFFMANN, Heinrich	30	Sachsen	53-0590
Therese 29, August 21			
HOFFMANN, Henriett	25	Oerlinghausen	50-0472
HOFFMANN, J. (m)	30	Erdmannsrode	52-0652
HOFFMANN, J. (m)	28	Altmannshause	48-0453
HOFFMANN, Jacob	31	Almen	52-1580
HOFFMANN, Jean	20	Frankfurt	49-0912
HOFFMANN, Johann	40	Chlodenschlos	53-1016
Procop 6, Johann 3			
HOFFMANN, Johann	24	Alten Koensta	51-0500
HOFFMANN, Johanna	27	Bettrum/Sax	52-1423
HOFFMANN, Juliane	30	Langenleube	54-1168
HOFFMANN, Juliane	27	Neustadt	53-0928
HOFFMANN, Kunig.	21	Steinbach/Bav	53-0628
HOFFMANN, Lewis	25	Veckerhagen	50-0323
HOFFMANN, Louise	22	Coburg	52-0895
HOFFMANN, Ludwig	22	Hildburghause	48-0887
Therese 24			
HOFFMANN, Magdalen	28	Bueg	48-1179
HOFFMANN, Margaret	23	Roetha	53-0267
HOFFMANN, Margaret	19	Grub	54-1554
HOFFMANN, Maria	25	Ohrenbach	51-1438
HOFFMANN, Marie	31	Muenchberg	54-1341
HOFFMANN, Martin	29	Seiferts	52-0370
HOFFMANN, Nicolaus	26	Rodach	54-0053
HOFFMANN, Oscar	22	Berlin	53-0161
HOFFMANN, Peter	27	Gruenberg	54-0850
HOFFMANN, Robert	43	Ruplau/Pr.	50-0323
HOFFMANN, Wilhelm	23	Allerdorf	54-1282
HOFFMEISTER, Georg	24	Heilfeld	53-0324
HOFFMEISTER, Mich.	57	Alkhofen	54-1371
HOFFMEYER, Adam	25	Babber	53-1086
Caroline 21, Christoph 15, Heinrich 4			
HOFFMEYER, H.	41	Babber	53-1086
Engel 44, Johann 17, Leonore 10, El. 9m			
HOFFSTAETTER, Mich	24	Baiern	52-0895
HOFMAN, Andreas	53	Ilm	52-1304
Anna Marg. 50, Charles 21, August 20			
Theresia 16			
HOFMAN, Georg Mich	19	Herrenthierba	53-1062
HOFMAN, Kunigunde	16	Steinweisen	53-0914
HOFMANN, Andreas	42	Steppen	52-0279
HOFMANN, Anna	37	Bremen/Boeh.	54-1092
Elisabeth 15			
HOFMANN, August	32	Kamstaedt	53-0652
Louise 27			
HOFMANN, C. (m)	24	Stollberg	47-0868
Auguste 34			
HOFMANN, Elisabeth	26	Garbenteich	52-0807
HOFMANN, Friedrich	23	Dachstadt	52-0693
HOFMANN, Friedrich	34	Haina	51-1639
HOFMANN, Georg C.	18	Mittelruessel	49-0737
HOFMANN, Joh.	23	Gresmes	54-1283
HOFMANN, Johann	25	Laufe	54-1647
Barbara 25			
HOFMANN, John	23	Baiern	54-1724
Barb. 21			
HOFMANN, Minna	22	Charlottenbur	54-1371
HOFMANN, Wilh.	36	Langensalza	54-1094
HOFMEIER, C.H. (m)	21	Essen/Hann.	52-0960
Elisb. 18			
HOFMEYER, Wm.	28	Rodenberg	48-1114
HOFNER, Solomon	24	Baden	47-0672
HOFSCHNITZER, Barb	36	Rothweid	51-1438
HOFSFELD, Johannes	38	Schweina	52-0095
HOGE, Wilhelm	56	Lienen/Pr.	52-1432
Elisabeth 46, Elisabeth 17, Heinrich 14			
Ernst 9, Minchen 6, Bandine 9m			
HOGER, Carl	36	Rothenoven	54-0987
Christiane 22, Carl 4, Jette 1, August by			
HOGER, Gottfried	40	Rothenoven	54-0987
Christiane 40, Christiane 22			
Gottfried 19, Johann 14, Marie 9			
Caroline 3			
HOGREFE, D. (m)	26	Hohenaverberg	49-0383
HOGREFE, Jacob	35	Hatzeln	54-1297
HOHENBERGER, Mich.	47	Eferding	53-0991
Susanna 34, John 14, Theresa 12, Anna 11			
Julian 8, Elisabeth 6, Sebastian 5			
Magdalena 3			
HOHENSTEIN, C. (f)	21	Weildenstadt	54-1341
HOHENSTEIN, Johann	33	Hungen	53-0557
Margretha 25			
HOHL, Georg	44	Herrenberg	53-0914

NAME	AGE	RESIDENCE	YR-LIST
Catharine 30, Georg 6, Elise 4, Ernst 18m			
HOHL, Louis	21	Lobenstein	54-0987
HOHLE, Margarethe	58	Kaub	54-1371
Christiane 25, Sophie 18			
HOHLFELDER, Ad.(m)	19	Hamberg	52-0515
Fr. (m) 20, Joh. (m) 24			
HOHLFELDER, John	39	Hamberg	52-0515
Marg. Anna 41, Margaret 7, Friedrich 6			
HOHLSTEIN, Eva	25	Mainz	52-0699
HOHLSTEIN, Wilhelm	22	Saalfeld	52-0699
Eva 25			
HOHM, v. August	22	Richmond	53-0161
Heinrich 19			
HOHMANN, Catharina	23	Haibach	52-0515
HOHMANN, Diedr.	15	Achim	51-0326
HOHMANN, Joh.	25	Wehren	50-0472
HOHMANN, Sebastian	42	Obernbernharz	51-0500
HOHMEISTER, Christ	26	Weissenborn	51-1725
Anna Elisab. 27, Heinrich 11m			
HOHMEISTER, Elise	18	Orfrode	54-1717
HOHMEYER, Adam	20	Milden	48-1131
HOHMEYER, J.U.	27	Clausthal	54-1419
HOHN, James C.	20	Eslangen	49-0737
HOHNAGEL, Christ.	34	Hieben	53-0905
Hanna 24			
HOHOFF, Theodor	45	Werl	48-0260
HOHR, Joseph Rupp.	36	Leingruben/A.	53-0628
HOHRENWEISER, Aug.	28	Altenwottinge	53-0267
HOISE, Caspar	28	Oberleuchnigs	54-0850
HOK, Christiana	21	Riedenhopf	49-1517
HOLB, Leo	18	Baiern	49-1106
Henriette 45, Michael 18			
HOLBAUER, Anna	30	Teich Wolfram	51-1084
HOLBORN, Johann	36	Schairinghafe	53-0838
HOLD, Jonas	26	Pr. Minden	52-0351
HOLDEMEYER, Friedr	24	Petershagnerh	54-0930
Sophie 26, Heinrich 5			
HOLEINBEIN, G. (m)	29	Hamberg	52-0515
HOLKAMP, Fried.		Borenby	54-1419
Anna 49, Christian 17, Wilhelm 14			
Heinrich 9, August 21			
HOLL, Anton	31	Schegingen	52-1580
HOLL, Johann	29	Frudenkog	48-1184
HOLLAND, Anna	23	Bamberg	51-1035
HOLLAND, Catharina	29	Bamberg	52-1362
HOLLAND, G.M.	26	Walddorf	53-0914
Margr. 24			
HOLLANDT, Carl	23	Seligenthal	50-0472
HOLLEMANN, Meta	25	Heuslingen	50-1071
HOLLEN, Barbara	27	Eisenach	53-0942
HOLLENBECK, Jane	23	Dissen	53-1164
HOLLENROTH, Andr.	22	Mittelruessel	49-0737
HOLLER, August	32	Luebbeke	51-1686
HOLLER, Carl	42	Burscheid	54-1371
Samuel 20			
HOLLER, Charlotte	21	Destel	53-1023
HOLLER, Doris	10	Stolzenau	51-1035
HOLLERS, Michael	36	Heldburg	49-0781
HOLLING, Doris	17	Misselwarden	54-0987
HOLLING, Heinrich	16	Spaden	51-0756
HOLLINGSTEDT, Hein	21	Altenbruch	50-0366
HOLLIZ, Louis	32	Breslau	54-0987
Louise 34, Elisabeth 2, baby 1			
HOLLMANN, Eman.	33	Breslau	50-1071
HOLLMANN, Heinr.	22	Battelsdorf/H	52-0351
HOLLMANN, Henry	9	Buttel	53-1164
HOLLMICH, Gottlieb	53	Mehnen	53-0942
Anna 50, Henriette 14, Heinrich 11			
Wilhelmine 7			
HOLLSTE, Wilhelm	32	Danzig	49-1106
HOLLSTEIN, Friedr.	25	Bothmer	54-1168
HOLLSTEIN, Joh.	20	Hesdorf	49-0574
HOLLSTEIN, Michael	28	Niederzimmern	50-0292
HOLMS, Marie	21	Schlausingen	54-1078
HOLO, Kurt	27	Springen	53-0652
HOLSETEN, Lorenz	57	Abensberg	53-0825
Anna Maria 54			
HOLSK, Ferd.	23	Solingen	48-0406

NAME	AGE	RESIDENCE	YR-LIST
HOLST, Wilhelm	42	Schaumburg	54-1297
HOLSTE, Heinrich	48	Stadthagen	54-1168
HOLSTEIN, Adolphus	34	Muenster	50-0840
HOLSTEIN, Dorothea	23	Vockerode	54-1554
Anna 19			
HOLSTEIN, Jul.	23	Glogau	51-1796
HOLSTEIN, W. (m)	19	Gotha	48-0445
HOLSTEN, Geerd	27	Rothenburg	54-1649
HOLTE, Josephine	21	Bremerhaven	53-1164
HOLTER, Johann	23	Siedenburg	54-0987
Albert 17, Friedrich 16			
HOLTER, Marie	33	Fexen	53-0492
HOLTERS, Hedwig	38	Mohrsdorf	51-1101
HOLTHAUS, Peter W.	28	Ohle/Pr.	48-0053
HOLTHAUSEN, Heinr.	25	Leiste	48-1355
HOLTHUSEN, Peter	21	Oldenburg	51-1084
HOLTHUSEN, Wuebke	20	Leste	51-0405
HOLTMANN, Christ.	24	Neu Arensberg	51-0352
Johann 24			
HOLTMANN, Heinrich	23	Osterkappeln	47-0762
HOLTMANN, Joh Phil	19	Heepen	54-1647
HOLTSCHEN, Wilhelm	28	Capellan	53-1016
Gertrude 24, Peter 32			
HOLTSCHER, Louise	51	Elberfeld	48-1355
Johanna 20			
HOLTZ, W.	23	Darmstadt	49-1358
HOLTZ, Wm.	39	Lodingsen	51-1588
Dorothy 39, Elisabeth 9, Anna 6, Henry 20			
HOLTZMANN, F.	31	Hausen	53-0492
HOLTZSCHUER, Conr.	7	Niederstetten	54-1168
HOLUB, Franz	37	Rottweis	54-0053
Catharina 31, Barbara 6, Puntranella 3			
Joseph 3m, Anna 26			
HOLWEG, Diedr.	19	Bederkesa	50-1317
HOLZAMER, Valentin	28	Worms	53-0991
HOLZAPFEL, Cath.	3-	Weimar	48-0565
HOLZAPFEL, Chr.	18	Eschwege	54-0600
HOLZAPFEL, Friedr.	47	Immenrode	52-1410
HOLZBAUER, J.	53	Hartkirchen	54-1094
Catharina 38, Joseph 16, Anna 14			
Georg 12, Franz 10, Catharina 7, Johann 5			
HOLZBERGER, Babett	20	Diesfuck	50-0840
HOLZBERGER, Marg.	50	Possenheim	54-1371
HOLZBORN, G.A.	23	Braunschweig	51-1160
HOLZGREBE, Casp.	30	Spenge	52-1321
HOLZHAUER, Carol.	24	Sooden/Hess	52-1423
HOLZHAUER, Chris.		Aurich	54-0987
HOLZHAUER, Eliza	19	Marburg	53-0991
HOLZHAUER, Friedr.	21	Soden	53-0838
HOLZHAUER, James	28	Wolferbuett	52-1304
HOLZHAUSEN, Com.	24	Letell	52-1321
HOLZINGER, Emanuel	24	Ermreuth	48-1179
HOLZMANN, Barbara	30	Dormitz	51-1245
Anna 6			
HOLZMANN, Chr.	26	Stetten	53-0492
HOLZMUELLER, J.(m)	26	Loewen	52-0652
HOLZNER, Simon	38	Greiz/Baiern	53-0475
HOLZRICHTER, J.H.	57	Lansberg	48-0453
HOLZWARTH, Cathr.	20	Steinfurth	52-0370
HOLZWARTH, Matth.	30	Unterbruender	49-0352
HOMANN, Diedr.	23	Brinckum	49-0324
HOMANN, Ferdinand	21	Braunschweig	52-1620
HOMANN, Fr.	20	Braunschweig	54-1011
HOMANN, H.	47	Minden/Pr.	48-0053
HOMANN, Heinrich	41	Spreinberg	53-1000
Johanne 40			
HOMANN, Marie	18	Boerstel	54-1443
Dietrich 14			
HOMBURG, O. Jos.	30	Romeswil/Swit	51-1796
Cath. 35, Jos. 9, Bernh. 6, Pauli 2			
HOMEYER, Barbara	20	Schmalenbuehl	54-1566
HOMMEL, Christ.	58	Croelpa	53-0914
C. 25, G. 17			
HOMMERT, Alexander	24	Ilvese	52-0807
Rudolf 17			
HONER, Georg	19	Markseid	52-1661
HONERPEIK, Heinr.	42	Bolk	52-1129
HONIG, Eduard	25	Wettlingen/Ba	52-0117

NAME	AGE	RESIDENCE	YR-LIST
HONS, Meta	18	Sievern	52-0699
HONSCHMEYER, Chr.	28	Waldenhorst	54-0987
HOOKS, Reinhard	27	Solingen	48-0406
HOOSEN, W. A.	57	Malsum	53-0905
Anna 16			
HOPER, E (m)	38	Rolfsbuttel	52-0558
Wilhelmine 19, G. (f) 28, J. (m) 18			
F. (m) 15, H. (f) 2			
HOPF, Dorothea	50	Oberkatz	52-1321
Rosien 19, Nicol.(f) 16, Georgine 9			
HOPF, Michael	51	Oberkatz	52-1321
HOPF, Michael	32	Weihmar	53-0942
HOPF, Valentin	27	Liebenstein	54-0987
Anna Christ. 27, Marie Ernest by			
HOPFF, Barbara	43	Spielberg	54-1078
Catharine 5			
HOPFF, Kunigunde	13	Weissmein	52-1362
HOPFFELD, Cathrin	25	Dinklage	53-0492
HOPFGARTEN, v Fr'z	24	Gr. Breitenba	53-0585
HOPPE, Auguste	20	Bekerhagen/He	51-1796
HOPPE, Conrad	33	Hannover	51-1725
Augusta 30			
HOPPE, F.	24	Langenleuba	53-0914
D. 30, T. 22			
HOPPE, Florentine	18	Stotel	53-1023
HOPPE, Johanne	24	Bekerhagen/He	51-1796
HOPPE, Moritz	21	Burk	49-1106
Charles 5			
HOPPENBURG, John	17	Salzwedel	54-1591
Catharine 19			
HOPPORT, Francis	23	Harkenstein	53-0914
Lische 28			
HOPS, Ludwig	23	Ottersberg	49-1358
HORBACH, Herm.	26	Philadelphia	53-0991
HORBACH, Theod.	39	Hannover/Hann	51-0048
Wilhelmine 28, Lina 4			
HORCHER, Philipp	30	Pfaffendorf	48-1184
Franz 32			
HORDMER, Henry	28	Schmalkalden	51-1588
HOREIS, William	23	Oberndorf	48-0887
HORGANG, Joseph	45	Bohemia	50-1236
HORLING, Heinr.	26	Holzhausen	49-0383
HORMANN, Heinrich	28	Rothenburg	51-0757
HORMING, Constant	24	Ballenberg	54-1371
HORN, Adalbert	31	Weimar	50-0021
HORN, C. (m)	18	Hanau	49-0416
G. (m) 17			
HORN, Christiane	25	Reschnitz	54-1647
HORN, Elisabeth	18	Bonnland	54-0053
HORN, Ernst	25	Gera	53-0320
HORN, Friederike	34	Soemmerda/Pr.	51-1532
HORN, Gottl.	39	Bavaria	50-1317
HORN, Joh Pet Carl	25	Gerolsgruen	53-1062
HORN, Joh. H.	25	Stebin	48-1184
HORN, Johann	29	Schrecksbach	51-1160
A. Elise 24			
HORN, Johann	25	Bavaria	53-0628
HORN, Johann	25	Brode	53-0905
Friederika 26, Carolina 2, Carolina 27			
Henriette 17			
HORN, Johannes	18	Langenbach	48-0284
HORN, Valentin	18	Braash	54-1443
HORN, Wilhelm	39	Cassel	51-1160
HORN, Wilhelm	26	Hersberg	54-0987
HORN, Wilhelmine	16	Lobenstein	49-0383
HORN, Wolf	22	Geisa	54-0903
Haendel 24			
HORNAEFFER, Eduard	17	Wilterode	53-0888
HORNER, Elisabeth	24	Gt. Britian	48-1015
HORNER, Heinr.	23	Beuthen	49-0781
Auguste 24, baby			
HORNING, Barbara	22	Trieb/Bav.	51-1532
HORNING, H.(m)	25	Seidelshapt	50-0746
HORNING, Ludwig		Beineburg	54-1716
HORNSCHER, M. (m)	27	Gorga	50-0746
HORNSCHUH, Friedr.	35	Abtswind	54-1371
HORNSTEIN, Adam	16	Rambach/Hess	52-1620
HORNUNG, Anna Marg	58	Mosbach	53-1070

NAME	AGE	RESIDENCE	YR-LIST
HORNUNG, Elisabeth	18	Lichtenfels	53-0637
HORNUNG, Georg	28	Mosbach	52-1321
HORNUNG, Gustavus	30	Bremen	53-0991
Pauline 24			
HORNUNG, Jac.	32	Mosbach	52-1321
HORNUNG, John		Hamburg	52-0515
HORNUNG, Lenghon	25	Ballenberg	53-1164
HORNUNG, Leonhard	17	Feirenbronn	52-0515
HORNUNG, Regina	21	Heidelberg	53-1164
Emma 5, James 4, Lenghon 25			
HORNUNG, Veronika	54	Bamberg	54-1168
Emilie 19			
HORRENTER, Abraham	17	Sulz	54-1168
HORRMANN, Georg	31	Birke/Hann	52-1332
HORRMANN, J.H.	34	Bremen	53-0161
HORSCHTMANN, Elis.	27	Mohra	53-0942
HORST, Caroline	22	Koenigshofen	53-0590
HORST, Elise	27	Bleidenrode	54-0830
HORST, Ernst Heinr	26	Buer	54-1371
HORST, Georg	33	Aschach	53-0320
HORST, Wilh.	35	Harpstedt	48-0284
HORSTMAIER, W. (f)	44	Grosshersen	47-0868
W. 18, Heinr. 12, Ludwig 6			
HORSTMAN, Friedr.	31	Hanoveri	52-0351
HORSTMANN, Anna M.	20	Mehringen	52-1452
HORSTMANN, J. (f)	24	Ostbevern	50-0746
HORSTMANN, Johann	26	Scharmbeck/Ha	51-1532
HORSTMANN, Johann	32	Scharmbeck	51-1245
HORSTMEYER, Adolph	26	Kolstadt	52-0775
Wilhelm 28			
HORWITZ, Rosalie	31	Berlin	54-1371
Heinrich 6, Otto 3, Maria 5, Antonia 10m			
HOSBACH, Wilh'mine	18	Hauda	53-1164
Auguste 16			
HOSE, Eduard	28	Oldelsde	54-0600
HOSE, Elisabeth	25	Homberg	51-1101
HOSENHAINER, G.(m)	39	Munster	54-1341
Franziska 28, Georg 4, John 3, son 10m			
HOSER, Anna M.	18	Suzburg	51-1455
HOSFELD, Georg	25	Fischbach	51-1245
HOSFELD, George	48	Gehaus	54-1341
A.M. (f) 19, Catharine 11, George A. 9			
HOSS, Theodor	29	Oleff	54-0987
Catharine 25, Marie by			
HOSSENS, Conrad	33	New York	54-0872
Henriette 32			
HOSSFELD, Carl	22	Cassel	54-0053
HOSSFELD, Elisab.	19	Salzungen	53-1000
Richard 15			
HOSSMANN, Henry	28	Lesumstotel	51-0048
HOSSOLD, Adelbert	45	Neustadt	54-1078
Babette 36, Ludwig 9, Louise 8, Babetta 6			
Ernst 4, Caroline 3			
HOSST, Carl	22	Marburg	48-1131
HOSTMAIER, W. (f)	44	Grosshersen	47-0868
W. 18, Heinr. 12, Ludwig 6			
HOSTMANN, August	35	Buetzow	54-0987
HOTZELE, Sophie	19	Schernberg	54-1554
HOVEN, Friedrich	26	Aukum	51-0352
HOVING, Bernhard	2-	Coesfeld/Pr.	49-0365
HOWALD, Fr. (m)	21	Braunschweig	54-0918
HOYA, Adam	52	Burkersreuth	53-0637
Margaretha 50, Johann Georg 12			
HOYEMEYER, Thomas	30	Reichsbach	47-0918
Barb. 40, Thomas 1			
HOYEN, Albert	34	Wagenfeld	51-1084
HOYER, Carl	21	New York	54-1649
HOYER, Emilie	16	N.Y.	51-1686
HOYER, Ernst	26	Hoever	54-1371
HOYER, Gottlieb	28	Wuestenselbit	53-0637
Elisabeth 27, Joh Albrecht 8			
Anna Marg. 6, Johann 2			
HOYER, Jacob	26	Ahornis	54-1554
HOYERMANN, Cath.	23	Bremen	51-1084
HRNITSCHKO, Joseph	26	Doll/Boehmen	52-0807
Anna 25, Anna 6			
HUBBERT, Jette	26	Frohnheim	48-0260
HUBEL, A.M. (f)	18	Schopfloch	50-0746

NAME	AGE	RESIDENCE	YR-LIST
HUBEL, L.B. (m)	24	Berlin	48-0453
W. (f) 24			
HUBENER, Ernst	22	Altenburg	48-0269
HUBER, Anton	39	Kempten	52-1512
Maria 38			
HUBER, Anton	35	Tuchling	52-1200
HUBER, Caroline	19	Bilfingen	51-0352
HUBER, Catharine	42	Mundenheim	54-1717
Catharine 14, Anna Maria 9			
Margaretha 11m			
HUBER, Ferdinand	27	Rienau	52-0279
HUBER, Gustavus	26	Vegesack	53-1164
HUBER, Jacob	26	Brochord	54-0850
Maria 28, Ursula 9			
HUBER, Johann	36	Baiern	53-0324
HUBER, John	25	Fahrenhaus	54-1341
HUBER, Leonhard	28	Openau/Baden	52-0351
HUBER, Lorenz	40	Wolferstadt	52-1200
HUBER, Martin	30	Birkenfeld	52-1304
HUBER, Michael	28	Landshut	54-1452
HUBER, Peter	18	Bruick	53-0905
HUBER, Rosa	24	Insbruck	53-0888
HUBER, Tarteus	34	Waldstetten	53-0914
HUBERSTEIN, Barbra	21	Finnemuende	49-0345
HUBERTHAL, Anna M.	24	Tremding	51-1245
HUBLER, Magarethe	23	Heibuer	52-1464
HUBMANN, Ernst	64	Sulzbach	48-0887
Conrad 34, Magdalene 63, Kunigunde 22			
HUBNER, Conrad	61	Klevershausen	47-0672
HUBNER, Gottfr.	29	Muhlendorf	54-1716
Marie 31			
HUBNER, Joh. G.	25	Eichenberg	51-1455
Christina 28, Maria 6, Margarett 3			
HUBNER, Margaretha	19	Memelsdorf	52-0515
HUBSCHIN, Mar Marg	21	Dentlein	52-0515
HUCH, Mary	20	Sand	54-1341
HUCHTHAUSEN, E.	36	Eimen	48-0951
Friedrich 24, Charles 9, August 7			
William 3, August 24			
HUCK, Caroline	49	Dankersen	52-1321
Caroline 15, Henr. 12, Carl 2			
HUCK, Chr.	55	Berenbusch	52-1321
HUCK, Daniel	65	Kamstaedt	53-0652
HUCK, Hermann	29	Bremen	53-1164
HUCKE, Hermann	18	Ridenburch	53-0590
HUCKE, Nicolaus	17	Lendorf	48-1179
HUCKSHOLT, Friedr.	23	Ostendorff	49-0413
HUDENG, Georg	56	Greisbach	52-1452
Maria 44, Georg 18, Franz 9			
HUEBENER, Fr. Aug.	17	Bremervoerde	51-1725
HUEBER, Joh.	23	Buch	49-0324
HUEBNER, Christian	17	Ehringen	53-0557
HUEBNER, Christine	24	Coburg	53-1013
HUEBNER, Christine	17	Eringen	53-0557
HUEBNER, Cunigunde	26	Baiern	52-1362
HUEBNER, Emilie	25	Camenz	54-1297
HUEBNER, Georg	37	Reichelsheim	53-0838
Elisabeth 29, Fr. Wilhelm 8, Marie 3			
HUEBNER, Joh. Gott	36	Leidsmansdorf	53-1062
Carolina Ch. 37			
HUEBSCH, Hermine	17	Triffshausen	51-1686
HUEBSCHMANN, Kunig	30	Dachstadt	52-0693
HUEDEPOHL, Louise	21	Bruchhausen	53-1070
Caroline 19			
HUEHMSTADT, Julius	32	Harzburg	54-0850
Gottfried 13, Elisabeth 20			
HUEHNER, Therese	46	Empfingen	52-0279
HUEHNS, Heinr.	17	Nordhausen	49-1358
HUELL, Joh. Heinr.	30	Marksuhl	51-1796
HUELLER, Christ.	35	Hannover	50-1317
HUELMANN, Herm.	23	Lingen	54-1297
HUELSEBERG, Cath.	14	Hagen	51-1245
HUELSEBERG, Nicol.	19	Donnering	54-0987
HUELSEMANN, Carl	34	Niederroden	51-1438
HUELSEMANN, Friedr	30	Bieren	54-1452
HUELSHORST, Bernh.	25	Senden	54-1554
Dora (died) 56, Agnes 17			
HUELSKOETTER, Wilh	26	Muenster	53-0473

NAME	AGE	RESIDENCE	YR-LIST
HUELSS, Bernhard	3	Coburg	49-0352
HUELTHAU, Joh. H.	51	Oberzell	53-0435
Barbara 48, Philipp 23, Elisabeth 21			
Heinrich 16, Wilhelm 14, Kunigunde 12			
Johann 6, Barbara 3			
HUEMANN, J.C. (m)	24	Osnabrueck	52-1512
HUEMER, John	29	Lichtenfels	48-0887
HUEMMELMANN, Elis.	21	Gruenden	50-0379
Catharine 19			
HUEMMER, Johann	29	Weidach/Sachs	52-1332
HUEN, Carl	24	Berlin	48-1243
HUENAU, Friedrich		Elberfeld	54-1168
HUENECKE, Friedr G	19	Bremen/Hann.	54-1092
HUENING, J. Heinr.	48	Kirchtimke	50-1132
Christine 48			
HUENKEN, Herrm.	22	Thedinghausen	51-1640
HUENNE, Heinrich	30	Niederhoerlen	52-1452
Elisabeth 30, Anna 5, Jacob 9, Johannes 3			
HUEPNER, C. (m)	24	Bernstadt	49-1358
HUER, v. der Herm.	29	Leer	50-0292
HUERBEIN, Georg	36	Canton Aargau	51-1245
Otilie 32, Reinhard 6, Fridolin 2			
HUESEMANN, Marie	25	Babber	53-1086
HUESER, Jonas	19	Niederkaufung	54-1078
HUETER, Georg	21	Malsfeld	51-1062
HUETHER, Catharine	30	Aschaffenburg	51-1438
HUETTE, Georg	25	Zendern	50-0292
HUETTE, Wilh.	24	Hoxter	49-0324
HUETTEBRECHER, Pet	42	Luedenscheid	49-0053
Henriette 29, Ewald 1			
HUETTEN, G. (m)	18	Coeln	49-0416
HUETTER, Josepha	35	Kipfenberg	54-1297
HUETTING, Joh Gott	35	Weimar	52-0895
HUFE, Johann	34	Lichtenhaid/S	53-0628
Amalia Louis 10			
HUFFMANN, August	15	Fuerstenhause	51-1639
HUFNAGEL, Charles	17	Darmstadt	53-0991
HUFNAGEL, Conr.	17	Thuisbrunn	52-0693
HUFNAGEL, Daniel		Aschaffenburg	52-0279
HUFNAGEL, L. (m)	26	Harberg	48-0445
G. (f) 25, L. (m) 2			
HUFSCHMIDT, El.	19	Rotenburg	54-1575
HUGE, Anna	17	Essen	53-1086
HUGE, Ernst	56	Babber	53-1086
Marie 49, Anna M. 23, Maria L. 19			
Maria 13, Louise 9, Adolph 29			
HUGE, Herman Math.	27	Essen	53-1062
HUGE, J.H. (m)	57	Essen	53-1086
HUGE, K.	51	Boebber	53-1086
Dorette 31, Ernst 13, Heinr. 10, Louise 9			
Friedrich 7, August 4, Elisabeth 23			
Engel 22, Jette 18			
HUGELACK, Jos.	28	Eldenstedt	49-0324
HUGER, Francisca	21	Ottersweier	53-1164
HUGLER, Andrew	39	Langenbrink	48-0951
HUHBOM, Carl	29	Roetha	53-0267
HUHN, Alex	18	Klesberg	54-1419
HUHN, Catharina	26	Heilbach	52-1101
Cerenka 19			
HUHN, Christian	23	Goodelsheim	50-0379
HUHN, Friderike	22	Remstadt	54-0053
HUHN, Joseph	28	Hauswurz	54-1282
HUHNBAUM, Conrad	47	Roetha	53-0267
Elisabeth 43, Friedrich 13, Catharina 12			
Elisabeth 12, Carl 8, Wilhelm 6			
Gottlieb 6m, Carl 29			
HUHTLAN, Friedrich	20	Rheren	53-1086
HUKE, H.	52	Meerane	54-1341
Louise 52, Dorretha 18, F. (m) 57			
HULDMANN, Therese	27	Donauwoerth	54-0872
Mina 26			
HULK, Daniel	65	Kamstaedt	53-0652
HULL, Andr.	24	Obertrippach	54-1078
HULL, Margaretha	24	Uettlefroth	48-1184
HULLENMANTEL, Bern	59	Humrechtshaus	54-1283
HULSEBERG, Diedr.	27	Hannover	50-1067
HULTHOFER, Maria	22	Rahlbirken/Bv	53-0628
HUMBOLD, August	41	Gera	52-1661

NAME	AGE	RESIDENCE	YR-LIST
HUMBORG, Christian	23	Dorenhagen	54-0930
HUMBURG, Theodor	17	Telze	54-1566
HUMDLEY, Lucy	30	Wien	53-0652
HUMFOKE, Louis	22	Hameln	54-0930
HUMM, Anton	31	Baden	51-1438
HUMMEL, Chr.	33	Niederstolzin	54-0600
Barbara 32, Christ. 5			
HUMMEL, Michael	22	Coburg	52-0895
HUMMITSCH, Carl W.	24	Hoefendorf	54-1371
HUMMITSCH, William	23	Hoekendorf	53-1164
HUNCKEL, Otto	20	Bremen	51-0326
HUND, Elisabeth	34	Gilsenberg	51-0352
HUND, Franz	26	Frankenhausen	50-0379
HUND, Gottlieb	32	Gruenfeir	52-0563
Rosine 33, Wilhelmine 18, Ernestine L. 4			
Friedr. Aug. 2, Andreas 27			
HUND, H.S.	29	Bautzen	50-1071
HUND, Joh. Fried.	53	Bohmte	52-1200
Anna Maria 53, Charlotte 16			
HUND, Luc.	14	Frankenhausen	49-1358
HUNDESHAGEN, Adolf	25	Geesen	51-1438
HUNDSBERGER, Mose	17	Sanding	52-0558
HUNDT, Anton	36	Allendorn	48-1355
HUNEBEL, Maria	36	Michelotstadt	52-1101
HUNECKE, Peter	22	Freyburg	53-0473
Josephine 27, Georg 6, Ignaz 3			
HUNEKE, H.	25	Bassum	51-1084
HUNGER, Vincent	35	Beil	51-1686
HUNICH, David	44	Breslau	54-1419
Paul 14			
HUNKE, Joseph	20	Zeidler	53-0324
HUNKER, Conrad	52	Morsum	52-0515
Josina 53, Johan 25, Joshema (f) 26			
Rebecca 19, Catharina 22, Herman 21			
Josunah (f) 14			
HUNSCHKOL, B. Fr.		Triptis	53-0942
HUNSTMANN, Elise	36	Arzberg	53-0557
HUNTEMANN, Diedr.	19	Brinckum	49-0324
HUNTING, Ernst	20	Ottersberg	52-1362
HUPFER, Fried.	15	Molsdorf	50-1132
HUPFER, Johann	24	Baiern	53-0585
HUPFF, Bernhard	19	Danzig	54-1168
HURWALD, Carl	26	Luninghausen	54-0882
HUS, Anna	22	Bramsche	54-0987
HUS, Elisabeth	63	Appelhusen	49-0912
HUSCHEN, Sophie	24	Lienen	54-1371
HUSEMANN, Ludwig	29	Warendorf	50-0292
HUSMANN, Johann	23	Sulingen	53-1000
HUSPENBANN, G. (m)	44	Stuttgart	49-0329
HUSSE, H. (m)	28	Ostenwald	54-1341
HUSTEDT, Justus	24	Hamburg	52-0960
HUTFILTER, Fr.	25	Hannover/Hann	51-0048
HUTH, Adolph	31	Minden	53-1023
Sophia 32			
HUTH, C. (m)	26	Bremen	47-0762
HUTH, Catharine	24	Schoeltgruppe	53-0825
HUTH, Conrad	30	Bavaria	53-0628
Osta 35, Adam 8			
HUTH, Maria	23	Mehrholz	53-0888
HUTH, Michael	19	Ober Rodenbac	51-0352
HUTH, Rudolph	18	Gesell	52-1321
HUTH, Theodor	18	Ruplau/Pr.	50-0323
HUTMACHER, Carl H.	30	Brandenburg	54-1649
HUTMANN, Heinr.	32	Melle	51-1739
HUTT, Margaretha	28	Schoenau	50-0292
HUTTINGER, Samuel	19	Weissenburg	52-0095
HUXHALD, Jette	24	Heimsen	48-1131
Lisette 24			
HYRENBACH, Jacob	39	Lindau	48-0887
IBACH, Christ.	37	Fischbach/Pr.	51-0048
IBORG, Joh. Wilh.	27	Hannover/Hann	51-0048
IBSELE, Barbara	23	Suess	48-0887
IDE, Conr.	18	Schellbrock	51-0405
Marg. 22, Anna Elise 24			
IDE, J.G.	38	Lohne/Hessia	51-0048
IDE, Wilhelm	40	Salzwedel	54-1297
Marie 32, Anna 9, Carl 7, Wilhelm 5			
Minna 2			
IDING, Johann	29	Badbergen	54-0987
IFERT, Heinrich	18	Mernes	52-0563
IFFERFT, Martin	32	Dankmarshause	48-0284
IFLAND, Justus	29	Beberah	51-1686
Anna 29, Heinrich 9, Elisabeth 10m			
IGLAUER, M.	14	Burg Cunstadt	50-0439
IGNATZ, Christian	32	Groschlatengr	53-0928
IHLETZ, Carl	23	Hohenberg	50-1236
IHLKING, Caroline	21	Minden	52-1410
IHMSEN, Heinrich	46	Mansbach	50-0379
Wilhelm 23			
IHNE, Theodor	27	Roehnsaal	51-0326
IHRIG, Adam	22	Rusbach	54-0987
IHRING, August	20	Hannover	53-0590
IKE, Johannes	53	Niedenstein	52-1105
Johann 14			
IKLER, J.	21	Sand	54-1341
ILGEN, J.E. (m)	23	Fambach	51-0517
ILGENFRITZ, Conrad	25	Weidelbach	53-1000
ILKENHANS, Friedr.	34	Hessen	50-0021
Wilhelmine 28, William 8, Carl 5			
Auguste 2			
ILKO, Jos.	21	Baden	50-1317
ILLGEN, Hein.	27	Scherboer	47-0868
ILLIG, Eva	24	Fahnbach	49-0413
ILLIG, Johs.	30	Pforzheim	48-0269
ILLIZER, Martin	47	Weingerstreid	54-1717
ILLNER, Robert	22	Hildesheim	50-0021
ILSE, Louis	18	Muenden	53-0590
ILSEMANN, C.F. (m)	28	Stadthagen	52-1321
ILSNENSEE, Philipp	30	Hedingen	54-1649
IMENICK, Frieda	44	Aahausen	47-0672
baby bob			
IMMEL, August	14	Frankenberg	53-1016
Louise 25			
IMMEL, Christiane	23	Treisbach	52-1452
IMMEN, Anne C.	22	Sievern	48-0951
IMMEN, John	15	Dingen	48-0951
IMMENTHUN, Gerhard	18	Kneheim	54-1371
IMMER, Joseph	33	Fremdingen	52-1362
Theresia 32, Barbara 4, Joseph 9m			
IMMERMANN, H.	37	Sielleben	54-1341
Mary C. 36, Edward 10, Charles 6			
Aurora 8, Eda 4			
INACKER, J.J.	20	Dednau	52-1512
INHOFF, Heinrich	28	Raden/Pr.	51-1796
INSELMANN, Heinr.	18	Klinkendorf	50-0292
Anna 16			
INTEMANN, Claus	24	Ummel	54-0987
INTEMANN, Heinrich	15	Hassendorf	51-1101
IPFLAND, Georg	18	Eichenberg	52-1661
IRBER, Joseph	32	Triftern	47-0828
Andreas 29			
IRLBAUER, Kunigund	36	Neuhaus	48-0951
Conrad 2			
IRMSCHER, Carl Geo	18	Chemnitz	52-1362
IRSCHITZ, Math.	42	Wien	53-0905
ISAAC, Joseph	20	Hanover	47-0987
ISCHERMANN, Eduard	20	Eberschuetze	54-0930
ISEDOR, Edward	17	Muenden	53-0590
ISELI, J.	28	Osterwaal	54-1419
ISENSTEIN, Salomon	22	Hannover	54-1168
ISERMAN, Heinrich	27	Ebergoetzen	54-0882
ISERMANN, Wilhelm	38	Fredilslohe	51-0405
Caroline 24			
ISLEI, Adam		Storndorf	54-1575
ISLEIB, V.	24	Springen	51-0517
K. (f) 27, F. 6m			
ISMAEL, Georg	18	Muenden	53-0590
ISRAEL, Imul	25	Koblegura	54-0882
ISRAEL, Rosa	22	Strassburg	49-1358
ISSERTEL, C. Heinr	52	Carlshafen	54-0053
ISSERTELL, Justus	22	Schoeneberg	54-0965
ITICH, Minna	24	Herdecke/Pr.	52-1620
Auguste 10m			
ITSCH, Andreas	24	Hochstraf	52-1101
ITTIG, August	27	Schleusingen	52-0807
ITTIG, Carl Christ	19	Schleusingen	54-0903

NAME	AGE	RESIDENCE	YR-LIST
ITTINGER, Crescent	36	Follmersdorf	51-0384
Johann 15, Catharina 13, Mathilde 2			
Johann 17, Catharina 19			
IVAS, Wilh.	61	Solingen	50-0439
Ald. (f) 61			
IVEMEYER, Ernst	25	Hapenfeld	54-0965
Elisabeth 23, Heinrich 1, Catharine 16			
JACH, Paul	28	Krisczin	54-1282
JACKEL, Andreas	23	Neumark	51-0460
JACKEL, W. (m)	22	Leipzig	54-1341
JACOB, B.	20	Kleinsteinach	54-1283
JACOB, Caroline	21	Grafenau	54-0830
Regine 22			
JACOB, Charlotte	22	Volkershausen	54-0918
JACOB, Christoph	38	Oberheldrunge	53-1164
JACOB, Gottfried	27	Boehl/Bav.	52-0351
JACOB, Heinr.	17	Eichshausen	50-0439
JACOB, Hermann	27	C. Ulm	54-1591
JACOB, John	31	Lichtenau	52-0804
M. (f) 25, Ann (died) 4m			
JACOB, John	33	Ulm	53-0991
JACOB, Justus	27	Retterode	52-1580
JACOB, Peter	17	Einberg	54-1168
JACOB, Peter	26	Zeune/Bav.	48-0053
Magdalena 24			
JACOB, W. (m)	22	Jesberg	50-0746
JACOBEN, Anna	26	Oeslau	54-1282
JACOBI, Charles	17	Willingen	52-1304
JACOBI, Eduard	34	Spreinberg	53-1000
Gottliebe 29			
JACOBI, Jacob	17	Hartum/Pr.	52-0351
JACOBI, Jost	45	Oberklein	52-1321
JACOBI, Mary Elise	25	Ansefar/Hess.	49-0365
JACOBS, Catharine	24	Eitze	54-1566
JACOBS, Ferdinand	30	Neu-Brandenbu	52-1423
JACOBS, Gesche	24	Wekhausen	54-1094
JACOBS, Henry	16	Nesselrode	54-1716
JACOBS, Joh Gevert	18	Waakhausen	53-0557
JACOBS, John	14	Cofferhausen	51-1455
Cacharia 9			
JACOBS, Peter	22	Elzerath	51-1062
JACOBSEN, Bernhard	20	Miselwaren	53-0838
JACOBSMEYER, Anna	39	Niedertudorf	50-0379
Anton 9, Bernhard 7, Joseph 4			
JACOBSMEYER, Joh.	36	Salzkotten	51-1245
JACOBSOHN, August	30	Itzehoe	54-1554
Katharine 26, Heinrich 3			
JACOBSON, Mathilde	17	Osterode	52-0895
JACOBY, Christian	38	Mittenwald	54-0872
Maria 30, Friederike 17, Minna 8, Carl 9			
Wilhelm 5, Auguste by			
JAEBKE, Wilhelmine	24	Hildesheim	54-1297
Franz 2			
JAEGER, Andrea	30	Kitzingen	53-0324
JAEGER, Anna	23	Gilverberg	50-0366
JAEGER, George	51	Eltmann	53-0991
Susanna 50, Josepha 27, Brigetta 18			
John 16			
JAEGER, Gesina	27	N.Y.	52-1580
JAEGER, Godfrey	22	Oberheldrunge	53-1164
JAEGER, Hein Deric	22	Achim	48-1209
JAEGER, Heinrich	26	Gifhorn/Hann.	53-0475
Johanne 21, Wilhelmine 23			
JAEGER, J.	19	Bamberg	51-0405
JAEGER, J.(m)	24	Storndorf	52-0652
M. (f) 22			
JAEGER, Jacob	25	Bremen	49-0324
JAEGER, Joh Friedr	17	Heidelsheim	53-0991
JAEGER, Johann	37	Wuechern	53-1016
Barbara 31, Joseph 7, Anna 4, Joseph 9m			
JAEGER, Johann	18	Sellstedt	51-0756
JAEGER, Johanne	20	Bremen	48-1209
JAEGER, Joseph	38	Undernach	48-0565
JAEGER, Louise	18	Pr. Minden	53-0267
JAEGER, Margar.	43	Bussendorf	54-1078
JAEGER, Mayer	16	Gelnhausen	53-0914
JAEGER, Philipp	18	Holzheim	54-0830
JAEHRLING, Christ.	33	Crimmitschau	53-1023

NAME	AGE	RESIDENCE	YR-LIST
Maria Ros. 31, Carl Louis 5, Friedrich 3			
JAEKEL, Conrad	22	Vahlen/Hess.	50-0323
JAEP, W. (m)	23	Mengerhausen	48-0453
JAESIGER, Johann	26	Neuhof	52-0699
JAGEHORN, D. (m)	21	Bremen	52-0775
JAGER, Casper	18	Alsfeld	54-1341
JAGER, Christ. A.G	57	Immenrode	48-0951
Dorothea 53, Carl A. 29, Friedrich 18			
JAGER, Conr.	21	Haibach	52-0515
JAGER, D. (m)	19	Marburg	48-1131
E. (m) 23			
JAGER, Gesche	20	Knarenburg	53-0905
JAGER, W.	53	Dorstadt	54-1341
Dorretha 36			
JAGODZINSKY, Valt.	29	Gebenizky	52-1304
JAHN, Adolph	30	Grosshirschen	49-0365
JAHN, Chr. Heinr.	21	Bucha	51-0352
JAHN, Elisabeth	17	Erfurt	54-0850
Wilhelm 19, Gustav 11, Emma by			
JAHN, Ernst	36	Grafenthal	54-0850
JAHN, Gustav	38	Lichtenstn/Sx	52-1332
JAHN, Heinrich	19	Geilhain	53-0652
JAHN, Joh. Heinr.	39	Erfurt	54-0850
Julie 42			
JAHN, Marie	30	Belza/Wuertt.	52-1332
Regine 17			
JAHN, Otilia	21	Gossau	53-0320
JAHN, Robert	32	Guetinburg	54-1282
JAHNER, John Conr.	25	Unterusselbac	52-0515
JAHNS, August	27	Schoningen	47-0872
Charlotte 21, Ferdinand 21m			
JAHNS, Conrad	28	Othfresen/Han	52-1332
JAHR, Th.	36	Frankenhausen	53-0492
JAKOB, Adam	37	Pukelheim	53-0435
JAKSON, Alexander	24	Coeln	51-0500
JAMES, Joseph	30	Gt. Britian	48-1015
JAMM, Adam	46	Niederlenden	52-0558
JANASCH, Carl	30	Zittau	49-0574
Amelia 22			
JANECECK, Franz	22	Hodyna	54-1647
Joseph 21			
JANECEK, Adalbert	40	Sedlitz	54-1647
Marie 27, Anna 32, Martin 5, Wenzel 2			
JANIASCH, Carl	30	Zittau	49-0574
Amelia 22			
JANKE, Heinrich	25	Einbeck	54-1283
JANSEN, Andreas	30	Mohrlach	54-1716
JANSEN, Friedr.	38	Eidewurden	54-0053
Marg. Cath. 49, Helena Fried 9, Betty 8			
JANSEN, Heinrich	52	Emden	53-0652
Johanna 46, Henricus 19, Hermann 18			
Nilla 16, Catharine 8, Nicolaus 4			
JANSEN, Henry	18	Dingen	48-0951
JANSEN, Hermann	16	Dorum	49-0345
JANSEN, Johann	24	Bederkesa	52-1580
JANSEN, Louis T.	27	Mittelruessel	49-0737
Agatha 23			
JANSEN, Peter	46	Leichlingen	53-0888
Catharine 59, Julie 18			
JANSON, Andreas	50	Witzmansberg	53-0637
Barbara 52, Eva Margreth 38			
Margaretha 34, Michael 12			
JANSSEN, Heinrich	52	Emden	53-0652
Johanna 46, Henricus 19, Hermann 18			
Nilla 16, Catharine 8, Nicolaus 4			
JANSSEN, Jacob	36	Hannover	50-0311
JANSSEN, Johann	43	Etzel	51-1160
P. (m) 10, Cath. 3			
JANSSEN, Ulrike	35	Sillenstedt	54-0872
JANTZEN, Eibe (f)	22	Dingen	52-0699
JANZEN, Wilhelm	21	Osnabrueck	53-0652
JARL, Michael	21	Koenigshelf	54-1297
JARVIS, Mary	43	Gt. Britian	48-1015
Franziska 22, Sarah 14, Richard 16			
Robert 10			
JASGER, Henry	16	Kleinensee	48-0284
Barbara 20			
JASPER, Ernst	36	Lengerich/Pr.	52-1432

NAME	AGE	RESIDENCE	YR-LIST
Sophie 36, Wilhelm 9, Sophie 5			
Rudolf 10m, Wilmne(died) 3			
JASPERSEN, Theodor	23	Kiel	54-1371
JATHO, Conrad	17	Holzhausen	51-1245
JAUGERMANN, Christ	19	Treysa	49-0345
JECKEL, Cath.	30	Wustendorf	52-0515
JEDDECKEN, H.J.W.	33	Lancaster	48-1015
JEGLINGEN, Sophie	22	Bieberach	54-1282
JEKEN, Elise	20	Waddenwarden	50-0323
JELKMANN, Anton	36	Wandersloh	54-0918
JELLIES, Joh Bern.	45	Hohenkirchen	54-0872
Maria 51, Maria 13, Johanne 9, Henrich 20			
Johann 16			
JELLNOR, Henry	19	Halsdorf	52-0515
JENEMANN, Peter	26	Kurhessen	53-0628
JENNA, Christiane	30	Arzberg	53-0557
JENSCH, Joh. Georg	64	Koetschbroda	54-1297
Johanne 54, Otto 20, Hulda 17, Maria 16			
Robert 13, Francisca 13, Reinhold 12			
Johann 9			
JENSEN, Georg	24	Arendal	49-0324
JENTSCH, Ern. Jul.	20	Oberspaar	48-1131
JENTZSCH, Fr. Aug.	26	Dresden	48-1355
JERABECK, Joseph	42	Holitz	53-1016
Franziska 17			
JESEKER, Sophia	15	Scheeren	54-1341
JETTER, Marie	20	Gochsheim	50-0292
Carl 5, Susanne 15			
JILTER, Heinrich	25	Sielhorst	53-0905
JOACHIM, Ricka	19	Neustadt	51-0756
JOAS, Barbara	24	Engen	51-1455
JOB, Anne Marg.	20	Metzgels	53-0582
JOCH, Andreas	27	Ebrach	52-1200
JOCHMUS, Anton	55	Siemerswald	51-0460
Mauter (f) 17, Johann 15			
JOCHNER, Carl	24	Knurbach	53-0324
JOCHUM, Joh. H.	24	Treisbach	48-0269
JOCKRACKS, Henry	21	Gannitz	54-1724
JOERG, Jacob	62	Huetten	54-1168
JOERGEN, Jacob	21	Koenigshelf	54-1297
JOERGER, Catharine	29	Baden	52-1625
JOERGES, Joseph	33	Koenigshelf	54-1297
Peter 23			
JOERING, F. (m)	24	Bodenfelde	52-0652
JOHANNES, Doris	17	Misselwarden	54-0987
JOHANNES, Heinrich	36	Dorum	53-1013
Maria 25, Christian 25, Heinrich 2			
Rebecca 3			
JOHANNES, P.E. (m)	27	Hannover	50-0311
JOHANNESS, Mich.	35	Mittelstreu	47-0868
JOHANNING, W. (m)	25	Buehne	52-0652
Ann 20			
JOHANNOOSMANN, C.	64	Bissendorf	48-1114
Cath. 20, Herm. 18			
JOHANNSMEYER, Mar.	24	Babber	53-1086
JOHANNY, Philip	53	Bayedorf	54-1716
Johann 17, Elisabeth 28			
JOHN, Bernhard	17	Schwartzau	53-0585
JOHN, Franz	53	Powitzko	54-1575
Elisabeth 41, Carl 25, Anna 22			
JOHN, Franz	58	Powitzko	54-1575
Elisabeth 41, Carl 25, Anna 22			
JOHN, Friedrich	36	Sillau	50-0840
JOHN, Heinrich W.	22	Wanna	51-0756
JOHN, J.B.	22	Stohlen	49-0324
JOHN, Joh. Eberh.	40	Offenwarden	54-1297
JOHN, Johanne	21	Nordhausen	54-1575
JOHN, Julius	23	Rudolstadt	50-1067
JOHN, Wilh.	30	N. Preussen	51-1084
JOLEIM, Christian	26	Wachtenbrunn	53-0637
JONAS, David	18	Kairlindach	51-1245
JONAS, Hirsch	17	Kaiserlindach	53-0320
JONAS, Lina	22	Kalender	48-1184
JOOS, Joseph	47	Schoeffau	52-1362
Josepha 41, Joseph 16, Marianne 12			
Xaver 6, George 4, Veronica 32			
Sebastian 14, Veronica 7			
JOOS, Martha	20	Amt Amertinge	51-1686
JOOST, Albert		Cassel	48-1355
JOOSTMANN, Wilh.	17	Bramsche	54-0600
Margarethe 20, Heinr. 24, Mathilde 25			
JORDAN, Jul. Th.	35	Leipzig	52-1625
JOSENHANS, Wilh.	30	Stuttgart	52-0370
JOSEPH, Diane	32	Wien	53-0652
JOSEPH, Heinrich	45	Allendorf	53-1062
Catharina E. 53, Christ Heinr 25			
Louise 21, Carl 12			
JOSHUA, Cath.	19	Feuchtwangen	52-0515
JOST, Bernhard	16	Mackenstedt	51-0460
JOST, Catharina	22	Ullersbach	51-0384
JOST, Hans	23	Mackels	49-0329
Herm. 19			
JOST, Johann	31	Bellmuth	52-1200
JOST, Johannes	23	Warburg	54-1649
JOST, Mar.	47	Ulrichstein	47-0868
JOST, Margareth	25	Holstein	52-1620
JUBREN, Peter	24	Weydenberg	52-0804
JUCHBRUNNER, J.	50	Langnau	54-1419
JUDT, Ludwig	25	Wahlbach	53-0590
JUECHTERN, Ernst	36	Tecklenburg	52-1432
JUENGERICH, Christ	45	Giesen	52-0699
Wilhelmine 17, Jacob Juls 21			
Catharine 10, Helene 8, Juergen 6			
Jacob 60			
JUENGERICH, Johann	46	Giesen/Hess.	52-0699
Helene 34, Wilhelm 10, Greta 9m			
JUENGERICH, Mich.	56	Giesen/Hess.	52-0699
Helene 40, Jacob 19, Otto 15, John 10			
JUENGERWIRTH, J.G.	22	Rudolstadt	50-0021
JUENGLING, Henry	27	N.Y.	52-1620
JUENGLING, Wilhelm	18	Bremen	52-1332
JUERGEN, Jacob	23	Lippe	49-0329
JUERGEN, Joh. H.C.	21	Braunschweig	50-0021
JUERGENS, Anna	18	Muenster	54-1575
JUERGENS, Heinr.	16	Binden/Hann.	52-0960
JUERGENS, Sibelt	40	Wittmold	53-1164
JULIUS, Joh.	45	Oberndorf	53-0492
Marg. 48			
JUNG, Ant.	32	Herbornselbac	49-0574
Elisab. 27			
JUNG, Anton T.	18	Bremen	52-1148
JUNG, August	26	Niedersalzbru	53-1062
JUNG, Carl	23	Darmstadt	53-0590
JUNG, Conrad	25	Holzheim	54-0830
Elisabeth 24, Conrad 18, Conrad 23			
JUNG, Engel (m)	29	Maier	48-1131
Catharina 20			
JUNG, Ernst V.	23	Weissenberg/N	52-0807
JUNG, Georg	34	Siegen/Pr.	51-1725
Catharina 39, Catharina 13, Louis 4			
JUNG, H. (f)	27	Kahla	50-0746
JUNG, Heinrich	20	Hernshausen	52-1512
JUNG, Heinrich	30	Freiburg	53-1062
JUNG, James	23	Donassenheim	53-0582
JUNG, Johannes	38	Bersrod	52-1105
Elisabeth 11, Margarethe 9, Maria 7			
JUNG, Joseph	32	Weinhelmsdorf	53-0637
Maria 29, Joseph 2, Anna Maria 3m			
JUNG, Marie	52	Giesen	53-1000
JUNG, Th.	27	Trunoal	54-1676
JUNGBLUT, Heinrich	19	Neuhaus	52-0699
JUNGBLUT, Susanna	24	Darmstadt	50-1067
JUNGE, Gottlieb	49	Seiderdorf	49-1106
Helene 45, Christiana 20, Carl 4			
JUNGE, Joseph	50	Paritz	54-1297
Johanne 40, Franciska 22, Josepha 19			
Johann 14, Carolus 12, Maria 2, Joseph 7			
Julius 5, Heinrich 30, Michael 30			
JUNGE, Martin	54	Kempenich	50-0292
JUNGER, Barbara	23	Hinterweiler	53-0320
JUNGERMANN, M. (m)	26	Mehlen	54-0918
JUNGH, August		Cassel	53-0914
JUNGHEN, Julius		Roeddenau	53-0942
JUNGHK, August	15	Baermichswald	54-0872
JUNGINGER, J. Ludw	32	Heidenheim	49-0352
JUNGK, Caspar	21	Auerbach	54-0600

NAME	AGE	RESIDENCE	YR-LIST
JUNGKER, John	37	Negelsheh	49-1517
wife 34, August 14, Friedr. 11, Bertha 9 Charlotte 7, Gustav 4, Martha 6m			
JUNGMANN, John	36	Neuenkirchen	49-0781
JUNGNIKEL, Albert	17	Berlin	51-1796
JUNKER, August	20	Eisenberg	53-0942
JUNKER, Ernst	29	Erfurt	54-1443
JUNKERMANN, Julie	19	Manrode	51-1160
JURGENS, Diedrich	30	Dorum	50-0366
JURGENS, Elise	23	Dingen	48-0951
JURGENS, Franz	23	Grossfuerste	53-0324
JURGENS, Henry	33	Dingen	48-0951
August 27			
JURGENSMEYER, Jos.	24	Elsen	48-0269
JURY, Maria Magd.	18	Berlin	54-1647
JUSCHHOLD, C.	18	Toensnitz	54-1283
JUST, J.G.	40	Hornburg	49-0383
Louise 39, Robert 12, Albert 6			
JUST, Joh Gottlieb	44	Langenlaube	54-0930
Rosine 37, Sophie 17, Therese 15 Wilhelm 9, Auguste 12, Gustav 3 Pauline 1			
KAAS, Wilhelm	20	Lehnsted	49-0345
KABCHEL, Joseph	42	Boehmen	52-0699
Anna 24			
KADDEN, A.	27	Halsdorf	51-1455
KADERA, (m)	54	Kanzenberg	54-0987
KADSKENESKEY, Carl	29	Geagua	54-1341
KAEFER, Joh. Geo.	23	Buechelberg	54-1371
KAEHLER, Otilla	30	Kirch Ortbach	53-1013
Anna 3, Friedr. 3m, Mathilde 53			
KAEMINGA, Margaret	32	Loquard	53-0888
KAEMMERER, Barbara	24	Bavaria	50-0021
KAEMPER, Wilhelm	28	Plantlunne	54-1371
KAEMPF, Charles	47	Meerholz	53-0888
Therese 48, Susanne 42, Margaretha 39			
KAEMPFE, Carl	25	Roschuetz	54-0872
KAEMPFER, Joh Bapt	19	Steinweisen	53-0914
KAENFTLE, Wilhelm	24	Karlsruhe	52-1580
Wilhelmine 45			
KAEPEL, C. H. (m)	21	Osnabrueck	52-1512
KAEPPEL, F. (m)	25	Selb	52-0652
KAERLE, Conrad	45	Zennern	48-1179
Anna 41, Lieschen 14, Catharine 12 Maria 10, Hermann 4, Heinrich 34			
KAESE, August	2	Gossbach	52-0279
KAESE, Chr.	26	Halle	51-1640
KAESE, Conrad	33	Steinbrexen	52-0279
Karoline 23, August 2			
KAESEBERG, Wilhelm	36	Sain	51-1640
Cath. 30, Simon 6, Joh. 4, Adolph 9m			
KAESEMANN, Friedr.	25	Kleinberg	53-1164
KAESINGER, Val.	24	Ziegenhain	54-1078
Joh. 18			
KAESSMANN, Friedr.	18	Asch	53-1062
KAESTNER, Herrmann	27	Neustadt	49-0345
KAETHNER, Christ.	26	Wiegeln	50-0379
Friedrich 28			
KAEUFEL, Michael	24	Schweinfurth	54-1283
KAEUTGEN, Theodor	19	Bremen	53-1086
KAFUNKEL, Rosalia	24	Kimpen	54-0882
KAGER, Joseph	31	Stettfeld	54-1554
KAHKE, Heinrich	24	Fehlenburg	50-0379
KAHL, Johannes	35	Werra	49-0345
KAHLE, Emil	28	Dessau	52-1580
KAHLE, John	47	Wien	53-0914
Catharine 42, Barbara 17, Rosalin 15 Helen 12, Petronella 6, Amalia 3			
KAHLE, L. (m)	17	Fuchtholz	52-1512
KAHLEN, Mary	25	Schneeren	54-1341
KAHLENBACH, Heinr.	30	Lenabach	51-1739
KAHLENBACH, Heinr.	21	Salzingen	53-0324
KAHLENBERG, Otto	16	Aerzleben	53-0492
Emilie 24			
KAHLENBERGER, Ant.	24	Kleinlegerste	54-1716
Christian 18			
KAHLETTE, Heinrich	26	Othfresin	53-0905
KAHLHOEFER, Wilh.	28	Siegen	52-0563

NAME	AGE	RESIDENCE	YR-LIST
KAHLMANN, Marie	27	Verden/Hann.	52-0807
KAHLS, Fanny	24	Saaz	49-1106
KAHMANN, Louisa	18	Neunkirchen	54-1470
Catharine 24			
KAHN, Alois	38	Pesth	49-0574
KAHN, Juergen	19	Latrum	52-1580
KAHNBACH, J.C.	25	Kirchosten	50-1071
KAHND, Joh.	23	Reichstaedt	50-1071
KAHRS, Johann	19	Karlshoeven	53-0905
KAIL, Gabriel	20	Memmingen	51-1245
KAILER, Anna	25	Klein Auheim	52-1512
KAIMPF, Charles	47	Meerholz	53-0888
Therese 48, Susanne 42, Margaretha 39			
KAIN, George	29	Podhuns	54-1341
KAISENBEIN, Amalie	19	Siedenburg	54-0987
KAISER, Anna	24	Hoxter	48-1015
KAISER, Anna Cath.	27	Immelrode	52-0563
KAISER, August	30	Calbsried	50-0379
Christine 28			
KAISER, Bertha	23	Breslau	54-1371
KAISER, Carl	46	Weimar	50-0021
KAISER, Caspar	19	Tiefenort	53-0942
Catharina 26			
KAISER, Catharina	26	Luesche	52-0563
Wilhelmine 22			
KAISER, Charles	18	Wiesbaden/Nas	48-0447
KAISER, Christoph	21	Guenzerode	54-1554
Maria (died) 57			
KAISER, Conr.	19	Herrmannsroda	51-1084
KAISER, Eva Marie	24	Rosa	49-0781
Barbara E. 22			
KAISER, Franz	59	Norten	53-1164
Sophia 59, Doris 4			
KAISER, Heinrich	21	Gehrde	50-0292
KAISER, Joh.	21	Wulfeck	49-0574
KAISER, Johann	33	Eppsdorf/Kurh	53-0628
KAISER, John	25	Etlendorf	48-0565
KAISER, Louise	26	Dieren/Pr.	52-1620
KAISER, Margaret	30	Neuess	51-1588
KAISER, Michael	22	Gleichenberg	54-1283
KAISER, Petra	28	Schwarza	53-0905
KAISER, Walpurga	27	Pilgersdorf	54-0850
KAISER, Wilh.	23	Prussia	54-1724
Charlotte 54, Rudolph 17			
KAISER, Wilhelm	21	Iserlohn	54-1566
KAISINGER, Mary	28	Opladen	48-0406
KAITHE, Catharine	21	Frankenau/Hes	50-0323
KALB, Friedr.	31	Nuernberg	50-1317
KALB, Georg	23	Ruttenheim	52-0370
KALB, Guido	28	Gross Weisand	51-0352
KALB, Louise	13	Zweibruecken	52-0699
KALB, Susanna	22	Herzogenwind	52-0693
KALBENBACH, Georg	55	Gumbelstadt	52-0563
KALBFLEISCH, Heinr	31	Giessen	49-0912
Maria 27			
KALBFLEISCH, Jos.	21	Altenburg	51-0500
Margaretha 24			
KALBFLEISCH, Maria	27	Gernsbach	49-0912
KALFUER, Carl	19	Minden	52-1410
KALKMANN, August	26	Parretz	53-0825
KALKSTEIN, Louis	29	Berlin	54-1297
KALLE, August	28	Wesel	48-0951
Friedrich 24			
KALLE, Joseph	26	Carlsruhe	54-0987
KALLE, Philipp	26	Ringelheim	52-1625
KALLENBACH, Adam	45	Salzingen	53-0324
Magdalene 32, Joseph 9, Ernst 7, Elise 1			
KALLENBACH, Johann	44	Sachsen	49-0413
KALLENBERG, Fr. W.	36	Breslau	54-1092
KALLENBUCH, Johann	28	Mohra	53-0942
KALLENSEE, Friedr.	41	Herzberg	53-1023
Ernestine 30, Carl 2, Fritz 1			
KALLIN, A.	30	Dumburg	51-0517
KALLMANN, Jul.	16	Gunzenhausen	50-0439
KALLMEIER, Joh. H.	19	Osnabrueck	50-0021
KALLMEYER, J. Herm	13	Osnabrueck	50-0021
KALTENHAEUSER, Wm.	18	Coblenz	54-0850
KALTENNEGGER, Ant.	20	Wertingen	52-0279

NAME	AGE	RESIDENCE	YR-LIST
KALTENSCHNEE, Adam	30	Mauswinkel	53-1062
Margaretha 33, Melchior 9m			
KALTHOFF, H.W.	24	Neunkirchen	54-1470
KAMARIT, Franz	45	Pilgramm	54-1094
Anna 38, Matthias Alb 4, Anton 2			
KAMBROCK, Anton	20	Loeningen	53-1062
KAMINSKY, Theodore	24	Berlin	48-1243
KAMLAH, Otto	28	Groningen	53-1086
KAMMACH, Albertine	23	Posen	51-1062
Challie by			
KAMMER, Eliese	19	Rainrod	52-1321
William 16, Julius 10, Jacob 7			
KAMMER, Jacob	46	Rainrod	52-1321
KAMMER, Konrad	39	Oberhofen	52-1105
Wilhelm 28, Anna 26			
KAMMER, Louis	24	Alsfeld	54-1443
Louise 32, Johanna 5, Linna 11m			
KAMMERER, Elisabet	56	Schwarzenbach	53-0475
Georg 17, Sophie 18			
KAMMERER, Fr. Chr.	21	Zich	51-1455
KAMMERER, Theodore	25	Berlin	48-1243
KAMMEYER, Johann	18	Hainsfarth	52-1200
KAMNER, Herm.	26	Leeste	50-0439
KAMP, AUF DEM Ern.	21	Ottersberg	52-1362
Clara Elise 23, Friedr. 28			
KAMP, Andreas	23	Reime/Pr.	52-0117
KAMP, Johann	18	Sandstedt	50-1067
KAMP, Sophie	18	Oblaten/Prss.	52-1332
Peter 22			
KAMPE, Heinrich	21	Schweringen	53-1000
KAMPE, Joseph	25	Welda	52-1304
KAMPEN, Friedrich	15	Wersabe	52-0048
KAMPF, Wilhelm	30	Homburg	53-0825
KAMPFERT, Wilhelm	26	Warsin	54-1168
Johann 24, Emilie 19			
KAMSS, Gertrud	21	Beser	49-0912
KAN, Hermann	21	Geldern	49-0912
KANEFEND, August	25	Halle	47-0672
KANES, Fr. Aug.	26	Bansa	51-1640
KANN, Bernh.	48	Niederwerbe	52-1200
KANN, Johanna	56	Berlin	53-0324
Fanny 23			
KANNENBLEY, Chr'ne	30	Schweringen	48-1209
KANNENBLEY, Henry	28	Schweringen	48-1209
Dorette 34, Wilhelm 45, Jane 36			
Friedrich 9m, Friedrich 36			
KANNENGIESER, H(m)	23	Rohrberg	50-0311
M. (f) 24			
KANNENGIESSER, J H	28	Fardinghausen	52-0563
KANSCHAM, Joseph	25	Abterode	47-0872
KANSCHER, Heinr.	19	Katel--f	50-0439
KANSSEL, Dorothea	23	Waechtersbach	52-1625
KANSTEIZER, Johann	24	Neuburg	53-0324
KANTELMEIER, J.(m)	42	Salzburg	49-1358
KANUSKY, Johann	38	Schlawentzig	51-0757
KANZE, Georg	26	Binsfoerth	54-1716
KANZELMANN, G.A.	24	Fruchtelfinge	51-1640
KANZLER, Christian	41	Thonrode	52-1101
Christiane 34, Theodor 12, Fritz 10			
Wilhelmine 8, Anna (died) 5, Minna 1			
KAPELLER, Michael	30	Biswangen	54-1168
KAPER, Eduard	36	Treptow	54-0872
Caroline 27, Adolphine 9, Otto 8, Emil 2			
Anna by			
KAPKA, Tresia	24	Illiconete	54-0918
KAPPES, Caspar	26	Griesheim	51-1640
KAPPHAUFF, Maria	25	Berlin	54-1371
Anna 11m			
KAPS, Christoph	51	Sindewiese	54-1717
Veronica 42, Joseph 20, Ignaz 18			
KARAS, Mathias	34	Schrewska	54-1591
Mary 35, Mary 3, Barbara 11m			
KARBACH, Peter	28	Badenhard	53-1164
Catharine 27			
KARG, Barbara	31	Deiningen/Bav	51-1532
KARG, Joh.	18	Forschheim	54-1168
KARGER, Anton	30	Maehren	53-1000
Anna 28, Anna 3, Therese 1			

NAME	AGE	RESIDENCE	YR-LIST
KARGER, Michael	44	Vollmersheim	50-0311
KARKECK, Meta	28	Bruchhausen	49-0413
KARKHECK, Marg.(m)	18	Neundorf	48-0284
KARL, Franz	22	Coburg	52-0895
Wilhelm 21, Eduard 19			
KARL, Lorenz	31	Reichsbach	47-0918
Ursula 39, Alois 4, Franziska 2			
Anne Marie 9m			
KARL, Wilhelm	39	Gotha	52-0895
Johanne 42, Johann 15, Hermann 11			
Bernhardine 6, Mathilde 9m			
KARMANN, Gustav	23	Bueckeburg	54-1168
KARNASS, Karl	38	Breslau	54-1554
KARNAUER, Simon	28	Erlangen	49-0574
KAROLD, Ernst	25	Gern	54-1452
KARPE, Friedr. Wm.	42	Brembach	54-0872
Wilhelmine 42, son 16, Charlotte 9			
Emilie by			
KARPE, Georg Andr.	47	Brembach	54-0872
Louisa 38, Friedr. Gust 19, Alma 14			
KARSCH, Georg	28	Reichenbach	54-1283
Ernestine 27			
KARSHLER, Maria	19	Dresden	53-1062
KARTEMANN, Charlot	26	Versmold	48-1355
KARTHEHAUSEN, Thos	54	Schlossheltru	49-0781
KASBERGER, Elis.	32	Michingen	54-0903
KASCHENREUTER, Joh	32	Herdorf	48-1179
KASE, John	30	Armstorf	52-0804
Elisabeth 25, Martha 4m			
KASEKAMPF, Herm.	27	Ibbenbuehren	48-0269
KASEMEYER, Joh.	40	Gr. Wertz	48-0445
E. (f) 18, J. (m) 16, M. (m) 14			
F. (m) 11, G. (m) 9			
KASPAR, Charlotte	23	Bieren	54-1452
KASPER, Catharine	17	Sulzbach	48-0887
KASSEBAUM, Hein.	19	Luebke	52-1321
KASSEBOM, Wilhelm	32	Tellsdorf	52-1625
KASSEBOOM, J.C.(m)	21	Bremen	47-0104
KASSHOLA, Anna	19	Weydenberg	52-0804
KASTEN, Catharine	20	Ottendorf	54-1452
KASTEN, Franz	25	Dedinghausen	54-0053
KASTEN, Theodor	32	Mordheim	54-1168
KASTENDIECK, Lewis	28	Osnabruck	53-1164
KASTENDYK, Dorit	26	Osnabrueck	53-1164
KASTENS, Heinr.	23	Loehe	52-1512
Ludwig 16			
KASTENS, Henry	16	Schweringen	48-1209
KASTNER, Heinrich	18	Oberfranken	53-0557
KATHAN, Bernhard	25	Aschen	53-1062
KATHOLING, Georg	36	Eger	54-1283
KATHREIN, Joseph	43	Tyrol	48-0887
Remiges 12, Jacob 11			
KATMANN, H. Wilh.	24	Ladbergen	48-0260
Friederike 24, Wilhelm 6m			
KATTEN, Betti	17	Oberasbach	54-1371
KATTENDAM, Nicol.	26	Moller	47-0828
KATTENHORN, Alb.	24	Schwarmbeck	53-0991
KATTENHORN, John H	34	New York	53-0991
Alb. 24			
KATTNER, Joseph	38	Forbach	51-1796
KATZ, Amalie	38	Hatzbach/Hess	52-0960
Rosa 15			
KATZ, Bonum	19	Hilshau	52-1101
KATZ, Constant	25	Hermanrode	53-1016
KATZ, Ewald	16	Dillenburg	53-1023
Eduard 22			
KATZ, Franz	24	Rippenberg	52-1101
Maria 28, Franz 28			
KATZ, Julius	22	Saxony	50-0021
KATZ, S. (m)	25	Hermanrode	53-1016
KATZENBERGER, Joh.	26	Reichenbach/B	53-0628
KATZENBERGER, Nic.	32	Sommersdorf	48-0260
KATZENSTEIN, Alb.	18	Hoeringhausen	54-0987
KATZENSTEIN, Berta	24	Voelkershause	53-0942
Ester 21			
KATZENSTEIN, Helen	25	Werda/Hess.	50-0323
KATZMANN, Cathrina	35	Rotenburg	54-1649
KATZMANN, Eva	27	Muellershause	51-0460

NAME	AGE	RESIDENCE	YR-LIST
KATZMANN, Georg W.	40	Iba	54-0930
Barbara Elis 30, Anna Maria 11			
Heinrich 9, Elisabeth 1, Anna Cath. 59			
KAUCKY, Franz	50	Boehmen	53-1000
Marie 51, Joh. 19, Elisab. 12, Ant. 16			
KAUCKY, Wenzel	23	Boehmen	53-1000
Friederike 23			
KAUERBACH, Balth.	19	Salzingen	53-0324
KAUFELD, Ernestine	18	Minderwald	54-1371
Auguste 16			
KAUFFEL, Nanny	26	Calm	53-1164
KAUFFMANN, Marie	20	Bremen	54-1168
KAUFFOLD, Auguste	23	Wendthoehe	52-1321
KAUFHOLD, Minette	23	Schildhorst	54-0987
KAUFHOLDT, Heinr.	29	Elberfeld	48-0565
KAUFMAN, August	25	Osterode	54-1419
KAUFMANN, Bonavy	24	Schwarzbach	50-1067
KAUFMANN, Bonum	58	Steinberg	54-1647
KAUFMANN, Cathar.	24	Hofheim	54-0930
KAUFMANN, Dorothea	30	Cassel	54-1716
Joseph 6			
KAUFMANN, Franz	18	Fuhrbach	54-0053
KAUFMANN, Friedr.	30	Helmessen	49-0574
KAUFMANN, Georg	23	Birkenfeld	49-0352
KAUFMANN, Heinr.	20	Eidorf	51-0460
KAUFMANN, Henry	20	Werninghausen	50-0840
KAUFMANN, Joh. G.	20	Mittelruessel	49-0737
KAUFMANN, Lazarus	29	Beuersdorf	54-1647
KAUFMANN, Minna	37	Baiersdorf	52-1200
Babette 13			
KAUFMANN, Moses	25	Hannover	52-1410
KAUFMANN, Nenne	60	Altenstein	48-1179
Carl 24, Babette 20			
KAUFMANN, W. (m)	29	Sontra	52-1512
KAUKE, Wilhelm	19	Hagenburg	53-0492
KAUL, Samuel	33	Herzberg	54-0053
KAULA, Johann	46	Muichowitz	54-1575
Theresia 46, Franziska 7, A. (f) 5			
Maria 2			
KAULA, Jos.	27	Muichowitz	54-1575
Maria 24, Franziska 5			
KAUPER, Walburga	27	Pilgersdorf	54-0850
KAUPERT, Anna	19	Oberlindenbac	52-0693
KAUS, Gerhard	37	Haseloh	53-1000
KAUSCHER, Christ.	29	Mittelruessel	49-0737
KAUSSEL, Dorothea	23	Waechtersbach	52-1625
KAUTELMEIER, J.(m)	42	Salzburg	49-1358
KAUTH, Johann	36	Kamp/Nassau	52-1332
KAUZ, Christoph	44	Gotha	53-0473
KAVUT, Barbara	20	Neuhof	52-0699
KAYSER, Bernh.	33	Warz---r	50-0439
KAYSER, Christian	18	Bilshausen	53-1016
KAYSER, Christian	48	Muehlhausen	53-1023
KAYSER, Christian	50	Heimssen	54-1566
Louise 49, Anton 18, Friedrich 12			
Sophie 2			
KAYSER, Elise	17	Roetha	53-0267
Dorothea 22, Antonetta 26			
KAYSER, Fr. (m)	35	Berge	54-0918
KAYSER, Heinrich	33	Bremen	52-1362
Meta 24			
KAYSER, Heinrich	21	Detmold	54-0918
KAYSER, Joh. Georg	50	Illhausen	52-1625
Catharine 46, Heinrich 23			
KAYSER, Mayer	44	Schwarza	54-1078
Caroline 46			
KAYSER, Nicolaus	51	Roetha	53-0267
Margaretha 41, Christian 9, Johann 8			
Jacob 4, Friederika 2, Dorothea 1			
Sophia 11m			
KAYSER, Wilhelm	24	Dassel	49-0345
KAZISCHEK, Wenzel	62	Kopullo	54-1647
Anna 50			
KEANE, Friedr.	24	Mittelruessel	49-0737
KEBERLEIN, Andreas	27	Ahornis	54-1554
KEBLE, Margarethe	40	Hernnsfeld	50-0944
Eduard H. 8			
KECK, Friedrich	45	Duermenze	53-1164
KECK, Marie Cath.	26	Hermeringen	49-0352
KEDDERMANN, Heinr.	24	Hannover	51-1101
KEECK, Maria	28	Bachenau	49-0345
KEEK, Christian	28	Libingen	49-0345
KEEN, James	24	Canada	48-1243
KEFER, Johann	22	Munster	52-1362
KEFERSTEIN, Wilh.	25	Tinsleben	54-0987
KEGEL, Bernhard	44	Baiern	54-1724
Rosalie 30, Eduard 21, Mary 9, Tekla 6			
August 6m			
KEGEL, Rosine	39	Zeitz	54-1649
KEGHELE, Anna	20	Friedrichshof	53-0637
KEHL, Elisabeth	20	Mengers/Hess.	51-1532
KEHL, Johannes	47	Awaillenburg	53-0825
Anna Barbara 21, Anna Elis. 19			
Anna Maria 19			
KEHLENBECK, Claus	19	Kirchweih/Han	54-1092
KEHLING, Andreas	34	Waldorf	49-0574
Henriette 28			
KEHR, Nicolaus	54	Steinbach	53-0914
Hanna 44, Cath. 19, Barbara 10, Jacob 18m			
KEHRER, Agnes	28	Sondelsingen	54-1575
KEHRER, Joh. Geo.	32	Kustebingen	51-0352
KEHRES, Joh.	24	Fritlos	50-1236
KEICH, Charlotte	58	Urach	54-1341
F. (f) 24			
KEIDEL, Anna	21	Torgau	52-1661
KEIERBERGER, J.(m)	23	Mannheim	48-0453
KEIFER, Gesina	28	Bamberg	49-0345
KEIL, Andreas	37	Langeleben	51-1640
Friederike 26, Henriette 19, Elisabeth 64			
Andreas 6, Friederike 4, Sophie 2			
Elise 9m			
KEIL, Anna	26	Delmenhorst	49-0574
KEIL, Carl	23	Nordhausen	49-0574
Anna 26			
KEIL, Cath. Elis.	22	Frankenberg	48-1355
KEIL, Christiane	28	Giessen	53-0991
KEIL, Conrad	22	Feltkuecken	51-1101
KEIL, Friederike	21	Langeleben	51-1640
KEIL, Georg	28	Neukirchen	54-0850
Kunigunde 27			
KEIL, Hugo	13	Frankenberg	47-0828
KEIL, Joh.	48	Billerthausen	51-0460
Margaretha 39, Elisabeth 13, Catharine 1			
KEIL, M.	26	Altendorf	51-0517
KEIL, Marg.	56	Utrictshausen	52-0515
KEIL, Wilhelmine	27	Lennep	50-1236
KEIL, William	29	Molsdorf	53-0991
KEILIG, F.A.	38	Zeitz	53-1000
Wilhelmine 35, Max 12			
KEILMANN, Ludwig	28	Busserode	48-0284
KEIM, Valentin	50	Neumuehle	54-1554
Anna 52			
KEINER, Wolfg. Erh	45	Bayern	53-0557
Margarethe 43, Magdalena 20, Sabine 17			
Michel 10, Cathrine 5, Erhard 2			
KEINER, Wolfgang E	45	Bavaria	53-0557
Margrethe 43, Magdalene 20, Sabine 17			
Michel 10, Cathrine 5, Erhard 2			
KEIPER, M. (f)		Schermede	54-1575
Joseph			
KEISEN, Augustus	20	Gehaus	54-1341
KEISER, Anna Marg.	19	Emmerloh	53-0324
KEISLING, Christ.	40	Sulzfeld	51-1588
Sabina 36, Herman 10, George 7			
Caroline 5, Anna 3			
KEISSMINGER, Cunig	10	Kuebs	51-1084
KEISTEN, Fritz	27	Hannoveri	52-0351
KEITZ, v. Heinrich	45	Lauterbach	51-1101
KEK, G.	37	Zeeland	49-0912
Adriaantje 32, Willem 6			
KEKER, George	22	Ansbach	49-0912
KELB, Heinrich	24	Hagenburg	53-0492
Sophie 22			
KELBE, Carl	21	Linsen	49-0345
KELL, Barbara	63	Schleisingen	50-1132
KELLENBECK, Ferd.	20	Ochtrup	51-0352

NAME	AGE	RESIDENCE	YR-LIST
KELLENBERGER,	29	Paderborn	50-0021
KELLER, B. (m)	26	Vantungen	48-0453
KELLER, C. August	19	Bietigheim	53-0838
KELLER, Caspar	29	Klein Auheim	52-1512
Elisab. 25, Johann 17			
KELLER, Elisabeth	25	Willofs	53-1000
KELLER, Ernst	48	Meiningen	54-0918
Dorothea 41, Gothard 21, Carl 20			
Hermann 6, August 2, Christine 9, Emma 4			
KELLER, Friederike	32	Langenbrandt	54-1078
Friedr. 9, Fritz 7, Carl 5			
KELLER, Friedrich	25	Zwickau	52-1580
KELLER, Georg	33	St. Gallen	51-1686
KELLER, Gustav	36	Rutesheim	52-1200
KELLER, Jacob	58	Wuertt	53-0557
Euphemia 58			
KELLER, Jacob	16	Neustadt	54-1470
KELLER, Johann	27	Kautenbach/Pr	52-1620
KELLER, Johann	25	Roslein	51-1588
KELLER, Johannes	38	Bietigheim	53-0838
KELLER, Johs.	40	Greiffenstein	49-0574
Magdalene 34, Louis 18, Genoveva 6			
KELLER, Juliane		Willofs	54-1575
KELLER, Kunigunde	19	Handorf	53-0492
KELLER, Mathilde	25	Constanze	53-1164
KELLER, Michael	45	Wiesenfeld	48-1355
Anna 34			
KELLER, Sholastica	23	Eiterfeld/Hes	51-1532
KELLER, Theod. Hch	31	Weissenfels	50-1132
KELLER, Wm.	32	Meiningen	47-0762
KELLER, v. Rud.	29	Solingen	48-0101
KELLERBASSEL, C(m)	32	Ibbenbahren	49-0416
G. (f) 31			
KELLERMANN, Johann	28	Crimmitschau	53-0928
Christian 23			
KELLIN, William	42	Hamburg	53-0914
KELLING, Dorothea	21	Hof/Baiern	53-0475
KELLING, Ernestine	17	Herford/Pr.	51-1725
KELLNER, Anna Barb	24	Lamershof	54-0903
KELLNER, Emelius	17	Hannover	53-0991
KELLNER, Heinrich	25	Schweina	52-0095
KELLNER, Veit	28	Sommerhaus	48-1355
KELZ, Valentin	18	Baiern	52-0370
KEMBEL, Georg	19	Cordes	54-1282
KEMELE, Christiane	19	Bethmar	54-1283
KEMLAGE, Leopold	22	Osnabrueck	52-1661
KEMLEIN, G.M.	40	Wiesenbach	52-0515
KEMLEIN, Maria M.	25	Weisenbach	52-0515
KEMMER, Joh. Adam	28	Kirchenlainit	54-0930
KEMP, Jacob	32	Leonberg/Wuer	52-0351
Friedericke 30, Friedericke 5, Gottlieb 3			
Maria (died) 6m			
KEMPE, Wilh.	27	Altenberge	53-0585
KEMPEL, Ernst	16	Grossen----	50-0439
KEMPER, Mathilde	18	Prussia	53-0628
KEMPF, Conrad	55	Giessen	53-1062
Johanetta 47, Sophia 22, Carolina 18			
Theodor 12			
KEMPF, Friedrich	18	Bruennau/Bav.	52-0807
KEMPF, Hermann	15	Cassel	54-1371
KEMPFER, Georg	53	Crimmitschau	54-0987
Henriette 16, Marie 4			
KEMPKEN, Jacob	25	Asperg	47-0872
KEMPKEN, Maria	55	Repelen	54-0053
Elisabeth 15, Sophie 13, Margaretha 9			
Anna 6			
KEMPLER, Jacob	6m	Germany	51-0460
KEMPNER, Anne	27	Gannitz	54-1724
KEMPTEN, H. (m)	23	Lansberg	48-0453
KENLEIN, G. (m)	23	Dirbelspiel	50-0746
KENNIG, Gertrud	21	Alfhausen	51-1160
KENSING, Hermann	30	Schledehausen	51-1588
Louisa 28, Fried. 10m			
KEOB, Carl	23	Dorum	54-1078
KEPFEL, J.G.	40	Gehaus	53-1013
Margareth 28			
KEPMECK, Christoph	27	Wuertenberg	53-0557
KEPNECK, Christoph	27	Wuertt	53-0557

NAME	AGE	RESIDENCE	YR-LIST
KEPPE, Friedr.	33	Winhausen	51-1084
KEPPLEMANN, A.	25	Gt. Britian	48-1015
KEPPLER, Friedrich	36	Wuertenberg	53-0557
KEPPLER, Joh.	23	Bergenweiler	54-0600
KERHEBEN, Augustus	30	Gronau	50-0840
KERL, Joseph	27	Friebenzog	50-0840
KERL, Louise	24	Rosenrohde	50-0366
KERLE, Daniel	20	Waldeck	52-1105
KERLE, Heinrich	25	Sachsenberg	53-0838
KERLING, Franz	26	Weissenfels	49-0324
KERLING, Lorentz	53	Michelau	52-1625
KERN, Anton	2-	Ansefar/Hess.	49-0365
KERN, Caroline	32	Gablonz/Oest.	52-1620
KERN, Caspar	47	Nauheim	54-0830
Ludwig 17, Jacob 16, Johannes 9, Carl 3			
Elisabeth 37, Justine 10, Elisabeth 6			
Marie 2, Christian 9m			
KERN, Catharine	50	Robern	51-0384
Michael 29, Auguste 21, Famingus (f) 11m			
August 18, Johann 15			
KERN, Elise	27	Schleusingen	52-1362
KERN, Helena	15	Rippenberg	52-1101
KERN, Joh.	30	Wien	49-0324
wife 27			
KERN, Joh. Leonh.	30	Wettringen	52-0515
Margaret 33			
KERN, Johannes	17	Bayreuth	51-1739
KERNER, Barbara	29	Schildhutter	53-0435
KERNER, Barbara		Schildhutter	53-0435
KERNER, Joseph	27	Weidennang	49-0781
KERPER, Heinrich	41	Tommerichhaus	54-1717
KERRES, Johannes	34	Bakenau	49-0345
KERSON, Jane	21	Breitenbach	54-1470
KERST, Adolph	29	Saxony	53-0628
KERST, Johannes	34	Niederkaufung	50-0292
KERSTEN, Heinr.	18	Cassel	54-0987
KERSTING, Lewis	26	Cassel	50-0323
Antonia 25			
KERTCHER, Sophia	21	Ziegelheim	54-0930
KERZ, Elise	22	Cothen	53-1086
KESES, (m)	36	Mansbach	53-1086
Bertha 13, Wilhelmine 11, Bianka 9			
Emil 7			
KESES, Joh. Christ	24	Erfurt	49-0352
KESPLER, Joh. Conr	39	Eberschuetz	51-0460
Marie Elise 38, Conrad 13, Friederike 11			
Friedrich 10			
KESSEL, Feit	23	Coburg	53-0324
Margarethe 25, Dorothea 9			
KESSLER, A. Cath.	18	Hausen	51-1160
KESSLER, Andreas		Aschenhausen	50-0323
KESSLER, Anna Barb	19	Ndr. Altheim	52-1423
KESSLER, Barbara	60	Schweinfurt	50-1317
Victoria 25, Veronica 27			
KESSLER, Carl	23	Noerdlingen	51-1245
KESSLER, Conrad	62	Stiebach/Bav.	52-1332
Barbara 58			
KESSLER, Georg	36	Laaga	54-1282
Anna 28, Franz 6			
KESSLER, Heinr.	38	Gotha	52-0895
Elisabeth 36, Christoph 15, Theodor 29			
Elisabeth 31, Heinrich 9			
KESSLER, Heinr.	28	Bringhausen	54-0600
KESSLER, Heinr.	16	Ackerhausen	50-0472
KESSLER, J.G.	20	Hermansrode	52-0370
KESSLER, Joh.	31	Frehenhorst	51-1084
KESSLER, Mariane	23	Waltbach	52-0095
KESSLER, Michael	21	Bavaria	50-0311
KESSLER, Seibert	25	Hessen	52-0699
KESSLER, Sophie C.	22	Ndr. Altheim	52-1423
KESSLER, Tobias	22	Unterelbe	54-1575
KESSNER, C.	21	Rheinsdorf	54-1283
KESSNER, Carolina	24	Gotha	53-0473
KESTEL, Johann	35	Schmelz	53-1000
Kunigunde 19			
KESTNER, Carl	26	Waltershausen	49-1358
Traugott 19, Gustav 17			
KESTNER, Georg	26	Lobenstein	49-0383

NAME	AGE	RESIDENCE	YR-LIST
KETTELKAMP, H. (m)	24	Prussia	50-0311
KETTLER, Heinrich	64	Wahmbeck	47-0872
Wilhelm 18, Tienchen 16			
KETTLER, Maria	15	Hunteberg	52-1580
KETTRITZ, Amalie	42	Zeitz	53-0324
Alwine 6			
KEUB, Gottlieb	16	Buch/Bav.	52-1620
KEUBER, Barbara	41	Langenleube	54-1168
Ida 12			
KEUCHER, J. Gottfr	42	Untergreistau	49-0324
KEUG, Paul	25	Lageloh	49-0742
KEUH, Lud.	20	Dresden	54-1419
KEUPER, Heinr.	17	W. Ollendorf	52-0960
KEYBOER, Mathias	51	Portslut	49-0912
Mantze 39, Jan 24, Machiline 9			
Janne Cath. 11m			
KEYENHAGEN, Friedr	35	Engter	47-0762
Christ. Lud. 25, Gerh. Heinr. 19			
Elis. Sophie 17, Herm. Heinr. 11			
KEYENHAGEN, Gerd.	65	Engter	47-0762
Anna Marie 55			
KEYERS, August	33	Mittelruessel	49-0737
KEYSER, Asmus	23	Grossenglis	52-0775
KEYSER, Friedrich	32	Katrinhagen	53-1086
KEYSER, P. (m)	26	Lauterbach/He	52-0960
KHUERY, Wenzel	20	Bilsen	54-1443
KIEBEL, Johannes	48	Marburg	53-1000
Cath. 49, Johs. 23, Cath. 21, Heinr. 19			
Elisab. 17, Cath Elisab. 16, Cath. 6			
KIEBER, Barbara	28	Ebnat	52-0515
KIEFHABER, Conrad	35	Bleck/Bav.	52-1620
KIEFHABER, John	27	Baiern	54-1724
KIEGLE, Rudolf	24	Stuckhard	53-0324
KIEL, Christian	28	Ottberg	52-0095
KIEL, Ferdinand	23	Rottenberg/He	52-1620
KIEL, Friedrich	16	Winzlar	53-1164
KIEL, Heinrich	57	Winzlar	54-1371
Margarethe 54			
KIEL, Heinrich	26	Winzlar	54-1371
KIEL, Wilhelm	30	Winzlar	54-1371
Sophie 24, Wilhelm 3, Caroline 2			
Wilhelmine 6m			
KIELGUS, Mathias	19	Baden	53-0590
KIELMEIER, Heinr.	28	Affinghausen	52-1512
Dorothea 20			
KIELMEYER, Carsten	48	Affinghausen	53-1016
Marie 52, Anna 25, Heinrich 11			
KIELMEYER, Hermann	14	Brockhausen	52-1512
KIELMEYER, Joh. H.	34	Affinghausen	53-1016
Meta 30, Sophia 9, Marie 2, Hermann 3			
Sophie 6m			
KIEM, Eduard	44	Ignitz	52-1105
KIENAPFEL, Emma	20	Schwerin	54-1297
KIENZLER, Gottlieb	41	Ohringen	49-0352
KIEPEL, Johannes	37	Hessen	54-1649
KIESEL, Theod.	25	Bremen	51-1725
Emilie Maria 25, Georg Herrm. 7m			
KIESEL, Valentin	38	Waldaschbach	54-1371
Rosina 39			
KIESELSTEIN, Fr. C	19	Nuernberg	52-0095
KIESHAUER, Jane Ch	58	Grossenstein	53-1164
KIESLING, Johann	19	Quellenreuth	52-0351
KIESS, Friedrich	28	Bergmann	54-1591
KIESSELBACH, C.(m)	25	Markuhl	52-0558
KIESSELSTEIN, Fr'd	26	Meiningen	48-1355
Friederike 21			
KIESSHAUER, Heinr.	28	Crimmitschau	52-1410
KIESSLING, Friedr.	24	Gersdorf/Sach	52-0960
KIESTE, Baptiste	22	Ottersweier	53-1164
KIETZINGER, Nic.	30	Leipzig	54-1575
KIFFE, B. (m)	21	Germany	49-0413
KILIAN, Aug.	20	Biedenkopf	48-1179
KILIAN, Chr.	29	Obernlippach	48-0447
KILIAN, Christian	27	Konnerstadt	50-0840
KILIAN, Franz	25	Bremen	53-1164
KILIAN, Joh Heinr.	47	Grossenruette	52-1362
Anna 44, George 17, Heinrich 7, Hermann 5			
Elisa 2			

NAME	AGE	RESIDENCE	YR-LIST
KILLER, Charles	23	Duermenz	53-1164
Adolphus 19			
KILLIAN, Ludw.	23	Cuxhaven	54-1724
KILLMER, August	25	Warburg	53-1070
KILLSCHELL, Karl	30	Brausnitz	54-1283
KILSSLEINER, John	25	Dilmannsdorf	50-0840
Anna 23, Bernhard 31			
KIMM, C. (m)	27	Sand	54-1341
KIMM, Mrs.	29	New York	48-0078
Elise 3, Anna 3, Gottfr. 1			
KIMME, Isaak	58	Sand	54-1341
Elisabeth 56, Anna 25, Leonard 31			
Jacob 9, son 9m			
KIMPEL, Johs.	28	Lauterbach/He	52-0960
KIND, Charles	24	Neukirchen	53-0991
KIND, Franz	26	Steinfeld	54-1716
KINDER, Caroline	30	Atens	53-1070
KINDER, Friedrich	20	Rotenburg	54-1649
KINDERMANN, D. (m)	34	Wahlen	54-1724
KINDERWATER, Soph.	22	Lippe	54-0882
KINNING, Wilh'mine	2	Bordel	51-1588
KINOLD, Christian	52	Willingen	52-1304
KINS, Richard	32	Roemhild	53-1164
KIPKE, Carl	26	Biegedorf	54-1716
Ernst 24, Franz 14, Rosine 20			
KIPP, Ludwig	40	Weiningen	54-1371
Christine 38, Engel 60, Sophie 11			
Heinrich 8			
KIPPHIN, Heinrich	22	Cassel	49-0413
KIRBERG, Caroline	23	Nienburg	50-0439
KIRCHDENKER, Joh.	28	Gotha	54-1554
KIRCHECK, Joh.	25	Hanau	49-1358
Cath. 24, Anna 8			
KIRCHENSTERNER,	24	Pasberg	53-0825
KIRCHHEIM, Cath.	19	Langenstein	54-1566
Anna 17			
KIRCHHOF, Georg	50	Nidda	52-1512
Friedr. 16, Hardtmann 21, Sophia 19			
KIRCHHOF, Georg	21	Niederorschel	53-0267
Dorothea 22, Adam 11m			
KIRCHHOF, Jacob	23	Niederoschel	52-0279
Ignatz 35			
KIRCHHOFF, Chr. Fr	18	Wolfersdorf	54-0930
KIRCHHOFF, Friedr.	19	Petershagnerh	54-0930
KIRCHHOFF, Henriet	21	Hildburghause	50-1132
KIRCHHOFF, William	44	Burlington	54-1168
KIRCHMAIER, Theres	36	Breitenloh	54-0872
KIRCHMEYER, Christ	32	Ottenburg/Bav	52-1332
KIRCHMEYER, Johana	21	Oldenburg	49-0329
KIRCHNER, Andreas	20	Meiningen	53-0590
KIRCHNER, Cath.	18	Elmshausen	52-0699
KIRCHNER, Charles	31	Neutorf	54-1470
Elisabeth 30, Caroline 6, William 4			
Louisa 2, Charles 2m			
KIRCHNER, Conr.	28	Liederbach	54-0600
KIRCHNER, Eva	29	Coburg	50-0379
KIRCHNER, H.	29	Carlshaven	51-0460
Christine 20			
KIRCHNER, Johannes	43	Wernshausen	53-1000
KIRCHNER, Johannes	38	Kaltensensfel	49-0781
Anna Cath. M 38, Eva E. 8, Elizabeth 4			
baby			
KIRCHNER, Kilian		Althausen	53-0942
KIRCHNER, Magdalen	24	Stettbach	48-0260
KIRCHNER, Margaret	22	Cadolzburg	50-0439
KIRCHNER, Pauline	20	Birkenfeld	49-1358
Charlotte 31			
KIRCHNER, Peter	17	Hessen	52-0699
KIRCHNER, Rudolph	42	Aschersleben	54-1297
Otto 8			
KIRCHNER, Wm.	20	Lauchroeden	53-1013
KIRKENBERG, Sophie	25	Nienburg	50-0021
KIRMSE, G.H.	26	Altenburg	52-1129
KIRRSIG, Herm.	17	Tarman	49-0574
KIRSCH, Barbara	28	Fulda	51-0405
KIRSCH, John	23	Wuerzburg	47-0158
KIRSCHBAUM, Andr.	29	Rodach	54-0053
KIRSCHBAUM, J. Geo	28	Borbath	54-1371

NAME	AGE	RESIDENCE	YR-LIST
KIRSCHBAUM, Johann	26	Salzbach/Bav.	54-1092
KIRSCHER, Ludwig	31	Huenfeld	52-0563
KIRSCHFELD, Eduard	26	Nordhausen	52-0095
Louise 28			
KIRSCHLING, George	30	Tiegenhagen	51-1588
Christine 24			
KIRSCHNER, Nicolas	23	Schmalzdorf	52-1362
KIRSCHNER, Philipp	25	Biebrich	47-0672
KIRSTEN, Ludwig	18	Mannstadt	51-1101
Gotthold 17			
KIRTING, Anna	9		53-0928
KISCHER, Friedrich	18	Hoya	52-1410
KISELKA, Joseph	33	Andryone	54-1676
Barbara 32, Jakob 10			
KISKETHIEN, Rud. L	22	Machtnung	47-0672
Louis 20			
KISSEL, Philippine	45	Schwalbach	51-1035
Heinrich 16			
KISSLING, Edward	28	Altenburg/Sax	48-0053
KISSLING, Johann	34	Bayern	53-0557
Anna Barbara 30, Anna Cath. 3			
Eva Margaret 6m			
KISSNER, (m)	31	Bettenhausen	54-0918
Anna Cha. 26, Christian 4, Gustav L. by			
KISSNER, Maria	14	Bulfenrode	54-0830
KISTER, Aug.	25	Boelen	50-1071
KISTER, J. Fr. Wm.	37	Bremen	51-0352
KISTER, Kolban	44	Grafenhausen	52-1105
KISTNER, Charles	26	Washington	53-1164
KITTEL, Adam	19	Hinterweiler	53-0320
KITTEL, Ferd.	54	Berlin	53-1164
KITTEL, Maria	60	Halle	54-0987
KITTLEIN, Ana Barb	20	Schrokenloh	53-0324
KITTLER, Gust. A.	19	Leipzig	52-1321
KITZELE, Wilhelm	22	Unterturkheim	53-0320
KITZER, Johann	39	Hottenbach	51-1062
Caroline 44, Friedrich 12, Caroline 7			
KITZING, Gottlieb	29	Calbsried	50-0379
Carl 19			
KITZINGER, Joseph	34	Obermoessring	54-1554
KITZLER, Anna	58	Andressen/Boh	54-1676
Franziska 26, Barbara 20			
KLABUNA, Christ. F	29	Steinweisen	53-0914
KLAENER, Gerard	35	Streck	53-0991
KLAFFEIER, Conr.	25	Barkdrup	52-1321
KLAFFER, Friedr.	55	Weitersheim	51-1588
Leonore 44, Leonore 22, Carloline 15			
Friedr. 11, Wm. 9, Christian 5, Mary 4			
Anton 2			
KLAFFKY, Andreas	21	Preussen	52-0699
KLAFFTLEISS, Fried	28	Esperstaedt	50-0379
Ernestine 27			
KLAGES, Aug.	27	Einbeck	50-0472
KLAGES, Friedrich	26	Hollenstedt	53-1164
KLAGES, Minna	27	Rethen	49-1358
KLAGETER, B. (m)	25	Haver	48-0453
KLAHOLZ, Franz	29	Bomkirchen	54-0053
KLAHRE, Theodor	50	Naumburg	52-1200
Henriette 46, Theodor 24, Oscar 10			
Anna 8			
KLAMHOF, Johann	37	Buxtehude	54-0882
KLAMM, Bernhard	48	Schwetzingen	51-0384
Catharina 45, Barbara 13, Catharina 6			
Maria 7			
KLAPDOR, Peter	32	Muenster	54-1371
KLAPPER, Carl	34	-adfeshausen	54-1341
KLAPPERT, Jacob	25	Hersfeld	53-0652
KLAPPROTH, F. (m)	29	Holzminden	54-1566
KLAPPSTEIN, Mayer	26	Altenburg	54-1717
KLAPROTH, Martin	44	Saalfeld	52-0699
Marta 40			
KLAR, Christ.	28	Nidda	48-1131
Gretchen 22			
KLAS, Johannes	45	Fischbach/Nas	53-0628
Catharine 41, Johann Adam 23, Heinrich 13			
KLASS, Philipp	24	Bornich/Nass.	48-0447
KLASSE, Julius	25	Merseburg	53-0652
KLATTE, Gosselke	19	Bremen	50-1236

NAME	AGE	RESIDENCE	YR-LIST
KLATTE, Hermann	18	Zaur	54-0987
Heinrich 21			
KLAUDER, Anna	19	Misselwarden	50-0366
KLAUER, Heinrich	46	Erfurt	54-1649
Clara 50, Ernst 15, Theodor 13			
Caroline 4			
KLAUER, Johann	29	Schleusingen	52-0807
KLAUFF, Andreas	25	Berghuelen	53-0838
KLAUK, Elise	23	Homberg	54-1168
KLAUNINGER, C. (m)	22	Walpenreuth	54-1341
KLAUS, August	17	Wittlage	49-0413
KLAUS, Conrad	39	Halmshaus	51-1062
Wilhelm 29			
KLAUS, Gerhard	18	Stapelfeld	54-1371
KLAUSFELDER, Siegm	22	Nuernberg	53-1000
KLAUSING, Caroline	26	Wiersen	54-1282
Caroline			
KLAUSMEYER, Friedr	38	Gramberg	53-1086
Catharine 34, Marie 58			
KLAUSSEN, Jette	24	Bremen	49-1358
KLAUSSNER, Cath.	31	Brand/Bav.	53-0628
KLAUSSNER, Kunigun	29	Duisbrun/Bav.	53-0628
KLEBE, Wilhelm	19	Hofgeismar	52-1321
KLEE, Christian	30	Oestheim	49-0781
Christine 35, baby			
KLEE, Conr.	17	Ottersberg	49-1358
KLEEMANN, Robert	32	Ulm	54-1566
Magdalena 27, Robert 5, Heinrich 4			
Elise 9m			
KLEEMANN, Wilh.	31	Coburg	52-1304
KLEFF, William	53	Ruppigrath	53-0991
KLEHMANN, Johann	33	Hof a.Steinac	53-0324
Anna Margret 36, Ludwig 17			
Anna Margret 12, Nicolaus 9, Margrethe 4			
Johann 1			
KLEIER, Christoph	36	Hoerlach	54-1554
KLEIM, John	19	Augsburg	50-0840
KLEIMANN, Philipp	26	Wisloch	51-1686
Gesine 30			
KLEIN, Carl	38	Freiberg	52-1512
Maria 24			
KLEIN, Carl Peter	32	Geilsheim	52-0279
Louise 4			
KLEIN, Conrad	22	Volkerthausen	54-1554
KLEIN, Conrad	23	Gemunden	50-0379
KLEIN, David	21	Westheim	53-0928
KLEIN, Elisabeth	60	Marburg	49-0912
KLEIN, Emil	20	Bertelsdorf	53-0825
KLEIN, Fr.	39	Lennep	53-1016
Margarethe 27, Friedrich 6, Carl 2			
Ida 9m			
KLEIN, Friedrich	32	Wirtenbach	53-1070
KLEIN, H.	27	Ziegenhain	51-1160
KLEIN, Heinrich	16	Marburg	52-0699
KLEIN, Herman	40	Nordhausen	51-1588
Catherine 40, John 19, Herman 18, Anna 17			
Louisa 16, Catherine 14			
KLEIN, Hermann	23	Frankfurt/M.	54-1092
KLEIN, Isaac	31	Koengen	51-1640
KLEIN, J. (m)	20	Buellenbach	49-0416
KLEIN, Joh. Th.	27	Wasungen	53-0905
KLEIN, John James	18	Krammenau	53-0991
KLEIN, Joseph	22	Muenchen/Bav.	54-1092
KLEIN, Leonhard	27	Ohrenbach	51-1438
Friedrich 25			
KLEIN, Louise	30	Breslau	54-1078
KLEIN, Marie	21	Kreinsfeld	53-1070
KLEIN, Nicolaus	24	Bebra	51-0352
KLEIN, Peter	18	Sietzenhofen	54-1371
KLEIN, Philipp	27	Loedel	53-1023
KLEIN, Wilhelm	36	Leidhecken	53-1086
Barbara 40, Margaretha 50, Georg 11			
Elisabeth 5, August 3, Anna M. 40			
Katharina 5, Kaetchen 3			
KLEINE, Charlotte	22	Severns	53-0942
KLEINE, Charlotte	18	Ostenholze	50-0944
KLEINE, Heinrich	35	Magdeburg	52-1148
KLEINE, Heinrich	40	Enger	52-1452

NAME	AGE	RESIDENCE	YR-LIST
KLEINECKE, Wilhelm	29	Lauterberg/Ha	52-1332
KLEINEIBST, Adolph	26	Baltimore	54-1371
KLEINERT, John		Arzberg/Bav.	50-0323
KLEINFAHL, Philipp	26	Rembeck	51-0352
KLEINGUENNER, Adel	20	Dornheim	52-1304
KLEINHAND, Barbara	38	Wien	54-0987
Barbara 7, Andreas by			
KLEINHAUER, H.	27	Hessen	51-1084
KLEINHAUS, Friedr.	28	Morlingen	50-0944
Louisa 25			
KLEINHAUS, Jacob	32	Tringhausen	52-0563
Martha E. 38			
KLEINMANN, Louis	27	Hildburghause	52-0117
KLEINMAYER, Gabr.	26	Pappenheim	54-0850
KLEINMEYER, Salmon	30	Pappenheim	50-0311
KLEINPETER, Franz	34	Ulrichstal	54-1371
KLEINROTH, Auguste	26	Glatz	52-1661
KLEINSCHMIDT, Fr.	30	Schleusingen	54-0903
Carl 22			
KLEINSCHMIDT, Frke	25	Vilsen	48-0406
KLEINSCHMIDT, G.	25	Humburg/Hess	47-0987
KLEINSCHMIDT, Gert	5	Wellingholzha	51-0352
KLEINSCHMIDT, Jean	20	Niederschelds	53-1016
KLEINSCHMITZ, Ad.	28	Unterheinach	53-0905
KLEINSCHROTH, Joh.	32	Knottstadt	51-1796
KLEINSTAUBER, Chr.	20	Warburg	54-1283
KLEINSTEUBER, Abb.	29	Ruhla	50-1071
KLEINSTEUBNER, H.	23	Gotha	52-1332
KLEIPPER, Charlott	19	Sand	54-1341
KLEIPPERT, Valent.	20	Eiterfeld	54-0053
KLEIS, Heinrich	25	Leer	50-0366
KLEIS, Theodor	28	Drensteinfurt	54-1371
KLEISNER, W.	21	Braunschweig	54-1283
KLEIST, Gerhard	19	Lingen	51-1101
Caroline 17, Lisette 23			
KLEMIN, Conrad	21	Ruettenau	53-0585
KLEMM, August	30	Oldendorf/Han	52-1423
KLEMM, Carl Fr.	40	Baussa	50-1236
Caroline 30, Anna 10, Lina 8, Franz 5			
Carl 2			
KLEMM, Joh. Ant.	25	Happenbach	53-0435
KLEMME, Christine	45	Oerlinghausen	54-1297
Charlotte 16, Louise 20			
KLEMME, Ernst	26	Verliehausen	54-1371
KLEMME, Ludwig			50-0944
KLEMME, Therese	17	Oerlinghausen	54-1297
KLEMMER, Alb.	23	Wiesenstein	54-1283
KLENE, Margarthe	15	Cincinnati	48-0101
KLENNIG, Ed.	22	Alfhausen	51-1160
Gertrud 21			
KLEPPER, Emil	19	Cassel	54-1371
KLEPPER, Heinr.	28	Bielefeld	51-1686
KLESSIG, Ernst	22	Schlagwitz	50-0323
August 20			
KLETT, Augustus	25	Suhl	53-1164
KLEWITZ, Ludwig	32	Dessau	48-0101
KLEYER, Rosine	23	Bayern	54-1649
KLIE, Friedrich	44	Friedland	54-1297
KLIE, G.F. (m)	16	Doerigsen	54-1168
KLIEBENSEHER, Anna		Muenchen/Bav.	50-0323
KLIEBER, Joh Jacob	21	Malchis/Hess.	51-1532
KLIEKAMP, Marie	32	Wolsa	47-0762
Agnes 24, Marie 18, Elisabeth 14, Anna 9			
Gerhard 6			
KLIER, Joh. Friedr	26	Elberfeld/Pr.	51-1725
KLIN, Elisabetha	58	Nidda	54-1717
KLINE, Herman	40	Nordhausen	51-1588
Catherine 40, John 19, Herman 18, Anna 17			
Louisa 16, Catherine 14			
KLING, Ludwig	59	Schoemberg	54-0903
Caroline 48, Friederike 16, Ludwig 7			
KLINGE, Joh.	25	Goettingen	50-0311
KLINGE, Marianne	21	Schwarzbach	50-1067
KLINGELHOEFER, Con	21	Hessen	53-0590
KLINGEMANN, Georg	28	Bassum	50-1071
KLINGER, Wilhelm	25	Neu Oltmansdo	53-0324
KLINGERNELE, C.	29	Wiesenstein	54-1283
KLINGHAMMER, Fried	32	Rosswein	48-1179
KLINGHOLZ, Richard	33	Sprockhoevel	53-0991
KLINGSTON, Theod.	18	Borgfeld/Pr.	51-0048
KLINKE, Anna	24	Brueckenheim	49-0329
KLINKEL, Georg	24	Buttershausen	54-0965
Cathrine 22, Elisabeth 2			
KLINKER, Ludwig	17	Elsoff	52-0563
KLINKERMANN, Heinr	32	Ringerhare	49-1517
KLINKLE, John	23	Meimler	49-1517
KLINZMAN, Friedr.	32	Ballin	53-0905
Friederika 31, Maria 4, Christian by			
KLIPPERT, Conrad	17	Rupperhausen	51-0352
KLIPPSTEIN, Louis	26	Battenberg	54-1371
KLOBUS, Heinrich	28	Hesserothe	51-1062
Cath. Elis. 24, Jacob by			
KLOCKE, Caroline	23	Leopoldsthal	48-0565
KLOCKEMEYER, Henry	29	Harpenfeld	54-1470
Ann 30, Ann 4, Henry 2			
KLOCKENBRINK, Wilh	19	Osnabrueck	54-0850
KLOEFFLER, Heinr.	24	Cassel	50-0021
KLOEGER, Lewis	46	Durlach	53-1164
KLOEPFER, Rosine	22	Aichenbach	49-0352
KLOEPPER, C. (m)	24	Frille	52-1321
KLOES, Marie	24	Ockersdorf	52-0807
KLOFFER, Wilhelm	17	Kirchheim	54-0053
KLOFT, Heinrich	27	Luesche	52-0563
KLOKA, Hanna	25	Detmold	52-0804
KLOOGORN, Maria	29	Stoode	49-1517
KLOPFER, Elise	17	Heueben	54-0872
KLOPPENBERG, T.(m)	28		54-1591
KLOPPENBURG, Alb.	22	Oldenburg	50-0311
KLOPPENBURG, Bernh	32	Emsdetten	48-0260
Herrmann 19			
KLOPPENBURG, Chas.	20	Mittelruessel	49-0737
KLOPPENBURG, John	17	Salzwedel	54-1591
Catharine 19			
KLOSE, Wilhelm	18	Rotenburg	54-1575
KLOSS, Anna	34	Reichenberg	53-0905
KLOSS, Lebrecht	32	Friedeberg	50-1132
Marie 33, Bertha 9			
KLOSSE, J.	45	Breslau	54-1716
Hedwig 38, Juliane 7			
KLOSSMANN, Marie	23	Schildesche	54-1554
KLOSTERKAMPER, A.	21	Amelsbuehren	49-1358
KLOSTERMANN, Franz	23	Steinfeld	48-1355
KLOSTERMANN, Marg.	21	Steinfeld	49-0324
KLOTEN, L. (m)	28	Camp/Pr.	48-0447
KLOTHUSEN, Heinr.	14	Stotel	53-0590
KLOTSCH, Franz	33	Goselitz	51-1084
KLOTT, Philipp	22	Oberwaldstadt	49-0383
KLOTZ, Catharina	29	Schorndorf	53-0320
KLOTZ, Christiane	26	Crimmitschau	53-1164
KLOTZ, Ignaz	44	Tyrol	48-0887
Johanne 37, Cresenze 8, Nicolaus 6			
Ignaz 5, Catharine 1			
KLOTZBACH, Heinz	38	Geyer	49-1106
Margr. 38, Heinr. 16			
KLOTZBACH, Johann	22	Lengers	48-0260
KLOTZBACH, Marie	46	Lengsfeld	53-0942
KLUEBER, Gottfr.	28	Baiern	52-0370
KLUEBER, Justine	31	Elters	51-0500
KLUENDER, William	33	Schwartau/Old	50-0323
KLUEPER, Adolph	28	Lippe	52-0048
KLUESEKAMP, Georg	27	Ahrhaus	54-0600
KLUEVER, Heinrich	38	Hohne	50-0292
KLUG, Minna	18	Niedenstein	52-1105
KLUG, Wilhelm	25	Vatterode	54-0850
KLUGE, Michael	21	Zagkwitz	54-0930
KLUMP, Bertha	20	Kappelroda	51-0352
KLUMP, Johanna	23	Langenzlan	48-0951
Johanette 16			
KLUMPP, Friedrich	33	Philadelphia	53-0991
Friedrich 7			
KLUSING, Charles J	24	Herdingen	54-1470
KLUSS, Julius	22	Schlesien	52-1620
KLUTE, Christine	20	Hannover	50-0311
KNAB, Conrad	18	Lockney	52-0095
KNABE, Alexander	21	Zwickau	53-0267
KNACK, Catharine	26	Oberwarf	52-1580

NAME	AGE	RESIDENCE	YR-LIST
KNAEKUELS, Maria	18	Schledehausen	51-1588
KNALL, Simon	32	Weitzenhofen	52-1321
Mary 30			
KNAP, Carl	47	Burg	53-0267
Johanne 48			
KNAPP, Angelica	19	Bohmte	52-1200
Friederike 17			
KNAPP, Christian	37	Ulm/Wrt.	54-1092
Maria B. 42, Johann C. 7			
KNAPP, Elisabeth	47	Essen	50-0292
Elisabeth 21			
KNAST, Marie Engel	28	Essen	53-0825
KNAT, Lambert	21	Baiern	52-0370
KNAUER, Kunigunde	20	Niendorf	48-1355
KNAUER, Peter	23	Coburg	52-0895
KNAUF, Heinrich	18	Cassel	52-0699
KNAUF, Ludwig	19	Udenhausen	54-1554
KNAUS, Carl	26	Hanau	49-1106
Louise 29, Lud. 24			
KNAUS, E. (m)	24	Fesseldorf	52-0558
KNAUS, Thomas	40	Kln. Langheim	52-1423
KNAUSER, Cath.	20	Markseid	52-1661
KNAUSS, Chr. Fried	32	Schorndorf	49-0352
KNEBEL, Dorette	32	Hildesheim	53-0652
Heinrich 15			
KNEBEL, Maria Cath	53	Laasphe	54-0903
Alf. Friedr. 25, Friedrich 16			
KNECHT, Carl	24	Geislingen	54-0987
KNECHT, Daniel	27	Rullen	48-0406
KNECHT, Friederike	21	Augsburg	54-1001
KNEER, H.	27	Herdingen	54-1470
KNEES, Joh. Carl	58	Rodenberg	48-1114
Cath. Doroth 54, Wm. 17, Louis 13			
Heinr. 18, Sophia 25			
KNEFELI, Henry	25	Wiesbaden/Nas	48-0447
Marie 22			
KNEITZ, Joh. Leonh	19	Culmbach	54-1371
KNETSCH, Heinrich	27	Monterbach	52-0807
KNETZLE, Benedict	37	Wemding	52-1200
Walburga 34			
KNIBBE, William	20	Bodenfelde/Ha	50-0323
KNICK, Andr.	67	Muenden/Bav.	51-0048
KNICKMANN, Diedr.	26	Bassum/Hann.	52-1332
KNIEBEL, Heinr.	16	Neuenkirch	51-1245
KNIERIEN, Justus	27	Lengsfeld	49-0413
KNIERNSCHILD, Fr'd	31	Muehlberg	53-1062
Augusta 35, Emilia 7			
KNIES, Richard	32	Roemhild	53-1164
KNIES, Valentin	22	Buchenheim	52-1661
KNIESE, Adam	23	Fussen Erfurt	53-0942
KNIESEL, Marie	44	Handingen/Bad	52-1332
KNIESS, Anna Marta	22	Sues	48-0284
KNIESS, Georg	39	Nied	54-1717
Marie 34, Georg 10, Johannes 7			
Heinrich 5			
KNIEST, Eduard	35	Brunswyk	51-1725
KNIEWASSER, Joh. G	23	Schwabach	50-1071
Amalia 26			
KNIGGE, Andr.	47	Brunswick/Br.	51-0048
Johanne 54, Heinr. 26, William 24			
August 21			
KNINBEL, Franz K.	24	Mittelruessel	49-0737
KNIPP, Friedr.	25	Waldeck	50-0021
KNIPPENBERG, Chr.	28	Neuhaus/Hann.	52-0960
KNIPS, Conr.	38	Fulda	50-0472
KNIRIEMEN, Friedr.	31	Eiderhofen	51-1796
KNIRL, Friedrich	19	Unternbribert	50-0379
KNISE, Heinrich	32	Niederurff	48-1184
Friedrike 36, Elise 3			
KNITTEL, Heinr.	45	Huettenguss	53-0914
Anna 43, Christine 19, Marie 13, Henry 21			
Rosine 12, Margr. 7			
KNITTEL, Silvester	27	Muehlhausen	52-0699
KNIZEKI, Joseph	35	Andryone	54-1676
Anne 30, Marie 6			
KNOB, Jacob	18	Reutlingen	49-0329
KNOBLAUCH, August	18	Steinau	54-1168
Marie 14			

NAME	AGE	RESIDENCE	YR-LIST
KNOBLAUCH, J.H.(m)	25	Twellake	49-0324
KNOCH, Heinrich	49	Salzungen	49-0413
Adam 24, Catharina 15			
KNOCHENHAUER, Hein	29	Halberstadt	54-1168
KNOCK, A. (m)	21	Neundorf	49-1358
KNOCK, Adam	27	Hessen	51-1245
KNOEBEL, Margareth	25	Wohnsgehaig	54-0850
KNOELKE, Adolph	53	Hardegen	48-1355
Louise 23			
KNOENER, Conrad	33	Minden	52-0563
KNOEPFEL, Adolph	17	Cassel	53-0888
KNOFF, Anna Cath.	31	Helmbrecht	54-0930
KNOLBL, Carl	42	Schoenlind	54-1566
KNOOP, Dan. Deric	19	Bremen	53-1164
KNOOR, Joseph	54	Heinrichsdorf	50-0439
Andr. 27, Franz 23, Anna 22, Luise 23			
Martha 51, Ernst by			
KNOP, Conrad	35	Hessendorf	51-1640
Anna 31			
KNOR, Andreas	48	Lichtenfels	50-0379
Barbara 48, Margaretha 20, Marianne 10			
Georg 8			
KNOR, Nicolaus	34	Nitelbach	53-0324
Barbara 37, Georg 4, Barbara 51			
KNORLG, Marg.		Rochlitz	48-1131
KNORR, Benedict	-1	Torbau/Bav.	50-0323
KNORR, M. (m)	24	Tauberzoll	52-0558
KNORR, Martin	34	Cassel	53-1023
Margarethe 34, Georg 5, Barbara 2			
KNOSCH, Georg	23	Hansendorf/Bv	53-0628
Johann 28			
KNOTZ, Michael	52	Weissbrunn	48-0101
KNUEBEL, Bekka	28	Utlehde	50-1067
KNUEDDEL, Christ.	39	Neuhaus/Bav.	53-0475
Anna 32, Margarethe 7			
KNUEPFEL, Adam	41	Niedenstein	52-1105
Maria 41, Georg 14, Heinr. 9, Elisab. 5			
Johannes 3, Carl 1			
KNUEPFER, Gottlieb	28	Elsnitz/Sax.	54-1092
KNUEPFER, Hermann	24	Redenitz/Sax	54-1092
Ernestine 17			
KNUEPFER, Pauline	23	Gera	53-0590
Henriette 18, Moritz 29			
KNUEPPER, F.	25	Beckum	51-0517
KNUEPPLING, Friedr	17	Aschen	53-1062
KNUETTEL, Margaret	25	Finkler	52-0370
KNUOF, Wilhelm	29	Backnang	49-1517
KNUPFER, H. (m)	20	Langenstade	49-0383
KNUST, Wilhelmine	42	Magdeburg	53-1070
KOBER, Johann	23	Augsfeld	51-0352
KOBI, Sara	27	Wiseck	54-1554
KOBISCH, Maria	60	Brake	50-1071
KOBMANN, Friedrich	20	Altendorf	53-0637
KOBMANN, Sophie	26	Egloffsheim	54-0987
KOBOLD, Joh. Chr.	52	Naundorf	50-1071
KOBROCK, Rebecca	21	Suess	48-0269
KOBSTAED, Ernestin	25	Friedrichsrod	54-1282
KOCH, Ad.	37	Nonnenroth	47-0868
Susanne 30, Heinrich 7, Jost (died) 2			
KOCH, Adam	40	Treysa	51-0352
Leonhard 33			
KOCH, Adolph	17	Carlsruhe	52-1362
KOCH, Albert	22	Barn	54-1297
KOCH, Alois	28	Preussen	53-0590
KOCH, Anna	38	Sondershausen	53-0473
KOCH, Anton	45	Frille	51-1588
Mary 40, John 12, Anna 8, Louisa 4			
KOCH, August	23	Biebrach	49-0352
KOCH, August	29	Geldershausen	47-0672
KOCH, Balthasar	40	Nentershausen	48-0269
Daniel 39, Margaretha 36, Wm. 10, Fr. 8			
Sophie 3			
KOCH, Bernhard	36	Paderborn/Pr.	51-1532
KOCH, C. Friedr.	26	Cassel	48-0101
KOCH, Caecilie	18	Prag	48-1131
KOCH, Carl	26	Stolzenau	54-1716
KOCH, Carl	31	Frille	51-1588
KOCH, Carl	19	Peterfeld	52-0699

NAME	AGE	RESIDENCE	YR-LIST
KOCH, Carl	3m	Germany	51-0460
KOCH, Cas.	27	Alsfeld	53-0905
KOCH, Cath. Margr.	29	Melle	52-0872
KOCH, Chr. Fr.	29	Marbach	54-1575
KOCH, Christ.	31	Peine	51-0405
Doroth. 33, Wilhelm 8			
KOCH, Christian	39	Langensalza	54-0987
KOCH, Christian	16	Paderborn	54-1371
Wilh. Anton 57			
KOCH, Christine	23	Dankersen	52-1321
Henr. 2, Henr. 74			
KOCH, Christoph	40	Gebstedt	52-1148
Marie 35, Hermann 14, Carl 11, Gustav 6m			
KOCH, Conrad	18	Jesburg	54-1168
KOCH, Conrad	20	Treysa	49-0345
KOCH, Diedr.	33	S. Deich/Hann	52-0960
KOCH, Eduard	21	Braunschweig	48-1355
KOCH, Elisabeth	28	Wedelbach/Hes	52-1620
Martha 28			
KOCH, Elisabeth	35	Eldersdorf	53-0320
KOCH, Elisabeth	16	Grossenglis	53-0942
KOCH, Elise	19	Warenrode	52-0652
KOCH, Ernest	21	Bayreuth	53-0888
KOCH, Ernestine	28	Erfurt	51-0460
Fritz 3, Wilhelm 2			
KOCH, F. (m)	36	Welsede	48-0445
G. (m) 24, Louise (m) 26			
KOCH, Ferdinand	32	Schleusingen	52-1362
Friedrike 21			
KOCH, Ferdinand	28	Buczkowo	54-1297
KOCH, Franz Otto	33	Paderborn	54-0903
KOCH, Friedr.	43	Zweibruecken	54-1566
KOCH, Friedr.	19	Nuttenbusch	48-0053
KOCH, Friedr.	27	Versmold	49-0352
KOCH, Friedr. Wm.	18	Hildburghause	49-0352
KOCH, Friedrich	27	Nordheim	53-1086
Marie 27			
KOCH, Friedrich	46	Frille	51-1588
Christine 42, Christian 11, Carle 7			
Christine 24, Leanore 20, Sophie 18			
KOCH, Friedrich	18	Muehlhausen	52-0699
KOCH, Friedrich	31	Bruchhausen	49-0413
KOCH, Gertrud	28	Sendenhorst	53-0585
KOCH, H.	35	Niederbessing	47-0868
M. 27, M. 5, S. 3, H. 1			
KOCH, Heinr.	19	Aschersleben	54-0600
Andreas 24, Hermine 28			
KOCH, Heinr.	20	Hannover	51-1160
KOCH, Heinr.	30	Dankersen	52-1321
KOCH, Heinr. Aug.	26	Rannetze	48-1131
KOCH, Heinrich	21	Grossenglis	52-0775
KOCH, Heinrich	22	Scharmbeck	50-0366
KOCH, Herm.	22	Bremen	53-0991
KOCH, J.H.	43	Hammeln	53-0161
KOCH, Jacob	17	Piepen	51-0500
KOCH, Joh. Heinr.	20	Gerach	54-1649
KOCH, Johann	36	Schmalzgruben	53-1016
Catharine 39, Joseph 9, Michael 7			
Georg 4, Margrete 12, Anna 2			
KOCH, Johann	21	Mehlen	54-0918
KOCH, Johann	22	Kaltenbach	54-1554
Gertrud 24			
KOCH, Johann	34	Oesdorf	53-0825
Elisabeth 36, Catharina 9, Franzisca 3			
Johannes 9m			
KOCH, Johann	34	Tagewerkshaus	51-0352
KOCH, John	26	Mittelruessel	49-0737
KOCH, Joseph	23	Reuhendorf	54-0600
KOCH, Joseph	24	Emsdetten	48-0260
KOCH, L.	28	Brackel	51-0517
KOCH, Ludwig	49	Destel	52-1200
Anna Maria 53			
KOCH, Ludwig	25	Treysa	49-0345
KOCH, Ludwig	21	Alsfeld	51-0352
KOCH, Ludwig	39	Eberschuetz	51-0460
Maria 32, Anna 15, Caroline 13			
Dorothea 6, Wilh. 4			
KOCH, M. (f)	22	Limburg	50-0746

NAME	AGE	RESIDENCE	YR-LIST
KOCH, Marie	18	Niederstolzin	54-0600
Sidonie 16			
KOCH, Marie Elis.	19	Obermoellrich	48-1179
KOCH, Marie Georg.	21	Eisfeld	53-0914
KOCH, Rebecca	25	Werder	53-0991
KOCH, Sophie	27	Marburg	52-0699
Wilhelm 2			
KOCH, Theo.	23	Neersen	52-0095
KOCH, Therese	20	Wemptingen	53-0320
KOCH, Therese	27	Schmichten	51-1245
August 23, Wilhelm 19, Marie 16			
Franziska 6, Ludwiga 11m			
KOCH, Therese	31	Haidhausen	54-1297
Anna 5, Caroline 11m			
KOCH, Wilhelm	36	Gebstedt	52-1148
Maria 30, Oswald 3, August 2			
KOCH, Wilhelm	46	Weimar/Weimar	51-1725
Anna Elisabe 44, Barbara 14, Emma 9			
Maria 6, Wilhelm 3			
KOCH, Wilhelm	21	Berka	48-0284
KOCH, Wm.	18	Ilserhaide	51-1588
KOCH, v. William	30	Hohegeis/Brun	51-0048
KOCHLE, Anna	20	Weisenhaide/B	53-0475
KOCHLING, Martin	25	Borgholz	51-1101
KOCHMANN, Georg	28	Bliesewach	53-0905
Catharina 29, Anna by, Catharina 4			
Maria 18			
KOCHSEL, Conrad	49	Kirchdorf	47-0672
Dorothe 36, Heinrich 18, Sophia 11			
Friedrich 9, Conrad 7, Wilhelm 4			
KOCI, Joseph	32	Boehmen	53-1000
Marie 38, Roesel 3			
KOCK, Diedrich	28	Doehlen	53-0888
KOCK, Heinr.	18	Neukirchen	52-1105
KOCKBERG, Louis	26	Osterode	48-0887
KODER, Joh.	25	Bavaria	50-0311
KOEBEL, Marg.		Telbershausen	54-1575
KOEBER, Georg	33	Rineck	52-1625
KOEBER, Joh. Chr.	28	Gera	53-0905
Joh. Sophie 32, August Ed. 9			
Johanne Emma 2, Johanna Soph by			
KOECHELN, Math.	26	Obergensburg	49-0324
KOECHER, J. (m)	25	Rabers	50-0746
KOECHFLETH, Julius	20	New York	54-0987
Elisabeth 23, Ida by			
KOEDEL, G.H. (m)	18	Langendorf/Bv	52-0960
KOEGEL, August	35	Sachsen	53-0590
KOEGEL, Carl Heinr	38	Stoessen	53-0888
Clara 25, Chr. Heinr. 58			
KOEGELMAIER, Andre	22	Schwabing	54-1168
Carl 28, Marie 26			
KOEHLER, Anton	20	Masslowitz	54-1566
KOEHLER, Bernhard	32	Wernigerode	51-1686
Johanne 28, Louis 3, Hermann 1			
KOEHLER, Carl	42	Radlazdorf	52-1148
Christ. M. 42, Ferdinand 13, Lina 11			
Robert 6, Therese 4, Anna 1			
KOEHLER, Caspar	30	Steelz/Darm.	50-0323
KOEHLER, Ferdinand	44	Boehnenwerda	53-0652
KOEHLER, Fr.	23	Frankenhausen	53-0492
KOEHLER, Fr. Ludw.	25	Fischbach/Nas	53-0628
Johannette 23			
KOEHLER, Franz	23	Brockhusen/Ha	51-0048
KOEHLER, Friedrich	31	Beersdorf	53-0652
KOEHLER, G.J. (m)	19	Neuwieter	49-0329
KOEHLER, Georg	26	Freiberg	51-1084
KOEHLER, H.	45	Bremen	50-0119
KOEHLER, Hein.	29	Bleicheralte	52-1321
KOEHLER, Heinr.	27	Osterhagen	50-1132
Marie 36			
KOEHLER, Heinrich	20	Sielen	54-1168
KOEHLER, J.G. (m)	18	Eisenberg	52-1512
KOEHLER, Joh Georg	26	Kleinherder	52-1625
KOEHLER, Joh. Chr.	36	Muehlhausen	50-1317
KOEHLER, Johann	34	Oberdiefenbac	53-0628
Catharina 33			
KOEHLER, Johann	31	Ahornberg	53-0637
Kunigunde 26, Adam 10m			

NAME	AGE	RESIDENCE	YR-LIST
KOEHLER, John	22	Heimertshause	50-0323
KOEHLER, Juliane	23	Herstelle	53-0585
KOEHLER, L. (m)	26	Giessen	53-1086
KOEHLER, Ludwig		Reckershausen	53-0942
Henry			
KOEHLER, Margareth	24	Rhomberg	52-1362
KOEHLER, Marie	27	Baiern	52-0895
KOEHLER, Mary	22	Buehne/Hann.	50-0323
KOEHLER, Mathias	40	Doeringstadt	54-0053
KOEHLER, Michael	32	Schmalkalden	51-1084
KOEHLER, Philipp	29	Wohlenhagen	50-1132
KOEHLER, Val.	25	Stummeroth	52-0652
KOEHLER, Veronika	22	Blankenau	53-0585
KOEHLER, Wilh'mine	25	Fritzlar	54-1554
KOEHN, Johann	19	Mittelheim	52-0563
KOEHN, Julius	24	Uernau	51-0500
KOEHNE, Louis	35	Sachsenburg	53-0492
Friedrike 29, Emilie 6, Therese 9m			
KOEHNERT, Johanna	22	Teich Wolfram	51-1084
KOEHNHOLZ, Herm.	23	Pasewalk	51-1686
KOEHNLEIN, C.B.		Barchlingen	54-1575
KOEHR, Nicolaus	24	Steinbach	52-1105
KOEHRMANN, J. Hein	38	Eitzen	47-0872
Marg. Adelh. 33, Joh. Heinr. 11, Dorthe 9			
Carsten 7, Johann 5, Diedrich 2			
KOEK, Anton	45	Frille	51-1588
Mary 40, John 12, Anna 8, Louisa 4			
KOEKE, Johann	37	Triptis/Weim.	52-1620
Auguste 31, Mina 5, Anna 3, Emma 6m			
KOELLE, Heinrich	26	Winzlar	54-1371
KOELLE, Heinrich	57	Winzlar	54-1371
Margarethe 54			
KOELLE, Wilhelm	30	Winzlar	54-1371
Sophia 24, Wilhelm 3, Caroline 2			
Wilhelmine 6m			
KOELLER, Johann	23	Soelsingen/Ha	53-0475
KOELLNER, Chr'tine	42	Marklissa	54-0987
Hermann 11, Gottlieb 9, Paul 6, Carl 5			
KOELN, Andreas	24	Ulm	53-0557
KOELZENDORFER, Ad.	26	Libochswitz	48-1184
KOELZLE, H.	20	Stuttgart	54-1575
KOENE, August	29	Braunschweig	54-1717
Lucie 28, Theodor 3, Otto 2			
KOENEMANN, H.H.(m)	27	Halle/Pr.	52-0960
KOENER, Anna	23	Wasmuthausen	53-1062
KOENIG, Abraham	29	Nurnberg/Bav.	53-0628
KOENIG, Adam	26	Rappelsdorf	54-0903
KOENIG, Aug.	43	Bafzen	49-0574
KOENIG, C. August	59	Schoenegg	54-1283
F. 27, Johann 26, Pauline 4, Gustav by			
KOENIG, Carl	27	Breslau	53-0557
KOENIG, Carl	26	Wittersheim	49-0329
KOENIG, Catharina	38	Arzberg	50-1236
Magdaline 15, Leonhard 12, Christoph 9			
Christian 7, Catharine 4			
KOENIG, Dorothe	20	Weiderode/Hes	51-1532
KOENIG, F.H.		Heyen	53-0942
male , male , male , female			
female , child , child			
KOENIG, Friedrich	25	Wuertenberg	53-0557
Louise 17			
KOENIG, Georg	26	Solingen	48-0406
KOENIG, Heinr.	22	Riede	51-1640
KOENIG, Jacob	27	Germersheim	49-0912
Maria 26			
KOENIG, Joh. Heinr	18	Gehrde	50-0292
KOENIG, Johann	17	Rotenburg	54-1649
KOENIG, Johanne	20	Rossfeld	53-0267
KOENIG, Ludw.	29	Heidenheim	49-0352
KOENIG, Margarethe	-7	Arzberg/Bav.	50-0323
KOENIG, Peter	52	Neukirchen	48-0406
Wilhelmine 42, Edward 18, August 17			
Hermann 15, Auguste 13, Alwine 11			
KOENIG, Philipp	25	Hungen	53-0557
KOENIG, Richard	21	Landshut	54-1443
KOENIG, Sim. Aug.	29	Exter	53-1000
Engel 23			
KOENIGER, Nicolaus	20	Wremen	54-1647

NAME	AGE	RESIDENCE	YR-LIST
KOENIGSBERGER, J.	38	Zell/Bav.	51-0048
KOENIGSREUTHER, G.	30	Frauenaurach	54-1647
Barbara 30, Georg 9m			
KOENKER, Joh Heinr	15	Oldendorf	53-0991
KOEPFORT, Eliese	20	Fuexten	49-1358
KOEPPEL, Joh.	22	Walpenrieth	49-1358
KOEPPLING, Andreas	33	Pischhausen	53-1062
Martha 23, Anna Cathr. 10m			
KOERBER, Barbara	56	Cur Hessen	53-0557
KOERBER, Barbara	56	Kur-Hessen	53-0557
KOERBER, Friedrike	29	Wuertt	53-0557
KOERBER, Friedrike	29	Wuertenberg	53-0557
KOERBER, H.F. (m)	22	Lemningerode	52-1512
KOERBER, Heinrich	36	Eloesen	53-0825
Hanna 33, Auguste 9, Friedrich 7			
Heinrich 5			
KOERBER, Michael	32	Cadolzburg	52-1410
Barbara 26			
KOERBER, Michael	28	Zochenreuth	52-1200
Cunigunde 2, Cunigunde 23			
KOERBILZ, Emil	28	Nordhausen	48-1209
KOERBURGER, Anton	37	Kempten	52-1512
J.B. 23			
KOERMANN, Heinrich	15	Affinghausen	53-1016
KOERN, Michael	32	Wedringen	52-0095
KOERNEFFER, Carol	21	Metzgels	53-0582
KOERNEFFER, Friedr	32	Metzgels	53-0582
Marie 33, Eliza 14, Anna Marie 9			
Friedr. Bern 2, Eliza 6m			
KOERNER, Christoph	24	Hohenberg	50-1236
KOERNER, J. Rosine	22	Volkmannsdorf	51-0352
KOERNER, Wilhelm	33	Roetha	53-0267
KOESEL, Emilie	22	Uenzen	51-1160
KOESEL, Th.	21	Bremen	51-1160
Emilie 22			
KOESTER, Carl	55	Hessen-Cassel	52-0048
Ludowine 44, Johanna 17, Carl 10			
KOESTER, Johann	17	Lockstedt	54-1094
KOESTER, John Fr.		Bokel	54-1470
Edert , Sally , Henry 4, daughter 9m			
KOESTER, Marie	24	Eimelrod	52-0807
KOESTER, Michael	24	Brinkum	49-0324
KOESTER, Wilh.	30	Steineck	52-1661
Meta 31, Carlne(died) 4, baby 3m			
KOESTERS, Salomon	30	Gildehaus	53-0991
KOESTNER, Andr.	38	Kirchlein	50-0439
Joseph 16, Ludw. 14, Margarethe 12			
Amalie 36, Heinr. 33			
KOETING, Mesina	21	Bremen	51-1035
KOFLER, Franz	35	Thanz	54-1717
KOFOD, J.	31	Denmark	47-0987
KOGLER, Rosa	18	Erlangen	52-1200
KOHL, Cath.	36	Oberolbach	51-0757
KOHL, Catharine	43	Kleinern	50-0840
KOHL, Diana	22	Steinbach	54-1566
KOHL, Joh.	28	Ellenbach	52-1129
KOHL, Joh. Heinr.	22	Schaabe	54-1168
KOHL, Joseph	32	Germershausen	53-0991
Dorothy 27			
KOHLBUSS, (m)	28	Freudelburg	52-1661
KOHLENBERG, Heinr.	29	Arensfeld/Han	54-1092
KOHLENBERG, Wilh.	26	Ahrenfeld	52-1512
KOHLER, Ant.	28	Bosserode	52-0558
KOHLER, Jacob	17	Elchingen	52-0515
KOHLER, Joh Martin	23	Thuningen/Wrt	52-0351
KOHLER, Johann	18	Hasberg/Bav.	53-0628
KOHLER, Marianna	27	Grossbuchen	52-0515
KOHLER, Nicolaus	28	Rothenoven	54-0987
Friederike 28			
KOHLER, Niel	20	Lageloh	49-0742
KOHLER, William	20	Mittelruessel	49-0737
KOHLES, Barbara	26	Grossbirkach	52-0807
Georg 6			
KOHLES, Kunig.	30	Vainwind	54-1078
Barb. 16, Juliane 14, Johann 9, Wilhelm 7			
Margaretha 2			
KOHLHAAS, Hartmann	33	Dankmarshause	48-0284
Johannes 19, Valentin 25, Martha 27			

NAME	AGE	RESIDENCE	YR-LIST
Caspar 3, Magdalena 1			
KOHLHEP, Joh Georg	18	Oberzell	53-0435
KOHLMANN, Anna M.	24	Rutesheim	48-1355
KOHLMANN, G.B. (m)	24	Bremen	50-0439
KOHLMANN, John	20	Osterholz	53-0991
KOHLMANN, Louise	17	Muenden	52-1200
KOHLMEIER, Johanna	23	Hehlen	53-1070
KOHLMEYER, Fr.	28	Bueckeburg	53-0492
KOHLMUELLER, Joh.	30	Haag	54-1283
KOHN, Bernhardt	41	Nordlingen/Bv	53-0628
KOHN, David	57	Bromberg	50-1236
Anna 57			
KOHN, Eduard	35	Gotha	52-0895
KOHN, Israel	14	Lubatch/Pr.	54-1092
KOHN, Joh.	24	Berwangen/Bd	52-0117
KOHN, Joseph	30	Bandorf/Wesse	53-0435
KOHN, Michel Moses	23	Nackel	53-1062
KOHNE, David	16	Mauneck	51-0460
KOHNE, Heinr.	37	Goettingen	54-1647
KOHNER, Caroline	24	Trosau	54-1078
KOHNLA, Joseph	32	Eichstaedt	54-1297
KOHRDRESS, Christ.	42	Boebber	53-1086
Anna M. 38, Marie 16, Friedrich 11			
Heinrich 9, Ernst Fr. 7, Marie Engel 3			
KOHRES, Adolph	33	Kohlenbeck	53-0825
Theresia 34, Adolph 4, Joseph 2			
KOHRES, Anton	24	Solingen	48-0406
KOHRING, Ernst	20	Buur/Hann.	52-0960
KOHRS, Catharine	25	Woltmershause	50-1067
KOHRS, Johann H.	15	Ottersberg/Ha	54-1092
Anna M. 20			
KOKE, Christian	18	Lingen	48-0887
KOLB, Adam	36	Neudorf	54-1168
KOLB, Andr.	19	Hamberg	52-0515
KOLB, Conrad	18	Wachternach	53-0652
KOLB, Crescens	26	Sullen	53-1013
KOLB, Ernestine	20	Gold	54-1443
KOLB, Joseph	36	Regenstein	53-1000
Anna 42, Andreas 16, Anna 12			
KOLB, Philip	30	Fulda	52-0699
KOLB, Wilhelm	19	Mesmerode	53-0492
KOLBE, Eibe (m)	15	Wremen	53-1000
KOLBE, Elisabeth	34	Hersfeld	47-0828
Georg 12, Friedr. 6, Hermann 3			
KOLBE, Henrietta	17	Marburg	53-0991
KOLBERG, Johann	30	Memerow	53-0905
KOLBRUNN, Auguste	47	Brake	48-1355
Adelheid 19, Minna 14, Emma 10			
Theodor 16, Fritz 12, John 7			
KOLBUS, Heinrich	34	Petershausen	54-1717
KOLBY, John C.	29	Bremen	50-0021
KOLEMANN, Sophie	26	Egloffsheim	54-0987
KOLER, Johanna	24	Hundsbach	53-0928
baby 6m			
KOLINGER, Lorenz	33	Leubelsdorf	47-0918
KOLL, P.	28	Rab	54-1724
KOLLE, Franz	17	Schleusingen	54-0903
KOLLER, Johann	23	Soelsingen/Ha	53-0475
KOLLER, Peter	42	Bergen/Hess.	52-0807
Elisabetha 36, Margaretha 18			
Catharina 15, Friedrich 14, Jacob 9			
Johann 9, Wilhelm 8, Elise 8, Maria 5			
Elisabetha 3, Christine 10m, Dorothea 63			
KOLLERMANN, Johann	34	Altenmarschen	52-1661
Dorothea 30, Anna 6, Catharine 3			
KOLLING, Heinr Aug	18	Bremen	51-1725
KOLLING, Sophie	22	Mesterode	53-0492
KOLLMANN, Caroline	35	Mittelruessel	49-0737
KOLLMANN, Chr.	20	Kohlenfeldt	53-0492
KOLLMANN, Elis.	20	Lispenhausen	53-1023
KOLLMANN, Rud.	35	Bruenn	50-1317
Magdalene 27			
KOLLMANN, Sophie	32	Iserlohn	52-0895
Diedr. 13, Emma 9, Hermann 4, Ernst 9m			
KOLLMEIER, J.W.G.	23	Herford	50-1317
KOLMANN, Otto	24	Langwedel	54-0987
KOMBER, Christ.	20	Niederkaufung	51-1640
KOMBRINK, Heinr.	26	Bockhorst	49-0352

NAME	AGE	RESIDENCE	YR-LIST
KOMENS, Louise	23	Obernkirchen	54-1282
KOMP, Nannie	20	Fulda	53-0585
KOMPELHAUS, Elis.	28	Bremen	54-1092
KOMPOSCH, Sebast.	47	Demingen	48-0887
Cresenze 46, Joseph 10			
KONATH, Heinr.	30	Oldendorf	50-0021
KONEN, Hermann	24	Lingen	48-0887
KONIG, Daniel	27	Hau/Hess.	52-0117
KONIG, Fritz	14	Bremerhafen	51-1084
KONITZER, Hein Geo	22	Schleiz	49-0352
KONLEI, Franziska	18	Wuertenberg	53-0557
KONOLACK, H.	24	Leipzig	54-1470
Louisa 23, Louisa 3			
KONPANDS, Johann	35	Beringenhause	52-1101
KONTER, August	27	Gotha	52-1620
KONTHER, Johann	34	Ortroff	52-1362
Rosalia 22, Louise 13, Riechhin (f) 4			
Emilie 3, Hermann 6m			
KONTSCH, Adolph	31	Magdeburg	52-1321
KONZELMANN, Margr.	28	Wuertenberg	53-0557
KOOL, Elanor	21	Unterlangerst	51-1588
KOOP, Georg	50	Coburg	53-0324
KOOP, Johann	24	Schiffdorf	52-1661
Catharina 27			
KOOP, Johannes	24	Beverstedt/Ha	51-1725
KOOPMANN, Auguste	20	Harpstedt	50-1067
KOOPMANN, Meinert	29	Strickhausen	52-1423
Johanna 24			
KOORT, Elisabeth	22	Berghorst	53-0585
KOOS, Elisabeth	28	Unterferdinan	51-0460
Philippine 11			
KOOSS, Carsten	20	Scharmbeck	52-1362
KOPER, E. (m)	38	Rolfsbuttel	52-0558
Wm. (f) 19, G. (f) 28, J. (m) 18			
F. (m) 15, H. (f) 2			
KOPEZKY, Fanny	29	Gmuend	53-0991
KOPF, Andr. H.	24	Belum	53-1164
KOPF, C.J.	27	Ihlienworth	51-1160
KOPF, Caroline	59	Hartdorff	54-1591
KOPFE, Babette	17	Burg Cunstadt	50-0439
KOPLIN, John	26	Priesewitz	53-1164
KOPMANN, August	25	Ludwigslust	51-0352
KOPP, Ferdinand	21	Ramrod/Pr.	49-0365
KOPPEL, Ida	29	Berlin	54-0987
Julius 9			
KOPPELSTETER, Nic.	28	Neuhaus/Bav.	52-1620
KOPPERBERG, Jul.	24	Huecksen	54-1168
KOPPING, Joh Fried	17	Sontra	54-1168
KOPPINGER, Conrad	25	Welfenbet	52-1304
Martha 16			
KORBACHER, Lud.	26	Londorff	51-1160
KORBEL, Franz	19	Bohemia	50-0311
KORBER, Michael	23	Steinach/Bav.	53-0628
Therese 42			
KORBER, Nicolaus	8	Steinach/Bav.	53-0628
Carl 13, Therese 48			
KORDES, Johann	26	Ahausen	54-0918
KORDING, Joh Heinr	22	Huntlosen	53-0888
KORMANN, Joh.	22	Cassel	49-0742
KORN, Johannes	20	Bayern	53-1000
KORN, Leonhard	33	Reinhausen/Bd	52-0117
Sophie 32, Auguste 12, Johannes 10			
Wilhelm 9, Maria 1			
KORNDORF, Joh.	42	Martinsreuth	47-0868
KORS, Heinr.	34	Stade	54-0600
KORTE, Emilie	26	Solingen	54-0872
KORTEJOHANN, Bernh	27	Everswinkel	50-0840
KORTEZ, Joseph	25	Hermansberg	52-1512
KORTLANG, Wilhelm	18	Duecke	50-0366
KORTZ, Geo. Adam	35	Klein Pisttst	51-0352
Maria Vict. 53, Chr. Auguste 9			
KORTZELIUS, Heinr.	28	Uslar	50-1317
Elise 32, Jette 9, Johanne 3, Ludwig 9m			
KOSCHWITZ, Carl	24	Jaura	54-0053
KOSEL, Conrad	24	Effeldeich/Bv	52-0960
KOSINSKY, Hermann	29	Koenigsberg	54-0903
KOSS, Friedrich	18	Lindenberg	54-0872
KOSS, Otto	17	Loebow	54-1649

NAME	AGE	RESIDENCE	YR-LIST
Johann 15			
KOST, Friedrich	25	Gummelstadt	48-0887
KOST, J.H. (m)	27	Bremen	48-0453
KOSTELMANN, Wilh.	22	Treptow	54-0872
KOSTER, Heinr.	26	Hechthausen	54-0053
KOSTMLATCK, Anna	15	Boehmen	53-1000
KOSTNER, Johann	22	Mistelfeld	48-0284
KOTHE, Bernhard	30	Bostel	52-0095
Mary Ann 31, Beta 22			
KOTHE, Heinrich	36	New York	47-0872
KOTHE, Johannes	29	Eichstruth	54-0850
Cath. Elis. 29, Elisabetha 5			
Maria Elis. 3, Magdalena by			
KOTHE, Nicol.	22	Achim/Hann.	48-0053
A. 21			
KOTLERRE, Charlott	16	Eldegson	51-1588
KOTLISK, Josepha	31	Prague	48-1015
Anna 6			
KOTTBAUM, Joseph	34	Gerpehof	53-1062
KOTTE, Anton	28	Wesuwe	49-0324
Herm 62, Lubertus 23, Gesine 26, Anna 22			
KOTTERHEINRICH, Ch	25	Tecklenburg/P	52-1432
KOTTLER, Carl	24	Breslau	54-0903
KOTTSIEPER, Wilh.	27	Barmen	48-0565
KOTZDENSEUTER, Joh	35	Neufand	51-1588
KOTZEBUE, Carl	60	Celle	53-1070
Anna 23			
KOUL, Johann	20	Churhessen	52-1620
KOWATS, Friederike	25	Detmold	53-0991
KOWATS, Martin	44	Tapolza	53-1164
Anna 17, Hermine 15			
KRAASS, John	24	Kalbbrunn	50-0944
KRABB, Friedrich	32	Secklendorf	54-1566
Pankratius 24			
KRACK, Diedr.	20	Hannover	50-0311
KRACKER, Jos. A.	18	Oberndorf	53-0492
KRACKER, Rosine	30	Oberndorf	53-0492
KRACKHARDT, John	34	Baiern	54-1724
Loise 31, Marg. 6, Rosa 5, Pf. 4, Emil. 3			
Rud. 6m			
KRAEMER, Andreas	43	Riethen	48-0260
KRAEMER, Cath.	54	Albertshausen	52-0563
KRAEMER, Friedr.	34	Wuertemberg	50-0021
KRAEMER, John	21	Oppertshausen	48-0447
KRAEMER, Sophie	18	Baden	54-1724
KRAEMER, Wilhelm	22	Stuttgart	48-1355
KRAEMERS, Fr'drke	24	Lienen/Pr.	52-1432
KRAEMERS, Peter	46	Vluyn/Pr.	48-0447
M. (f) 46, George 21, H. (m) 19, John 17			
Jacob 15, Wm. 13, A. (m) 11, Eliza 9			
Peter 7			
KRAETZES, Ferd.	20	Hottstedt	54-1452
KRAFFT, Joh. Wilh.	32	Barmen	48-0565
KRAFT, Cath.	21	Storndorf	49-0742
KRAFT, Charlotte	56	Hofgarte	52-1105
KRAFT, Elis.	23	Borgholz	54-0600
KRAFT, Elisab.	17	Mittelruessel	49-0737
KRAFT, J.C.	-8	Waldsachsen	49-1358
KRAH, Dorothea	20	Salzungen	49-0413
KRAHENWINKEL, Joh.	30	Riesel	54-0965
Elisabeth 20			
KRAHL, Joseph	17	Frankenstadt	49-0383
KRAHLERS, Charlott	29	Berlin	50-0292
Emma 9m			
KRAHN, B.	28	Schlottheim	53-0492
KRAHWINKEL, Ant.	20	Paderborn	51-0405
KRAINBACH, F.	29	Lohne	54-1716
KRAINBACH, Wil'mne	49	Steinfeld	54-1716
Therese 22, Gerhard 20, Franz 18			
Heinrich 16, Anton 14, Alwine 9			
KRAL, Anton	55	Kopullo	54-1647
KRALLINGER, Fritz	32	Carlsruhe	53-0905
Carl 35			
KRAMER, Adam	26	Fulda	53-0585
KRAMER, Adele	24	Bremen	51-1101
KRAMER, Albert M.	20	Mittelruessel	49-0737
KRAMER, Andr.	22	Nischwitz	54-1282
KRAMER, August	36	Prussia	53-0628

NAME	AGE	RESIDENCE	YR-LIST
KRAMER, Augustine	25	Bildechingen	50-1071
KRAMER, C.	19	Hessia	50-1317
KRAMER, Domicus	31	Kirchheim	54-0053
KRAMER, Heinrich	29	Rendeleben	54-0903
KRAMER, Heinrich	30	Braunschweig	54-1649
KRAMER, Henry	21	Mittelruessel	49-0737
KRAMER, Hermann	19	Turarve	53-0582
KRAMER, Joseph	28	Mauchen	49-0912
Anton 20			
KRAMER, Marie	26	Muehlhausen	54-0872
KRAMER, Robert	37	Haschhausen	53-0905
KRAMER, Theodor	20	Lehning	53-0267
KRAMER, Wilhelm	19	Plaue	51-1438
KRAMMENSCHNEIDER,H	33	Laemershagen	54-1371
KRAMMER, Joh.	16	Kleinsteinach	54-1283
KRAMMES, Margareth	24	Kirchberg	53-0991
KRAMPERT, Georg	26	Buchberg	54-1443
KRANBERGER, Chr'ne	36	Hungary	54-1724
Aug. 7, C. (f) 9			
KRANICH, Helmuth	19	Gr.Breitenbch	53-0585
Alwin 14			
KRANTZ, Friedr.	29	Detmold	47-0918
KRANZ, Adolf	29	Heidenheim	53-0928
KRANZ, C.	26	Rhoden	53-0582
Wilhelmine 31, Mary 11, Caroline 7			
KRANZ, Franz	18	Seidelsdorf	52-0370
KRANZ, Gette	21	Feueth	54-0872
KRANZ, Joh.	77	Grevensteinbe	47-0828
KRAPFER, Jacob	27	Siegen/Pr.	51-0048
KRAPFF, Lorenz	31	Schwimmbad	47-0918
KRAPPMAN, Anna	21	Costnitz/Bav.	51-1532
KRASEMANN, Friedr.	24	Wilzihn	54-0872
KRASS, Georg	54	Wien	49-0324
KRASS, Peter	29	Doernduerchhe	53-1086
KRASSER, Christian	24	Lichtenberg	48-1184
KRATCH, Joh Gottfr	45	Untergreistau	49-0324
KRATOCHWILL, Franz	28	Muichowitz	54-1575
Therese 32, Eg. (f) 9, Johanne 7			
Catharine 5, Franziska 3, Martha 9m			
KRATOCHWILL, Joh.	39	Andryone	54-1676
Katharina 20			
KRATOCKWILL, Franz	53	Muichowitz	54-1575
Catharine 55			
KRATSCH, Abraham	48	Langenlaube	54-0930
Christine 38, Ernestine 19, Gustav 17			
Reinhard 14, Johann 12, Hermann 9			
Emma Bertha 4			
KRATSCH, Julius	30	Monstab	54-0872
Sophie 19			
KRATSCHE, Herm.	27	Monstab	54-0872
Sophie 23			
KRATZE, Leonardine	52	Soltengreesba	49-0781
Marianne 47, Walpurgis(m) 7			
KRATZENBERG, Elis.	19	Vockerode	54-1554
KRATZENSTEIN, Brno	22	Wernigerode	50-1236
KRATZENSTEIN, Ferd	37	Quedlinburg	48-0887
KRATZER, Eva	30	Nuernberg	50-1317
KRATZGENER, H. (m)	50	Darmstadt	48-0453
W. (m) 15, Eva 7			
KRAU, Anton	50	Rosenberg/Ung	52-0117
Maria 33, Anton 12, Moritz 10, Marie 7			
Franz 1			
KRAUS, Adam	35	Fromberg	53-0582
Anne 31, Anne 10, Rose 7, Catharine 4			
KRAUS, Anna M.	23	Neises	52-0515
KRAUS, Auguste	18	Northheim/Han	51-1532
KRAUS, Chr.	22	Urach	54-0600
KRAUS, Erhard	25	Coburg	53-1013
KRAUS, Franz	25	Niederklein	51-0460
KRAUS, Friederike	43	Lobenstein	49-0383
KRAUS, Friedrich	25	Grotsch	49-1106
Ernestine 26, Henriette 6m			
KRAUS, Gregorius	24	Spral	51-0500
KRAUS, J.	30	Carlsbad	54-1575
Barb. 29, A. (m) 28			
KRAUS, Joh.	21	Dettendorf	52-0693
KRAUS, Joh.	28	Regensdorf	54-1282
KRAUS, Johann	20	Hofdorf	52-1452

NAME	AGE	RESIDENCE	YR-LIST
KRAUS, Johann	22	Oberwaldstadt	51-1532
KRAUS, Johann	21	Homes	52-0370
KRAUS, John	24	Mittelruessel	49-0737
KRAUS, Susanne	18	Suess	48-0269
KRAUS, Theresia	30	Prague	48-1243
Ludwiga 8, Mathilde 5			
KRAUSE, Ad. (m)	23	Flessburg	48-0447
KRAUSE, Barbara	22	Sues	48-0284
KRAUSE, C.D.(m)	48	Hagen	48-0453
Th. (m) 22			
KRAUSE, Carl	21	Fernrode	52-1321
KRAUSE, Hermann	32	Ponitz	54-1647
KRAUSE, Moritz	45	Breslau	53-1164
KRAUSE, P. (m)	22	Herrfeld	48-0445
KRAUSE, Therese	18	Jena	54-1297
KRAUSE, Traugott	18	Zugenrueck	48-1184
KRAUSE, Wilhelm	35	Klosterneudor	53-0652
KRAUSE, Wilhelm C.	25	Soemmerda/Pr.	54-1092
KRAUSENECK, Gustav	17	Coblenz	54-0850
KRAUSHAAR, Anna	35	Zeitloss	51-1101
KRAUSHAAR, Friedr.	36	Utrictshausen	52-0515
Cath. 31, Marg. 8, Cath. 5			
KRAUSHAAR, H.	19	Armsfeld	51-0405
KRAUSHAAR, Joh Geo	26	Utrictshausen	52-0515
KRAUSMUELLER, Conr	36	Rufenrode	54-0830
KRAUSNER, Alois	27	Eidenbach	52-1452
Franziska 37, Carl (died) 3			
KRAUSS, Albert	18	Bueckeburg	53-0888
KRAUSS, Babel	3m	Frohnheim	48-0260
KRAUSS, Barbara	24	Wuertenberg	53-0557
Cathrine 19			
KRAUSS, Behrend	35	New York	47-0872
KRAUSS, Carl	33	Coburg	53-0267
KRAUSS, Catharine	21	Nuernberg	48-0887
KRAUSS, Constanz	31	Oberschwandor	49-0352
KRAUSS, Friedr.	36	Schoningen	48-0112
Friederike 36, Henriette 10, Johanna 5			
Friedrich 3			
KRAUSS, Frit(died)	6m		53-0557
KRAUSS, Fritz	6m	(died)	53-0557
KRAUSS, Griself	31	Bayern	53-0557
KRAUSS, Isaac	24	G----nnsdorf	48-0260
KRAUSS, Jacob	45	Wuertenberg	53-0557
Christ. Herm 55			
KRAUSS, Justus	24	Reichelsdorf	48-0284
KRAUSS, M. (m)	40	Kemath	53-1016
KRAUSS, Nicolaus	36	Knetzgau	54-0053
KRAUSS, Rosa	26	Konradsreuth	47-0868
Joh. 5			
KRAUSSLOCH, Marie	28	Gumbelshausen	53-0320
KRAUT, Johann	19	Erfurt	54-1716
KRAUTER, David	46	Stuttgart	53-1016
KRAUTH, Gottf.	62	Weberstedt	51-1160
M.C. (f) 62, J.A. (m) 33, J.F. (m) 31			
KRAUTHEIM, Johann	33	Pasewalk	53-1023
KRAXBERGER, Martin	30	Wels	53-0991
Barbara 22, Anna 2, Elisabeth 56			
Michael 19			
KREBS, Carl	31	Verden	52-1101
Elise 23, Trina 9m, Carl 6			
KREBS, Conrad	48	Rheren	53-1086
KREBS, Elise	21	Braunschweig	50-0323
KREBS, Gerhard	23	Goettingen	54-1297
KREBS, Gottlieb	18	Cassel	54-1371
KREBS, Heinrich	25	Berleburg	53-1086
KREBS, Susanna	16	Frankenberg	53-1016
Maria 19			
KRECHTER, Wenzisl.	34	Baden	51-1245
Herw. 32, Joh. H. 2, Bertha 3m			
KRECHTING, John	16	Odenhausen	53-0492
KRECK, Caroline	19	Farmbach	51-1455
Louisa 9, Marsetta 7, Nicholas 4			
KRECKMEIER, J.E.	38	Wolmach	54-1419
KREDER, Jos.	43	Obernrieth	47-0868
KREFFT, Gerhard	21	Braunschweig	51-1160
KREFFT, Heinrich	27	Windheim	53-0825
KREGEL, Adolph	28	Brokeloh	54-1371
KREGEL, Marie	23	Marberg	53-0905

NAME	AGE	RESIDENCE	YR-LIST
KREGENHAGEN, Gerd	65	Engter	47-0762
Anna Marie 55			
KREGER, Louise	24	Landsberg/Han	51-1796
KREI, Peter	23	Klein Grabau	54-1168
KREIANIK, Georg	28	Boehmen	53-1000
Elise 24, Catharine 57			
KREIDE, Johann	15	Tollhaus	49-0912
KREIER, Johann	28	Springe	54-1554
KREIGER, Johanna	28	Dillenburg	52-1101
KREILE, Margarethe	25	Pfalz	54-1419
KREILING, Wilhelm	24	Rauschenberg	52-1464
KREINER, Johann	19	Eichen	52-1200
KREINER, Ludwig	28	Alten	52-0279
KREINERING, Lorenz	23	Haren	49-0324
KREINHAGEN, Louise	22	Osnabrueck	54-0987
Louis 17			
KREINSCHMIDT, Gert	5	Wellingholzha	51-0352
KREIS, Johs.	31	Oberweyd	49-0781
KREIS, Lorentz	25	Mernis	52-0563
KREIS, Sebastian	28	Canton Aargau	51-0048
Marie 27			
KREISCHMEIER, Aug.	19	Rothenburg	54-1283
KREISEL, Friedr.	26	Mittelruessel	49-0737
KREISER, Elisabeth	31	Brakenheim	54-1371
KREISER, Franz	32	Elbingenalf	49-1358
Ther. 9, Joseph 3			
KREISS, Henry	24	Hofhausen/Hes	50-0323
KREISSEL, Val.	49	Grevenitz	49-0737
KREISSMANN, Ch. H.	29	Breitenhein	52-1625
KREITLER, Joh. (m)	38	Salzstetten	52-0370
KREIZER, Ernst	20	Hirschfeldt	52-0699
KRELING, Barbara	24	Seissen	52-0370
KRELL, George	22	Sues	48-0284
Anna Elise 22			
KRELN, Albert	16	Rebbra	49-0737
KREMER, Friederike	24	Eisenberg	54-1470
KREMER, Heinrich	32	Collinghorst	52-1452
Imkelin 27, Trienjen 18, Harm 15			
Remmert 12, Gerhard 10, Johann 8, Liena 7			
KREMKE, Franz	23	Fronhausen	50-0292
KREMPEL, Carl	30	Sainerholz	54-1297
KREMPEL, Joh. Ad.	42	Sainerholz	54-1297
Anna 14, Margarethe 7			
KRENBERGER, Gotth.	19	Lintersdorf	52-1321
KRENIS, Kunigunde	18	Knetzgau	54-0053
KRES, M. (f)	20	Frankmanshaus	51-0517
KRESS, Conrad	24	Muenchen	54-1371
KRESS, Johannes	27	Wallrod	52-1625
Margarethe 32, Carl (died) 6m			
KRESSE, Anton	34	Hirschfeld	53-1164
Anna 34, James 17, Florence 16			
Hermann 13, Lina 9, Olga 7, Otto 5			
KRETCHER, Vinc.	19	Boehmen	54-1724
KRETSCH, Mart.	34	Pilberg/Bav.	51-1796
KRETSCHMAR, Carlne	25	Leipzig	53-0888
KRETSCHMAR, Henry	27	Reiss	54-1724
KRETSCHMER, Carl	56	Sachsen	52-1432
Gottlieb 46			
KRETZER, Jette	21	Wildeshausen	50-0323
KRETZSCHMAR, Fr. W	23	Sachsen	53-1000
KRETZSCHMAR, Wilh.	19	Vogelsang	54-0872
KREUSING, Heinrich	21	Nienburg	53-0905
KREUTZ, Johann	35	Preussen	53-0590
KREUTZ, Ludwig Fr.	57	Minden/Pr.	51-1725
KREUTZBERG, Joh.	26	Volkmarsdorf	48-0269
KREUTZBURG, Carl	20	Cassel	51-0352
Maria 25			
KREUTZER, Barbara	54	Humelsmoder	48-0101
Caspar 18, Maria 20, Barbara 15			
KREUTZER, Marg.		Willofs	54-1575
KREUTZPEINTNER, G.	64	Moosberg	49-0574
Magdalene 58, Johann 30, Nicolaus 29			
Simon 19, Sebastian 15, Anna 32, Maria 28			
KREUZER, Anna Marg	18	Seisenhausen	50-0292
KREUZER, Babette	17	Hambach/Bav.	53-0628
KREUZKAMPS, Doris	21	Hoya	53-1000
KREYE, Georg	26	Oederan	54-1575
KREYENHAGEN, Fried	35	Engter	47-0762

NAME	AGE	RESIDENCE	YR-LIST
Christ. Lud. 25, Gerh. Heinr. 19			
Elis. Sophie 17, Herm. Heinr. 11			
KRICK, Barbara	24	Dietershausen	52-1200
KRICK, Herm.(died)	-0	Darmstadt	50-0021
KRICK, Lebrecht	32	Lennep	54-1371
KRIEBEL, Barbara	17	Unterkuebes/B	52-0351
KRIECHENDORF, Ant.	30	Sarden	49-0912
KRIECK, Andrew	35	Munich	53-0991
KRIEG, Ernst	22	Naumburg	54-0987
KRIEG, Waldburge	26	Grossendolft	48-1184
KRIEGBAUM, Anna	30	Ermreuth	52-0693
KRIEGE, Franz A.	28	Hagen	54-1371
KRIEGE, Heinr. Wm.	58	Lienen	54-1371
Maria 41, Wilhelm 14, Ernst 18			
Hermann 11, Heinrich 9, Bernhardine by			
Friedrich 40			
KRIEGER, Rosine	25	Werrenburg	54-1297
KRIEGSMANN, Martin	51	Esens/Hann.	51-1725
Adrian 45			
KRIESELMEIER, Joh.	22	Dettwang	49-0352
KRIESS, Anna Maria	24	Deitz	53-0267
KRIGEL, Johann	20	Baiern	53-0324
KRIMMELBEIN, Carl	17	Lauterbach	53-1000
KRING, Christ	24	Luesche	52-0563
KRINGEL, Wilhelm	17	Grossen--	50-0439
KRIPPNER, Walburge	58	Neustadt	52-1105
KRISCHE, Elise	24	Goettingen	52-0563
KRISCHKER, Carolin	28	Delmenhorst	53-0590
KRITSCHKE, Carl	32	Breslau	54-0053
KROEBER, Theod.	24	Altenburg	50-1071
KROEGER, Chr. H.	26	Hannover	50-0311
KROEGER, Dominik	42	Wien	53-0905
Anna 35, Wilhelm 13			
KROEGER, Wilh.	24	Frohnhausen	54-0600
KROEGER, Wilhelm	19	Strohhausen	54-0903
KROEHL, Friedrich	26	Roben	54-0872
KROEHNUNG, A.	43	Welkers	54-1575
KROENER, Adam	28	Hoechstedt	51-1438
KROENKE, P.H.	28	Otterndorf	51-1160
Caroline 26, Heinr. 5, Fritz 3, Carl 2			
Otto (died) 9m			
KROERL, George	52	Lolitz	52-1101
Maria 52, Georg 23, Elisabeth 26			
Johann 21, Anna 19, Johann 13, Paul 9			
Margrethe 9m			
KROGER, Peter	35	Mittelruessel	49-0737
KROH, Ulrike	20	Krotoschin	53-1023
KROHER, Johann	26	Froschenreuth	54-1443
KROHNE, Julius	31	Dresden	49-0574
KROKENBERGER, Geo.	24	Theusenbronn	52-0515
KROLB, Christ.	33	Bilshausen	52-1625
Margarethe 29, Regina 1			
KROLL, Anna Elis.	24	Oberbeissheim	51-1062
KROLL, Anton	27	Volkmarsen	54-1554
KROLL, Auguste	22	Bohmte	52-1200
KROLL, Carl	29	Landau	50-1071
KROLL, Catharina	35	Reiderhausen	54-0882
Louise 32			
KROLL, Henriette	25	Prussia	53-0628
Julie 23			
KROLL, Hermann	29	Reidershausen	54-0882
KROLL, Simon	18	Selchow	54-1168
KROLLBERG, Ferd.	24	Tannenhausen	51-1035
KROLLMANN, August	26	Stotel	53-1023
KROLLPFEIFFER, Wm.		Grebenstein	54-1575
Agnes			
KROME, A.H. (m)	48	W. Ollendorf	52-0960
Catharine 52, M.E. (f) 17			
KROME, Ferdinand	17	Einbek	54-1717
KROMER, Caspar	31	Harthausen/Pr	54-1001
Marie 31			
KRONBERGER, Eva	25	Albstadt/Bav.	52-1423
KRONE, Carl	29	Magdeburg	53-1013
KRONE, Doris	30	Hagen	51-1101
KRONE, Gotthilf	50	Graevinghagen	48-1355
Louise 56, Julius 19, Franz 16			
Hermann 14, Hermine 20			
KRONE, Heinrich	28	Holzminden/Br	51-0500
KRONE, Josephine	23	Thanhausen	52-0279
KRONE, Theodore	25	Mittelruessel	49-0737
KRONE, Wilhelmina	27	Ohle/Pr.	48-0053
KRONENBURG, Franz	16	Werden	54-0600
KRONENFELD, Anna M	18	Osnabrueck	52-1512
KRONHEIMER, Regine	36	Triest	53-0838
KRONHEIMER, Regine		Triest	53-0838
KRONIE, Friedr.	28	Leene	47-0918
KRONS, Henry	25	Mittelruessel	49-0737
KRONWALD, Cath.	29	Wildflecken	51-1796
KROPF, Ludwig	38	Coten	49-1517
KROPF, Wilhelm	41	Wenigendopt	48-1131
KROPP, Amand	16	Blankenau	52-1200
KROPP, Johann	29	Bayern	53-0557
KROPP, Nicolaus	29	Neuhaus	54-1078
KROSCH, Joh Gottfr	55	Gessnitz	54-0903
Joh Rosina 53, Joh August 21			
Meintwold 19, Gustav 11, Henriette 16			
KRUEBEL, Friedr.	16	Neuenkirchen	49-0352
KRUEBER, Elizabeth	23	Niederbiber	49-0365
KRUEGER, A. (m)	19	Erzien	48-0453
KRUEGER, Adolphus	34	Doemitz	53-0991
Jane 21			
KRUEGER, Carl	32	Zina	53-0652
Dorothea 35, Elisabetha 6, Wilhelm 2			
KRUEGER, Carl	33	Rostock	54-1297
KRUEGER, Charlotte	19	Melle	52-0872
KRUEGER, Emil	26	Goerlitz	54-1297
Caroline 26, Lina 2, Fanny by			
KRUEGER, Friedrich	30	Nienburg	53-1070
Caroline 32			
KRUEGER, Heinrich	4	Dillenburg	52-1101
Ludwig 9m			
KRUEGER, Jane	16	Lingen	53-0991
KRUEGER, Lewis	24	Rothenuffeln	48-1209
KRUEGER, Rudolph	42	Lingen	50-0292
KRUEGER, Theodor	24	Frohausen	50-0379
KRUEGER, Walburga	26	Stuttgart	53-1016
KRUEGER, Wilhelm	22	Pyrmont	51-1101
KRUEKEBERG, Carl	20	Hameln	48-0887
KRUEMMERICH, Joh.	33	Eisnach	52-0370
KRUEMPEL, Herm Did	51	Pueppen	53-1062
Anna Elis. 51, Elisabeth 15, Adelheid 9			
KRUENELKE, Friedr.	25	Prussia	50-0021
KRUENING, Fr.	24	Ledde	48-0269
KRUEPPEL, Joh Hein	41	Coburg	52-1423
KRUEPPNER, Friedr.	25	Rossdorf	49-0574
KRUETLY, Friedrich	31	Hildesheim	53-1070
KRUETZMANN, Caspar	31	Hagen	54-1371
KRUG, Georg	30	Buchfeld	54-1717
KRUG, Heinrich	22	Grifte	54-1566
KRUG, Jakob	27	Unterzella	54-1283
Elise 27, Georg 1			
KRUG, Johann	28	Fichtelberg	54-0903
KRUG, Samuel	19	Tringhausen	52-0563
KRUGER, Geo Peter	27	Schnelldorf	52-0515
KRUGHEBEL, Chr'tne	5	Armsfeld	51-0405
KRUKEBERG, Wilh.	42	Bueckeburg	50-1317
Dorothea 40, Carl 13, Philippine 11			
Christine 9			
KRUKENBEER, Wilh.	3	Bueckeburg	50-1317
Caroline 9, Heinr. 7m			
KRULL, Johann	18	Buehne	50-0379
KRUMBECK, William	17	Bederkesa	54-0987
KRUMDICK, Sophia	21	Hannover	53-0590
KRUMER, Heinrich	22	Michelsdorf	52-0872
KRUMM, Heinrich	26	Wahlbach	53-0590
KRUMM, Jacob	21	Frohenhausen	51-0048
KRUMME, Anton	19	Frille	52-1321
KRUMMERICH, Christ	14	Muhlhausen/Pr	53-0628
KRUMMERICH, Johann	22	Geertingen	53-0267
KRUMMRAD, Carl	23	Bueren	48-0887
KRUMMWIEDE, Wilh.	24	Woelpe	54-1443
Heinrich 24			
KRUMSIECK, Aug.	47	Koenigslutter	53-0492
Aug. 23, Marie 19, Georg 17, A. 15, H. 7			
KRUMWIEDE, Friedr.	32	Elsbruecken	53-0914
Dorothea 34, Dorothea 9, Heinrich 7			

NAME	AGE	RESIDENCE	YR-LIST
Christine 5, Sophie 3, Caroline 14			
KRUMWIEDEL, Ludwig	31	Rodewald	47-0762
Sophie 24, Louise 5, Friedrich 4, Marie 2			
KRUNHAGEN, Louise	22	Osnabrueck	54-0987
Louis 17			
KRUNZ, Conrad	28	Hersfeld	50-0944
John 14			
KRUSBER, Heinr.	18	Bavaria	50-1317
KRUSE, Conrad	28	Riepen	47-0672
KRUSE, Conrad	40	Cassel	54-1371
KRUSE, Eleonor	35	Frille	52-1321
KRUSE, F.	32	Brackel	51-0517
A.(f) 34, B. 2			
KRUSE, Fr. Wilhelm	20	Doehren	54-1443
KRUSE, Francis	25	Neualtmannsdo	53-0914
(m) 24			
KRUSE, Franz	22	Heilstadt	49-1517
KRUSE, Friedrich	23	Hanoveri	52-0351
KRUSE, H. (m)	55	Steinberg	48-0453
C. (f) 50, J. (m) 13, A. (f) 7			
KRUSE, Joh.	28	Burnstof	50-0472
KRUSE, Johann	45	Koenigsberg	54-1452
Caroline 27, Heinrich 13, Pauline 7			
KRUSE, Joseph	18	Heyden	53-0628
KRUSE, Sophie	18	Riepen	50-1132
Johann 50			
KRUSSE, Johann	32	Schorst	48-1131
KRUST, Marie	23	Steimke	47-0762
KRUSTER, Louise	15	Bakenau	49-0345
Catharina 20			
KUBESCH, F. (m)	32	Radowitz	54-0918
Magdalene 45			
KUBLER, Jacob	26	Reichenberg	49-0352
KUCH, Friedrich	25	Thema	54-1676
KUCH, Wilhelmine	30	Tecklenburg	52-1432
Ernst 25			
KUCHER, Carl	37	Schneeren	54-1341
Doretha 30, Caroline 8, Henry 9			
child 10m			
KUCKUCK, Conrad	39	Grossenberkel	53-0914
KUCSHIF,	41	Heldenfingen	52-0515
KUDDER, Jobst	40	Buer	48-0445
Fr. (m) 38			
KUDLING, Johann	31	Heustreu/Bav.	53-0628
KUEBLER, John	26	Goeppingen	50-0840
KUECHENMEISTER, An	40	Oechsen	53-0942
Martha 16			
KUECHER, Dorothea	20	Nentershausen	53-0942
KUECHLER, Friedr.	56	Weimar	51-1245
Rosine 56, Aug. Wilh. 31			
KUECK, Diedr.	33	Schmalenbach	49-0574
KUECKE, Joh.	20	Fendorf	51-0460
KUEEB, Martin	21	Tindorf	51-1035
KUEFERLE, Franz.	21	Ravensberg	54-1371
KUEFFLE, Johannes	28	Koechingen/Wr	54-1092
KUEHL, Aug. Fr. W.	28	Braunschweig	49-0324
KUEHLE, Ludwig	35	Hannover	52-0699
KUEHLKOPF, Cath.	33	Sparwissen	52-0095
KUEHLTREIBER, Joh.	29	Wien	49-0324
Mrs. 20			
KUEHLWEIN, Carl	35	Graefen Tonna	49-0324
KUEHLWEIN, Georg	29	Muenken	49-0324
KUEHMSTADT, Julius	32	Harzburg	54-0850
Gottfied 13, Elisabeth 20			
KUEHN, C.J. (m)	18	Altenburg	50-1067
KUEHN, Charles	20	Lindenau/Sax.	48-0447
KUEHN, Christiane	25	Hellmers	52-1321
KUEHN, Ernst	25	Stadt Ilm	52-1464
KUEHN, Heinr Traug	20	Gera/Prussia	49-0365
KUEHN, Joseph	33	Krenzeler	54-0850
Magdalena 32			
KUEHN, Sophia	25	Jever	50-0379
KUEHN, Wilhelm	30	Stadt Ilm	52-1464
Auguste 38			
KUEHNE, Adelheid	21	Munster	52-1362
KUEHNE, Adolf	16	Muenster	51-1438
KUEHNE, Franz	26	Obergimpern	49-0912
Dorothea 24			

NAME	AGE	RESIDENCE	YR-LIST
KUEHNEL, Winzelaus	36	Reichertshofe	52-1304
Theresia 35, Joseph 8			
KUEHNER, Friedrike	22	Brakenheim	54-1371
KUEHNER, Georg	26	Hessia	50-1317
KUEHNER, Henry	34	Erligheim	48-0447
KUEHNERT, Carl	20	Ebeleben	54-1168
KUEHNERT, Carl	34	Ruegen	49-0345
August 21, Albert 28			
KUEHNHOLZ, Jab. J.	48	Niederwilling	48-0269
KUEHNLE, Christine	20	Brackenheim	54-1371
KUEKER, Elega	10	Otterndorf	51-1160
KUELING, Caroline	20	Luesche	52-0563
KUELP, Babette	34	Westerhausen	54-1647
KUELTHAU, Joh. H.	51	Oberzell	53-0435
Barbara 48, Philip 23, Elisabeth 21			
Heinrich 16, Wilhelm 14, Kunigunde 12			
Johann 6, Barbara 3			
KUEMMEL, Carl	19	Bellingsbach	54-1443
KUEMMEL, Cassimir		Ginternberg	49-0365
child 2, Flora 4			
KUEMMEL, Johann	19	Frankenau	53-1016
KUENECKE, Christ.	18	Nuisberg	49-1106
KUENELLER, Gabie	20	Wiesbaden/Nas	48-0447
KUENOTH, Th. (m)	28	Daublitz	49-1358
KUENSTING, H.	42	Exter	53-1086
Wilhelmine 32, Wilhelm 11, Louise 8			
Heinr. 5, son 2			
KUENSTLER, Carolin	32	Ettenheim	51-0352
KUENSTLER, Mathaus	33	Hohhaltheim	54-0872
KUENZEL, Christian	23	Selb	53-1062
KUENZEL, Wilhelm	18	Eisenberg	52-1512
KUENZLER, Joh.	19	Fendenheim	52-0370
KUENZLER, Nanny	24	Weinsberg/Wrt	54-1092
KUEPANTNER, Elis.	24	Neubau/Bav.	52-1423
KUEPPE, M. (f)	28	Ofen	51-0517
KUERBIS, Ad.	42	Berlin	49-0383
KUERMEIER, Joh.	28	Obersteinach	49-1358
Ther. 25, Ther. 11, Ther. by			
KUERSCHNER, Mart.	34	Mohra	53-0942
KUERTEN, Julius	20	Stubben	53-0161
KUERTZER, Jacob	19	Rotenburg	54-1649
KUESCHE, Julius	18	Praumetz	54-0918
KUESPERT, Carl	17	Arzberg	53-0557
KUESPERT, Nicol.	27	Seuzen	53-0557
KUESTER, Franz	47	Hohen-Hameln	53-0492
F. 36, Marie 9, Alwin 5			
KUESTER, Friedr.	22	Bockhorst	49-0352
KUESTER, George	32	Lueneburg/Han	52-1620
Herman 27			
KUESTER, Johann	30	Arzell	52-1661
Regina 28, Sabina 4, Catharine 2			
KUESTER, W.	19	Bueckeburg	54-1470
KUESTER, Wilh.	21	Posen	49-0574
KUESTNER, Elise	26	Cassel	54-1717
KUETHEN, Maria	27	Ankum	53-1070
KUETTER, Carl	25	Crimmitschau	54-0987
KUEZTEN, Heinr.	19	Ratingen	49-0324
KUGEL, F. (m)	18	Singmarn	52-0558
KUGELMANN, Michael	31	Schweckhausen	53-1070
Minna 28, Marie 1			
KUGER, Georg	17	Lutzenreuth	52-0558
KUGLER, Carl	3	Welzheim	54-1566
KUGLER, Fr.	27	Preussen	51-1160
KUGLER, Sixtus	19	Busch	53-0267
KUHAGEL, Johann	22	Wien	54-1591
KUHHIRT, Otto	24	Viernau	54-0600
KUHL, Christian	24	Putzbach	50-1067
KUHLAU, Wilh.	28	Bielefeld	49-0352
KUHLIG, Ernestine	26	Saalfeld	54-1297
Auguste 20, Wilhelm 17			
KUHLING, Wilhelm	30	Benkenstein	54-0987
KUHLMANN, Adolph	34	Gruenberg	47-0840
KUHLMANN, Anna	29	Verden	53-0628
KUHLMANN, Bernd	26	Nordwalde	49-0324
KUHLMANN, Christ.	30	Dornstadt	54-1283
KUHLMANN, Davy	17	Schweringen	48-1209
KUHLMANN, Eberhard	24	Osnabrueck	52-1512
Elise 25, Georg 6m			

NAME	AGE	RESIDENCE	YR-LIST
KUHLMANN, Elise	23	Alfhausen	51-1160
KUHLMANN, Georg	27	Wunstorf	47-0762
Georgine 24, Henriette 7			
KUHLMANN, Gerhard	34	Neustedt	53-0888
KUHLMANN, H. (m)	19	Dankersen	52-1321
KUHLMANN, Heinr. F	17	Lingen	51-1101
KUHLMANN, Heinrich	18	Hoya	52-1362
KUHLMEYER, Heinr.	40	Kohlstedt	54-1371
Louise 30			
KUHN, David	20	Inowraclaw	53-0320
KUHN, Franz	31	Altenburg	54-0930
KUHN, Gottlob	25	Tauchhausen	54-1443
KUHN, Heinr.	31	Billeben	50-0439
KUHN, Jacob	21	Schoenau	50-0292
KUHN, Joh. Jac.	28	Amt Gehren	47-0918
KUHN, Seibert	58	Halsdorf	54-1575
KUHNE, Aug.	22	Prussia	50-0311
KUHNER, Elisabeth	27	Unterscheffen	48-0269
KUHNER, Joseph	25	Bachenau	47-0918
KUHNERT, Fransus	32	Koppendorf	53-0582
Anne Marie 27			
KUHNHENNE, Christ.	24	Goodelsheim	50-0379
KUHRT, H. (m)	25	Bebra	52-0652
KUICHLER, Christ.	61	Lauchstedt	52-0699
KULBE, August	26	Pollwitz	53-1062
KULEMANN, Peter	28	Huenfeld	52-0563
Ottilie 28			
KULL, Joh.	26	Hirschheim	54-1283
E. 8			
KULMANN, D. (f)	29	Amt Kloppenbu	50-0476
KULZKG, Charles	24	Eichfuhr	50-0840
KUMBALEK, Math.	46	Muichowitz	54-1575
Josepha 37, An. (f) 6, Anna 4			
KUMEROLL, Herman	24	Berlin	53-0590
KUMEROW, Hermann	24	Berlin	53-0590
KUMMEL, Carl Heinr	46	Cassel	54-1371
KUMMEL, Gerh.	26	Schliengen	52-0370
KUMMELMANN, Hugo	22	Meiningen	48-1131
A. (m) 40, B. (f) 30, C. (f) 19			
KUMMER, Bernh.	20	Alfhausen	51-1160
KUMMER, Beta	21	Wuerttemberg	54-1724
KUMMER, Marie	24	Wimmer	53-1086
Marie Elis. 20			
KUMMY, John	31	Switzerland	54-1724
Sibilla 32			
KUMPE, Moritz	47	Hornburg	49-0383
Justine 42, Justine 13, Marie 9, Minna 7			
Carl 4, Wm. 1			
KUMPEL, Ernstine	24	Erfurt/Pr.	52-1432
Magarethe 11m			
KUMPF, Sebastian	34	Krefeld	54-0903
Anna 26, Emilie 3, Eduard 1			
KUNATH, Franz Rob.	28	Dresden	53-1164
KUNATH, Nic.	48	Wuertt.	54-1724
Ernestine 50, Ernestine 20, Gottlieb 18			
Caroline 9			
KUNBERGER, Carolin	23	Marchard	53-0928
KUNDEL, Joh.	53	Aue	47-0918
Catharina 43, Joseph 22, George 21			
Matias 19, Gregor 16, Maria 13			
Franciska 11, Waldburga 9			
KUNDERT, A.	24	Farmbach	51-0517
KUNDIGER, Jean	19	Tuer	54-1297
KUNG, Friedrich	26	Carlsruhe	54-0987
KUNGLER, Carl	24	Gnadenberg	50-1071
KUNICKE, Emma	27	Mittelruessel	49-0737
Fanny by			
KUNIGE, Lud.	32	Arken/Pr.	51-1796
KUNKEL, Balthasar	28	Babenhausen	54-0987
KUNKEL, Heinrich	33	Gerstungen	53-0324
Johann 24			
KUNKEL, Michael	32	Schoellkrippe	54-0903
Barbara 32, Wendelin 4, Michael 56			
KUNKEL, Wilhelm	32	Nieder Rodenb	51-0352
Rosine 31, Maria 4, Margaretha 6m			
KUNLE, Anton	21	Oetdorf	51-1035
Franziska 16			
KUNOLD, Maria	40	Brichum	49-0574
KUNOTH, Georg	19	Bremen	51-0326
KUNSCH, Albert	13	Magdeburg	53-0991
KUNSTMANN, Elise	36	Arzberg/Bav.	53-0557
Joh. Nikolas 52, Eva Cathrine 52			
Wolfgang 26, Ferdinand 24, Susanne 20			
Cathrine 18, Andreas 16, Johann 27			
KUNSTMANN, Herm.	32	Grafenthal	50-1071
KUNSTMANN, Joh Nik	52	Bayern	53-0557
Eva Cathrine 52, Wolfgang 26			
Ferdinand 24, Susanne 20, Cathrine 18			
Andreas 16			
KUNSTMANN, Johann	27	Bayern	53-0557
KUNTZ, Gustav	20	Voelkershause	54-0987
KUNTZ, Otto	21	Braunschweig	51-0326
KUNTZE, August	25	Sterbehausen	52-0563
KUNTZE, Franz	46	Guestrow	54-1371
KUNTZE, Hartus	35	Wernigerode	51-1455
KUNTZEL, Johann	18	Arzberg	53-0557
KUNZ, August	49	Schneeberg	48-1184
Caroline 41, August 9			
KUNZ, Carl	30	Warburg	50-0021
KUNZ, Friedr.	42	Westphalia	50-0021
Carl 17, John 12, Georg 10, Marie 6			
KUNZ, Josepha	26	Bielesthal	49-0329
KUNZ, Louise	20	Stuttgart	53-0838
KUNZ, Marg.	63	Rinzenberg	50-0439
KUNZ, Philipp	31	Dillenburg	53-1023
KUNZ, William	27	Warburg	50-0021
KUNZE, Cathr. E.	19	Herbehausen	54-1647
KUNZE, Ernest	39	Gewitz	53-0652
Wilhelmine 35			
KUNZE, Friedr. Alb	7	Gewitz	53-0652
KUNZEL, Christ.	25	Mehmels	53-0914
KUNZELMANN, August	35	Uslar	54-1297
Friederike 37, Johann 2			
KUNZMANN, H.	26	Altendorf	54-1168
Martin 37			
KUNZMANN, Michael	34	Zafringen	53-0435
KUPERT, Heinrich	26	Flammersheim	54-0987
KUPFER, Mina	20	Baiern	48-0887
KUPFERSCHMIDT, Ph.	29	Schwetzingen	51-0384
Jacobine 24, Barbara 6, Catharina 4			
Joseph 3			
KUPFNER, Th.	28	Rohr	53-0942
KUPP, Johann	23	Barfelde	53-0590
KURA, Carl	23	Neuettingen	52-1452
Crecencia 28, Anna 3			
KURFUERST, Robert		Oberweiler	54-1554
KURLICH, Wenzel	29	Woidain	54-1282
Franz 59, Barbara 54, Leopold 23			
Johanne 22, Marie 18, Franz 14			
Ferdinand 12, Anton 16, daughter by			
KURSBURG, Albert	24	Mittelruessel	49-0737
KURSCH, Carl	17	Hirschheim	54-1283
Friedrich 16			
KURT, Carl	34	Alsfeld	53-0905
Auguste 29, Pauline 9m			
KURT, Friedrich	30	Alfeld	51-1639
KURTZE, William	20	Froeschershau	50-0840
KURZ, A.	25	Schecksbach	51-1160
KURZ, Anna	36	Weissenborn	52-1129
KURZ, Charlotte	32	Egeln/Prussia	53-0628
Rosette 8, Adolph 5			
KURZ, Johann	48	Eschenfeld	54-0930
Leonhard 17			
KURZ, Joseph F.	26	Witzenhausen	52-0563
KURZBACHER, Joh.	28	Perg	54-0987
KURZE, Rosine	34	Langenlaube	54-0930
KURZENAKER, Christ	30	Wiesbaden	54-1452
KURZGER, Gottfried	41	Freiburg	53-1062
Auguste 42, Friedrich 15, Clara 12			
Moritz 10, Marie 8, Emma 6, Alfred 4			
Natalie 9m			
KURZMANN, Eduard	27	Gruenberg	47-0828
KUSCHKAE, Fritz	26	Hambro	50-1317
KUSCHNICK, Nicolas	30	Rakelwitz	53-1062
Magdalena 28			
KUSINGER, W.	42	Munster	54-1341

NAME	AGE	RESIDENCE	YR-LIST
Therese 44, Therese 14			
KUSSLING, J. (m)	23	Sparnek	47-0868
KUSTNER, Johann	23	Koderitz	48-0887
Barbara 25			
KUTEMEYER, Sophia	18	Meinsen	51-1588
KUTN, M. (m)	19	Mondenhausen	54-1341
KUTSCHER, Wilhelm	39	Wernigerode	53-0557
Elisabeth 46, Henriette 17, Carl 16			
Johanna 14, August 9, Louise 6, Auguste 4			
KUTZER, Erhard	19	Bayern	53-0557
KUTZHEL, Eduard	26	Wochselsdorff	48-0284
KUUK, Wilh.	35	Hanover	51-1084
LAATZE, Charles	18	Minden	49-1517
LABEL, Albert	16	Berlin	48-1243
LABER, Joh. P.H.	17	Mittelruessel	49-0737
LABES, Wilhelm	40	Harburg	49-1517
LABJUHN, Wilh'mine	16	Vlotho	54-1647
LABMAIER, Anton	26	Baiern	53-0585
Victoria 28, Therese 5, Barbara 2			
LACHER, Joseph	22	Ravensberg	49-0574
LACHMANN, August	37	Burg	53-0267
Dorothea 27, August 5, Wilhelm 7m			
LACHMANN, Eduard	50	Bertelsdorf	53-0825
LACHMANN, Elias	41	Breslau	54-0987
Amalie 29, Salzig 4			
LACHMANN, Gabriel	24	Lissa	54-0987
LACHMANN, Sal.	25	Altenmuhr	51-1160
LACHMEYER, Cath.	30	Bamberg	51-1245
LACHNER, Henry	25	Switzerland	54-1724
Bertha 27			
LACHS, Mathias	22	Lesering	53-0914
LACHS, Ribchen	23	Breslau	54-1297
Friederike 20			
LACHS, Wilhelm	51	Greiz	54-0987
Johanne 50, Carl 29, Friedrike 22			
Antonia 17, Caroline 7, Louise by			
LACKLI, Johann	32	Ettlingen/Wrt	52-1332
Rosine 26			
LACKMANN, H.A.	20	Bremen	51-0326
LACKNER, Hugo	19	Glogau	49-0781
LADA, Franz	39	Lenzela	54-1676
Anna 37, Anna 4, Catharina 9m			
LAEMMEL, Chr. Gott	60	Chemnitz	53-0991
Amalia 55, Richard 14			
LAEMMERHIRT, Ernst	58	Mohra	53-0942
Friederike 58, Marie 33, Heinrich 26			
Christian 24, Christine 18, Gottlieb 8			
Nicolaus 24			
LAEMMERMANN, Conr.	21	Adelsdorf	51-1245
LAEMMLE, Philip	27	Stuttgart	53-0991
LAERMEYER, Joseph	2	Eichendorf	52-1452
LAFT, Robert	35	Breslau	53-0637
Caroline 32, Ida 7, Hugo 5, Maria 4			
LAGEMANN, Heinrich	33	Bardhausen	49-0352
Fried. H'tte 44, Cath'ne Char 10m			
LAGEMANN, Hermann	21	Menninghausen	52-0563
LAGENGOP, William	22	Wigfelden	48-0406
LAHAGEN, Adam	37	Leipzig	48-1131
M. (f) 27, N. (m) 30, O. (m) 19			
P. (f) 16, S. (m) 13			
LAHMANN, Fr.	20	Iloese	54-1470
LAHMEYER, August	23	Kiel/Oldbg	50-0323
LAHNERS, Maria	45	Accum	52-0370
Johann 18, Friedr. 12, Elisabeth 8			
Maria 6m			
LAHRMANN, G.H. (m)	24	Engter	48-0445
LAHUSEN, Johannes	22	Bremen	51-1101
LAIBACH, Dorothea	23	Klein Auheim	52-1512
LAITSCH, Carl	28	Zelle	53-1023
LAKMANN, F. Carl	30	Barmen	48-0565
LAM, Wilhelm	53	Oberhelmer	52-1661
LAMBECK, Emilie	37	Erfurt	54-0850
LAMBERTSBERG, Balt	36	Nordlingen/Bv	53-0628
LAMBRECHT, J.	18	Natzugen	53-0435
LAMERS, Friedr.	18	Hilter/Hann.	51-1532
LAMKER, Louise	17	W. Ollendorf	52-0960
LAMKER, M.E. (f)	15	W. Ollendorf	52-0960
Cath. L. 14			

NAME	AGE	RESIDENCE	YR-LIST
LAMM, Edmond	19	Huettenbach	53-0991
LAMM, Elisabeth	18	Roodenau	50-0379
LAMM, Friedrich	31	Waldeck/Wald.	52-0807
LAMMERMEIERS, C.E.	22	W. Ollendorf	52-0960
LAMMERS, Franz	26	Gothenfelde	54-1566
LAMMERS, Harm. H.	23	Neu Schoenbec	49-0324
LAMMERS, J.H.	21	Buxtehude	51-1455
LAMMERS, Joh. H.	31	Hannover	50-1317
Johanna 32			
LAMMERS, Nihl	17	Holsen	51-0756
LAMMET, Heinrich	29	Hoeringhausen	54-0987
LAMPARTER, Mich.	19	Urach	54-0600
Chr. 22			
LAMPE, Bertha		Charleston	53-0888
LAMPE, Heinrich	38	Gehren	52-1362
Dorothea 41, Heinrich 12, Ernst 10			
Louise 5, George 2			
LAMPE, Henry	22	Dingen	48-0951
LAMPEL, Kunig'de	19	Furth	49-0352
LAMPERT, Heinr.	20	Reichenbach	54-0872
Caroline 18, Jacob 24, Wilhelm 18			
LAMPERT, Heinr.	20	Elmhausen	54-0872
LAMPKE, Henry	-8	Niederholzen	50-0323
LAMSON, Julius	31	Mobile	53-1164
LAMY, Chr.	18	Oldenburg	48-0269
LANDAU, C.F.	4	Ernsthausen	52-1321
Elise 4			
LANDAU, Carl	30	Nordhausen	49-1358
LANDAU, Chr.	19	Waldeck	50-0021
LANDAU, Gerh.	35	Ernsthausen	52-1321
LANDAUER, Emilie	27	Allendorf	50-1236
LANDECK, V. (m)	28	Ofen	51-0517
LANDENBACH, Jos(f)	46	Hait	47-0868
LANDES, Jan Berend	21	Neu Schoenbec	49-0324
LANDFELD, Just.	18	Niederkaufung	54-1078
LANDGRAF, Conrad	54	Willmars	53-1164
Elisabeth 50			
LANDGRAF, Georg	36	Altenstein	48-1179
LANDGRAF, Johann	23	Tannhausen	54-0903
Rosine 23, Marianne by			
LANDGRAPH, Georg	20	Bayern	53-0590
LANDGREBE, Johann	35	Grebenau	54-0930
Catharine 35, Jacob 9, Anna Elis. 4			
Paulus by			
LANDHERR, Johann	25	Waldshut	51-1686
Teobald 20, Mariane 46, Liberate 22			
Wilhelm 13, Cacilie 1, Catharine 9			
LANDLSPERGER, Wolf	28	Parkstetten	52-0558
LANDSBERG, Wilhelm	24	Umstedt	54-0987
LANDSBERGER, Wolfg	29	Emhof	54-0965
Joseph 30			
LANDSIDEL, Heinr.	39	Borken/Hesse	51-1796
LANDSIEDEL, Georg	9	Bargen	54-1566
LANDSMANN, Johann	36	Krumpenwin/Bv	52-1423
Barbara 36			
LANDSRATH, Fr'drke	22	Wiesbaden/Nas	48-0447
E. (f) 9m			
LANDWEHR, Adam	24	Markelsheim	54-1371
LANDWEHR, Adelbert	35	Sudwalde	53-0928
Margareth 33, Hermann 32, Sophie 24			
Hermann 5, Marie 3, Wilhelm by			
LANDWEHR, Heinr.	17	Badbergen	50-0292
LANDWEHR, Heinr.	30	Ellingerholz	49-0352
LANDWEHR, Heinrich	17	Arkum	54-0987
LANDWEHR, Henry	23	Melle	53-0991
LANDWEHRMANN, Hein	26	Minden	52-1410
LANG, Anna	19	Lynsdorf	49-0737
John 19			
LANG, Anton	33	Elbingenalf	49-1358
Johanne 27			
LANG, Anton	22	Schwetzingen	51-0384
LANG, Barbara	22	Flochburg	54-0872
Catharina by			
LANG, C.	22	Buch	54-1419
LANG, Catherika	17	Bamberg	51-1035
LANG, Catherina	30	Mittelruessel	49-0737
LANG, Charles	19	Cassel	54-1724
LANG, Conrad	26	Grafsolms	53-1000

NAME	AGE	RESIDENCE	YR-LIST
LANG, Esther	27	Freudenberg	47-0868
LANG, Friederike	27	Beerfelden	54-0987
Elisabeth 28			
LANG, Gustav	27	Baiern	52-1512
LANG, Isaac	14	Fritzfeld	48-0887
LANG, Johann	49	Mainroth/Bav.	52-1332
Anna Marie 46, Michael 16			
LANG, Johanna	27	Elbingenalf	49-1358
LANG, John	19	Eslangen	49-0737
LANG, Juliane	21	Themar	53-0590
LANG, Margarethe	24	Rachelhausen	52-1452
LANG, Rosina	24	Mittelruessel	49-0737
LANG, Sarah	20	Treuchtlingen	54-0850
Jette 22			
LANGBEIN, Nicolaus	32	Steinfeld	53-0324
Anna Margret 24, Chicka 3m			
LANGDON, John B.	27	New York	48-1015
LANGDORF, Adolf	24	Baden	54-1297
LANGE, August	33	Hildburghause	53-0914
LANGE, Bertha	22	Goling	54-1676
LANGE, Carl	23	Goldberg	53-0324
LANGE, Carl	25	Grafenhain	54-1168
LANGE, Carl	26	Daspe	50-1132
LANGE, Casp.	27	Suhl	49-1358
LANGE, Catherine	24	Bissendorf	51-1588
LANGE, Christian H	33	Wimpften	53-0267
Joh. Lorenz 32			
LANGE, Doris	25	Nordheim	53-1164
LANGE, Elise	23	Abterode	51-1796
LANGE, Elise	16	Gramberg	53-1086
LANGE, Ernest Ferd	30	Zwieschiritz	53-0888
LANGE, Franz	25	Auscha	49-0574
Anna 22			
LANGE, Franz	30	Hennersdorf	54-1371
LANGE, Georg	31	Hintersteinen	52-0370
LANGE, George	29	Wiesbaden	52-1580
LANGE, Gottlieb	28	Farme--	51-0757
LANGE, H.W. (m)	27	Essen/Hann.	52-0960
LANGE, Henry	20	Schaapen	53-0991
LANGE, Henry	22	Steltge	48-0284
LANGE, Johann	31	Marzdorf	48-1179
LANGE, Johann Ant.	20	Bremen	53-1070
LANGE, John	35	Hettenhausen	50-0840
LANGE, John H.	40	Hannover	51-0500
Charlotte 40, Heinrich 15, Elise 5			
Gustav 3			
LANGE, Lenhardt	26	Wittringen/Bv	54-1092
LANGE, Leo	18	Meerane	53-0435
LANGE, Marg.	22	Seggen	54-1470
Gertrude 20			
LANGE, Marie	28	Bayern	51-1245
Carl 7, Heinr. 2			
LANGE, Marie	20	Breitbach	54-1283
LANGE, Mathias	46	Kaedingen	52-0699
Anna 42, Catharine 20			
LANGE, Nicolaus	22	Bremen	47-0672
LANGEMANN, Heinr.	22	Bremen	53-0324
LANGEN, William	33	Felsburg	50-0944
Mary 26, Mary 3			
LANGENAU, Adelheid	21	Rhaden	50-1317
LANGENBERG, Heinr.	21	Bockhorst	49-0352
LANGENKAMP, J.W.	17	Schinkel	54-1470
LANGENOHL, August	19	Burscheid	54-0987
LANGENSTRASSE, (m)	28	Calbestadt	54-0987
Wilhelmine 22			
LANGER, Anton	45	Breslau	54-1078
LANGER, Chr. Benj.	50	Poembsen	53-0628
Henriette , Caroline 12, Paul 4			
baby 10m			
LANGER, Thomas	47	Sedlitz	54-1647
Maria 46, Joseph 21, Barbara 18			
Josepha 16, Anna 11, Veronika 7			
LANGERMANN, Christ	19	Treysa	49-0345
LANGERT, Joh. G.	27	Oberod	53-0914
LANGERT, Maria	27	Oberroth	52-1321
LANGES, Johann	17	Dissen	52-1661
LANGESCHUTTE, A C	18	Schaabe	54-1168
LANGFRITZ, Johann	17	Duisbrunn/Bav	53-0628

NAME	AGE	RESIDENCE	YR-LIST
LANGFRITZ, Marg.	20	Kalkreuth	53-0320
LANGGUTH, Ernst	18	Rappelsdorf	54-0903
LANGGUTH, Georg	25	Hildburghause	54-1078
LANGGUTH, Johann	34	Bischwend	52-1321
LANGHANS, Marg.	29	Knetzgau	54-0053
LANGHAUS, Heinrich	27	Edelsheim	51-0352
LANGHELD, W. Fried	24	Muehlhausen	52-1304
LANGHOFF, Friedr W	29	Witstock/Pr.	54-1092
LANGHORST, Carl	19	Wagenfeld	51-1101
LANGHORST, Fried.A	24	Strohen/Pr.	48-0053
LANGHORST, H. (m)	20	Wagenfeld	49-0742
LANGHUT, Joh Adam	34	Weilsdorf	53-0324
Dorothea 23, Martin 8, Carl 4, Caroline 6			
LANGKAMIR, Anna M.	23	Heilbronn	52-0515
LANGKNER, Louis	13	Bergen	54-0600
LANGSDORF, Johann		Pohlgoens	53-0942
(m) , (m) , (f) , (f)			
LANGSDORF, Selig	25	Rennertehause	54-1371
LANGSTORF, Johann	26	Kirchgoens	54-0965
LANGUTH, Casp.	32	Holzhausen	53-0320
LANNET, Ludw.	25	Doerborn	49-0324
LANSBERG, Alex.	19	Regensburg	54-1724
LANSING, Bernh.	32	Stadtlohn	54-0987
LANSTEDEN,	28	Eggerfeld	54-1419
Cath. 30, Anna 6			
LANTERWASSER, J.	21	Erdmannsheim	48-0453
LANTZEL, Friedr.	25	Christgarten	49-0574
LANZ, Jacob	32	Medenbrechen	49-0912
Catherina 37			
LANZER, Basil	29	Loerrach	49-0912
LAPP, Anna B.	23	Schwarzenborn	54-0600
LAPP, August	26	Schleisingen	50-1132
LAPP, Johann	31	Bodes	52-1410
LARENZ, Marie Soph	24	Muckefeld	51-1455
LAROCHE, Anton	20	Dalhausen/Pr.	51-1796
LAROSE, Adolph	25	New Orleans	48-1015
LASAR, Erh. (m)	21	Russ	48-1131
LASCH, F. (m)	37	Nurtingen	49-0416
LASMULER, Friedr.	27	Bieren	54-1452
LASS, Louis	23	Luhra	51-1686
LASSEN, Catharina	19	Griesbach	52-1452
LASSEN, Wilhelm	17	N.Y.	51-1245
LATERBACH, Fr'drke	31	Mettwitz	53-0324
LATTERMANN, Julie	23	Fretterode	51-1245
Wilh. 33			
LATTERMANN, Phil.	22	Bremen	50-1067
LATTMULLEN, Elise	24	Gesmold	47-0762
LAUBACHER, Cath.	19	Marburg	49-0383
Elisabeth 20			
LAUBRICH, Fritz		Grapzig	50-1067
Mathilde 27			
LAUCKMANN, Ge. (m)	27	Reithberg	52-0515
LAUDABER, Johann	26	Rembech	51-0352
LAUDENBACHER, Fid.	47	Rukestetten	53-0914
LAUE, Heinr.	26	Gr. Monra/Pr.	52-0960
LAUEN, Caroline	50	Bayersdorf	54-0903
Adolph 12, Abraham 28			
LAUENSTEIN, J.F.	53	Essenhagen	50-1067
G.W. (m) 14, S. Juliane 11			
J. Ferdinand 8			
LAUER, Amann	18	Ulmbach	54-1419
LAUER, Florian	31	Remscheid	51-1160
Anna 23, Franz 4			
LAUER, Georg	39	Ulmbach	52-1625
Eva 20, Regina 19, Wilhelm 17			
LAUER, Georg	37	Prussia	50-1317
Louise 35, Emilie 4, Mathilde 2			
Ad. Rud. 24, Moritz 26			
LAUER, George	42	Berkelurg	51-1588
LAUER, Johann	27	Ulmbach	52-1625
Johann 37, Christine 28, Juliane 8			
Elisabeth 27, Anton 6, Marcus 3			
Wilhelm 6m			
LAUER, Levi	25	Gehaus	53-0942
Meier 19			
LAUER, Nicol.	38	Wiembach/Bav.	48-0053
LAUERHAUSE, Susann		Stiberlimbach	54-1554
LAUFER, Kunigunde	18	Neuses	52-0693

NAME	AGE	RESIDENCE	YR-LIST
LAUFER, Michael	31	Stosestedt	52-0563
LAUG, Gottl.	32	Hohnstadt	54-1078
Louise 42, Adolph 9			
LAUGEMANN, Friedr.	27	Osterhage	49-0352
LAUING, Heinrich	18	Hasbergen	53-1000
LAUN, G. Chr.		Mittelhausen	53-0942
LAUN, Stina	23	Geste	47-0828
LAURANN, Conrad			51-1455
LAURICH, Franz	28	Grottkau	52-1321
LAUSCHE, Charles	34	Uttstadt	54-1724
LAUSE, Alexander	18	Friederichsdo	51-1035
LAUSTERT, W. (m)	27	Elberfeld	48-0565
LAUTENBACHER, Alb.	19	Bavaria	53-0628
LAUTENSCHLAEGER,	26	Heidelberg	53-0267
LAUTENSCHLAEGER, T	22	Baiern	54-0903
LAUTENSCHLAGER, A.	27	Coln	48-0951
LAUTER, B.	31	Holzborn	51-1160
LAUTERBACH, Carl	19	Bremen	52-0095
LAUTERBACH, Cath.	22	Ermerdings	52-1105
LAUTERBACH, Conrad	19	Ernteiss	54-1566
LAUTERBACH, Ester	38	Geltern	49-0912
Matagay (m) 12, Isaac 4, Adelhaid 6			
Bette 2, Annchen 26			
LAUTERBACH, Heinr.	20	Heeringen	48-0284
LAUTERBACH, Henry	45	Eisfeld	53-0914
Ernest 17			
LAUTERBACH, Justus	25	Emeteis	51-1640
Martin 30			
LAUTERBACH, Marg.	22	Lindenhof	53-0492
Elisabeth 20			
LAUTERBACH, Wilh.	20	Bremcke	51-0460
LAUTERWASSER, J.	21	Erdmannsheim	48-0453
LAWISDROWSKI, Aug.	34	Seehausen	54-0987
LAZARUS, Betha	54	Karwendeich	54-0830
Betha 17, Rebecca 15, Raphael 9			
LEBACH, Samuel	28	Pekelheim	50-1067
LEBERLE, Andreas	25	Wingenhausen	53-0585
LECHERMAIER, Peter	26	Maasburg	54-1647
LECHINSKY, Lewin	17	Rogarsen	54-1297
LECHNER, Friedrich	22	Buchenwald	53-0320
Margaretha 24			
LECHNER, Jac.	29	Weinberg	52-0515
LECHNER, Margareth	24	Carlshafen	53-0320
LECKER, William	23	Oldendorf	53-0991
LEDERER, David	18	Dasslaw	53-1070
LEDERER, Emanuel	33	Fereshau	48-1131
LEDERER, Joh Nikol	19	Arzberg	53-0557
LEDERER, Joh. Nikl	19	Bayern	53-0557
LEDERER, Joseph	22	Rzucholau	54-1078
LEDERER, Judith	18	Pauter	54-1566
LEDERER, Saul	29	Meseritz	53-1023
LEDERHOF, Karl	27	Arolsen	54-1554
LEDERMANN, Bertha	24	Auerbach	48-1131
LEDERMANN, Fanny	23	Hannover	54-1724
LEE, Heinrich	46	Packenheim	53-1000
LEES, Anna	24	Hofheim	54-0930
LEFFLER, J. (m)	38	Hamburg	49-0416
LEGATH, Conrad	29	Reuth/Bav.	52-1423
LEGENHAUSEN, Chr.	24	Wachtendorf	53-1164
LEGER, Babette	32	Oberreichenba	54-0850
Katharina 9			
LEGLER, Amalie	29	Punzlau	54-0053
LEHETGERN, Cath.	32	Walduern	52-1580
LEHMANN, Ar.	29	Guben|Pr.	54-1001
LEHMANN, Carl	22	Frensdorf	52-0370
LEHMANN, Ch. Aug.	48	Wanfried	53-0888
LEHMANN, Christine	56	Erfurt/Pr.	53-0475
LEHMANN, Daniel	32	Posen	49-0413
LEHMANN, Fr.	30	Berlin	54-1575
LEHMANN, Franz	33	Altenburg/Pr.	52-1423
LEHMANN, Georg	32	Danzig	53-0324
LEHMANN, Gustav	32	Sommerfeld	54-1371
LEHMANN, Heinr.	22	Werden	52-1129
LEHMANN, Henriette	25	Berlin	49-0742
LEHMANN, Joh. Gott	38	Sorgau	53-1062
Ernestine 28			
LEHMANN, Julius	25	Dresden	51-0405
LEHMANN, Louise	18	Burghaslach/B	53-0628

NAME	AGE	RESIDENCE	YR-LIST
LEHMANN, Moritz	38	Lohbau	51-1084
LEHMANN, Rosine	57	Wittenberg	52-1200
LEHMANN, Wilh.	20	Fossens	51-0460
LEHMEYER, C. (f)	24	Broechterbeck	49-0416
LEHMHASE, Louise	25	Berlin	54-1371
LEHMKER, Heinrich	22	Esel/Hannover	51-1725
LEHMKOHL, Friedr.	27	Mehringen	52-1452
LEHN, Louis	14	Meerholz	53-0888
LEHNER, Andreas	36	Grueb	52-0095
LEHNER, Vitus	28	Gumpenhof	54-1078
Cath. 22			
LEHNGRING, Alonzo	21	Mittelruessel	49-0737
LEHNLER, Friedrich	50	Camstadt	52-1580
LEHR, Jobst	29	Inheiden	53-1070
Susanne 27, Carl 8, Hermann 6, Heinrich 5			
Christian 3, Margaretha 9m			
LEHR, Jobst	55	Inheiden	53-1070
Elisabeth 45, Carl 18, Georg 12			
LEHR, Marie	28	Feuchtwang	48-0887
LEHR, Peter	24	Schwalbach	51-1035
LEHRER, Johannes	33	Bergdorf	51-0757
Maria 32, Anna 9, Louise 7, Caroline 3			
LEI, Magarethe	28	Hendershofen	51-1686
LEIB, Henry	29	Hannover	47-0158
LEIBBE, Martin	22	Lippspringen	48-0284
LEIBER, Heinrich	36	Wippersheim	51-0757
Elisabeth 26, Elisabeth 24, Johannes 5			
LEIBER, Karl	21	Engen	52-1105
LEIBIG, Andreas	27	St. Gilgen	54-1168
Susanne 24			
LEIBIN, Sophie	23	Gratz	54-0987
LEIBOLD, Maria	27	Schluchtern	54-1297
LEICH, August	24	Anstadt	51-1101
LEICHEN, Carl	21	Hagen	50-1067
LEICHNITZ, Friedr.	46	Hirschberg	53-1023
Bernhardine 33, Herrmann 15			
LEICHT, Adam	31	Hirschberg	54-1443
LEICHT, Johannes	20	Steinberg	53-1000
LEICHTFEIN, A. (m)	24	Trienz	50-0746
LEICHTFUSS, Carl H	20	Gera	53-0905
LEIDEL, Auguste	30	Erfurt	49-1106
Charlotte 3, Caroline 9m			
LEIDENBERG, Chr.	27	Emmetzheim	47-0868
LEIDENBERGER, Anna	28	Unmenzheim	52-1512
LEIDENBERGER, Anna	23	Degingen	52-1512
LEIDENROTH, Sophie	17	Bremen	50-0366
LEIDNER, Marg.	22	Kalchreuth	52-0515
LEIDSCHER, J.G.(m)	36	Tuebingen	49-0383
LEIDSCHUCK, Peter	31	Selchers	47-0828
Pantalon 37			
LEIER, Doroth.	56	Lichtenfels	51-0405
LEIER, Gottfr.	19	Reichenberg	49-0352
LEIM, F. (m)	29	Alsfeld	54-1341
Elisabeth 26			
LEIMANN, Daniel	20	Roodenau	50-0379
LEIMBACH, Heinrich	33	Hau	53-1062
Henriette 31, Wilhelm 5			
LEIN, Friederike	18	Klein Ansbach	51-1686
LEINBERGER, Adam	27	Rozstoll	47-0828
Joh. 17			
LEINE, Barbara	16	Gaffeldorf	54-1283
LEININGER, Adam	21	Hosenfeld	53-0320
LEIPPER, Heinrich	28	Koenigsberg	53-0590
Christian 17			
LEIRER, Chr. Wilh.	28	Leispendorf	49-0352
LEIRER, Franz	28	Mistelfeld/Bv	51-1532
Barbara 34, George 4, Friedrich 10m			
Andreas 22, Margretha 25			
LEISCHED, Cathr.	21	Strang/Hess.	51-1532
LEISEBERG, Wilhelm	24	Katrinhagen	53-1086
Hanne 22			
LEISINGER, Johann	34	Hessen	53-1013
Elisabeth 28, Conrad 9m			
LEISLER, Joseph	31	Hochwartel	53-0914
Marie 31, Marie 11, Anna 6, Margaretha 3			
LEISNER, Caspar		Bucksdorf	53-0942
male , female , baby			
LEISNER, Heinrich	26	Mucheln	52-0117

NAME	AGE	RESIDENCE	YR-LIST
LEISS, Joh.	25	Westheim	47-0918
Eva 22, Barbara 17			
LEISTENBERGER, Joh	39	Broetzingen	51-1438
LEISTER, Anna	24	Lindenau	54-1168
LEISTER, Sebastian	32	Einhausen	53-0582
Elisabeth 42, Matthew 9, Andrew 5			
LEISTNER, Johann	28	Blech/Bav.	52-1620
LEITHAEUSER, Barb.	30	Neuhaus	53-1062
LEITHEIZ, John	19	Coburg	53-0324
LEITHEUSER, Heinr.	24	Waldeck	50-0311
LEITNER, Johann	22	Coburg	52-1321
LEITNER, Joseph	28	Coeln/Pr.	52-0960
LEITNER, Margareth	27	Kalkreuth	53-0320
LEITNER, Math.	36	Bubenreuth	48-1179
Barbara 32, Friedrich 8, Catharine 7			
Barbara by			
LEITSCH, George	29	Reichstadt	53-0492
LEIVE, Emily	20	Melle	53-1070
LEIVERSTEIN, Moses	25	Gutensberg	50-0472
LEIWITZ, Margareth		Lorenzreuth	50-0323
LELL, Anna	24	Bayern	53-1013
LEMBACH, Heinrich	52	Weyke	54-1168
LEMBKE, Heinr.	18	Oerel	51-1245
LEMBURG, Fette	50	Muenchen/Bav.	53-0475
Joseph 17			
LEMIEN, Margaretha	32	Holdersteten	49-1517
Margaretha 4			
LEMKUHL, A.H.F.	29	Berne	52-1148
LEMME, Charles	28	Boston	53-0991
Agnes 25			
LEMMERMANN, Cath.	19	Achim	52-1512
LEMMERMANN, Friedr	20	Ottersberg	52-1362
LEMPER, Joseph	25	Klandorf	52-1464
LENERT, Johann	22	Widelshofen	53-1000
Maria 23			
LENGEL, Barbara	28	Stadel	51-1062
LENGELSEN, H.D.	49	Rupeljan/Pr.	48-0053
Christiana E 50, Peter Friedr 23			
William 21, August 18, Caroline 13			
Louise 8			
LENHAM, Fr.	47	Eichenberg	51-0460
LENK, Ernst C.	50	Bernsbach/Sax	54-1092
LENK, Georg	27	Kocheim	48-0269
LENKERODT, Aug.	29	Halzganz	52-1321
LENNOWITZ, Carl	46	Erfurt	53-1023
Dorothea 33			
LENSING, J.D.	51	Hannover	50-0021
LENTZ, Fr. Joh.	23	Allendorf	51-1686
LENTZ, Johann	24	Salzingen	53-0324
LENZ, Emilie	25	Magdeburg	48-1015
LENZ, Friedrich	29	Schleising	54-1282
Johanne 26, Anna by			
LENZ, Georg	38	Braunschweig	54-1282
LENZ, Johanna	34	Halle	50-1071
LENZ, Wilhelmine	15	Trysothe	54-0903
LENZ, William	36	Tattenfeld	53-0991
LEONARD, Adolphus	19	Mittelruessel	49-0737
LEONARD, Barthel	29	Ferdinandsdor	51-0384
LEONARD, Hub.	27	Bayern	54-1282
LEONHARD, Christ.	33	Prussia	53-0628
Elisabeth 31, Alwina 9, Dorothea 6			
Friederike 2			
LEONHARD, Johann	15	Eschenfeld	54-0930
Barbara 11			
LEONHARD, Mathias	30	Waltendorf	50-0379
LEONHARDT, Auguste	18	Gildehaus	54-1371
Amalie 26			
LEONHARDT, Carl	27	Mittweida	52-1321
LEONHARDT, Carl G.	27	Kirchbach	49-0781
LEONHARDT, Ch.	27	Alzey	53-0582
LEONHARDT, H. (m)	28	Todtemann	52-1321
LEONHARDT, Michael	42	Frankenhausen	53-0492
LEONHARDT, Siegm.	36	Windelheim	53-0492
LEONRE, Dorothea	53	Coburg	53-1013
LEOPOLD, Franz	28	Schkeuditz	54-1371
LEOPOLD, G.	20	Schernberg	53-0492
LEOPOLD, H.	19	Boebber	53-1086
LEOPOLD, Heinrich	35	Boebber	53-1086

NAME	AGE	RESIDENCE	YR-LIST
Leonore 34, Marie 6, T. 6m			
LEOPOLD, Theodor	21	Bueckeburg	54-1001
LEOPOLD, W.	30	Boebber	53-1086
Marie 30, Marie 4, Friedr. 9m			
LEPINSKI, Anton	28	Germernik	50-1071
LEPPER, G.	50	Stromberg	51-0517
LEPPERT, Joh. Geo.	26	Redwitz	47-0918
LEPPERT, Magaretha	24	Oberwerre	48-0260
LEPRINCE, Riquet	36	France	48-1243
LER, Johann	52	Treptow	52-0872
Otto 23, Ferdinand 22, Minna 24			
LERCH, Andreas	28	Reusendorf	51-0352
LERCHTFEIN, E. (m)	17	Trienz	50-0746
J. (f) 20, M. (f) 34, E. (f) 3m			
LERNER, Casper	25	Bamberg	50-1071
LEROY, Adolph	29	Elberfeld	48-1184
Mathilde 19, Mathilde Fr. 2			
LESCHING, Anna	29	Kleinwichberg	49-0574
LESEBERG, J.F.	35	Lauenburg	50-1071
LESEDIG, B. (m)	24	Lothe	49-0416
LESEMANN, Elise	17	Bremen	50-0366
LESIK, August	20	Sieke	54-1575
LESNER, Philip	28	Mannheim/Bad.	52-0117
LESS, Conrad	30	Zeitloss	53-1062
LESSEBERG, F. (m)	13	Wendenborstel	54-1341
H. (m) 31, Mary 34, W. (m) 26			
LESSING, Aug.	31	Sera	51-1686
LESSING, Franz	27	Schkeudiz/Pr.	52-0807
LESSLER, Johann	-0	Forst	52-1464
Jos. 32			
LESSMANN, Franz	25	Voerden	54-1443
LETTENMEIER, Barb.	33	Schmehingen	54-1282
LETZING, Johann	19	Quentil	54-1554
LETZING, Peter	47	St. Olilien	53-0928
LEUBERT, Rosa	25	Wuerzburg	53-0590
LEUCKERT, Joh Hein	47	Pornitz	49-0352
LEUDNER, W. (f)	18	Budingen	49-1106
LEUEINIEGER, Mor.	25	Bayern	53-0590
LEUERINIEGER, Mor.	25	Bayern	53-0590
LEUKING, Heinrich	32	Ludlohn	54-0987
LEUNER, F. Ed.	30	Koenigsheim	53-0582
LEUPERT, Johann	26	Schleusingen	54-1168
LEUPOLD, And.	15	Grafenberg/Bv	51-1796
LEUSSNER, Christ.	35	Marburg	49-0912
Elisabeth 36, Sophie 6			
LEUTE, Nicolaus	23	Winterthur	51-1725
Susanne 23, Johannes 7m			
LEUTELT, Adolphus	20	Kratzau	53-0991
LEUTERMEYER, Ludw.	56	Oberrheren	53-1086
Wilhelmine 57, Friedrich 17, Heinrich 11			
LEUTNER, Joh.	29	Rosenberg	51-0757
LEUTPOLD, Johanna	29	Karlsruhe/Bad	53-0628
LEVENSSTERN, Isaac	27	Obermoellrich	50-0472
LEVERENZ, Gesine	29	Warftith	50-1071
LEVERSTEIN, Moses	25	Gutensberg	50-0472
LEVI, Dav.	24	Bromberg	54-1575
Rosa 23			
LEVI, Mayer	23	Celle	51-1686
LEVI, Reese (f)	22	Koenigsberg	48-1179
LEVI, Rosalie	23	Adelsdorf	51-1245
LEVIBERG, Moses	44	Oberurff	54-1716
Jette 45, Therese 10, Jacob 8, Blumchen 6			
Malchen 4			
LEVIE, Moritz	18	Buttenhausen	48-0887
LEVIE, Roeschen	17	Berfa	54-0830
LEVINGER, Joh.	24	Himmelkron	51-1084
LEVISON, Jacob	31	Bromberg	50-1236
Rose 34, Helene 4			
LEVISTEIN, Sabine	23	Geisa	54-0987
LEVY, Joseph	24	Rotenburg	51-0405
LEVY, Schaft.	25	Waldeck	54-0918
Jettchen 18			
LEVY, Veronica	21	Canitz	54-1371
LEWEDAG, Heinrich	8	Lengerich/Pr.	52-1432
LEWEO, Friederike	20	Uslar	50-0439
LEWY, de Eduard	16	Emden	48-1184
LEYBACH, Catharina	27	Kitzingen	52-0807
LEYBOLD, Johann	23	Schopback	51-1639

NAME	AGE	RESIDENCE	YR-LIST
LEYHAUF, Joh. Geo.	44	Lirritzhofen	52-1101
LIBERT, Anton	30	Niedendorf	54-1717
Ida 42, Therese 7			
LICHT, Franz	21	Brunshusen	53-0825
LICHT, Georg Hugo	40	Berk	50-0292
LICHT, Killian	32	Beureth/Hildb	53-0628
LICHTENBERG, Eva	18	Utendorf	49-0574
LICHTENFELD, E.B.	21	Rudolstadt	50-1067
Emi 21			
LICHTENFELD, Edm.	35	Mittelruessel	49-0737
LICHTENHAUSEN, Ad.	24	Dankmarshause	48-0284
LICHTENSTEIN, Jul.	22	Meerane	54-1168
LICHTENSTEIN, Sim.	30	Tollub	49-1358
LICKHARDT, Martha	18	Fussen Erfurt	53-0942
LICKMANN, Lucas	19	Waldeck	53-1016
LIEB, Barbara	25	Staffelstein	52-1129
LIEB, Franz	34	Hettingen	54-0053
Pauline 39			
LIEB, Ignatz	22	Wolfertschwen	49-0365
LIEB, Joh (m)	19	Lanzendorf/Bv	52-0960
LIEBAU, Friedrich	44	Keula	51-1101
Dorothea 44, Carl 16, Bertha 14			
Christoph 9, Wilhelm 7, Ottomar 3			
LIEBAU, Ottomar L.	6m	Reula	51-1101
LIEBE, Heinr.	38	Bavaria	51-0405
Cathr. 76, Maria 37			
LIEBE, Peter	20	Duesseldorf	54-1092
LIEBECK, Elisabeth	19	Dettelferde/K	53-0628
LIEBEL, Ernst	28	Leissneg	48-1179
LIEBENBERG, Chr'ne	50	Bovenden	53-0888
Bernard 20			
LIEBENHAAR, Cath.	30	Redles	51-1160
LIEBER, Elise	22	Cassel	54-1297
LIEBER, Herm.	20	Duesseldorf	53-0585
LIEBERMANN, Abr.	73	Bischberg	47-0672
Fanny 63, Babette 23			
LIEBERMANN, Fanny	63	Hatenberg	47-0672
LIEBERMANN, Paul	38	Gipfendorf	52-0279
Margaretha 46, Joh Nikolaus 8, Heinrich 3			
LIEBETREU, Gust.	24	Friedrichwert	50-0439
LIEBIG, Leopold	25	Gera	54-0987
LIEBING, Andreas	42	Leiperzell	53-0590
Maria 40, Caroline 15, Marie 13, Carl 9			
Christian 6			
LIEBSTAETTER, Behr	15	Hattenhausen	54-0987
LIEDER, Carl Aug.	30	Gera	53-0838
LIEDER, Ernst	3	Gera	53-0838
LIEDKE, Franz	21	Gosfeld	50-1236
LIEGE, Franz		Chum	53-0942
(f) , child , child			
LIEGEL, Joh. A.	48	Spielberg	54-1078
LIEHAN, Philipp	20	Hechelmannski	51-1640
Adam 23			
LIEHAU, Georg	37	Bruchheim	52-0563
Simon 29			
LIEKHARDT, Martha	18	Fussen Erfurt	53-0942
LIENHARDT, Chr.	20	Lageloh	49-0742
LIENKESSER, C. (m)	27	Altona	48-0453
LIEPOLD, Christoph	42	Rosenthal	53-0267
Concordia 41, Friederich 17, Eduard 13			
LIERD, Cath. Elise	54	Kleinensee	48-0284
Anna Barb. 20, George 14, Margaretha 20			
LIERD, Peter	30	Hoenebach	48-0284
Anna 30, Christina 6, Johannes 3			
Wilhelm 24, Anna Cath. 26			
LIERE, Joh. H.	26	Gehrde	50-1236
LIESBERGER, Robert	23	Lich	53-0825
LIESCHE, Lebrecht	23	Goelpau	49-0324
LIESE, Dorothea	22	Walburg	54-1168
Heinrich 18			
LIESENISS, Chr.	28	Auhagen	53-0492
Dor. 24			
LIESON, Anton	24	Berlin	49-0352
LIEST, Jette	22	Naurnberg	53-0590
LIEST, Jette	22	Nuernberg	53-0590
Selma 20			
LIETIN, Meta	24	Scharmbekstot	50-1067
LIFERLING, Con.	21	Bisingen	51-1796

NAME	AGE	RESIDENCE	YR-LIST
LILGE, Ph. (m)	29	Meissenheim	52-0960
LILIENFELD, Math.	50	Lipstadt	48-0951
LILIENTHAL, Friedr	18	Osterholz/Han	54-1092
LILIENTHAL, Friedr	16	Holzeln	50-0366
LILLPAPP, C. (f)	24	Muenster	49-0416
LIMBERG, Carl Aug.	23	Elberfeld	48-0565
LIMBERG, Chr.	26	Martinvode	52-0370
LIMBERG, Lene	28	Blomberg	54-1168
LIMBORG, E. (m)	23	Dotmold	48-1131
LIMBURG, Conrad	19	Volkerthausen	54-1554
LIMBURG, Kon.	29	Unterbreutzba	51-1796
LIMKUGEL, Joseph	39	Bergmann	54-1591
Gertrude 38, Betty 14, John 10, Franz 8			
Mary 5, Gertrud 2			
LIMMEMANN, J Heinr	24	Wesuwe	49-0324
LIMPERT, August	22	Rosenthal	54-1452
LINCK, Alex	25	Grossbuchen	52-0515
LINCK, Andreas	24	Gr Sachsenhag	53-0435
LINCKER, Joh.	18	Extorf	50-0439
LIND, Anton	65	Fischbach/Nas	53-0628
Elisabeth 64, Friedr Jacob 34, Johanne 35			
Catharine 10, Peter 3			
LINDAHL, Isaac	31	Stockholm/Swd	50-1071
LINDE, v.der Jacob	36	Aschaffenburg	53-1000
LINDEGREN, Carl	22	Gottland/Swed	50-1071
LINDEL, Anton	37	Pasberg	53-0825
LINDEMANN, Carsten	25	Wildeshausen	51-0500
LINDEMANN, Elise	37	Elberfeld	53-0557
Emma 11, Guido 9, Gustav 7			
LINDEMANN, Fr'drke	24	Dessin	52-0652
LINDEMANN, Gesine	28	Twiess	49-0324
LINDEMANN, Henry	27	Teplinghausen	50-0323
LINDEMANN, Henry	33	Neustadt	48-1209
LINDEMANN, Joh.	25	Bremen	52-1661
LINDEMANN, Peter	14	Maden	52-1661
LINDEN, Gertrud	29	Wipperfuerth	54-1371
LINDENBAUM, Hirsch	16	Oberlistingen	53-0991
LINDENBERG, Carl A	28	Hannover	50-0311
LINDENHAUER, Aug.	22	Braunschweig	54-0987
LINDENHEIN, Herman	35	St. Louis	48-1243
LINDENSTRUCK, Pet.	37	Zwingenberg	54-1371
LINDERMANN, H. (m)	27	Ruhrort/Pr.	48-0447
C. (f) 18			
LINDERSCHMIDT, Cat	18	Mengsdorf/Hes	52-0960
LINDERT, Cl. Fr. J	25	Robbert	53-0825
LINDHORST, Chr.	52	Philadelphia	53-1164
LINDIG, August	18	Wilhelmsdorf	54-0872
LINDIG, Ferdinand	16	Ferdinandsdor	54-0872
LINDIG, J.F. (m)	23	Limburg	49-0416
LINDIG, Jacob	48	Farmbach	51-1455
Adam 14, Rosina 42, Margaretha 17			
Anna M. 9, Eliza 5, Rosina 3, Anna 9m			
LINDIG, Willian	45	Gaumor	53-0991
Jane 34			
LINDLER, Franz Sim	44	Wagenschwendt	51-0384
Eva Magdalen 43, Johann 24, Catharina 22			
Caroline 19, Simon 14, Leonhard 12			
Appolonia 7, August 3, Ottilie 11m			
Franz Carl 11m			
LINDNER,	50	Glashuetten	51-1084
Joh. 18, Joh. 16			
LINDNER, Aug.	28	Burgstadt	53-1016
LINDNER, Fr.	26	Ebenharz	54-1575
LINDNER, Friedr.	35	Castell	54-1371
Joh. Caspar 32			
LINDNER, Georg	36	Rappelsdorf	54-0903
LINDNER, Johann	36	Waldsachsen	53-0475
Marianne 33, son 3m			
LINDNER, Joseph	41	Floth	52-0095
Margaretha 41, Anna 9, Conrad 6			
LINDNER, Otto	41	Dresden	48-1184
LINDNER, Paul	23	Kreisel	54-1282
LINDSTADT, Friedr.	40	Buetzow	54-0987
Charlotte 26			
LINDWURM, Louis	29	Burg	53-1062
LINE, Ludw.	26	Bremervoerde	54-0600
LINET, Marie	30	Unterbert	49-0912
LINGE, M.	22	W. Ollstein	52-0558

NAME	AGE	RESIDENCE	YR-LIST
LINGEL, Maria	23	Steinberg	54-0965
Georg 28			
LINGELBACH, Friedr	54	Cassel	54-1724
Henry 17			
LINGELBACH, G. (m)	22	Rothenditmold	52-0652
LINGEMANN, Emilie	17	Sontra	51-0405
LINGEMANN, Michel	14	Niederwarschu	54-0930
LINGEMEYER, Marg.	24	Bockhorst	49-0352
LINHARD, Margareth	23	Wilmersreuth	53-0637
LINK, Anton	50	Rokitzau	54-1575
Johanna 47, Maria 17			
LINK, Friederike	26	Leipzig	49-0345
Mina 6, Emil 4, Maria 2			
LINK, H.	27	Schrecksbach	51-1160
M. Cath. 19			
LINK, Nick.	31	Walbur	53-0590
LINK, Wilhelm	29	Thueringen	52-0095
LINKE, August	60	Buchholz	54-1566
August 31, Emilie 30, Minna 7, Anna 4			
E. (m) 20, M. 16			
LINKE, Conrad	24	Ostford	51-1084
LINKEN, Adelheid	32	Eberfeld	50-0439
Heinr. 11, Conrad 9, Friedr. 7, Christ. 5			
Hermann 3			
LINKHOHL, Christ.	44	Niedermoellri	49-0345
LINMANN, Anna	16	Utlehde	50-1067
LINN, Conr.	33	Istorndorf	47-0868
Els. 36, Ko. 9, Hein. 9m			
LINN, Joh.	29	Storndorf	47-0868
Els. 29, Mar. 8, Ka. 6, In. 4, John. 2			
LINN, Sophia	23	Wallenroth	51-1101
LINNECKE, Dorothea	22	Diepholz	53-0557
LINNEMANN, Arnold	22	Rodach	53-0914
LINNEMANN, Claus	31	Eichedorf	49-0574
LINNEMANN, Heinr.	35	Riepen	50-1132
Anna 35, Heinrich 4, Christian 9m			
LINNEMANN, W.	32	Herford	54-1575
LINNEMEYER, Geo H.	59	Petershagnerh	54-0930
Sophie 59, Heinr. Conr. 30, Diedrich 20			
Friedrich 18, Anna 15, Sophie 29			
Heinrich 1			
LINS, Barbara	22	Oberzell	53-0435
LINSEBACH, Fr'drke	20	Gera	51-0757
Emilie 62			
LINSENMAIER, Marie	22	Borgau	49-0324
LINSER, Julius	20	Sachsen-Meini	53-1013
LINSLER, Franz	32	Schegingen	52-1580
LINSTEDT, August	26	Obereisen	52-1321
LINTNER, Georg	11	Kreiselbach	54-0930
LINZ, Simon	20	Steinbach	54-0882
LINZ, Wilhelmine	15	Trysothe	54-0903
LINZE, Henry	25	Hannover	54-1724
LINZE, Wilhelm	19	Minden	54-1371
LINZNER, Andr.	27	Feuschatz	54-1575
LIONHARD, Anton	30	Neukirchen	54-0882
LIPP, Susanne	28	Alsfeld	54-0830
LIPPEL, Adam	37	Sontra	52-1304
LIPPELT, August	26	Braunschweig	52-1200
LIPPERT, Adam	25	Arzberg	50-1236
LIPPERT, Barbara	16	Limback	50-0840
LIPPERT, Johannes	17	Eidorf	51-0500
Anna E. 22			
LIPPHARD, Reinhard	44	Sontra	52-1304
Anna 33, John 8, Conrad by			
LIPPLER, Carl	25	Domburg	52-0279
LIPPMANN, Friedr.	28	Kroge	47-0918
LIPPMANN, Moses	17	Schwarza	54-1078
LIPPMEIER, J.A.	28	Brackel	51-0517
F. (f) 28, L. 4, M. 6m			
LIPPOLD, Friedr.	27	Altenberge	53-0585
LIPPOLD, Friedr.	44	Hannover	54-1724
Henrt. 38, Eml. 18, Georg 16			
Friederike 1, Cr. (f) 14			
LIPPOLD, Lewis	33	Zwickau	53-0991
Henrietta 29			
LIRCHNER, Johann	22	Langroten	50-1067
LISCHEWSKY, Gust.	19	Graudenz	54-1371
LISSAUER, Mary	2-	Ungedanken/He	50-0323

NAME	AGE	RESIDENCE	YR-LIST
LIST, Friedrich	22	Erbach	53-0991
LIST, Peter	29	Boxdorf	52-0693
LISTMANN, C. (f)	22	Alsfeld	54-1341
LITSCHHAUER, Ignaz	24	Wien	50-1132
LITT, Johannes	46	Holzheim	54-0830
Conrad 11, Clara 42, Juliana 17, Clara 15			
LITTAUER, Meyer	31	Breslau	53-0888
LITZ, Philipp	35	Meckbeuren	54-1168
LITZELMANN, Carl	42	Waldkirch	53-0991
LITZKENDORF, Wilh.	48	Obereichstaed	48-0887
Elisabeth 42			
LOBEN, Carl	20	Rennafeld	48-0951
LOBENSTEIN, Elise	24	Brake	50-1071
LOBER, Carl	26	Erfurt	54-1716
LOBS, A.C. (f)	18	Arnsheim	51-0517
LOCH, Pankratz	38	Zeckindorf	49-0574
Marg. 30, Joh. 9, Barb. 7, Michael 26			
LOCHNER, Conrad	24	Flusnitz	54-1554
Catharina 25			
LOCHNER, Georg	27	Paffeldorf	54-1283
LOCHSTAMPKER, J.M.	37	Schnelldorf	52-0515
LOCKBELER, J.M.		Vorderburg/Bv	49-0365
LOEB, Adolph	24	Giessen	52-1512
LOEB, Anna Maria	44	Friedrichsdor	51-0384
Jacob 24, Anna Cath 15, Valentin 8			
LOEB, Eva Catharin	30	Friedrichsdor	51-0384
Wilhelm 14			
LOEBE, Elias	35	Schwarza	54-1078
Regine 39			
LOEBENSTEIN, Levi	27	Fritzlar/Hess	52-0807
LOEBER, Emilie	19	Cassel	52-1410
LOEBER, Fr.	30	Bolhorn	51-1160
LOEBER, Friedr. Wm	47	Steinbach	54-1647
Clothilde 38, Lina 5, Carl 3, Emilie 1			
LOEBER, Helena	34	Connefeld/Hes	48-0053
Catharina 9			
LOEBL, Therese	22	Schoenlind	54-1566
LOECHFELTH, Elis.	25	New York	54-0987
Ida by			
LOECHLE, Carl	19	Kirchberg	49-0352
LOEFFLER, Caroline	26	Wuertenberg	53-0557
LOEFFLER, Elis.	19	Steinweisen	53-0914
LOEFFLER, Ernst	19	Heilbronn	49-0912
LOEFFLER, Friedr.	48	Seebach	52-1304
Wilhelmine 46, William 27, Wilhelmine 19			
Johanna 17, Augusta 11, Dorothea 20			
LOEFFLER, Leonh.	27	Wolfsdorf	52-1129
Anna 36, Elisab. 8, Peter 6, Kunigunde 9			
LOEFFLER, Theo	23	Bardburg	54-1724
LOEHDEN, Claus	22	Wennebostel/H	53-0475
LOEHMANN, Friedr.	29	Gardelegen	53-0652
LOEHR, Hieron.	35	Erckeln	54-0600
LOEHR, J. (f)	28	Reddagshausen	48-0453
LOEHRDING, Heinr.	27	Hannover	51-1725
LOEHRMANN, Georg	32	Ebersbruenn	51-1245
Cath. 30, Joh. Georg 37, Georg 37			
Cathar. 27			
LOEHRPABEL, M. (m)	27	Guetersloh/Pr	48-0447
Christine 30			
LOENING, Angelina	29	Lingen	53-0991
LOEP, Joh.	21	Emsdorf/Hess.	52-0960
LOERITZ, Friedrich	30	Langenrode	52-1148
Maria 38, Pauline 2			
LOERZEL, Maria	17	Hilders	52-1625
LOERZING, Conrad	35	Eishausen	53-0320
LOESCH, Anna	19	Oberhoechstad	54-1575
LOESCH, Johann	43	Tatschenbrunn	48-0101
Magdalene 34, Catharine 12, Margarethe 5			
Barbara 2			
LOESCH, Ludwig	22	Wuerzburg	50-0292
LOESCH, Traugott	24	Coburg	53-1013
Barbara 32, Carl 7, Amalie 9m			
LOESCHER, Carl	32	Destel/Pr.	54-1092
LOESCHER, Carl	23	Splau	54-1168
LOESCHER, Simon	27	Schauerheim	49-1106
LOESER, Anna	48	Coburg	52-1620
LOESSEL, Carl	26	Heinrichsgrue	53-0585
LOESSEL, Georg	37	Baiern	53-0585

NAME	AGE	RESIDENCE	YR-LIST
LOESSEL, Johann	29	Ortenburg	50-0292
LOEVER, Anna	28	Frankenberg	53-1016
Elisabeth 22			
LOEWE, Caroline	24	Minden	52-1661
LOEWE, Fr. August	28	Siebenlehn	54-0987
LOEWE, Gertrude	46	Melsungen	53-1000
Cath. Elis. 17, Cath. 13, Anna Cath. 6			
LOEWE, Robert	19	Reichenbach	54-1371
LOEWEN, Catharine	28	Gehus	53-0652
LOEWEN, Henry	29	Wiesbaden/Nas	48-0447
LOEWENBACH, Bernh.	23	Gueterslohe	51-1245
LOEWENBERG, Eva	18	Waechtersbach	52-1625
LOEWENHAUSEN, Aug.	25	Muenchen/Bav.	53-0628
Margaretha 18			
LOEWENHEIM, Friedr	25	Berlin	53-0888
LOEWENSTEIN, Eva	20	Lichtenstadt	54-1371
LOEWENSTEIN, Isrel	37	Altenbrock	50-1067
LOEWENSTEIN, J.(m)	30	Lengerich	49-0416
LOEWENSTEIN, M.	18	Cassel	54-1724
Wilh. 17			
LOEWENSTEIN, Mar.A	50	Peckelsheim	54-1371
LOEWENSTEIN, Meyer	16	Muehlhausen	53-0928
Bernhard 17, Wilhelm 17			
LOEWENSTEIN, Sam'l	20	Waldeck	53-1013
LOEWENTHAL, Heinr.	17	Forth	50-0439
LOEWENTHAL, Julius	22	Berlin	54-0965
LOEWITT, Joseph	20	Hohen Elbe	49-0324
LOFF, H. (m)	14	Mulsenn	48-0453
LOFFLER, Eduard	35	Beuthen	49-0781
Amalie 35, baby			
LOFFLER, John	18	Kehlbach	52-0515
LOGEMANN, Carl	34	Oldenburg	53-0267
LOGEMANN, William	28	Strohen/Pr.	48-0053
Ann Margaret 43, Mary Carolin 9			
Mary Sophia 6, Henry Wm. 5, Friedr. Wm. 2			
Mary Wilh'mn 3m			
LOGEMANN, William	70	Stroehen	50-1071
LOH, Dorothea	25	Barmen	53-1164
LOHBAUER, Gottfr.	35	Schmaehingen	52-1200
LOHDE, Ernst	32	Berlin	53-0492
LOHEYDE, Oskar	20	Herford	48-0406
LOHFING, Heinr.	20	Eiterfeld/Hes	51-1532
LOHMANN, F.H.	25	Emden	53-0473
LOHMANN, Friedrich	25	Kalhorn	51-0352
LOHMANN, G.A.	30	Altenberg	52-0563
LOHMANN, Heinrich	46	Wollten	52-1625
Friederike 43, Caroline 14, Wilhelmine 12			
August 10, Conrad 7, Heinrich 3			
Wilhelm 9m			
LOHMANN, Meta	47	Leer	51-0757
LOHMEYER, Fritz	21	Rechtenfleth	52-0699
LOHMEYER, Heinr.	18	Wiedersheim	52-1321
LOHMEYER, Ludwig	54	Stroehen	50-1071
Mina 24, Maria 16, Wilhelm 18			
Friedrich 22, Dorothea 8			
LOHMEYER, William	16	Pente	53-0991
LOHMUELLER, Anton	15	Hettingen	54-0053
LOHNASSER, Georg	26	Carlsbad	51-1160
LOHNER, Simon	62	Solingen	48-0406
Barbara 38			
LOHNERT, J.	56	Pordirf	54-1419
Barbara 56, Georg 15			
LOHR, Andr.	27	Linzler	51-0757
Maria 26, Heinr. 7			
LOHR, August	21	Riestert	54-1283
LOHR, Catharine	20	Lendorf	48-1179
LOHR, Emma	18	Eisenberg	52-1512
LOHR, Maria	30	Kauseln	49-0352
LOHRBERG, August	37	Kohlen	49-0329
LOHRENGEL, Marg.	22	Bilshausen	52-1625
LOHREY, Barbara	19	Wiesenthal/S.	53-0475
LOHRMANN, W. (m)	29	Tesberg	49-1358
LOHWIED, Georg Ad.	24	Follmersdorf	51-0384
LOLZE, Johann	15	Wilhelmshause	53-0590
LOOBOLD, Mathias	16	Klesberg	54-1419
LOOS, J. (m)	33	Eschenbach	48-0445
LOOS, Joh.	25	Weingarts	52-0693
LOOS, John	23	Hegendorf	53-0888

NAME	AGE	RESIDENCE	YR-LIST
LOOS, Kunig.	26	Dettendorf	52-0693
Leonh. 9, Kunigund. 5			
LOOSEN, Friedr. D.	27	Gross Hamburg	54-1371
LOOTMANN, Otto	23	Osnabrueck	52-0699
Gustav 28			
LORBER, Carl	46	Blankenhain	54-1297
Carolina 40			
LORBER, Elias	22	Kuelberg	53-0652
Barbara 22, Barbara 56			
LORBER, Fried. Wm.	38	Pfiffelbach	52-1148
Adelheid 35, Auguste 10, Carl 8, Emil 4			
Minna (died) 2			
LORBER, Michael	23	Steinach/Bav.	53-0628
Therese 42			
LORBER, Nicolaus	8	Steinach/Bav.	53-0628
Carl 13, Therese 48			
LORCH, Amalie	20	Nuernberg	52-0693
Emilie 21			
LORCH, Carl	24	Stuttgart	54-1341
LORCH, Catharina	58	Fischbach/Nas	53-0628
Christian 21, Wilhelm 19			
LORCH, Heinrich	27	Fischbach/Nas	53-0628
Elisabeth 29, Heinrich 8, Johannette by			
LORCH, Joh. Peter	33	Fischbach/Nas	53-0628
LORCH, Lorenz	31	Worbis	52-0279
Elise 33, Adolph 9, Ferdinand 6, Eduard 4			
LORE, Heinr.	14	Brakel	51-1796
Theresa 10, Gertrude 8, An. Marie 5			
LORENTZ, Conrad	30	Herda	48-0284
LORENTZ, Johann	40	Schiredorf	52-0775
Margaretha 41, Johann 15, Clemens 11			
Margaretha 9, Margaretha 5			
LORENZ, Carl	19	Weidenthal	54-0600
LORENZ, Carl	39	Barmen	48-0565
LORENZ, Conrad	32	Bayern	53-0590
LORENZ, Dorothee	26	Bayern	53-0590
LORENZ, Herm.	28	Dresden	50-1071
LORENZ, Johann	17	Oberlis	52-1200
LORENZ, Theodor	17	Aschen	50-0379
Carl 16			
LORENZ, Xaver	23	Zwiesel	54-1341
LORG, Philippine	23	Fischbach/Nas	53-0628
LORING, Georg Mich	36	Aalen	54-1371
Christiane 37, Catharine 3			
LORK, Alois	27	Wanssen	54-1676
LORK, Susanne	53	Freiderhausen	49-0781
LORSCH, Eleonora	22	Alsfeld	54-1443
LOSS, Conrad	36	Harmrode	53-0324
LOSS, Joh.	33	Taublitz	52-1129
Eva Cath. 30, baby			
LOTFELD, Lotte	26	Uchte	51-1084
LOTH, Joseph	26	Evelter	50-1067
Maria 21			
LOTH, Louisa	42	Bibra	53-0991
Gustavus 25, Louisa 18, Rudolph 15			
Minna 13			
LOTHHOLZ, Marg.	21	Wuertt.	54-1724
LOTICHIUS, Ernst	40	Wiesbaden	54-1297
LOTZ, Charles	18	Dillenburg	53-1164
LOTZ, Georg	24	Hosolms	52-0699
LOTZ, Herm.	30	Hessen	50-0021
Anna B. 21			
LOTZ, Joseph	28	Fulda	51-0405
LOTZ, Marie	25	Basel	54-0987
LOTZE, Ernst Ad.	29	Meissen	54-1297
LOTZGESELL, Geo. H	23	Wattenbach	52-1105
LOUNG, Mathias	16	Buchdorf	54-0903
LOUSS, Elise	20	Dorum	52-0699
LUBAR, Heinrich	36	Wippersheim	51-0757
Elisabeth 26, Elisabeth 24, Johannes 5			
LUBER, Friedr.	38	Kalckreuth	52-0693
Cathar. 38, Johann 4, Christine 2			
LUBESCH, Helene	16	Berlin	53-0825
LUBLASSER, Jacob	29	Erdmannsdorf	54-1168
LUBNITZ, Lousia	26	Mittelruessel	49-0737
LUCHMANN, August	37	Burg	53-0267
Dorothea 27, August 5, Wilhelm 7m			
LUCHTERLAND, Carl	24	Moabit	52-1304

NAME	AGE	RESIDENCE	YR-LIST
Ernestine 26			
LUCK, Caroline	27	Berghausen	52-1321
Friedrich 3, Wilhelm 1			
LUCKE, Carl	8m	Willebadessen	50-0472
LUCKE, Casper H.	24	Paderborn	48-0951
LUCKEN, Marie	20	Osterkappeln	47-0762
LUCKHAUPT, John	23	Umstedt	53-0991
LUCKING, J.		Wilde	51-0517
LUCKNER, Paul	24	Zchippach	52-1105
LUDFING, Charlotte	20	Wunstorf	52-0095
LUDIG, Fritz	27	Hannover	53-0628
LUDOLF, Cathrine	40	Minden	49-1517
Maria 16, Eliza 8			
LUDOLPH, Charles	22	Minden	52-1304
LUDOLPH, Joseph	30	Prussia	49-0329
LUDORF, Julius	32	Muenster	49-1358
LUDOVICI, Heinrich	21	Cassel	51-1245
LUDT, Ludwig	25	Wahlbach	53-0590
LUDWIG, Caethchen	24	Friedberg	54-0987
LUDWIG, Conrad	28	Baltimore	51-0352
Elisabeth 24			
LUDWIG, Ferdinand	8	Nordhausen	49-1106
LUDWIG, Friedrich	43	Leipzig	51-1640
LUDWIG, Friedrich	29	Luegde	51-1101
Wilhelmine 35, Anton Friedr 3			
LUDWIG, Gotte	26	Sondheim	51-1160
LUDWIG, Jacob	36	Gellmern	51-1245
LUDWIG, Jacob	22	Friedberg	54-0987
LUDWIG, John A.	34	Offershausen	51-1455
Lora D. 24			
LUDWIG, Joseph	54	Meinbach/Pr.	53-0628
LUDWIG, Nicolaus	35	Schwarzenbach	53-0475
Eva 38, Auguste 13			
LUDWIG, Wilhelmine	6m	Luegde	51-1101
LUEBBE, Bern.	29	Brunswick	50-1317
LUEBBECKE, Ludwig	29	Waldeck	54-0053
LUEBBEN, Heinr.	26	Bremen	50-1236
Cathr. 24			
LUEBCKE, Ernst	32	Heiligenstadt	52-0699
Margarete 27			
LUEBING, Anna	56	Sontra	52-0699
LUEBKE, Luer	16	Hannover	49-0329
LUEBKE, Sophie	14	Polle	53-1086
LUECK, Carl	30	Berghausen	52-1321
LUECKE, Elisabeth	55	Papenhoefen	48-1355
Elisabeth 16, Friedrich 11, Anton 9			
August 6			
LUECKE, J.	19	Billendisen	51-0517
LUECKE, Johanne	20	Ringelheim	52-1625
LUECKEL, Catharina	23	Kleinern	54-1566
Marie 20, Maria 9m			
LUECKEN, Elisab.	66	Dardesheim	51-1062
LUEDDECKE, C.	23	Beverungen	51-0517
LUEDEKE, Dorothea	23	Beverungen	53-0585
LUEDERS, C. (m)	50	Eitzen	48-0453
LUEDERS, Emil	23	Braunschweig	54-0600
LUEDERS, Heinrich	38	Chemnitz	54-1554
Caroline 34			
LUEDERS, Louise	36	Braunschweig	53-1062
Emil 14, Otto 13			
LUEDERS, M.J.W.	18	Braunschweig	49-0324
LUEHMANN, Joh. Fr.	30	Volkmarsen	54-1371
LUEHNEMANN, Jac.	36	Veckerhagen/H	50-0323
LUEHNEMANN, John	33	Veckerhagen	50-0323
LUEHRS, Anna	20	Lahmstedt	51-1035
LUEHRS, Christian	38	Achum	54-0903
LUEHRS, Claus	19	Spaden	50-0366
LUEHRS, Heinrich	24	Scheppe	54-0872
LUEHRS, Joh. H.	28	Ottersberg	51-1245
LUEHRS, Nicolaus	34	Dorum	49-0345
Albert 17			
LUEKE, A.M. (f)	48	Hammelsberg/P	51-0048
Oswald 17, Aug. 10			
LUEKE, Joh.	40	Willebadessen	50-0472
Theresia 33, Sophie 8, Carl 8m			
LUEKE, Joseph	35	Istrup/Pr.	54-0965
LUELKE, Joh. Heinr	58	Strosel	54-1452
Marie 48, Heinrich 46, Hermann 26			
Carl 20, Charlotte 26			
LUELLMANN, Christ.	18	Achim	54-1297
LUEMMER, Heinrich	24	Gera	54-0987
LUENEBRINK, Friedr	18	Bohnde	49-0352
LUENEMANN, Stephan	48	Plantelinne	51-0352
Dominicus 16			
LUENING, Julia	19	Hannover	50-1317
LUENSEMANN, Martin	58	Rothenburg	51-0405
Marie 52			
LUERESSEN, Johann	17	Scharmbeck	52-1580
LUERING, Ernst	20	Rotenburg	54-1649
LUERS, Doris	24	Rehton	47-0158
LUERSSEN, Hermann	24	Hannover	54-1649
LUESSEN, Christoph	35	Wiegeln	50-0379
Friederike 6			
LUETJEN, John	22	Bergedorf/Han	51-1725
LUETTER, John	53	Pohlhausen	48-0406
LUETTGEN, Gustav	42	Elberfeld	54-0872
Julie 40, Louise 11			
LUETZ, Carl	23	Ludwigshalle	51-0460
LUETZ, Christoph	35	Baiern	53-0585
LUETZ, Helene	26	Freudenberg	51-0352
LUFT, Catharine	46	Langenheim	52-1625
LUFT, Conrad	23	Albertshausen	52-0563
LUFT, Johannes	54	Lauterbach	51-1101
LUHEMHOEP, Ludwig	46	Brau	53-0914
Sophie 40, Marie 16, Minna 9, Louise 7			
Sophie 5, William 3, Christine 3m			
LUHRMANN, Heinr.	20	Neuenkirchen	49-0383
LUHRMANN, Herrm.	34	Fischerhude	51-1245
LUITJEN, Hermann	15	Schwarmbeck-S	53-1070
LUITLEN, Ludw Bern	26	Heilbronn	53-1062
LUK, Fr.	19	Beverstedt	48-1114
LULL, Joh.	46	Hirschheim	54-1283
LUMBACH, Heinrich	18	Niedernebuch	54-0930
LUMBERGER, Georg	30	Fernaubrunst	54-1282
LUMP, Conrad	36	Willofs	54-1575
Margareth 35, Barb. 49, Johannes 9			
Barbara 5			
LUMP, Joh. Carl O.	20	Burghaun/Hess	49-0365
LUMP, Metta	24	Hannover	53-0590
LUMPE, Johann	29	Niederdorf	52-1101
LUNDMACHER, Heinr.	18	Weselow	47-0872
LUNESCH, Georg	35	St.Louis	54-1371
LUNG, Carl	23	Darmstadt	53-0590
LUNGNIEKEL, Thomas	25	Fichtelberg	54-0903
Anna 27			
LUNSMANN, Franz	35	St. Louis	54-1371
LUPPENPLATZ, Joh.	18	Meinsheim	52-0370
LURBORN, Heinrich	17	Quakenbruck	54-0987
LURCH, Ernst	23	Nordhausen	52-0279
Ferdinand 27			
LURCH, Lorenz	31	Worbis	52-0279
Elise 33, Adolph 9, Ferdinand 6, Eduard 4			
LUS, Minna	24	Adelsdorf	54-1297
LUSCHER, Heinrich	29	Wildeshausen	48-0260
LUSCHER, Siegfried	20	Cassel	52-1620
LUSEMHOEP, Ludwig	46	Brau	53-0914
Sophie 40, Marie 16, Minna 9, Louise 7			
Sophie 5, William 3, Christine 3m			
LUSSMEYER, Heinr.	24	Brunen	53-1062
Maria 22			
LUST, Adam	46	Prussia	50-1317
Martha 41, Mathilde 18, Carl 16			
Hermann 16, Friederike 14, Marie 14			
Wilhelmine 12, Auguste 10, Wilhelm 6			
Heinr. 3			
LUTEMANN, Christ.	29	Ost Friesland	54-0903
LUTHER, Catharina	24	Oldenburg	52-1362
LUTHER, Charles Th	19	Salzungen	53-0991
LUTHER, Friedrich	36	Heubach/Sax.	51-1796
LUTHER, Joh. Andr.	32	Eisfeld	53-0914
Eva 35, Catharine 53			
LUTJES, Eduard	16	Dorum	52-0895
LUTTCHEN, Hermann	19	Leichlingen	52-1580
LUTTER, Carl	19	Muehlenkamp	49-0345
LUTTRUPP, Heinrich	21	Harelshausen	54-0930
LUTZ, Anna	23	Lehrberg	53-0991

NAME	AGE	RESIDENCE	YR-LIST
LUTZ, Dorothea	23	Obertheers	54-1554
LUTZ, Franz	24	Muehldorf	54-1649
LUTZ, Joh.	50	Niederbessing	47-0868
A. 43, M. 14, W. 3			
LUTZ, Leonhard	29	Dambeck/Wuert	52-1332
Francisca 23, Margrethe 9m			
LUTZ, Michael	34	Hochstetten	52-1423
LUTZ, Michel	47	Mettwitz	53-0324
Anna Margret 40, Johann 13, Catharina 8			
LUTZ, Ursula	25	Zeil	54-1554
LUZ, Georg (died)	38	Oberthiers	54-1554
LUZ, Gottl.	20	Wuertt.	54-1724
LUZ, Vict. Georg	25	Kirchentellin	52-0351
Gottl. Fried 22			
LUZE, Berthold	27	Minden/Hann.	51-1796
LYAN, Betty	18	Cassel	49-0742
MAAG, Anna	23	Oberdingenhei	50-0840
Albert 2			
MAAG, Barbara	18	Ebingen	53-1164
MAAK, Sophie	18	Wuertenberg	53-0324
MAAS, Heinr.	24	Hannover	50-0439
MAAS, Wilh.	25	Dinslaken	48-0565
MAASEN, Joseph	21	Dieren/Pr.	52-1620
MAASS, Christian	52	Treptow	54-0872
Friederike 22, Bertha 20			
MAASS, Fried. Herm	14	Naumburg	53-0888
MAASS, Frommet	44	Luebbecke	53-0492
Jeannette 13, Abraham 9, Bella 7			
MACH, Anna	19	Hass	54-0987
Cunigunde by			
MACHENNAU, L. (m)	18	Trienz	50-0746
Sh. (m) 37			
MACHETANZ, Marie	24	Vacha	54-1371
Caroline 17			
MACKE, Georg	28	Ellingerode	52-0095
Wilhelm 23			
MACKENNAU, A. (m)	39	Wrinech	50-0746
MACKRODT, Maria	54	Immenrode	54-0903
MACOMBER, E.D.	16	Brooklyn	48-0112
MADEL, Marg.	25	Bischofsreith	54-1283
MADER, Bernhard	25	Langenau	52-1362
MADER, Joseph	29	Obenricht/Bav	49-0365
Marianne 22			
MADER, Lud.	25	Eningen	49-0329
MADMER, August	27	Boston	53-0914
MADS, Edward	26	Laumberg	51-1588
MAEDER, Cath.	24	Wildenberg	51-1160
MAEGERLEIN, Steph.	23	Jacobsmuehl	53-0914
MAEHL, Balthasar	51	Giesen	53-1000
Elisab. 39, Cath. 15, Marie 12, Friedr. 7			
Georg 5, Carl 3			
MAEHLHAUSEN, Elise		Homberg	54-0930
MAENEL, Anna	22	Bayern	53-0557
Barbara 45, Sophie 15			
MAER, Michael	38	Langenbruch	54-1419
MAERTEN, Friedr. C	23	Wahmbeck	47-0872
Charlotte 24			
MAERZ, Friedr.	24	Kappel	52-1129
MAERZ, Georg	35	Buerenfels	48-1179
MAERZ, Heinrich	41	Wurtzbach	53-1070
MAERZ, Joh.	24	Graefenberg	49-1358
Reg. 20			
MAERZ, Joh.	36	Retterbach	47-0868
MAETKE, Julius	26	Andreasberg	53-0928
MAEULE, Catharine	18	Brenz	54-0600
MAG, Friederika	20	Giessen	54-0850
MAGELSEN, Istela	9	Schower	49-0912
MAGENBURG, Heinr.	18	Kispeldamm	49-1517
MAGFARTH, A.E. (f)	22	Gospenrode	51-0517
MAGFAUTH, C.	24	Franckensel	51-0517
J. (f) 27, F. 1			
MAHLAND, C.W. (m)	17	Hannover	50-0311
MAHLER, Charlotte	26	Brellingen	50-1067
MAHLER, Heinr.	31	Neuenkirchen	54-0987
MAHLMANN, Aug.	42	Barmen	48-0565
Bernh. 27, Wilh. 7			
MAHLMEIN, Ludw.	28	Rehlenz	52-1321
MAHLSTEDT, Fr.	26	Leeste	50-0439

NAME	AGE	RESIDENCE	YR-LIST
MAHLSTEDT, H.	60	Harssstedt	54-1716
Anne 49, Heinrich 21, Anne 24			
MAHNCKE, F. (m)	19	Salzwedel	54-1591
MAHNKE, Heinrich	22	Rheine	51-1455
MAHNKE, Joh.	19	Osterholz	51-0326
Ludw. 16			
MAHNKE, Ludwig	19	Scharmbeck/Ha	54-1092
MAHNKEN, Diedrich	18	Kamstein	48-0887
MAHNKEN, Hermann	29	Rothenburg	52-1362
MAHNKEN, J.J.	16	Worpswede	51-0460
MAHR, Barbara	23	Muehlhausen	49-0352
MAHR, Georg	27	Wenigendoft	48-1131
MAHR, Wilh.	27	Hof	52-1321
MAIER, Catharina	29	Follmersdorf	51-0384
Lorentz 4, Anton 19			
MAIER, Christian	29	Fischingen	52-0279
MAIER, Johann	45	Bremerhaven	53-0825
Barbara 42, Georg 10			
MAIER, Margaretha	19	Frauenaurach	53-0991
Barbara 16			
MAIER, W. (f)	38	Harienstadt	47-0868
Do. 13, W. 7, Died. 4, Mic. 2			
MAIERHOFEN, Joseph	14	Staurling	54-1341
Anna 19, Theresa 19			
MAINER, Kunigunde	19	Arzberg	53-0557
MAINTHAU, Carl	16	Forth	53-0320
MAINZ, Chr.	23	Oldelsde	54-0600
MAINZ, Elisabeth	27	Rotbach	52-0370
MAIR, Gangolf	26	Pfaffenschwen	52-1625
MAIWALD, Franz	35	Boehmen	52-0895
MAIWALDT, Reinhold	33	Gruenberg	54-1168
MAKE, August		San Francisco	53-1016
MALDER, Cath.	22	Wildenberg	51-1160
MALENHAUER, Johann	50	Prussia	53-0628
Wilhelmine 52, Carl 27, August 22			
Christian 19			
MALER, Caroline	27	Bueren	48-0887
MALHISEN, Trena	20	Beverstedt	51-1084
MALKMUS, Franz Jos	25	Hunfeld/Hesse	49-0365
MALLICKH, Carl	40	Warmbrunn	54-1297
MALSCH, Emil	23	Cassel	53-0888
MALTHESER, Jacob	35	Bayern	53-0557
MALZSCHE, Rob.	25	Neise	51-1640
MAMAY, Daniel	28	Riga	51-1725
MAND, Mathilde	25	Meinertshagen	53-0557
MANDEL, Lisette	22	Langenzen	49-0912
MANDELBAUM, Anna	25	Langenzlau	48-0951
Henry 18m			
MANDELBAUM, David	15	Grabenstein	51-0352
MANDLINGER, Carl	28	Eichstaedt	54-1297
MANGELS, Berthold	36	Labstaedt	50-1236
MANGELS, Heinrich	17	Flugeln	54-0987
MANGELSDORF, Carl	49	St. Louis	54-1371
MANGER, Victor	21	Holstadt/Bav.	52-1620
MANGLER, Antonie	26	Mecklenburg	54-0903
MANGOLD, Anna	30	Reichenbach	53-0320
MANGOLD, H.	15		54-1716
MANGOLD, Joseph	28	Hochberg	54-1716
MANGOLD, Margareth	25	Hepsisau/Wuer	52-0351
MANGOLD, Theresia	31	Balder	53-0435
MANN, Hirsch	17	Schlesingen	53-0628
MANN, Joh. Christ.	49	Nordhausen	52-0279
MANNHEIMER, Wilh.	35	Hermannmilste	54-1297
MANNS, Georg	42	Wuertenberg	53-0557
Margretha 38, Peter 12, Johann Georg 9			
Rosina 6, Anna 2			
MANNS, Georg	36	Buchenag	54-0930
MANNS, George	24	Dens	52-1304
MANNS, Johann	25	Buchenau	52-1661
MANNS, Johann	51	Wuertenberg	53-0557
Barbara 43, Joh. Friedr. 13			
MANS, Georg	34	Oldensachsen	54-1647
MANS, Marg.	44	Buchenau	51-1796
Marie Frick 16			
MANTEL, A. Elis.	18	Oberschmitten	53-0838
MANTEL, Christian	24	Wolpe	48-0887
MANTEL, John	62	Muhlbach	48-0951
Anne B. 18, Conrad 12, Eva Cath 7			

NAME	AGE	RESIDENCE	YR-LIST
Cathrine E. 2			
MANTEL, Joseph	26	Fischbach/Bav	53-0628
Regine 20			
MANTEL, Rosalie	27	Langenzlau	48-0951
MANTERS, T. (f)	18	Bakfram	48-0453
MANTKEMEYER, Heinr	19	Fuerstenberg	49-0574
MANTYCK, Jules	27	France	48-1015
MANUS, George	24	Dens	52-1304
MAR, Conrad	20	Hessen	53-1013
MARASS, Anna	23	Gablonz/Oest.	52-1620
MARBURGER, Georg	32	Elsoff	52-0563
MARC, Nicolaus	17	Arolsen	52-0699
MARCHL, Andr.	22	Postau	49-0574
MARCKEL, Mich.	30	Sittling	54-1078
MARCOTTE,	29	France	48-1243
MARCOWITCH, M. (m)	18	Pretoria	49-0413
MARCUS, Carl Heinr	23	Brakel	54-1452
MARCUS, Jeanette	20	Crefeld	51-0352
MARCUS, Joseph	26	Graez	52-1625
MARCUS, Max	19	Butin	54-1078
MARDFELDT, Wm.	26	Hudenmuehlen	52-1625
MARDORF, Conr.	21	Remsfeld	50-1071
MARECK, Johann	38	Triptis	54-1283
Theres 39, Theres 17			
MARGHOLF, H. (m)	21	Waldeck	54-0918
MARGRAF, Fr. Wm.	22	Stadtilm	48-0269
MARGRAF, Friedrich	31	Muehlberg	53-1062
Elisabeth 32, August 3, Paulina 1			
MARGRI, Heinrich	26	Gunzenheim	52-1661
MARGUISON, Martin	29	Posen	53-1086
MARISCH, Joseph	32	Boehmen	53-1000
Anna 34, Joseph 8, Wenzel 7			
MARIUS, Max	36	Krotoschin	53-1023
Friederike 34, Helene 18			
MARK, v. J.H.	25	Hannover	54-1470
MARKART, Fritz	27	Hannover	52-0699
MARKEL, Peter	33	Niederkaufung	54-1078
MARKER, Wilhelm	28	Sawaburg	53-1070
MARKERT, At.(died)	16	Holzhausen	48-1131
MARKEWITSCH, Hen't	19	Eulm	54-1283
Johanna 18			
MARKGRAF, C.	23	Gotha	54-1283
MARKGRAF, Eliza	25	Goettingen	53-0991
MARKGRAF, Guenther	17	Schernberg	54-1554
MARKMINDER, Marg.	24	Marburg	51-1588
Caspar 30			
MARKOWSKI, Matilde	18	Driesen	53-1023
MARKS, Catharina	35	Marburg	48-1355
Elisabeth 28, Balthasar 10, Elise 5			
Heinrich 3			
MARKS, Charles	25	Charleston	53-0991
MARKSCHEFFEL, Carl	45	Gehrden	49-0383
Carl 17, Emma 18, Dor. 41, Anna 13			
Wilh. 11, Emilie 4			
MARKWALTES, Mich.	23	Braunschweig	51-0756
MARKWALTES, Peter	16	Holweide	51-0756
MARKWALTES, Wilh.	19	Holweide	51-0756
MARMEL, M.	56	Ostbevern	50-0746
Clara 51, O. (m) 22, C. (m) 20, F. (m) 19			
Fr. (m) 17, L. (f) 23, C. (f) 23			
P. (f) 16			
MARPE, Carl	20	Dinker	51-1084
MARPE, Louise	16	Zeven	48-1114
MARR, Friedrich	24	Goettingen	52-0563
MARR, Michael	46	Stolzenrode/B	48-0053
Dorothy 44, Catharine M. 13			
Marg. Elis. 9, Barbara 6			
MARSCH, Gerhard	28	Heinstetten	54-0903
MARSCHALL, Gottl.	43	Jena	51-1245
Friedr. 37, Minna 16, Therese 2			
MARSCHALL, Henry	30	Dresden	53-1164
Helena 29			
MARSCHALL, Lenid	23	Kattenrundt	50-0472
MARSCHUETZ, Henr't	17	Wambach	50-0366
MARSCHUETZ, Max	15	Wambach	48-1131
MARSHALK, Joh. Chr	42	Osten	51-1101
Margaretha R 38, Friedrich 12			
Adele Emilie 10, Christian Em 8			
Amandus 6			
MARSHALK, Therese	6m	Osten	51-1101
MARTE, Martin	22	Steinfeld	54-1716
MARTEN, Friedrich	27	Kolfeld	47-0672
MARTENS, Friedrich	21	Kl. Berkel	52-1304
MARTENS, Heinrich	20	Ebersdorf	49-0345
MARTENS, Heinrich	19	Bremervoerde	54-1297
MARTENS, Hermann	26	Ebersdorf	49-0345
MARTENS, Joseph	28	Luetgeneder	52-1661
MARTENS, M.	26	Farven	54-0918
Jacob 44, Anna M. 34, Jacob 11			
MARTER, Nicolaus	55	Weigelen	50-0379
MARTH, Charles		Woelsaw	53-0888
MARTH, Nicol.	22	Tann	51-0405
MARTHREY, de F.	36	France	48-1015
MARTIN, Albert	24	Braunschweig	54-1001
Marie 21			
MARTIN, Anna	28	Buchenrod	50-0379
Martin 7, Dorette 6			
MARTIN, Elisabeth	49	Helldrit	53-0267
Johanne 23, Catharina 18			
MARTIN, Erhard	36	Walsloch	53-0637
Margaretha 28, baby 10m			
MARTIN, Gottfr.	24	Saxony	50-0021
Carl 21			
MARTIN, Heinrich	31	Wehlheiden	54-0930
Joh. Christ 20			
MARTIN, Joh Georg	18	Coburg	52-1423
MARTIN, Joh. Carl	19	Erfurt	54-1078
Joh. Wilh. 21			
MARTIN, Joh. Chr.	38	Untergreistau	49-0324
MARTINE, Carl	19	Buchel	54-0053
MARTINI, Constant	21	Riedlingen	48-1355
MARX, Ferd.	34	Rottweil	53-1164
MARX, G.	22	Baden	49-1358
Emil 23			
MARX, Leonhard	24	Kurwalden	54-0872
Elise 23			
MARX, Matheas	28	Esch	47-0672
MARZ, Jacob	18	Nidda	48-1131
MARZ, Philipp	26	Celle	52-0095
Charlotte 27, Gottfried 9			
MASBACH, Jonatan	33	Neuwied	54-0987
Emilie 28			
MASCHE, Elise	19		51-0756
MASCHMEIER, G.H.	18	Osnabrueck	52-1512
MASKE, Albertine	19	Lobsens	48-1355
MASON, Friedrich	20	Mittelruessel	49-0737
MASSICH, Joh	25	Fernbreidenba	52-0558
G. (f) 20			
MASSLE, Johannes	48	Wuerttemberg	54-1716
MAST, Catharina	29	Openau/Baden	52-0351
MASTE, Louisa	29	Hannover	53-1164
Otto 2			
MASTIN, Joh. Carl	19	Erfurt	54-1078
Joh. Wilh 21			
MATEHT, John	34	Wasserknoden	54-1341
MATER, Carl	18	Frankenberg	53-0492
MATERER, Elizabeth	28	Mittelruessel	49-0737
MATERN, Friedrich	30	Memel/Pr.	54-1092
MATHAIE, Claude	26	Cassel/Hesse	51-1725
MATHAU, Friedrich	34	New York	48-1015
MATHE, Isidor	20	Wahlen	54-1724
MATHEIS, Doris	24	Hannover	50-0366
MATHEIS, Jacob	36	Hungen	54-1282
Elise 31, Louise 6, Rudolph 3			
MATHER, George	42	Erlangen	49-1517
MATHERIN, August	23	Mittelruessel	49-0737
MATHERS, Margareth	28	Michlbach	53-0838
MATHES, Christ.	28	Wolfsbaum	53-0825
MATHES, Georg Mich	31	Abensberg	53-0825
Mariana 21, Mariana 9m			
MATHIAS, Henry	27	Solingen	48-0406
MATHIAS, Joh. Chr.	31	Estedt	54-1371
Sophie 33, Mathias 9, Louise 7			
MATHIAS, Martin Ed	34	Hayna	47-0872
MATHIAS, Regina	19	Oberschlichti	52-0895
MATHIES, Caroline	20	Bederkesa	50-1317

NAME	AGE	RESIDENCE	YR-LIST
MATHIES, Marie	19		54-1716
MATHIS, Friedrich	28	Fulda	51-1101
MATHIS, Georg	22	Braunschweig	51-1796
MATTERN, Carl	28	Brunswyk	51-1725
MATTERN, Johannes	30	Bisses	54-1717
Heinrich 22			
MATTFELD, Diedr.	19	Armsen	54-1647
MATTFELD, Hermann	32	Rothlacke	54-1647
MATTFELD, Margreth	27	Rothlacke	54-1647
MATTHAEUS, Friedr.	26	Goettingen	53-0324
Friederike 27, Sophie 4, Louis 10m			
MATTHEES, Nicolaus	24	Oberlimbach	54-1554
MATTHESER, Jacob	35	Bayern	53-0557
MATTHEWS, James	43	United States	48-1243
Miss. 37			
MATTHEY, Philipp	19	Radenberg	53-0590
Georg 18			
MATTHIAE, Adolph	24	New York	52-0095
MATTHIAS, Wilh.	19	Riepen	50-1132
MATTHOUSE, Cathar.	22	Chlodenschlos	53-1016
MATTLAGE, Charles	18	Versmold	53-1164
MAU, Valentin	36	Brandlis	50-0379
MAUCHERT, Ernst	22	Pforzheim	48-0269
MAUCK, Joh.	23	Carlsruhe	51-0460
MAUER, Bruno	21	Coburg	54-1371
MAUER, Chr. Fr.	32	Gleicherwiese	52-1304
Elise 28, Martin 4, Friedrich 2			
MAUERS, Herm.	22	Gera	51-0757
MAUK, Wilhelm	16	Wuertenberg	53-0557
MAUL, Caecilie	19	Ried	54-1168
MAUL, Catharina	17	Frankenberg	53-1016
MAUL, Eduard	36	Bilingsleben	50-1071
MAULIK, H. (m)	19	Strauffen	54-1341
MAUREDE, Johann	22	Unterdanbach	52-0095
MAURER, Adam	24	Ellingshausen	50-0366
MAURER, Albert	32	Heilbronn/Wrt	54-1092
MAURER, Andreas	18	Lesering	53-0914
MAURER, Diedrich	37	Wittlehn	53-0838
Diedrich 2			
MAURER, Franz	57	Churhessen	52-1620
Christine 55, Georg 19, Helena 16			
Eduard 13			
MAURER, Henriette	52	Schweppenhaus	54-0987
MAURER, Joh.	27	Niederurff	48-1184
MAURER, John	32	Deisingen	53-0914
MAURER, Marie	25	Cassel	54-1078
MAURIN, Carl	26	Loeka	54-1341
MAUS, Adam	35	Finkenhain	51-0500
MAUS, Augustin	28	Elters	51-0500
Adam 35			
MAUS, Elisabeth	20	Sandhausen	52-1661
MAUS, H.	19	Schonstadt	52-0515
MAUSCHUND, Peter	25	Baumbach	52-0563
MAUSHARDT, Max	24	Dietmannsried	52-1512
MAUSSNER, Marg.	29	Dachstadt	52-0693
MAY, Andreas	30	Eltmann	52-1321
MAY, August	17	Treisa	49-0345
MAY, C.W. (m)	21	Muenchenberns	52-1321
MAY, Elisabeth	19	Maysfelde	54-1341
MAY, Johann	30	Cassel	52-1620
Anna 29			
MAY, Johann	19	Frankfurt	49-0413
MAY, Lea	54	Ebelsbach	52-0807
MAY, Leon	35	Cassel	54-1724
Wilh. 11			
MAY, Martin	29	Meleringstad	52-1580
MAYER, Adam	23	Bayern	51-1686
MAYER, Albert	30	Stuttgart	54-0987
Christian 20			
MAYER, Andreas	37	Bayern	54-1717
Barbara 25			
MAYER, Claus	27	Sellstedt	51-0756
MAYER, Conrad	50	Reichelsdorf	52-1464
Elisabeth 46, Dorothea 15			
MAYER, Ernst	53	Zimmern	52-1304
MAYER, Friedrich	23	Keynichin	51-1035
MAYER, G.	26	Lauingen	53-0582
MAYER, Georg	27	Neundorf	52-0693

NAME	AGE	RESIDENCE	YR-LIST
Cath. 29, Georg (died) 2, Conr. (died) 3m			
MAYER, Heinrich	21	Rechtenfleth	51-0756
MAYER, Jacob	28	Pudenz	52-1464
MAYER, Joseph	44	Neuferdingen	54-1371
Marie 44, Mathias 17			
MAYER, Levi	18	Bockenheim	49-0912
MAYER, Louise	46	Grubenhagen	52-0807
MAYER, Louise	30	Storklfeld/He	51-1796
MAYER, Marie	22	Hochberg	52-0370
MAYER, Mina	22	Gettern	49-0912
MAYER, Regine	38	Bayreuth	54-1297
MAYER, Susanna	19	Bayern	53-0585
MAYER, Wilh. Heinr	27	N.Y.	52-1620
MAYER, Wilhelm	15	Gustendorf	53-0838
MAYFAHRT, Ben.	24	Drigleben	47-0868
MAYLAENDER, Caspar	57	Buende	54-1452
Anna Maria 50, Heinr. Wilh. 20, Herman 15			
August Fried 13, Heinrich 11			
Elisabeth 21, Johanna 17			
MAYLAENDER, Wilh.	45	Buende	54-1452
Marie Louise 44, Elisabetha 24, Maria 19			
Ilsebein 11, Anna 9			
MAYRER, Therese	17	Elzenfeld	54-0987
MAYWALD, Alexander	22	Berlin	54-1168
MECHEL, Catharine	14	Mittelruessel	49-0737
MECKFESSEL, W. (f)	30	Dessin	52-0652
H. (m) 24			
MEDER, Catharine	51	Voes	51-1686
MEDHOLD, Philip F.	27	Mittelruessel	49-0737
MEESE, Heinrich	18	Selsingen	54-1647
Marie 21			
MEESEN, Helene	28	Badbergen	50-1132
Cath. Marie 4			
MEESTER, Johann	29	Lindach	54-0930
MEGGENHOFEN, Adolf	37	Frankfurt	51-1532
MEGNERS, D.	25	Bramel	54-1716
Meta 25			
MEGNERS, Meta	25	Langendam	54-1716
MEHDEN, v.d, Henry	31	New York	53-1164
Mary 19			
MEHL, D. (f)	21	Hahn/Nassau	48-0447
MEHL, Eberhardine	48	Koechingen/Wt	54-1092
MEHLER, Carl	22	Neuenkirch	49-0345
MEHLER, Johann	43	Neustadt/Bav.	53-0475
Ottilie 40, Margarethe 20, Johann 17			
Bonifatius 3			
MEHLKOP, Heinrich	28	Weselop	53-1016
MEHNIRTZ, Moller	24	Mittelruessel	49-0737
MEHR, Ernst	19	Dreisa	52-0279
MEHRDORF, Charles	54	Apelnstedt	53-0888
Jane 34, Henry 9, Ahrina 8, Mary 5			
MEHRMANN, Ferd.	26	Glattbach	54-1575
MEHRTENS, Cathr.	33	Neuenlande	54-1647
MEHRTENS, Catrina	20	Hagen	51-0326
MEHRTENS, Gesine	20	Hagen	52-0699
MEHRTENS, Joh Hein	28	Bremervoerde	51-1725
MEIDINGER, Xaver	58	Neuburg	53-0914
Victoria 56, Anna 16			
MEIENBERG, C.	22	Heiligenrode	52-0558
MEIER, August	44	Egeln/Prussia	53-0628
Christiane 49, Wilhelm 17, Carl 12			
Eduard 10			
MEIER, Auguste	28	Bremen	53-0161
MEIER, Auguste	15	Hildesheim	53-0324
MEIER, B.	20	Luekbergen	51-0517
MEIER, Catharine	35	Freirittenbac	48-1179
Margaretha			
MEIER, Christ.	18	Fruchtelfinge	51-1640
Jacob 16			
MEIER, Christoph	18	Landborstel/H	53-0475
MEIER, Dietr.	33	Riede	51-1640
Anna Elis. 25			
MEIER, Elisabeth	30	Brand	54-1168
MEIER, Ernst	18	Stierberg	54-0987
MEIER, Florian	14	Nienburg	49-1358
MEIER, Franz	23	Fardel	49-1517
MEIER, Friedrich	24	Soltau	48-1131
MEIER, Gottlieb	49	Hirschheim	54-1283

NAME	AGE	RESIDENCE	YR-LIST
Christoph 16, Louise 14			
MEIER, Heinrich	21	Lippe	49-0352
MEIER, Heinrich	28	Altwist	50-0366
MEIER, Herm.	18	Rodenwedel	50-0472
MEIER, Herrm.	20	Wien	51-1640
MEIER, Joh.	40	Neuendorf	52-0693
MEIER, Joh.	42	Indiana	50-1236
MEIER, Joh. Casper	27	Kirchhatten	47-0872
Alida 29			
MEIER, Johann	19	Kolheim/Hann.	53-0475
MEIER, Johann	14	Schwarzenbach	53-0475
MEIER, Johanne	22	Neckarsweinma	52-0117
Marie 15			
MEIER, Johannes	27	Bergenweiler	54-0830
MEIER, John	28	Heinersberg	53-1164
MEIER, John Martin	-3	Lorenzreuth/B	50-0323
Mary Barbara -8, John Michael -7, Mary			
John Martin			
MEIER, Jul.	22	Teuringen	49-1358
MEIER, Louis	19	Rethem	51-0405
MEIER, Ludwig	22	Ostereistedt	53-0475
MEIER, Marg.	34	Rothenburg	54-1283
MEIER, Margarethe	17	Rhade/Hann.	53-0475
MEIER, Marianne	21	Bibra	48-1131
MEIER, Oskar	18	Braunschweig	50-0379
MEIER, Wolfgang	23	Nabburg	54-1283
MEIERHOFF, Joseph	35	Niesburg	49-1517
MEIERREISS, H. (m)	26	Storndorf	52-0652
MEIKA, Fr. Wilhelm	24	Helsa	53-0838
MEILNER, Joh.	24	Mosenberg	49-0324
MEIN, Diedrich	41	Neuhaus	52-0699
MEINECKE, Gottfr.	57	Gewitz	53-0652
MEINEKE, Friedrich	26	Lohnde/Hann.	51-1532
MEINEKE, Th.	26	Woldegk	53-0905
MEINEKE, Wilhelm	23	Braunschweig	54-0872
MEINHARD, Carl	28	Gera	51-0460
MEINHARD, Friedr.	21	Freudenstein	52-0515
MEINHARDT, H. (m)		Upmannsfeld	54-1575
MEINHARDT, Herrman	22	Weissbach	54-1168
MEINHARDT, Isaac	17	Burghaslach	53-1000
MEINHARDT, Jakob	20	Westfalen	52-1620
MEINHOLTZ, Joh Gus	19	Harlingrode	49-1358
Mad. (f) 41, B. (m) 20, C. (f) 18			
Joh. C. 14, Mad. 29			
MEINING, Sophie	22	Sontra	53-1070
MEININGEN, Christ.	56	Schleisingen	50-1132
Fried. 32, Johanne 22, Johanne 23			
MEINKE, Fr.	42	Betel	50-1071
MEINKE, Joh. Heinr	29	Drangstedt	50-0366
MEINKEN, Johann	19	Bremen	51-1532
MEINKEN, Meta	23	Bollen	53-0991
MEINKING, Fritz	21	Hannover	53-0590
MEINS, Adelheid		Wueppel	54-0872
MEINSCHEIN, Beta	16	Wersabe	52-0048
MEINZEN, W.	63	Neuen Syhl	47-0868
K.K. (f) 27, R. 5, Chr. 2, M. 1			
MEISCHNER, Joh.	26	Schierding	52-1129
MEISEKOTTEN, Fr.	34	Barmen	48-0565
MEISEL, Catharine	24	Waldeck	54-1443
MEISEMANN, Carolin	49	Schlawenzis	51-0757
MEISMER, Catharina	25	Helferoth/Bav	52-0351
MEISNER, Nicolaus	24	Helfenroth/Bv	52-0351
Margaretha 25, Catharine bob			
MEISS, Georg	16	Pommern	49-0574
Anna 18			
MEISS, Georg	17	Pommern	52-0693
Nicol. 14, Johann 13			
MEISS, Johann	16	Gehaus	54-1341
MEISSEL, Anna Marg	25	Sanderreuth	53-0825
MEISSEL, Marg.	18	Kalchreuth	52-0515
MEISSELBACH, Elise	45	Hofheim	53-1086
MEISSGEIER, Marie	52	Lobenstein	54-1371
MEISSMANN, Chr.	52	Schlawentzig	51-0757
Friederike 15, Carl 13, Hermann 11			
Joseph 9, Ernst 7, Elise 4			
MEISSNER, Thomas	30	Bamberg	51-1245
MEISSNER, W. (m)	42	Schwabhausen	52-0960
MEISSNER, Wilhelm	22	Dessau	52-1200

NAME	AGE	RESIDENCE	YR-LIST
MEISTER, Anna	27	Kirchheim	54-0053
Wilhelm 3, Hermann 11m			
MEISTER, Caspar	34	Kirchheim	53-0267
MEISTER, G.	32	Ettendorf	48-1184
Elisabeth 30, Elisabeth 8, Margareth 6m			
MEISTER, H.C.	24	Thueringen	51-0517
MEISTER, Johann	27	Gillershausen	53-0320
MEISTER, Johann	26	Oechsen	53-0942
Anna 23, baby			
MEISTER, John G.	51	Langensalza	53-0582
John G. 25, Cath. Eliza 52			
MEISTER, Marg.	32	Thalheim	52-1129
MEITHE, Ernst	32	Dessau	50-0439
Christine 26			
MEJA, Oskar	18	Braunschweig	50-0379
MELBIR, Xaver	24	Mittelruessel	49-0737
MELCHER, William	27	Hohegeis/Pr.	51-0048
MELCHERS, Const.G.	24	Muenster	53-0991
MELCHERSMANN, Fr'z	19	Westphalen	54-1554
MELCHIOR, Conrad	22	Darmstadt/Hes	52-0351
MELCHOR, A. (m)	24	Stierling	48-0453
MELCHOR, Johann	21	Schadenbach	54-0918
Catharine 23			
MELCKE, J.H. (m)	36	Wolfenbuettel	48-0453
MELEY, Heinrich	31	Sachsen	53-0557
MELICHAR, William	21	Prag/Oest.	52-1620
Henrietta 16			
MELLWIG, Johann	25	Warburg/Pr.	53-0475
MELZER, Joseph	31	Wischke/Pr.	54-1092
MEMLER, Joh.	24	Michelbach	51-1686
MEMMLER, Soph.	28	Meiningen	52-1321
MEMPFER, Michel	32	Bayern	51-1686
MENDEL, A.	2	Dresden	54-1419
MENDEL, Bartholome	20	Stierbaum/Bav	49-0365
MENDEL, Elisabeth	21	Knetzgau	54-0053
MENDLEN, Catharina	27	Schoenfeld	49-0574
Franz 3			
MENDLER, Joh. Ant.	19	Freihalden	49-0352
MENGE, Anna	26	Reichstadt	53-0492
MENGE, Carl	39	Gebstedt	52-1148
Rosina 42, Auguste 8, Carl 5, Wilhelm 3			
MENGE, Friedrich	21	Lichtenau	54-1554
MENGEDOTH, Wil'mne	26	Marsbroch	47-0872
MENGEL, Ludwig	20	Elsoff	52-0563
MENGEN, E. (m)	27	Bochler	48-0453
MENGER, Ida	19	Kopelsdorf/Me	51-1796
MENGER, Johann	56	Niederscheid	52-1620
MENGER, Mathias	24	Rotenburg	51-0405
MENGER, Oscar	22	Weimar	50-1317
MENGER, Wilh. Ferd	52	Leipzig/Sax.	51-1796
El. Marg. 42, Ida 19, Carl Luis 16, Max 9			
Hein. 5			
MENGERS, Adolph	17	Bremerlehe	51-0500
MENGERT, Heinr.	29	Sophienthal	52-0960
MENHEL, Johann	30	Buchel	48-1184
Helena 22, August 2			
MENING, Friedrich	47	Osterwick	47-0672
Minna 16, Teresa 13, Gustav 11, Barbara 9			
MENINGER, Therese	27	Schneiderhof	53-0905
MENKE, Engel	25	Seggen	54-147
MENKE, Fr.	34	Cassel	52-1625
Margarethe 28			
MENKE, Friedrich	26	Neudoerfen	54-1371
MENKE, G. (m)	19	Osterholz	49-1517
MENKE, John	38	Uxhausen	54-147
Martha 18			
MENKEL, Heinrich	20	Ramrod	51-035
MENKEN, Lena	17	Misselwarden	47-087
MENNEMANN, Heinr.	50	Ratingen	49-032
Agnes 46			
MENNICH, Wm. Marg.	56	Neuenkrug	51-116
Chr. 31, Friedr. 29, August 19			
Bernhard 16			
MENSCH, Ludwig	59	Solingen	54-091
Maria 26, Dorothea 26, Marie Christ 24			
Ludwig 22, Christian 19, Friedrich 17			
Johannes 13			
MENSCHING, Christ.	18	Nordbruch	54-116

NAME	AGE	RESIDENCE	YR-LIST
MENSCHING, Christ.	54	Idensen	53-0492
Dorothea 44, Friedrich 20, Heinrich 18			
Wilhelm 8			
MENSCHING, Heinr.	32	Sachsenhagen	50-1236
MENSEN, Tina	19	Salzwedel	54-1591
MENSHAUSEN, Henry	27	Hardegsen	53-1164
MENSING, Christian	54	Idensen	53-0492
Dorothea 44, Friedrich 20, Heinrich 18			
Wilhelm 8			
MENSKE, August	20	Bielefeld	50-1317
MENTER, Adolf	19	Gutenberg	54-1283
MENTZEL, Friedrike	30	Treusin	54-1371
Caroline 20			
MENTZEL, Luise	18	Minden	50-0021
MENZE, Sophie	21	Fresdorf/Hann	52-1332
MENZEL, Aug.	18	Schneeberg	53-0320
MENZEL, August	26	Treusin	54-1371
Johann 18			
MERGEL, August	14	Brenken	52-1129
MERGEL, Heinr.	55	Grossengels	52-1129
August 14			
MERGELE, Andreas	22	Knollgraben	49-0574
MERGELE, Joh.	29	Kirchhofen	49-0574
Andreas 22			
MERGERLS, Aug.	25	Knollgraben	49-0574
MERGLER, Franz	34	Mainstockheim	52-0807
Anna 3, Ernestine 2, Marie 9m			
MERK, Georg Friedr	25	Daubersbach	54-0930
MERK, Joh. Friedr.	31	Neustetten	54-0930
Anna Barbara 27			
MERKA, Fr. Wilhelm	24	Helsa	53-0838
MERKEL, Catharina	24	Ramrode	54-0850
MERKEL, Christ.	25	Schnabelweid	54-1078
MERKEL, Elise	18	Ahlfeld	50-1236
MERKEL, Fritz	29	Gruenenplan	54-1575
MERKEL, John	31	Mitteldorf	49-0737
MERKEL, Karl	32	Muenchen	52-1512
Cath. 32, Karl 44			
MERKEL, Kunig.	19	Grossenbach	52-0693
MERKEL, M.	26	Gruenenplan	49-0324
Gottfr. 23			
MERKER, A. (f)	23	Worms/Hessen	48-0447
R. (f) 21			
MERKER, August	21	Mittelruessel	49-0737
MERKLIN, Edmund	35	Urach/Wuertt.	52-1512
MERREM, Otto	24	Prussia	51-1725
MERSCHEL, Tobias	30	Ilbenstadt	53-0320
MERTE, Heinrich	40	Lixfeld	52-1105
Margr. 28, Margr. 5			
MERTENS, Charles	29	Osterode	53-0914
MERTENS, H.F.	37	Woebsen	53-1016
Anna Marg. 42, Joh. Friedr. 9, Heinrich 6			
Louise 5, Margarethe 20, Christian 35			
MERTENS, J.	19	Billerndisen	51-0517
MERTENS, John	22	Osteranden/Ha	50-0323
MERTENS, Lorenz	26	Germany	50-0472
MERTENS, Meth. (f)	22	Wayer	54-1094
MERTZ, Adalbert	26	Gossau	53-0320
MERTZ, Rosine	25	Hotzberg	52-0370
MERX, Jacob	19	Roth	52-0563
MERZ, Conrad	34	Kl.Sindelbach	51-1245
MERZ, Elise	27	Stangenrod	53-1086
MERZ, Ernst	31	Oberalba	52-1580
Anna 29, Minchen 6m			
MERZ, Gertrude	56	Hannberg	54-1575
Marie 30			
MERZ, Ignatz		Muehlactz	53-0942
MERZ, Louise	24	Fulda	53-0585
MERZ, Peter	28	Alsheim	52-0095
MERZ, Robert	22	Chemnitz/Sax	54-1092
MESCH, Ant Lew Edm	18	Judenbach	53-0991
MESCKE, Eilert	49	Oldenburg	51-1245
MESS, John	20	Wahlen	54-0053
MESSER, John D.	32	U.S.A.	49-0329
Eibe 16, Marie 20			
MESSER, Nicolaus	34	Hochheim	54-1168
MESSING, Christian	24	Eisenach	54-1717
MESSINGSCHLAGER, M	30	Frensdorf	52-0370

NAME	AGE	RESIDENCE	YR-LIST
MESSLENGER, F. (m)	29	Fambach	54-1341
MESSLER, Franz Jos	28	Ferdinandsdor	51-0384
MESTER, H. (m)	31	Campen	54-1078
MESTZER, Georg	26	Ilsensdorf	49-0737
METIUS, Gottlieb	59	Eisenberg	52-1512
Julius 30			
METIUS, Julius	30	Philadelphia	52-1512
Gottlieb 59, Anton 32, Marie 58, Selma 34			
Otto 8			
METIUS, Theodor	22	Eisenberg	52-1512
Constanze 18			
METRO, S.		Marburg	48-1355
METT, Hermann	21	Luebeck	54-1371
METTENHAUSEN, Elis	23	Gilten	50-1132
METTLER, Joh.	27	Offenhausen	54-1575
METZ, Albert	26	Isny	54-1371
METZ, Anna Marie	36	Heuenhag	53-0914
METZ, Ant.	26	Regensburg	49-1358
METZ, Balthasar	25	Harle	51-1062
METZ, Bertha	30	Frankfurt	50-1317
METZ, Conrad	20	Dickershausen	51-1062
METZ, Elisabeth	23	Blankenbach	48-0284
Catharina 19			
METZ, Johann	51	Esslingen	48-1355
METZ, Lorenz	16	Ober Fleiden	47-0840
METZ, Margret	20	Hessen	53-0590
METZ, Wilhelm	19	Harly	54-0930
METZ, William	18	Mittelruessel	49-0737
METZER, Marg.	22	Baeldingen	54-1282
METZGER, Georg	49	Nordlingen	49-0574
Regina 33, Catharina 16, Carolina 11			
Rosine 1			
METZGER, Johannes	21	Mittelruessel	49-0737
Joh. G. 30			
METZGER, John	26	Freiburg	52-0699
METZNER, Bertha	24	Coburg	53-1013
MEUCKE, William	19	Germany	48-1015
MEUER, Johann	19	Kolheim/Hann.	53-0475
MEULE, Carl	18	Prag	48-1131
MEUSEN, H. (m)	23	Boushave	50-0746
MEUSER, Philipp	25	Mengeringhaus	50-0323
MEUSSEN, Aloys	48	Wiedenau	50-0840
MEUTH, Theodor	25	Bamberg	53-0267
MEWERS, Caroline	19	Hackshorst	51-1588
MEY, Sebastian	28	Egingen/Bav.	53-0475
Therese 37			
MEYBAUM, Carl	23	Bremen/Hann.	54-1092
MEYBECK, Heinrich	23	Munster	49-0413
MEYBERGER, Barb.	39	Cassel	51-1588
MEYBERGER, Phillip	14	Berstein	51-1588
Joseph 12, Geronemas 6			
MEYENBORG, Heinr.	15	Wremen	53-1000
MEYER, Adelheid	21	Brinkum	49-0324
MEYER, Albert	16	Suestedt	54-0872
MEYER, Am. (f)	20	Stoudel/Hann.	51-1796
MEYER, Anna	28	Frille	51-1588
Louisa 7			
MEYER, Anna Barb.	25	Reichelsdorf	52-1129
Marg. 2			
MEYER, Anna C.	56	Bederkesa	52-0048
Maria 19			
MEYER, Aron	22	Lippehne	54-0903
Johanne 24			
MEYER, Aron	22	Chicago	54-1371
MEYER, Aug.	33	Heydorf	51-0326
MEYER, August	18	Bruchhausen	53-1070
MEYER, August Jac.	23	Dahlenburg	51-0500
MEYER, Auguste	30	Hannover	50-1067
MEYER, B.	20	Buhren	49-0383
MEYER, Barbara	21	Wiedenau	50-0840
MEYER, Bruene	19	Otelsen	53-0838
MEYER, C.F. (m)	20	Hasenkamp	49-0329
MEYER, C.H. (m)	22	Dankersen	49-0329
MEYER, C.P. (m)	23	Bruende	49-0416
MEYER, Carl	29	Hannover	54-1078
MEYER, Carl	42	Weimer	54-1716
MEYER, Carl	38	Ballendorf	54-1168
Helme 38			

NAME	AGE	RESIDENCE	YR-LIST
MEYER, Carl	20	Hausbergen	52-1321
MEYER, Carl	26	Hanover	51-0500
MEYER, Carl	20	Oldenburg	48-0269
MEYER, Carl	29	Neustadt	54-1371
MEYER, Carl	29	Fallersleben	54-1647
Caroline 32			
MEYER, Carl W.	25	Uelzen/Hann.	54-1092
Minna 25			
MEYER, Caroline	35	Brakenheim	54-1371
Carl 26, Pauline 13, Christoph 9			
MEYER, Carsten	16	Gestendorf	51-1035
MEYER, Casper	32	Hochberg	54-1716
MEYER, Cath.	23	Muenster	54-1575
MEYER, Ch. F.	27	Lageloh	49-0742
MEYER, Charles	17	Osnabrueck	53-0991
Eliza 21, Amanda 19, Julia 14			
MEYER, Chr.	28	Heidenheim	49-0352
MEYER, Christ.	27	Gehrda	53-1016
Elise 29			
MEYER, Christ.	27	Katrinhagen	53-1086
MEYER, Christ.	18	Brinckum	49-0324
MEYER, Christian	30	Bremen	53-1164
MEYER, Christian	36	Dorschen	53-1164
MEYER, Christian	47	Rodenberg	47-0672
MEYER, Christiane	58	Letell	52-1321
MEYER, Christoph	26	Eiterfeld/Hes	51-1532
MEYER, Conr.	39	Osterwicke	53-1013
Josepha 19, Friedr. 8, Carl 6			
MEYER, Conrad	28	Muenchen	53-0267
MEYER, Conrad	48	Osnabrueck	52-1101
Heinrich 9, Johann 14, Elisabeth 20			
Engel 18, Elisabeth 16, Maria 18			
MEYER, Davy	15	Schweringen	48-1209
MEYER, Diedr.	27	Batsum	54-0987
MEYER, Diedrich	48	Hasbergen	53-1000
Marie 46, Doroth. 17, Marie 14, Sophie 11			
Heinr. 9			
MEYER, Dietrich	24	Bremen	51-1725
MEYER, Doris	35	New York	48-0406
Rebecca 10, Elise 6, Adelhaid 4			
Henriette 2			
MEYER, Dorothea	20	Reichhausen	53-1016
MEYER, Dorothea	39	Norden	51-0500
Johann 12, Carl 5m			
MEYER, Eberhard	18	Bicken	50-1067
MEYER, Eduard	20	Braunschweig	53-0590
MEYER, Eduard	23	Prussia	49-0329
MEYER, Elanor	18	Belm	51-1588
MEYER, Eleonore	18	Dankersen	52-1321
MEYER, Elise	24	Bremen	49-0329
MEYER, Eliza	34	New York	53-0991
Dora 2m			
MEYER, Engel	25	Sandbostel	54-0918
MEYER, Engelbert	29	Gellmern	51-1245
MEYER, Ernest	29	Haag	53-0888
MEYER, Ernestina	33	Roden/Hess.	48-0053
Joh'a Charl. 18			
MEYER, Ernst	31	Salzungen	53-1000
MEYER, Ernst	22	Bielefeld/Pr.	51-0048
MEYER, Ernst A.	30	Burgholzhause	48-0951
MEYER, Ernst Heinr	30	Loisebech	47-0918
MEYER, Ester	20	Treuchtlingen	53-0905
MEYER, F.A.H. (m)	23	Vlotho	49-0329
MEYER, F.L.	44	Meckel	53-1086
Friedricke 46, Friedrich 17, Ludwig 6			
MEYER, Ferdinand	21	Michelsdorf	54-0872
MEYER, Fr.	17	Braunschweig	54-1001
MEYER, Franciska	34	Utzwingen	54-1297
MEYER, Franz	30	Muenchen/Bav.	54-1092
MEYER, Franz	24	Knurbach	53-0324
MEYER, Friedr.	21	Bremerhafen	54-0053
MEYER, Friedr.	30	Undrup	48-0101
Wilh. 20			
MEYER, Friedrich	25	N.Y.	52-1580
MEYER, Friedrich	40	Magdeburg	53-0267
Wilhelmine 44, Friedrich 5			
Wilhelmine 11m			
MEYER, Friedrich	27	Bieberbach	53-1062

NAME	AGE	RESIDENCE	YR-LIST
Elisabetha 30, Margaretha 4			
MEYER, Friedrich	16	Schotten	53-0991
Philippina 20			
MEYER, Friedrich	54	Braunschweig	54-0872
Sophie 46, Julius 25, Anna 15			
MEYER, Friedrich	54	Idensen	53-0492
Chr. 44, Dorothee 17			
MEYER, Friedrich	30	Hoya	53-1164
MEYER, Friedrich	24	Hagen	52-0095
MEYER, Friedrich	30	Oldendorf	54-0987
MEYER, Friedrich	20	Buecken	48-1209
MEYER, Fritz	18	Buecken	50-0366
Wilhelm 17			
MEYER, G. (m)	32	Welsede	48-0445
MEYER, Geo. Friedr	20	Plattleg	51-0352
MEYER, Georg	17	Bederkesa	52-0699
MEYER, Georg	26	Bremen	50-0292
MEYER, Georg	29	Muenchen	54-1649
Helene 26			
MEYER, Gustav	19	Hamburg	49-0324
MEYER, H.	21	Krumen	51-1160
MEYER, H. (m)	26	Loewen	52-0652
MEYER, Hein	23	Buchholz	52-1321
MEYER, Hein.	27	Dorum	49-0329
MEYER, Heinr.	30	Hannover	50-1317
MEYER, Heinrich	20	Hasbergen	53-1000
Sophie 22			
MEYER, Heinrich	43	Mehringen	52-1452
Dorrethe 46, Wilhelm 18, Heinrich 16			
Carl 9, Rebecca 5			
MEYER, Heinrich	29	Mehringen	52-1452
Margarethe 32, Mienchen 5, Wilhelm 3			
Heinrich 8m			
MEYER, Heinrich	29	Hostel	54-0918
D. 22			
MEYER, Heinrich	26	Auma	54-1566
MEYER, Heinrich	34	Grubenhagen/H	52-0807
Caroline 34, Caroline 13, Heinrich 10			
Fritz 9, Charlotte 7, Wilhelm 10m			
Louise 46			
MEYER, Heinrich	30	Kirchlengern	51-0352
Rebecca 32			
MEYER, Heinrich	24	Hannover	51-1101
MEYER, Heinrich	29	Bumberg	48-1179
MEYER, Heinrich	19	Kleinensee	48-0284
MEYER, Heinrich	62	Insen	50-1067
Maria 52			
MEYER, Heinrich	23	Hoya	52-1625
MEYER, Heinrich Wm	50	Rodewald	47-0762
Dorothea 43, Sophie 21, Louise 17			
Wilhelm 6			
MEYER, Heinz	41	Eversdorf	54-0987
Clara 29, Louise 12, Hulda 8, Heinrich 6			
Friederike 7			
MEYER, Helene	18	Wremen	50-0366
MEYER, Heloise	20	N.Y.	53-0991
Leonora 18			
MEYER, Henrika	24	Braunschweig	48-0053
MEYER, Henry	28	Blender	53-0888
MEYER, Henry	34	Oldendorf	50-0840
Margarethe 30, Sophie 3, John 1			
Caroline 4m			
MEYER, Henry M.	29	New York	53-0991
MEYER, Herm. Heinr	21	Engter	54-0987
MEYER, Hermann	30	Bremen	53-1000
MEYER, Hermann	19	Osterode/Hann	48-0053
Henrika 24			
MEYER, Herrmann	23	Wollings	52-1625
MEYER, Herrmann	25	Bodenfelde	50-1132
MEYER, Herrmann	34	Hannover	50-1067
MEYER, J. (m)	25	Creba-k	50-0439
MEYER, J.H.	26	Bremen	52-1148
Johanne E. 18			
MEYER, Jacob	19	Humdweitz	52-1101
MEYER, Joh Wilhelm	16	Siedenburg	54-0987
MEYER, Joh.	26	Ellenbach	52-1129
MEYER, Joh.	25	Liritzhofen	52-1129
MEYER, Joh.	19	Neuhaus	51-1245

NAME	AGE	RESIDENCE	YR-LIST
MEYER, Joh.	36	Breslau	54-1283
MEYER, Joh.	41	Steinfeld	49-0574
MEYER, Joh. Friedr	26	Adolphhausen	50-0292
Elise Immar 25, Heinrich 21			
MEYER, Joh. Heinr.	21	Baden	48-0887
MEYER, Johann	25	Schwarzenfels	53-1016
Anna 24, Margarethe 22			
MEYER, Johann	31	Chaen	54-1078
Marie 21			
MEYER, Johann	27	Farven	54-0918
MEYER, Johann	19	Ritterhude	52-0048
MEYER, Johann	18	Hannover	52-0699
MEYER, Johann	22	Achendorf	54-0987
MEYER, Johann	19	Bruchhausen	51-0352
MEYER, Johann	27	Hallenstedt	50-0472
MEYER, Johannes	40	Notzingen/Wue	52-0351
MEYER, Johannes	63	Schwabach	48-0260
A. Maria 26, G. Johann 22, Dorothea 19			
Mathias 1m			
MEYER, John	19	Veldrow	53-0492
MEYER, John	30	Estenbach	50-0944
MEYER, John	38	Waltersberg	50-0840
Catharine 43, John 8			
MEYER, John Georg	28	Hofstaetten	49-0365
MEYER, John H.	18	Schinkel	54-1470
MEYER, John Henry	27	New York	53-0991
Eliza 29			
MEYER, Johs.	23	Rothenburg	51-0757
Heinr. 28			
MEYER, Joseph	17	Oldenburg	50-0311
MEYER, Joseph	27	Solothurn	50-0439
Franz 33			
MEYER, Joseph	21	Prussia	50-0311
MEYER, Joseph	16	Niederurff	52-1101
Sarah 18			
MEYER, Josephine	17	Herrenwies	53-0928
MEYER, Julius	17	Osnabrueck	54-1297
MEYER, Kunig.	24	Hilmannsberg	52-1129
MEYER, Kunigunde	19	Schneidebach	54-0965
Joseph 28, Therese 33, baby			
MEYER, Leonor	19	Glasenbach	54-1470
MEYER, Louis	22	Coburg	53-1013
MEYER, Louis	17	Burgholzhause	48-0951
MEYER, Louise	24	Dielmissen	50-1132
MEYER, Ludwig	24	Burhofe/Old.	51-1725
MEYER, Male (f)	27	Londorf	54-1168
MEYER, Margareth	24	Schnelldorf	52-0515
MEYER, Maria	30	Goettingen/Ha	51-1532
MEYER, Maria	18	Luneberg	51-1101
MEYER, Maria	22	Mittelruessel	49-0737
John C. 21			
MEYER, Marie	17	Boebber	53-1086
MEYER, Michael	17	Ottingen	52-0279
MEYER, Peter	36	Rinteln	52-0563
MEYER, Simon	20	Schwarza	53-0888
MEYER, Sophie	21	Stockdorf	48-1179
MEYER, Susanna	19	Bayern	53-0557
MEYER, Theodor	34	Crimmitschau	53-0928
Christine 41, Wilhelm 14, Carl 9			
MEYER, Theodor	34	Frohburg	53-0928
MEYER, Therese	26	Ottenhofen	54-1443
MEYER, Thomas	30	Itzum/Hann.	52-0960
MEYER, W.	26	Omdorf	54-1470
MEYER, W. (m)	17	Rothenburg	49-0329
MEYER, W. (m)	30	Wolpe	48-0453
MEYER, Wendelen	31	Rettingen	54-1371
Theresa			
MEYER, Wilh.	59	Weste	54-1078
Friederike 56, Auguste 31			
MEYER, Wilh.	20	Nurenberg	48-0101
MEYER, Wilh.	29	Achim	50-1132
Marie 31, Louise 6m			
MEYER, Wilhelm	57	Relingen	54-0053
MEYER, Wilhelm	27	Obernkirchen	54-1168
MEYER, Wilhelm	18	Vusshude	48-1184
Henriette 28			
MEYER, Wilhelm	24	Brake	48-0887
MEYER, Wilhelm	22	Schweringen	54-0987

NAME	AGE	RESIDENCE	YR-LIST
MEYER, Wilhelmine	30	Boebber	53-1086
MEYER, Wilhelmine	22	Roringen	52-0563
MEYER, William	30	Frille	51-1588
MEYERDING, Christ.	64	Vechelde/Br.	54-0903
Henriette 45, Christian 17, Henriette 15			
MEYERDIRKS, J.K.	23	Bremen	48-0453
MEYERFELD, Isaac	19	Beverungen	52-1148
MEYERFELD, Salomon	26	Beverungen	53-1023
Julie 30, Mathilde 2			
MEYERHOEFER, Joh.	34	Lehrburg	54-1566
MEYERS, Elisbth.	21	Essen/Hann.	52-0960
MEYERSTEIN, J. (m)	19	Hagenburg	53-1016
MEYNE, Franz F.	27	Mittelruessel	49-0737
MEYNE, W Chr. Ferd	44	Braunschweig	53-0888
MICHAEL, Albin	22	Dresden	53-0161
MICHAEL, Eduard	30	Targau	52-1580
MICHAEL, Friedr.	39	Steinau	50-1071
MICHAEL, Henry	21	Froeschershau	50-0840
MICHAEL, William	28	Neustadt	53-0888
MICHAELIS, Albert	22	Goettingen	52-0699
MICHAELIS, Emil W.	28	Marietto	53-0888
Auguste 27			
MICHAELIS, Georg	16	Bevern/Hann.	53-0475
MICHAELIS, H.	26	Rengsters	51-0757
MICHAELIS, Sabina	30	Prussia	51-1532
MICHEL, Angelin	53	Achenbach	52-1452
Adam 27, Georg 17			
MICHEL, Augustus	28	Doerenthe	53-0991
MICHEL, Christoph	42	Bernstein	51-1588
Eliza 41, Catherine 14, Ernestine 7			
MICHEL, Friedr.	15	Dettendorf	52-0693
MICHEL, Friedrich	26	Siebertswolkw	54-1371
Johann Carl 30			
MICHEL, Georg	26	Bordorf	52-1105
MICHEL, George	45	Fischborn	51-1588
Catherine 42, Catherine 16, Mary 14			
MICHEL, Hanna	10	Lisberg	53-0324
MICHEL, Helena	21	Fulda	54-1554
MICHEL, J. (m)	19	Achenbach	50-0746
MICHEL, Johann	18	Fischborn	48-1184
MICHEL, Jos. Georg		Luetterz/Hess	49-0365
Johann Adam			
MICHEL, Margarethe	38	Erdmannsroth	52-1661
Blasius 11			
MICHEL, Maria	21	Gerstungen/Sa	54-1092
MICHEL, Nicol.	18	Fulda	51-0405
MICHEL, Stephan	25	Belzheim	54-0872
MICHEL, Therese	16	Lisberg	53-0324
MICHEL, W. (f)	23	Buhlersell	54-1341
child 6m			
MICHEL, Wilhelmine	57	Bissendorf	51-1640
Herm. Heinr. 3			
MICHEL, Wm.	19	Knauer	52-1625
MICHELBACH, Martha	22	Homberg	54-0930
MICHELS, Andreas	32	Bayern	53-0557
Margrethe 33, Johann Georg 10, Johann 3			
MICHELS, Anna Mar.	25	Osnabrueck	52-1512
MICHELS, Ant.	32	Luebbecke	52-1321
MICHELS, Ignaz	28	Arken/Pr.	51-1796
MICHELS, Johann	20	Nassau	53-0838
MICHELS, Juliane	48	Hottenbach	51-1062
MICHEN, Joseph	25	Curhessen	52-1432
MICHLER, Johann	39	Berghueten	53-0838
Magdalene 43, Ursula 10, Anna 9, Michel 5			
Margarethe by			
MICHLER, Margareth	22	Markelsheim	54-1371
MICK, Anna	22	Preussen	52-0370
MIDDENDORF, Adam H	54	Oldendorf	53-0991
Catharina 44, Louisa 19, Maria 16			
Gertrude 12, Wilhelmine 4, Catharina 8			
John 11m			
MIDDENDORF, Bernh.	48	Luthen	54-1078
Lisette 44, Franz 18, Catinka 16			
August 14, Anton 12, Agnes 10, Hermann 7			
MIDDENDORF, Henry	23	Oldendorf	53-0991
Louisa 23			
MIDDER, Christoph	34	Dasseln	53-0324
MIDERER, Johann	35	Dinzing	52-1410

NAME	AGE	RESIDENCE	YR-LIST
Johanne 40, Beno 10			
MIEDEL, Cath.	21	Walkofen	54-1282
MIEHE, C. (f)	50	Brunswick	50-1317
Sophia 18			
MIEHE, Doris	35	Hannover	53-0991
MIEHE, Mathilde	19	Braunschweig	49-0383
MIERSCH, Wilhelm	52	Cottbus	53-0928
MIESEGADER, Friedr	20	Doldorf	47-0828
MIESEL, Carl Gottl	42	Auglich	54-0053
MIETHER, Friedrich	33	Magdeburg	50-0944
Johanna 27			
MIHM, B.	18	Lingolshof	54-1575
J.P. 27			
MIHM, Ferdinand	32	Frankhof	53-0838
Catharine 36, Gertraut 9			
MIHM, Georg	73	Dreschhoff	51-1455
Caspar 26, Margareth 37, Elisabeth 32			
Matilda 29			
MIHM, Martin	23	Tann	51-0405
Michael 25			
MIHR, John	30	Eichensell	51-1588
MIKE, Ernst	34	Freiburg	53-1062
Carolina 29, Emil 7, Bertha 5, Paul 11m			
MIKM, Martin	23	Tann	51-0405
Michael 25			
MILCHSACK, Ph'pine	42	Hottenbach	51-1062
Sophie 18, Johanne 13, Wilhelm 7			
MILDER, Ferdinand	31	Niederosche	54-0053
MILHOEFE, Johann	27	Osnabrueck	52-1512
MILITZ, Johann	40	Mittelwalde	54-1078
Albertine 40, August 49, Carl 9			
MILKING, Dorette	33	Marburg	48-1209
MILLER, Anna Cath.	25	Oberngluehn/He	50-0323
MILLER, Carl	24	Rothe	52-0279
MILLER, Caroline	28	Zweibruecken	52-0699
Helene 8, Friedr 6, Ludwig 3, Carl 9m			
MILLER, Ernst	30	Eimen	48-0951
MILLER, Gustav	22	Borgena	54-0882
MILLER, Joh.	12	Baden	50-1317
MILLER, Johann	36	Nindorf/Boehm	52-1332
Veronica 24			
MILLER, Johann	37	Nixdorf	54-1371
MILLER, Joseph	34	Bavaria	53-0628
MILLER, Minna	20	Gelnhausen	51-1455
MILLER, Peter	18	Kindenheim	49-0912
Leopold 23			
MILLER, Wm.	30	Peppinghausen	51-1588
MILTZ, Chr.	31	Lindenberg	49-1358
MILTZ, Chr. Ferd	39	Bielefeld	53-1013
Sophie 25, Fr. Wm. 9m			
MINCKLER, Carl		Heidenheim	54-1575
Max , Georg			
MINDER, Anna	22	Wiesbaden/Nas	48-0447
MINDING, Aug.	22	Braunschweig	51-1796
MINGERMANN, Victor	32	Wernigerode	52-1512
Friederika 31, Gustav 5, Emma 4			
Bertha 6m			
MINIUS, Joh. N.	23	Nuernberg	50-1317
MINKE, Heinrich	19	Alendorf	53-1000
MINOR, Wilhelm	30	Schwerin	54-1371
MINSSEN, Henriette		Wayens	54-1297
MIRLING, Conrad	25	Seivershausen	53-1164
wife 17			
MISCHE, Johann	31	Neukirche	54-0882
MISCHEL, Georg	19	Barntrupp/Lip	51-1725
MISLIWITZ, Joseph	42	Czakowitz/Boe	54-1092
Maria 37, Wenzel 8, Catharina 12			
Joseph 2			
MISSELHORN, H.C.	25	Osnabrueck	53-1016
MISSLER, Johann	25	Herrenbreidun	52-1410
MIST, Catharine	20	Mittelruessel	49-0737
MIST, Sophia Ann	14	Mittelruessel	49-0737
MISTELI, Bernhard	45	Gerolfingen	51-1438
Elisabeth 28, Gottlieb 3, Rosa 1, Amme 3m			
MITEBECH, Charles	61	Minden	49-1517
Mrs. 42, Albert 16, George 14			
MITH, Eduard	52	Radewitz/Sax.	51-0048
MITIG, Stephan	30	Johannistahl	53-0928
Anna 28			
MITIG, Stephan	30	Oberbertsdorf	53-0928
Anna 28			
MITS, Henry	19	Schonstadt	52-0515
MITSCHELE, George		Mittelruessel	49-0737
MITTE, Friedrich	24	Osnabrueck	54-1371
MITTENDORF, J Bern	27	Schaabe	54-1168
MITTENDORF, Mita	29	Bremen	48-1184
MITWEDE, Heinr.	53	Wernigerode	51-1686
Elisabeth 53, Louis 22, August 20			
Gustav 18			
MLESYWA, Jacob	22	Menghof	53-1016
MODENSCHATZ, Chr.	29	Marlesreuth	54-1283
MODER, Fried.	24	Coburg	53-1013
MODER, Georg	45	Schoenlind	54-1566
Joseph 22, A. (m) 18			
MODEROCH, Johann	29	Doll	52-0699
MOEBUS, Anna Fried	18	Herrnschoellb	49-0352
MOEDERMEYER, Aug.	bob		54-1297
MOEHLE, A.	28	Holzminden	49-1358
Her. (m) 30			
MOEHLE, Friedrich	40	Stroit	54-1554
Engel 36, Ernst 32			
MOEHLE, Henrietta	25	Burgdorf	53-1164
MOEHLENKAMP, J Did	34	Menslage	54-0053
MOEHLING, Carl	26	Muender	50-0292
MOEHRING, Adolph	29	Bremen	54-1078
MOEHRING, Eduard	15	Eistruff	54-1554
MOEHRS, Heinrich	25	Meinberg	52-0775
MOEHRSBERGER, Carl	18	Baiersdorf	49-1106
Mich. 15			
MOELCK, Casp. Hein	30	Melle	54-0872
MOELLER, B. (m)	27	Elte	49-0416
MOELLER, Conrad	16	Stade	54-0987
MOELLER, Elisabeth	30	Waldeck	54-1566
MOELLER, H.	44	Olfen	54-1566
Elisabeth 45			
MOELLER, Heinr.	36	Naumburg	52-1200
Gertrud 32, August 8, Margaretha 3			
Anton 1			
MOELLER, Henry A.	29	Rodach	53-0914
Johanna 59, Johann H. 34			
MOELLER, J. Math.	18	Riemsloh	54-1443
MOELLER, J.H. (m)	21	Neuhaus/Hann	52-0960
MOELLER, Joh Georg	30	Eiterfeld/Hes	51-1532
Maria Barb. 24, Leonhard 3, Carolina 8m			
MOELLER, M.	18	Frankmanshaus	51-0517
MOELLER, Nic.	26	Altendorf	50-1071
MOELLER, Pet.	29	Hannover	50-1317
MOELLER, W.	44	Lauterberg	54-1566
MOELLERS, Wil'mine	28	Tecklenburg	50-0840
Johanne 3			
MOELLMANN, Heinr.	15	Badbergen	50-1132
MOENCH, Andreas	26	Rossfeld	53-0590
MOENCH, Friederike	29	Dilstadt	52-1464
MOENCH, Georg	32	Coburg	51-0405
MOENCH, Joh Friedr	42	Hirschberg	54-0850
Marg. Babett 42, Ern. Henr'tt 15, Max 16			
Ernestine 8			
MOENKEMEYER, Carl	22	Gittelde/Brun	51-1725
MOENKHOFF, Wm. Ch.	51	Ebersen	52-1304
MOENNICH, Gerhard	37	Becke	54-0987
Anna 32, Gerhard 5, Marie 3, Heinrich by			
MOENTEMANN, Fr. W.	26	Riemsloh	54-0872
MOERGEL, Carl	26	Wilderstadt	54-0053
Marie 27			
MOERINGER, Johann	30	Heppberg	53-0267
MOERKING, Heinr.	17	Bramsche	54-0600
MOERLINS, Julie	30	Pattensen	54-1371
MOERNIG, Agnes	30	Dringenberg	51-1035
MOERSCHEL, Peter 1	21	Ilbenstedt	49-0383
MOERSCHEL, Peter 2	21	Ilbenstedt	49-0383
MOERSCHEN, C. (m)	26	Heborn	52-0652
MOESELL, Math.	21	Rothenberg	49-1358
MOESSINGER, Cath.	26	Reutlingen	53-0991
MOETTING, Friedr.	23	Prussia	47-0987
MOHLENHOFF, J. Alb	16	Freudenberg	49-0413
MOHLMANN, Cath.	25	Rinbath	51-1588

NAME	AGE	RESIDENCE	YR-LIST
baby			
MOHNBERG, Heinrich	50	Dissen	52-1661
Elisabeth 40, Louis 16, Magdalena 14 Johannes 14, Heinrich 12, Justus 6 Johannes 5			
MOHNBERG, Johann	44	Ndr. Wuerschn	52-1661
Anna 22, Adam 17, Justus 15, Elise 13 Magdalena 12, Heinrich 6, Minna 8 Ferdinand 3			
MOHNBERG, Peter	28	Melsungen	52-1661
MOHR, Andreas	28	Geisa	54-1649
MOHR, Anna	20	Bargten/Hann.	51-1532
MOHR, Chr.	24	Cadolzburg	47-0828
Georg 19			
MOHR, Conrad	20	Seidelsdorf	51-0460
Maria 25			
MOHR, H.	18	Wallerod	51-0517
MOHR, Henry	26	Endorf/Darm.	50-0323
MOHR, Joseph	30	Friessenhaeus	49-0365
MOHR, Lorenz	22	Kolmsdorf	51-1160
MOHR, Marie	22	Lobenstein	49-0383
MOHR, Peter Nicol.	20	Bremerhafen	51-1725
MOHRING, James N.	20	Mittelruessel	49-0737
MOHRING, Joh. Mich	22	Weilheim/Wuer	52-0351
MOHRMANN, Friedr.	20	Bremervoerde	50-0366
MOHRMANN, J Joach.	62	Woldegk	53-0905
Christel 52, Johann 29, Ernst 28 Friedrich 26, Hermann 21, Mina 19 Lothe 17, Friederika 28, Sophie 28 Rudolph by			
MOHRMANN, J.H. (m)	22	Hanstadt	48-0453
MOHRMANN, Johann	22	Sieden/Hann.	53-0475
MOHRMANN, Theodor	26	Damme	48-0101
MOLEIN, Leonhard	27	Westheim	49-0912
MOLKENBORN, Cath.E	28	Osnabrueck	52-1512
MOLKENBUHR, Wilh.	26	Minden	52-1625
MOLKENBURG, Christ	30	Kronsundern	54-1554
MOLL, J.A.	21	Marburg	49-0383
Barb. 21			
MOLL, Johs.	51	Rauschenberg	52-1200
Heinrich 18, Johann 17			
MOLL, Ulrich	56	Forstenbach	53-0825
MOLLENBERGER, Conr	40	Osnabrueck	52-1512
MOLLENHAUER, Heinr	22	Ebbersdorf	50-1067
MOLLENKAMP, J Fr'd	40	Engter	47-0762
Elisabeth 30, Elisabeth 3m			
MOLLER, Carl	23	Seligenthal	50-0472
MOLLER, Elisabeth	55	Naumburg	52-1200
MOLLER, Elizabeth	11	Sulzfeld	51-1588
Catherine 16			
MOLLER, Heinr.	21	Eisenberg	49-0324
MOLLET, Edward	28	Charleston	48-1015
MOLLITOR, Joseph	20	Bremcke	52-0370
MOLLMANN, Th. (m)	27	Gottingen	51-0757
MOLLMANN, Wm.	32	Iserlohn	54-1078
MOLTER, Wilhelm	20	Allenbach	51-1062
MOLWITZ, Thomas	38	Mittelruessel	49-0737
MONAT, Johann	55	Grossengesche	52-0693
Elisabeth 42, Conrad 25, Joh. Conrad 17 Stephan 12, Leonh. 2, Barbara 20 Elisabeth 13, Margareth 8, Gertrude 6 Catharine 6m, Marg. Elis. 4, Sophie 22 Elise 17			
MONATH, August	35	Rudolphstadt	54-1724
MONFEES, Hermann	27	Scharmbeck	52-0048
MONGLER, C.W.	22	Laubau	54-1283
MONICH, Ferdinand	21	Woldegk	53-0905
MONIKE, August	21	Friedrichschw	54-1717
MONINGER, Anna Cl.	26	Niederklein	52-1321
MONKEMEYER, Wm.	26	Verwalle	52-1129
MONS, Wm.	59	Hagenburg	49-0324
MONTAG, Caspar	40	Gaustadt	48-0887
Franziska 34			
MONTAG, Franz Jos.	34	Duren	54-0987
MONTAG, Henry	44	Worms	48-0951
Elisabeth 34, Hellena 6, Phillip 4 Adam 2, Melchior 33, August 10m			
MONTAG, Julius	34	Pforzheim	48-1015

NAME	AGE	RESIDENCE	YR-LIST
MOOG, Christian	47	Hessen	53-0590
Elisabeth 47, Martha 22, Georg 18 Catharina 14, Anna 9			
MOOJER, George	25	Fromershausen	53-0991
MOOS, Adelheid	24	Fechlin	49-0324
MOOS, George	48	Donsbach	52-0807
August 15, Ferdinand 7			
MORATH, Johann	26	Grafenhausen	52-1105
MORAWETZ, Paul	49	Strimelitz	54-1676
Katharina 46, Johann 16, Barbara 14 Wo. (m) 9			
MORD, Jacob	23	Lengsfeld	52-1661
MORELL, Anna	28	Friedrichsdor	54-1554
MORGENBAUM, Marg.	37	Hildburghause	53-1023
MORGENROTH, Adolph	18	Bischberg	48-0269
MORGENROTH, Fen.	19	Hildburghause	51-1084
MORGENROTH, Friedr	36	Volkmersdorf	54-1371
MORGENROTH, Justus	51	Lautersdorf	49-1358
Cath. 49, Eduard 24, Marie 23, Julius 22 Amalie 18, Luise 16, Mariane 14 Rudolph 11, Richard 7			
MORGENROTT, Lis.	24	Altenburg	51-1084
MORGENSTEIN, Clara	18	Prague	48-1243
MORGENSTERN, Alex.	32	Mariendorf	47-0828
Wilhelmine 30, Bertha 11, Lina 3, Alex. 1			
MORGENTHAL, Heinr.	35	Beverungen	52-0279
Christine 22			
MORHAN, Georg	27	Scheinfels	51-1084
Margarethe 25			
MORISSE, Elisabeth	22	Schwanewedel	53-1070
MORISSE, Fr. (m)	32	Neuenfeld	48-0453
MORITRE, Johann	21	Rahde	47-0872
MORITZ, Caspar	38	Bielefeld	50-0379
Heinrich 9			
MORITZ, Catharina	30	Ziegenhain	53-1013
Heinrich 14			
MORITZ, D. Chr.	14	Beverstedt	47-0872
MORITZ, Doretta	33	Hannover	53-0991
MORITZ, Georg	24	Selzthal	52-0095
MORITZ, Heinr.	18	Beverstedt	49-0324
MORITZ, J. Adam	26	Accum	52-0370
MORITZ, Lucie	44	Eberfeld	50-0439
Minna 22, Heinr. 20, Wilh. 18, Ludwig 12 Emma 9, Johanne 7			
MORITZ, Theodor	20	Hannover	52-1410
MORKEL, Joh Lorenz	50	Auerbach	54-1371
Christine 60			
MORKEN, Hermann	17	Bremervoerde	52-1580
MORLANG, Christ. L	38	Mittelruessel	49-0737
MORLOCH, Wilh.	24	Baden	51-1084
MORRELL, A. (m)	24	Kelze	52-0652
MORSTAEDTER, Jacob	23	Daggenheim	51-0352
MORUS, Martin	28	Fulda	54-1554
MOSCH, Martin	22	Lobenstein/Re	52-1332
MOSCHENHEIN, Monz	32	Cassel	54-1717
MOSEL, G. (m)	20	Bremen	50-1317
MOSER, An. Mar.	33	Michelfeld	51-1796
MOSER, Friedrich	30	Lobenstein	53-1070
MOSER, Johann	21	Bern	51-1686
MOSES, Clara	19	Koppershausen	53-0590
MOSES, Ernestine	29	Posen	50-1067
MOSLER, Ida	17	Grossrippenha	54-1092
MOSSER, Ch. Jacob	26	Unterkremmach	48-0447
E. (f) 28			
MOSSNER, Paul	25	Maebenberg	53-0905
Catharina 25, Maria by			
MOST, Georg	30	Merks	51-1455
MOTSCHMANN, Gottfr	22	Coburg	53-1013
MOTSCHULSKY, Vict.	42	Petersburgh	53-0991
MOVIUS, Joseph	20	Brilon	52-1200
MOYSAS, Ernst	29	Prussia	51-1725
Sophie 27			
MUCKE, Maria E.	35	Haenberg	51-1455
Maria E. 9			
MUDROCH, Franz	32	Doll/Austr.	52-0807
Carl 17, Theresia 32, Catharina 8, Anna 5 Franz 9m			
MUECKE, Franz	23	Hildesheim	48-0887

NAME	AGE	RESIDENCE	YR-LIST
MUECKE, Magdalena		Schoenbrunn	54-1554
MUEHLBACH, Carl	24	Habenshausen	54-0918
MUEHLENDER, Joh.	65	Louisenhof	54-1078
Anna Maria 60			
MUEHLENKAMP, Conr.	26	Schale	51-0352
MUEHLENSTEDT, Hein	19	Bremen	54-1452
MUEHLENSTEIN, C.H.	42	Saxony	51-0405
Herm. 14, Franz 9, Nanny 16			
MUEHLENWEG, Ferd.	35	Quelle	52-1625
MUEHLER, Franz Ant	42	Bavaria	50-1317
MUEHLHAUS, Georg	55	Ebersfeld	54-1554
Marg. 25, Maria 20, Anna 15, Marianne 13			
MUEHLHAUS, Maria	20	Nentershausen	53-1070
MUEHLHAUSEN, Eman.	26	Waldkablossen	51-1686
MUEHLHEIMER, Joh.	23	Goepmannsbuel	54-1554
MUEHLHEUSER, B	25	Lauf	53-0582
MUEHLKE, Heinr.	20	Riepen	50-1132
MUELDNER, Doroth.	24	Waldcappel	51-1160
Elise 6			
MUELLER, Elisab.	30	Weigersdorf	52-1580
Sebastian 3			
MUELLER, Wm.		P--rod/Nas	48-0447
MUELLER, A. (f)	22	Waldkappeln	52-0652
MUELLER, Ad.	36	Dresden	49-0574
MUELLER, Adam	38	Geibshausen	54-0850
Christina 32, Otto 5, Helena by			
MUELLER, Albert	35	Kuhla	53-1062
MUELLER, Albert	14	Maroldsweisac	54-0872
MUELLER, Andreas	20	Westerbrook	53-1016
MUELLER, Andreas	50	Pappendorf	54-1078
MUELLER, Andreas	54	Buettstedt	54-0987
Christine 46, Amalie 16, Carl 12			
Rudolph 8, Louise 1			
MUELLER, Andreas	16	Lehnbach	50-0379
MUELLER, Andrew	25	Bautzen	53-0888
MUELLER, Anna	54	Kreutzburg	52-1464
Joh. 20, Elisabeth 23			
MUELLER, Anna	22	Coburg	53-1013
MUELLER, Anna	26	Hohenschwarz	52-0693
MUELLER, Anna	33	Brunn	49-0574
Anna 3			
MUELLER, Anna Cath	22	Conradsreuth	53-1062
MUELLER, Anna Mar.	23	Debach	52-0279
MUELLER, Anthony	27	Wasseralfinge	53-0991
MUELLER, Anton	26	Homburg	52-1625
Marie 20, Carl 9m			
MUELLER, Anton	35	Langoens/Hess	54-0965
Catharina 33, Conrad 8, Catharina 3			
Maria 16, baby			
MUELLER, Aug.	26	Grochwitz	49-0574
MUELLER, August	29	Cassel	52-1620
MUELLER, August	34	Rupperdorf	54-1717
Marie 37, Pauline 2			
MUELLER, August	27	Dresden	54-1717
MUELLER, August	17	Ahldorf	52-1101
MUELLER, Auguste	26	Mittweida	53-1070
Clemens 27			
MUELLER, Augustus	23	Hannover	53-0991
MUELLER, B.		Mainz	54-1297
Elisabeth			
MUELLER, B. (m)	23	Vantungen	48-0453
MUELLER, Babette	25	Langenburg	54-1554
MUELLER, Barb.	22	Weismain	52-1321
MUELLER, Barbara	23	Zafringen	53-0435
MUELLER, Barbara	40	Westhausen	54-0600
MUELLER, Barbara	32	Soerzefeld	53-0320
MUELLER, Benedikt	22	Grafensburg	54-0600
MUELLER, Benjamin	26	Solothurn/Sw.	51-1725
MUELLER, Bernh.	29	Borstel	52-1512
MUELLER, Bernh.	38	Zeitz	52-1321
MUELLER, Beruk	22	Ahden	47-0918
MUELLER, C.	52	Hellingen	53-0582
M. 20, D. 18, M. 41, El. 13, M. 10, Eva 8			
Andreas 6			
MUELLER, C.	23	Genterskirche	51-0517
MUELLER, Carl	21	Letell	52-1321
MUELLER, Carl	20	Wolfenbuettel	48-1355
MUELLER, Carl	25	Brakel	51-0500

NAME	AGE	RESIDENCE	YR-LIST
MUELLER, Carl	28	Stadtilm	49-0324
MUELLER, Carl	35	Cronigfeld	52-1101
Auguste 32, Hugo 8, Rudolph 7			
Cushut (m) 2, Conkordia(m) 10m			
Forbst (f) 2m, Friedrich 58			
Wilhelmine 54			
MUELLER, Caroline	39	Nennrueck/Han	52-1332
MUELLER, Casper	30	Carlstadt	53-0991
MUELLER, Catharina	24	Spangenberg	52-0563
MUELLER, Catharine	27	Mehlen	53-0492
MUELLER, Catharine	17	Saroth	52-1101
MUELLER, Catharine	22	Emden	52-0895
MUELLER, Catharine	20	Daspe	50-1132
MUELLER, Ch. (m)	30	Bremerhafen	48-0453
MUELLER, Christ.	32	Stuttgart	53-1016
MUELLER, Christ.	20	Motzfeld	51-0352
MUELLER, Christ.	30	Sprendlingen	53-0582
Anne 23			
MUELLER, Christ. F	44	Minden	52-0563
Charlotte 38, Minna 7			
MUELLER, Christian	19	Gotha	53-0590
MUELLER, Christian	52	Willingen	52-1304
MUELLER, Christian	27	Wuelferode	48-0284
Anna 28			
MUELLER, Christian	42	Linden	54-1371
Anna 40			
MUELLER, Christina	29	Selb	53-0991
MUELLER, Christine	18	Ottersberg	52-1362
Charlotte 16, Anna 14, Elise 9			
MUELLER, Christine	19	Alsfeld	51-0352
MUELLER, Christine	27	Steinau	51-0352
MUELLER, Christine	21	Wiedersheim	52-1321
Anton 18			
MUELLER, Christoph	19	Baiern	53-0324
Barbara 39			
MUELLER, Conr.	35	Bederkesa	53-1000
MUELLER, Conr.	14	Angenrode	50-1236
Elise 18			
MUELLER, Conrad	15	Ahlfeld	50-1236
MUELLER, Daniel	22	Fachingen	52-0807
MUELLER, David	30	Hirschberg	49-1106
Lina 28, Paline 21			
MUELLER, Ed. Gust.	19	Nordlingen/Bv	53-0628
MUELLER, Eduard	21	Eisenberg	52-1512
MUELLER, Eduard	30	Eibenstok	54-1452
Jobst 46			
MUELLER, Elisabeth	43	Neukirchen	54-0930
MUELLER, Elisabeth	29	Herolds	53-1164
MUELLER, Elsie	17	Muenden	53-0590
MUELLER, Ernest	17	Neuhaus	48-0406
MUELLER, Ernst	25	Goslar	54-1591
MUELLER, Ernst	33	Schneidemuehl	54-1443
MUELLER, Eva	9	Meinrode	52-1321
MUELLER, F.G.	53	Lobenheim/Sax	51-0048
Franziska 26			
MUELLER, Ferd.	25	Grafenhain	54-1168
MUELLER, Ferdinand	21	Reitersbach	52-1661
MUELLER, Fr.	25	Pommern	52-1661
MUELLER, Fr.	18	Rothenburg	49-1358
MUELLER, Fr.	24	Luebbecke	50-1071
MUELLER, Fr. W.	26	Gera	53-1164
MUELLER, Franz	25	Hallenberg	53-0585
Franz 18			
MUELLER, Franz	19	Werl	52-1321
MUELLER, Franz	20	Neustadt	54-0987
Georg 20			
MUELLER, Friedr.	27	Kleinern	54-1566
Nanette 26, Elisabeth 2			
MUELLER, Friedr.	27	Gich	48-0053
MUELLER, Friedr.	29	Wischhausen	50-1236
MUELLER, Friedrich	20	Ostheim	51-0405
Friederike 20			
MUELLER, Friedrike	18	Wagenfeld	53-0585
Carl 15			
MUELLER, Fritz	41	Alzey	51-1739
MUELLER, G.	24	Leimberg	53-0582
MUELLER, G. H.	32	Henfenfeld	52-1129
MUELLER, Geo. Hein	36	Hohenschwarz	54-1419

NAME	AGE	RESIDENCE	YR-LIST
Margaretha 38, Friederike 16, Doris 2			
MUELLER, Georg	18	Wallesburg	52-1200
MUELLER, Georg	17	Nidda	54-1717
MUELLER, Georg	44	Forgheim	54-1282
MUELLER, Georg	25	Hannover	49-0383
MUELLER, Georg	29	Elberfeld	48-0565
MUELLER, Georg	55	Fischbach	51-1640
MUELLER, Georg Ph.	28	Meiningen	52-1423
MUELLER, Gerhard	32	Popens	52-1304
Hesschen 35, Fooke (f) 11, Diake (f) 9			
Herman 7, Sophia 5, Rinne (f) 3, John by			
MUELLER, Gerhard	48	Ankum	54-1371
MUELLER, Gustav	18	Burgsfleth	52-1512
MUELLER, Gustav	16	Milren	49-1517
MUELLER, H. (m)	17	Gotha	48-0445
MUELLER, H. Chr.	30	Lelm	51-1160
Maria 28, Maria 4			
MUELLER, Heinr.	28	Redwitz	52-1200
MUELLER, Heinr.	19	Hannover	50-0021
MUELLER, Heinrich	28	Appeln	52-1625
MUELLER, Heinrich	55	Bengshausen	54-0930
Gertrude 50, Catharine 24, Marie Elis. 17			
Cath. Elis. 1			
MUELLER, Heinrich	36	Bingenheim	54-1717
Margaretha 40, Heinrich 14			
MUELLER, Heinrich	32	Katrinhagen	53-1086
MUELLER, Heinrich	21	Hohenaverberg	53-0838
MUELLER, Heinrich	17	Heidelbach	53-0905
MUELLER, Heinrich	30	Ebersdorf	54-0987
Richard 13			
MUELLER, Heinrich	30	Weissenfeld	54-1297
MUELLER, Heinrich	18	Frestorf	48-1355
MUELLER, Heinrich	39	Koenigsbetten	50-0292
Rieke 20, Heinrich 6, Friedrich 4			
Andreas 18m			
MUELLER, Heinrich	21	Hohenaverberg	53-0838
Hermann 25			
MUELLER, Henriette	32	Crimmitschau	54-1078
Albrecht 3, Oscar 6m			
MUELLER, Henry	28	Erfurt/Sachs.	52-1620
MUELLER, Henry	44	Oberod	53-0914
Catharine 48, Johannes 18, Peter 16			
Anna 14, Louise 12, Conrad 9, Cath. 6			
Elisabeth 3			
MUELLER, Henry	24	New York	53-1164
MUELLER, Henry	30	Burgsteinfurt	48-0284
MUELLER, Henry Chr	27	Schlangenbad	53-0991
Augusta 24			
MUELLER, Herm.	26	Noerdlingen	54-0987
MUELLER, Herrmann	25	Berlebech	48-0260
MUELLER, J.C.	47	Hofgeismar	54-1566
Caroline 17, Adolph 11			
MUELLER, Jacob	23	Borsum	53-0652
MUELLER, Jacob	31	Backnang	49-0352
MUELLER, Joh Georg	26	Wahlburg	50-0292
MUELLER, Joh.	52	Schwarzwinkel	53-0825
Eva 24, Margaretha 2			
MUELLER, Joh.	28	Hedersdorf	52-0693
MUELLER, Joh.	57	Greissen	54-1282
MUELLER, Joh.	24	Osnabrueck	50-1236
Cathr. 25			
MUELLER, Joh. Chr.	56	Ottersberg	52-1362
MUELLER, Joh. Chr.	26	Herbehausen	54-1647
MUELLER, Joh. Hein	20	Roedinghausen	54-1452
MUELLER, Joh. Jac.	26	Wimpften	53-0267
MUELLER, Joh. M.	30	Grub	50-0439
MUELLER, Johann	25	Schoenweissba	53-1023
MUELLER, Johann	26	Lenderscheidt	54-0930
MUELLER, Johann	19	Bremen	54-0930
MUELLER, Johann	31	Gosmansroth	53-0320
Barbara 32			
MUELLER, Johann	25	Bueckeburg	52-0095
MUELLER, Johann	24	Michelfeld/Bd	52-0351
MUELLER, Johann	19	Osterholz	54-0987
MUELLER, Johann	25	Spaden	50-0366
MUELLER, Johann	18	Estrup/Hann.	52-0807
Anton 15			
MUELLER, Johann	45	Mohringen	52-0279
Wilhelmine 33, Marie 9, Christian 7			
MUELLER, Johanna	21	Plate	54-0850
MUELLER, Johanne	22	Herbartswind	53-0267
MUELLER, Johanne	22	Suhl	52-1105
MUELLER, Johanne	25	Brunk	49-0742
MUELLER, Johannes	20	Muelsam/Hann.	51-1725
MUELLER, Johannes	42	Deuz/Preussen	53-0475
Anna 32, Catharine 15, Johann 12			
Heinrich 9			
MUELLER, John Mich	27	Albingshausen	53-0991
MUELLER, Joseph	32	Simmern/Wrt.	54-1092
MUELLER, Joseph	23	Grafensburg	54-0600
MUELLER, Joseph	25	Steinach	52-1321
MUELLER, Joseph	47	Haugsdorf	53-0888
Anna 27, Anna by			
MUELLER, Kunigunde	21	Fleinkheim	54-1283
MUELLER, Leonhardt	29	Almoshof	53-0267
MUELLER, Leopold	15	Marisfeld	52-1200
MUELLER, Levy	17	Eiserfeld	54-1168
MUELLER, Lorenz		Helsa	53-0838
MUELLER, Lotte	21	Ottersberg	53-0557
MUELLER, Louise	18	Schleising	54-1282
MUELLER, Ludw.	25	Bavaria	50-1317
MUELLER, Ludwig		Trohe	53-0942
MUELLER, Ludwig	35	Dillenburg	52-1101
Cathrina 38, Minna 7, Christiane 9m			
Johanne 4			
MUELLER, Maria	25	Plattenhardt	52-1580
MUELLER, Maria El.	25	Ballhausen	52-0279
Anna Maria 20			
MUELLER, Marie	20	Rothen	52-1625
MUELLER, Marie	12	Maehren	53-1000
Monika 20			
MUELLER, Marie	23	Schwartzau	53-0585
MUELLER, Martin	43	Harburg	54-1341
F. (m) 42, Johanna 38, Wilhelmina 13			
Auguste 6, Johanna 9			
MUELLER, Martin	24	Frankfurt	50-0311
MUELLER, Martin	17	Goldkronach	52-1101
Johann 23, Heinrich 22			
MUELLER, Mathias	37	Weissenstadt	48-1209
MUELLER, Matth.	39	Brind	49-0324
MUELLER, Meta	22	Warpedorf/Han	54-1092
MUELLER, Meta	24	Ottersberg	51-1084
MUELLER, Michael	39	Salz	52-1580
MUELLER, Oscar Jul	30	Leipzig	48-0101
MUELLER, Oswald	17	Speigitz	52-0279
MUELLER, Otmar	38	Krumbach	53-0324
MUELLER, Paulus	22	Thalheim	51-0352
Margar. 24, George 4m			
MUELLER, Peter	19	Kurhessen	53-0324
MUELLER, Peter	34	Meinrod	52-1321
MUELLER, Peter	20	Hunger	54-1282
MUELLER, Peter	24	Samborn	51-0352
MUELLER, Peter	43	Canton Aargau	51-0048
Christine 43, Conrad 11, Susanne 8			
Emilie 3, Nicol(died) 9m			
MUELLER, Philipp	22	Neustadt	54-1168
MUELLER, Philipp	23	Fertheim	54-0987
MUELLER, Philipp	23	Diepholz	48-0260
MUELLER, Raimund	22	Wolfsberg	54-0872
MUELLER, Samuel	46	Erfurt/Pr.	53-0475
MUELLER, Sebastian	13	Niederhagen	54-0930
Abraham 21			
MUELLER, Simon	31	Strallendorf	54-1554
Cathar. 32			
MUELLER, Sophie	27	Hainweiler	54-1419
MUELLER, Theodor	21	Sachsen	53-0590
MUELLER, Therese	25	Farnbach	53-0585
MUELLER, W.	21	Langenhausen	53-0905
MUELLER, W. C.	24	Larrelt	53-0991
MUELLER, Wenzel	19	Reichenberg	53-0905
MUELLER, Wilh.	19	Gera	54-0600
MUELLER, Wilh.	24	Wolkersdorff	51-1796
MUELLER, Wilhelm	28	Vaihingen	52-1580
MUELLER, Wilhelm	21	Sachsen	53-0590
MUELLER, Wilhelm	58	Wallershausen	54-0987
Marie 43			

NAME	AGE	RESIDENCE	YR-LIST
MUELLER, Wilhelm	28	Iserlohn	52-0895
Heinr. 22			
MUELLER, Wilhelm	31	Erfurt	54-1371
MUELLER, William	33	Crimmitschau	53-1164
MUELLER, Xaver	30	Ingolstadt	53-0492
MUELLER, Xaver	34	Fautenbach	48-1355
Magdalene 43			
MUELLERS, J.H. (m)	25	Telgte	50-1236
MUELLERS, Sophia	26	Wiedersheim	52-1321
Christine 22			
MUELLERWEISS, Geo.	26	Mittelstadt	47-0672
Johannes 23, Johanne 18			
MUELLICH, Juliane	42	Weimar	50-1317
Franziska 8, Anton 5			
MUELVERSTEDT, Aug.	20	Eichenrode	53-0942
MUENCH, A.	22	Etterhausen	51-0517
MUENCH, Anton	17	Wetzlar	53-0590
MUENCH, August	29	Hannover	52-1580
MUENCH, Conrad	39	Berka	54-1649
Ernestine 39, Sophie 10, Henriette 5			
Rosine 3			
MUENCH, Heinrich	17	Hirschberg	53-1062
MUENCH, Henry	25	Gellershausen	50-0840
MUENCH, Johann	34	Barmen	48-0565
Marie 32, Marie 1, Jacob 27, Heinr. 25			
Christian 22			
MUENCHHAUSEN, Adlf	21	Alsfeld	53-1070
MUENCHHAUSEN, Hein	25	Hagen	54-1443
MUENICH, Adam	30	Baaden	52-1620
Ludwig 20			
MUENIH, Franz	35	Schachten	53-0905
MUENNING, Heinrich	17	Bieren	54-1452
MUENSTER, Joseph	22	Paderborn	50-0021
MUENSTERBERG, Hugo	24	Muenster	48-0269
MUENSTERMANN, Herm	48	Unzen	54-1297
Anna 42, Adelheid 15, Diedrich 12			
Heinrich 9, Johann 4			
MUENSTERMANN, W.	45	Herdingen	54-1470
MUENTINGA, Wilhelm	29	Potshausen	52-1148
MUENZEMEYER, Luise	14	Zweibruecken	52-0699
MUENZENMEYER, G.	25	Rothenburg	54-1078
Mich. 27			
MUENZHAUSEN, Heinr	32	Ohr/Hannover	51-1725
Friederike 31, Wilhelmine 10, Louise 10m			
MUENZINGER, Phil.	28	Noerdlingen	54-0872
MUERSBERGER, Lor.	29	Ebersbach	51-1160
MUESSEL, Christ	40	Arzberg	52-1129
MUESSIG, Carl	34	Affaltrach	48-1355
MUESZEL, Christine	28	Arzberg	53-0557
Cathrine 9, Ludwig 7, Wilhelm 5			
Christian 3, Jette 2			
MUETZE, Helene	20	Homershausen	53-0320
Marie 24, Wichand 23			
MUETZE, Ludwig	22	Hummershausen	53-0320
MUETZEL, Christine	28	Arzberg	53-0557
Catharine 9, Ludwig 7, Wilhelm 5			
Christian 3, Jette 2			
MUHLER, Seb.	22	Mittelruessel	49-0737
MUHLHAUSEN, Mart.	19	Altenstadt	54-1341
MUHLICH, John	29	Wismar	54-1724
Marg. 29, Marg. 6m			
MUHR, Jacob	47	Muenchen	54-1717
MULENBROOK, Cath.	18	Sloppin	51-1588
MULICH, Robert	23	Oetlingen	49-0574
MULL, Johs.	46	Rauschenberg	47-0918
MULLBERG, Chr'tine	23	Wissenbach	52-0807
MULLEN, J.H.	17	Neudorf	51-0517
MULLENER, Kunig.	24	Coburg	52-1129
MULLER, Adam	22	Guntersblum	52-0117
Elizabeth 20			
MULLER, Anna	33	Kirchheim	54-1716
Heinrich 5			
MULLER, Anne M.	21	Mittelruessel	49-0737
MULLER, August	13	Kentald	48-1131
MULLER, Barl (f)	28	Remschlitz	51-1588
MULLER, Charles	28	Prussia	54-1724
MULLER, Christ.	22	Mittelruessel	49-0737
MULLER, Christ.	30	Kahla	47-0918

NAME	AGE	RESIDENCE	YR-LIST
MULLER, Conrad	27	Angenrod	51-0757
Hans 31, Elisabeth 36			
MULLER, Eduard Gus	19	Nordlingen/Bv	53-0628
MULLER, F. (m)	33	Urach	54-1341
Rosina 22			
MULLER, Georg	22	Bruennstadt	47-0672
MULLER, Georg	25	Bamberg	52-0515
Margaretha 24			
MULLER, Gertrude	24	Schachen	51-1035
MULLER, Gotthilf	28	Berlin	48-1243
MULLER, Gustav	42	Linden	48-1015
MULLER, Heinrich	19	Nuckel	54-0987
MULLER, Herman	30	Baltimore/Md.	48-1015
MULLER, Joh. Peter	19	Haibach	52-0515
MULLER, Julius	28	Pofferthausen	51-1455
MULLER, Ludwig	24	Lengsfeld	49-0413
MULLER, Magdalene	23	Bruchhausen	49-0413
MULLER, Marg.	48	Fischbach	47-0918
Andres 22, Andres 8			
MULLER, Mathilde	22	Hamburg	49-0781
MULLER, Michael	45	Aslebach/Bav.	53-0628
Anna Maria 44, Joh. Michael 19			
Michael 16, Anna Maria 14, Marianne 9			
Margarethe 9			
MULLER, Philipp	15	Alsfeld	51-1455
MULLER, Richard	22	Geis	51-0500
MULTHAUPT, Jacob	60	Worms	48-0951
Charlotte 60, Friedrich 26, John A. 25			
Hellen 27, Catherine 3m			
MUMFORD, Charlotte	11	New York	48-1015
B.A. (m) 35, Mrs. 27			
MUNCH, Margrette	36	Wetzlar	51-1455
MUNCK, Richard	21	Mittelruessel	49-0737
Barbara 56, Clara 23			
MUNCKWITZ, Carl J.	22	Keschau	47-0672
MUND, Hermann	35	Mansbach	53-0942
Marie 30, Juliane 42, August 5, Anna 4			
Conrad 2			
MUNDERLOH, Gerhard	33	Neuenhuntdorf	54-0987
Anna 32, Georg by			
MUNDSING, Caspar	20	Wuertenberg	53-0557
MUNGER, Jacob	27	Hollstadt/Bav	48-0053
MUNSCHKE, G. (m)	28	Nowitz	49-0416
MUNSTER, Catharine	45	Bederkesa	54-1078
MUNSTER, Friedrike	30	Sulzfeld	51-1588
Appolonia 3, Augusta 2			
MUNTER, August	15	Bederkesa	48-0887
MUNZINGER, Babette	22	Averdlingen	54-0872
MURDORF, Bernhard	19	Ulenborn	50-0840
Minna 23			
MURITFELD, Carolin	25	Bueckeburg	54-0987
MURMANN, Johannes	22	Kronach	52-1661
MURR, Maria Barb.	19	Noerdlingen	54-0903
MURRER, Isaac	45	Steinhart	48-0951
Mary 40, John 12, Jacob 10, Cathrine 6			
Barbara 3			
MURY, Julius	26	Blankenhausen	49-1106
Carl 29			
MUSCHALECK. Wolf.	29	Weiden	54-1283
MUSCHWERK, Carl	31	Muenchen	54-1168
MUSGEDANT, Wilhelm		Duesseldorf	54-1092
MUSSINGER, Philipp	27	Oberwahlstadt	49-0383
Catharine 22, Julie 11m			
MUSSMANN, Heinrich	32	Hannover	47-0672
Auguste 27, Christian 1			
MUSSMANN, W.	34	Steinke	54-1341
Sophia 26, daughter 10m			
MUSSMANN, W.	58	Wrakalohe	54-1341
Doretha 48, Sophia 15, Johanna 15			
Christina 13, Henry 8			
MUTH, Casper	37	Steinau	54-1716
Johannes 17, Georg 9			
MUTH, Heinrich	43	Fischbach/Nas	53-0628
Philippine 39, Joh. Wilhelm 19			
Joh. Philipp 15			
MUTH, Johannes	23	Hessen	53-0590
MUTH, Nicolaus	25	Ettenhausen	54-0053
MUTH, Wilhelm	48	Fischbach/Nas	53-0628

NAME	AGE	RESIDENCE	YR-LIST
Margaretha 36, Peter 17, Philipp 4			
MUTSCHLER, Joseph	32	Hechingen	50-0840
MUTT, Carl	23	Detmold	47-0918
MUTTER, Louise	20	Muenster	51-0326
MUTZBAUER, Georg	25	Forst	54-0965
Sabine 50, Elisabeth 50			
MUZAK, Joseph	29	Neuhof	52-0699
Johanne 24, Josepha 6m			
MYER, Friedr.	32	Obberhibbe	47-0762
Dorothea 26, Ernst 2			
MYER, Henry	32	Minden	50-0944
MYLEAR, Rebecca	49	Ottersberg	52-1362
NAAF, John	28	Wartscheid/He	48-0447
NABER, Andreas	33	Bayern	53-1013
NABER, John Diedr.	56	Saunum	53-0888
Anna 50, Margarethe 25, Anna 24			
Gerhard 21, Sophie 19, Henry 11			
Charles 9, Mary 7, Catharine 3			
NACHRIEMER, Mich.	36	Waldmuenster	54-1078
Franziska 29, Joseph 8, Alice 6, Johann 2			
Michel 9m			
NACHTIGALL, Heinr.	18	Hessen	52-0895
NACHTMANN, Mart.	15	Roetterbach	51-1160
NADERMANNS, Rebeka	22	Hannover	50-0311
NADLER, Anna	35	Oberfranken	54-1554
NADLER, Theresia	41	Senderhausen	54-1554
Anna 35			
NAECHTER, Johann	40	Utshausen	48-1131
NAEDEL, Heinrich	26	Hofgeismar	53-1062
NAEGEL, Georg	52	Dormitz	53-1023
Anna 52, Barbara 19, Johann 13			
Michael 10, Johann Georg 10, Conrad 24			
NAFZIER, Cath.	26	Kaemeln	52-0699
NAGEL, Adam	21	Lemwerder	48-0887
NAGEL, Adam	17	Grossassach	49-0352
Elisabeth 20			
NAGEL, Andreas	18	Gmuend/Wrt.	54-1092
Xaver 17			
NAGEL, Andreas	53	Kupferbra/Bav	53-0628
Barbara 46			
NAGEL, Bina (f)	23	Wesuwe	49-0324
NAGEL, F.O.	20	Laubau	54-1283
NAGEL, Friedr.	22	Offenbach/Hes	54-1092
NAGEL, Georg	26	Trochtelfinge	54-1297
NAGEL, Jacob	19	Andershausen	51-0460
NAGEL, Johannes	28	Bavaria	51-1725
Babette 23			
NAGEL, Ludwig	32	Rohrbach	49-1106
Friederike 9m, Katharine 24			
NAGEL, Wilhelm	34	Kaierde	54-1371
NAGELER, Barbara	20	Daubersbach	54-0930
NAGELMEYER, Friedr	21	Kohlstedt	54-1371
NAGELSCHMIDT, Cath	18	Schwarzenfels	52-1625
NAGELSMANN, Gerh'd	36	Neustadt	54-0987
NAGENGAST, Cath.	24	Troilsdorf	54-1554
NAGIL, Fr.	26	Beverstedt	48-1114
NAGILL, J.H. (m)	45	Cassill	48-1114
NAHRGAN, Jac.		Lerbach/Hess.	50-0323
NAHRUNG, Carl	26	Altenstedt	54-1282
Philip 22			
NAHRWOLD, Eliza	30	Celle	53-0991
Charles 6, William 3			
NAPP, Jacob	35	St Goarshause	49-0345
NAPP, Peter	24	Berlinrode	47-0868
NARY, Th. Julius	27	Ballenstedt	54-1078
NASH, Samuel B.	36	New Orleans	48-1015
NATHAN, N.	28	Hohtsch	54-1283
Samuel 37			
NATHANCHER, Carl H	30	Brandenburg	54-1649
NAU, Ludwig	25	Rensdorf	48-0565
NAU, Nicolaus	28	Pfaffenrod	53-0320
NAUER, Therese	23	Rotenburg	51-0352
NAUHOLZ, Georg	30	Weifenbach	53-0838
Rosina 33, Ludwig 9			
NAUL, Ch. (m)	26	Dankersen	49-0329
NAUMAN, Catherine	26	Dresden	51-1739
NAUMANN, Adolph	23	Hassefelde	53-1086
NAUMANN, Christian	30	Wetter	51-1101

NAME	AGE	RESIDENCE	YR-LIST
NAUMANN, Joh.	37	Dresden	51-1640
NAUMANN, Johannes	25	Didenshausen	53-1000
NAUMANN, Victoria	20	Winterfingen	54-0903
NAUMANN, Wilhelm	28	Schlesien	54-1724
Wilhelmine 49, Albertina 18, August 12			
NAW, Conrad	55	Leithofen/KHe	53-0628
Conrad 18			
NEANDER, Theodor	15	Geestendorf	49-0329
NEBEL, H.	35	Omdorf	54-1470
Susan 30, Charles 5			
NEDDEN, Gustav	29	Hattingen	54-0965
NEDER, Barbara	27	Windheim	52-0515
NEDVIDECK, Joseph	32	Neuhof	52-0699
NEDVIDECK, Joseph	33	Neuhof	52-0699
Josepha 28, Wenzel 30, Barbara 60			
Anton 9, Gottfried 6, August 6m			
NEEF, Georg	36	Woerth	51-1639
NEFFE, Wilh.	27	Baden	50-1317
NEGELE, Jacob	19	Stuttgart	54-1092
NEGER, Friedr.	53	Rodewald	47-0762
NEHER, Margareth	31	Memmingen	47-0828
NEHMER, Heinr.	27	Wulfhagen/Hes	52-0960
NEHRR, Joseph	42	Neresheim	52-1101
NEIDENBERGEN, Anna	27	Dorfguting	52-0515
NEIDHARD, Christ.	25	Bernick	50-1236
NEIDHARDT, Anna	24	Bayern	53-0557
Christoph 27			
NEIDHARDT, Cath.	32	Floss	52-0095
NEIDTHARDT, Anna	27	Bayern	53-0557
Christoph 27			
NEINERT, Rosalie	23	Gosfeld	50-1236
NEISING, Bernard	45	Emsdetten	51-1455
Catherine 45, Joseph 13, Rosa 11			
Bernard 5			
NEISSER, Wolff	24	Breslau	53-0888
NEITHARD, Ad. (m)	18	Grossendaste	52-0370
Sabine 23			
NEITHART, Leonard	34	Knurbach	53-0324
NEITZ, Lisette	17	Heilbronn	52-1580
NELLER, Georg	35	Bamberg	54-1717
NEMELMANN, H.	17	Soxten	53-1070
NEPERT, Anna B	27	Lehrberg	54-1575
NERIG, Therese	26	Abaffersdorf	53-0928
NESS, Ludwig	27	Copenhagen	49-1517
NESSE, J. (f)	21	Arnstadt	49-0416
NESSELS, G.H. (m)	26	Bremen	52-0775
NESSENTALF, Joh'a	24	Wollburg	49-1106
NESSLAGE, Diedrich	18	Kl. Mimmelage	51-0352
Joh. Heinr. 19			
NESSLAGE, Joh Hein	19	Natrup	51-0352
NESSLER, Johannes	24	Herrenreitung	53-1062
Conrad 55, Anna Marg. 34, Wilhelm 32			
August 16, Eva Cath. 11			
NEST, F.	28	Bremen	53-0914
NETTACK, Eduard	40	Magdeburg	53-0914
NETTE, Wilhelm	24	Niederrumpf	54-1554
NETTER, Anna Mary	25	Stierbaum/Bav	49-0365
Eva 30, Walspurga 29			
NEUBAUER, Friedr.	17	Gotha	52-1512
NEUBAUER, L. (m)	20	Trienz	50-0746
G. (m) 28			
NEUBENTZ, Mary	16	Donebach	48-1131
NEUBER, Caroline	17	Kaunstein/Sax	50-0323
NEUBER, Moritz	28	Wolkenstein	47-0828
NEUBERGER, Alb.	48	Schoeningen	54-1078
Jeanette 47			
NEUBERGER, Emanuel	21	Wilhelmsdorf	48-0887
NEUBERT, Barbara	19	Mainstockheim	52-0807
NEUBERT, Joh. Fr.	19	Bayern	53-0557
NEUBRAND, Jos.	24	Windelheim	53-0492
NEUBURG, Leonhard	25	Bielefeld	54-1297
NEUBURGER, Leopold	22	Wilhelmsdorf	53-1070
NEUDEKER, Elis.	21	Eue	54-1717
NEUDOLD, Em. (f)	29	Baden	54-1724
NEUENSTEIN, Cath.	21	Tatschenbrunn	48-0101
NEUGEBAUER, Jane	18	Liegnitz	53-1164
Jane 20			
NEUGEBAUER, Johann	18	Gr.Breitenbch	53-0585

NAME	AGE	RESIDENCE	YR-LIST
NEUHAEUSER, Adam	28	Echtrup/Pr.	52-1423
Ferdinand 24			
NEUHAEUSER, Carl	19	Neustadt	54-0930
NEUHAUS, August	18	Burgprepach	54-0872
NEUHAUS, Conrad	50	Wiedenbrueck	54-1554
Caspar 13, Anna 40, Johanne 6			
NEUHAUS, F.	28	Hoya	54-1716
NEUHAUS, Joh. Wilh	49	Ahden	47-0918
Mathilde 39, Anne Marie 14, Ludw. Aug. 12			
Marie 8, Marie 5, Friedr. 3			
Franz Carl 34			
NEUHAUS, Johann	30	Eickhorst	51-1438
NEUHEIN, J.	23	Buch	54-1419
NEUHIERE, A. (f)	33	Regensburg	53-0888
NEUHOFF, Fried.	20	Mulsum	49-0329
NEUKIRCH, Anton	10	Medenbrechen	49-0912
Joh. 7			
NEUMANN, Augst.	24	Neuhaus	54-1716
NEUMANN, Caroline	27	Maroldsweisac	54-0872
NEUMANN, Franz	26	Gunzendorf	52-0370
Magareta 23, Magareta 9m			
NEUMANN, Fried Aug	44	Trebach	51-1101
NEUMANN, Georg	54	Westphalia	50-0021
Christina 42, Ferdinand 19, Pauline 16			
NEUMANN, Gertrude	20	Emsdetten	54-0903
NEUMANN, Joh.	26	Carolatte	54-1575
NEUMANN, John	40	Gelnhausen	54-1724
Thr. 36, L. 4			
NEUMANN, L. (m)	18	Hagen	48-0453
NEUMANN, Ludwig	21	Driesen	54-1554
NEUMANN, Rosine	19	Bavaria	53-0628
NEUMANN, Rosine	20	Honitz	54-1371
NEUMANN, Simon	31	Montgomery	53-0991
NEUMEISTER, C Herm	30	Schweinbach	48-1355
NEUMEISTER, George	33	Heidelberg	53-0991
NEUMEISTER, H.	27	Lindenau	52-1661
NEUMEISTER, J. Fr.	45	Schmiedebach	48-0887
Catharine 36, Christian 12, Dorothea 9			
Ernestine 4			
NEUMEYER, Willigis	25	Fritzlar	54-0053
NEUNER, Johann	25	Wohnsgehaig	54-0850
Kunigunde 19			
NEUNER, Nicolaus	56	Zochenreuth	52-1200
Eva 21, Georg 27, Margaretha 29			
Catharine 4			
NEUNERT, Fritz	42	Waldorf	52-1105
NEUNERT, Hanchen	25	Walldorf	52-1105
NEUPERT, Adam	17	Frauensee	53-0942
NEUSCHAEFER, Chr'e	19	Frankenberg	50-0379
NEUSCHAEFER, Jul.	14	Frankenberg	53-1016
NEUSCHLER, Ferd.	28	Mittelstadt	47-0762
Friederike 20			
NEUSENGER, A.B.	32	Darmstadt	50-1067
Anna Maria 10, Elisabeth 7, Mina 3			
NEUSER, Julius	24	Neu Oltmansdo	53-0324
NEUSINGER, Michael	24	Freiensteinau	53-1000
Gertrude 28			
NEUSS, Carl	23	Cassel	53-0628
NEUSTADT, Sophie	24	Borgholz	53-1164
NEUSTADT, Zacharia	32	Walsrode	54-1371
NEUSTADTL, Jacob	29	Prague	48-1243
Julia 28, Clara 4, Hedwig 3, Emily 15m			
NEUSTIEL, Ludwig	27	Heimboldhause	54-1647
NEUSTRUM, Sophie	53	Siedenburg	54-0987
NEUWAHL, Simon	19	Meschede	54-1371
NICANDER, Fr.	22	Jena	52-1625
NICHOFF, Heinrich	31	Everod	54-1283
NICHOLAI, Gustav	27	Hamburg	49-0781
NICHTER, Andreas	20	Oberbreitbach	50-0323
George 19			
NICKEL, Andreas	38	Regensburg	53-0557
NICKEL, Gustav	29	Sagau	53-0838
NICKEL, Heinrich	30	Hungen	53-0557
NICKEL, John	33	Wiesbaden/Nas	48-0447
NICOLAI, J.W.	24	Weberstadt	51-1160
NICOLAI, Wilhelm	21	Osterlinde/Br	52-1423
August 15			
NICOLAUS, Carl	40	Bielefeld	51-1739

NAME	AGE	RESIDENCE	YR-LIST
NICOLAUS, Chr'tine	23	Mehlen	53-0492
NIEBEGELE, Tiedem.	26	Eisenach	51-1739
NIEBEL, Johann	24	Koethen	51-0500
NIEBELING, Carolne	23	Neidernhof	54-0882
NIEBORN, L. (f)	5m	Ostbevern	50-0746
NIECK, Wilh.	24	Laitkirchen	51-0326
NIEDEMUELLER, Hein	31	Burgholzhause	54-0053
NIEDERBRENNER, H.	20	Bieren	54-1452
NIEDERMAYER, Seb.	17	Bamberg	52-1304
NIEDERMEIER, Joh.	21	Einarzhausen	54-1282
NIEDERMEYER, J Vin	36	Hammelburg	54-1297
Margarethe 33			
NIEDERREUTHER, Jos	29	Landsberg	49-1106
Anton 30, Nepomuck 27			
NIEFHAUS, Ignatz	29	Buckard	54-1297
NIEGEL, Johann	31	Baiern	52-0370
NIEHAUS, H. (m)	12	Ibbenbuehren	48-0445
NIEHAUS, J. Friedr	23	Melle	54-1297
NIEHAUS, John A.	32	Culm	54-1470
NIEHOF, Caroline	21	Ochtrup	50-0840
NIEHOF, Joh.	23	Muenster	54-1078
NIEHOLF, Theresia	19	Soltengreesba	49-0781
NIEK, Chr.	17	Thalheim	54-1078
NIELK, Joh.	25	Hessen	51-1686
NIEMANN, Andreas	27	Feldheim	47-0672
NIEMANN, Fr. Lor.	30	Prussia	51-1725
NIEMAUNT, Wilhelm	27	Prilon	53-1062
NIEMEIER, Heinrich	28	Bruchhausen	49-0413
NIEMER, Emilie	23	Everwinkel	53-0888
NIEMES, Louise	38	Holzhausen	53-0585
Rieckchen 15, Fritz 7, Anna 5, Dorette 2			
NIEMEYER, Adolph	31	Braunschweig	50-0292
NIEMEYER, Carl	30	Hannover	50-1317
NIEMEYER, Christ.	15	Holtorf	48-0887
NIEMEYER, Christ.	18	Lingen	54-1371
NIEMEYER, Emil	18	Braunschweig	54-1470
NIEMEYER, Heinr.	19	Braunschweig	50-1132
NIEMEYER, Johann	21	Lederfohers	51-1639
NIEMEYER, Johann	43	Meinberg	52-0775
Wilhelmine 47, Ludwig 26, Wilhelmine 25			
Henriette 23, Friedrich 17, Heinrich 12			
Louise 9, Sophie 1			
NIEMEYER, Juliane	19	Hornburg	49-0383
NIEMEYER, Louise	17	Gr. Schwuelfe	54-1297
NIEMEYER, Sophie	26	Buxtehude	54-1371
Johann 1m			
NIEMEYER, Therese	17	Hildesheim	50-0439
NIEMEYER, Wilh'mne	24	Homburg	49-0781
Christine 22			
NIEMS, Auguste	24	Mixhausen/Han	48-0053
Jane 3			
NIENHUSER, J.A.E.	32	W. Ollendorf	52-0960
J.H. (m) 14			
NIERBAM, Georg	32	Reichendorf	52-1580
Magdalena 28, Adolph 5			
NIERMEYER, Hein. D	25	Luebbecke	50-0292
NIESAR, Otto	29	Breslau	51-0352
NIESS, Joh. G.	30	Reichenbach	52-0563
Clara 36			
NIESS, Johannes	30	Stirnfelz	53-0267
NIESS, Lena	24	Warenrode	52-0652
NIESSNER, Marie	27	Spandau	54-1371
NIETERS, G.H. (m)	29	Apeldorn	49-0324
NIETMANN, Wilh'mne	53	Roringen	52-0563
NIEWEINER, Anna	25	Schildesche	54-1554
Johann 34, Katharina 35			
NIEWOERNER, Johann	34	Schildesche	54-1554
Katharina 35, Anna 25			
NIGGEL, B. (m)	29	Bischofsreith	54-1283
Georg 37			
NIKOLAI, Carl	16	Langoens/Hess	54-0965
NILS, Christ.	24	Neufels	52-1625
NILSCHE, Sophie	21	Nilschka	50-0840
NILSEN, Christ	24	Neufels	52-1625
NIMEYER, Wilh'mine	24	Homburg	49-0781
Christine 22			
NIMM, Lud.	36	Luechow	50-1236
NIMMEIER, Casper	37	Schweine	53-1023

NAME	AGE	RESIDENCE	YR-LIST
Friederike 28			
NINNBACH, Andr.	15	Mummelsdorf	54-0872
NIPOLD, Nicolaus	25	Birkenfeld	53-0324
NIPPER, Catherine	33	Oldenburg	50-0311
NIPPER, John C.	28	Luesche	52-0563
NIPPLING, Peter	22	Gerschfeld	52-1362
NISSE, Carl Ed.	32	Naumburg	54-0872
NISST, Anna	30	Puchberg	54-1443
NITSCHE, Ernst	19	Freiberg/Sach	51-1725
NITSCHE, Friedrich	32	Leipzig	53-1000
Helene 30, Friedr. 5, Emil 2			
NITTELMAIER, John	43	Muenchen	54-1724
Anne 20			
NITZEL, Anna	30	Cadolzburg	52-1580
NITZKE, Johanne	36	Luetzenau	50-1132
Ludwig 7, Julius 5, Marie 2			
NITZSCHE, J. Carl	27	Gr. Boehle	48-1179
Amalie 23, Carl Hermann 2			
NOACH, Anna Maria	20	Kalitz	49-0574
NOAH, Carl Traug.	17	Freyburg	54-1371
NOBBE, Heinr.	26	Barkhausen	49-0329
NOBBERS, Sophia	22	Fremersheim	54-0882
NOCH, Friedr.	53	Jena	54-1297
Johanne 53, Ernst 30			
NOELK, Heinr.	24	Suess	48-0269
NOELKE, Conrad	25	Sontra	52-1304
Anna 25			
NOENECKE, Sophie	22	Nienburg	51-1160
NOERDEMANN, Ernst	18	Goettingen	48-0887
Charlotte 25			
NOERGE, J. Wilh.	41	Minden	50-1067
NOETH, Mathias	36	Greuth	51-0352
NOHE, Andreas	16	Ferdinandsdor	51-0384
NOHE, Franz	60	Friedrichsdor	51-0384
Catharina 26, Franz 32, Andreas 16			
NOHN, F.M.	33	Ferdinandsdor	51-0460
NOHR, Friedr.	24	Gotha	54-1716
Louise 22			
NOLBRICHT, Mar.(f)	21	Thedinghausen	52-0515
NOLDENBORG, August	22	Munster	49-0413
NOLKE, Conrad	25	Sontra	52-1304
Anna 25			
NOLL, Adolph	31	Steinhaus	47-0828
Adolph 22, Scholastica 14			
NOLL, Caroline	21	Wuertenberg	53-0557
NOLL, Cath.	26	Giessen	54-1470
NOLL, Christian	24	Hessen	50-1067
NOLL, Conrad	40	Bughofen	54-1470
NOLL, Elise	20	Rhina	54-1647
Franz 17			
NOLL, Fr.	21	Hersfeld	51-0405
NOLL, Georg	36	Waldkappel	52-1321
NOLL, Heinrich	40	Giessen	47-0872
NOLL, Henry	14	Kalbsburg	50-0840
NOLL, Louise	16	Buttenhausen	53-0825
NOLL, Maria	19	Giessen	54-1443
NOLL, Wilhelm	46	Churhessen	52-1620
NOLL, Wilhelm	21	Kaufungen	51-1640
NOLTE, Clamer	54	Wehrenberg	52-1362
Maria 53, Anna 15			
NOLTE, Conrad	58	Meinberg	52-1661
Berh. 56, Sophia 38, Minna 10, Carolina 7			
August 3			
NOLTE, Elise	35	Ellerberg	53-1070
NOLTE, Friedr.	25	Offensen	54-1371
NOLTE, Georg	29	Arensberg	52-0699
NOLTE, Heinr.	27	Branders/Hess	51-1532
NOLTE, Heinr.	23	Kolsharn	50-0439
NOLTE, Henry	35	Borgentreich	50-0323
NOLTE, Maria	28	Hannover	51-1639
NOLTE, Schwibart	28	Brilon	54-0600
NOLTE, Wilhelm	36	Hochstedt	51-0756
NOLTEMEIER, Fr.	19	Wunstorf	50-0439
NOLZHEIM, Casp.	21	Oberzell	53-0435
NONNERBER, Cath.	8	Eichendorf	52-1452
NOPHUD, Conrad	21	Oberuffhausen	52-1105
Melani 23			
NORDEN, Heinrich	27	Tellsdorf	52-1625

NAME	AGE	RESIDENCE	YR-LIST
NORDENSCHILD, Feis	19	Boenstadt	52-0807
NORDHAUER, Sophie	29	Stolzenau	51-1035
Wilhelmine 24			
NORDHAUS, Wilhelm	18	Osnabrueck	52-0095
NORDHAUSEN, Anna	30	Wittmund	53-0838
NORDHEIM, Doris	22	Hengsfeld	54-1341
NORDHEIM, Friedr.	19	Cassel	54-1724
NORDHOFF, Amandus	24	Hannover	51-1438
NORDHOFF, Friedr.	42	Herzfeld	51-1101
NORDMANN, Luer	45	Hannover	50-1317
NORDMEYER, Carolin	16	Buchen	54-0987
NORDSIEK, Metha	28	Varel	51-1160
NORTBRUCH, Dorothe	29	Habstaedt/Han	52-1423
NORTH, Peter	23	Gelnhausen	51-1796
NORTMANN, Joseph	31	Bilshausen	52-1625
Magdalene 31			
NOST, Friedr. Aug.	32	Freyburg	54-0872
NOTBROK, Wilh.	27	Burgholzhause	49-0352
NOTHDURFT, An Dor.	24	Asel	49-0352
NOTHLING, Emanuel	24	Niederdorla	51-1455
Caroline 21			
NOTT, Christian	37	Meinberg	52-0775
Sophie 40, Wilhelmine 10, August 9			
Hermann 6, Wilhelm 4, Louise 18m			
NOTTE, Veronika	23	Fuhrbach	51-1084
NOVACK, Albert	21	Ravende	54-1168
NOWACK, Franz	35	Breslau	51-0352
NOWAK, Franz	46	Londsel	54-1676
Katharina 26			
NOWAK, Joseph	44	Londsel	54-1676
Barbara 3, Wenzel 8, Franz 5			
NOWETNI, J. (m)	36	Malschwitz	50-0746
NOWOTNE, Carl	20	Bautzen	49-0574
NUCKE, Joh. Phil.	36	Geseke/Pr.	48-0053
NUECHTERLEIN, Joh.	36	Rosstall	47-0828
Margaretha 34, Johann 9			
NUEHR, Johann	24	Rotherod	52-1625
NUENNING, Heinr.	18	Dassel	50-0292
NUERNBERGER, Carl	30	Rastenberg	54-0600
NUERNBERGER, Elis.		Cleppach	54-1717
Lina , Louise , Emilie , Traugott			
NUERNBERGER, Luise	22	Hoya	53-0652
NUESSLE, Ilfriede	37	Machtolsheim	53-0838
NUESSLEIN, Johann	30	Reitzendorf	54-1554
NUETING, Wilhelm	26	Fuerstenhagen	51-1639
NUETZEL, J.G.	38	Forkendorff	51-0517
NUFF, John	26	Frohnlach	51-1588
NUHN, Conrad	41	Niederaula	48-0951
Cath E. 38, Anne E. 11, Elisabeth 3			
NURSCHELER, Andr.	24	Altenstedt	47-0828
NUSLERMANN, Bernh.	26	Everswinkel	50-0840
Theodor 21			
NUSS, Magdalene	22	Riedheim	54-1717
NUSSBAUM, (m)	33	Unterriedberg	54-0987
NUSSBAUM, Betty	24	Geisa	54-0903
NUSSBAUM, Fr.	24	Duennen	54-1283
NUSSBAUM, Joseph	16	Hausen	52-1105
NUSSBAUM, Levi	27	Gehaus	54-1341
M. (f) 19			
NUSSBAUM, Lina	26	Hessen	52-0895
NUSSLER, Ch. (m)	42	Henneberg	54-0918
Athilda 44, Lorenz 14, Elisabeth 9			
NUTT, Johs.	53	Detmold	48-1114
Cath. 45, Sophia 19, Geo. 17, Doris 12			
Gust. 10, Minnie 7			
OBENAUF, Heinr. Ch	54	Trepnitz	54-0872
Eduard 16, Ferdinand 14, Louis 11			
Pauline 12, Emma 4			
OBERGEN, Marie	22	Prussia	50-1317
OBERHAUS, W (m)	20	Brake	52-1321
OBERHAUSER, Ig. M.	31	Westheim	54-1371
OBERHAUSER, Joh. L	28	Unterschwanin	54-1371
OBERLAENDER, Sam.	32	Muehlfeld	53-1086
OBERMANN, Aug.	21	Hannover	52-0370
OBERMEYER, Barbara	40	Eichendorf	52-1452
Catharina 36, Anna 54, Franziska 9m			
OBERNDOERFER, Isak	22	Archshofen	54-0053
OBERNDORFER, Soph.	23	Breitzfeld	49-0742

NAME	AGE	RESIDENCE	YR-LIST
OBERSEIDER, Conrad	27	Wendsbach	50-0366
Isabella 69			
OBERSTEDT, Caspar	27	Brilon/Preuss	53-0475
OBERSTENWILMS, F.W	25	Warmbel	49-0352
OBFENNIT, D. (m)	24	Quackenbrueck	48-1015
OBLIE, Wollega	26	Stuttgart	54-1341
Adolph 5			
OBRCK, Louis	24	Wittlage	52-1410
OBST, Fr.	29	Eisenberg	52-1661
Aug. 28, Wilh. 3			
OCHER, Anton	30	Wetzgau	53-0914
OCHIM, Wilhelm	30	Biegedorf	54-1716
OCHNK, Hermann	20	Ochtrup	50-0840
OCHS, Adam	34	Heinchen	54-0882
OCHS, Chr.	29	Riskirchen	54-1078
Cath. 19, Christine 2			
OCHS, Conrad	50	Lanzenheim	52-1304
OCHS, Elise	19	Quentil	54-1554
OCHS, Franz	34	Saaz	49-1106
OCHS, Joh. G.	47	Frankfurt/M.	52-1661
Charlotte 43			
OCHS, Johann	37	Guttenberg	52-0693
OCHS, Jost	28	Argenstein	51-0352
OCHS, L.	30	Pforzheim	52-1661
Dorothea 32, Anna 9m			
OCHS, M.	58	Sollenberg	54-1419
OCHS, Sabina	39	Ehlmannsfurth	49-1106
OCHSE, Anna Cath.	20	Roemershausen	53-1016
OCKER, August	17	Diepholz	53-0557
ODENSTEDT, Jacob	57	Gebhardshagen	54-1443
Catharine 55, Heinrich 30, Minna 19			
Louise 17			
ODENWAELDER, Maria	22	Weinheim	53-0991
OECHSLER, Michael	26	Bayreuth	54-1591
OECKLER, Stephan	27	Hafenpreppach	50-0379
Catharine 22			
OEDEMANN, Henry	16	Preussen	52-1620
OEDERER, Johann	48	Ermenreuth	52-0693
OEDERS, Dorothea	30	Wesseloh	54-1371
Anna 3m			
OEFELEIN, Barbara	24	Knetzgau	54-0053
OEH, Marie	25	Hemmersheim	54-1575
OEHLER, Georg	22	Zell	52-0370
OEHLER, Heinr.	22	Grochwitz	49-0574
OEHLER, Valentin	37	Groebern	54-0872
Marie 21			
OEHLESKING, Henry	59	Brasse	53-0914
Friedrich 48, Dorothea 50, Henry 18			
Christine 16, Friedrich 14, Sophie 11			
OEHLMANN, Heinr.	35	Wernigerode	51-1686
Cath. 29, Heinr. 3			
OEHLMANN, Johanne	40	Hof	54-1554
OEHLSCHLAEGER, Em.	23	Erfurt/Pr.	53-0475
OEHS, Christian	17	Steierhof	53-0905
OEKS, Joh. Georg	37	Schimmerdorf	53-0324
OELEMANN, Henriett	21	Bielefeld	54-1371
OELKERS, Ernst	33	Huepede	54-1443
OELLERMANN, Friedr	20	Dielingen/Pr.	48-0053
J. 23			
OELRICHS, Claus	32	Tarmstedt	49-0574
Margarethe 27, Marg. 16			
OELRICHS, Friedr.	23	Bremervoerde	52-1580
OELRICHS, Joh.	25	Tarmstedt	49-0574
Gretchen 23			
OELS, Siegmund	24	Edershausen	51-1639
OELSCHLAEGER, Mart	24	Reiselberg	53-0914
Barbara 22, Catharina 9m			
OELSNER, Friedrich	37	Breslau	54-1092
Minna 36, Paul 7, Rudolph 4, Martha 2			
OELSNEY, Fanny	22	Bautzen	54-1649
OELSON, Caspar	40	Twistringen	48-1184
Anna 30, Gerhard 16, Engel 14			
OELTZE, Marie	34	Referlingen	48-1355
Hermann 7			
OENTRICH, Maria	26	Lersen	53-0928
Heinrich 20			
OERDEL, Georg	26	Bayreuth/Bav.	52-0960
OERTEL, Auguste	20	Anstadt	52-1464

NAME	AGE	RESIDENCE	YR-LIST
OERTEL, F. (m)	34	Goettingen	51-0517
L. (f) 34, M. 9			
OESER, v. B.	15	Luneberg	54-1716
OESMANN, Jac.	1-	Hohenaverberg	50-0323
OEST, Johann	18	Quentel	54-1554
OESTEREICHER, Mich	26	Schleerieth	52-1512
OESTERMEIN, Ch.(f)		Wittlage	50-0746
OESTING, Carl	20	Minden	52-1410
OETEL, Emil	34	Eisenberg	52-1661
Henriette 30, Gustav 6, baby (died) 3m			
OETTEL, Gottl. Fr.	22	Cospeda/Sax	52-1423
OETTGEN, Christian	20	Hannover	49-0329
OETTING, Friedrich	23	Uchte	48-0101
OETTINGER, Adolf	23	Ederhaim	51-1796
OFEN, Elenore	20	Rischberg	52-0515
OFENIUS, Soph.	20	Quakenbrueck	50-1132
Bernhard 9m			
OFF, H.W. (f)	21	Germany	49-0413
OFF, Jacob	53	Rammelshausen	53-0267
Catharine 37, Gottlieb 8, Johann bob			
OFINGEN, Georg	18	Itzlingen	54-1371
OGGER, Rosine	24	Schegingen	52-1580
OHAUS, J. (m)	24	Limburg	49-0416
OHBE, Michael	25	Markuhl	52-0558
OHDE, Georg	26	Behns/Prussia	53-0628
Wilhelmine 27			
OHENHAUSEN, Joh.	20	Scholgripen	52-1101
OHL, Martin	24	Umstedt	53-0991
OHL, Valentin	34	Herzstein	52-0095
Margaretha 8			
OHLAND, Johann	15	Debstedt	50-0366
OHLAND, Levin	15	Bederkesa	52-0699
OHLANDT, Herm.	14	Bederkesa	54-0987
OHLENDORF, Joseph	25	Sellum	53-1086
Johanne 22			
OHLHOFF, Anna	16	Bremervoerde	51-1035
OHLICH, Sophie	39	Sachsen	52-1432
Gustav 7, Emma 6, Emil 5m			
OHLIG, Carl Johann	36	Stelzendorf	53-1070
Amalia Nanna 34, Wilhelmine 14, Alwine 11			
Wilh'm Franz 7, Carl 3			
OHLING, Rolf Kr.	57	Loquard	53-0888
Behrntje 55, Heike 33, Paul 33			
Janneke 30, Thekla 22			
OHLSEN, Aug. Herm.	28	Bremerlehe/Ha	50-0323
OHLWERTHER, Barb.	23	Liling	52-0693
OHM, Carl	19	Minden	50-1067
Auguste 23			
OHM, Ed.	18	Bueckeburg	49-0329
OHM, Heinr.	36	Kirchbrak	49-0324
OHM, Herrmann	28	Hannover	52-0699
OHMSTEDE, Eibe	31	Jever	54-0987
OHMSTEDE, Johann	20	Gr. Meer	49-0574
OHNE, Carl	47	Schwarzfeld	53-0637
Friederika 52, Wilhelm 23, Charlotte 21			
Georg 22			
OHNE, Georg	22	Schweisdorf	53-0637
OHNTROP, Angelica	17	Osnabrueck	52-1512
OHRMANN, Wilhelm	30	Westphalen	54-1717
OHRSCHING, Joseph	33	Borsum	53-0652
Apollonia 22			
OHST, H. (m)	20	Otterndorff	50-0746
OKEL, Christian	26	Giessen	54-1676
OLDEHOFF, Dorethea	22	Bassum	53-0557
OLDEKOSS, Georg	32	Hannover	51-0460
OLDENBURG, Georg	26	Ederwind	53-1000
OLDENBURG, Wilhelm	22	Duecke	50-0366
OLDENDORF, Georg	19	Obergrenzbach	51-1035
OLDIGS, Hermann	30	Tungeln	53-0888
OLDINBUTTEL, Cath.	16	Scharmbeck	52-1362
OLIVET, Georg	28	Brunstein	53-0590
Louis 31			
OLLERICHS, Johann	24	Retterode	52-1580
OLTMANN, Joh. Died	25	Dohlen	47-0872
OLTMANN, Marie	24	Wildeshausen	51-0500
OLTMANNS, Carl	20	Oberwarf	52-1580
OLZENDAMM, Albert	26	Barmen	48-0565
OMERLE, Wil'mine D	23	Rochingen	48-1355

NAME	AGE	RESIDENCE	YR-LIST
OMMEN, Joh. Becker	55	Sillenstedt	54-0872
Margarethe 46, Eduard 37, Jacob 27			
Elisa 14, Alfred 17, Albert 7, Anna 22			
Tina 14			
OORS, Hermann	16	Bargel	49-0345
OPERMANN, Amalia	19	Gena	52-1101
OPFERKUCH, Chr.	27	Almen	52-1580
OPITZ, Franz	16	Twittringen	54-1168
OPITZ, Raimund	23	Heurode	54-1297
OPP, Markus	18	Boehmen	48-1179
Adam 17			
OPPEL, Anton	22	Emberg	54-1371
Joh. 14			
OPPEL, Catharina	35	Gilfershausen	53-0320
Barbara 28			
OPPEL, Charles Aug	27	Scheibe/Schwb	48-0053
Friederike 29, August 3, Barthold 1			
OPPENHEIM, Michael	47	Burgkundstadt	51-0460
Sarah 46, Lene 12, Bertha 5			
OPPENHEIM, Salamon	26	Brilon/Preuss	53-0475
OPPENHEIMER, Jette	19	Huettenguss	53-0914
OPPENHEIMER, Moses	24	Esens	54-1371
OPPER, Anna	28	Hessen	52-0699
OPPERMANN, Fr.	53	Mehle	49-0352
OPPERMANN, Heinr.	19	Berka	54-1554
OPPERMANN, Joseph	26	Erckeln	54-0600
OPPERMANN, M.C.(f)	28	Halle/Pr.	52-0960
ORDING, Heinrich	19	Bremervoerde	54-1371
ORDNUNG, Catharine	21	Witrelshofen	53-0492
ORDNUNG, J.C. (m)	24	Weidenbach	54-1341
ORFF, Caspar	40	Mendhausen	51-1640
ORLOPP, Alexander	36	Dresden	48-1243
ORSING, Hen.	17	Appel/Hann.	51-1796
ORSTERHELD, Jacob	22	Bischausen	54-0882
ORT, Sebast.	55	Oberreichenba	52-0693
Kunig. 52, Kunig. 16, Sophia 10			
ORT, Wilhelm	18	Nidda	52-1321
ORTEGEL, John	16	Frauenaurach	53-0991
ORTENAN, David	26	Fuerth	52-1625
ORTH, Dorothea	20	Uslar	50-1317
ORTH, Ernst	36	Herford/Pr.	51-1725
Friedrich 6			
ORTH, Friedrich	27	Breitenbach	51-0352
ORTH, Heinr.	27	Bamberg	48-1114
ORTHMANN, Joh. Chr	33	Berlin	54-1168
ORTJENS, Charles	19	Wellen/Hann.	50-0323
ORTMANN, A.W.	25	Warburg	51-0405
ORTMANN, Gottlieb	20	Gumbelstadt	52-0563
ORTMANN, Philipp	21	Nortingen	50-1067
ORTNER, Joh.	32	Eichenberg	47-0828
ORTWEIN, Conrad	24	Hessen	53-0590
ORTWEIN, Philipp	31	Frankenberg	53-1016
Auguste 10, Catharina 7, Heinrich 4			
OSCHMANN, Friedr.	56	Frankfurt/M.	53-1000
OSELEIN, C.	29	Elbingen	49-1358
OSMANN, Joh. Stef.	19	Grafenberg/Bv	51-1796
OSMERS, Depper	30	Bollen	53-0991
OSMERS, Friedrich	18	Achim	53-0991
OSSEBEL, H.	29	Breslau	54-1283
OSSENBERG, Henry	28	Rupeljan	48-0053
Ann Ch. 31, Wilhelmina 7, Friedr. Wm. 5			
Arnold Wm. 3, Caroline 9m			
OSSENKOPP, Christ.	42	Hildesheim	53-1070
OSSMANN, Anna	14	Ruesselbach	52-0693
OSSMANN, Kunig.	14	Ermreuth	53-0320
Anna 21			
OSSWALD, Elisabeth	22	Coburg	52-0895
OST, Christian	18	Steinau	51-0500
OST, Johann	20	Odesheim	51-0500
Christian 18			
OSTENBACHER, M.Ann	17	Schegingen	52-1580
OSTENBERG, Fr.	32	Elberfeld	48-0565
D. 66			
OSTENWALD, H.C.(m)	28	Vlotho	49-0329
OSTER, H.	32	Polck	54-0987
OSTERLOH, Margaret	24	Hatten	52-1362
OSTERMANN, Friedr.	25	Brevoerde	51-1101
OSTERMEIER, Sophie	30	Kohlenfeldt	53-0492
OSTERMEIER, W.	40	Hofgeismar	51-0517
O. (f) 40, W. (f) 10			
OSTERMEYER, Joh.	45	Bamberg	54-0053
OSTERMEYER, Johann	16	Meinsen	52-1321
OSTERMEYER, Lenore	46	Meinsen	52-1321
Caroline 22, Engel 18			
OSTERMEYER, Ludwig	38	Weitersheim	51-1588
Christine 32, Christine 58, Louise 17			
Friedrich 24, Caroline 8m			
OSTERMEYER, W. (m)	49	Warlem	52-1321
OSTERMEYER, Wilh.	28	Bergdorf	52-1321
OSTERNDORF, H.W.	42	Dorum	53-0905
Maria 37, Friederika 15, Eibe Henni 10			
Maria Doroth 6			
OSTERRIED, Veronka	26	Schlingen	53-0492
OSTHAM, Franz	30	Woeltingerode	52-0095
Minna 20			
OSTHEIM, Georg	18	Echzel	54-1717
OSTHEIM, Jenny	19	Brakel	51-1101
OSTHEIM, Levi	25	Munster	49-0413
OSTHEIM, Philipp	23	Harsewinkel	48-0260
OSTHOLZ, Louis	20	Hannover	51-1438
OSTHUM, Georg	18	Echzel	54-1717
OSTLER, Elisabeth	28	Eisenach	54-1649
OSWALD, Alex	26	Merseburg/Pr.	52-0960
OSWALD, Herrmann	28	Ried	54-1168
OSWALD, Joseph	19	Hagen	51-1686
OTT, Barbara	21	Geffingen/Wue	52-1620
OTT, Friedrich	22	Priesewitz	53-1164
OTT, Joh.	59	Schottsteinac	50-0746
OTT, Joh. Georg	30	Leiheim	54-0903
OTT, Johann	37	Zuerich	51-1686
OTT, Margarethe	31	Wittenberg	53-0652
OTTE, Carl	49	Meinberg	52-0775
Friedrike 56, Simon Heinr. 21, Conrad 17			
Heinrich 26			
OTTE, Friedrich	41	Leopoldsthal	52-0775
Louise 38, Friedrich 11, Simon 5			
Wilhelmine 2			
OTTEN, Anna	24	Wetzbach	53-0590
OTTEN, Cath. Marg.	24	Thedinghausen	52-0515
OTTEN, Diedr.	18	Alt Lueneburg	47-0828
OTTEN, Hermann	17	Rachereissted	53-0475
OTTEN, J. (m)	24	Kaltenhof	49-0324
OTTEN, Joh.	21	Felde	54-1647
Diedr. 14, Friedr. 17			
OTTENWALTER, Mich.	31	Baiern	52-0895
OTTERBEIN, Barb. J	21	Grossenlueder	49-0365
Joseph by			
OTTERBEIN, Bendikt	21	Grossenlueder	50-0323
Mary 26			
OTTO, Amalie	50	Handorf	54-1371
OTTO, Anton	18	Seisheim	49-1106
OTTO, August	50	Oerlinghausen	54-1297
Charlotte 45, Caroline 22, August 9m			
OTTO, Carl	42	Preussen	52-1620
Friedrike 40			
OTTO, Casper	35	Falzdorf	53-0324
Heinrich 22			
OTTO, Charles	20	Rodenberg	53-1164
OTTO, Christian	30	Weilsdorf	53-0324
Magretha 35, Carl 8, Daniel 5, Paul 3			
Dorothea 11m			
OTTO, Conrad	25	Ulenborn	50-0840
Wilhelmine 21, Elise 11m			
OTTO, Franz Ed.	17	Siebenlehn	54-0987
OTTO, Friedrich	26	Crimmitschau	54-0987
OTTO, Friedrich	44	Lauterberg	54-0987
Henriette 47, Emilie 19, Marie 9, Minna 6			
Elisa 3, Adolph by			
OTTO, Friedrich	19	Schwarzburg	53-0928
Al. 22			
OTTO, Georg	28	Bolle	54-1282
OTTO, Heinrich	60	Weilsdorf	53-0324
OTTO, Heinrich	20	Carlshafen	52-0563
OTTO, Heinrich	29	Duderstadt	52-0563
OTTO, Johann	28	Churhessen	52-1620
OTTO, Johann	41	Heiligengrab	54-0872

NAME	AGE	RESIDENCE	YR-LIST
Henriette 34, Carl 14			
OTTO, Johann	24	Sachsen	53-0590
OTTO, L. (m)	21	Estrup	48-0453
OTTO, Maria	28	Ziegenhain	53-1013
Martha Soph. 57			
OTTWEIN, Catharine	22	Wallenrode	51-0352
OUELL, Peter	17	Hagen	50-0366
OUENTIN, Lisette	22	Dransfeld	48-0887
OVERLACH, Minna	27	Brandenburg	52-0699
OVERLACH, Theodor	37	Braunschweig	52-0699
Minna 27			
OVERWETHER, Carl H	19	Osnabrueck	48-1131
OWEN, Admiral W.W.	69	Gt. Britian	48-1015
Mrs. 59			
OWERN, Louisa	32	Kemrode	54-1470
Louise 58			
OZWALD, F.	20	Steinewald	54-1419
Barbara 56			
PAAR, Marie	33	Pukelheim	53-0435
PABSCH, August	24	Heurode	54-1297
PABST, Caroline	25	Coburg	50-1067
Hugo 9m			
PABST, Lorenz	39	Staffelstein	52-1129
Cath. 42, Marg. 17, Anna Mar. 15			
Barbara 13, Christoph 11			
PACHHALER, Johann	18	Bokel	49-0345
PACHTMANN, Henriet	39	Wernigerode	54-1371
Friedrich 5			
PACKE, Carl Aug.	38	Castrop	50-1071
PACKKAEFER, Johann	24	Letten	54-1554
Susanne 22			
PACTOBL, Conrad	28	Wedelbach	48-1131
PADBERG, Heinr.	20	Gruenebach	53-1000
PADE, Aug.	18	Burgholzhause	49-0352
PAECKEL, Johannes	21	Gruenberg	47-0840
PAECKEL, Julius	28	Goerlitz	54-1297
PAEPELKE, Carl	40	Treptow	54-0872
Johanna 34, Hermann 9, Fritz 9, Rudolph 5			
August 2, Sophie by			
PAETZ, Alois	34	Wallerdorf/Bv	49-0365
PAETZ, John	21	Foellingen/He	50-0323
PAETZ, Louis	17	Leeten	53-1000
PAETZSCH, C.G.	32	Saxony	50-0311
PAEZ, Joh. Casp.	19	Hanau	48-1131
PAFFENBERG, Joseph	31	Brengberg	52-1101
Hetes (m) 22			
PAHLKE, Rudolph	32	Pr. Holland	54-1282
Catharine 29			
PAITSE, Chr.	34	Walldorf	51-0757
PAKE, A.D.	16	Frischluneber	51-1160
PAKTOBL, Conrad	28	Wedelback	48-1131
PALM, Carl	22	Nebeling	47-0672
PALMER, Ludowina	27	Emsdetten	54-0903
PALSCHER, Fanny	20	Fuerth	50-0840
PAMM, Johanne	58	Neustadt	54-1297
PAMPEL, Chr. Fried	33	Schmoelln	53-0914
Christian 27, Emma 2, Minna by			
PANCK, Herm. Heinr	29	Kirchlengern	51-0352
Anna Maria 21			
PANDORF, Carl H.	20	Bremen	51-0326
PANER, Fred. Wm.	27	Oelsnitz	53-0991
PANGRATZ, Georg	54	Friedrichstha	53-0905
PANKOW, Friederike	56	Mecklenburg	54-0903
PANNEMANN, John A.	19	Neusuedland	54-1470
PANNING, Christ.	28	Walsroede	51-1245
PANNING, Heinrich	23	Hunzig	50-0366
PANNOT, Jean	18	Hanau	53-1164
PANSE, Christian	48	Artern	50-0379
Pauline 44, Maria 19, Christiane 18			
Therese 16, Christian 10, Gustav 7			
Caroline 5			
PANSE, Gustav	20	Nordhausen	48-1184
Julius 18			
PANTHOEFER, Cathr.	52	Schulzbach/Pr	51-0048
Helene 19, Cathr. 26			
PANZER, Eduard	38	Grossen	53-1013
Amalie 45, Friederike 26			
PAPE, Auguste	25	Diepholz	53-1062

NAME	AGE	RESIDENCE	YR-LIST
PAPE, Cord	21	Selsing/Hann.	51-0048
PAPE, Elisabeth	30	Gotha/Sachsen	51-1725
PAPE, Engel	23	Stroit	54-1554
PAPE, Louise	20	Grossen---	50-0439
PAPENDIECH, Ferd.	19	Lauchsted	49-0345
PAPENSCHLAEGER, J.	22	Reitlingen	49-0345
PAPENSIEDER, Lina	25	Lippstadt	51-0500
Marie (died) 3m			
PAPIER, Anne	22	Koppendorf	53-0582
PAPPE, Albert	24	Brockhausen	52-1512
PAPPE, Friedrich	37	Hagen	52-0048
PAPPENBERG, A.	22	Braunschweig	49-1358
PAPPENDICK, Marg.	38	Erfurt	54-1001
PAPPLER, Mich.	44	Burchsalach	52-1321
PAPPON, Georg	23	Hochdorf	54-1371
PAPROTH, Carl	35	Magdeburg	53-0267
Christiane 42			
PAPST, Const.	22	Boelen	50-1071
PAPST, David	22	Langenstein	49-0352
Wilhelm 22			
PARCHEN, Georg	43	Vatterode	48-1355
Marie 39, Christian 17, Louise 14			
Heinrich 10, Catharina 71			
PARGOUD, Jean	29	France	48-1243
PARNDECKER, Henry	37	Vluyn/Pr.	48-0447
PASCAL, Alexander	44	Grenoble	50-0311
PASCHOLA, Wenzel	56	Luze	52-0699
Anna 48, Franz 27, Alouise 22			
PASKUWITSCH, Vinz.	27	Gratz	54-0987
PASSOLT, Heinr.	18	Hirschberg	54-0987
Sophie 26			
PASTERT, Christine	29	Elberfeld	48-0565
PATTERSON, James	40	Philadelphia	50-0021
PATZ, Carl	16	Seehausen	50-0379
PATZ, Georg	21	Bernau	52-0095
PATZ, Georg	24	Gerach	54-1649
Josepha 25, Barbara 5			
PATZELT, Vinzenz	41	Thurnau	53-1164
PATZIG, Gott.	35	Cassel	54-1724
PAUDLER, Joh. Mich	25	Coburg	51-1640
PAUDY, Emil	26	Weissenfels	54-1649
Louise 23			
PAUL, Anton Franz	34	Oberginna	53-1062
PAUL, August	20	Emsdorf/Hess.	52-0960
PAUL, Bernhard	23	Muenster	49-0324
Lotte 28, Johanna 26			
PAUL, Carl	24	Wernigerode	53-0942
PAUL, Casper	19	Laer	53-0991
PAUL, Conrad	29	Schlitz	51-0352
PAUL, Heinrich	31	Niederurf	54-0053
PAUL, Herm.	22	Luttehausen	52-0370
PAUL, J.F. (m)	32	Cassel	52-0652
PAUL, John	14	Wanfried	53-0888
PAUL, Lotte	28	Bremen	49-0324
Johanna 26			
PAUL, Martin	28	Besen	52-1105
PAUL, Sara	28	Hessen	52-0895
PAUL, Wilhelm	24	Hannover	50-1317
PAUL, Wilhelmine	35	Schwalenberg	51-1062
PAULA, Ernst	33	Lampersdorf	49-1517
Mrs. 30			
PAULE, Ignaz	35	Krumbach/Bav.	51-1532
Maria Magd. 19			
PAULI, Henriette	23	Friedrichsdor	53-1023
PAULI, Joseph	19	Zaeuschen	53-0585
PAULIG, Friedrich	42	Sommerfeld	54-1371
PAULING, Friedrich	32	Drebber	50-1132
Christine 21, Sophie 2, Heinrich 6			
PAULING, Friedrich	58	Drebber	50-1132
Marie 61, Diedrich 27, Dorothea 25			
Marie 22, Anna 19			
PAULMANN, Caroline	25	Ludwigshalle	51-0460
PAULMANN, E.	32	Brunk	49-0742
PAULSEN, Ernst	25	Blamberg	49-1358
PAULY, Chr.	24	Oberod	53-0914
PAULY, Nicolaus	25	Ochtendung	53-0652
PAUS, Joseph	26	Prussia	53-0628
PAUS, Louisa	42	Neustadt	48-1209

NAME	AGE	RESIDENCE	YR-LIST
Mary 20, Mary Sophie 17, Dorette 14			
PAUSE, Julius	30	Neischs	50-0840
PAUTSCH, F.	24	Oberlangenau	53-0582
PAWLUS, Georg	26	Leithen	54-1443
PAYEKEN, R.	16	Bremerlehe	53-0582
PEAUT, Salomon	16	Rauschenberg	54-1168
PECH, August	26	Wallwitz	54-1283
PECHERE, Johann	19	Gotenberg	53-0324
PECHMAYER, Louise	38	Raden	51-1796
PECK, Gerhard	19	Kneheim	54-1371
PECKEN, Meint Harm	40	Wittmund	54-0872
PEDER, Jacob	26	Steinbach	52-1105
PEETZ, Johann	46	Puentzfeld	54-1554
PEFFERKORN, Ernst	21	Glauchau	52-1580
PEFFERKORN, Sevill	28	Kreuzburg/Wei	52-1620
PEICKE, Ad.	22	Hannover	50-1317
PEIFER, Johannes	24	Kirchoff	53-1000
PEIKERT, Johann	25	Glatz	54-1297
PEINER, Friedrich	22	Coburg	53-0267
PEINKOFER, Peter		Waldmuenchen	53-0942
PEIPENBRING, Carl	23	Brunswick	51-1532
PEISEL, Gerth.	31	Thalenmais	53-0435
PEISINGE, Margreth	21	Leimberg	53-0582
PEISKER, Johann	25	Gebharddorf	50-1067
PEITZ, Joh. Bernh.	21	Westerlohe	52-0563
PEITZSCH, Joh Ant.	17	Altenburg	53-0942
PELEG, H. (m)	25	Hunfeld	54-1341
PELKE, Friedrich	16	Russ	48-1131
PELLAZINO, Joseph	26	Notteln	54-1078
PELSTER, B. (m)	24	Sassenberg	49-1358
PELZ, Johann	32	Tocksbach	52-1452
PENNA, Christiane	30	Arzberg	53-0557
PENNENGROTH, Carol	21	Petershagnerh	54-0930
PENNING, Peter M.	40	Helegoland	53-0991
Mary 38, John 17, Anna 13			
PENZEL, August	28	Berlin	54-0965
Amalia 23			
PEPER, Christ.	15	Bederkesa	51-1084
PEPPELHAUS, Gerh.	55	Solingen	48-0406
PEPPER, Carl Heinr	25	Eickhorst	47-0762
PEPPER, Hermann	38	Eickhorst	47-0762
Elise 39, Elisabeth 13, Louise 10			
Marie 8			
PERCK, Elisabeth	23	Assbach	52-1625
Catharina 21			
PERGERIL, Marg.	20	Feuchtwangen	52-0515
PERKING, Georg	24	Spassberg	54-0987
PERLBACH, Lena	22	Bederkesa	48-1015
PERLSCH, Cath.	34	Leyern	47-0918
PERNACHEL, J. (f)	32	Schwarzenau	48-0453
Ch. (f) 7, Christine 5			
PERNFUSS, Joseph	31	Iglan	53-1070
Catharina 31, Franz 10m			
PERSONN, Christian	36	Aurich	53-0942
PESCHECK, Jacob	48	Boehmen	54-1724
Cath. 40, Franz 15, Rosalia 9, John 4			
Joseph 2			
PESCHEL, Gottl. W.	35	Sachsen	51-1725
Clara 36			
PESHIK, C.	27	Andressen/Boh	54-1676
M. 35, Carol. 2			
PETER, Anna C.	21	Immelborn	53-0320
PETER, Carl	30	Andreasberg	48-1355
Charlotte 34			
PETER, Catharina	21	Rapoltshausen	53-0267
PETER, Catharine	32	Niederwildung	53-1086
PETER, Christine	33	Kahla	54-1297
PETER, Georg	24	Cassel	53-0825
Hugo 33, Franz 18			
PETER, Hermann	23	Colbe	54-0930
Carl 20			
PETER, Heronimus	39	Netphen	53-1062
Eckhardt 27			
PETER, J. (m)	22	Aschen	48-0453
PETER, Johann	21	Overschuetz	48-1179
Catharine 14			
PETER, Johannes	24	Uttenhausen	52-1105
Maria 21, Conrad 2			

NAME	AGE	RESIDENCE	YR-LIST
PETER, John	21	Switzerland	54-1724
PETER, Lorenz	37	Illicornete	54-0918
Marie 27, Paul 12, Johann 10, Franz 2			
Marie 8, Catharine 5			
PETER, Marg. Elise	18	Unterelbe	54-1575
David 22			
PETER, Nick	26	Wellingerrode	53-0320
PETER, Peter	20	Marburg	51-1796
PETERJOHANNE, Soph	23	Tecklenburg/P	52-1432
PETERMAN, George	45	Meiningen	51-1588
Catherine 40, Maria 16, George 11m			
PETERMANN, Ad. (m)	25	Dresig/Pr.	52-0960
PETERMANN, Chr. Fr	32	Gera	53-1164
Jane 40			
PETERMANN, J.H.	28	Osterholz	48-0112
Diedrich 17, Bertha 24			
PETERMANN, Joh.	38	Jochaus	54-1282
Kunigunde 38, Johannes 6, daughter by			
PETERS, Anton	24	Bremerhafen	54-1092
PETERS, Auguste	20	Treusin	54-1371
PETERS, Catherine	50	Bremervoerde	51-1035
PETERS, Chr.	46	Herges-Vogtei	52-0370
Anna 43, Georg 18, Kasper 10, Auguste 1			
PETERS, Diedrich	20	Steinkirchen	54-0987
Johann 17			
PETERS, Friederike	24	Lengerich/Pr.	52-1432
PETERS, Heinrich	14	Deedesdorf	50-1067
Christian 12			
PETERS, Johann C.J	25	Witstock/Pr.	54-1092
PETERS, John	50	Schwerin	53-0991
Dorothy 49, Henry 21			
PETERS, Leonhardt	18	Duderstadt/Ha	53-0628
PETERS, Metta	20	St.Magnus	51-0326
PETERS, Philipp	20	Wingslar	51-1455
PETERS, Th. Lutter	25	Voeln	53-0888
PETERS, Theodor	31	Soest/Prussia	51-1725
PETERSEN, Adelheid	38	Wachendorf	50-0292
PETERSEN, Alexis	19	Copenhagen	54-1566
PETERSEN, August	20	Gottland/Swed	50-1071
PETERSEN, Caroline	37	Halle	54-0987
PETERSEN, Christ.	18	Neuenkirchen	50-0366
PETERSEN, Johann	26	Gothland/Swed	50-1071
PETERSOHN, Wilhelm	49	Bamberg	54-1717
Margaretha 46, Conrad 18, Margaretha 16			
Christian 10, Heinrich 8, Mina 6			
Henriette 3			
PETERSON, Jess.	30	Dannewerk	54-1297
PETERSSEN, Doris	41	Flensburg	52-0699
Jens 18, Nicolai 16			
PETRAIN, Mathias	58	Zamrsk/Bohm.	52-1304
Anna 45, Anna 22, Marie 20, Josepha 18			
PETRI, Bernhard	22	Eisenach	50-1132
PETRI, Friedrich	25	Milden	48-1131
PETRI, Theodor	21	Ohrdruff	52-1321
PETRI, Therese	24	Darmstadt	54-1371
PETRIST, Cresentia	27	Eckenthal	50-0379
PETRUS, Simon	28	Krotoschin	53-1023
Caroline 26			
PETRY, Wilhelm	26	Preussen	53-0590
PETTENHAUSEN, Wilh	14	Cassel	54-0930
PETTER, Ant.	17	Rotenkirchen	52-0515
PETTERS, Oscar	25	Weimar	48-1184
PETTINGER, Jeanett	31	Mainsfarth	53-1062
PETTRY, Leonhard	26	Gunzburg	52-0370
PETZ, Thomas	40	Puentzfeld	54-1554
PETZOLD, A.	21	Langenleuba	53-0914
PETZOLD, Andreas	48	Gotha	54-1649
PETZOLD, Theresa	52	Breslau	54-1078
PETZOLD, Wilhelm	19	Kleinbundorf	54-1371
PEUSER, Carl	42	Berlin	49-0352
PEUSTER, August	25	Rullen	48-0406
PEUTTER, Johann	25	Reutlingen/Wu	52-1620
PEZOLD, A.	21	Langenleuba	53-0914
PFADENHAUER, Heinr	40	Bayern	52-1620
Barbara 34			
PFADENHAUER, Veron	33	Mainek	54-1168
Johann 23			
PFAF, Elise	20	Nordeck	53-1013

NAME	AGE	RESIDENCE	YR-LIST
PFAFF, Andreas	23	Tiefenort	52-1410
PFAFF, Anna	24	Lauchrieden	54-0053
PFAFF, Carl	25	Zwota	52-0095
PFAFF, Charlotte	18	Giesen	53-1000
PFAFF, Emilie	18	Vacha	47-0828
PFAFF, Gotth.	22	Odenhausen	51-1160
PFAFF, Wilhelm	29	Sinna	47-0828
Emilie 18			
PFAFFENBACH, Anna	20	Tangerode	54-1566
Barbara 19, Catharine 17			
PFAFFENWIMMER, P.	20	Wels	53-0991
PFALLER, Josepha	16	Wintersdorf	54-1647
PFANNKUCH, Johann	19	Burg	47-0828
PFANNKUCHEN, Carl	20	Ebersholz	50-0379
PFANNSCHMIDT, Andr	24	Borg/Pr.	52-1620
PFANSTIEL, Carl		Curhessen	52-1620
Elisabeth 46, William 12, Auguste 10			
Caroline 8, Marie 5, Robert 2			
PFARER, Mich.	25	Schildhutter	53-0435
Barbara			
PFARR, Elise	22	Heringen	52-0370
PFARR, Heinrich	25	Heringen	52-1148
PFARR, Johann A.	26	Nuernberg/Bav	54-1092
PFEFFER,	24	Unterfarnbach	54-1419
PFEFFER, Anna Barb	23	Sachsen-Mein.	53-0324
PFEFFER, Elisabeth	20	Staufenberg	54-1470
PFEFFER, Joh.	23	Rothenburg	54-1283
PFEFFER, Joseph	32	Flettau	54-1716
Margareth 27			
PFEFFERHORN, Adam	28	Stockheim	50-0472
PFEFFERKORN, Sevil	28	Kreuzburg/Wei	52-1620
PFEFFERMANN, Wilh.	43	Kreiensen	54-1371
Johanne 33			
PFEFFLE, Martha	34	Theilfingen	52-1580
PFEIFER, Marg.	26	Warenrode	52-0652
PFEIFER, Stephan	44	Birkel	48-1184
PFEIFFER, Amalia	24	Cassel	48-1243
PFEIFFER, Anton	40	Rudelsdorf	54-0872
Barbara 48, Johann 15, Eduard 9			
Mathilda 18, Emilie 7			
PFEIFFER, Balthas.	21	Angberg	47-0672
PFEIFFER, C.W. (m)	18	Crabfeld	49-0416
PFEIFFER, Chr'tine	50	Rotenburg	54-1649
PFEIFFER, Christ.	24	Schraplau	47-0672
Barbara 28			
PFEIFFER, Daniel	28	Unzittel/Bav.	52-1620
PFEIFFER, Elis.	26	Gotha	52-1332
PFEIFFER, Friedr.	22	Steinburg	52-1148
PFEIFFER, Friedr.	36	Schweina	52-0095
PFEIFFER, Georg	20	Rotenburg	54-1649
PFEIFFER, Heinrich	24	Kleinhainsdor	54-1371
PFEIFFER, J.	14	Mennberg	51-0517
PFEIFFER, Joh. Fr.	25	Katzenelnboge	54-1371
PFEIFFER, Johanne	19	Rotenburg	51-0352
PFEIFFER, Joseph	35	Bombs	52-1625
PFEIFFER, Joseph	33	Bruex	53-1070
PFEIFFER, Marie	30	Grosskarfeld	54-1168
PFEIFFER, Pauline	18	Koechingen/Wr	54-1092
PFEIFFER, Sophie	20	Rothenburg/Wu	51-1532
PFEIFFER, Sophie	30	Darmstadt	48-1355
Margarethe 13, Philipp 4			
PFEIL, August	24	Wernigerode	48-1179
PFEIL, Dorothea	30	Bakenau	49-0345
PFEIL, Eva Kunig.	32	Lohm	51-1640
PFEIL, Friedr.	33	Wernigerode	54-1168
PFEIL, Georg Ludw	30	Dahle	52-0563
PFEIL, Johannes	50	Niedermoellri	49-0345
Catharina 48, Catharina 18, Elisabeth 15			
Bernhard 14, Conrad 10			
PFEIL, Valentin	16	Muese/Hess.	50-0323
PFEIL, Wilh.	19	Cassel	54-0053
PFENNING, Heinrich	44	Gutstedt	54-1443
Elisabeth 30, Christian 8, Elisabeth 9			
PFERDEORT, Elustin	21	Detmold/Lippe	50-0323
Henriette 18			
PFERMANN, Carolina	20	Rhaunen	53-1062
PFEUFFER, Johann	19	Wulfershausen	52-1321
PFICHTS, C. (f)	39	Limbach	50-0746

NAME	AGE	RESIDENCE	YR-LIST
C. (m) 19, M. (m) 17			
PFIKS, Jacob	31	Tobbens	54-0872
PFILLN, Wilhelmine	22	Oberr---	50-0840
PFINGSTEN, Christ.	27	Buhler	52-0279
PFINGSTEN, Conrad	31	Hannover	53-0652
PFINGSTEN, Heinr.	28	Gruemmer	50-0439
PFISTER, Anna	23	Ballhof	48-1179
Margaretha by			
PFISTER, Georg	25	Werners	54-1554
PFISTER, Joseph	21	Herbersdorf	52-0693
PFISTNER, Georg	54	Lauterbach	54-0903
Joseph 15, Margaretha 14, Margeret 20			
PFITZEG, Johann	34	Herriden	50-0379
Marie 28, Catharine 4, Georg 3			
PFITZENMEYER, Ludw	21	Mittelruessel	49-0737
PFITZENREITER, Ign	32	Niederorschel	53-0267
Anna 32, Barbara 9, Joseph 7, August 2			
Catharina 10m			
PFITZMEYER, Jacob	28	Backnang	49-0352
PFLANZ, M. (m)	35	Seidelshapt	50-0746
PFLEGER, Henriette	23	Bauscheidt	54-1371
PFLUEGER, Caroline	17	Mengeringhaus	49-0383
PFLUEGER, Jacob	16	Elingrode	52-1362
PFLUEGER, Joh.	41	Lichterfeld	53-1013
Franciska 29, Herm. 6, Lisette 4			
Regina(died) 3m			
PFLUG, Anna Cath.	27	Elders/Hessen	49-0365
PFLUG, Johann	28	Grosenlieder	53-0320
PFLUG, Lorenz	37	Hofhausen/Hes	50-0323
PFLUG, Rud. H.	21	Altenburg	51-1245
PFLUGARDT, Georges	29	Leipzig	48-1209
PFLUGRADT, Georges	29	Leipzig	48-1209
PFLUMM, Ludwig	28	Ohmden/Wuertt	52-0351
PFOELLEN, Gottlieb	48	Rottweil	54-0053
Marie 29, Wilhelmine 6			
PFOERTENER, Henr't	27	Seesen	54-0987
Wilhelm 27			
PFORDT, Margaretha	20	Heeringen	48-0284
Heinrich 19			
PFORST, Margaretha	20	Heeringen	48-0284
Heinrich 19			
PFUHL, Christian	16	Ritterode	50-0379
PFUHLER, Heinrich	24	Rasch	50-0311
PFULLER, Adam	25	Artern	50-0379
Carl 20, Andreas 23			
PFULSCHMIDT, Kath.	26	Munster	49-1106
PFUND, Georg Mich.	34	Rammelshausen	53-0267
PFUSCH, Johann	50	Filke	54-0053
Anna Elise 40, Caroline 9			
PHIELER, Christine	37	Gerstungen	51-1640
Anna Barb. 8			
PHILIPPBAR, Cath.	37	Selters	54-0872
Hermine 9, Friedrich 8, Rudolph 7			
PHILLIPS, Gott.	27	Mittelruessel	49-0737
Wilhelmina 28			
PHOLIUS, Friedrich	23	Germany	51-1588
PHOMANN, Jacob	35	Isny	54-0872
PICARD, Johann	53	Groenberg	54-1371
Carl 18, Friedrich 26, Carl 19			
PICHEL, Franz	23	Sachsen	53-0590
PICHERT, Julius	27	Fuerth	54-1297
PICK, Nicolaus	31	Harbruch	51-1062
PICKARD, Henriette	24	Lennep	50-1236
PICKEL, Anna Barb.	34	Kirchenhameln	52-1129
PICKEL, Joh. Fried	53	Brunnersthaus	52-0370
Sophie 35, Elisabeth 4, Barbara 9m			
PICKEL, Leonh.	33	Tuernried	52-1129
Anna Barb. 34, Jacob 8, Cathar. 7			
Gabriel 4, Margaretha 1			
PICKERT, Paul	18	Lutterg/Hess	50-0323
PIECHATZER, Alois	31	Breslau	53-0637
Pauline 31, Louise 6, Pauline 4			
PIECKER, Joh. Chr.	23	Ruettigheim	48-1209
Anna Elise 26, Elizabeth 25			
PIEHTMAYER, Mina	34	Pyrmont	51-1101
PIEKER, Wilhelm Fr	20	Tharnbach	53-0838
PIEL, Carl	41	Hainschen	51-1639
Friederike 41, Carl 15, Gotthard 10			

NAME	AGE	RESIDENCE	YR-LIST
Guido 7, Friederike 6			
PIENEBERGE, Christ	25	Windheim	50-0944
PIEPER, Christoph	44	Helsdorf	54-1443
PIEPER, Conrad	19	Reinsdorf	53-1086
PIEPER, Diedrich	17	Bremen	49-0383
PIEPER, Margaretha	57	Bettinghausen	54-0053
Heinrich 21			
PIEPER, Wilhelm	26	Osterode	53-1000
PIEPKO, Christ.	25	Rodenberg	52-1580
PIETMEYER, August	32	Pyrmont	51-1101
PIETSCH, Carl	22	Altenburg	48-0269
PIETSCHMANN, Joh.	28	Nixdorf	54-1371
PIKE, Fritz	26	Hannover	49-1517
Mrs. 25			
PILLATH, Joh. Th.	43	Neustadt	52-1105
Rosine 36, Cath. 8, Barbara 5			
Friedrich 3, Elisab(died) 58			
PILLMANN, Johanne	40	Salzgitter/Ha	52-1332
PILSING, Peter	26	Rauschenberg	52-1464
PILZ, Carl	36	Reichenberg	54-0987
Caroline 21			
PILZ, Carl	17	Friedland	54-1371
PILZ, Emma	18	Grossen	53-1062
Rosalie 29			
PILZ, Fr.	30	Hainspack	48-1179
PILZ, Joseph	33	Reichenberg	54-1647
PINDIG, August	18	Wilhelmsdorf	54-0872
PINDIG, Ferdinand	16	Ferdinandsdor	54-0872
PINEHMIB, Henry	20	Schonstadt	52-0515
PINGEL, Maria	19	Bremervoerde	54-1371
PINKERT, Chr.	23	Cassel	54-1724
PINZER, Johann	30	Trevesen	54-1078
PIPER, Georg	23	Emden	53-0324
PIPO, August	21	Caklenfeld	50-0311
PIPPER, Marie	29	Goettingen	54-1078
PIPPERT, Martha E.	21	Niedermoellri	54-0930
PIRMER, Johann	24	Glashuetten	51-1084
PIRSCH, Mathias	47	Steiermark	53-0267
PIRSECH, Ferdinand	38	Pasewalk	53-1023
Dorothea 36, Gustav 9, Reinhold 3			
Laura 2			
PIRTZ, Anton	23	Krainburg	49-1358
PISSERT, Samuel	47	Breslau	54-1554
PISTLER, Friedrich	27	Mehnen	53-0942
PISTLER, Henriette	27	Severns	53-0942
PITET, J. Conrad	31	Cassel	54-1371
Maria Reb. 25, Maria Leont. 4			
Elisabeth 2, Conrad 3m			
PITSCH, Sophie	23	Schwetzingen	54-1371
PITZEL, Theresia	26	Fornbach	54-1168
PITZER, Johann	30	Heng	52-1464
PLACH, Catharine	23	Cassel	51-0352
PLACH, Christoph	28	Sera	51-0352
Catharine 23			
PLACHT, Franz	33	Schoenbach	49-0574
PLADT, Hieronymus	28	Iglau	54-1371
PLAESING, Lorenz	32	Almen	52-1580
PLAMBECK, John	41	Berlin	54-1724
PLAN, Leonh.	28	Ellenbach	52-1129
PLANER, Theresa	23		50-0944
PLANQUE, de Fr.	40	Crefeld	50-1071
PLANSON, Anna	18	Bremerlehe	51-1245
PLANSON, Helene R.	23	Bremerlehe	50-1236
PLASS, Theodor	20	Verden	54-1297
PLATE, Claus	24	Bremenhafen	52-0279
PLATSCHER, Chr'tne	19	Wuertenberg	53-0557
PLATTNER, Cath.	54	Harbach	52-1452
PLATZER, Joh.	30	Langenbrueck	54-1078
PLAUNITZER, Anton	16	Sachsen	53-0585
PLAUTS, B. (m)	28	Tyrol	49-1358
PLAUTZ, Liebmann	14	Nordhausen	54-1168
PLAUTZ, Matheus	28	Lachims	53-1023
PLECHEMER, Michael	22	Hetzstadt	48-0269
PLEITNER, Heinrich	23	Weissenstadt	54-0965
PLESS, Theodor	29	Hamburg/Hess.	50-0323
PLESSING, Marie	20	Steinreinaach	54-0872
PLETSCH, Johannes	23	Muekelsberge	51-0352
PLETTNER, Theodor	28	Wolfenbuettel	52-1332

NAME	AGE	RESIDENCE	YR-LIST
PLETZER, Georg	20	Gemen	53-0914
Marg. 20			
PLEUSS, Heinrich	19	Hannover	52-1362
PLISTER, Rudolph	23	Ratingen	49-0324
PLOBIG, Herm.	17	Dresden	51-1686
PLOCH, Heinrich	21	Kamrod	50-0292
PLOCH, Johann	25	Alsfeld	50-0292
PLOEGER, Joh Conr.	48	Steinburgdorf	54-0850
Ernst Heinr. 17, Anna Mar Chr 38			
Heinr Conrad 14, Hermann Hein 8, Louise 3			
PLOEGER, Lewis	46	Durlach	53-1164
PLOESSER, Georg	25	Obernzell	54-0930
PLUMP, Givert	19	New York	54-1716
Henry 24			
PLUMP, Heinrich	17	Ritterhude	51-0326
POCK, Friederike	56	Warendahl	54-1575
August 27, Otto 18, Ferdinand 15			
POCK, Friedrike	56	Wahrendahl	54-1575
August 27, Otto 18, Ferdinand 15			
POCK, H.	46		54-1716
Caroline 38, Auguste 12, Charlotte 9			
Caroline 4			
POEBEL, Johann	18	Kreutzburg	52-1464
POECKLEIN, Barbara	30	Lofeld	53-0267
POEHLER, Carl	26	Braunschweig	54-0872
POEHLER, Johanna	25	Raetzheim	54-0930
POEHLER, Johannes	43	Berghuelen	52-1200
POEHLING, Heinrich	42	Mehringen	52-1452
Marie 44, Marie 15, Elisabeth 13			
Philipp 7, Heinrich 3			
POEHLMANN, Wm. B.	19	Redwitz	53-0888
POEHLMANN, Elis.	27	Hohenberg	53-0557
POEHLMANN, Gottfr.	18	Lorenzreuth	53-0888
POEHLMANN, Johann	46	Bayern	53-0557
Eva Kunigund 38, Margrethe 20, Barbara 18			
Andreas 15, Christian 10, Wolfgang 8			
Christian 5, Abraham 3m			
POEHLMANN, Johann	40	Bayern	53-0557
Eva Kunig. 38, Margrethe 20, Barbara 18			
Andreas 15, Christian 10, Wolfgang 8			
Christian 5, Abraham 3m			
POEKEL, Julius	19	Eschwege	51-0652
Gertrude 23			
POETH, Ernst	18	Homberg	51-0405
POETSCHNER, Franz	27	Poepeln	54-0872
POGGENBURG, Geo. F	20	Barrien	54-1371
POHL, Friedrich	18	Gleimenheim	54-0830
POHLANZ, Marie	36	Steiermark	53-0267
POHLER, Joh Heinr.	18	Heepen	54-1647
POHLERT, Ludwig	28	Frille	51-1588
Christoph 13, Louisa 28, Friedrich 11m			
Christof 3			
POHLIG, Stephan	27	Meiningen	52-0895
POHLMANN, August	40	Ebersfelde	54-0600
POHLMANN, Heinr. F		Renig	49-0781
Mine 20, baby			
POINTER, Sebastian	31	Berg	54-1371
POLAND, Edward	33	Berlin	48-1243
POLCKHAUS, Gottfr.	24	Ronneburg	53-1013
Rosine 24			
POLEN, Issak L.	21	Rzchuhlau	54-1078
POLET, Marie	19	Riveling	52-1464
POLGEMEYER, C.	35	U.S.	48-1243
POLHEIM, v. August		Lennep	54-0930
POLL, Dorothea	21	Giessen	53-1086
POLLACK, Joseph	27	Lachowitz	48-1131
POLLCHRISTOFFER, H	31	Verl	52-1625
POLLITZ, Mary	20	Oldenburg	53-1164
Amanda 18			
POLMANN, Wilhelm	22	Brunswick	50-0311
POLS, Christian	14	Wannberg	48-1209
POLSCH, Anna	28	Tonnern	51-1084
POLSTER, Andreas	25	Eichstaedt/Bv	54-1092
POLSTER, Georg	19	Egloffsteinho	49-0352
POLSTER, Joh. Geo.	24	Egloffsteinho	49-0352
POLSTER, Margareth	25	Untersambach	54-0850
POLSTER, Tobias	23	Falsoe Leoe	54-1716
POLTERMANN, C.	29	Freren/Hann.	51-0048

NAME	AGE	RESIDENCE	YR-LIST
POLTZ, Johannes	48	Konnefeld	53-1000
Anna 45, Heinr. 18, Justus 15, Conr. 3			
POLZE, J. (m)	24	Vantungen	48-0453
POLZIN, Wilhelmine	27	Bremen	51-0500
POMMER, Theophilus	28	Groeningen	53-0991
POMPA, Wilhelm	26	Aergen	53-0435
Fritz 30, Georg 25			
POMPER, Augustus	29	Schneeberg	53-1164
POMPLITZ, Fried. W	37	Braunsrode	54-0903
Rosine Fried 32, Wilhelm F. 9			
Wilhelm Rob. 6, Pauline A. 2			
Wilhelm Hein by			
POOS, Heinrich	53	Darmstadt	53-1000
Marie 48, Elisab. 17			
POPHEN, Anna	30	Jever	54-0872
POPMEIER, Cath.	21	Steinbach	53-0637
POPP, Barbara	36	Ebrach	52-1200
POPP, Barbara	23	Ebnath	48-1179
POPP, Cath.	32	Taubersschenb	52-0558
POPP, George	29	Darmstadt	53-0991
POPP, Gottlieb	17	Birkenfeld	50-1132
POPP, Joh.	25	Muehlhausen	49-0352
Susanna 25, Margarethe 2			
POPP, Joh. Heinr.	25	Taunersreuth	47-0918
POPP, Johann	30	Flusnitz	54-1554
POPP, L. (m)	26	Hagenbuechen	52-0652
POPP, Marg.	36	Schneeberg	54-1575
POPP, Margaretha	20	Steinbach	53-0637
POPP, Wolf.	26	Frensdorf	52-0370
POPPE, Carl	20	Fuerstenberg	49-0574
POPPE, Ernst	17	Vollbrechshau	50-0439
POPPE, Johann	18	Linder	54-1716
POPPE, Johann	33	Lageloh	49-0742
POPPE, Johann	31	Eichenzell	54-1647
POPPE, Wilhelm	15	Vollbrechshau	50-0439
POPPEL, Simon	19	Prag	53-0473
POPPEN, Marie	25	Hannover	50-0311
POPPENBERGER, J.	22	Breitenbach	54-1575
POPPER, Emanuel	27	Raudnitz	54-1647
POPPER, Hermann	26	Prag	54-0987
Rosalie 30			
POR, Joseph	23	Philadelphia	53-1164
PORCHERT, Kunig'de	46	Furth	49-0352
PORCK, Georg	56	Schotten/Hess	52-0807
Louise 52			
PORCK, Theodor	22	Umstadt/Hess.	52-0807
PORNHAGEN, Marg.	20	Hannover	50-0021
PORSTEL, Peter	20	Otterndorf	54-0053
PORTELE, Rosalie	23	Strzitech	52-0699
PORTH, Geo. Philip	28	Eckenheim/Hes	52-0807
PORTNER, Charlotte	23	Melle	54-0872
PORTWIG, Friedrich	26	Lesering	53-0914
PORTZ, Adam	36	Rindelfeld	52-1101
PORWITH, (m)	21	Batschel	53-0914
PORZELT, Christoph	19	Cronach	53-0914
POSENER, Pauline	43	Lubatch/Pr.	54-1092
Hermann 6			
POSER, Fritz	35	Bremen	51-0500
Adelheid 25, Wilhelmine 3, Fritz 9m			
POSSAVANT, Carl	22	Frankfurt	54-1371
POST, Gottfried	56	Wuekenberg	48-0406
Ann Cathrine 50, August 21, Justine 17			
Mathilde 14, Alwine 7			
POTERING, Christ.	24	Tretterode	53-0838
POTINNS, F. (m)	37	Neusitz	50-0746
POTRIR, Charlotte	20	Kirchensitten	49-0574
POTRIR, Louis	31	Meinberg	49-0574
Charlotte 20			
POTTHARDT, Dorothe	25	Blomberg	54-1168
Amalie 21			
POTTINGER, Sebast.	44	Reichsbach	47-0918
Anna 31, Elise 10, Marie 6, Barthold 3			
Joseph 6m			
POTTS, Heinrich	44	Belm/Hann.	52-1332
Anna Marie 42, Marie Elis. 16			
Augustine 12, Elise 10, Auguste 7, Adam 5			
POTZINGER, Johann	24	Cronach	53-0825
POVESSE, Marie	48	Bahr	52-1362

NAME	AGE	RESIDENCE	YR-LIST
Franz Heinr. 19			
PRAEGER, Caroline	23	Waldkirchen	51-1035
Oswald 1			
PRAESLER, Ernst	30	Leer	51-0757
Meta 29, Marie 4			
PRAGER, Joh Friedr	25	Hegersbronn	49-0352
PRALLE, Carl	23	Bederkesa	49-0345
PRANTZ, Joseph	30	Fichtelberg	50-1236
PRASSER, Georg	38	Sarkwitz	53-0825
Therese 28, Therese 3, Franzisca 3m			
PRAUSINGER, Carl	22	Osnabrueck	47-0158
PREBUSCH, Theodor	31	Werse	51-1245
PRECHT, Charles	30	Bremen	53-0991
Ida 23			
PREDIGER, Johann	19	Coburg	50-0439
PREGNITZ, Carl	32	Lindenberg	47-0672
PREGNITZ, Chr'tine	31	Marburg	49-0324
Marthe 27			
PREGOT, August	31	Switzerland	54-1724
PREHLER, Georg	19	Salzschlirf	51-1101
PREIGER, Gustav	22	Neustadt	53-0914
PREIN, Marie	25	Hub	54-1168
PREISE, Carl	20	Frankenhausen	50-0379
PREISING, Leonhard	25	Remstadt	54-0053
PREISS, Bernhard	15	Weisslitz	54-0053
Moritz 17			
PREISS, Joseph	39	Regen	54-1341
J. (m) 13			
PREISSER, Joseph		Chum	53-0942
PRELL, Elisabeth	25	Bamberg	50-0292
PRELLBERG, Sophie	23	Schulenburg	52-0563
PRENTZEL, J.G. (f)	41	Cohler	50-0746
J. (m) 40, F. (f) 17, A. (m) 15			
H. (m) 10, B. (m) 6			
PRENTZEL, Rosine	28	Coburg	53-1013
PRENZERS, Johs.	20	Rauschenberg	52-1200
PRETTIG, Adam	18	Neustadt	53-0991
PRETZEL, Leonhard	37	Eldmann	48-0053
Elisabeth 40			
PREUN, Theodor	24	Altenluenne	53-0991
PREUSSE, Christof	40	Alberode	51-1796
Maria 30, Christine 2, Elise 7m			
PRIEBON, Gottlieb	22	Neurofelifro	53-0652
PRIGERT, Florian	33	Pulbach	53-0825
PRIGGE, Heinrich	15	Osterholz	53-1086
Rebecca 20			
PRINDER, Elisabeth	28		53-0838
PRINDER, Elisabeth	28	Echzell	53-0838
PRINZ, Andreas	30	Kirtorf	51-0352
PRINZ, Anton	22	Frankenhausen	50-0379
PRINZ, Marie	48	Mengeringhaus	49-0383
PRINZ, Melchior	28	Laibach	51-0460
Emanuel 30			
PRIOR, Gustav	26	Dortmund	51-1245
PRISTER, Herrm.	26	Detmold	51-1640
PRIX, Johann	38	Gmuenden	54-1575
Maria 58			
PROBST, Elisabeth	34	Coburg	51-0405
PROBST, Ernst	30	Greene	54-1371
PROBST, Heinrich	19	Naensen	54-1371
PROBST, Wilh.	43	Herdecke	54-0600
Louise 36, Wilh. 21			
PROBST, Wilhelm	28	Bockenheim	53-0324
Louise 25			
PROBSTER, Johann	33	Terrogsberg	54-0930
PROCHASKA, Anton	48	Austria	51-1084
PROEBENER, George	21	Scharmbeck	50-0366
PROEDEL, Johann	39	Bayern	53-1013
Anna 34, Christian 13, Sabine 9, Georg 8			
Michel 5, Ferdinand 5, Monika 6m			
PROETZ, Heinr.	29	Almerode/Pr.	51-1160
Marg. 29, Marg. 2, Anna Elise 58			
PROFETTLICH, Urban	34	Rolandswerth	51-1455
PROLERT, Joseph	21	Regen	54-1341
PROMBERGER, John	30	Wochdalaun	54-1470
PRONOLD, Marg.	25	Floetz	54-1078
PROPFE, Friedr.	66	Bremke	49-1517
Louis 21, Emilie 19, Julia 17, Carl 11			

NAME	AGE	RESIDENCE	YR-LIST
Georgina 8, Edward 6			
PROSCHINGER, Wenz.	49	Triesch	54-1371
Anna 38, Ignatz 11, Wenzel 9, Johanne 4m			
PROTH, Franz	39	Reinbeck	51-0352
Lorenz 28			
PROTT, Catharina	29	Frankfurt/M.	53-0991
PRUCHHAUSEN, Cath.	26	Kleinwichberg	49-0574
PRUEFER, Fritz	32	Leipzig	52-1101
PRUEGEL, Wilhelm	29	Gernshofen/Bv	52-1332
PRUEGER, Joh. Mich	47	Dorna	53-1013
Eva Marie 42, Johann 9, Fr. Aug 8			
Bertha 4			
PRUENERT, Gottfr.	46	Behringen	52-1304
Christiana 48, Pauline 24, Amalie 21			
Albert 18, Emilie 15, Herman 13			
Hermine 12			
PRUESCHER, Heinr.	19	Lockstedt	53-0590
PRUESER, Johannes	23	Langwedel	52-1105
Herm. 15, Herm. Friedr 23			
PRUMING, Matthias	19	Schledehausen	52-1148
PRUSCHAWER, Isak L	17	Inowraklow	53-1016
PRUTSCHER, Jos.	26	Hindelang	53-0492
PUCHEL, Johann	38	Mittelruessel	49-0737
PUCHTA, Lorenz	18	Martinlamitz	52-0351
PUCKHABER, Johann	16	Wallhofen/Han	51-1532
PUEHMER, Otto	24	Steinbachhall	53-1070
PUELL, Ernestine	29	Schleiz	52-1512
PUERRIES, H. Chr.	20	Braunschweig	49-0324
PUETKER, Eberhard	25	Leiden	50-0292
PUFF, Carl	21	Eisenberg	53-0942
PUHLHORN, Margr.	49	Keise	53-0914
Johann 24, Falk 19, Sophie 15, Mayer 10			
Friedr. 7			
PUHN, Anton	25	Schlossberg	52-1129
PUHS, Heinrich	23	Hersfeld	49-1517
PULT, Johann	19	Natzungen	53-0435
PULVERMANN, Bernh.	17	Krotoschin	53-1023
PUMPERIN, Dorothea	30	Molverstadt	51-1796
PUNDSTEIN, Ludwig	29	Salzderhelden	51-1532
PUNDT, Heinrich	20	Eckwarden	51-0460
PUPO, Aug.	27	Hameln	51-0757
Louise 28			
PURHENNE, Georg	51	Wizenhausen	54-1717
Conrad 22			
PURKNER, John	44	Kohlberg	48-0951
Brigitta 34			
PURNKER, Eva Marg.	22	Oschwitz	51-1640
PURRUCKER, Eva Cat	24	Arzberg/Bav.	53-0557
Johann bob			
PURRUCKER, Joh And	36	Weissenstadt	53-1023
Elisabeth 38, Joh. Michael 14, Barbara 9			
Margarethe 7, Johanna 6m			
PURRUCKER, Johann	28	Arzberg/Bav.	53-0557
Johann 26, Anna 30, Eva Cathrine 4			
Lorentz 6m			
PURRUCKER, Johann	26	Arzberg/Bav.	53-0557
Johann 28, Anna 30, Eva Cath. 24			
Lorentz 6m, Eva Cath. 4, son bob			
PURUZ, Franz	18	France	48-1015
PURZEL, Gertrud	22	Breitenbach	47-0918
PUTTNER, Joh Georg	30	Puchitz	48-1131
L. (f) 25, Q. (m) 14, X. (f) 10			
PUVOGEL, D. (m)	39	Harstede	52-0515
Gesina Marg. 28, Catherine 3			
PUVOGEL, Heinr.	48	Donnerstadt	52-0515
Gesina M. 42, Cath. 10, Johann 7			
Gesina 3			
PYCHLAU, H.W.	20	Riga	54-0830
QUAITSCH, Andreas	34	Klicks	49-0574
QUANK, Johann	14	Landwerhagen	53-0590
QUAST, Christine	23	Heidelberg	49-0324
QUEERNER, Heinrich	16	Muenden	53-0590
QUELL, Peter	17	Hagen	50-0366
QUENTEL, Charles	22	Duenzebach	48-0053
Julius 23			
QUENTIN, Georg	27	Goettingen	53-0991
QUENTIN, Hermann	27	Goettingen	54-1371
Elise 25, Louise 4m, Henriette 25			

NAME	AGE	RESIDENCE	YR-LIST
QUENTIN, Lisette	22	Dransfeld	48-0887
QUERNETHER, Carl H	19	Osnabrueck	48-1131
QUINT, Louis	27	Berlin	51-1245
QUIS, Wenzel	40	Nienburg	50-1067
Ludmille 34, Franz 58, Herwicke 18			
Schwadink 6, Wratika 4, Ludmilla 6m			
RAAB, Eberh.	31	Oberquembach	54-1078
Cath. 29, Georg 8, Jacob 6			
RAAB, Franz	29	Nordwalle	53-0585
Maria 30			
RAAB, Friedrich	27	Baiern	53-0324
Friederike 23			
RAABE, Elisabeth	24	Lobenhausen	54-0930
RAABE, Emilie	24	Prussia	51-1725
RAAKE, Carl	28	Bettrum/Sax.	52-1423
RAAKE, Heinrich	46	Dietzenrode	51-0048
RAAP, Jacob	24	Pirkach	53-0324
RABBA, Friedrich	22	Doehren	53-1164
RABE, Carl	28	Essen	53-1086
RABE, Friederike	30	Ehrdrissen	53-0888
RABE, G. (m)	30	Greffen	49-1358
RABE, Johann	50	Artern	50-0379
Maria Sophia 42			
RABENSTEIN, Cathr.	19	Bayern	53-0557
Christian 17			
RABENSTEIN, Christ	17	Arzberg/Bav.	53-0557
Cathrina 19			
RABENSTEIN, Conr.	26	Bayreuth	51-1245
RABERDING, Friedr.	8	Bremen	50-0021
RABICH, Henry	32	Marktstuhl	52-1304
RABITZ, Christian	30	Bilra	51-1588
RACHE, Carl	31	Seyffertsdorf	54-1566
Dorothea 54, Therese 25, Eduard 4			
Carl 9m			
RACHSCHMIDT, Chr.	31	Kempten	53-0492
RACK, Theodor	35	Appelhulsen	49-0912
Maria 26, Theodore 1			
RADECK, Charles Fr	37	Steinkunzendo	53-0582
Caroline Ch. 31, Caroline Ch. 7			
Charles Fr. 4			
RADEMACHER, J Hein	39	Bremen	50-0292
RADEMACHER, Theod.	38	Wohlau	51-1062
RADER, Gustav	18	Burscheid	54-0987
RADESTOCK, Charles	29	Halberstadt	54-1724
RADIGEN, Rosine	39	Neu Schoenfel	49-0574
RADMANN, Eduard	18	Hersfeld	51-0405
RAEBER, Philippine	2-	Muenden	49-1358
RAEDEKER, Caroline	19	Kl. Berkel	52-1304
RAEDLEIN, Adam	21	Hafenpreppach	53-0320
RAERODE, Johann	27	Severns	53-0942
Catharina 26			
RAESNER, Gustav	21	Frankenhausen	52-1105
RAESTLER, Carl	18	Schelinde	49-0574
RAETHE, J. Heinr.	43	Frielingen	54-1297
Sophie 33, Heinrich 14, Doris 11			
Friedrich 9, Wilhelm 6, August 3, Carl 9m			
RAETHER, Conr.	23	Weissenbrunn	51-1160
RAETZER, Gustav	24	Loensdorf	54-1282
RAEZEK, Joh.	41	Polna	54-1297
Marie 31, Heinrich 11, Carl 8, Gottlieb 6			
Sophie 4, Adalbert 5m			
RAFBERG, Therese	58	Chemnitz	52-1580
RAFF, Joh.	19	Esslingen	54-1371
RAFFENIER, Joseph	47	Germany	48-1243
RAFFER, Conrad	30	Eutendorf	54-1341
RAGER, Anton	31	Prag	53-1016
Theresia 29, Joseph 9, Anton 7, Tobias 2			
Carl 9m, Franzisca 5			
RAHE, J.H.(m)	21	Osnabrueck	52-1512
Maria 22			
RAHENKAMP, Eberh.	40	Schledehausen	51-1588
RAHL, Hermann	23	Versmold	53-0825
Heinrich 20			
RAHM, August	21	Roden	52-0563
RAHMM, Friedrich	38	Paris	51-0326
RAHN, Abel	27	Meiningen	52-1620
RAHN, Elisabeth	19	Halle	54-1554
RAHN, J.	55	Lenheim	51-0517

NAME	AGE	RESIDENCE	YR-LIST
RAHN, Johannes	61	Schmitte	51-1101
Heinrich 25, Christine 21, Elisabeth 2			
RAHNEFELD, A. (m)	32	Arneburg/Wuer	48-0447
RAHNER, Friedr.	25	Niederlangdor	54-1554
RAHTJE, Claus	54	Beven/Hann.	51-1725
Caroline 45, Josephine 14, Charlotte 12			
Doris 8			
RAIBEL, Joh. (m)	18	Fruchtelfinge	51-1640
Jacob 18, Heinr. 17			
RAICHEL, Anna	19	Helmbrecht	54-0930
RAILHOFER, Rosine	20	Autenz	54-1078
RAITHEL, Joh.	20	Schwarzenbach	51-1160
RALTHER, Conr.	23	Weissenbrunn	51-1160
RAMEISS, Friedrich	42	Sachs.-Gotha	50-1236
Johanne 33, Georg 16, Heinrich 13			
August 11, Louis 4, Hermann 2			
RAMENIG, Heinrich	18	Untersteinach	53-1062
RAMHOLT, Elisabeth	23	Bavaria	50-0311
RAMIEN, Ch.	25	Strichhausen	49-1358
RAMM, Wilhelm	34	Blomberg	51-0326
RAMP, G.	15	Fockenroth	51-0517
RAMPAU, Theodore	22	Braunschweig	48-1015
RAMPE, Wilhelm	20	Hoxter	49-0324
RAMS, Tillmann	20	Toenisberg	54-1371
RAMSTAEDT, Peter	34	Hessen	50-1067
Anna Maria 32			
RAMUS, Charles	18	Mittelruessel	49-0737
RANDORF, Fritz	24	Alfeld	54-1297
RANGE, Christian	50	Tringhausen	52-0563
Anna G. 50, Cath. E. 22, Johannes 20			
Elisabeth 18, Samuel 16, Georgine 14			
M. Elisabeth 12, Christian 10			
RANKE, Friedrich	24	Ljhren	47-0672
Sophia 24, Caroline 2			
RANKE, Sophia	24	Beckersdorf	47-0672
RANKOW, Elise	30	Bremen	50-1317
RANNEBERG, Heinr.	58	Hartzberg	54-1575
Wilhelmine 22, Carl 20, Friedr. 26			
RANO, Albert	18	Rippen	49-0345
RANSSEL, Dorothea	23	Waechtersbach	52-1625
RANZEN, Diedrich	23	Horsten/Hann.	54-1092
RANZMEYER, Michael	42	Linz	54-1371
Elisabeth 27, Johann 13, Joseph 5			
RAPKE, J.W. (m)	34	Hameln	47-0762
RAPLER, Heinr.	25	Rauschelshaus	54-0600
RAPP, Gottfried	33	Vaihingen	54-1168
Sophie 24, Louise 2, Wilhelmine by			
RAPP, Johann Georg	39	Feldsteten	53-0838
Anna Marie 39, Anna Marie 10, Christine 8			
RAPP, Marie	29	Augsburg/Bav.	52-1332
RAPP, Matthias	28	Bremen	54-0830
RAPPE, Chr.	16	Hannover	54-1724
Anne 18			
RAPPERT, Johann	24	Oessingen	48-1355
RASCH, Doris	25	Peine	51-0405
RASCH, Jacob	22	Budingen	49-1106
RASCH, Joh.	27	Hirschheim	54-1283
Jacob 55, Georg 26			
RASCH, Therese	36	Greisbach	54-1078
RASCHE, Heinrich	16	Grossminden	54-1717
Friederike 14			
RASCHER, Carl	31	Crimmitschau	51-1640
Herrm. 22			
RASE, Wilhelmine	28	Oldenburg	49-0345
RASIER, Michael	27	Winckels	51-1438
RASSAU, Emil	24	Bernburg	54-0987
RASSMANN, W.	31	Melzel	54-1283
RASSNER, Christ.	24	Hippoldstein	52-1129
RAST, Carl	32	Woerlitz	50-1132
Sophie 24			
RAST, Philipp	20	Erlangen	49-0574
Babette 23, Elisabeth 26			
RATENSTEDT, Andr.	28	Bayern	52-0370
RATH, G.	24	Sparnek	47-0868
RATH, Kunigunde	21	Bamberg	52-1362
RATH, Louis	19	Stolzenau/Han	54-1092
RATH, Peter	24	Coeln am Rh.	50-0292
RATHER, Franz	27	Boston	53-0914

NAME	AGE	RESIDENCE	YR-LIST
RATHGEBER, Dorothe	21	Mohrlach	54-1716
RATHGEBER, Jacob	18	Treisen	53-0161
RATHGEBER, Salomon	37	Dortrecht	49-0912
Gertrud 57			
RATHJEN, Friedrich	48	Rodewald	48-1209
Mary 50, Lewis 11, Sophia 5			
RATHMANN, Heinrich	30	Battenhaus	52-0370
RATHMANN, Wilhelm	32	Osterode	54-1591
RATHSEN, Conradine	46	Bremen	52-1661
Heinr. 20, Wilh. 16			
RATSCH, Wilhelm	25	Pretzsch	53-0652
Caroline 25			
RATZO, Wilhelm	22	Stargard	53-1000
Sophie 23			
RATZOW, Friedrich	27	Stargard	53-0905
Friederika 19			
RAU, Carl	31	Hirschberg	54-1443
RAU, Christ Adolph	25	Nuernburg	53-1016
Anna Maria 20			
RAU, Friedrich	15	Hof/Baiern	53-0475
RAU, Gustav Franz	20	Stressenhause	50-0379
RAU, H. (m)	17	Fuerth	49-0416
RAU, Joh. Michel	66	Longstein	53-1013
Heinr. 32, Johanna 36			
RAU, Johann	17	Hof/Baiern	53-0475
RAU, Joseph	22	Wohnfurt	52-0807
Benjamin 17			
RAU, Louise	49	Rothfelden	52-0095
RAU, Peter	52	Fischbach/Nas	53-0628
Elisabeth 51, Peter 14			
RAU, Samuel	17	Friesen/Bav.	53-0628
RAUCH, Christ.	21	Hof	52-1321
RAUCH, Christoph	16	Coburg	53-0324
RAUCH, Friedrich	37	Kaltensundhei	50-0323
Friedrich 25			
RAUCH, Georg	29	Prussia	54-1724
Ernst 24			
RAUCH, Margareth	61	Steinnis	54-1282
RAUCH, Maria	19	Wallis	52-1321
RAUCH, Wilhelmine	23	Nuernberg	50-1317
RAUCHFELD, Gustav	22	Zerbst	49-0324
RAUDE, Anna Elis.	23	Leiterode	54-0930
RAUE, Eliese	37	Hannover	51-0460
Dorothea 17, Gottfried 34, Wilhelm 9			
RAUH, Jacob	47	Wink	54-1078
Georg 5, Caroline 5, Anna 3, J. (m) 6m			
RAUH, Joh. Mich.	28	Fronhofen	54-1371
RAUH, Marg. Barb.	20	Oberkzau/Bav.	52-0351
RAUHE, Christ.	29	Schleiz	49-0352
RAUKE, Franz	20	Saleborn	54-1716
RAUPOLD, Anna M.	7	Holzguenz	52-1321
RAUPOLD, Walpurga	30	Halzganz	52-1321
RAUSCH, Heinrich	44	Bobenhausen	53-1023
Andreas 16, Conrad 14, Elisabeth 9			
Heinrich 8, Johannes 6			
RAUSCH, Heinrich	21	Colbe	54-0930
RAUSCH, J. (m)	30	Storndorf	52-0652
RAUSCH, Joh. Heinr	32	Heidengrun	50-1071
RAUSCH, Pauline	26	Gotha	54-0987
RAUSCHENBERG, C.J.	32	Marbach	47-0672
RAUSCHENBERG, Jos.	48	Steinbach	47-0672
RAUSCHER, Jacob	19	Cadolzburg	47-0828
RAUSCHER, Nicolaus	22	Lambrechtshau	53-0267
Margaretha 48, Catharina 27, Caroline 24			
Susanna 26, Caroline 4, Andr. (died) 10m			
Carl (died) 2			
RAUSER, Basilius	27	Alendorf/Wrt.	54-1092
RAUSER, Leopold C.	25	Wuerttemberg	54-1092
RAUSSEL, Dorothea	23	Waechtersbach	52-1625
RAVE, Gerd	15	Meyerburg	50-1067
RAVENSBERG, Wilh.	24	Glinde	49-0345
RAVENSBURG, Anna	19	Bremervoerde	52-0807
RAVENSBURG, Nics.	21	Beversfleth	52-1512
RAYT, Ludw. Heinr.	54	Lingen	50-0292
REBEL, Catharina	21	Freirittenbac	48-1179
REBELE, Joseph	20	Wolferstadt	52-0279
REBER, Catharina	15	Tollnusshoff	51-0384
Genoveva 26			

NAME	AGE	RESIDENCE	YR-LIST
REBHAHN, John	18	Coburg	50-0840
REBNER, Joh. D.	51	Schoenbade	51-1160
Carl 20, Friedr. 17, Rosine 45, Hanna 23			
Caroline 12, August 7			
REBRECHT, Carl	27	Halle	49-1358
RECH, John James	12	Bundenbach	53-0991
RECKAM, Adolphus	34	Osnabrueck	50-0840
RECKENBEIN, Marg.	26	Herrenreitung	53-1062
RECKNAGEL, Johann	38	Obersteinbach	51-1062
Mar. Salome 36, Cath. Marie 9			
Caroline by			
REDE, N. (m)	34	Lichtenberg	50-0746
REDEMANN, August	28	Warburg	48-0269
REDEMANN, Wilh.	21	Klanstreet	52-1661
REDER, Claus	25	Staphorst	49-0912
REDER, Nicolaus	30	Hafferstedt	50-0472
REDLICH, Albert	24	Austria	53-0628
REDLICH, Marie	20	Muenchen	54-1297
REDLICH, Otto	23	Chemnitz	54-1297
REDO, J. Chr.	45	Prussia	49-0383
REDTKAM, Therese	30	Mauchen	49-0912
Thekla 5, Appolonia 3			
REDWITZ, B. (f)	23	Walsdorf	47-0868
REED, Andrew	27	Gt. Britain	48-1015
REED, Mrs.	31	Gt. Britain	48-1243
REER, Joseph	32	Berghorst	53-0585
REES, Anna Cath.	19	Koeppel	53-1070
REESE, Carl	27	Bibra	52-1148
Ernestine 33			
REESE, H.F.	30	Pagesloaf	54-1470
REESE, Herm. Aug.	23	Todenmann	52-0563
REESE, Joh Heinr.	30	Riepen	50-1132
REGAMB, Bernh.	19	Boitzenburg	52-1512
REGEINHART, F. (m)	26	Fredine	54-1341
REGEL, Georg	19	Cronach	53-0825
REGELUM, John	40	Dorfgutinger	52-0515
REGENSBURGER, Geo.	28	Laubregen	53-1164
Catharina 26			
REGGEMANN, Ger.	25	Hoerstel	48-0269
REGIES, Joh Ulrich	28	Egloffsheim	54-0987
REGLE, Georg	27	Schmehingen	54-1282
REGNER, Friederike	21	Bayern	53-0557
REGNER, Joseph	25	Bertusgaren	47-0672
REGNET, Michael	29	Aschbach	52-1464
Marianne 28, Georg 8, Kunigunde 5			
Joseph 3, Joh. 2, baby 4w, Franz 27			
REGUS, Joh. Ulrich	28	Egloffsheim	54-0987
REHBACKER, Joseph	31	Schomburg	54-1591
Barbara 33, Johanna 8, Mary 6, Joseph 3			
Anna 11m			
REHBEIN, August	23	Carlshofen	53-1062
REHBEIN, Johannes	60	Vatterode	54-0850
Margaretha 48			
REHBEIN, Maria	16	Vatterode	54-0850
REHBOHN, Fr.	20	Celle	51-1084
REHDANTZ, Charles	22	Mehmels	53-0582
REHFUSS, Matth.	32	Sulz	51-1640
REHKLAU, Michael	30	Arlesried	49-0365
REHKOPF, Ernst	25	Goettingen	50-0021
REHL, Georg	22	Schauberg	53-1013
REHLING, Diedrich	19	Ilvese	48-1179
REHLING, E. Maria	35	Riepen	47-0672
Conrad 10, Hermann 7			
REHLING, Friedrich	25	Kreienhagen	52-1452
Elise 26			
REHM, Augustin	33	Burggriesbach	49-0365
Regine 25, Regine 35			
REHM, Carl August	26	Memmingen	50-1071
REHM, Caroline	26	Gersfeld	53-1023
REHM, Conrad	42	Voellinghause	52-1423
REHM, Johannes	21	Frankenheim	54-1371
REHMANN, Maria	24	Istrup/Pr.	54-0965
REHMKE, Catharine	22	Brodersdorf	54-1297
REHMKEN, G.H.	23	Farven	54-0918
REHSE, Heinrich	26	Riepen	50-1132
REHZE, Sebandr.	35	Seebach	51-1455
Martha 30, Bernard 5, Wm. 1			
REIBER, Elisabeth	23	Magdlos	51-0352

NAME	AGE	RESIDENCE	YR-LIST
REIBSTEIN, Georg	40	Heringen	52-0370
REICH, Heinrich	21	Prussia	50-0021
REICH, Kunigunde	11	Weissbrunn	48-0101
REICHARD, Chr.	20	Ostheim	49-0574
REICHARD, Friedr.	24	Cassel	52-0699
Dorothea 23, Gertrude 2, Christian 9m			
REICHARD, Johannes	22	Oberaula	54-1566
REICHARDT, Adolph	23	Muehlhausen	53-1070
Elise 24, Carl 5m			
REICHARDT, Caspar	52	Dreffurt	53-1070
Georg 18			
REICHARDT, J.	22	Sehautn	51-0517
REICHAUF, Georg	19	Coburg	53-0585
REICHE, August	29	Gruenenplan	53-0435
August 16			
REICHE, Heinrich	18	Gruenenplan	52-0279
REICHE, Heinrich	45	Gruenenplan	51-0352
REICHE, Heinrich	18	Gruenenplan	54-1371
REICHE, Hermann	18	Gruenenplan	54-1575
August 16			
REICHEL, Caroline	51	Nyskey	49-0383
E. 10, Antonia 24			
REICHEL, Ignatz	68	Berlin	48-1243
REICHEL, Johann	18	Wasserkurt	52-1332
Dorothea 27			
REICHEL, Johannes	28	Biberach	53-0557
REICHEL, Johannes	28	Biberbach	53-0557
REICHEL, Joseph	23	Bergatreite	51-0352
REICHEL, Katharine	23	Geisberg	53-0435
REICHEL, Louise	24	Muenchberg	53-1062
REICHENBACH, Fried	24	Scharmbeck	51-1101
REICHENBECHER, T.	28	Warnstein--dt	50-0746
REICHENBERGER, Mic	29	Kirmhess	52-1200
REICHENEDER, M.(m)	27	Schwarach	54-1341
Mary 27, baby 6m			
REICHENICKER, Joh.	45	Sundelfing/Wu	52-0351
Dorothea 44, Regina 18, Joh. Michael 13			
Barbara 8, Dorothea 2			
REICHERL, Charles	25	Lengfeld	54-1724
Bertha 32, Charles 4, Lina 6m			
REICHERS, A.	21	Clausthal	54-1419
REICHERT, Benj.	44	Goetringen/Wu	52-0960
REICHERT, Christ.	31	Carlsruhe	54-0987
REICHERT, Elise	25	Hofgeismar	51-1062
Louise 3, Carl 15m			
REICHERT, Franz'ka	38	Rengensricht	52-1464
REICHERT, Gottlieb	2-	Bersten	49-1358
REICHERT, Gottlieb	25	Carwusen	50-0840
REICHERT, Jacob	21	Odenstadt	54-0053
REICHERT, Johanne	21	Weimar/Sachs.	51-1725
REICHERT, Julius	27	Fuerth	54-1297
REICHERT, Mathias	44	New York	54-1297
REICHHARD, Marie	24	Cassel	52-1410
REICHHOF, Ernst C.	19	Chrislos	51-1062
REICHL, Barbara	21	Neudorf	54-0965
REICHL, Joh.	31	Niederkaufung	54-1078
REICHLOHEN, Marg.	19	Neubrunn	49-1358
REICHMANN, Elis.	27	Willsdorf/Pr.	53-0475
REICHMANN, Jacob	28	Landsberg	52-1625
REICKERT, Christ.	23	Perka	50-0311
REID, Johanna	28	Schweinfurt	50-1317
REIDEKE, Carl	54	Roden/Waldeck	54-1092
Caroline 27			
REIDEL, Lorenz	16	Schwarzenbach	53-0475
REIF, Caroline	18	Salzingen	53-0324
REIF, Friedrich	28	Sinterfingen	53-1070
REIF, Johann	28	Baiern	53-1070
Margarethe 25			
REIF, Mary A.	37	Steinhart	48-0951
Michael 17, Andrew 15, George 9			
Margreth 12			
REIF, Math.	37	Baiern	52-0370
REIFENSEN, H.	22	Gunzenhausen	54-1419
REIL, Johannes	26	Niederohmen	52-1452
REIM, August	39	Eckartsberge	48-1355
REIM, Johann	25	Allendorf	51-0460
REIMALD, Cath.	17	Cassel	52-1321
REIMANN, Christine	22	Naumburg	51-0352

NAME	AGE	RESIDENCE	YR-LIST
Louise 26			
REIMANN, Emma	17	Naumburg	54-1078
Caroline 19			
REIMANN, Georg	23	Augsfeld	51-0352
REIMANN, Johann	21	Forme	49-0742
REIMANN, Nicolaus	22	Sachs.-Altenb	54-0903
REIMANN, Thomas	26	Canton Aargau	51-1245
REIMBOLT, Paul	30	Muenchen	48-0101
REIMDIECK, Wilhelm	22	Halle/Pr.	52-0960
REIMER, August	19	Rodenberg	48-1114
REIMER, Gottlob	28	Tilsit	54-1452
Amalie 29, Emma by			
REIMERS, Sophia	23	Raden	51-0326
Caroline 21			
REIMERS, Wilhelmne	70	Hanover	51-0500
REIMKE, Gerhard	22	Luenninghause	54-0882
REIMUND, Therese	22	Langenzlau	48-0951
REINATH, Wilhelm	21	Winterhingen	49-0574
REINBACH, Jacob	21	Iba	54-0930
REINBACKEL, G. (m)	24	Leitz	52-0652
REINBOLD, Constant	42	Neustadt	48-0406
REINBOTT, Wilhelm	17	Hessen	53-0590
REINCKIN, Marie	20	Oldenburg	49-0329
REINDEL, Lorenz	34	Moosburg	52-1200
Catharina 27			
REINDEL, Philipp	25	Erlangen	52-1200
REINDERS, Trina	24	Danner	52-0048
REINECKE, Carl	34	Weiningen	54-1371
Johanne 28, Heinrich 4, Minna by			
REINECKE, Chr.	17	Schweina	54-0987
REINECKE, Wilhelm	22	Severns	53-0942
REINEKE, Heinr.	26	Dreye	52-1105
REINEKE, Sophie		Bassum	50-0323
REINEMANN, Georg	28	Barken	53-1013
REINEMANN, Moses	17	Altenmuhr	51-1160
REINER, Franz	43	Schoffstadt	49-1106
REINER, Levi	23	Vo--fen	52-0279
REINERS, Bruene	25	Uphusen	53-0991
REINERS, Caroline	22	Rahden	50-0292
REINERS, Claus Alb	22	Uthlede	53-0991
REINERS, Heinrich	21	Lilienthal/Ha	52-1620
REINERT, Adalbert	29	Grossenlutter	50-0323
REINERT, August	21	Naensen	52-1304
Christian 33			
REINERT, Johann	24	Chovtau	54-1649
Henriette 22			
REINFELDER, Max	33	Muenchen	54-1452
Arminia 27			
REINHARD, Amalie	18	Gruenenplan	51-1438
REINHARD, Babette	20	Lichtenfels	51-0405
REINHARD, Barbara	30	Arnshausen	49-0912
REINHARD, Carl	21	Bingstaedt	52-1321
REINHARD, Christ.	36	Trier	50-0366
Dorothea 23			
REINHARD, Dorothy	21	Ottervind	53-0582
REINHARD, Georg	21	Beyersdorf	52-1148
REINHARD, Heinrich	48	Sudwalde	51-1062
Margarethe 47, Johann 23, Wilhelmine 20			
Magdalene 17, Sophie 14, Adelheid 11			
Friedrich 9, Margarethe 5			
REINHARD, Johann	28	Witzmansberg	53-0637
REINHARD, Mariane	25	Waldueren	52-1101
REINHARD, Melchior	37	Scheinbach	54-0930
Christine 36, Therese 7, Ernestine 4			
Auguste 3, Abraham 20			
REINHARD, Moritz	17	Rosa	49-0781
REINHARD, Peter	25	Armshausen	49-0912
REINHARD, Valentin	25	Busselheim/Bv	47-0987
REINHARD, Wilhelm	29	Neuwied/Prss.	52-1332
REINHARDT, Anna	29	Limbach	54-1554
REINHARDT, Carl	24	Islau	53-1000
Margarethe 20			
REINHARDT, Eva Mar	24	Dorfgutingen	53-0590
REINHARDT, Ferd.	42	Neuschoenfeld	49-0574
REINHARDT, George	37	Lichtenau	54-0987
REINHARDT, H(died)	50	Guenzerode	54-1554
Christ. 26, Maria 23, Friederike 18			
Auguste 13			

NAME	AGE	RESIDENCE	YR-LIST
REINHARDT, J. Mich	25	Lehrberg	54-1566
REINHARDT, Johanna	19	Burgheim	54-1168
Josepha 16			
REINHARDT, Louis	21	Steinfurth	50-1132
Carl 19			
REINHARDT, Rebecca	20	Lengsfeld	52-1321
REINHARDT, William	18	Neustadt	53-0991
REINHOLD, Eduard	20	Hamburg	54-0872
REINHOLD, Justus	19	Bremervoerde	54-1297
REINHOLT, Gottlieb	21	Seeling	54-1676
REINIKE, Joseph	40	Nieheim	51-1101
REINING, Elisabeth	32	Ruppertenroth	51-0500
Johannes 14, Johann 9m			
REINISCH, Ludw.	24	Obbach	52-1321
REINKEN, Heinrich	20	Leste	49-0324
REINKEN, Magdalene	37	Leeste	47-0828
Albert 6, Johann 1			
REINKER, Catharine	23	Holte	54-0872
REINKING, Auguste	21	Nordhammern	53-0888
REINLEIN, Leonhard	32	Ansbach	54-1566
Marie 24			
REINSCHMIDT, Simon	25	Ottersweier	53-1164
REINSHSMA, M. (m)	33	Oldersum	52-1148
REIS, Johann	24	Bayern	53-1013
REISBERGER, Georg	19	Boxdorf	52-0693
Magdalena 33, Magdalena 9			
REISCHER, Eberhard	31	Verba	52-1362
REISCHLER, Martha	23	Mittelruessel	49-0737
REISENHOFER, Peter	30	Graetz	51-0500
REISIGER, Margaret	22	Lengsfeld	49-0413
REISING, Friedrich	21	Minden	53-0473
REISLER, M.	22	Hofstein	54-1419
REISNER, Gottl.	40	Weisenne	54-1575
REISNER, Johann	25	Gerlingen	49-1106
REISS, F.	24	Rhueme	50-0840
Ann 26			
REISS, Marg. Clem.	21	Erbach	54-1566
REISS, Rosine	20	Alstadt	51-1588
REISSBERGER, Mand.	38	Mittelruessel	49-0737
REISSER, Kunig.	24	Weingarts	52-0693
REISSER, Maria	31	Leutkirch	52-1580
REISSHAUER, Louis	26	Prussia	54-1724
REISSNER, Conrad	56	Bensen	51-1084
REISTBERGER, Mart.	32	Rieselback	48-0951
Barb. 32			
REIT, S.	42	Wuettenfingen	52-1661
Josepha 35, Joseph 11, Michael 8			
Varena 7			
REITEMEYER, Friedr	38	New York	51-0048
REITEN, Mah.	33	Obermeyershei	47-0868
REITEN, Maria	25	Wolffstein	54-1094
REITER, M.	24	Unteressen	54-1419
REITER, Margaretha	44	Hoehringen	53-0838
REITH, Anna	27	Kappel	54-0918
REITH, Joseph	26	Elters	51-0500
REITH, L. (m)	27	Hattenbach	52-0652
REITH, Margareth	21	Deidershausen	51-1455
REITH, Peter	20	Grossenlueder	54-1554
REITH, Victoria	24	Deiningen	54-0903
REITHEL, Elisabeth	27	Markschrey	52-1362
REITS, Johann	19	Franzenburg	50-0366
REITZ, Conrad	55	Holzheim	54-0830
Conrad 18, Theodor 16, Heinrich 9			
Juliana 42, Susanna 22, Catharina 15			
Margarethe 6			
REITZ, G.H.		Bernhausen	54-1575
REITZ, Peter	47	Holzheim	54-0830
Johannes 20, Conrad 18, Catharine 47			
Catharina 16, Susanne 12, Adam 10			
Margarethe 2			
REITZ, v. Heinr.	45	Lauterbach	51-1101
REIZENSTEIN, Selig	20	Muehlhausen/B	52-0351
REMBALDT, Christof	27	Wuertenberg	53-0557
REMBOLDT, Christof	27	Wuertt	53-0557
REMERT, Hermann	21	Boge	54-1452
REMME, G.H. (m)		Engter	48-0445
REMMERS, H.W.	31	Mariensiel	53-1164
Catharina 27			

NAME	AGE	RESIDENCE	YR-LIST
REMMERT, Carl	32	Minden	52-1410
REMMLER, Wilhelm	24	Brome	53-0652
REMOLI, Heinrich	27	Gewenitz	53-0652
Auguste 23, Dorothea 1, Friedrich 24			
REMP, Jacob	32	Leonberg/Wuer	52-0351
Friederike 30, Friederike 5, Gottlieb 3			
Maria (died) 6m			
REMP, Maria	25	Natzungen/Pr.	51-1725
REMPE, Johann	20	Natzugen	53-0435
REMPF, Johann	28	Neuses	53-0825
Margarethe 24, Conrad 2			
RENBACH, Martha El	22	Iba	54-0930
RENDINGS, Caroline	18	Brinkum	51-0405
RENG, Christian	21	Schaffhausen	52-0370
RENGSHAUSEN, Conr.	30	Nidda	48-1131
RENILLA, Antoinett	35	Teesen	54-1078
RENJES, Beta	18	Schiffdorf/Ha	54-1092
RENK, Fridolin	35	Herthen	52-1625
RENKE, Rosalie	36	Schlawenitz	51-0757
RENKEN, Heinrich	24	Horsten/Hann.	54-1092
RENKEN, Johann	17	Langenhusen	50-0292
RENNEMANN, Wilhelm	21	Korbach	52-0095
Margarethe 26, Wilhelmine 23			
RENNER, C. (m)	21	Reichenbach	49-0383
RENNER, Eduard	20	Jena	53-0492
RENNER, Joh.	24	Reichhardshof	49-1106
Stephen 17			
RENNER, John	18	Coburg	50-0840
RENNER, Theo. Ern.	26	Jena	53-0991
RENNERT, Henry	30	Salzufeln/Lip	51-0048
RENNERT, Mich.	23	Winghausen/He	52-0960
RENSEL, Conrad	26	Hameln	51-0352
RENZ, Andreas	25	Ermmingen	49-0574
RENZAK, Stephan	28	Stettin	49-0352
REPLITZ, Joh. G.	28	Siegelsdorf	51-1160
Marg. 26			
RERN, Catharina	50	Robern	51-0384
Michael 29, Auguste 21, Famingus (f) 11m			
August 18, Johann 15			
RESE, Lina	23	Misselwarm	52-1580
RESEMANN, Wilh.	22	Bringhausen	54-0600
Gertrud 23, Heinr. 6m			
RESNER, Gehardine	52	Alsfeld	54-0830
RESSLER, Kunigunde	54	Rottenshein	54-0930
RESSNER, Anton	43	Bergmann	54-1591
RETTER, Emma	18	Winterbach	54-0987
RETTER, F. (f)		Regensburg	53-0888
RETTEWITT, Wilh.	16	Baden	54-1724
RETTING, Friedrich	28	Redewisch	54-1297
RETZ, Justine	16	Cloppenburg	50-1067
RETZIG, And.	25	Anhalt	51-1160
REUBOLD, Eva M.	23	Stockheim	53-0991
REUER, Balthasar	23	Ulfen	54-1168
REUHLE, David	24	Wallenstadt/W	52-1332
REULEIN, Anna	18	Lesering	53-0914
Marie 14			
REULEIN, Barbara	32	Lemmingen	50-0840
John 28			
REUMANN, Heinrich	35	New York	48-0887
REUNINGER, Georg	36	Schwabach/Bav	52-1423
Margarethe 32			
REUS, J.	26	Licht	51-0517
REUSCHEL, Christ.	24	Blankenheim	52-1101
REUSCHEL, Loise(m)	23	Cronigfeld	52-1101
Christian 24			
REUSCHLER, Michael	30	Wuertt.	54-1724
Barbara 28, Joseph 9, Adam 7, Anne 4			
Barbara 9m			
REUSENER, Ernst	31	Nordholz/Lipp	51-1725
REUSENWEBER, Nicol	28	Wirlsdorf	50-0840
REUSS, Adam	31	Keldingsdorf	50-0840
Barbara , Anna			
REUSS, Anna	25	Schellenberg	51-1160
Georg 9m			
REUSS, Heinrich	22	Liech	53-1000
REUTEL, Wilhelmine	23	Grabzow	54-0872
REUTEN, M. (f)	25	Batfram	48-0453
REUTER, Carl	32	Greiffenstein	49-0574

NAME	AGE	RESIDENCE	YR-LIST
Catharine 8			
REUTER, Conrad	20	Cassel	52-0699
REUTER, Daniel	42	Breitenbach	52-1105
Albertine 46, Elisabeth 18, Georg 9			
Heinr. 5			
REUTER, Doroth.	5-	Ade--msbg.	50-0439
Johann 25, Peter 17, Hans 16, Rob. by			
REUTER, Felix	26	Wiesenscharte	52-0279
REUTER, Ferdinand	34	Berlin	54-1452
Friederike 50			
REUTER, Fritz	23	Aerzen	53-0435
REUTER, Herbert	48	Hochheim	50-0840
Catharine 46, Henry 14			
REUTER, Johannes	22	Edesheim	52-1200
REUTER, Margarethe	56	Sulingen	53-1000
REUTER, Michael	23	Gerrelshofen	50-0323
REUTER, Valentin	25	Finkler	52-0370
REUTER, Wilhelm	22	Melle	52-1512
REUTHEL, Marg.	28	Egloffsheim	54-0987
REUTNER, Lucas	31	Eltmannshause	51-1686
REUTPATH, H. (m)	30	Kleinern	54-1566
REUTTER, Barbara	23	Lindenau	53-0320
REUTTER, Sal. (m)	18	Heinsforth	51-1796
REWE, Gertrud	23	Bromskirchen	53-0492
REWERTS, Fritz	31	Emden	50-1067
REY, Cyrus	29	New York	48-1015
REYBOER, Matheus	51	Portslut	49-0912
Mantze 39, Jan 24, Machiline 9			
Janne Cath. 11m			
REYMER, Christian	24	Gothenberg	54-0987
REYNMUELLER, Joh.	24	Stargard/Pr.	54-1092
Auguste 17			
RHADE, Joh.	18	Fuhrbach	51-1084
RHEIN, Louise	23	Amoeneburg	54-1566
RHEIN, Peter	18	Germany	50-0472
RHEKOPF, Georg	22	Altona	50-0366
RHINO, Julius	23	Frankfurt	50-0311
RHODE, Adolfine	26	Luede/Pr.	52-1620
RHODE, Friedrich	24	Minden/Hann.	52-1620
RHODE, Heinrich	20	Neuenkirchen	50-0366
RHOEDER, Michel	40	Bayern	53-1013
Anna 37, Anna 6, Sabine 4, Catharine 6m			
RHUEDEN, Jos. V.	48	Heerdorf	51-1084
Johann 24, Anton 18, Theresia 16			
Friederike 12, Maria 9, Agate 50			
RIACGG, Ludwig	24	Thuestingen	54-1717
RIBBE, Friedrich	18	Trarbach/Pr.	54-1092
RICHARD, C.B. (m)	34	New York	51-0352
RICHARD, Johann	30	Strutt	52-0563
Therese 29, Michael 26, Catharine 3			
Barbara 9m			
RICHARD, Luise	21	Volkershausen	54-0918
RICHARDS, F.B.	38	New York	48-1015
RICHARDT, Heinr. C	25	Treffurt	54-1297
Anna 24			
RICHART, H.	28	Halberstadt	54-1470
RICHEL, Wm.	29	Hessen	53-1013
Elisabeth 26, Johannes 6m			
RICHERT, Friedrich	26	Scharel	48-0284
RICHHAUS, Peter	40	Marienfeld	52-1512
RICHTER, Adolph	30	Schoenwalde	54-1649
RICHTER, Anton	39	Walawitz	47-0672
Barbara 37, Anna 14, Leodewila 11			
Elisabeth 7, Anton 3			
RICHTER, Carl	23	Breidenbach/S	53-0475
RICHTER, Charlotte	21	Blomberg	54-1168
RICHTER, Christian	27	Dillenburg	52-1101
RICHTER, Christine	26	Blomberg	54-1168
RICHTER, Elias	25	Noerdlingen	54-1168
Wilhelm 15			
RICHTER, Emma	24	Pforzheim	53-1086
RICHTER, Fr. J.		Geisselbach	54-1575
RICHTER, Francisca	21	Grossendorf/H	51-1532
RICHTER, Friedr. A	33	Leipzig	53-1023
RICHTER, Friedrich	32	Sachsen	53-0652
RICHTER, Gottlieb	22	Grossau	54-0882
RICHTER, Gustav	17	Selchow	54-1168
RICHTER, Gustav	44	Dresden	48-1209

NAME	AGE	RESIDENCE	YR-LIST
RICHTER, Heinrich	27	Muenster	51-1101
RICHTER, Helene	26	Hannover	49-0329
Gottlieb 4			
RICHTER, J. Traug.	23	Krohle	54-1168
RICHTER, Jacob	26	Elingrode	52-1362
Maria 25, Eduard 9m			
RICHTER, Johann	22	Kirchendorf	53-0590
RICHTER, Johann	40	Wistenzellwit	53-0652
Catharine 31, Christian 13, Margarethe 9			
Elisabethe 4			
RICHTER, Johann	22	Strutt	52-0563
Gertrud 22			
RICHTER, Joseph	19	Saaldorf	53-0267
Johanne 21			
RICHTER, Joseph	40	Austria	50-1317
RICHTER, Julius	13	Petershausen	53-1023
RICHTER, Kath.	17	Regensfeld	54-1554
Anna 15			
RICHTER, Wilhelm	49	Regensfeld	54-1554
Johann 19, Catharine 21, Margarethe 47			
Anna 46			
RICHTUNG, Friedr.	24	Tanne	47-0762
RICK, Fr.	21	Brake	49-1358
RICK, Georg	17	Sachsen	53-0590
Margaret 36			
RICK, Joseph	29	Forbach	53-0928
Seraphina 20, Catharina			
RICK, Lorenz	31	Ebersporn	53-0928
Friedrike 29, Maria 9, Fris. 18m			
RICK, Seraphina	20	Hundsbach	53-0928
RICKEL, Adr.	26	Bamberg	50-1071
RICKELS, Heinrich	28	Cappel-Altend	50-0366
RICKENBERG, Henry	26	Bissendorf	48-0951
RICKER, Margaretha	30	Andervenne	54-0053
RICKERT, Gustav	25	Rottorf	48-1355
RIEBEL, Bernhard	28	Hohentann	52-0095
RIEBEL, Christian	40	Floth	52-0095
Margaretha 36, Salome 9			
RIEBELING, Heinr.	15	Hengsberg	54-0930
RIECHARD, Geo Hein	16	Neukirchen	52-1105
RIECHEIMER, Rosa	24	Aschenhausen	48-1114
Regina 23			
RIECHERS, Johannes	22	Hohenassel/Br	51-1725
RIECHMANN, Friedr.	25	Pr. Minden	53-0267
RIECK, Christiane	39	Vorderburg/Bv	49-0365
Christiane 9			
RIECKE, Luise	25	Goettingen	50-0021
RIECKE, Wilhelm	19	Muenster	49-1358
RIED, Juliane	25	Nidda	53-1164
RIED, Ludwig	27	Hofgeismar/He	51-1532
Luise 28			
RIED, Peter	34	Friedewald	52-1661
RIED, Rosina	25	Friedrichsdor	51-0384
RIEDEL, August	19	Berlin	53-1164
RIEDEL, Barbara	30	Baiern	54-1724
RIEDEL, Cath.	21	Walkofen	54-1282
RIEDEL, Charles	44	Trebbin	53-1164
RIEDEL, Joh Caspar	35	Zughofstetten	53-0825
RIEDEL, Joh Jacob	27	Langenlaube	54-0930
RIEDEL, Joh.	38	Kairlindach	52-0693
RIEDELBAUCH, Sigm.	32	Hoeschstedt	53-0825
Eva 23			
RIEDEN, Friedrich	16	Bremervoerde	51-1035
RIEDER, Augustus	27	Hofkalbsburg	50-0840
Hermann 25, Trina 23			
RIEDER, E.	21	Stetten	53-0492
RIEDER, Friedrich	19	Raitzenhayer	48-1184
RIEDER, Johanna	38	Drossenhausen	52-1512
Juliana 45			
RIEDER, Stephania	20	Waldkirch	51-1455
RIEDERER, Paul	28	Donau	53-0905
Maria 26			
RIEDERER, T. (f)	28	Regensburg	53-0888
RIEDIGER, Christ.	28	Wieblingen	51-0460
RIEDLINGER, Xaver	31	Wasserburg/Bv	54-1452
Marie 28			
RIEDMANN, Cath.	21	Osnabrueck	52-1512
RIEF, Gottlieb	23	Drieburg	52-0370

NAME	AGE	RESIDENCE	YR-LIST
RIEGEL, Anton	26	Adelgosslitz	50-0439
RIEGELER, Anna	32	Wien	53-0888
RIEGER, Anton	26	Schlesien	52-1620
RIEGER, Egidius	36	Ansbach	54-1566
RIEGER, Joh. Heinr	34	Falkenburg	54-0987
RIEGER, Vinz	27	Ruppesdorf	53-0928
RIEHL, Barbara	22	Grossenglis	52-0775
RIEHL, Friedrich	21	Cassel/Hessen	51-1725
RIEHL, Fritz	21	Hagen	50-1067
RIEHM, Friedrich	31	Moringen	52-1625
RIEHME, Johanne	44	Camenz	54-1297
RIEKE, Gertrude	27	Bekum	51-1035
RIELAG, Franz	28	Osnabrueck	52-1105
Anna 31			
RIEM, Chr.	18	Siebenstein	52-0960
RIEM, Heinrich	27	Borstel	48-1131
RIEMANN, Alb.	30	Weissenfels	54-1078
Caroline 27			
RIEMANN, Caspar	21	Rotenburg	54-1649
RIEMANN, Clemens	38	Alfhausen	49-0329
RIEMANN, H. (m)	23	Berlin	50-0311
RIEMANN, Ludwig	21	Langenberg	53-0585
RIEMEKASTON, Augte	30	Gunstedt	54-1371
Carl 7			
RIEMEN, Martin	34	Grebenstein	50-1067
RIEMEN, Philippina	28	Steinberg	52-1321
RIEMENSCHNEIDER, A	23	Nordhausen	49-0737
RIEMENSCHNEIDER, F	27	Eimbeck	53-0991
RIEMENSCHNEIDER, G	30	Eimbeck	53-0991
RIEMENSCHNEIDER, L	28	Alipsen	53-1000
RIEMSCHNEIDER, Joh	19	Wabern	51-0460
RIEMSCHNEIDER, Lud	38	Blankenbach	52-1148
Elisabeth 31			
RIEMSCHNEIDER, Wm.	33	Neukirchen	54-1078
Henriette 34			
RIENACKER, Carolin	39	Tanne	48-1179
Emilie 20			
RIENACKER, E. (m)	54	Tanne	47-0762
Elisabeth 30, Ernst 12, Henriette 10			
Carl 8			
RIENECKER, Johann	20	Wiesenfeldt	53-1062
RIENFANG, Johann	28	Sensler	47-0672
RIEPE, Casper Hein	19	Poedinghausen	53-1062
Hanna Fried. 20, Betha Heinr. 9			
Anna Marie 25, Anna 49			
RIER, E.	16	Bremerhaven	53-0914
J.P. 18			
RIES, Carl	28	Pettendorf	51-0517
RIES, Charles	35	Wiesbaden/Nas	48-0447
RIES, Joh.	30	Kuehlenfels	52-0693
RIES, Johann	20	Bayern	53-0557
RIES, Johann	20	Arzberg/Bav.	53-0557
RIES, Johann	17	Pommersfeld	47-0918
RIES, Mathias	39	Forkenhofen	53-0991
Josepha 23			
RIESCHE, August	23	Hannover	54-1566
RIESE, Ernst	24	Forste	50-1071
RIESE, Friedrich	36	Zeitz	52-1512
RIESENBACH, Johann	30	Muelheim	49-0324
RIESENBECK, Chr.	28	Oldenburg	50-1317
RIESENER, Friedr.	19	Fuerth/Bav.	51-1725
RIESENWETTER, Casp	23	Roetha	53-0267
RIESLING, Johann	19	Quellenreuth	52-0351
RIESS, Dietrich	21	Gunzenhausen	53-0905
RIESS, Johanne	27	Wunsiedel	47-0868
RIESS, Peter F.	25	Fliede	52-1625
RIETHAMBER, Maria	50	Osnabrueck	52-1512
RIETHMANN, Dorothe	19	Nordheim	52-1105
RIETHMANN, Maria	28	Osnabrueck	52-1512
RIETZEL, C. (m)	48	Gr. Glogau	50-0746
E. (f) 47, G. (f) 9, F. (m) 3			
RIEVE, Carl	28	Barmen	48-0565
Elise 28			
RIEXINGER, Johann	21	Suppingen	52-1200
RIFFMEYER, G. (m)	28	Recke	48-0445
RIHA, Wenzel	45	Kopullo	54-1647
Maria 33, Wenzel 5			
RIMBACH, Conrad	23	Aufenau	53-0435

NAME	AGE	RESIDENCE	YR-LIST
RIMBACH, Martin	19	Blankenbach	48-0284
RIMBACH, Rosalie	42	Halle	54-0987
RIMMEL, C. (m)	38	Bernbach	48-0445
H. (f) 36, M. (f) 5			
RINCH, Johannes	31	Kl. Altenstad	49-0574
Catharina 26			
RINCK, Reinhard	57	Wahlhausen	54-0872
Margareth 54, Eduard 21, Alexander 20			
Emil 3, Louise 24			
RINCKE, Julie	32	Stadtilm	48-1179
Dorothee 32, Caroline 12, Therese 8			
Henriette 4			
RINDELAUB, Conrad	15	Frankenberg	53-1016
RINDL, Joseph	58	Pasberg	53-0825
RINDLER, Babette	22	Wolitz	54-1647
Abraham			
RING, Friedrich	35	Dothen	52-1200
RING, Johann		Frischborn	54-1575
RING, Leonore	28	Empfingen	52-0279
RINGBACH, Johann	45	Dietz	53-0825
RINGE, Christ.	26	Daspe	50-1132
RINGE, J. (m)	23	Hanstadt	48-0453
RINGEL, Elis.	54	Wismar	54-1724
RINGEL, Heinrich	16	Ermreuth	53-0320
RINGELBERG, Chr'ne	37	Marburg	49-0912
RINGEN, Peter	20	Rhadereissted	53-0475
RINGHAUSEN, Conrad	54	Nidda	52-1512
Maria 47, Caroline 19, Ludwig 14			
Elisabeth 7			
RINGLEB, Elisabeth	21	Walhausen	54-0850
RINGLEBEN, Martha	60	Hessen	50-0021
Martha E. 30			
RINGSCHNEIDER, Am.	38	Hannover	54-1649
Georg 11, August 9, Heinrich 2			
RINITZ, Gerhard	19	Jever	51-1686
RINK, Gottfr.	38	Womartshausen	52-1304
RINMUELLER, W'mine	27	Grohnde	52-0775
RINNERT, Elisa		Zwesten	53-0942
RINNOW, August	28	Chemnitz	52-1362
Dorothea 28			
RIOK, Gerhard	37	Ost Dewelane	49-0912
Andriane 32, Wilhelm 6, Saerbus 10m			
RIPKE, Elisabeth	18	Vatterode	48-1355
RIPP, Theodor	24	Warburg	53-1070
RIPPE, Hermann F.	21	Vegesack/Brem	54-1092
RIPPEL, Anna	17	Beitenbach	52-1580
RIPPERGER, Johann	14	Gold	54-1443
RISCH, Lorenz	23	Forchheim/Bav	52-0960
RISCKE, Daniel	23	Magdeburg/Pr.	52-1332
RISEMANN, Gustav	24	Bersenbruck	48-1209
RISIUS, Heinr.	30	Neust Sadens	51-1686
Gretke 37, Jacob 9m, Marie 4			
RISSNER, Maria	14	Bulfenrode	54-0830
RIST, Balthasar	43	Wolmedingen	54-1443
Therese 50, Alois 19, Nepomuk 20			
Ursula 15, Catharina 13, Crescenza 11			
RITHWERGER, Marie	24	Hildburghause	54-1078
RITTER, Barbara	49	Maar	54-0053
RITTER, Conrad	27	Bleidenrod	54-0053
Anna Marie 31, Anna Elis. 7			
Catharina 11m			
RITTER, Friedrich	24	Langwedel	53-1000
RITTER, Friedrich	25	Gotha	47-0828
Elisabeth 49, Catharina 18, Maria 12			
RITTER, Georg	28	Schwarzenbach	51-1160
Marg. 25, Johanna 3, Friedr. 6m			
RITTER, Heinrich	14	Altendorf	54-0987
RITTER, J. (m)	27	Tyrol	49-1358
RITTER, Joh Gottfr	36	Immenrode	54-0903
Caroline 31, Carl 9, Ferdinand 4			
Friedrich by			
RITTER, Joh. Conr.	27	Pfalz	50-0021
RITTER, Johanne	19	Melle	54-1297
RITTER, Ludwig	31	Wolfhagen	48-0284
RITTER, M. (m)	34	Taubersschenb	52-0558
A. (f) 44, E. (f) 12			
RITTER, Theo.	28	Hetschburg	51-1084
RITTERSHAUS, J Wm.	28	Barmen	48-0565

NAME	AGE	RESIDENCE	YR-LIST
RITTERT, Christine	42	Wendich	54-0987
RITTL, Anton	42	Cekanic/Boehm	52-0960
Marie 40, Joseph 9, Anna 7, Marie 2			
RITTLER, Rosalie	45	Altenburg	54-1566
Louise 15, Elvira 13, Anton 11, Ernst 10			
Helena 9, Laura 3, Clara 19			
RITZ, Genofefa	21	Kurhessen	53-1000
RITZEL, Barbara	23	Gelnhausen	53-0914
RITZEL, Friedrich	20	Wiesbaden/Nas	48-0447
RITZERT, Georg	37	New York	53-0475
RITZMANN, August	17	Klosterneudor	53-0652
ROBECK, Andreas	22	Calau	52-0895
ROBETT, Barbara	16	Languterstadt	53-0652
ROBLE, George M.	27	Ramsreuth	48-0951
Marie 8m			
ROBSING, Wilh'mine	24	Berlin	51-1438
Carl 3			
ROCHMANN, Gotth. M	28	Stuerzelbach	52-1105
ROCHMANN, Simon	18	Korbach	51-1160
ROCHOTSCH, Carol.	16	Gratz	54-0987
ROCICH, Joh.	23	Vilseck	54-1078
ROCKE, Aug. Herm.	20	Fischortan	51-0352
ROCKMANN, Fr.	20	Todtenhausen	51-0757
RODDE, Friedrich	30	Huemme	53-1164
RODE, Heinrich	30	Bodenburg	53-1070
Helene 31, Johanna 3, Otto 2, Heinrich 4m			
RODE, Maria	21	Cassel	54-1371
RODEHAU, Joseph	28	Schlesien	50-0021
RODEHR, Henriette	15	Hepen	51-1101
RODEMEIER, Heinr.	36	Westphalia	51-0405
RODEN, v. Fr. Ludw	58	Pattensen	54-1371
Eduard 24, Auguste 28			
RODENER, Elisabeth	19	Fichtelberg	54-0903
RODERER, Franziska	35	Trevesen	54-1078
RODERER, Therese	22	Neubau/Bav.	52-1423
Anna 14			
RODEWALD, Ernst	31	Marsbroch	47-0872
RODEWALD, Sophie	33	Drebber	50-1132
RODEWIG, Ernst	17	Fuerstenreuth	54-1554
RODI, Gustav	22	Neuhof	49-0352
ROEBER, Jacob	33	Geestendorf/H	50-0323
Anna , Friederike , Louise 6, William 3			
Emilie 7m			
ROEBER, Pauline	22	Mietzlau	52-1661
ROEBKE, A. (m)	17	Grimmen	49-0383
ROECKNER, Julius	17	Dissen	54-1371
ROEDEL, Charles	28	Pittsburg	53-0991
ROEDEL, David	25	Isny	49-0352
ROEDEL, Franz	20	Zeulenroda	50-1071
ROEDEL, Johann	23	Steinach/Bav.	52-1620
ROEDEL, Margaretha	28	Ermreuth	53-0320
ROEDENBECK, Friedr	18	Berenbusch	52-1321
ROEDER, A. (m)	24	Heinboldhause	52-0652
ROEDER, Andreas	19	Hoehstaedt	53-0557
Georg 14			
ROEDER, Conrad	18	Nordecke	54-1566
ROEDER, Conrad	43	Maryoss	52-0095
Anna Maria 41, Johannes 9			
ROEDER, Fr. Carl	25	Nora	51-0352
ROEDER, J. Cathar.	26	Wunsiedel	53-0888
ROEDER, Robert	32	New York	53-0888
ROEDER, v. Sigism.	21	Essen	54-0930
ROEDERER, Georg	29	Coburg	54-0930
ROEDL, Ferdinand	30	Leipzig	52-1620
ROEDL, Xaver	22	Diedeldorf	54-0965
Margaretha			
ROEFFS, Joh.	30	Canten	51-1245
ROEGAL, Arnold	34	Coeln	53-0914
ROEGE, Ammerie	22	Essen	53-1086
ROEGELMAIER, Andre	22	Schwabing	54-1168
Carl 28, Marie 26			
ROEHER, Franz	44	Wiehe	52-1148
Henriette 37, Albert 17, Franz 15			
Hermann 12, Rosalie 5			
ROEHLER, Johann	24	Bodenburg	52-0095
ROEHLMANN, Heinr.	28	Doerrigsen	53-0825
ROEHNERT, Friedr.	33	Gotha/Sachsen	51-1725
Maria 32, Elise 18m			

NAME	AGE	RESIDENCE	YR-LIST
ROEHR, Eugen	39	Weimar	53-0161
ROEHREN, Georg	53	Killede	51-1686
Susanna 46, Armantus 9			
ROEHREN, Therese	25	Neuenbecken	54-1452
ROEHRIG, A (m)	-6	Limburg	49-0416
ROEHRIG, G. (m)	24	Wald	49-0416
ROEHRING, Adam	2-	Flieden/Hesse	49-0365
ROEHRING, Friedr.	26	Grossen---	50-0439
ROEHRMANN, Therese	29	Sueddesen/Pr.	52-0351
ROEHRS, Christian	26	Beverstedt	53-1164
ROEHRS, Fried Conr	15	Stuckenbostel	51-1101
ROEHRS, Heinrich	47	Verden	49-0413
Margarethe 42, Catharine 19, Gesche 15			
Heinrich 9			
ROEHRS, Wilhelm	19	Osterwede	53-0905
Heinrich 16			
ROEHS, Chr.	26	Hannover	50-1317
ROELER, Gottlieb	21	Auma	52-1661
Caroline 22			
ROELVER, Theod.	34	Altenberge	53-0585
ROEMER, C.W.A.	22	Braunschweig	49-0574
ROEMER, E.B. (f)	30	Elgersberg/Co	52-0560
ROEMER, Eliza	23	Alzey	53-0582
ROEMER, Georg	27	Oftershein	52-0095
ROEMER, Georg	25	Petershagen	48-1179
ROEMER, Mathilde	23	Pr. Minden	51-1245
Marie 2			
ROEMMLEIN, Johann	43	Mainroth/Bav.	52-1332
Anna Marie 40, Barbara 10, Andreas 14			
Adam 12			
ROENNEBERGER, Fr.	31	Triptis	52-1661
Wilh 29, Minna 2			
ROENNEMANN, John	34	Bremen	52-0699
ROENNER, Carl	26	Reichenbach	49-0324
ROENNING, Conr.	23	Boxdorf	52-0693
ROEPE, Friedrich	17	Schweringen	53-1000
ROEPETER, Heinrich	25	Bodenfeld	54-1282
ROEPKE, Adelh.	28	Wiedersheim	52-1321
ROEPKER, Wilhelm	20	Filingen	53-1062
ROEPPER, Dietrich	31	Kustendorf	52-0693
ROERICH, Franz	24	Scheinfeld	54-0830
ROES, Johanne	21	Wremen	52-0699
ROES, Anna	27	Lintig	51-1084
Meta 17			
ROESCHES, Burchard	15	Wallings	49-0345
ROESE, Conr.	15	Weiler	51-0405
ROESE, Conr.	18	Armsfeld	51-0405
ROESE, Heinr.	20	Frankenberg	53-1016
ROESELER, Wm.	36	Immenthal	50-1071
Auguste 28, Carl 4, Alwine 9m			
ROESENER, Anton	28	Wiedersheim	52-1321
ROESENER, Chr'tine	23	Meinsen	52-1321
William 19			
ROESENER, H. (m)	27	Petze	52-1321
ROESENER, Heinrich	22	Wiedersheim	52-1321
ROESIGER, Fr. Wilh	15	Zeitz	53-1016
ROESLER, Franz	26	Schoenlinde	54-0872
ROESLER, Ignatz	45	Baden	52-1625
ROESLER, Joh. C.	20	Oechingen	54-1078
ROESMANN, T.	25	Verden	54-1470
Isabe 22			
ROESSLE, Catharina		Pfaffenreuth	50-0323
ROESSLER, Joh. Chr	22	Oberthoelein	51-1640
ROESSNER, Cath.	17	Birkenfeld	54-1078
ROESSNER, Nicolaus	28	Leopoldsgruen	52-1362
ROESTER, Franz	26	Schoenlinde	54-0872
ROETING, Mesina	21	Bremen	51-1035
ROETTGER, Angler	23	Neustadt	53-1062
ROETTGER, Heinr.	24	Binden	51-1640
ROETTGER, Hermann	2-	Hohenauerberg	50-0323
ROETZEL, Adam	25	Curhessen	51-1686
ROEWER, Caroline	53	Meinsen	52-1321
Friedrich 9			
ROEWER, E. (m)	18	Meinsen	52-1321
Pf. (m) 14, W. (m) 54			
ROEWER, Ernst	17	Meinsen	52-1321
C. (m) 24			
ROEWER, Marie	16	Tueringen	52-1432

NAME	AGE	RESIDENCE	YR-LIST
Martin 32, Matilde 35, Marie 7, Fritz 5			
Anthoni 2			
ROFIGNER, Friedr.	27	Rothmuelle	52-1101
ROFSGEN, Carl	31	Oberosberg	52-1101
ROGGE, Henry	17	Seefeld	48-0887
William 14			
ROGGE, Johannes	25	Bremen	53-0473
ROGGENKAMP, Wilh.	20	Guethersloh	52-1410
ROHDE, Christian	25	Muenden/Hann.	50-0323
ROHDE, Henry	38	New York	54-1371
ROHDE, Johann	39	Rosenhagen	54-0053
Marie 26			
ROHDERS, Heinrich	16	Beverstedt	51-1084
ROHHAUER, Anton	33	Obermoessring	54-1554
ROHKAMP, Minna	23	Langenhain	53-0324
ROHLER, Caspar A.	25	Friedrichsdor	51-0384
ROHLES, Margarethe	22	Dorgen	49-0324
ROHLFING, Carol.	22	Hahlen	54-1282
ROHLFS, Richard	38	Kluss	53-1164
Adelheid 34, Sophia 2			
ROHLING, Anton	72	Cloppenburg	50-1067
Anton 42, Dorothea 32, Theodor 17			
Wilhelm 15, Leonhard 8, Engelbert 4			
Antonette 9m			
ROHLMOOS, J. (m)	19	Egesel	49-0383
ROHM, M. (m)	30	Geisinge	50-0746
ROHM, Victoria	25	Tammerspach	51-0352
ROHMANN, Caroline	26	Hannover	53-0582
ROHMES, Andrew	37	Frauenaurach	53-0991
Anna 33, Anna 14, Magdalena 11, Babetta 8			
Friedrich 6, Lorenz 4, Catharina 9m			
Balthasar 29			
ROHN, Aug.	26	Wunstorf	53-0585
ROHN, Christoph	21	Nufrengen	51-0757
Dorothee 58, Johannes 10			
ROHN, Conrad	29	Gilverberg	50-0366
ROHRBACH, Anna Cat	22	Meckburg/Hess	52-0351
ROHRBACH, Ern'tine	22	Gotha	54-0872
ROHRBACH, Heinrich	20	Bergen/Hess.	52-0807
ROHRDRESS, Christ.	42	Boebber	53-1086
Anna M. 38, Marie 16, Friedrich 11			
Heinrich 9, Ernst Fr. 7, Marie Engel 3			
ROHRIG, Wilhelm	27	Homburg	47-0762
ROHRMESEN, John	26	Bolsterlang	53-0492
ROHRS, Elisa	25	Surtchen	52-0804
ROHRS, Joh. Heinr.	23	Verden	49-0413
ROHRS, Wilhelm	16	Osterwedel	50-0292
ROHRSCHEID, Christ	50	Melsungen	53-0942
Elise 15, Heinrich 14, Nicolaus 11			
Helene 6, Sophie 3			
ROHRSTROH, Gotth.	14	Darflas	48-1131
ROHSE, O. (m)	25	Arombach	49-0416
ROHWEDEL, Chr. (m)	28	Wiesenfeld	54-0918
ROL, Adolph	25	Veldrom	54-0872
ROLAND, Antonette	58	Tiefenort	52-1410
ROLAND, Johann	22	Obermarburg	51-0352
ROLAND, Nicolaus	18	Allendorf	50-0472
ROLF, Jacob	26	Reutlingen	49-0329
ROLFE, Joseph		Berlingerode	48-1355
ROLFE, Josephine	55	Berlingerode	47-0828
Wilhelmine 23			
ROLFS, Joseph		Berlingerode	48-1355
ROLFS, Josephine	55	Berlingerode	47-0828
Wilhelimine 23			
ROLING, A. (m)	33	Muenster	49-0416
ROLL, Eduard	40	Neustadt	54-0882
ROLLBERG, Theodor	21	Schwarzburg	50-0311
ROLLER, Christiana	20	Wuertenberg	53-0557
ROLLMANN, C.	24	Hamm	54-1470
ROLOFF, Christian	28	Wreschen	53-0905
Johanna 27			
ROLSING, Wilh'mine	24	Berlin	51-1438
Carl 3			
ROLTMAN, Anna	25	Spoaren	52-0515
ROLZE, Friedrich	43	Goltren	48-0951
Dorothea 28, Friederike 4			
ROLZE, H. (m)	43	Wienhagen	47-0762
Marie 16, Heinrich 14, Wilhelm 10			

NAME	AGE	RESIDENCE	YR-LIST
Friedrich 5, Louise 3			
ROMMEISS, August	21	Thorey	53-0492
Ferdinand 19			
ROMMEL, Erig	31	Wickers	52-0370
ROMMEL, Gerhard	25	Baiern	52-0370
ROMMEL, Heinr.	40	Rossdorf	48-1131
ROMMINGER, Andreas	21	Dutlingen	50-0840
ROMSTAEDT, Carol.	29	Aberniest/Hes	52-0960
ROMUELLER, Heinr.	20	Zeitloss	53-1062
RONBACH, Henriette	20	Prussia	50-1317
RONENBANNER, W.(m)	29	Kahla	50-0746
S. (f) 30, T. (m) 3			
RONNINGER, Anna	22	Wohnfarth	54-1554
RONSCH, Caroline	18	Prussia	53-0628
RONSCH, Henriette	25	Gnadenfeld	53-0914
RONSICK, Caspar	55	Benthe	52-1661
Anna 58, Anna Marie 28, Louise 24, Anna 5			
Anna Cath. 3			
ROOS, Barbara Elis	28	Kerrenhausen	54-0930
ROOS, M.	25	Windelheim	53-0492
ROOS, Nathan	21	Munster	49-0413
ROPER, John	15	Gehaus	54-1341
ROPIEQUET, Hugo	24	Kirchheimtola	54-0987
ROPKEY, John H.	32	America	47-0987
Anna M. 20			
ROPPEL, J. Sim.	20	Birkenbuehl	54-0053
ROPPLER, Seb.	25	Windelheim	53-0492
RORICH, J. (f)	23	Lingen	50-0746
ROSA, Alexander	43	Roth	52-1200
ROSA, Johann	29	Kozanaz	54-1676
Barbara 33, Maria 3			
ROSBACH, Heinrich	30	Ladenberg	51-1438
Julius 4			
ROSBACH, Margaret	17	Ohrenbach	51-1438
ROSCH, Elise	23	Osnabrueck/Ha	52-1332
ROSE, Augustus	18	Oldenburg	53-1164
ROSE, Carl	15	Eidewarde/Old	54-1092
ROSE, Doris	18	Hannover	53-0628
ROSE, Ferdinand	34	Bosen/Hann.	51-1532
ROSE, Fr.	28	Roesebeck	54-1282
Anton 30			
ROSE, H.A. (m)	35	United States	48-1015
ROSE, Heinrich	22	Neuhaus	53-0585
ROSE, Hermann	34	Waldenburg	51-1035
ROSE, Herrman	21	Hannover	52-0807
ROSE, Jacob	39	Thormhosbach	47-0840
ROSE, Jacob	27	Munster	49-0413
ROSE, Louis	34	Noerdlingen	54-0987
Emilie 37, Clara 5, Emil 2, Marie by			
ROSECHER, Georg	18	Gr. Walbur	52-0370
ROSEI, N. (m)	40	Stuttgart	54-1341
Ludwig 14			
ROSELER, Martin	29	N.Y.	50-0366
ROSEMEYER, Fr'drke	26	Eichholz	49-0352
ROSEN, Peter	19	Lennep	54-1371
ROSENAU, Samuel	18	Gunzenhausen	50-0439
Gertrude 16			
ROSENBACH, Moses	18	Unsleben	53-0888
ROSENBACHER, Isid.	22	Bamberg	53-0888
ROSENBAUER, J. Geo	43	Unterweichelb	53-0590
ROSENBAUM, Diedr.	25	Erwitte/Pr.	51-0048
ROSENBAUM, Fanny	16	Lichtenstadt	48-1179
ROSENBAUM, Isaac	33	Schoenlind	54-1566
Barbara 26, Sophie 2, Sophie 6m			
ROSENBAUM, Jette	25	Grevenstein	54-1078
ROSENBAUM, Julius	12	Cunreuth	53-0991
ROSENBAUM, Moses	46	Brittsfeld	52-1362
ROSENBAUM, Selig	20	Borgentreich	51-1160
ROSENBAUM, Simon	15	Kuep	53-0888
Elisabeth 24			
ROSENBAUM, Wil'mne	19	Bremen	54-1078
ROSENBAUMER, Suemn	29	Baumbach/Kurh	53-0628
ROSENBERG, Albrect	21	Amoeneberg	54-1168
ROSENBERG, Charles	23	Bueckenberg	49-0912
ROSENBERG, Elise	27	Aurich	52-1304
ROSENBERG, Friedr.	22	Bueckenberg	49-0912
ROSENBERG, Marcus	35	Erwitte	48-0269
ROSENBERG, Minna	20	Inowraklow	53-1016

NAME	AGE	RESIDENCE	YR-LIST
ROSENBERG, Salomon	15	Niedermeisser	53-0991
ROSENBERGER, Carol	22	Altenstein	54-1647
ROSENBERGER, Fried	23	Sindelbach/Bv	48-0053
ROSENBERGER, Joh.	26	Sommersdorf	48-0260
ROSENBERGER, Joh.	6w	Gristhal	48-0260
ROSENBLATT, Lewi	19	Werda/Hessen	51-1796
ROSENBLATT, Mendel	27	Hebel/Hessia	51-0048
ROSENBLUETH, Eman.	21	Koenigshof/Bv	54-1092
ROSENBOHM, Johann	16	Debstedt	50-0366
Maria 20			
ROSENBOKEN, Johann	16	Debstedt	50-0366
Maria 20			
ROSENBROCK, G.F.	30	Wettorf	48-0284
ROSENBROCK, Heinr.	14	Sobrum	51-1101
ROSENBUSCH, Carol.	24	Borken	50-0840
ROSENER, Sophie	18	Eldegson	51-1588
ROSENFELD, Fran'ka	16	Deut. Chotter	54-1297
ROSENFELD, v. H.	32	Muenster	51-0326
ROSENFELDER, Georg	27	Loerrach	52-1512
ROSENFELDT, Wilh.	29	Zerbst	52-1200
Johanna 52			
ROSENGART, Abraham	25	Buttenhausen	53-0991
ROSENHEIMER, Max	19	Dormitz	53-0320
ROSENHEIN, Maurice	20	Jebenhausen	53-0991
ROSENKRANZ, Anne C	20	Appenfeld	48-0951
ROSENKRANZ, Johann		Altenkirchen	54-1371
ROSENMEYER, Cecil.	20	Danzig	54-1371
ROSENTHAL, Carolin	22	Geisa	54-1168
ROSENTHAL, Ernst	27	Worbis	52-0279
Anna 27			
ROSENTHAL, Jeremia	21	Friedewald	53-0942
ROSENTHAL, Leopold	20	Hainsfahrt/Ba	52-1423
ROSENTHAL, Leopold	22	Berleburg	53-1086
ROSENTHAL, Marie	19	Budingen	49-1106
ROSENTHAL, Mich.	17	Prag	48-1131
ROSENTHAL, Salomon	30	Langenzlan	48-0951
Barbara 24			
ROSENTHAL, Samuel	18	Pyrmont/Wald.	51-1532
ROSENTHAL, Wil'mne	53	Bovenden	53-0888
ROSENTHAL, William	15	Koenigsberg	50-0840
ROSENWASSER, H.	46	Boehmen	54-1724
Ros. 40, P. (f) 19, P. 13, J. (f) 7, A. 5			
R. (f) 3, P. 6m			
ROSENZWEIG, Jeanet	31	Burgdorf	53-1164
Bernard 13, Siegmund 10, Albert 7			
Alwina 5, Bertha 18m			
ROSENZWIEG, Joh.	32	Bamberg	52-1321
ROSER, Catharine		Volhurheim	53-0914
ROSILOH, Simon	29	Schlawentzis	51-0757
ROSINE, Anton	54	Peppinghausen	51-1588
Mary 45, Christine 11, Mary 9, Carl 4			
Christian 4			
ROSINSKY, Hermann	29	Koenigsberg	54-0903
ROSKAMP, F. (f)	58	Belhaven	50-0746
R. (f) 24			
ROSS, Carl Friedr.	30	Bueckeburg	53-0991
ROSS, Elisabeth	17	Vockerode	54-1554
ROSS, Marg.	24	Rauzenthal	54-1078
ROSSBACH, Eduard	17	Emberg	54-1371
ROSSETER, Friedr.	18	Hevensen	50-0366
ROSSGER, Fried Aug	25	Voigtsberg	54-0987
ROSSKOPF, Michael	42	Moehren	52-1200
Margaretha 48, Barbara 18, Joseph 16			
Rosa 10, Michael 8, Anton 7			
ROSSKOPF, Walburga	46	Wolferstadt	52-1200
Anton 18, Crescentia 16, Joseph 10			
Walburga 6			
ROSSMANN, Ed.	18	Braunschweig	53-1000
ROSSMANN, Hermann	32	Stublach	54-0872
ROSSNER, Friedrike	19	Grafenberg/Bv	53-0628
ROSSNER, Magd.	20	Schweintal	52-0693
ROST, C. (m)	28	Manheim	48-1179
ROST, Carl	27	Bremen	53-0928
Doris 25			
ROST, Franz	20	Bremen	54-1566
ROST, Friedr. Aug.	32	Freyburg	54-0872
ROST, Philipp	20	Erlangen	49-0574
Babette 23, Elisabeth 26			

NAME	AGE	RESIDENCE	YR-LIST
ROST, Wilh.	21	Doebeln	49-0574
ROSTDEUTSCHER, J.M	36	Buerthen	51-0500
ROTENBACHER, Carol	37	Calw	54-1164
ROTERMUND, Joh.	28	Werden	54-0600
ROTH, Eva	21	Gocklingen	54-1371
ROTH, Franz	26	Angenrod	52-1625
ROTH, G.	28	Standorf	51-0517
ROTH, Georg	21	Utterode	52-1321
ROTH, Georg Math.	26	Ebersbach	47-0672
Margarethe 46, Elisabeth 10, Dorothea 7			
ROTH, Johann	56	Tiefenort	53-0320
Catharina 52, Veronika 24, Barbara 20			
ROTH, Johannes	15	Gundernhausen	52-0807
Johanna 20			
ROTH, John	28	Saxony	50-0021
ROTH, John	36	Lobenheim/Bav	51-0048
ROTH, Joseph	51	Heuntsbach	53-0928
Albertine 40, Wilhelmine 13, Maria 10			
Barbara 22, Caroline 17, Amalie 19			
ROTH, Margarethe	46	Harmersdorf	47-0672
ROTH, Margarethe	29	Kirchberg	49-0352
ROTH, Maria	21	Neustadt	53-0628
ROTH, Maria	18	Hettensroth	51-1588
ROTH, Mart.	38	Schmalfelden	49-0574
Barb. 40			
ROTH, Oswald	25	Marienthal	52-1580
ROTH, Theodor	19	Sonneberg	53-0557
ROTH, Vitis	58	Wolersdorf	48-0951
Elisabeth 51, John 21, George P. 18			
Magdalen 15, Christ. 11			
ROTH, Wilhelm	19	Gundernhausen	52-0807
ROTH, Wilhelm	16	Eisenach	51-0352
Elisabeth 20			
ROTHARDT, Amalie	32	Gorsleben	53-1164
ROTHE, August Noah	26	Calau	54-1566
ROTHE, Carl	34	Osterwick	54-1078
ROTHE, Conrad	30	Lippe	54-0882
Caroline 18, Wilhelmine by, Louise 53			
ROTHE, Ernst	23	Millwitz	54-0872
ROTHE, Friederike	23	Erfurt	49-0383
ROTHE, J.G. (m)	46	Glauchau	49-0383
ROTHE, Joseph	32	Schoenlinde	54-0872
ROTHENBACH, Georg	22	Klienkenbach	49-0574
ROTHENBECK, Elis.	36	Quetzen	52-0807
Wilhelmine 16			
ROTHENBERG, Loewe	38	Polle	50-1236
ROTHENHACKER, Fr.	42	Baiern	54-1724
ROTHENHAUSER, Fr.	42	Baiern	54-1724
ROTHGER, Amalie	18	Ilm	52-1304
ROTHHAGER, Abraham	26	Oberhofen	49-0912
ROTHHAUPT, Heinr.	28	Herph	49-0574
ROTHHOF, Albert	23	Brakel/Pr.	51-1796
ROTHMANN, Franz	18	Muenster	49-1358
ROTHMUND, Margaret	27	Grafenburg	48-0887
Joh. Michael 3			
ROTHSCHILD, Abrah.	17	Krautheim	54-0053
ROTHSCHILD, Carol.	54	Muehlhausen	53-0928
Henriette 32			
ROTHSCHILD, Jacob	25	Goodelsheim	50-0379
Moses 27			
ROTHSCHILD, Johana	36	Goddelsheim	53-1086
Fanny 9, Emil 8, Julius 6, Leopold 5			
ROTHSCHILD, Meyer	23	Igelheim	49-1106
ROTHSTEIN, William	20	Elberfeld	53-0991
ROTT, August	25	Tammerspach	51-0352
ROTTMANN, Fr. Gott	47	Isny	49-0352
ROTTMANN, Georg	15	Meilinghausen	52-0563
ROWALD, Altmann	33	Oldenburg	49-0352
ROWER, Wilhelm	27	Meinsen	52-1321
ROWERS, Sophie	20	Peppinghausen	51-1588
ROX, Carl Fr.	22	Hohenmelzen	48-0269
RUAAS, Conrad	41	Schneeren	54-1341
Mary 40, Caroline 8			
RUBEL, Johann	26	Hulbach	52-1101
Elisabeth 24, Florian 3, Theodor 10m			
RUBKER, Bernh.	27	Berg	52-1512
RUBSAM, Const.(f)		Geisselbach	54-1575
RUCHLE, Albertine	19	Herrenwies	53-0928

NAME	AGE	RESIDENCE	YR-LIST
RUCKDAESCHEL, Sab.	26	Weissenstadt	49-1106
RUCKDASSEL, Lor.	32	Dehlau	52-1129
Anna 36, Joh. 4, Nicol. 2			
RUCKERT, Henriette	17	Werdau/Sax.	52-1332
RUDEL, Emma R.	23	Mittelruessel	49-0737
RUDER, Cornelius	28	Haus	49-0737
RUDER, Georg	28	Winsberg	48-1199
RUDHARDT, Georg	18	Leutkirch	53-0435
RUDLER, L.M.	20	Danzig	54-1419
RUDOLF, Bern.	32	Magdeburg	51-1796
RUDOLPH, Adam	38	Heringen	51-1062
RUDOLPH, Anna Elis	21	Aue	54-0930
RUDOLPH, Aug.	30	Garrey	53-0585
RUDOLPH, Carl	25	Ruppertenroth	51-1101
RUDOLPH, Chritzia	24	Eisne	52-1101
RUDOLPH, Conrad	32	Mansbuch	53-0942
Elisabeth 32, Catharine 9, Friedrich 7			
Juliane 5			
RUDOLPH, Conrad	50	Frauensee	53-0942
Mathilde 23, Lewis 21, Jacob 18			
Dorothea 16, Gertrud 12			
RUDOLPH, Friedr.	27	Gemberg	51-1245
RUDOLPH, Fritz	36	Arnstadt	48-1184
RUDOLPH, Georg	25	Hoheneichen	52-1661
Elisabeth 28			
RUDOLPH, Georg	32	Kleinsteinach	54-1283
Kunigunde 31			
RUDOLPH, H.	24	Hessen	51-1084
RUDOLPH, Heinr Gus	25	Schleiz	49-0352
RUDOLPH, Heinrich	34	Langenstein	49-0352
RUDOLPH, Herm.	16	Oleff	54-0987
RUDOLPH, Herrmann	18	Buende	54-1566
RUDOLPH, Joh. H.	33	Arnstadt	48-0269
RUDOLPH, Johann	50	Leimbach	48-0284
Anna Christ. 19, Johannes 9			
RUDOLPH, Joseph	24	Ratchez	49-0574
RUDOLPH, Joseph	41	Hengsfeld	54-1341
Doretha 40, Joseph 15, Elisa 9, George 2			
RUDOLPH, Peter	23	Elberberg	50-0292
RUDOLPH, Philipp	43	Magenburg	54-0987
RUDOLPHSEN, (m)	21	Hamburg	48-1243
RUDORF, Oswald	37	Werdau	54-1168
RUEBE, J.B. (m)	19	Loesche	48-0445
RUEBEN, David	20	Peine	50-1317
RUEBENSAHL, Marg.	17	Lichtenfels	51-0405
Marg. 60			
RUEBENZAHL, Doro.	21	Lichtenfels	50-0379
RUEBESAM, Friedr.	19	Lindenau	54-1168
RUEBNER, Joh Georg	51	Brucke	53-0825
Anna Marg. 50, Joh. Georg 28			
RUEBSAM, Ludwig	17	Amoeneburg	52-0699
RUECK, Katharina	21	Rechenberg	54-1554
Rosine 27			
RUECKERT, Pauline	25	Berka	52-0699
RUEDEMANN, Martin	30	Emeteis	51-1640
RUEDINGER, Anton	30	Frauenrod	53-1062
Elisabetha 33			
RUEDL, Joseph	58	Pasberg	53-0825
RUEGER, Barbara	23	Bibera	54-1566
RUEGGEN, Chr.	22	Husberra	52-1321
RUEGNER, Nicolaus	37	Roetha	53-0267
Barbara 37			
RUEHER, Heinr.	12	Burgham	50-0472
RUEHL, Andreas	21	Hoffgarten	53-1000
Christine 22			
RUEHL, Carl	17	Rittberg	53-0473
Peter 25			
RUEHL, H. (f)	20	Villingen	47-0868
RUEHL, Maria	30	Moening	52-1464
RUEHL, Math.	40	Volhesgau	52-1464
Cath. 36, Johann 10, Georg 6, Peter 3			
baby bob			
RUEHL, Nick	36	Ansbach	53-0320
RUEHLING, Jacob	18	Vatterode	54-0850
RUEMER, Tobias Em.	23	Eisenberg	52-0563
RUEMPEL, Heinrich	28	Boerge/Hann.	52-0807
RUEPING, William	42	Essen	53-0991
wife 43, William 18, Friedrich 16			

NAME	AGE	RESIDENCE	YR-LIST
Lewis 14, Alwina 8, Charles 6, Bertha 2			
RUEPPEL, Joh.	15	Niederaula	51-1160
RUERKLEIN, Elis.	19	Fuerth	54-0850
RUESCHE, August	23	Hannover	54-1566
RUESNER, Franz	18	Sachsen-Meini	53-1013
RUESTIG, Heinrich	23	Engelat	53-1062
RUETEL, Franz	29	Fulda	53-0473
Chatarina 36			
RUETER, Adelbert	25	Moers	50-1236
RUETMACHER, C.W.J.	42	Wermelskirche	49-0329
Albert 18, Julius 17, August 17			
RUFFINSTAHL, J.	32	Braunschweig	54-1470
RUFSWURM, Andreas	19	Arzberg	53-0557
RUFTZ, Joh.	27	Lichtenfels	50-0439
Catharina 24			
RUFZ, M.	18	Steinewald	54-1419
RUGE, Just.		Vilsen	53-0942
RUGEN, Eleanor	26	Vilsen	50-0944
RUGEN, Heinrich	22	Hepstedt	54-0987
RUGER, Valentin	32	Mansbach	54-0053
Sophie 28, Georg 11m			
RUGLER, Nic.	15	Boehmen	54-1724
RUH, Franz	18	Birchstadt	49-0912
RUHL, Kuhlenbahn	30	Herpstein	51-1101
RUHLAND, Margareth		Waldmuenchen	53-0942
RUHRED, Theodor	22	Siedenburg	54-0987
Ernest 16			
RUITIGER, Fr.	27	Oberloehmersd	54-1470
Mary 23, baby 1			
RUKOWITZ, Georg	23	Luckow	53-1023
RULING, H.C.A. (m)	28	Hannover	49-1358
RUMFELTH, Margaret	59	Bremen	52-1432
RUMKE, Caroline	26	Stemmen	54-0872
RUMMEL, Andreas	30	Zumhaus	52-0515
Eva Rosina 28, Georg Fried. 3			
Eva Carstrin 26			
RUMMEL, Eduard	21	Etlingen	52-0370
RUMMEL, George	18	Darmstadt	53-0991
RUMMEL, John G.	33	Wildenholz	52-0515
Eva Marg. 36, Anna Rosanne 6			
Anna Cath. 4			
RUMMEL, Paul	30	Grosback	51-1639
RUMMELMEIER, Mich.	35	Gerabrunn	48-0887
RUMMLER, Georg	23	Bernick	50-1236
RUMONIE, John	18	Lippspringen	48-0284
RUMPF, Amalia	19	Minden	52-0563
RUMPF, Friedrich	28	Giesen	54-0830
RUMPF, Monika	24	Osterberg	54-1554
RUMPOST, M. Agnes	23	Telgte	50-1236
RUMPSFELD, Herrm.	16	Leeste	51-1160
RUMPSFELD, Joh.	19	Leeste	51-1160
RUNDEL, Xaver	27	Ravensberg	49-0352
RUNECKE, Wilhelm	22	Severns	53-0942
RUNG, Augustus	33	Wulfenlutter	50-0944
RUNGE, Agnes	18	Marburg/Hesse	54-1001
RUNGE, Anton	26	Hallenberg	53-0585
RUNGE, Friedrich	31	Hannover	54-1011
RUNGE, Heinr.	25	Holte/Hann.	52-0960
RUNGE, Heinrich	25	Steimke	47-0762
Friederike 24, Heinrich 6m			
RUNGE, Hermann	38	Mehringen	52-1452
Elisabeth 38, Wilhelm 4, Louise 8m			
RUNGE, J.A.	32	Bremen	51-0352
RUNGE, Philipp	32	Hofgeismar	53-1062
RUNGE, Wilhelm	22	Freudenberg	49-0413
RUNGEN, Tina	21	Germany	54-1591
RUNKELSHAUS, Conr.	15	Kestrich	53-0905
RUNSCH, J.H.	38	Chemnitz	50-1067
RUOF, Johannes		Balingen	54-1575
RUOFF, Mart.	59	Tuebingen	52-1321
RUPERT, Heinrich	26	Flammersheim	54-0987
RUPERT, Joseph	42	Kleinbach/Bav	53-0628
RUPP, Georg		Frischborn	54-1575
RUPP, Johann	23	Barfelde	53-0590
RUPP, Johann	29	Weismir	51-1438
Elisabeth 24			
RUPP, John	27	Biebrich/Nass	48-0447
RUPPEL, Conr.	44	Utrictshausen	52-0515
Catharine 47, Charles 9, Eleonor 7			
Casper 5			
RUPPEL, H.	68	Biebern	47-0868
An. (f) 58, Elisabeth 24, K. (f) 21			
RUPPEL, Heinrich	22	Niederaula	51-0352
RUPPEL, Heinrich		Frischborn	54-1575
RUPPER, Jacob	19	Winklach	52-1464
RUPPERSBERG, Edw.	46	N.Y.	48-1243
RUPPERT, Elise	30	Schrecksbach	51-1160
RUPPERT, Georg	51	Amoeneburg	54-1717
Katharine 26, Anna 20			
RUPPERT, Johann	40	Rineck	52-1625
Anna 38, Eva 14, Alexander 11, Philipp 8			
Anna 5, Gertraud 3, Michael 9m			
RUPPERT, Michael	43	Sunzenhausen	52-1304
RUPPRECHT, James	35	Leutkirch/Wue	49-0365
RUPPRECHT, Mariane	30	Feldorf	53-0825
RUPRECHT, Joh.	33	Prussia	50-1317
Susanna 34			
RUPRECHT, Wilh'mne	22	Wienhagen	47-0762
RUSCH, Andreas	22	Widdershausen	53-0942
RUSCH, M. (f)	27	Seidelshapt	50-0746
RUSING, Caroline	17	Warburg	54-1649
RUSL, Therese	23	Neustadt	54-1078
RUSS, Antonia	18	Freiamt	52-1362
RUSS, Wilhelm	18	Reckelsdorf	54-1282
RUSSE, Albert	17	Minden	54-1566
RUSSEL, Otto	18	Weissenfels	52-0095
RUSSWURM, Andreas	19	Arzberg	53-0557
RUST, Amande	37	Schlesingen	53-0590
RUST, Anton	32	Wien	54-1724
RUST, Christian	23	Idensen	53-0492
RUST, Conrad	32	Hannover	50-1067
RUST, Heinrich	26	Mismerode	53-0492
RUTENBECK, Ferd.	24	Braunschweig	50-1317
RUTH, Eli	54	Baiern	54-1724
RUTH, Margareth	45	Garitz	51-1455
Marg. 15, Martin 9, Teckla 2			
RUTKA, Johann	34	Boehmen	53-1000
Anna 28, Marie 2			
RUWITTEL, Elis.	30	Frankenau	54-1554
RYOR, Eduard	24	Edinburg/Scot	54-1717
SAAL, Johs.	21	Lengsfeld	52-1321
SAALFRANK, Henr.	20	Naila	48-0565
SAAM, Johann	62	Blankenbach	48-0284
SAAR, Donat	35	Prague	48-1243
Appollonia 34, Wilhelm 9, Philippine 3			
Clothilde 15m			
SAAR, Elisabeth	56	Prague	48-1243
SAAR, Solomon	33	Prague	48-1243
SAAR, W. (m)	19	Hannover	49-0329
SABATH, Carl	25	Iserlohn	48-0260
SABELIN, Sophie	28	Eisenshamm	51-1245
SACHS, Andreas	46	Wiegeln	50-0379
Marie 48			
SACHS, August	16	Frankenberg	53-1016
SACHS, Georg	27	Nuernberg	50-1317
SACHS, Wilhelm	51	Greiz	54-0987
Johanne 50, Carl 29, Friedrike 22			
Antonia 17, Caroline 7, Louise by			
SACHSE, Henn.	54	Erfurt	52-1321
SACHSE, Joh Friedr	49	Pfiffelbach	52-1148
Christiane 33, Carl Fried. 8			
Maria Rosine 7, Amalia F. 4			
Auguste P. 9m			
SACHSE, Simon	45	Berlin	48-0260
SACHSE, Wilhelm	30	Sachsen	53-0590
SACK, Adam	45	Bayern	53-0557
SACK, Wilh.	39	Utphe	47-0868
Els. 40, H. 11, Elsa 13, Hein. 9, Georg 7			
Lud. 3			
SACKMANN, Friedr.	25	Braunschweig	53-0590
SACKMANN, J.H.	30	Nordthauen	49-1358
SACKMANN, Joh Wilh	20	Hassendorf	51-1101
SADLER, Johannes		Dittlingen	54-1575
SADLER, Johs.		Dettingen	54-1575
SAEBKE, Wilhelmine	24	Hildesheim	54-1297
Franz 2			

NAME	AGE	RESIDENCE	YR-LIST
SAELZEN, Elise	20	Lodingsen	51-1588
SAEMANN, Ad.	28	Ruekerss	47-0868
An. 20			
SAEMANN, An.	20	Ramssthal	47-0868
SAENGER, Ernst	32	Gotha	52-1362
Friederike 28, Alex 2, Minna 11m			
SAENGER, F.C.	43	Wien	53-1000
Alosia 53			
SAENGER, Joh Gottl	23	Doehnholzdorf	51-1686
SAENGLER, Carl	19	Eimen	49-1358
Aug. 26, Caroline 21, Aug. 38, Joh. 35			
Minchen 10, Hannah 8, Aug. 5			
SAFES, Friederike		Strelitz	54-0987
SAFFRAN, Marg.	21	Worchheim	54-1554
SAFT, Robert	35	Breslau	53-0637
Caroline 32, Ida 7, Hugo 5, Maria 4			
SAGEBIEL, C.H.A.F.	18	Braunschweig	49-0324
SAGER, Susanne	23	Prussia	53-0628
SAGMASTER, Mich.	31	Jederberg	54-1078
Magdal. 41			
SAHL, Wilhelm	20	Wolfenbuttel	54-1168
Auguste 19			
SAHLMANN, Carsten	16	Rechtenfleth	50-0366
SAITER, Marianne	22	Baiern	54-1554
SALAMONSKY, Paulne	23	Schmiegel	53-0590
SALATIN, Herm. Joh	28	Kampen	49-0912
Anna Marie 27, Peter 64, Ursula 37			
SALBERG, Isaak	25	Gershagen/Pr.	52-1423
SALBERG, Salomon	19	Bracke	50-1132
SALEN, Peter	35	Bechte	48-1015
SALIG, Henry	26	Norten	53-1164
SALIG, Mathias	28	Follmersdorf	51-0384
Georg Adam 26			
SALIMON, Christine	37	Vichlach	53-0825
SALING, H.	22	Schoenegg	54-1283
SALINGER, Benjamin	19	Stargard/Pr.	54-1092
SALLMANN, Ernst	22	Cassel	50-0439
SALLMANN, Sigmund	16	Cassel	51-0500
SALOME, Bienchen	36	Lengsfeld	53-0942
Rueschen 21			
SALOMON, Hanchen	20	Ottendorf	52-1129
SALTZMANN, J. Otto	26	Fulda	51-1796
SALZER, Carl	22	Barmhausen	48-1184
SALZER, Gottlieb	20	Neuhaus	53-1070
SALZKOETTER, Meyer	23	Warstein	48-0951
SAMBERLICH, Ant.	68	Putzenteuch	51-1796
SAMELSON, David	34	Mittelruessel	49-0737
SAMISCH, Josephine	19	Lichtenstadt	48-1179
SAMMEL, Franz	18	Luebbecke	52-1321
Ludwig 17, Gerth 11, Friedr. 8			
SAMMS, G.L.	34	Bremerhaven	48-0887
SAMMY, Ismael	33	Pyrmont	49-0345
SAMSBIER, Heinrich	29	Schwerin	52-1362
SAMSE, August	33	Litzenade	52-1129
Friederike 20, Auguste 3, Heinr.			
SAMSE, Friederike	20	Stadoldendorf	52-1129
SAMSON, Julius	31	Mobile	53-1164
SAMUEL, Ester	21	Obermuchestad	49-0912
SAMUELSON, David	34	Mittelruessel	49-0737
SAMUS, August	18	Groeningen	54-1717
SAND, Joh. Heinr.	27	Havelbeck	49-0324
SAND, Marg.	47	Trappstadt	51-1640
SANDAU, Christ.	35	Rothenfeld	47-0918
Caroline 36, Friedr. 18, Ludwig 16			
Conrad 11			
SANDER, Carl	20	Carlshafen/He	52-0117
SANDER, Carl	28	Pforzheim	48-0269
SANDER, Christoph	36	Othfresen/Han	52-1332
SANDER, Conrad	49	Schlossholte	51-1084
Bertha 32, Theodor 10, Adolph 7, Carl 5			
Bertha 3			
SANDER, Dina	24	Neuhaus	51-1686
SANDER, Friedrich	32	Oldendorf	52-1512
Elisabeth 24, Caroline 3m			
SANDER, Friedrich	52	Luebke	54-1282
Charlotte 50, Friedrich 19, Wilhelm 9			
SANDER, Gottlieb	22	Haeverstaedt	52-1410
SANDER, Gottr.	38	Ndr.Sachswerf	48-0269

NAME	AGE	RESIDENCE	YR-LIST
SANDER, Heinrich	43	Bremerhafen	48-1184
Anna 44, Diedrich 9			
SANDER, Joh Friedr	21	Peine	49-0324
SANDER, Julius	26	Kitzingenl	50-0439
SANDER, Ludwig	25	Osnabrueck	52-0095
SANDER, Wilhelm	26	Hoheneggelsen	54-0965
Rika 20			
SANDER, Wilhelm	31	Lomferde	48-1184
SANDERMANN, Heinr.	15	Alsfeld	53-0905
SANDERS, Carl	29	Breichtebeck	48-0260
SANDERS, Friedrich	19	Versmolt	51-1639
SANDERS, H. (m)	26	New York	50-0311
SANDERS, Margareth	27	Twiess	49-0324
SANDERS, Wilhelm	24	Oesenbrok	49-0345
SANDERSFELD, Amal.	19	Weserdeich	52-0095
SANDIG, Ernst	26	Sachsen	53-1000
SANDKER, John	37	Negelsheh	49-1517
Mrs. 34, August 14, Friedr. 11, Berta 9			
Charlotte 7, Gustav 4, Marta 6m			
SANDMANN, Johannes	21	Lauterbach	51-1101
SANDROCK, Conrad	31	Affelde	53-0914
SANDTROP, Georg	20	Reichensachse	51-1686
SANG, Anton	33	Elbingenalf	49-1358
SANGER, Carl	29	Bielefeld	51-1739
SANGERHAUSEN, Wilh	25	Wiegeln	50-0379
SANLER, (m)	19	Berlin	48-1243
SANNAFELDER, Sigm.	21	Scharrenweisa	48-1184
SANTROCK, Adam	22	Friedewalde	50-0311
Marie 24, Catherine 5			
SAPPE, Franz Wilh.	19	Wehe	54-0987
SAROHR, L.V. (m)	22	Carlsruhe	49-1517
SARTONI, Herrm.	35	Neuwied	49-0912
SASS, C.	28	Rotenburg	53-1016
Sophie 27, Maria 9m, Heinrich 9m			
SASS, Conr.	22	Gerolzhofen	47-0918
SASSE, Eduard	18	Eberschuetz	54-1168
SASSE, Heinr.	17	Lohe	50-0021
SASSEN, J.W. (m)	26	Holden/Pr.	48-0447
SASSNAHL, Christ.	16	Dollern	47-0828
Maria 18			
SATOR, Heinrich	48	Wahlbach	53-0590
Catharine 30, Sophie 14, Helene 11			
Bernhold 7, Pauline 4			
SATOR, Ludwig	44	Wahlbach	53-0590
Marie 42, baby 4m, Wilhelm 14, August 12			
Leohard 10, Heinrich 8, Mathilde 6			
Alwina 3			
SATTLER, A. (m)	40	Teweln	50-0746
SATTLER, Johann	46	Langenau/Bade	54-1092
SATZEN, v. Heinr.	23	Bederkesa	49-0574
Cath. 26			
SAUDER, C.J. (m)	21	Herrenberg/Wu	48-0447
SAUDERS, Dor. (f)	27	Hannover	54-1724
SAUER, B. (m)	26	Mehmels	53-0914
Johann 22			
SAUER, B. (m)	40	Avesing	50-0746
SAUER, David	18	Mainz/Darm.	52-1332
SAUER, Georg	16	Homberg	54-0930
SAUER, Joh.	24	Frensdorf	52-0370
SAUER, Johann	48	Fischborn	48-1184
Anna 51, Conrad 26, Hannes 16			
SAUER, Lewis	29	Darmstadt	53-0991
SAUER, M. (m)	29	Hackerode	48-0453
SAUER, Phil.	17	Lohne/Hess.	51-0048
SAUER, Stefan	16	Marburg/Hesse	51-1796
SAUERBIER, Anton	23	Grossendorf	54-1566
SAUERBIER, Marcus	20	Grossendorf	54-0053
SAUERBREG, Friedr.	44	Lenbach	54-0903
Wilhelmine 40, Friedrich 24			
Friederike 16, Ernst 12, Bertha 10			
Wilhelm 8			
SAUERBREI, Theodor	35	Alsbach	54-1371
SAUERMANN, Carolne	22	Lichtenfeld	52-1321
SAUERMANN, Conrad	19	Stambach	53-0492
Johann 16			
SAUERMANN, Georg	32	Lichtenfeld	52-1321
SAUERTEIG, Caspar	49	Rodach	53-0585
SAUERWALD, Pauline	40	Berlin	48-1015

NAME	AGE	RESIDENCE	YR-LIST
SAUKEL, August	34	Berka	54-1554
Wilhelmine 28, Auguste 4, August 1			
SAUL, C. (m)	31	Hasfurt	52-0652
SAUL, Eduard	22	Herford	51-0352
SAUL, Johockel	50	Hopfgarten	54-0987
Heinrich 20, Wilhelm 18, Theodor 15			
Friedrich 5			
SAUL, K.	32	Erfurt	47-0868
SAUL, Louis	17	Cassel	52-0699
SAUPE, Anton	29	Landwerhagen	53-0590
SAUPERT, Heinr.	28	Ulrichstein	52-1321
SAURS, Heinrich	54	Unterowesheim	51-1455
SAUTER, Ernst	24	Almen	52-1580
SAUTERMEISTER, Jul	19	Osnabrueck	48-0951
SAUWALD, Gottlieb	22	Sulzbach/Stgt	53-0435
SAWISDROWSKI, Aug.	34	Seehausen	54-0987
SCHAAD, Christ.	26	Struempfelbac	49-0352
Jacob 22			
SCHAAD, Georg	17	Hildesheim	54-1297
Johannes 15			
SCHAAD, J.	27	Landenhausen	51-0517
T. (f) 21			
SCHAAF, Heinr.	27	Holte	49-0324
SCHAAF, Heinrich	24	Eisin	50-0379
SCHAAFFS, Louis	26	Verden	53-0652
SCHAAFSTALL, Maria	28	Hunteburg	53-1016
SCHAAP, Lewis	25	Driesbach	54-1470
SCHAARMANN, Joseph	33	Senden	54-1554
SCHAB, Louise	25	Zweibruecken	54-1566
Catharine 27			
SCHABBEHAR, Fr. W.	18	Hannover	51-1532
SCHABER, Wilhelm	29	Bredenbeck	54-1282
SCHACH, Carl	22	Grosspueschue	54-1297
SCHACH, Nicolaus	33	Wiegeln	50-0379
Christina 22, Anna 35, Maria 13			
SCHACHT, Wilhelmin	22	Braunschweig	53-0928
SCHACHTEL, Anna	23	Gansendorf	52-0095
SCHACK, Friedr.	20	Burgholzhause	49-0352
SCHACKWITZ, Heinr.	21	Berlin	50-0292
SCHAD, Anna	23	Bayern	53-0590
SCHAD, Anna Maria	26	Bruekenau	53-1062
SCHAD, Elisabeth	17	Dankmarshause	48-0284
Christian 27			
SCHAD, Joh. Georg		Gresselgrod	53-0942
SCHAD, Johann	23	Hennebach	52-1148
SCHAD, Mary	26	Bremen	53-0991
SCHADE, Christiane	19	Hannover	50-0311
SCHADE, Christine	36	Homberg	52-0279
SCHADE, Christoph	28	Bosserode	52-1304
Anna Elis. 20			
SCHADE, Ernst Fr.	32	Lautmannsdorf	53-1062
SCHADE, Gottlieb	55	Luechow	54-1297
Auguste 35, Friedrich 26, Gottlieb 12			
Wilhelmine 13, Pauline 8			
SCHADE, Heinr.	40	Frankenberg	47-0828
Elisabeth 34, Conrad 13, Heinr. 4			
Reinhard 11, Martin 6, Johann 1			
SCHADE, Heinrich	26	Neukirchen/He	52-1423
Elisabeth 24			
SCHADE, Johann	25	New York	50-0379
SCHADE, Karl	34	Gruenenplan	51-1796
SCHADE, Michael	54	Neptenitz	54-1282
SCHADE, Rudolph	24	Braunsche	53-1000
SCHADECK, Franz	13	Collin	51-0352
SCHADECK, Joseph	26	Kuttenberg	51-0352
Antonia 22, Franz 13			
SCHADER, Conrad	22	Geilsdorf	54-1566
SCHADER, Johann	29	Marburg/Hess.	52-1620
Elisabeth 27			
SCHADL, August	23	Gruenenplan	53-0435
SCHADT, Susanna	26	Kitzingen/Bav	52-0807
SCHAECKER, Wilhelm	30	Minden	53-0473
SCHAEDEL, Adolph A	30	Altenburg/Sax	54-1092
SCHAEFEL, Hermann	29	Berlin	54-0987
SCHAEFER, Agnes	27	Wuertt.	54-1724
SCHAEFER, Amalie	21	Blomberg	54-1168
Fette 21			
SCHAEFER, Anna	25	Scholen	53-1016

NAME	AGE	RESIDENCE	YR-LIST
SCHAEFER, Anton	21	Uschlacht	50-0379
SCHAEFER, Aug.	13	Eiderhagen	54-1297
SCHAEFER, August	20	Schaumburg	52-1620
SCHAEFER, August	19	Lage	54-0987
Hermann 17			
SCHAEFER, August	22	Vogelsberg	54-0987
SCHAEFER, C. (m)	24	Reichelsdorf	52-0652
Johanna 22			
SCHAEFER, Carl	2-	Cassel	49-1358
SCHAEFER, Carl Got	28	-eibendorf	54-0987
Christiane 29, Carl 7, Juliane 5, Ernst 3			
Ernestine by			
SCHAEFER, Casper	25	Ilbenstedt	49-0383
SCHAEFER, Cath.	21	Bleitenrod	54-0053
SCHAEFER, Cath.	22	Geilsdorf	54-1566
SCHAEFER, Cathar.		Telbershausen	54-1575
SCHAEFER, Ch. (m)	28	Barkhausen	49-0329
SCHAEFER, Chr'tine	47	Zella/Sachsen	54-0965
SCHAEFER, Christ.	27	Fulda	52-1661
SCHAEFER, Christ.	54	Hartum	54-1554
Christina 41, Christina 17, Louise 13			
Engel 7			
SCHAEFER, Conrad	28	Oberauroff	52-1512
SCHAEFER, E.H. (m)	20	W. Ollendorf	52-0960
SCHAEFER, Elias	18	Arnheim	52-1410
SCHAEFER, Elis.	20	Niederaula	53-0942
SCHAEFER, Elis. D.	24	Thormhosbach	47-0840
SCHAEFER, Elise	22	Fulda	51-0405
SCHAEFER, Fr'drike	32	Langenbrandt	54-1078
SCHAEFER, Fr.	15	Bielefeld	54-1011
SCHAEFER, Franz	24	Reichenberg	54-1647
SCHAEFER, Friedr.	39	Hartum	54-1554
Elis. 39, Chr. 15, Carol.(died) 13			
Heinr. 12, Gottlieb 8			
SCHAEFER, Friedr.	32	Hildesheim	50-0021
SCHAEFER, George	23	Nenndorf	53-1164
SCHAEFER, Hein.		Lissberg	51-1739
SCHAEFER, Heinrich	21	Roeddenau	53-0585
Anna 20			
SCHAEFER, Heinrich	23	Debach	52-0279
SCHAEFER, Heinrich	45	Mohlenfelde	52-1362
Elisabeth 43, Lorenz 12, Heinrich 10			
SCHAEFER, Heinrich	21	Sachsen	53-0590
SCHAEFER, Henry		Zwesten	53-0942
SCHAEFER, Herrmann	21	Cassel	51-1245
SCHAEFER, Jacob	19	Bronweiler	53-0320
SCHAEFER, Jacob	19	Robern	51-0384
SCHAEFER, Joh Jos.	26	Fochen/Pr.	49-0365
SCHAEFER, Joh.	25	Springfield	53-1086
SCHAEFER, Johann	27	Leipsingen/Sw	51-1725
SCHAEFER, Johanna	24	Hofgeismar/He	51-1532
SCHAEFER, Joseph	27	Rhina	52-0279
SCHAEFER, Joseph	29	Hausen	51-0500
Margarethe 28, Caroline 3, Caecilie 33			
SCHAEFER, Joseph	19	Reichenberg	54-1647
SCHAEFER, Jost	47	Mandeln	52-1105
Elisabeth 44, Wilhelm 14, Christine 12			
Philippine 5			
SCHAEFER, Louise	42	Laaspke	54-1168
Carl 12			
SCHAEFER, Luise	16	Einbeck/Hann.	51-1532
SCHAEFER, M. (f)	19	Bodenheim/Hes	48-0447
SCHAEFER, Marg.		Pfordt	54-1575
SCHAEFER, Margaret	47	Troelingen	53-0942
Elise 15			
SCHAEFER, Marie	38	Detmold	50-0379
Caroline 14, Christine 11, Emilie 8			
Carl 5, Ernst 3			
SCHAEFER, Nicolaus	30	Wiesenthal	54-0903
Barbara El. 27, Cath. Elis. 8, Caspar 5			
Joh. Christ. by			
SCHAEFER, Peter	56	Quentel	54-1554
SCHAEFER, Ph.	31	Fraurombach	54-1575
wife 25, daughter 5, son 9m, Christina			
SCHAEFER, Philipp	24	Dalheim	52-1410
Catharine 24			
SCHAEFER, Valentin	64	Durnberg	54-1724
SCHAEFER, Wilhelm	22	Oldenburg	50-0311

NAME	AGE	RESIDENCE	YR-LIST
SCHAEFER, Wilhelm	30	Lippe	49-0329
Wilhelmine 27			
SCHAEFERS, J.	26	Brackel	51-0517
SCHAEFFEL, Friedr.	18	Kitzingen/Bav	52-0807
SCHAEFFER, Andreas	19	Arnheim	53-0652
SCHAEFFER, Georg	26	Auenheim	53-0652
SCHAEFFER, Wilhelm	26	Preussen	53-0590
SCHAEFLE, Caspar	36	Solothurn/Sw.	51-1725
Elisabeth 35, Marie Louise 8, Adelheid 8m			
SCHAEFLER, Cath.	29	Lamershof	54-0903
Johann 32			
SCHAELER, Cath.	23	Perlsberg	51-0460
SCHAELER, Johann	25	Coburg	54-1282
SCHAELER, Simon	25	Schwanfeld	52-0807
SCHAER, Christoph	47	Lauterbach	51-1101
SCHAETZNER, Joh	39	Mittelruessel	52-0693
SCHAF, Gertrude	25	Gossau	53-0320
SCHAFER, August	23	Prussia	54-1724
SCHAFER, Bernhard	32	Muenster	52-0699
SCHAFER, C. (m)	27	Hackerode	48-0453
M. (f) 27, E. (m) 2			
SCHAFER, Friedr. W	43	Detmold	47-0918
Wilhelmine 12			
SCHAFER, Josephine	23	Hessen	50-0021
SCHAFER, Martha	25	Mittelruessel	49-0737
SCHAFER, Mich.	64	Brammingsweil	51-1455
Jacob 34			
SCHAFER, Wilh. Aug	21	Mittelruessel	49-0737
SCHAFER, Wilhelm	25	Kohlgrund/Wal	53-0628
SCHAFERS, Anna	27	Doessel	52-1304
SCHAFFENORT, A.	46	Gotha	53-0905
SCHAFFER, Michael	36	Sunzenhausen	52-1304
SCHAFFER, Thomas	42	Wilda/Bavaria	53-0628
SCHAFFERT, Cath.	37	Schanalfelden	54-0872
SCHAFFNER, George	24	Gerau/Hessen	48-0447
Peter 26			
SCHAFFSTAEDT, Geo.	25	Giessen	53-1086
SCHAFROTH, John	33	Munich	53-0991
SCHAFUSS, Theodor	44	Braunschweig	53-0905
Antonia 45, Louise 15, Mathilde 13			
Georg 10, Margarethe 23			
SCHALE, Michael	57	Gereuth	53-0825
Dorothea 50, Joh. Georg 24			
SCHALENTZKY, Louis	22	Ratzeburg	53-1062
SCHALFER, William	34	Sachsenhausen	48-0053
SCHALL, Anna	23	Pasewalk	51-1686
SCHALLA, Friedr.	34	Marksdorgart	49-1517
SCHALLE, Diedr.	27	Iserlohn	48-1355
SCHALLENBERG, Carl	42	Moers	52-1200
SCHALLENBERGER,v.G	25	Trennfurt	51-1455
SCHALLER, Leonhard	38	Lach	52-0693
SCHALLHASE, Chr.	37	Kofferhausen	51-1455
Magertta 48, Eva Eliz. 26, Catherine 12			
SCHALLMAIER, A.M.	26	Rehr	54-1419
SCHAM, Georg	28	Wessendorf/Bv	52-0117
SCHAMBACH, J. Chr.	59	Beinstedt	49-0574
Johanne 24			
SCHAMBECK, Georg	23	Ohrenbach	51-1438
SCHAMEL, Christ.	25	Blankenhausen	49-1106
SCHANDER, August	20	Eisenach	48-1184
SCHANLOT, Margaret	18	Kreuzburg/Wei	52-1620
SCHANNING, Friedr.	40	Rodsenburgerh	53-0652
Anna Marie 29			
SCHANZ, Hein.	32	Schwarzenberg	51-1084
SCHANZE, Joh. Chr.	41	Rada	48-1131
SCHAPEL, Carl	34	Paderborn	52-1101
SCHAPER, Amalie	24	Doerigsen	54-1168
SCHAPER, Herrmann	24	Hohnsen	52-0095
SCHAPER, Johanne	25	Berka	54-1554
Wilhelm 18			
SCHARER, Henry	50	Niedertreten	48-0951
Margreth 50, Elisabeth 23, Henry 16			
Cathrine 13, Margrethe 9			
SCHARER, J. Georg	50	Kleinwichberg	49-0574
Marg. 20, Barb. 19, Marg. 11, Georg 15			
SCHARF, Jacob	19	Wuertenberg	53-0557
SCHARF, Margaretha	23	Bimbach/Bav.	52-0807
Barbara 18			

NAME	AGE	RESIDENCE	YR-LIST
SCHARFENBERG, Magd	30	Leierbach	53-0324
SCHARFENBERGER, M.	29	Troilsdorf	54-1554
SCHARFF, Friedrich	25	Soitzich	54-1282
Wilhelmine 24			
SCHARFF, William	25	Dessau	52-1304
SCHARKE, Christian	23	Waldeck	52-0807
SCHARLACH, Friedr.	35	Schwerstadt	48-1184
SCHARMANN, August	30	Schoeningen	54-1371
SCHARMANN, Georg	32	Koedingen/Aus	52-0807
SCHARMANN, J. (m)	20	Stummeroth	52-0652
SCHARMBECK, Friedr	42	Bockhorn	52-0095
SCHARNHADE, H. (m)	23	Steinke	54-1341
SCHARNHORST, Dietr	59	Woelpe	54-1443
Dorothea 54, Dietrich 22, Dietrich E. 21			
Friedrich 14			
SCHARNHORST, Ed.	24	New York	49-0413
SCHARNHORST, Georg	36	Salzgitter/Ha	52-1332
SCHARRER, C. (f)	28	Vorra	48-0445
SCHARZ, Franz	45	Schwarzkossel	54-1676
Barbara 37, Joseph 14, Maria 10			
Elisabeth 7, Johann 5, Anna 9m			
Veronika 23			
SCHASBERGER, J. Fr	49	Elberfeld	54-1575
Joh. Fr. 15			
SCHASBERGER, Mich.	60	Binswangen	48-0951
SCHASBERGES, J. Fr	49	Elberfeld	54-1575
Joh. Fr. 15			
SCHATEL, Mich.	20	Kitzingen	50-0439
SCHATTENBERG, Wm.	27	Quedlinburg	54-1371
SCHATTERER, Marg.	27	Mittelruessel	49-0737
SCHATZ, August	28	Ortrof	50-1132
SCHATZ, Georg	24	Wohnsgehaig	54-0850
SCHATZ, Joh W'mine	22	Neustadt	52-0370
SCHAU, Charlotte	26	Kahla b/Gena	52-1580
Amalia 2			
SCHAUB, Bernhard	26	Brueggenau	52-0279
Ludwig 24			
SCHAUB, Conrad	16	Albertshausen	52-0563
SCHAUB, Emil	33	Blasbach	54-0830
Elisabeth 23, Catharine 23			
SCHAUB, Friedr.	18	Balthorn	51-1739
SCHAUB, Philipp	37	Hoenebach	48-0284
George 36			
SCHAUER, J.G.	38	Kappel	52-1129
Helene 35, baby			
SCHAUER, Johann	44	Hilpoltstein	53-0628
SCHAUFLER, Conrad	20	Halsdorf	52-0515
Gustav 16			
SCHAUMBERG, Georg	18	Wallerode	54-1078
SCHAUMBURG, Aug'ta	20	Cassel	54-0930
SCHAUMBURG, Franz	29	Cassel	52-0699
Pauline 23			
SCHAUMLOEFFEL, AnM	22	Holzhausen/KH	52-1332
SCHAUMLOEFFER, AnM	17	Ostheim	52-0563
SCHEBE, Jacob	36	Cassel	54-1470
Elisabeth 36, Elisabeth 10, Mary 11			
Elisa 8, Friedrich 6			
SCHECHT, Auguste	20	Dresden	52-1321
SCHECK, Adam	19	Hugenfeld	51-1245
SCHECK, Gottlob	20	Stammheim	52-1580
SCHECK, Nic.	31	Grettstadt	49-1358
SCHECKER, Johann	24	Bayern	53-0557
SCHECKERMANN, Leo.	37	Neustadt	50-0366
SCHEEL, Johannes	55	Salzum	53-1000
SCHEELE, August	21	Braunschweig	51-1639
SCHEER, Dorothee	53	Muenden/Hann.	50-0323
SCHEFFEL, Carl	23	Osnabrueck	52-1105
SCHEFFEL, J.C.	18	Bremen	51-0405
SCHEFFER, Adam	27	Felsburg	50-0944
SCHEFFER, J. Heinr	52	Engter	47-0762
Elisabeth 51, Marie 65, Gertrude 25			
Herman 5, Wilhelm 15, Elisabeth 25			
Anna Marie 20, Catharina 9			
SCHEFFERLE, A.	32	Thalenmais	53-0435
SCHEFFLER, Joh.	32	Bohingen	54-1168
SCHEHR, Anne E.	24	Roth	48-0951
C. Charles 33			
SCHEHR, C. Charles	33	Elschwege	48-0951

NAME	AGE	RESIDENCE	YR-LIST
SCHEIBE, Friedrich	33	Eisenberg	52-1661
Chr. 27, Hermann 7, Julius 5, baby 6m			
SCHEIBEL, Anna	52	Hofdorf	52-1452
Kresens 18, Johann 16, Joseph 14 Johann 13			
SCHEIBEL, Gottfr.	36	Creves	51-1686
Christine 26, Caroline 3, Friederike 11m			
SCHEIBEL, Kunigund	34	Oefingen/Bad.	51-1725
SCHEIBEL, Matth.	36	Grafenhausen	52-1105
SCHEIBENPFLUG, Wm.	34	Freiburg	49-0383
SCHEIBERT, H. (m)	32	Weisenberg	54-1341
SCHEIBLE, William	28	Duermenz	53-1164
SCHEIBLER, Conr.	24	Schoenau	54-1078
Joh. 18			
SCHEIBLER, Joh.	18	Breuna	54-1078
SCHEICH, Cathr.	26	Horas	52-0370
SCHEICH, Victoria	26	Eiterfeld/Hes	51-1532
SCHEICKEL, Friedr.	21	Wiedersheim	52-1321
SCHEIDEMANN, Fried	37	Haina	51-1639
Christine 30, Maria 5, Franz 2 Theresia 11m			
SCHEIDEMANN, Henr.	31	Hillmarstein	50-0472
Georg 4			
SCHEIDEMANT, Marg.	19	Bamberg	49-0345
SCHEIDER, Georg	19	Hoechstedt	51-1438
Lorenz 19			
SCHEIDLER, Alois	16	Oetdorf	51-1035
SCHEIDLER, Heinr.	35	Oetdorf	51-1035
Johann 4, Joseph 2			
SCHEIDLER, Johann	18	Peckelsheim	51-1035
SCHEIDLER, Martin	21	Salzingen	53-0324
SCHEIDT, Ant.	24	Prussia	50-1317
SCHEIDT, Wilhelm	28	Kiesselbach	53-0320
Dorothea 28, Johannes 4			
SCHEIDT, Wilhelm	28	Tiefenort	53-0320
Dorothea 28, Johannes 4			
SCHEIFLER, Adolph	21	Bleicherode	54-1554
SCHEIKER, Johann	24	Scharmbeck	53-0942
SCHEIN, Heinrich	52	Blankenbach	48-0284
Cornelius 22, Martin 18, Dorothea 14 Anna Cath. 7			
SCHEIN, Johann	40	Blankenbach	48-0284
Dorothea 45, Henry 18, Anna 16 Cornelius 14, Catharine 4, Conrad 2			
SCHEINEMANN, Heinr	27	Hessen	53-1023
SCHEINERT, Carolin	36	Langenlaube	54-0930
SCHELAND, Lena	20	Rogasen	52-1105
SCHELBACH, Jacob	18	Hivenhard	49-0912
SCHELE, J. Nepomuk	48	Allach	54-1297
Rosine 38, Johann 9, Marie 8			
SCHELER, Andreas	24	Unterwalzbach	52-1332
SCHELER, Friedrich	32	Buch	48-1355
Elise 25			
SCHELK, Chr.	29	Baudeloh	53-0492
Charl. 32, Wilhelm 3			
SCHELKE,			52-1200
SCHELL, Christine	24	Friedrichsdor	51-0384
Carl 2, Caroline 21			
SCHELL, Johann	27	Bischofsheim	52-1620
SCHELL, Peter	39	Cur Hessen	53-0557
Theresia 37, Jacob 14, Maria 25			
SCHELL, Peter	39	Kur-Hessen	53-0557
Theresia 37, Jacob 14, Maria 25			
SCHELLBERG, Magd.	52	Dahlhausen	51-1035
Christine 9			
SCHELLBERGER, R.	15	Eggerhausen	54-1419
SCHELLE, Conr.	32	Hannover	50-0439
L. (m) 24			
SCHELLENBERGER, C.	18	Ruthrohr	54-0872
SCHELLER, Bernhard	18	Gumbelshausen	53-0320
SCHELLHAASE, A.	16	Vockerode	52-0558
SCHELLHAN, Wilhelm	44	Eschwege	54-1716
Margarethe 46, Heinrich 15, Friedr. 12			
SCHELLHASS, Gustav	21	Bremen	53-1164
SCHELLHAUS, Chr'ne	22	Vechta	54-1341
child 3m			
SCHELLHEIM, Carl	31	Minden	52-1410
SCHELLING, Jacob	17	Openau/Baden	52-0351

NAME	AGE	RESIDENCE	YR-LIST
SCHELLKOPF, Cath.	23	Wemding	52-0279
SCHELLMANN, Joh.	21	Nied.Berndorf	52-0370
SCHELP, Friedrich	21	Hagen	53-0825
SCHELPP, Wilh'mine	26	Loewenstein/W	54-1092
SCHELTER, Cath.	54	Arzberg	53-0557
SCHELTER, Chr'tine	21	Arzberg	50-1236
Marie 23			
SCHEMBS, George	24	Edelsheim/Wue	48-0447
SCHEMM, Georg	30	Hannover	52-0095
Louise 26			
SCHEMMEL, Heinr.	16	Asslar	49-0574
SCHEMPP, Louise	25	Fruchtelfinge	51-1640
SCHENCKE, M. (m)	33	Baltimore/Md.	48-1015
SCHENDEL, Gottfr.	35	Oberdzilsen	49-0742
illeg. 27, illeg. 5			
SCHENK, Heinr.	27	Ermreuth	52-0693
SCHENK, Joh. (m)	25	Sain	51-1640
Ludw. 21, Anton 19, Elisabeth 50, Anna 17 Maria 12			
SCHENK, Johann	32	Tannhausen	54-0903
SCHENK, Philipp	53	Obergimpern	49-0912
Philipp 23, Regina 52, Michael 18 Catharine 26, Johann 4, Carl 21 Blondine 16			
SCHENK, Wilhelm	21	Woldegk	53-0905
SCHENKE, Frz. Jos.	18	Pissighaim/Bd	51-1796
Joh. Ant. 16			
SCHENKEL, Christ.	28	Jochtfeld	53-0652
SCHEPE, Hermann	18	Zeitz	53-0324
SCHEPEN, Henry	15	Dingen	48-0951
SCHEPPELMANN, Hein	25	Nienburg	53-1062
SCHER, C.F. (f)	26	Grossarchbach	48-0453
SCHERER, Angelin	24	Niederhoerlen	52-1452
SCHERER, Appolonia	20	Schoellkrippe	54-0903
SCHERER, Friedr.	19	Schwabach	48-1355
SCHERF, Carl	30	Saxony	50-0311
SCHERF, Frederick	33	Savannah, Geo	48-1015
SCHERF, Gottl.	35	Dresden	49-0742
B. (f) 27, T. 3			
SCHERF, Jacob		Horchheim	54-1575
SCHERFF, Trina	20	Marssel	53-1164
SCHERLE, Cathrine	18	Wuertenberg	53-0557
SCHERM, Anna	32	Steinach	54-0903
SCHERP, Joh.	16	Glaudorf	50-0472
SCHERR, Wilhelm	29	Frebershausen	53-1023
SCHESSBERGER, J.M.	36	Mittelruessel	49-0737
Sophia 28, Gustav 2			
SCHETTER, Ludwig	43	Lossens	54-0872
Tabeta 42, Elisa 16, Christoph 14 Maria 9, Julius 8, daughter 4			
SCHEUBER, Wilh.	47	Neuwied	49-0912
Louise 57, Adolph 16, Bertha 19, (m) 26			
SCHEUNERT, Johann	54	Greifendorf	53-0590
Friedericke 46, Friedrich 24, August 20 Caroline 16, Therese 11, Amalia 9			
SCHEUSING, Martin	33	Schweckhausen	52-1625
SCHICK, Peter	30	Mardorf	53-0585
Anna 25			
SCHICKLER, J. Mich		Altbach	48-1355
SCHIEBLER, Carl	28	Goslar/Hann.	52-1332
Louise 23			
SCHIEBLER, L.	28	Nidda	54-1283
SCHIECH, C. (f)	19	Cohler	50-0746
SCHIEFENS, J.	28	Osnabrueck	48-1355
SCHIEFER, Georg	22	Markelsheim	54-1371
SCHIEFFER, Wm.	33	Lese	51-1455
Charlotte 34, Caroline 9, Friedr. 6 Sophie 3			
SCHIEKLER, Hermann	20	Buehne	53-0905
Mariana 56			
SCHIEL, Henry	27	Bundenbach	53-0991
SCHIELER, August	39	Gebstedt	52-1148
Aurelia 35, Julius 12, Edmund 10 Hermann 8, Otto 6, Richard 4 Hugo (died) 6m			
SCHIEMENZ, Carl A.	26	Senftenberg	53-0991
SCHIERHOLZ, C.F.W.	25	Heddinghausen	49-0329
SCHIERHOLZ, Carl	21	Detmold	52-1410

NAME	AGE	RESIDENCE	YR-LIST
SCHIERHORST, Joh.	26	Riede/Hann.	52-1332
SCHIERLOH, Hermann	22	Bremen	52-1105
SCHIERSTEIN, Ferd.	30	Bremen	52-1661
SCHIESLER, Brokop	33	Luze	52-0699
SCHIESS, Brigitte	34	Alpirsbach	54-1371
SCHIEVER, John B.	28	Rorup	48-0951
SCHIFF, Caroline	24	Geisa	54-0987
Jane 20			
SCHIFFBAUER, Heinr	28	Schiffarth	54-1371
SCHIFFER, Gabriel	13	Reckendorf	48-0887
SCHIL, Anna	28	Rothenbach	50-1236
SCHILBE, Christian	25	Grosensee	48-0284
Sophie 28			
SCHILD, Bernhard	44	Bellenberg	48-0565
Sophie 44, Friederike 16, Louise 26			
Caroline 24, Sophie 13, Bernhard 11			
Henriette 8, Wilhelmine 3			
SCHILD, Heinrich	19	Kilbe	52-0370
SCHILD, Johann	19	Colbe	54-0930
SCHILD, Peter	49	Friedrichsdor	51-0384
Marianna 46, Georg 26, Heinrich 21			
Eliese Cath. 15, Ludwig 12			
Marie Elisab 8			
SCHILDEMEYER, Chr.	24	Letell	52-1321
SCHILDKNECHT, Elis	21	Kirchheim	54-1716
SCHILDKNECHT, Rud.	30	Sacramento	54-1297
Rosalie 21, Rosalie 1			
SCHILDMEYER, Joh.	47	Kerm	47-0872
Sabina 43, Georg 19, Anna Maria 15			
Joseph 11, Johann 9, Therese 8			
SCHILEME, A. (m)	17	Buhlerthal	54-1341
SCHILL, Joseph	34	Waldkirch	52-0095
SCHILLE, Peter	26	Stockhausen	54-0882
SCHILLER, August	20	Sproetchen	48-0101
SCHILLER, Charles	38	Cannstadt	53-0991
Wilhelmine 38, Hermann 9, Carolina 8			
Charles 5, William 9m			
SCHILLER, Ferd.	35	Gebstedt	52-1148
Dorothea R. 29, Auguste 7			
SCHILLER, George	37	Asch	52-1101
Margretha 29			
SCHILLER, Gottfr.	27	Regensburg	52-1580
SCHILLER, Gustav	30	Halberstadt	48-0260
Auguste 20			
SCHILLER, Heinr.	24	Emptinghausen	52-0515
SCHILLER, Johann	18	Schwingen/Bav	52-0351
SCHILLER, John	22	Wuertt.	54-1724
Barbara 18			
SCHILLING, August	23	Jena	53-0991
SCHILLING, August	50	Hassenrode	51-1686
Johanne 50			
SCHILLING, C.	23	Unterpaktbach	51-0517
SCHILLING, Carl	34	Hannover	52-1129
Soph. 28			
SCHILLING, Carl	20	Kappelsdorf	54-0903
SCHILLING, Cath.	54	Lauterbach	51-0352
SCHILLING, Conrad	26	Angersburg	52-0370
SCHILLING, Conrad	29	Elzhof	52-1101
SCHILLING, Edmund	28	Heiligenstadt	52-0699
SCHILLING, Fr. Wm.	27	Rehden	50-0292
Behrend 30			
SCHILLING, Friedr.	20	Melzel	54-1283
Herm. 17			
SCHILLING, Georg	30	Coburg	50-0379
Friederike 32, Alexander 8			
SCHILLING, Heinr.	27	Luenzenau	50-1132
Ernestine 28, Louise 9			
SCHILLING, Juliann	17	Follmersdorf	51-0384
SCHILLING, Louis	24	Heiligenstadt	52-0699
Wilhelmine 58			
SCHILLING, Peter	42	Schnekenlohe	51-1532
SCHILLING, Peter	26	Baltimore	48-0101
SCHILLING, Th. L.	20	Meiningen	49-0383
SCHIM, Alex	25	Widenburg/Pr.	51-1796
SCHIMEK, Joseph	40	Brandis	54-1676
Barbara 30, Anna 9m, Barbara 30			
SCHIML, Wenzel	25	Kopidlo	54-1647
Josepha 21, Wenzel 2, Franz 8, Franz 58			

NAME	AGE	RESIDENCE	YR-LIST
Anna 55			
SCHIMM, Cath.	22	Rittling/Bade	52-0960
SCHIMMEL, Joseph	42	Tirschenreuth	52-1423
SCHIMMEL, M. (m)	19	Limberg	50-0746
SCHIMMEL, Th. (f)	41	Limbach	50-0746
SCHIMMELBACH, A.	25	Dusseldorf	48-0565
SCHIMMIK, Wentz	38	Boehmen	53-1000
Anna 28, Anna 7, Wentz 1			
SCHIMONSKY, Stan.	27	Koenigsberg	51-0652
SCHINDELARS, Johan	17	Reichenbrg/Bo	54-1092
SCHINDLER, Adam	29	Braunschweig	53-0590
SCHINDLER, Cath.	26	----nberg	53-1062
SCHINDLER, G.	50	Biegedorf	54-1716
Elis. 50, Louise 18, Louis Theod. 15			
Julius 10, Gottlieb 25			
SCHINDLER, K.A.(m)	21	Darmstadt/Hes	48-0447
SCHINDLER, Robert	38	Hirchberg	49-1106
Caroline 34, Emilie 8, Emma 6, Robert 5			
SCHINDLER, Wentzel	25	Motsdorf	49-0574
SCHINER, Therese	22	Baiern	52-1512
SCHINKE, Carl	22	Zerbst	52-1200
SCHINKE, Ilsebein	19	Holsen	54-1452
SCHINKLER, J. (m)	33	Ratzberg	50-0746
S. (f) 27			
SCHINNER, Matias	27	Mittelruessel	49-0737
SCHIPPARD, Johanne	25	Weimar	50-1236
SCHIPPERLING, Joh.	44	Hausboden	52-0693
SCHIPPERT, Adolph	20	Wuertt.	54-1724
SCHIRK, Lisette	26	Essen/Pr.	53-0628
SCHIRMER, Carl	29	Bonn	54-0965
Gertrude 24			
SCHIRMER, Christne	48	Lauterbach	53-1000
SCHIRMER, Doris	42	Charleston	54-1371
Simon 4, Josephine 6			
SCHIRMER, Henriett	19	Sallburg	48-1184
SCHIRNER, Michael	19	Hohlenbrunn	47-0672
Johann 22			
SCHISTEL, Josephin	23	Essen	53-1086
SCHITTLER, Konrad	22	Rinsheim	52-0279
SCHLACHTE, Anne	24	Brockhusen/Ha	51-0048
SCHLAD, E.	21	Frankmanshaus	51-0517
SCHLADE, Jacob	27	Ibenhausen	51-0757
SCHLADE, Johs.	21	Ibenhausen	51-0757
SCHLAEGER, Auguste	33	Altenburg	50-1067
SCHLAEGER, Falther	41	Oberhausen	54-1282
SCHLAG, Nicolaus	19	Aschenhausen	52-0370
SCHLAGEL, Angelica	25	Wense	52-1512
SCHLAGENHOFS, Geo.	33	Obernkreutz	53-1013
Kunigunde 36, Margret 6			
SCHLAGENHOFT, Marg	24	Haid	54-1554
SCHLAGER, Franz	35	Mittelruessel	49-0737
SCHLAMAN, Georg	39	Niederwilling	52-1304
Eleanora 39, Marianne 9, Christiane 6			
Louis 4			
SCHLAMANN, Ludwig	22	Lingen	54-1297
SCHLATTER, Heinr.	17	Rotenburg	54-1575
SCHLATTER, Ludwig	41	Wien	52-1105
SCHLEBOHM, Henning	17	Cappeln-Altde	50-0366
SCHLECHT, Jacob	27	Muehlhausen	53-0942
SCHLECHTWEG, Hen't	24	Lengsfeld	49-0413
SCHLEDER, James	23	Salzungen	53-0582
SCHLEE, Adam	38	Bernek	52-0279
SCHLEEBAUM, Adam H	14	Schleckhausen	52-1304
SCHLEER, Joh Math.	21	Wuertt	53-0557
SCHLEFFEL, Anthony	18	Reichenau	53-0991
SCHLEGEL, Andreas	17	Kleinlegerste	54-1716
SCHLEGEL, Emilie	20	Frankenhausen	54-0918
W. (m) 26			
SCHLEGEL, Marg.	33	Kulmbach	53-1062
SCHLEGEL, Wm.	21	Laumberg	51-1588
SCHLEGELMICH, C.F.	41	Mansbach	53-1086
Henr. 42, Louise 19, Franciska 8			
Magdalena 61			
SCHLEGELMICH, Luis	27	Mansbach	53-1086
Carl 7, Jacobine 4, Bernhard 3			
SCHLEGELMILCH, Bar	25	Seil	54-0053
SCHLEGEMILCH, Hein	31	Gotha	52-0895
Henriette 28, Emma 9m			

NAME	AGE	RESIDENCE	YR-LIST
SCHLEICHE, Bernh.	56	Lengsfeld	49-0413
Catharina 52, Elisabeth 14			
SCHLEICHER, Herm.	18	Frankenberg	53-1016
SCHLEICHER, Kasper	28	Hotzberg	52-0370
SCHLEICHER, Mar.	24	Reulbach	47-0918
Elisab. 28			
SCHLEICHERT, Ther.	27	Elters	51-0500
SCHLEID, Franz	18	Sandhausen	52-1661
SCHLEIER, F.	24	Steffenbach	54-1419
SCHLEIF, R. (m)	31	Neuhoft	54-1341
SCHLEIF, Traugott	30	Roebsen	54-0872
SCHLEIM, Mar. Elis	23	Oberrellenbac	51-1084
SCHLEINING, Wilh.	26	Alsfeld	51-0352
SCHLEIR, Joh Math.	21	Wuertenberg	53-0557
SCHLEITER, Charles	36	Halberstadt	53-0914
SCHLEITZ, Anna	16	Naumburg	54-0600
SCHLEITZ, George	24	Schleusingen	52-1362
SCHLEMM, Auguste	19	Soden	53-0838
SCHLEMM, Friedrich	25	Braunschweig	47-0158
SCHLENCK, Barb.	24	Volla	48-0445
SCHLENKE, Friedr.	46	Mergenussen	50-0472
Marie 40, Friede 9, Louise 6, Maria 21m			
SCHLENZ, Wilhelm	26	Hoeffingen	51-0405
SCHLENZKER, Conrad	40	Hille	51-1588
Henry 15			
SCHLEPPEGRELL, Hrm	26	Dinklage	52-0699
SCHLER, Christian	52	Brug Marterse	52-0807
SCHLESBACH, Gustav	19	Nagold	49-0352
SCHLESINGER, F.(f)	22	Gotha/Sax.	52-1423
SCHLESINGER, Jacob	36	Eckardrode/He	48-0053
SCHLESINGER, Rosal	30	Kirchbrit/Boe	53-0628
SCHLESTEIN, Helene	19	Wilhelmsdorf	48-0887
SCHLETZ, Carl	23	Hohenberg	50-1236
SCHLEUDER, Heinr.	24	Pr. Minden	51-0405
SCHLEUKHEIM, Heinr	14	Minden	52-1661
SCHLEUSAG, Charles	44	Prussia	54-1724
Rebecca 38, G. 12, Wilh. 10, Anne 6			
Charles 3			
SCHLICH, Reinhard	22	Grosseneichen	52-0699
Carl 20			
SCHLICHTER, Wm.	25	Wiesbaden/Nas	48-0447
SCHLICHTING, Carl	20	Luebeck	50-0292
SCHLICHTING, Diedr	26	Rodenberg	49-0383
SCHLICK, Casper	32	Eckersbach	52-0563
SCHLICK, Eva	26	Reith	54-0930
SCHLICK, Gust.	28	Gera	54-1297
SCHLICKERIDE, Hein	22	Steyerberg	51-0500
SCHLICKHARDT, Jul.	24	Pommern	54-1591
SCHLIECK, Anton	39	Pladen	51-1438
SCHLIEDER, Carl	60	Gleina	54-1371
Caroline 58, Charles 9, Franz 5			
Friedr. Carl 25, Friederike 23			
SCHLIEPER, Wilhelm	27	Heiselbach	53-1000
SCHLIEPMANN, Herm.	30	Kolkebeck	48-1355
SCHLIESSLER, Georg	28	Lamershof	54-0903
SCHLIFFTER, Doroth	20	Barsinghausen	52-1410
SCHLIMM, Sophie	21	Lichtenborn	51-0500
SCHLIMNER, Julius	21	Dassel	49-1517
SCHLINGLOFF, Carol	25	Sickendorf	53-0435
SCHLINTHAL, Sam.	20	Allenmuhr	50-0439
SCHLIPPE, Cresc.	29	Darpfhein/Mue	53-0435
SCHLISSELMANN, Cat	27	Frankenbostel	53-0492
SCHLITT, Anna Elis	21	Heiligendorf	54-0053
SCHLITT, E. (f)	19	Rotenkirchen	51-0517
SCHLOETTLER, Anna	22	Drangstedt	50-1067
SCHLOSS, Aron	14	Schweinshaupt	53-0991
SCHLOSS, Hirsch	28	Cassel	54-1724
SCHLOSS, Michael	29	Beltslarz	49-0912
SCHLOSSER, Friedr.	34	Andreasberg	54-1566
SCHLOSSER, John	20	Fl---	54-1341
SCHLOSSER, Rud.	24	Munsterberg	49-0781
SCHLOSSTEIN, Carl	20	Kirchheimtola	54-0987
SCHLOTE, Johann	22	Goettingen	52-1661
SCHLOTHAUSER, Jos.	20	Wieblingen	51-1245
SCHLOTT, Agness	28	Barch	50-0944
Mary 4, Louisa 9m			
SCHLOTT, Chr. Herm	28	Suhl	53-0888
Rosamunde 28, Auguste 8, Bertha 2			

NAME	AGE	RESIDENCE	YR-LIST
SCHLOTTA, Friedr.	27	Gotting	49-1517
SCHLOTTERBE, John	31	Bremen	53-1164
SCHLOTTERBECK, Aug	24	Schorndorf	49-0352
SCHLOTTMANN, Heinr	21	Bremen	54-1566
SCHLOTZHAUER, Adam	30	Oechsen	53-0942
SCHLUCH, George	16	Mittelruessel	49-0737
SCHLUCKEBIER, Pet.	19	Dissen	52-1661
SCHLUEBEL, Carl	30	Sittling	54-1078
SCHLUER, Carl Wilh	30	Ostercappeln	54-1371
Anna 27			
SCHLUESSEL, Alex.	18	Frensdorf	48-0269
SCHLUETER, Anna	24	Essen	53-1086
SCHLUETER, Anton	32	Sommersell	54-0600
SCHLUETER, August	35	Greene	54-1371
Minna 20			
SCHLUETER, Carolin	19	Hille	53-1023
SCHLUETER, Fr'drke	25	Derental	54-1443
SCHLUETER, H. (m)		H------d	49-1358
SCHLUETER, Heinr.	24	Bolensen	51-0500
Wilhelmine 30			
SCHLUETER, Henry	34	Braunschweig	53-0991
SCHLUETER, Marie	26	Eininghausen	54-1554
SCHLUND, Carl	27	Schleiz	53-0652
SCHLUND, Carl	22	Baden	54-1371
SCHLUR, Joh Math.	21	Wuertenberg	53-0557
SCHLUTER, Georg L.	20	Braunschweig	52-0558
SCHLUTER, Louise	21	Hibbe	47-0762
SCHLUTZ, Jacob	37	Du-----d	50-0944
SCHLUZ, C. (m)	26	Altona	48-0453
SCHMAEDECKE, Fried	17	Drakenborch/H	52-1332
SCHMAEDEKER, J.H.	21	Drakenburg	50-1067
SCHMAEHL, Johanne	20	Iburg	50-0439
Louise 22			
SCHMAELING, Engelb	17	Bruekenau	53-1062
SCHMAKE, Wilhelm	29	Naggen/Baden	51-1725
Maria 25, Sophia 8m			
SCHMAL, Leonh.	23	Hammelberg	49-1106
SCHMALENBERG, J.	34	Linden	50-0379
SCHMALSTICH, Fried	28	Hannover	53-0991
SCHMALZ, Johann	24	Altershausen	54-1168
SCHMAND, Anton	32	Naumburg	52-1200
Margaretha 30, Catharina 1			
SCHMANDT, Jacob	21	Steinberg	54-0830
SCHMANGEL, Adam	23	Oggenhausen	52-0370
SCHMANN, Reinhard	33	Glauchau	48-0887
SCHMANZE, Marie	31	Heiderdorn	50-0439
SCHMATZ, Friedrich	32	Doms/Sachsen	53-0628
SCHMAUSS, Apolonia		Luhe	53-0942
P. (m)			
SCHMAUSS, Jos.	28	Schneitach	52-0693
SCHMEDA, Meta	27	Lohe	51-1101
SCHMEDES, Otto	19	Bramstaedt	51-1640
SCHMEERBAUCH, F.	26	Ellers	49-0383
SCHMEISER, Georg	29	Bavaria	50-0311
SCHMEISSEN, v.d E.	35	Altona	54-1371
William 9			
SCHMEISSER, Joh Fr	27	Degenbach	52-0515
SCHMELZ, Carl	21	Stadtberge	53-0492
SCHMELZ, Franz	33	Grottkau	52-1321
SCHMELZKOPF, Anna	24	Niemburg	52-1410
SCHMERBAUCH, Anton	18	Strutt	52-0563
Anton 38, B. Catharina 37, Christian 7			
Marianne 9m, Marianne 23			
SCHMERBAUCH, Barth	30	Struth	51-0352
SCHMERZ, Heinr.	22	Hatzbach	50-0439
SCHMETCHEN, Herm.	18	Bertstedt	52-1321
SCHMETZER, Margret	27	Bayern	53-0590
SCHMID, Friedrich	32	Augsburg	54-1092
Johanna 27			
SCHMID, Johann	33	Milda	48-1131
Weigand 28			
SCHMID, Joseph	28	Wittenberg	49-0345
SCHMIDLEIN, Johann	33	Dachharz	54-1717
Anna 25, Johann 5, Margretha 4, Elise 10m			
SCHMIDT,	bob	Hannover	50-0292
SCHMIDT, (m)	36	Mittelstreu	50-0439
SCHMIDT, A.	30	Ahus	51-0517
(f) 29			

NAME	AGE	RESIDENCE	YR-LIST
SCHMIDT, A. (f)	27	Anzelape	48-0453
SCHMIDT, Adolph	21	Henneberg	54-0987
SCHMIDT, Adolphus	33	Willmars	53-1164
Elisabeth 32, Charles 11, Guenther 9			
Edward 7, Lisette 5, Gustav 3, baby			
SCHMIDT, Agathe	32	Ravensburg/Wu	49-0365
SCHMIDT, Albrecht	24	Braunschweig	52-1620
SCHMIDT, Alexander	24	Nordheim/Bav.	53-0628
SCHMIDT, Alois	24	Landsberg	49-1106
SCHMIDT, Amalie	28	Breslau	53-1086
SCHMIDT, Andreas	25	Lichtenfels	52-1661
SCHMIDT, Andreas	24	Neuhaus	54-1716
SCHMIDT, Anna	21	Hoefles	52-1129
SCHMIDT, Anna	23	Alfa	52-1105
SCHMIDT, Anna Elis	22	Weissenhassel	52-1148
SCHMIDT, Anna Kath	21	Hilgershausen	51-1062
SCHMIDT, Anna Marg	23	Frossem	54-1297
Johanne 2			
SCHMIDT, Anton	33	Bayern	53-0590
SCHMIDT, Anton	52	Boehmenskirch	50-0840
Marianne 48			
SCHMIDT, Aug.	16	Philipsthal	47-0828
SCHMIDT, August	23	Borkersdorf/S	52-1423
SCHMIDT, August	23	Schlettau/Sac	52-1620
SCHMIDT, August	27	Soeder/Hann.	50-0323
SCHMIDT, Auguste	28	Prenzlau	52-0807
SCHMIDT, B.	19	Neustadt	53-0914
SCHMIDT, B. (f)	23	Teigh	50-0746
SCHMIDT, Barb. Els	30	Tennstaedt	48-1355
SCHMIDT, Barbara	25	Rettenbach/Bv	52-1620
SCHMIDT, Barbara	13	Kirchlein	54-1168
SCHMIDT, C. (f)	36	Einoedhausen	48-0445
SCHMIDT, C. (m)	26	Bittstadt	49-0416
SCHMIDT, C.F.A.G.	18	Neustadt	49-0329
SCHMIDT, Carl	18	Tuisbrunnen	52-0693
SCHMIDT, Carl	25	Naumberg/Pr.	51-0117
SCHMIDT, Carl	40	Bayern	54-1716
SCHMIDT, Carl	57	Budingen	49-1106
Jeanette 57, Heinrich 1-			
SCHMIDT, Carl	30	Schkeuditz	54-1371
SCHMIDT, Carl Geo.	32	Hildburghause	52-1620
SCHMIDT, Caroline	33	Minden/Pr.	54-1092
Carl 8, Wilhelm 3, A. 9m			
SCHMIDT, Caspar	50	Bayern	53-1013
Caspar 29, Caspar 27, Anna 25, Mathias 23			
Theodor 19, Catharina 21, August 17			
Adam 15			
SCHMIDT, Caspar Ad		Kaltensundhei	50-0323
SCHMIDT, Cath Elis	21	Neukirchen	54-0930
SCHMIDT, Catharine	28	Bordorf	52-1105
SCHMIDT, Catherine	24	Kaiserslauter	49-0912
SCHMIDT, Charl.	24	Maenen	54-1282
SCHMIDT, Charlotte	21	Tecklenburg	52-1432
SCHMIDT, Chr. (m)	52	Leimbach/Mein	52-0960
M.E. (f) 58, Ch. C. (f) 17			
SCHMIDT, Chr. Lebr	39	Schwarzburg	50-1236
SCHMIDT, Christ.	24	Gr.Breitenbac	53-0585
SCHMIDT, Christ.	20	Leimbach	51-1084
Heinr. 20			
SCHMIDT, Christine	18	Dreba	52-1625
SCHMIDT, Christine	19	Obervorschiet	54-0930
SCHMIDT, Christine	17	Pommern	52-0693
SCHMIDT, Conr.	16	Nienburg	49-1358
SCHMIDT, Conr.	22	Frankenberg	47-0828
SCHMIDT, Conrad	28	Kehlbach	49-0352
Elisabeth 28, Magdalene 26, Lisette 24			
Christ. 30			
SCHMIDT, Dorothea	17	Rosswalden	48-1131
SCHMIDT, E.T.	46	Neudorf	51-0517
C. 40, T. 8, H. 5			
SCHMIDT, Eduard	26	Meiningen/Sax	51-0048
Elisabeth 29			
SCHMIDT, Elisabeth	38	Blankenbach	52-1148
Caspar 16			
SCHMIDT, Elise	21	Bremen	54-1078
SCHMIDT, Emil	19	Niederzimmern	50-0292
SCHMIDT, Ernestine	23	Mohrlach	54-1716
SCHMIDT, Ernst	31	Laubau	53-0825

NAME	AGE	RESIDENCE	YR-LIST
SCHMIDT, Eustach	23	Trennfurt	51-1455
SCHMIDT, Felix	17	Bueckeburg	53-0888
SCHMIDT, Ferd. Wm.	19	Barmen	48-0565
SCHMIDT, Ferdinand	24	Arensberg	52-0699
SCHMIDT, Ferdinand	18	Leikistern	52-1105
Emil 14			
SCHMIDT, Ferdinand	26	Daiten	54-1717
SCHMIDT, Francis	19	Forchheim	53-0991
SCHMIDT, Franz	31	Bremen	50-0840
Sophie 25			
SCHMIDT, Franz Jos	35	Struemphelbru	51-0384
Barbara 42			
SCHMIDT, Friedr.	27	Bonnland	54-0053
SCHMIDT, Friedrich	28	Oberfranken	53-1000
SCHMIDT, Friedrich	29	Schleusingen	54-0903
SCHMIDT, Friedrich	19	Wanderleben	52-1321
SCHMIDT, Friedrich	36	Lobenstein	53-0637
Catharine 32			
SCHMIDT, Friedrich	34	Wiesbaden/Nas	48-0447
Elisabetha 31, Charles 9, Philipp 4			
Helena 11m			
SCHMIDT, Friedrich	19	Gera/Pr.	49-0365
SCHMIDT, Friedrich	29	Mobile	54-1371
SCHMIDT, Friedrike	28	Rohmild	53-1000
SCHMIDT, G. Gottl.	31	Gottingen	49-1358
SCHMIDT, G.F.	30	Lehrberg	53-0582
M.B. 27, M.B. 3, Marie by			
SCHMIDT, Georg	21	Trapendorf	53-1000
Cath 26			
SCHMIDT, Georg	34	Thuengfeld	54-0930
SCHMIDT, Georg	26	Bramke	51-1640
Friederike 26, Theodor 9m			
SCHMIDT, Georg	33	Holsdorf	51-1639
Elise 33, Gertrude 4			
SCHMIDT, Georg	52	Walsrode	54-0987
Henriette 54, Friederike 22			
SCHMIDT, Georg	20	Hersfeld	51-0352
SCHMIDT, Georg	35	Elberfeld	48-0565
Johanna 25			
SCHMIDT, Georg	40	Straussfurth	51-0352
SCHMIDT, George	22	Croelpa	53-0914
SCHMIDT, George	39	Hemhofen	51-0352
SCHMIDT, George L.	28	Mittelruessel	49-0737
Margaretha 22			
SCHMIDT, Gertrude	28	Oberzell	54-1168
SCHMIDT, Gott.	58	Neuenbruege	47-0868
El. 48, H. 19, W. 11, E. 9, Karl 6			
SCHMIDT, Gottfr.	26	Ehlen	48-1355
Elise 24			
SCHMIDT, Gottfried	57	Erfurt	54-1649
Catharine 50, Carl 23, Henriette 19			
Heinrich 17, Wilhelm 17, August 9, Emil 7			
Ernestine 5			
SCHMIDT, Gust.	32	Graefenberg	49-1358
And. 19			
SCHMIDT, Gust. E.	29	Weida	51-1160
SCHMIDT, Gustav	23	Bayern	53-0557
SCHMIDT, Gustav	29	Moerseburg	52-0279
Lina 29, Pauline 9, Karoline 7, Anna 5			
SCHMIDT, H.	49	Breitenbach	54-1716
Maria 29, Catharine 6			
SCHMIDT, H.	33	Hannover	51-0460
Juliane 30, Marie 4			
SCHMIDT, H. (m)	28	Weidelbach	52-0558
F. (m) 40, J. (f) 20, H. (f) 25			
J. (f) 25, E. (f) 45, J. (f) 10			
SCHMIDT, H. (m)	36	Strebendorf	49-0742
SCHMIDT, Heinr.	19	Hizles	52-0693
SCHMIDT, Heinr.	20	Zwesten	51-1245
SCHMIDT, Heinr.	31	Muenden	54-1297
Emilie 27, Wilhelmine 11m			
SCHMIDT, Heinr.	31	Gilten	50-1132
SCHMIDT, Heinr.	20	Leimbach	51-1084
Christ. 20			
SCHMIDT, Heinr.	32	Charleston	50-0366
Helene 24			
SCHMIDT, Heinrich	26	Rauschenberg	52-1464
Henriette 48, Martha 28, Conrad 24			

NAME	AGE	RESIDENCE	YR-LIST
Caroline 22, Johannes 21, Cath. 19			
Daniel 18, Dorothea 13			
SCHMIDT, Heinrich	26	Werrel	53-0324
SCHMIDT, Heinrich	36	Erfurt/Pr.	53-0628
Dorothea 8			
SCHMIDT, Heinrich	24	Gotha	53-0473
SCHMIDT, Heinrich	20	Leiberg	51-0352
Anton 23			
SCHMIDT, Heinrich	25	Hoelle	49-1106
Lina 26			
SCHMIDT, Henrica	22	Homeberg/Bav.	53-0628
SCHMIDT, Herm.	25	Weimar	54-1297
SCHMIDT, Hermann	25	New York	47-0872
SCHMIDT, Hermann	30	Halberstadt	54-1371
SCHMIDT, J.	25	Cassel	51-0517
SCHMIDT, J.B.	24	Kunel	54-1419
SCHMIDT, J.G.L.	16	Cassel	54-1470
Chr. 16			
SCHMIDT, J.H. (m)	28	Walpenreuth	54-1341
M.S. (f) 22			
SCHMIDT, Jacob	22	Reinboldshaus	52-1625
SCHMIDT, Jacob	16	Schwalbach	51-1035
SCHMIDT, Jacob	21	Budingen	49-1106
SCHMIDT, Jacobine	17	Koengen	52-0095
Sophie 20			
SCHMIDT, Joh Georg	27	Noerdlingen	54-0987
SCHMIDT, Joh Georg	46	Kirchlanitz	48-1209
Barbara 48, Michael 26, Margaret 14			
Michael 10			
SCHMIDT, Joh Gottf	55	Magdeburg	52-0279
Emma 40			
SCHMIDT, Joh.	24	Rauschelshaus	54-0600
SCHMIDT, Joh.	33	Schweinfurt	48-1184
Barbara 44			
SCHMIDT, Joh.	19	Hainbach	49-0352
SCHMIDT, Joh. C.	42	Halle	50-0379
SCHMIDT, Joh. G.F.	25	Obereuth	49-0781
SCHMIDT, Joh. Marg	25	Schleusingen	52-1362
SCHMIDT, Joh. Sic.	34	Unterlauten	52-1332
Elsbeth 39, Eduard 7, Heinr. 3m			
SCHMIDT, Johann	31	Fulda	53-1016
SCHMIDT, Johann	18	Bayern	53-0557
Friedrich 17			
SCHMIDT, Johann	18	Arzberg/Bav.	53-0557
Friedrich 17			
SCHMIDT, Johann	39	Oberehrenbach	52-0693
Margarethe 39, Margarethe 2, Conrad 9			
SCHMIDT, Johann	30	Drueggendorf	52-0095
SCHMIDT, Johann	16	Langensalza	54-0987
SCHMIDT, Johann	28	Halmshaus	51-1062
SCHMIDT, Johann		Elberfeld	48-0565
Marie 33, Marie 4			
SCHMIDT, Johannes	25	Damshausen	53-1000
SCHMIDT, Johannes	19	Schoenstadt	54-1566
SCHMIDT, Johannes	13	Bersrod	52-1105
Marg. 47, Louise 15			
SCHMIDT, Johannes	37	Holzheim	54-0830
Heinrich 3, Juliana 36, Catharina 6			
Heinr. Ern. 9m			
SCHMIDT, Johannes	28	Christerode	54-1575
SCHMIDT, John	34	Doemitz	53-0991
Friedrich 28			
SCHMIDT, John	30	Pyrbaum	54-0053
SCHMIDT, John	24	Calmitz	53-0914
SCHMIDT, John C.	29	Helbra	54-1341
Adaline 28, daughter 6m			
SCHMIDT, John Jul.	30	Tolitz	53-0888
Henriette 24			
SCHMIDT, Johs.	14	Lengsfeld	48-1114
SCHMIDT, Jost	23	Schoenstadt	53-1016
SCHMIDT, Julius	29	Braunschweig	53-0590
Henriette 25, baby 4m			
SCHMIDT, Julius	21	Sandershausen	50-0021
SCHMIDT, L. (m)	23	Gensenhausen	54-1341
SCHMIDT, L. (m)	31	Alsalla	48-0445
A.M. (f) 35, L. (m) 9m			
SCHMIDT, Leon.	37	Sack/Muenchen	53-0435
SCHMIDT, Lorenz	32	Wolfrain	53-1023

NAME	AGE	RESIDENCE	YR-LIST
SCHMIDT, Louis	33	Bruckenau	51-1455
SCHMIDT, Louisa	23	Bielefeld	53-0991
SCHMIDT, Lucas Fl.	19	Rotenburg	51-0352
SCHMIDT, Ludwig	44	Luebbecke	51-1160
SCHMIDT, Ludwig	18	Koenigsberg	53-0590
SCHMIDT, Ludwig	49	Hengsfeld	54-1341
Magdalene 34, Ludwig 17, Friedrich 14			
SCHMIDT, Ludwig	17	Mannheim	49-0912
SCHMIDT, Marg.	22	Egloffsheim	54-0987
SCHMIDT, Marg.		Hutzdorf	54-1575
SCHMIDT, Marg. C.	25	Niederklein	52-1321
Conrad 17			
SCHMIDT, Margaret	28	Unterlindelba	49-0737
Margareta 25, Margareta 2			
SCHMIDT, Margareth	56	Marburg	54-0987
Friederike 30, Gustav 13, Eduard 9			
Margr. 4			
SCHMIDT, Margareth	60	Zeil	48-0887
Marianne 26, Angeline 21, Angeline 13			
Conrad 3, Angeline 1			
SCHMIDT, Margarett	21	Engenthal	51-1455
SCHMIDT, Margrethe	28	Wilhelmst---	48-0887
SCHMIDT, Maria	68	Seehausen	54-0987
SCHMIDT, Maria	21	Bremen	51-0652
SCHMIDT, Maria	28	Mittelruessel	49-0737
SCHMIDT, Marianna	17	Ferdinandsdor	51-0384
SCHMIDT, Marie	28	Oberneissen	54-1566
SCHMIDT, Martha	32	Waldcappel	49-0352
Martha Cath. 68			
SCHMIDT, Mary	36	Fulda	54-1419
SCHMIDT, Max.	33	Pfaffenhaus	53-0435
Barbara 24			
SCHMIDT, Michel	40	Osthofen	51-1639
Magretha 39, Andreas 13			
SCHMIDT, Michel	24	Lohenfels	54-0987
SCHMIDT, Moritz	22	Grossenheim	54-0053
SCHMIDT, Ms. (m)	32	Unterkremmach	48-0447
SCHMIDT, Nicolaus	20	Homberg	54-0053
SCHMIDT, Nicolaus	23	Neuhaus/Bav.	53-0475
Anna 27			
SCHMIDT, Otto	24	Brueggenau	52-0279
SCHMIDT, Otto	25	Zarzig	54-1168
SCHMIDT, Peter	24	Wallenroda	51-0352
SCHMIDT, Peter	18	Lindenbach	51-1084
SCHMIDT, Peter	40	Gruenebach/Pr	51-0048
Theodor 10, Jacob 8, Peter 6, Johanne 3			
SCHMIDT, Phil.	25	Homberg/Nass.	51-0048
SCHMIDT, Philipp	24	Gemen	53-0914
SCHMIDT, Richard	21	Meiningen	51-0405
SCHMIDT, Rosina	17	Cronach	53-0825
SCHMIDT, Theodor	16	Gmuenden/Bav.	52-1620
SCHMIDT, Theodor	29	Blankenburg	53-0914
Sophie 20, Sophie by			
SCHMIDT, Valentin	52	Wohnau	52-1200
Christine 54, Johann 18, Michel 16			
SCHMIDT, Valentin	20	Oberlimbach	54-1554
SCHMIDT, Veronia	21	Weimar	52-0370
SCHMIDT, Vincent	30	Boehmen	53-0557
SCHMIDT, W Th. Aug	14	Obernkirchen	53-0888
SCHMIDT, W. Ferd.	25	Lukau/Prussia	51-1796
SCHMIDT, Wilh'mine	28	Eichholz	49-0352
SCHMIDT, Wilh.	32	Reurieth	49-1358
Elisabeth 35, Ernst 7, Barbara 5			
Georg 22			
SCHMIDT, Wilh.	37	Amt Gehren	48-1179
SCHMIDT, Wilhelm	20	Minden	52-1410
SCHMIDT, Wilhelm	32	Muenden	52-1410
Julie 32, Friedrich 4, Julius 3			
Theodor by			
SCHMIDT, Wilhelm	19	Hannover	52-1362
SCHMIDT, Wilhelm	39	Semien	53-1086
Marie 40, Clara 20, Anna 18, M. Ernst 11			
Marie 7, Leonore 16			
SCHMIDT, Wilhelm	29	Weissenfeld	54-1297
SCHMIDT, Wilhelm	18	Kemmenau	54-1371
SCHMIDT, William	35	Oberod	53-0914
SCHMIDT, William	30	Nunkhausen/Na	51-0048
SCHMIDT, Wolfgang	38	Hoestach	50-0292

NAME	AGE	RESIDENCE	YR-LIST
SCHMIDTKUNG, Jos.	24	Bayern	53-0557
SCHMIDTNAGEL, Andr		Schleusingen	54-0903
SCHMIDTNAGEL, Fr.	28	Wallenfels	54-0903
Anna 28, Johann 4			
SCHMIDTS, August	19	Baiern	53-0585
SCHMIDTS, Paul	37	Feuchtwing/Bv	52-1332
Christine 34, Friederike 14			
SCHMIDTZ, Anthony	23	Coblenz	54-0850
Betty 25			
SCHMIDTZ, Henry	45	Kurthen	48-0406
Ann Cathrine 48, Margareth 19			
Christian 14, Johannes 10			
Ann Cathrine 18m			
SCHMIED, Mariana	25	Behmenkirch	49-0345
SCHMIEDEL, Joh. Wm	42	Doebeln	52-1625
Mathilde 35			
SCHMIEDER, Lusia	19	Huntsbach	53-0928
SCHMIEDES, Friedr.	37	Eistrup	48-1209
SCHMIEDING, Caspar	40	Barmen	48-0565
SCHMIEDING, Wilh.	23	Bunde	54-0930
SCHMIEG, Georg	34	Bayern	53-0590
SCHMIKALZ, Julius	23	Berlin	54-1724
SCHMILLE, Franz	25	Bremerhafen	54-1092
SCHMINKE, Carl	29	Duben	51-1739
SCHMINKE, Herrmann	20	Bremen	52-0095
SCHMIT, Hermann G.	18	Bremen	51-0500
SCHMITH, Henry	38	Cassel	53-0914
SCHMITT, Anna	47	Landberg	54-1283
Caroline 14, August 12, Adam 10			
SCHMITT, Eduard	27	Kamstaedt	53-0652
SCHMITT, Hugo	23	Weissenfels	54-1283
SCHMITTENS, Mich.	32	Garitz	51-1455
SCHMITZ, Heinrich	22	Dortmund	51-1245
SCHMITZ, Heinrich	26	Boston	54-1371
SCHMITZ, Jette	17	Dingen	48-0951
SCHMITZ, Ludwig	19	Dortmund	51-1245
SCHMOESCHER, Jos.	38	Hirschfeld/Bv	53-0475
Anna 36, Therese 2, Nicolaus 58, Anna 11			
Catharine 8, Margarethe 5			
SCHMOLL, Jacob Fr.	21	Elsbruecken	53-0914
SCHMOLZ, Christian	15	Mohringen	54-1575
SCHMOLZE, Louis	27	Zweibruecken	53-1086
SCHMUCK, Andr.	39	Theissnert	48-1179
Kunigunde 38, Margarethe 4			
SCHMUCK, Georg	28	Theresenort	53-0825
Mariane 29, Margarethe 9w			
SCHMUCK, Georg	23	Meiningen	51-0405
SCHMUCKER, Joseph	45	Luftig	54-1168
SCHMUDING, Friedr.	24	Hernebache	50-0292
Elisabeth 25, child bob			
SCHMUTZLER, Georg	53	Lollgruen	51-1686
Sophie 53, Christian 21, Friedr. 19			
Ferdinand 17, August 10, Christine 28			
Marie 21, Johanne 15, August 9, Wilhelm 6			
Carol. 24, Carl 10m			
SCHMUTZLER, Gottl.	28	Mittelruessel	49-0737
SCHNABEL, Augst.	39	Altenburg	52-1321
SCHNADEL, Marg.	50	Mannheim	48-0445
H. (m) 23, G. (m) 14, E. (f) 19			
D. (f) 16, D. (m) 14, F. (m) 11			
SCHNAKE, A.	28	Unterhibbe	47-0762
Catharina 27			
SCHNAKE, Ernst	33	Schnathorst	49-0329
G. (m) 25			
SCHNAPP, Philipp	36	Forschheim	54-1168
Margrethe 22, Friederike 22, baby			
SCHNARR, Demetrias	31	Heinzell	53-0320
SCHNAS, Heinrich	19	Sinlikte	49-0345
SCHNATHORST, Carl	26	Boelhorst	49-0329
SCHNATSMEYER, C.D.	22	Prussia	50-0311
SCHNAUFFEN, Elise	21	Kohlberg	48-0951
SCHNEDEWIND, Andr.	24	Scharnach	50-0439
SCHNEEBERGER, Hein	24	Kaierberg	53-0320
SCHNEEGEBERG, Hein	15	Hessen	53-1013
SCHNEEMANN, Heinr.	25	Wischhausen	50-1236
SCHNEETLER, John D	54	Prussia	51-1725
Theodor 26			
SCHNEEWEISS, Edw.	21	Rinteln	50-1236

NAME	AGE	RESIDENCE	YR-LIST
SCHNEHEIM, Heinr.	25	Cassel	49-0413
SCHNEIAU, Carl	21	Nuernberg	53-0914
SCHNEIDACHER, G.	27	Enger	53-0492
SCHNEIDER, A.	22	Arnsheim	51-0517
SCHNEIDER, Andreas	23	Muehl	53-0267
SCHNEIDER, Andrew	53	Salmsdorf/Bav	48-0053
Barbara 43, Friedr. 26, Catharina 28			
John 8, Andrew 3, Louis 20			
SCHNEIDER, Anna	17	Grossenritt	54-0965
SCHNEIDER, August	30	Lengefeld	53-1070
SCHNEIDER, August	36	Elspe	52-1105
SCHNEIDER, Bertha	36	Freyburg	53-0991
SCHNEIDER, Carl	56	Vasbeck	54-0053
Marie Elis. 48, Marie 17, Antoinette 14			
SCHNEIDER, Carl	15	Niederschelde	49-0781
SCHNEIDER, Carolin	26	Rheda/Prussia	53-0628
SCHNEIDER, Cath.	28	Fernbreitenba	52-1661
SCHNEIDER, Cath.	-4	Jeverbach	52-1464
Elise 12, Carl 9			
SCHNEIDER, Cath.	17	Osnabruck	50-1071
SCHNEIDER, Christ.	20	Filingen	53-1062
SCHNEIDER, Christ.	4-	Dalwigsthal	49-0365
Friedrich 17, Mary 15, Mary 15			
SCHNEIDER, Conrad	31	Bavaria	53-0628
SCHNEIDER, Conrad	22	Goodelsheim	50-0379
SCHNEIDER, Elenor	19	Schleusingen	52-0807
SCHNEIDER, Elise	30	Ammerhausen	54-1443
SCHNEIDER, F.K.	32	Fesseldorf	52-0558
SCHNEIDER, Fran'ka	26	Lunen	47-0918
SCHNEIDER, Friedr.	32	Rosswein	51-1438
SCHNEIDER, Friedr.	27	Wahlhold	52-1101
SCHNEIDER, Georg	23	Milz	54-1716
Ernst 16			
SCHNEIDER, Georg	60	Merschenbach	51-1640
SCHNEIDER, H. (m)	27	Altona	48-0453
SCHNEIDER, Heinr.	33	Kirchlein/Bav	53-0628
Barbara 33			
SCHNEIDER, Heinr.	27	Langenstein	49-0352
SCHNEIDER, Heinr.	23	Niederhelt	54-1443
SCHNEIDER, J. (m)	17	Lohne	48-0445
F. (m) 16, J. (m) 11m			
SCHNEIDER, J. Hein	16	Lester	54-1297
SCHNEIDER, Jacob	19	Luhra	51-1686
SCHNEIDER, Jacob	21	Badenheim/Hes	52-0117
SCHNEIDER, James T	32	Duermenz	53-1164
SCHNEIDER, Joh.	24	Speckswinkel	50-0439
SCHNEIDER, Johann	40	Knueffelbach	54-1078
Marg. 16, Elisabeth 11, Margaretha 9			
Catharina 8			
SCHNEIDER, Johann	44	Rodsenburger	53-0652
SCHNEIDER, Johann	18	Tatschenbrunn	48-0101
SCHNEIDER, John	19	Prussia	54-1724
SCHNEIDER, Joseph	28	Netphen	53-1062
Elisabetha 24			
SCHNEIDER, L. (m)	22	Harberg	48-0445
Christine 64, Ch. (f) 24			
SCHNEIDER, Leonh.	29	Unterpirk	49-0912
SCHNEIDER, Louis	41	Giessen	52-1362
SCHNEIDER, Lud.	33	Prussia	54-1724
SCHNEIDER, Mathias	26	Rodsenburger	53-0652
Magdalene 37, Maria 4, Anna Marie 1			
SCHNEIDER, Michael	37	Bischofsreith	54-1283
SCHNEIDER, Monica	22	Bietingen/Bad	51-1725
SCHNEIDER, Peter	48	Frankenhausen	53-0492
SCHNEIDER, Richard	17	Hesselried	54-1554
SCHNEIDER, Sophie	26	Dillenburg	53-1023
SCHNEIDER, Terese	24	Curhessen	52-1432
SCHNEIDER, Therese	28	Altenburg	50-0311
Sylvester 5, Louis 3, Marie 11m			
SCHNEIDER, Valent.	32	Gera/Gotha	52-0960
H. (f) 28, E. (f) 7			
SCHNEIDER, Wil'mne	18	Pfuhl/Nassau	53-0652
SCHNEIDER, Wilh.	28	Hoeseter	50-1071
Carl 23			
SCHNEIDER, Wilhelm	17	Eicha	54-1554
Magdalena 10			
SCHNEIDER, William	26	Leutkirch/Wue	49-0365
SCHNEIDER, Xaver	28	Meckenbeuren	54-1168

NAME	AGE	RESIDENCE	YR-LIST
SCHNEIDERHEINZE, A	31	Chemmitz	53-0914
SCHNEIDERHEINZE, A	31	Chemnitz	53-0914
male 26			
SCHNEIDERIN, Maria	18	Glasshofen	53-0590
SCHNEIDLER, Friedr	22	Sachsen	53-0590
SCHNEIDT, Carl Got	27	Noerdlingen	54-1452
SCHNEIER, Franz	32	Rossfeld	53-0320
SCHNEIER, Friedr.	31	Rossfeld	53-0320
SCHNEIER, Georg	35	Rossfeld	52-1321
SCHNEIER, Maria	37	Rasfeld	52-1321
SCHNEIR, Albert	19	Bamberg	51-1035
SCHNEISHUHN, Theod	19	Wildberg	49-0352
SCHNEITNER, Cath.	21	Geislingen	54-1341
SCHNEITNER, Elise	24	Geislingen	54-1341
SCHNELL, Fr. W.	34	Herford	51-1245
SCHNELL, Hans.	19	Stade	47-0828
SCHNELL, Johann	42	Tuebingen	47-0828
Agathe 29, Albertine 8, Maximilian 6			
Theodor 5, Anna 2			
SCHNELLE, Fr. Wilh	45	Melle	54-1297
SCHNELLE, Herman	18	Bissendorf	51-1588
Catherine 19, Maria 20			
SCHNELLE, Wilh'mne	25	Grossenrode	54-0987
Carl by			
SCHNELLER, Christ.	44	Tyrol	48-0887
Cresenze 40, Catharine 5			
SCHNELLER, Eduard	24	Baden	48-1355
SCHNELLER, Ernst		Baden	48-1355
SCHNELLING, Heinr.	33	New York	47-0828
SCHNELT, Johann	20	Cassel	54-0930
SCHNEPEL, Heinrich	16	Doehren	50-0366
SCHNEPEL, Hermann	16	Arschwarden	54-0930
SCHNETTLER, Friedr	21	Armsfeld	51-0405
SCHNICKEL, Hyron.	16	Cur Hessen	53-0557
Daniel 18			
SCHNICKEL, Hyronim	16	Kur-Hessen	53-0557
Daniel 18			
SCHNICKER, Fr.	22	Koehlen	51-0460
SCHNIDER, Peter	29	Weissenbach	53-0435
SCHNIEDERIAN, Just	28	Westenholz	53-0267
SCHNIEDERMANN, Crl	17	Meinberg	52-0775
SCHNIEDEWIND, Hein	16	Bremen	52-1105
Gesine 19			
SCHNIER, Bernhard	25	Greven	47-0762
SCHNIER, Caroline	19	Barkhausen	49-0329
SCHNIERINGER, Joh.	34	Fexen	53-0492
SCHNIFFLIN, Philip	25	Barmen	54-1371
SCHNIKKE, Ernst W.	50	Gera/Reus	54-1092
Ottilie 37, Louise 18, Karl 15			
SCHNITER, Mich.	30	Dalkingen	53-0435
SCHNITGER, Herrm.	26	Eichholz	49-0352
SCHNITGER, Simon	21	Eichholz	49-0352
SCHNITKER, Anton		Osterwick	53-0942
SCHNITKER, Caspar	26	Bieren	54-1452
Louise 20			
SCHNITTER, Georg	28	Schweinfurt	50-0021
SCHNITTGER, August	19	Spork	52-0775
SCHNITTKEN, Cath.	16	Bordel	51-1588
SCHNITZER, M. (m)	26	Minden	48-1114
SCHNITZLER, Simon	22	Rothenberg	50-1071
SCHNITZLER, Wilh.	30	Buer	52-1101
Hermann 28			
SCHNOFER, Christ.	20	Stuttgart	53-0585
SCHNOPP, Adam	36	Doellbach/Hes	50-0323
SCHNORBUS, Joseph	28	Berlin	53-0585
SCHNORFAIL, Joseph	39	Frankenstein	54-1717
Carl 15			
SCHNUBER, Albert	22	Mittelruessel	49-0737
SCHNUPHASE, Friedr	21	Dermsdorf	51-1062
SCHNUR, Heinrich	30	Lutter	54-1452
Henriette 33			
SCHNUR, Vict.	21	Hundsbach	53-0928
SCHNURBUSCH, Anton	27	Hallenberg	54-1297
SCHOBACKER, Joh.	46	Lengloh	54-1168
Anna 43, Catharine 21, Elisabeth 16			
Heinrich 19			
SCHOBEL, Joh.	50	Hof	50-1071
Elisabeth 48, Catharina 18, Maria 12			

NAME	AGE	RESIDENCE	YR-LIST
Hanna 6, Elisabeth 3m			
SCHOBESLEIN, Joh.	36	Oberndorf	54-1283
Marie 36, Leonhard 5			
SCHOBESTEIN, John	32	Oberndorf	53-0492
SCHOBUK, Gregrico	28	Mittelruessel	49-0737
SCHOBURG, Friedr.	12	Churhessen	52-1620
SCHOCHER, Martin A	29	Zeitz	54-0850
Caroline 29, Oscar by			
SCHOCKE, Joh.	52	Wahnbeck	54-1297
Louise 52			
SCHOCKMEYER, Heinr	55	Loewendorf	48-1355
SCHODTEL, Conrad	36	Langenstein	52-1512
Elisabeth 36, Caroline 7, Conrad 4			
Heinr. 3, Elisabeth 6m			
SCHOEBEL, Johann	42	Seifensdorf	54-0882
Daniel 14			
SCHOEDEL, Adam	24	Quellenreuth	52-0351
SCHOELE, Christoph	47	Oberricksinge	52-0351
SCHOELEIN, Barbara	20	Sterpersdorf	54-1554
SCHOELLING, Maria	25	Kirchberg	49-0352
Margarethe 23, Johann 27			
SCHOEMBERG, Heinr.	32	Treysa	49-0345
SCHOEN, Adam	23	Buchenau/Hess	52-1620
SCHOEN, Alb.	23	Ciershausen	54-1470
SCHOEN, Andreas	25	Hubstadt	53-0320
SCHOEN, J.E.	48	Berlin	54-1575
Julius 21			
SCHOEN, Joh Joseph	21	Mengers/Hess.	51-1532
SCHOEN, Mathias	44	Millewitsch	53-0905
Margarethe 37, Ludwig 16, Franz 11			
Maria 9, Mathias 7, Jacob 4			
SCHOEN, Nicolaus	49	Wieblingen	51-0460
SCHOENAU, George	40	Reinsfeld	52-1304
Sidona 36, Rosalie 14, Henry 9			
SCHOENAUER, Peter	24	Konigsfeld	51-1035
SCHOENBERG, Chr.	22	Sachsenburg	53-0492
SCHOENBERGER, Ch.	19	Ermreuth	53-1164
SCHOENBERGER, Jos.	32	Fuschendorf	53-0905
Elisabeth 26			
SCHOENE, Carl	23	Mockrehna/Pr.	52-1620
SCHOENE, Dorothea	23	Darmstadt	52-0807
SCHOENE, Heinrich		Elbersberg	54-1168
SCHOENE, Mar. Cath	23	Eberschuetz	51-0460
SCHOENE, Teresia	24	Butterich	51-1686
SCHOENEBECK, Cath.	44	Giesen	53-1000
SCHOENEFELD, Chr.	39	Roda	54-1297
Therese 37, Eduard 15, Theodor 14			
Emilie 9, Hermine 6, Bertha 1			
Friedrich 1m			
SCHOENEMANN, Fanny	18	Hainsfarth	52-1200
Jette 16			
SCHOENEMEYER, A.	24	Handerold	54-1341
SCHOENEMEYER, Wilh	29	Hauterode	54-1443
SCHOENERT, Charles	30	Halberstadt	53-0914
SCHOENEWALD, Elise	23	Frankenberg	54-0918
SCHOENFELD, Carl	38	Woldegk	53-0905
Mina 32, Herman 4, Carl by, Christian 36			
Mina 24			
SCHOENFELD, Fr. Er	34	Koenigshain	53-1016
SCHOENFELD, Marine	33		54-0987
Lina 9			
SCHOENHALS, Conrad	42	Eidorf	51-0460
Elisabeth 43, Elisabeth 20, Conrad 17			
Johannes 12, Heinrich 5, Catharina 2			
SCHOENHAMMER, Amel	33	Wuerzburg	53-0991
SCHOENHEIT, Wilh.	24	Graefenthal	48-1184
SCHOENHERR, CC Geo	29	Weimar	52-0563
SCHOENHERR, Cath.	54	Carlsruhe	54-1371
Catharine 20			
SCHOENHERZ, C.C.G.	29	Weimar	52-0563
SCHOENHOLZER, Conr	40	Turgau	53-0888
Georg 14			
SCHOENIAN, Heinr.	23	Braunschweig	49-0383
SCHOENIG, Michael	36	Ferdinandsdor	51-0384
Franz 48, Catharina 38, Johann 11			
Marianna 4, Franz Jos. 1			
SCHOENIG, S. (m)	26	Trienz	50-0746
SCHOENINGMEYER, H.	25	Westerlohe	52-0563

NAME	AGE	RESIDENCE	YR-LIST
SCHOENLEBER, Doro.	22	Eimersleben	49-0352
SCHOENLEIN, Sebast	26	Bamberg	53-0267
Anna 23			
SCHOENPERLE, Cath.	21	Gerlingen	49-1106
SCHOENTHAL, Jacob	26	Brilon/Pr.	53-0475
SCHOENTHAL, Moses	17	Altenmuhr	51-1160
Adele 22			
SCHOEPF, Anna	23	Ahornis	54-1554
SCHOEPPEL, J.G.	27	Heinsdorf	53-1016
SCHOEPPEL, Peter	34	Solingen	48-0406
SCHOEPPNER, Joh.	43	Fulda	54-0987
SCHOERE, John F.	27	Bodenwerder	54-1470
SCHOERNER, Johann	23	Schwarzenbach	53-0475
Margarethe 22, Adam 7			
SCHOESCHE, Jacob	29	Nentershausen	48-0269
Fr. 26, Dorothea 21, Johanne 20, Clara 2			
Sophia 6m			
SCHOETT, Carl		Steinfurt	54-1575
SCHOETTELDREYER, W	17	Bueckeburg	53-0492
SCHOHEI, Veronica	53	Iglau	54-1371
Albert 14, Franz 28			
SCHOHLFELDER, Joh.	29	Bamberg	52-0515
Margaretha 30			
SCHOLE, John	27	Hessia	47-0987
SCHOLL, Catharina	24	Mallbach	54-0053
SCHOLLE, Heinrich	52	Kirchhod	51-1639
Elisabeth 41, Martha 16, Maria 12			
Cathrine 6, Anna 3			
SCHOLLE, John	22	Bischofgruen	49-1517
SCHOLLKOFF, David	51	Brunnenweiler	47-0828
Anna 32, David 21, Anna 24, Ludwig 19			
Johann 17			
SCHOLT, Joh Heinr.	18	Bayreuth	51-1455
SCHOLTZE, Am.	29	Nienburg/Hann	51-1796
SCHOLTZE, Rudolph	35	Baltimore	48-1184
SCHOLZ, Anton	40	Ongelsbug	54-1676
SCHOLZ, August	43	Breslau	54-1717
SCHOLZ, Wilhelm	38	Gera	54-0872
SCHOMAKER, Engel	15	Bohnde	49-0352
SCHOMBURG, Gust. A	20	Wehlau	50-0439
SCHON, Alexander	24	Eierhausen	52-1661
Juliane 29			
SCHONAD, Johann	29	Schlessliz	54-1717
Barbara 33			
SCHONBURG, Henry	50	Gotha	50-0323
John 24, August 18			
SCHONERT, Christ.	52	Griesheim	52-1304
Dorothea 44, Theodor 20, Wilhelmine 18			
Auguste 13, Heinrich 11			
SCHONERT, Joh. H.	45	Niederwilling	48-0269
Fr. 16, Clara 57, Maria 14, Auguste 12			
SCHOO, Therese	23	Lingen	51-1101
SCHOONE, Catharine	24	Gehrde	50-0292
SCHOORER, Xaver	28	Bertholdshafe	53-0492
SCHOPF, Friedrich	20	Stambach	53-0492
SCHOPPNER, Heinr.	20	Saalfeld	49-0574
SCHOPPNER, John	2-	Flieden/Hesse	49-0365
Anna 29			
SCHORCHMEIER, Jos.	28	Hoexter/Pruss	53-0628
SCHORING, Carl	36	Gronig	52-1101
Martha 36, Luise 7, Therese 5			
Anna (died) 9m			
SCHORK, V. (m)	23	Trienz	50-0746
A. (f) 21, C. (f) 17			
SCHORK, W. (m)	20	Trienz	50-0746
SCHORN, Lucas	15	Obermerzbach	54-0872
SCHORNAGEL, Joh.	30	Steinheim	54-1168
Franz 28			
SCHORR, Elisabeth	27	Frommers	52-1200
SCHORTSTEIN, Geo.A	22	Rabboldshause	54-1647
SCHOSSBERGER, J.G.	30	Mittelruessel	49-0737
SCHOSTER, Ernst	27	Rabber/Hann.	54-1092
SCHOTHORN, John	25	Nettelstedt	47-0762
Marie 22			
SCHOTT, Adam	24	Rhina	52-1661
Elisabeth 21			
SCHOTT, Anna	23	Bobenhausen	53-1023
SCHOTT, Augusta	34	Loessnitz	48-1179

NAME	AGE	RESIDENCE	YR-LIST
Amalie 13, Emilie 10, Gustav 4			
SCHOTT, Cathar. El	22	Hessen	53-1023
SCHOTT, Catherine	21	Munchhausen	54-1341
SCHOTT, Dorothea	22	Wiesenhaid	54-1554
SCHOTT, F. (m)	30	Rheden	54-1341
SCHOTT, Heinrich	25	Felda	54-0053
SCHOTT, J.M. (m)	28	Tauberschonba	52-0558
S. (f) 50, E. (f) 22			
SCHOTT, Marg.	40	Tauberschonba	52-0558
SCHOTT, Philipp	24	Muenchberg	52-1512
Charlotte 22, Catharine by			
SCHOTTE, Wilh.	24	Roemhild	54-0600
SCHOTTLER, Heinr.	25	Elmeloh	54-1297
SCHRAAGE, Gustav	22	Brandenburg	54-1591
SCHRADER, August	20	Hildesheim	52-0095
SCHRADER, C.H.	31	Schoenegg	54-1283
SCHRADER, Charles	25	Celle	52-1304
SCHRADER, Chr.	55	Hannover	50-0311
SCHRADER, Ernst. A	25	Celle	51-1084
SCHRADER, F. (f)		Stein	54-1341
SCHRADER, F. (m)	20	Padingbuettel	49-0329
SCHRADER, Friedr.	33	Itzum/Hann	52-0960
SCHRADER, Fritz	15	Lahmstedt	53-0838
SCHRADER, H. (m)	26	Bodenfelde	52-0652
SCHRADER, H. (m)	23	Wendelbarstel	54-1341
SCHRADER, Heinr.	46	Meinsen	52-1321
Hans 40			
SCHRADER, Herm.	18	Prussia	50-0021
SCHRADER, Johann	25	Borgendreich	53-1000
SCHRADER, Johanna	32	Einbeck/Hann.	51-1532
SCHRADER, John	27	Braunschweig	48-1209
SCHRADER, Maria	25	Niederdorf	52-1101
SCHRADER, Marie	23	Borgentreich	53-1000
SCHRADER, Sophia	54	Meinsen	52-1321
Soph. 18, Engel 14			
SCHRADER, Sophia	58	Wendenborstel	54-1341
Sophia 15, Ludwig 19			
SCHRADER, Sophie	22	Hildesheim	54-1297
SCHRADER, Theodor	23	Gernheim/Pr.	54-1092
SCHRADER, W.	27	Nordheim	54-1283
SCHRADER, Wilh.	24	Bleicheralte	52-1321
SCHRAEGEMEYER, J.H	32	Mettingen	48-0269
Fr. 27, Wm. 28, Maria 27, Catharina 28			
Lotte 26, Friederike 24, Sophie 3			
SCHRAFER, M.E.	19	Maskuhl	52-0558
SCHRAGE, John	30	Pewsum	53-0888
SCHRAM, Joh Jacob	19	Wuestenselbit	53-0637
SCHRAML, Simon	28	Helmrecht	54-0965
Barbara 28, baby			
SCHRAMM, August	22	Freisdorf	48-0951
SCHRAMM, Casper	25	Neustadt	53-1023
SCHRAMM, Catharina	50	Lothe	51-1062
Gottlieb 16			
SCHRAMM, Fr.	35	Wrexen	54-1575
Minna 25, Carl 5, son 3, Wilhelm 11m			
SCHRAMM, Johann	32	Rekendorf/Bav	52-1620
Sophie 25			
SCHRAMM, Johann	38	Coburg	53-1013
Catharine 32			
SCHRAMM, Johann	31	Eppenreuth	51-0352
SCHRAMM, Justius	33	Freiberg	52-1321
SCHRAMM, Marg.	24	Rockenhof	52-1105
SCHRAMS, August	bob		48-0951
SCHRAU, Anna Marg.	20	Rasdorf	48-0284
SCHRAUCH, B. (f)	21	Salzungen	54-1470
SCHRAUDER, Marg.	18	Buch/Bav.	52-1620
Conrad 30			
SCHRAUDORF, Franz	44	Imshofen/Bav.	53-0628
SCHRECK, Joseph	30	Grosskarfeld	54-1168
SCHRECK, Peter	33	Bendheim	51-1796
SCHREI, Joseph	34	Ripplin/Bav.	49-0365
Gesine 29			
SCHREIBE, Georg H.	56	Muehlberg	53-1062
Maria Christ 53, Johanne Mar. 24			
Christiana E 21, Johann A.R. 19			
Maria Louise 16, Ida Arora 14			
Christ. Aug. 12			
SCHREIBEIS, Wilh.	24	Mudau	51-0460

NAME	AGE	RESIDENCE	YR-LIST
Fr. Cathr. 26			
SCHREIBER, August	35	Celle	52-0095
SCHREIBER, B.	18	Zwickau	51-1160
SCHREIBER, Barbara	24	Salzungen	49-0413
SCHREIBER, Bern.	38	Hannover	54-1724
SCHREIBER, Ch. B.	24	Cassel	53-0905
SCHREIBER, Eduard	32	Siegen	48-0269
SCHREIBER, Fran'ka	22	Dusseldorf	51-0652
SCHREIBER, Gottl.	38	Chemnitz	53-1023
Maria Ros. 40, Maria Agnes 8			
Ernst Heinr. 4, Friedr.Gust. 9m			
SCHREIBER, Helene	20	Preussen	53-0590
SCHREIBER, Joh Got	26	Endschuetz	52-0563
SCHREIBER, Johann	29	Meissen	54-1371
SCHREIBER, Lorenz	57	Lolitz	52-1101
SCHREIBER, Max	25	Preussen	52-0370
SCHREIBER, Philipp	40	Duesseldorf	51-0652
SCHREIBER, Sabine	23	Sterbfritz	50-0840
SCHREIBER, Theodor	33	Bremerhaven	54-1092
Elisa 32			
SCHREIBERS, Wilh.	24	Mudau	51-0460
Fr. Cathr. 26			
SCHREIBERT, Henr't	16	Cassel	54-1470
SCHREIDER, Christ.	44	W---son	50-0944
Sophia 36, Christian Jr 17, Sophia 16			
Conrad 13			
SCHREIER, Amalia	25	Carlsbad	51-1160
Magd. (died) 73			
SCHREIER, Georg	33	Barchfeld	54-1554
SCHREINECK, Friedr	19	Meiningen	52-0895
SCHREINER, Caspar	35	Volkmarsen	50-0292
SCHREINER, Cath.	19	Noerdlingen	52-1625
SCHREINER, Fran'ka	39	Volkmarsen	53-0914
SCHREINER, Hein. R	28	Mord-gen	50-0944
SCHREINER, Heinr.	24	Feldkruecken	51-1101
Balthasar 27			
SCHREINER, Herm.	27	Rundshausen	50-0292
SCHREITER, David	20	Zwickau	54-0882
SCHREIVOGEL, Jacob	39	Rothenburg	48-0887
Rosalie 28, Sophia 2			
SCHREMBEL, Em. (m)	25	Stolten	52-1321
SCHREMMEL, Mathias	33	Dillenburg	54-0830
SCHREMPS, Caroline	16	Wissingen	54-1283
SCHREMS, August	43	Haag	48-0951
SCHREMS, Henry	39	Haag	48-0951
SCHRENK, Carl	44	Hachingen	54-1168
Gottliebin 38			
SCHRENKEISEN, Mart	13	Grossenglis	52-0775
SCHREPFERMANN, J.O	19	Steinweisen	53-0914
SCHREUER, Marg.	27	Fleisen	51-1035
Theodor 3			
SCHREY, Friederike	30	Herzberg	54-1649
SCHREYER, Ferdin.	26	Sachsen	53-0585
SCHREYER, Peter	29	Kraftsohms	54-1078
SCHRICKER, Cath.	19	Arzberg	50-1236
SCHRICKER, Margar.	19	Wunsiedel	53-0888
SCHRIDER, Christ.	44	W----son	50-0944
Sophia 36, Christian jr 17, Sophia 16			
Conrad 13			
SCHRIEBER, Friedr.	47	Woldegk	53-0905
Marie 48, Wilhelm 14, August 8			
SCHRIEFER, Claus	20	Sellstedt	51-0756
SCHRIEFER, Diedr.	15	Offenwarden	51-0326
SCHRIEFER, Reg.	22	Twendamm	51-0326
SCHRIEVER, Chr.	25	Hannover	50-0021
SCHRIEVER, Elert	22	Oldenburg	50-0021
SCHRIFFLIN, Philip	25	Barmen	54-1371
SCHRIRES, W. (m)	36	Wachbach	49-0329
SCHRIUS, Johannes	46	Anleben/Sachs	51-1725
SCHROD, Joseph	21	Klein Auheim	52-1512
SCHRODER, Anton	29	Jordanmouth,O	54-1716
Johanna 32			
SCHRODER, C.	25	Gotha	54-1716
SCHRODER, Cecilie	21	Bibergau	48-0951
SCHRODER, Friedr.	29	Langendam	54-1716
SCHRODER, H. (m)	24	Kuchen	52-0558
SCHRODER, Heinrich	30	Neidernhof	54-0882
SCHRODER, Heinrich	34	Westheim	47-0762

NAME	AGE	RESIDENCE	YR-LIST
Mary 24, Mary 3m			
SCHRODER, Johanna	32	Strechten	54-1716
SCHRODER, Marta	25	Mittelruessel	49-0737
SCHRODER, Wilhelm	22	Neidernhof	54-0882
SCHROEDER, Adelh.	25	Wachtendorf	53-1164
SCHROEDER, An Gert	65	Lenderscheidt	54-0930
Georg 33, Anna Elis. 23			
SCHROEDER, August	28	Hamburg	54-1371
SCHROEDER, Bernh.	23	Anruechte	51-1686
SCHROEDER, Casper	18	Bastel	50-0366
SCHROEDER, Chr Got	20	Welsdorf	52-1200
SCHROEDER, Derie	38	Buecken	53-0991
SCHROEDER, Dora	18	Dorum	53-1000
SCHROEDER, Doris	25	Bremen	51-1160
SCHROEDER, Doroth.	49	Detmold	51-1245
Ernestine 26, Emilie 19, Heinrich 13			
Paul 6			
SCHROEDER, Dorothe	26	Dedendorf	53-0492
SCHROEDER, Ferd.	20	Katrinhagen	53-1086
SCHROEDER, Friedr.	29	Burg	52-1200
SCHROEDER, Friedr.	19	Ritterhude	51-0326
SCHROEDER, Friedr.	49	Bockhorst	49-0352
Heinrich 11, Anna Elis. 16, Anna Marie 16			
Wilhelmine 21, Charlotte 9			
SCHROEDER, G.	25	Farven	54-0918
SCHROEDER, Georg E	55	Osterrode/Han	53-0475
SCHROEDER, Gertrud	36	Duderstadt	53-1013
Margareth 9			
SCHROEDER, Gottfr.	28	Nunheiligen	52-1321
SCHROEDER, Gottfr.	34	Duderstadt	51-0460
SCHROEDER, Heinr.	20	Kentrode	54-0930
SCHROEDER, Heinr.	42	Urbach	52-0699
Ernestine 44, August 21, Christoph 18			
Heinrich 15			
SCHROEDER, Heinr.	24	Dortmund	53-0652
SCHROEDER, Heinr.	18	Dorum	49-0329
SCHROEDER, Heinr.	18	Wuendenburg	51-0756
SCHROEDER, Hen Aug	25	Obereisen	52-1321
SCHROEDER, Henrike	28	Opendorf	54-1647
SCHROEDER, Herm. D	18	Bremen	52-1362
SCHROEDER, Hinr(f)	57	Obereisen	52-1321
SCHROEDER, J.	27	Volkerode	51-0517
SCHROEDER, J. Carl	39	Altisleben	49-1358
Bruno 21, Auguste 22, Luise 19, Berta 17			
SCHROEDER, J. Paul	16	Ernteiss	54-1566
SCHROEDER, Joh.	23	Mellebruch	54-0918
Mina 39, Rosalia 8, Rickchen 6, Anton 19			
SCHROEDER, Joh. D.	28	Wollings	52-1625
SCHROEDER, Johann	28	Seitendorf	49-1358
SCHROEDER, Johanna	32	Cassel	49-1106
SCHROEDER, Johanne	17	Muehlenheim	53-0475
SCHROEDER, John	30	Schledehausen	51-1588
SCHROEDER, Joseph	39	Zell	52-0370
SCHROEDER, Louis	26	Bennigenstein	52-0807
SCHROEDER, M. (m)	26	Gregelshausen	49-0416
P. (m) 29			
SCHROEDER, Maria	37	Niedenhof	54-0882
SCHROEDER, Marie	27	Zierow	54-1297
SCHROEDER, Minna	20	Wueffelringen	52-1332
Caroline 17			
SCHROEDER, Minna	29	Weissenfels	50-0311
SCHROEDER, Peter	32	Schwarzenfels	52-1625
SCHROEDER, Rebecca	21	Nordholz	50-0366
SCHROEDER, Sophie	26	Handemsen	52-0279
SCHROEDER, Th.	30	Hess. Oldendo	54-1078
SCHROEDER, Wilh.	15	Frelsdorfer M	49-0324
Rebecca 19			
SCHROEDER, Wilhelm	24	Meyenburg	51-1101
SCHROEDER, Wilhelm	28	Osterode	51-1062
SCHROEDER, William	59	Leichlingen	53-0991
SCHROEDKE, Chr. H.	33	Bayreuth	54-1297
Margar. 55			
SCHROEDTER, Bertha	26	Werdau	54-1168
SCHROENER, Michel	34	Bayern	51-1686
SCHROERLICKER, W.	24	Ladbergen	48-0445
SCHROETEL, Jacob	33	Neustadt	52-1105
Cath. 34, Georg 10, Barbara 6, Carl 30			
Barbara 34, Rosina 8, Barbara 4			

NAME	AGE	RESIDENCE	YR-LIST
SCHROETER, Carl		Leipzig	53-0942
SCHROETER, Chr. LH	34	Nassau	53-0652
Auguste 31, Anna 6, Moriz 3			
SCHROETTE, Georg	46	Ebesdienken	49-0574
SCHROETTER, Christ	33	Dietenborn	49-0352
Louise 29			
SCHROFF, Th. (m)	26	Narbendorff	50-0746
L. (f) 26			
SCHROFF, Victoria	25	Wolmedingen	54-1443
SCHROFFE, John	26	Markshagas	49-1517
SCHROTMEYER, A.(m)	18	Reuhenbach	49-0416
SCHRUMPF, Heinr.	40	Eichelsheim	50-1132
Johannes 15			
SCHUB, Catharine	28	Cassel	51-0352
SCHUBART, Johann	32	Coburg	52-1512
Kath. 32			
SCHUBART, John	26	Baiern	54-1724
SCHUBARTH, Herm.	34	Crimmitschau	51-1796
SCHUBBERT, Elenor	18	Aschendorf	51-1588
Joseph 28			
SCHUBBERT, Theodor	27	Neu Brandenbu	53-1000
Christiane 26			
SCHUBEL, Maria	29	Bamberg	54-1419
SCHUBERT, Adolph	18	Schlesien	54-1649
SCHUBERT, Amalie	20	Schweinfurt	52-0807
SCHUBERT, Anton	28	Andressone	54-1676
Maria 22, Franz 3, Josephine 6m			
SCHUBERT, August	20	Gotha	52-1580
Charlotte 24			
SCHUBERT, Auguste	21	Chemnitz	53-1023
SCHUBERT, Barb.	30	Gruen	51-1160
SCHUBERT, C.F.	32	Chemnitz	51-0405
SCHUBERT, Carl	24	Biegedorf	54-1716
SCHUBERT, Carl	38	Kleinbundorf	54-1371
Sophie 33, Ferdinand 15, Ernst 13			
Carl Aug. 11, Carl Ferd. 9, Marie 7			
Wilhelm 4			
SCHUBERT, Charles	18	Millwitz	52-1304
SCHUBERT, Erich	23	Wien	51-1640
SCHUBERT, Friedr.	34	Potsdam	52-0563
SCHUBERT, Georg	32	Grunner	52-1580
Richard 28			
SCHUBERT, Johann	38	Chemnitz	50-0379
SCHUBERT, Maria	18	Sommerstadt	52-1580
SCHUBERT, Robert	20	Mittweida	49-0574
SCHUBERT, Theophil	52	Tschene	53-0991
Elisabeth 53, Theophilius 23, Bertha 20			
SCHUBERT, Wilhelm	34	Debschwitz	54-0987
SCHUBERTH, Kunig.	25	Schneckenlohe	51-1588
Johan 24			
SCHUCHARD, Adam	11	Oberbernhard	48-1184
Wilhelm 9			
SCHUCHARD, Const.	24	Neisiss	50-0840
SCHUCHARDT, Friedr	27	Frankfurt	52-1105
SCHUCHARDT, Jakob	23	Widdershausen	48-0284
SCHUCHERT, Valent.	52	Eisenach/Pr.	52-1432
Magrethe 47, Peter 22, Jacob 14			
SCHUCHT, Emil	15	Buetzow	54-0987
SCHUDLER, Regina	22	Helmershausen	48-1114
SCHUEBEL, Gottlieb	23	Reichenberg	49-0352
SCHUEFFER, Wilhelm	18	Chemnitz	54-1297
SCHUELE, Carl	39	Stuttgart	48-1179
SCHUELER, Amand	19	Borsch	52-1200
SCHUELER, Aug.	17	Grossen----	50-0439
SCHUELER, August	39	Gr. Eisch	54-1371
SCHUELER, Charles	60	Guben/Pr.	48-0053
SCHUELER, Christ.	42	Sondershausen	54-1371
Caroline 38, Reinhard 14, Louis 12			
Carl 9, Ernst 4, Hugo 4			
SCHUELER, Elis.	34	Burgheim	54-0903
Walpurga 26			
SCHUELER, Heinr.	24	Lengsfeld	51-0405
Christ. 19, Joh. 18, Conr. 17, Marg. 19			
SCHUELTE, Franz	25	Schlip Rued	52-0370
SCHUENEMANN, Fried	24	Falgau	53-1164
Sophie 56			
SCHUENEMANN, Heinr	42	Polle/Hann.	54-1092
Johanna 36, Wilhelmine 16, Ernestine 14			

NAME	AGE	RESIDENCE	YR-LIST
Carl 12, Johanna 10, Heinrich 8, Emilie 7			
Louise 6, Auguste 2			
SCHUENHAMMER, Seb.	23	Salzbach	54-1443
SCHUEPHRUMPH, Herm	26	Friedewalde	50-0311
SCHUERER, Carl	16	Borenfeld	54-0882
SCHUERIN, Ferdinan	19	Keper	52-0095
SCHUERMANN, J.K.	30	Duisburg/Pr.	48-0447
F. (m) 29			
SCHUERNER, Barbara	27	Lamershof	54-0903
SCHUERZHOFF, Heinr	19	Muenster	54-1443
SCHUESSLER, Anna C	20	Mosheim	53-1016
SCHUESSLER, Joh.	18	Wiesenfeld	54-0918
SCHUETGE, Johannes	20	St. Louis	54-0987
SCHUETTE, A.	24	Bremen	48-0053
SCHUETTE, Amalie	32	Minden	53-0888
SCHUETTE, Bernhard	26	Lette/Pr.	54-1092
SCHUETTE, Friedr.	21	Leichtenborn	54-1297
SCHUETTE, Gertrude	29	Suedlohn	54-1371
SCHUETTE, Heinrich	47	Hurrel	48-1179
Metta 20, Diedrich 18, Heinrich 16			
Ahrend 12, Joh. Heinr. 10, Joh. Diedr. 6			
SCHUETTE, J.Fr.Dan	19	Bremen	49-0352
SCHUETTE, Ludwig	30	Oldenburg	53-0590
SCHUETTE, Wilhelm	29	Prusia	52-0351
SCHUETTLER, Marg.	32	Wiesenbach	54-0872
SCHUETZ, Anton	15	Langoens/Hess	54-0965
SCHUETZ, Christoph	23	Kaiserslauter	48-0101
SCHUETZ, Ernest	34	Iserlohn	53-0825
SCHUETZ, Franz	20	Reichenberg	54-1647
SCHUETZ, Georg	47	Effeltrich	53-1062
Margaretha 48, Anna 18, Barbara 16			
SCHUETZ, Herrmann	16	Berlin	52-0095
Mathilde 19, Maria 43			
SCHUETZ, Joh Heinr	25	Wilhelmshause	52-0351
SCHUETZ, Johann	22	Tauchingen	53-0324
SCHUETZ, Johannes	24	Speckswinkel	49-0345
SCHUETZ, Kunigunde	19	Eichenzell	54-1647
SCHUETZ, Simon	42	Baltenbruse	53-0825
Margarethe 32, Georg 11, Michael 10			
Erhard 7, Margretha 3, Johann 6w			
SCHUETZ, Theoph.	20	Ilsfeld	53-1164
SCHUETZ, Wilh.	26	Kochstedt	49-0352
SCHUETZE, Friedr.	27	Gardelegen	53-0652
SCHUETZE, Heinrich	35	Bodenfeld	52-0048
SCHUH, Joh.	26	Traukirch/Bav	52-1332
SCHUHMACHER, Anna	20	Rothenburg	49-1358
SCHUHMACHER, Carol	20	Vechelsdorf	53-1086
Louise 16			
SCHUHMACHER, Henry	38	Kirchweihe	53-1164
Sophia 32			
SCHUHMACHER, Joh.		Gronau	54-1575
SCHUHMACHER, Joh.	36	Haid	47-0868
Soph. 24, Jos. 5, P. 3			
SCHUHMACHER, Joh.		Gronau	54-1575
SCHUHMACHER, Lowoe	26	Mehringen	52-1452
Sophie 1			
SCHUHMANN, Carl	36	Ruecken	49-0352
SCHUHMANN, Dietr.	28	Muenden/Hann.	52-1423
SCHUHMANN, Gottl.	31	Mittweiler	53-1016
Marie Rosine 43, Ernst 14, Emilie 5			
SCHUIDHAZ, Chobine	30	Krizelbach	53-0652
Marianne 3, Clothilde 3, Johannes 15			
SCHUK, A.M. (f)	30	Neumarkt/Hock	53-0435
SCHULEN, R.	23	Mittelruessel	49-0737
SCHULENBERG, Phil.	25	Bassum	52-1512
SCHULER, L. (m)	24	Schopfloch	50-0746
SCHULER, Mathilde	21	Wriezen/Oder	48-0053
SCHULERT, Ed. (m)	20	Vachdorp	48-1131
SCHULFINS, Carl Th	36	Braunschweig	54-0872
Louisa 36, Caroline 9, Louise 8			
Wilhelm 5, Carl 7, Marie by, Hermann 17			
SCHULTE, Alb.	15	Leeste	51-1160
SCHULTE, Carl	28	Brenken	53-1000
SCHULTE, Carl	21	Prussia	51-1725
SCHULTE, Charlotte	34	Bremerhaven	53-1164
Friederike 13			
SCHULTE, Diedrich	27	Oldenburg	50-0311
SCHULTE, E. (f)	25	Emsdetten	49-0416

NAME	AGE	RESIDENCE	YR-LIST
SCHULTE, Ernst	36	Babber	53-1086
Marie 40, Marie 16, Joh. Friedr. 11			
Clara 9			
SCHULTE, Ernst	23	Bruckhausen	53-0825
Jobst Herman 19			
SCHULTE, Franz	35	Lippstadt	51-1245
Sabina 24, Anna 4, Joseph 28			
SCHULTE, Gert (f)	23	Ankrin	51-1686
SCHULTE, H. (m)	17	Feldtrup	48-0445
SCHULTE, Heinrich	22	Memminghausen	54-1717
SCHULTE, Herrmann	26	Warburg	54-1717
SCHULTE, Maria		Schermede	54-1575
SCHULTE, Mich.	48	Mittelruessel	49-0737
Margareth 15, Christiana 14, Rudolf 13			
Herold 6, August 22			
SCHULTE, Peter Fr.	29	Ohle/Pr.	48-0053
SCHULTE, Th.	30	Herdingen	54-1470
SCHULTE-VELRUP, J.	28	Emsdetten	49-0416
SCHULTEN, Anna	30	Ibbenbuehren	48-0269
SCHULTEN, C.	32	Meerane	54-1341
Caroline 25, Louise 3, Caroline 1			
SCHULTES, John	37	Mittelruessel	49-0737
SCHULTHEIS, August	32	Echzell	48-1131
SCHULTHEIS, Eva	25	Hafenpreppach	51-0048
SCHULTHEIS, Friedr	21	Heinevun	49-0912
SCHULTHEIS, Joh. G	15	Birkach	54-0872
SCHULTHEISS, F.A.	14	Cassel	54-1078
SCHULTHEISS, Fr'ke	20	Weidberg/Bade	52-0960
SCHULTHEISS, Joh.	30	Hof	53-0267
SCHULTHEISS, Val.	27	Fliede	52-1625
SCHULTHESS, Michel	18	Wilhelmsthal	53-0825
SCHULTZ, Bernhard	22	Muenden	48-1015
SCHULTZ, Carl	17	Cassel	54-1297
SCHULTZ, Friedr.	28	Mittelruessel	49-0737
Carolina 19			
SCHULTZ, Friedrike	30	Arolsen	48-1114
SCHULTZ, Hajo	21	Jever	53-1013
SCHULTZ, Heinr.	24	Beuthen	49-0781
SCHULTZ, Justus	23	Blankenbach	48-0284
SCHULTZ, M.W.	25	Bremerhafen	48-1114
SCHULTZ, Philipp	18	Coburg	52-0895
SCHULTZ, Rob.	20	Zorge	49-1358
SCHULTZE, Carl	27	Weissenfeld	50-1071
SCHULTZE, Elise	25	Bremen	52-1661
SCHULTZE, Emil	24	Herford	54-1297
SCHULTZE, Hermann	21	Iburg	54-0850
Elise 25, Dina 23			
SCHULTZE, Kunigund	23	Weissenfeld	50-1071
SCHULTZE, Wilh'mne	24	Peine	54-1297
SCHULZ, August	17	Habichtswall	53-0161
SCHULZ, Augustus	27	Schloppe	50-0840
SCHULZ, Cath.		Ruttershausen	54-1575
SCHULZ, Catherine	16	Hannover	50-0311
SCHULZ, Christian	24	Gross Fiden	53-0905
SCHULZ, Conrad	23	Breitzbach	48-0284
SCHULZ, Friedr.	20	Braunschweig	50-1236
SCHULZ, Gottlieb	31	Coburg	50-0379
SCHULZ, H.	19	Cassel	50-0021
SCHULZ, H. (m)	22	Rulsheim	52-0652
SCHULZ, H. (m)	39	Lobenstein	49-0383
H. (f) 33, Anna 9, Hel. 8, Joh. 2			
Chr. 9m			
SCHULZ, Heinr.	20	Wingerhausen	52-1321
SCHULZ, Heinrich	33	Cassel	54-1168
SCHULZ, Heinrich	18	Gutensberg	50-0379
SCHULZ, Lisette	32	Burgsteinfurt	50-1236
Mina 27			
SCHULZ, Maria	22	Hessia	50-0311
SCHULZ, Marie	29	Goerlitz	54-1297
SCHULZ, Minna	23	Hannover	53-0942
SCHULZ, Sophie	22	Gerstungen	52-1410
Christian 27			
SCHULZ, Susanna	25	Muehlhausen	49-0352
SCHULZ, Wilh.	19	Hannover	50-0311
SCHULZ, Wilhelm	19	Braunschweig	50-1236
SCHULZE, Adolph	26	Peine	51-0405
SCHULZE, Arnold	29	Dissen	53-1164
SCHULZE, Carl	17	Stargard/Pr.	54-1092

NAME	AGE	RESIDENCE	YR-LIST
SCHULZE, Christian		Nordhemmern	53-0942
SCHULZE, Conrath	31	Eisenach/Pr.	52-1432
SCHULZE, Elisabeth	22	Langenbach	53-0324
SCHULZE, Elise	39	Gr. Almerode	54-0930
SCHULZE, Friedrich	38	Bergedorf	52-1148
Maria 28			
SCHULZE, Friedrike	31	Dresden	52-1620
SCHULZE, Fritz	31	Leipzig	50-1067
Henriette 34			
SCHULZE, Harman	32	Stolberg/Pr.	48-0053
SCHULZE, Johann	24	Lohhof	53-0320
SCHULZE, Julius	27	Verden/Retene	53-0838
Louise 22			
SCHUM, Georg	18	Hirschhaid	54-0053
SCHUM, Sophie	23	Otterstedt/Ha	54-1092
SCHUMACHER, Adelh.	28	Bremen	48-0406
Hermann by			
SCHUMACHER, Anna	20	Schoellkrippe	54-0903
Michael 16, Johann A. 52, Maria 52			
Maria 21, Adam 15, Johann Ad. 13, Aisla 9			
SCHUMACHER, Anna	24	Elm	49-0345
SCHUMACHER, Anna	18	Cellstedt	51-1084
SCHUMACHER, Char.	14	Swering	54-1443
SCHUMACHER, Christ	41	Grossenrode	50-0366
Hanne 5-, Doris 16, August 13, Wilhelm 10			
SCHUMACHER, Henry	30	Bremervoerde	51-1725
SCHUMACHER, Herman	18	Ottersberg	52-1362
SCHUMACHER, Johann	21	Weilheim/Wuer	52-0351
SCHUMACHER, John	51	Dueddenhausen	51-0048
SCHUMACHER, Mag.	40	Germany	50-0472
Diedr. 18, Heinr. 10, Doroth. 16, Adam 7			
SCHUMAN, Conrad	32	Losenstein	54-1676
SCHUMANN, August	24	Frankenhausen	51-1035
SCHUMANN, August	31	Uslar	47-0872
SCHUMANN, Clara	21	Frankenhausen	54-0918
SCHUMANN, Elisab.	30	Scheubach	52-1625
SCHUMANN, Emilie	39	Bremen	48-0078
SCHUMANN, Fr. (m)	25	Maralderode	52-1321
SCHUMANN, Friedr.	24	Bay---	50-0439
SCHUMANN, Friedr.	27	Meiningen	47-0672
SCHUMANN, John	34	Darmstadt	53-1164
Doris 27, Hermina 3, Otto by			
SCHUMANN, W. (m)	21	Marolterode	52-1321
SCHUMANN, Wilh'mne	17	Reust	54-0872
SCHUMCKERMEYER, J.	30	Irlsbrunn	49-0574
SCHUMEBROGGE, M.	50	Geismar	47-0762
SCHUMM, Andreas	36	Wettern	54-1168
SCHUMM, Catharine	24	Donassenheim	53-0582
SCHUMPE, Friedrich	32	Essen	53-1086
SCHUMPF, Babette	30	Montabaur	54-1371
SCHUNCK, Cordula	19	Neustadt	52-1512
SCHUND, Joh.	50	Mangenroth	54-1283
SCHUNEMANN, M. (m)	37	Wersen	47-0672
Sophia 35, Caroline 9, Sophia 5			
Friedrich 18m			
SCHUNICHT, Friedr.	17	Nieheim	51-1101
SCHUNK, Carl	28	Fulda	54-0987
SCHUNKE, Gottlieb	38	Weissenfeld	54-1297
Louise 31, Louisa 6, Maria 4, Therese 11m			
SCHUPPART, Marie	24	Mengeringhaus	49-0383
SCHURENBERG, Aug.	44	Horn	53-0991
SCHURFF, Nik.	30	Michelau	51-1796
SCHURIG, H.	20	Altmuehlen	51-1084
SCHURMANN, Adolph	52	Groppel/Pr.	53-0628
Anna Maria 51, Friedrich 25, Elisabeth 18			
Wilhelm 14, Heinrich 10			
SCHURMANN, Conrad	27	Baiern	53-0585
SCHURMANN, Herm.	26	Bramsche	49-1106
SCHURMEISTER, Ad.	37	Osterfeld	52-1512
Wilhelmine 33, Otto 9, Gustav 8			
Charlotte 7m			
SCHURR, Philip	24	Grosskuckla	52-0515
SCHURRMANN, H.L.	22	Nesse	52-1512
SCHURUBEK, Reinh.	36	Steinhausen	51-1796
SCHURZ, Marie Anna	54	Bonn	53-0267
Anna 19, Antonia 17			
SCHUSSICHT, Marie	19	Nichaim	52-1321
SCHUSSLER, Charles	20	Marburg	54-1724

NAME	AGE	RESIDENCE	YR-LIST
SCHUSTER, Anton	38	Schwabsberg	53-0435
Marie 33, Magd. 35			
SCHUSTER, Cath.	24	Birnbaum	53-1023
SCHUSTER, Ed.	41	Frankenstadt	49-0383
Clara 41, Heinr. 13, Eduard 12			
SCHUSTER, F. (m)	35	Bielefeld	52-1512
Maths.(f) 29, Lenore 5			
SCHUSTER, Florent.	38	Hersfeld	48-1243
Auguste 34, Anna 11, Hermann 9, Adolph 8			
Hugo 6, Hedwig 3, Richard 2			
SCHUSTER, Heinr.	18	Bavaria	50-1317
SCHUSTER, Helias	24	Duisburg	54-1371
SCHUSTER, Jacob	20	Hottenbach	51-1062
SCHUSTER, Joseph	49	Oberndorf	52-1304
Anna Maria 37, John 7, Joseph 5			
Maximilian 1			
SCHUSTER, Margaret	26	Ballhof	48-1179
Eva 2			
SCHUSTER, Mich.	22	Bayern	53-1016
SCHUTT, (m)	23	Hamburg	48-1243
SCHUTTE, Ernst	23	Bruckhausen	53-0825
SCHUTTE, Friedrich	25	Versmold	52-1512
SCHUTTENHELM, Pet.	31	Mindersberg	53-1070
SCHUTTER, Casper	19	Waler	54-1341
SCHUTTER, Christ.	23	Hetteroth	52-1101
SCHUTTES, John	37	Mittelruessel	49-0737
SCHUTZ, Ernst	25	Robeck	48-0951
SCHUTZ, Ferdinand	26	Coburg/Sachse	51-1725
Barbara 25			
SCHUTZ, Friedr.	44	Obermoellrich	50-0472
Anna 34, Joh. 13, Anna 10, Heinr. 3			
SCHUTZ, Heinrich	22	Ruderts-hsdor	53-0585
SCHUTZEBERG, J.(m)	33	Utenhausen	50-0746
SCHWAB, A. (m)	30	Seidelshapt	50-0746
SCHWAB, Ernestine	18	Schwabach	52-1321
SCHWAB, Heinrich	27	Rinderbeck	53-0435
SCHWAB, Joh. Mart.	17	Bayreuth	53-0888
SCHWAB, Sophie	29	Metzbach	51-1035
SCHWAB, Valentin	21	Altenhambach	47-0672
SCHWABE, Adolph	22	Lammspringe	54-0830
SCHWABE, August	35	Weimar	48-1184
Wilhelmine 24			
SCHWABE, Conrad	24	Pischbrun/Bav	52-0351
SCHWABE, F.	26	Marbach	51-0405
Mathilde 21, Auguste 2, Ferdinand 6m			
SCHWABE, G. Adolph	27	Bautzen	49-0574
SCHWABE, Jachet	59	Hebenstransen	53-0838
Jette 24			
SCHWABE, Madame	63	New York	54-1566
SCHWABENLAND, Hein	37	Rossdorf	53-0582
SCHWACKE, Christ.	20	Hannover/Hann	51-0048
SCHWAGER, Michael	30	Leihenbach	50-0840
SCHWALB, G.H.	43	Staufenberg	54-1470
Catharina 50, Elisabeth 19, Mary 13			
SCHWALLER, Felix	33	Solothurn/Sw.	51-1725
Catharine 30			
SCHWALLER, Peter	47	Solothurn/Sch	51-1725
Barbara 46, Jacob 11, Joseph 10, Maria 8			
Otilla 6			
SCHWALM, Andreas	35	Undenborn	54-1716
Anna 40, Elisabeth 9, Anna 3, Heinrich 9m			
Anna Elis. 58			
SCHWALM, Elise	27	Carlshafen	54-1566
Louise 19			
SCHWAMBERGER, Jos.	23	Tyrol	47-0828
Therese 27			
SCHWAN, Anton	20	Treysa	49-0345
SCHWAN, Heinrich	17	Frannenberg	53-0652
SCHWANDNER, Georg	25	Dobl	48-1355
Therese 23			
SCHWANEWEDEL, Eibe	16	Dorum	50-0366
SCHWANKHAUS, Elise	24	Holte	52-1512
Dina 18, Adolph 15			
SCHWANSSMANN, Barb	20	Haus	49-0737
SCHWANWEDEL, Minch	20	Misselwarden	50-0366
Eibe 8			
SCHWANZARAUS, Fr'z	22	Carlsbad	51-1160
SCHWARDT, Caroline	20	Scherneck	53-0590
SCHWARRER, Cath.	26	Neubrunn	48-0887
SCHWART, Anton	39	Frille	51-1588
Leanora 63, Sophie 19, Carl 4, Anton 2			
SCHWART, Mariane	24	Grevenau	49-0912
SCHWARTING, Sophie	24	Warftith	50-1071
SCHWARTZ, Anna	18	Pommern	49-0574
SCHWARTZ, Elise	17	Lenabach	51-1739
SCHWARTZ, Gustav	18	Wuertenberg	53-0557
SCHWARTZ, H.F.	58	Vehrte	54-1470
Mary 57			
SCHWARTZ, Johann	32	Luesche	52-0563
SCHWARTZ, Johann	39	Margelbach	52-1105
Christine 32, Friedrich 11, Johann 9			
Marg. 8, Catharina 7, Georg 2			
SCHWARTZ, Joseph	25	Rudolphzelle	47-0672
SCHWARTZ, Margaret	72	Luesche	52-0563
SCHWARTZE, Christ.	17	Leiferte	52-1512
SCHWARZ, Andrew	46	Huhlbach	48-0951
Anne B. 33			
SCHWARZ, Anton	26	Hallenberg	53-0585
SCHWARZ, Carl	19	Minden	52-1410
SCHWARZ, Carl	28	Gera	51-0757
Emilie 32			
SCHWARZ, Carl Aug.	15	Negertmuenf/A	53-0435
SCHWARZ, Carl Gott	44	Penig	49-0352
SCHWARZ, Catharine	24	Moenchs	54-1443
SCHWARZ, Charles	33	New York	52-0095
SCHWARZ, David	29	Blanckenbach	51-0460
SCHWARZ, Eduard	36	Herzberg	52-1580
Caroline 36, Idla 5, Eduard 9m			
SCHWARZ, Ernst	29	Wolkersbrunne	52-0693
Marg. 23, Marg. (died) 6m			
SCHWARZ, Eva	27	Reles/Bav.	52-0351
SCHWARZ, F. (m)	24	Hagenbuechen	52-0652
SCHWARZ, Ferdinand	23	Schwabach	51-1438
SCHWARZ, Gustav	22	Hilford	54-1297
SCHWARZ, H. (m)	23	Herford	49-0329
SCHWARZ, Johannes	43	Oefingen/Bade	51-1725
Christine 43, Anna 18, Christine 16			
Johannes 14, Joh. Martin 12, Michael 6			
Ursula 4			
SCHWARZ, Johannes	29	Basel	51-1438
SCHWARZ, Joseph	31	Retzen	47-0872
Elisabeth 55, Wilhelmine 24, Juliane 20			
August 16			
SCHWARZ, Lebrecht	16	Roeddenau	53-0585
SCHWARZ, Lina	28	Salzwedel	54-1591
SCHWARZ, Louis	27	Brackwede	48-0053
SCHWARZ, Marie	26	Treysa	52-1200
SCHWARZ, Martin	23	Suess	48-0269
SCHWARZ, Math.	42	Kraftshof	52-0693
SCHWARZ, Michael	32	Warz--	50-0439
SCHWARZ, Peter	31	Almoshof	53-0267
SCHWARZ, Rosine	28	Hochdorf	48-1179
SCHWARZ, Simon	25	Gerston	54-1282
SCHWARZ, Stephen	22	Winterthur	51-1725
Barbara 24			
SCHWARZ, Walburga	26	Oberndorff	52-1304
SCHWARZ, Wilhelm	27	Niederurschel	49-0574
Margarethe 26			
SCHWARZA, Anton	24	Maedebach	53-0585
SCHWARZER, Johann	16	Grafenberg/Bv	53-0628
SCHWARZFAERBER, C.	29	Bug	52-0693
Marg. 20			
SCHWARZKOPF, Joh.	40	Urberach	53-1023
Catharine 47, Catharine 14, Adam 9			
SCHWARZKOPF, Joh.	24	Wisgarelingen	49-0345
SCHWARZMANN, Marie	26	Boebber	53-1086
SCHWARZWICH, Peter	24	Buhshausen	51-1639
Anna 22, Cathrina 6m			
SCHWECKE, Heinrich	57	Sicke	49-0413
Dorothea 48, Joh Heinrich 19			
Bertha Adelh 15, Anna Dorothe 13			
Maria 10, Cord Heinr. 6			
SCHWECKE, Sophie	21	Weetsen	48-0284
SCHWEDDER, Wilhelm	42	Burscheid	54-1371
SCHWEDEN, Christ.	28	Mehnen	53-0942
SCHWEDLER, Ferd.	48	Frankfurt/Pr.	51-1532

NAME	AGE	RESIDENCE	YR-LIST
Wilhelmine 31, Hermine 14			
SCHWEDLER, Marie	23	Lindenau	54-1566
Anna 4, Allwine 2			
SCHWEERE, Mad.	5-	Hohenroth	49-1358
Cath. Luise 18, Dorette 21, Phil. Paul 24			
SCHWEGEL, Ben.	24	Schweinfurt	50-1317
SCHWEGLER, Fr'drke	24	Dietfurt	54-0850
SCHWEIGER, Georg	28	Sellmuth	52-0515
SCHWEIGERT, Friedr	30	Baiern	53-0585
SCHWEIKERT, J. Pet	22	Markt Erlbach	48-1355
SCHWEINBERG, Peter	39	Fuerstenhagen	51-1639
Elisabeth 35, Nicklaus 17			
SCHWEINFEST, Jos.	25	Neusitz	53-1016
SCHWEISCHGUS, Elis	22	Londorff	47-0840
SCHWEISS, Friedr.	23	Baden	54-1724
SCHWEITZER, H. (f)	26	Rahmstadt	49-0383
SCHWEITZER, Heinr.	54	Tiefenort	54-1371
Emilie 43, Robert 18, Minna 17, Edmund 10			
SCHWEITZER, Johann	22	Gotha	54-1554
SCHWEIZER, Johann	23	Hansen/Heking	53-0435
SCHWEIZER, Mac.	18	Cronheim	52-0895
SCHWEIZER, Marie	14	Wiesenstadt	52-0279
SCHWEKER, Barbara	78	Michelbach	51-1686
SCHWELLER, Auguste	29	Kirchberg	49-1517
August 6			
SCHWELT, Oscar	22	Milren	49-1517
SCHWEMMLEIN, Joh.	29	Sichelreuth	51-1160
Georg Adam 24			
SCHWEN, Friedr.	22	Mengsdorf/Hes	52-0960
SCHWENCK, Eduard	26	Hecklingen	48-0284
SCHWENDNER, Joh.	29	Gunzendorf	54-1078
Marg. 22			
SCHWENGLER, Eva	33	Beckerndorf	54-1575
SCHWENGLER, John	27	Rekendorff	52-1304
SCHWENK, Christ.	49	Gerhausen/Wue	54-1001
Margr. 47			
SCHWENK, S.	45	Licht	51-0517
G. (m) 44, R. (f) 45, S. (f) 6			
SCHWENK, Sebastian	33	Frankenberg	53-1016
SCHWENKE, Ana Mar.	39	Feldsteten	53-0838
SCHWENKE, Friedr.	20	Arolsen	53-0825
SCHWENKE, Friedr.	30	Diepholz	50-0292
Gesene Imar 24			
SCHWENKE, Ludwig	55	Arolsen	53-0825
Ludwig Fried 27			
SCHWENKE, Theodor	24	Erfurt	52-1200
SCHWENTKER, Fried.	30	Hille	51-1588
Henrietta 28, Anna 2, Louisa 10m			
Henry 21, John 16, Ger. 15, Louise 14			
Anna 17			
SCHWENZER, John	33	Utrictshausen	52-0515
SCHWERDT, Elisabet	24	Tiefenort	52-1410
SCHWERDT, Ignatz	30	Prussia	50-0021
Sophie 22, Caroline 9m			
SCHWERMECKER, Wm.	18	Wannfried	54-1078
SCHWERTFEGER, Carl	20	Holterup	48-1209
SCHWESTER, JG Emer	30	Gehrenberg	52-0515
SCHWETJE, Fritz	27	Barfelde	53-0590
SCHWETTEN, Louise	16	Severns	53-0942
SCHWICKER, Wilhelm	22	Arensberg	52-0699
Georg 24			
SCHWIEBERT, Herman	24	Beverstadt/Ha	51-1725
SCHWIEGER, Justus	38	Berlin	54-1092
Emma 38, Elisa 2			
SCHWIEGER, Kath.	32	Grossheirath	52-0279
SCHWIEGERT, Leonh.	38	Schwabach	50-1071
Anna Maria 48, Anna Maria 8			
SCHWIER, Bernh.	54	Senden	54-1554
Gertrud 52			
SCHWIER, Heinrich	18	Wueffelringen	52-1332
Catharine 52			
SCHWIER, Louise	16	Barkhausen	53-1023
SCHWIL, Ernst Ludw	25	Grafgetzwitz	47-0672
SCHWIMMER, Marg.	38	Heidenheim	48-0887
SCHWIND, Georg Ad.	54	Follmersdorf	51-0384
Joh. Jos. 23, Theresia 21, Juliana 18			
Catharina 30			
SCHWIND, Johann	23	Follmersdorf	51-0460
SCHWIND, Michel G.	28	Wiesbaden	51-1639
SCHWIND, Valentin	34	Follmersdorf	51-0384
Margaret 6, Leon 3			
SCHWINDT, Gottfr.	28	Follmersdorf	51-0384
Genovefa 30, Kunigunde 11, Genoveva 6			
Adolph 4, Remicus 6m, Johann 38			
Catharina 30			
SCHWINGER, Ernst	40	Kreuzburg	53-1070
Christiane 34, Friedrich 8, Johannes 6			
Conrad 3, Christoph 6m			
SCHWIRINGER, Jos.	32	Klanstreet	52-1661
Franziska 34			
SCHWITZER, C. (m)	30	Welsede	48-0445
H. (m) 40			
SCHWOBEDA, Richard	14	Ebersdorf	54-0987
SCHWOMEYER, Hein.	22	Meinsen	52-1321
SCHWONWEDER, Herm.	29	Hannover	53-1013
SCHWUR, A.	22	Oggenhausen	54-1419
SCHWUTU, G. (m)	30	Emsdetten	49-0416
SCOTT, Chr.	23	Trimmersdorf	51-1455
SCOTT, Tabl.	29	Burla	49-1358
SEBALD, Joh Friedr	28	Castell/Bav.	52-1332
SEBALD, Joh. Chr.	28	Castell	54-0987
Joh. 23			
SEBALD, Joh. Fried	28	Castell/Bav.	52-1332
Carl 24			
SEBALD, John	26	Castle	53-0914
William 23, Barbara 31, Catharina 5			
SEBALD, Marg.	54	Castell	54-0987
Doris 20			
SEBASTIAN, Carol.	38	Altenburg	51-1084
Bertha 18, Clara 15, Lina 9			
SEBASTIAN, Hermann	16	Altenburg	50-1071
SEBBERT, J.W.	33	Breslau	51-1160
SEBECK, Roenke	19	Neuenkirchen	51-0405
SEBOLD, Gottlieb	22	Sommerhsn/Bav	52-0807
SECKER, Conrad	43	Marienbron/He	52-0960
SEEBACH, Am.	60	Waldcappel	49-0352
Anna 60			
SEEBACH, Christian	33	Gold	54-1443
Laurette 30, Raphine 6, Christiane 2			
Heinrich 3			
SEEBACH, Conr.	24	Weikersbrunn	51-1160
SEEBACH, Georg Jac	57	Gold	54-1443
Margarethe 55			
SEEBACH, Wilhelm	20	Ohren	54-0882
SEEBALD, Martin	22	Rosenheim	53-0585
SEEBOHDE, Christ.	24	Letzlingen	53-0324
SEEBORG, Jacob	28	Michelfeld/Bd	52-0351
SEECKEL, Wilhelm	21	Stroeen	51-0326
SEEDORF, Christian	18	Lehmstedt	54-0053
SEEGE, H.	36	Breslau	54-1078
SEEGER, Barbara	25	Wuertt.	54-1724
SEEGER, Elisabetha	21	Mundenheim	54-1717
SEEGER, Louise	40	Braunschweig	54-0600
Marie 27			
SEEGER, Marie	26	Oberndorf	54-1717
SEEGERS, Conrad	28	Esferode	53-0492
SEEHAUSEN, Fr.	13	Mesmerode	53-0492
SEEHAUSEN, Wilhelm	56	Mesmerode	53-0492
Cathrina 46, Wilhelm 29, Cathrina 25			
Heinrich 24, Dorothea 30, Heinrich 2			
Dorothea 9, Cathrina 7			
SEEKAMP, Adelaide	21	Uphusen	53-0991
SEEKAMP, Georg	22	Oberneuland	54-1092
SEEKAMPF, Heinrich	26	Bremen	54-1371
SEELDORF, Julius	47	Magdeburg	53-0267
Johanne 45, Dorothea 18, Marie 16			
Louise 14, Julius 12, Friedrich 8			
Herrmann 3			
SEELE, Carl	16	Kewohle	51-1640
SEELEMEIER, Fr.	25	Erschenburg	54-1575
SEELEN, Heinrich	24	Bayern	53-0590
SEELIGMANN, L. (m)	18	Gregelshausen	49-0416
SEELMANN, A. (f)	19	Herrenwies	53-0928
Wilhelm 30, Carl 26			
SEEMANN, Georg	18	Haertz	53-0590
SEEMANN, Heinrich	53	Wietzen	54-1575

NAME	AGE	RESIDENCE	YR-LIST
Anna 42, Heinr. 19, Eleonore 12			
Wilhelm 9			
SEEMANN, J. Heinr.	54	Brodersdorf	54-1297
Anna Maria 54, Henry 25, Johann 8			
Henrich 21			
SEEMANN, Joseph	21	Willebadessen	50-0472
SEESER, Wilhelmina	33	Berlingerode	48-0951
SEEWALD, Michael	34	Gruenstadt	53-1164
SEFLING, Ernst	27	Mittelruessel	49-0737
SEGANDER, August	30	Prussia	49-0329
SEGEBROCK, Gottl.	38	Katrinhagen	53-1086
Louise 34, Lina 10, Heinrich 8, Wilhelm 6			
August 3, Gottlieb 9m			
SEGELKEN, Maria	36	Gnoeren/Meckl	52-0807
SEGER, Babette	32	Oberreichenba	54-0850
Katharina 9			
SEGER, Friedrich	33	Hildesheim	52-1580
SEGER, Friedrich	18	Nuernberg	53-0557
Heinrich 18			
SEGER, Friedrich	18	Nurnberg	53-0557
Heinrich 18			
SEHEN, Anna Cath.	30	Mosbach	53-1070
SEHETGERN, Cath.	32	Walduern	52-1580
SEHKAMP, Joh Heinr	24	Hastedt	48-0887
SEIB, Carl Benj.	28	Goeldentram	53-0825
Maria Rosine 23, Carl Aug. W. 3			
SEIB, Catharina	27	Bisfeld	54-0053
SEIB, Joh.	18	Erbstadt	54-0987
SEIBEL, Carl Benj.	28	Goeldeutram	53-0825
Maria Rosine 23, Carl Aug. W. 3			
SEIBEL, Joh Casper	35	Frankfurt/M.	53-0324
SEIBEL, Johannes	36	Nieder Rossba	54-0830
Heinrich 18, Ludwig 4, Friedrich 9m			
Catharine 32, Catharine 10			
SEIBEL, Peter	19	Cur Hessen	53-0557
SEIBEL, Peter	19	Kur-Hessen	53-0557
SEIBERT, Conrad	16	Rauschenberg	54-1168
SEIBERT, Gustav	20	Prussia	50-1317
SEIBERT, Mich	32	Sickendorf	53-0435
Maria 22			
SEIBEUN, Catharine	22	Terrogsberg	54-0930
SEIDE, Julia	22	Berlin	48-1243
SEIDEL, August	26	Prussia	50-1317
SEIDEL, Eduard	44	Rosswein	49-1106
Julianna 45, Eduard 17, Wilhelm 14			
Hugo 10, Wilhelmine 3m			
SEIDEL, Friedrich	26	Lichtenstn/Sx	52-0807
SEIDEL, Julius	18	Fraustadt	52-1410
SEIDEL, Michael	40	Neumark	53-0905
Barbara 37, Catharina 10, Margaretha 9			
Anna 3, Michael 8, Wolfgang 9m			
Barbara 40			
SEIDEL, Michel	32	Rosenheim	53-0585
SEIDEL, Theresa	24	Alburg	52-0652
SEIDELBACH, Judel	55	Marolsweisach	53-0991
SEIDENSTUECKER, Ch	44	Schernberg	54-1554
Friederike 20, Valentin 8			
SEIDL, Charlotte	40	Armsdorf	52-1321
Sebastin 5			
SEIDL, Georg	37	Armsdorf	52-1321
SEIDLER, Alberd	23	Berlin	53-0590
SEIDLER, Emilie	20	Oberweyd	49-0781
SEIDLER, George	50	Ruhla	47-0828
SEIDLER, Louisa	32	Oberweyd	49-0781
SEIDLER, Wilhelm	20	Ziegenhain	52-0095
SEIDTS, Georg	36	Nentershausen	48-0887
SEIFARTH, Sophie	28	Vollmersheim	50-0311
SEIFER, J.G.	53	Lengsfeld	52-1661
SEIFERT, August	43	Triptis	52-1661
Johanne 36, Carl 6, Franziska 4			
SEIFERT, August	36	Waltershausen	54-0053
Carl 42			
SEIFERT, Carl Aug.	42	Chemnitz	53-1070
SEIFERT, Caspar	19	Sachs.-Mein.	52-1686
SEIFERT, Heinrich	29	Schleiz	53-0590
Pauline 25, Einana 3			
SEIFERT, Johann	22	Schwarzenbach	52-1148
SEIFERT, Johann	22	Saeusen	50-1236
SEIFERT, Johann	56	Mittelstreu	47-0868
Margaretha 54, Ba. (f) 21, Johann 18			
Mag. 10			
SEIFERT, Michael	20	Salzungen	49-0413
SEIFERT, Simon	41	Glashuetten	51-1084
Elisabeth 42, Kunigunde 14, Elisabeth 11			
Amalie 8, Margarethe 3, Kunigunde 18			
SEIFERT, Therese	35	Carlsbad/Bad.	51-1532
Carl 8, Theresia 5, Julius 11m			
SEIFERTH, A.P.	26	Stein	54-1341
SEIFERTH, Eva	20	Oberkotzau	54-1554
SEIFFAHRT, John	51	Angelhausen	52-1304
Johanna 47, Robert 11, Christian 4			
SEIFFER, Chr. Gott	16	Esslingen	48-1355
Wilh. Ferd. 15			
SEIFFERT, Gustav	17	Daspe	53-1070
SEIFFERT, Johann	25	Wiesenthal/Sa	53-0475
SEIFRIED, Johann	24	Oberelsbach	54-0053
SEIFRIED, Joseph	24	Wiesenau	53-1062
SEIGERS, H. (f)	32	Weheindorf	54-1341
SEILER, Maria	27	Eiterfeld/Hes	51-1532
SEILFUSS, Hermann		Bramsche	54-0987
SEIMANN, J. Heinr.	54	Brodersdorf	54-1297
Anne Maria 54, Henry 25, Johann 8			
Henrich 21			
SEIPEL, Ludolf	24	Herford	53-0324
SEIPERT, Joseph	35	Neuoltmannsdo	53-0914
Albertine 35, Pauline 8, Ida 7, Joseph 4			
Francis 2			
SEIPPEL, Friedrich	25	Butzbach	53-0888
SEISS, August	26	Eisennach	47-0872
SEITERS, Marie	22	Babber	53-1086
SEITZ, Anna	33	Andershausen	50-0021
Maria 11, Martha 6			
SEITZ, Catharina	25	Homberg	48-1184
Lina 3			
SEITZ, Franz	40	Gratz/Germ.	51-0352
Josepha 30, Maria 5, Franz 4, Johann 11m			
SEITZ, J. (m)	40	Trienz	50-0746
E. (f) 38, M. (f) 17, S. (f) 11			
F. (m) 13, A. (m) 9			
SEITZ, Joseph	33	Holzguerz	52-1321
SEITZ, Margarethe	24	Schleifhausen	52-0095
SEITZ, Therese	30		52-1321
SEKEIKER, Johann	24	Scharmbeck	53-0942
SELBERT, Dorothea	31	Abbach	48-0260
Cathrine 17			
SELBERT, F.F. (m)	23	Engter	48-0445
SELENKA, Gustav	19	Braunschweig	48-1355
SELGER, Chas. G.	24	Mittelruessel	49-0737
SELHEIM,	23	Moritzreuth	51-1084
SELIG, Gustav	18	Wichsthausen	54-0918
SELIG, Mine	26	Markt-Steft	52-0807
SELIGBERG, Martin	13	Medwitz	48-0887
SELIGER, Clamor	24	Osnabrueck	54-1470
SELIGMANN, E. (m)	24	Westhoven	47-0872
SELINGER, Carl	29	Gonsdorf	54-1566
SELKMANN, Emilie	23	Berlin	53-0888
SELLE, Heinrich	32	Eickhorst	47-0762
Marie 30, Louise 6, Joh Heinrich 5			
Fried. Wm. 2, Catharine 55			
SELLECKSON, Louise	26	Vollbrechshau	50-0439
SELLER, Ferdinand	26	Roth/Bavaria	53-0628
Michael 38, Eva 34			
SELSEMEYER, Anton	22	Almena/Lippe	52-1423
August 18, Carl 26, Friedrich 14			
Wilhelmine 46, Wilhelmine 20			
Henriette 16			
SELZ, Mathias	27	Ibenhausen	51-0757
SELZER, C.E. (f)	24	Seidelsdorf	51-0517
SELZER, Friedrich	36	Niederwildung	53-1086
SELZER, Leopold	17	Mannheim	49-0912
SELZLI, Joseph	29	Hausen	54-0600
SEMENTINGEN, Aug.	29	Urach	49-0912
Magdalene 21, Alwine 1			
SEMF, Johannes	53	Burkhardrode	54-0053
Nicolaus 26, Georg 16, Christiane 12			
Magdalena 23, Justin 9m			

NAME	AGE	RESIDENCE	YR-LIST
SEMIEN, Margaretha	32	Holdersteten	49-1517
Margaretha 4			
SENF, Emil	19	Leitz	53-1164
SENF, Wm.	28	Elze	51-0757
SENGEL, Friedrich	25	Wiesbaden/Nas	48-0447
SENGER, Carl	17	Greifendorf	53-0590
SENGER, Joh. Nikol	26	Landsberg	52-0279
SENGER, Joseph	40	Aschenbach	48-0951
Anne 38, John 14, Anne 16, Jacob 12			
Caroline 5, Elisabeth 3, Elizabeth 11w			
SENGNER, Christine	22	Pottigen	54-0987
SENKELAND, Johanne	22	Unterohn	51-0757
Chr. 4			
SENKIND, Conrad	45	Wallenstedt	51-1101
SENNA, John G.	39	Hernhausen	50-0944
Johanna 41, Pathold L. 10, Ernst W. 5			
Friedrich F. 11m, Christian E. 19			
John G. 63, Louisa F. 8, Theodor R. 3			
Christian F. 15, Amelia 21			
SENNE, Christoph	22	Winzlar	54-1371
Justine 20, Maria 17			
SENNEFIELD, Andr.	22	Hamberg	52-0515
SENNHOLZ, Friedr.	26	Bekedorf	52-1304
Marie 25, Henry 3			
SENNLER, Conrad	28	Kestrich	49-0742
SENNLER, Vict.	30	Limbach	49-0742
SENOR, Anna Cath.	25	Blankenbach	48-0284
SENTELBECK, Arnold	31	Bayreuth/Bav.	54-1092
SERBE, Wilhelm	28	Leipzig	53-1023
Ulrike 24, Maria 2, Carl 9m			
SERFLING, Auguste	18	Eisenberg	52-1512
SERFLING, Julius	23	Istrup/Pr.	54-0965
SERR, F. (m)	24	Rulsheim	52-0652
SERTH, Charles	20	Darmstadt	53-0991
SETTELMAIER, Elis.	38	Langenmosen	54-1371
SETZ, Michel	57	Reising	54-1554
Georg 15, Anna 11			
SEUBECK, Marianne	23	Gristhal	48-0260
SEUBERT, Rosa	25	Jewer	53-0590
SEUFER, Alex	24	Frankenhein	54-1283
SEUFERT, August	32	Plauen	48-0269
SEUFFERT, Elis.	77	Blumberg	54-0987
SEUFFERT, Eva	23	Kleinsteinach	54-1283
SEUSTER, Caspar	37	Luedenscheid	49-0365
SEVEDING, An Marie	21	Biberbach	53-0324
SEVERING, Carl	25	Altona/Holst	51-1796
SEVERLOH, Christ.	35	Weihaus	54-1283
SEYBOLD, John	37	Ehlmannsfurth	49-1106
Conrad 32			
SEYDELMANN, G.	29	Untermichlelb	47-0762
SEYFERT, Catherine	35	Hengsfeld	54-1341
Elisabeth 26			
SEYFERT, J. (m)	30	Nowitz	49-0416
SEYFFERT, Ernestin	26	Goessnitz	54-0987
SEYFURTH, William	19	Crimmitschau	53-1164
SEYLER, Ch. (m)	32	Seidelshapt	50-0746
SHILLING, Matheus	27	Mainstockheim	52-0807
SIBBEL, Margarethe	49	Wirlsdorf	50-0840
SIBERT, Elisabeth	38	Porkholz	52-0515
SIBOLD, Friederike	39	Renneberg	51-1686
Friedrich 16, Carl 8			
SICH, Therese	32	Freiburg	51-1686
Wilhelm 4			
SICHLING, John	29	Frauenaurach	53-0991
SICHT, J.G.	34	Heldburg	49-0324
W.H. (m) 19			
SICK, Dorothea	15	Wuertenberg	53-0557
SICKENMEIER, Maria	19	Holte	52-1512
SIDENTOPF, C. (m)	29	Quedlinburg	50-0439
SIEBEIN, J.H.	30	New York	51-0500
Caroline 18, Heinrich 6m			
SIEBEL, Rudolph	23	Ilbenstedt	49-0383
SIEBENBORN, Cath.	14	Bisses	54-1717
SIEBENHUETTER, Mat	54	Neuburg/Bav.	52-1423
Joseph 20, Xaver 6			
SIEBER, James	20	Ilsfeld	53-1164
SIEBERT, Anna	19	Maden/K.-Hess	52-1332
SIEBERT, Carl	26	Prussia	50-1317

NAME	AGE	RESIDENCE	YR-LIST
SIEBERT, Caspar	26	Fritzlar	54-0053
SIEBERT, Catharine	20	Neustadt	54-1716
August 16			
SIEBERT, Franz	15	Fulda	53-0628
SIEBERT, Friedrich	57	Hohenschoenau	50-1071
Dorothea 47, Friedrich 25, Gottl. 23			
Daniel 20, Dorothea 18, Herm. 15			
Emilie 13, Alwine 5			
SIEBERT, Henry	24	Waflik	54-1716
SIEBERT, Hermann	18	Neustadt/Hess	50-0323
SIEBERT, Maria	32	Marburg	50-0021
Leonhardt 9, Sophie 7, Catharina 4			
SIEBERT, Marie	15	Grossenglis	52-0775
SIEBERT, Martha	27	Cassel	54-1371
SIEBERT, Wilhelm	20	Bremen	52-1105
SIEBING, Andreas	42	Leiperzell	53-0590
Maria 40, Caroline 15, Marie 13, Carl 9			
Christian 6			
SIEBRASSE, Fr.(m)	23	Brake	52-1321
SIEBRECHT, Carl	26	Bruchhausen	53-1070
SIECHERT, Ann Barb		Ahornberg	53-0637
SIECK, Margarethe	24	Niederstolzin	54-0600
SIECKE, Johanne	30	Danzig	54-1371
Maria 4, Johannes 2			
SIECKERMANN, Joh.	46	Hoya	52-1362
Anna 45, Sophia 16, Elise 14			
Friedrich 12, Marie 10, William 6			
Heinrich 4, Dorothea 1			
SIECKMANN, Friedr.	39	Lesum	54-0600
Doris 36			
SIEDE, J.F.	32	Burgwedel	51-0460
SIEDENBURG, Carl	14	Achim	54-0872
SIEFKAN, Carl Ulr.	31	Hohenkirchen	54-0872
Meta 35, Anna 5			
SIEFKEN, Friedr.	20	Jever	54-0053
SIEFKEN, Tobias	30	Etzell/Hannov	51-1725
SIEGBERT, Heinrich	23	Kronheim/Bav.	52-1423
SIEGBRECH, Heinr.	50	Celle	50-1067
Maria 50, Charlotte 20, Morchen 16			
Heinrich 25, Carl 19, Conrad 13, Martin			
Teressa , Maria 10			
SIEGEL, Anna	20	Vegesack	49-0383
SIEGEL, Georg	26	Huttensteinba	53-1164
Barbara 29			
SIEGEL, Gertrude	26	Vockerath	48-0269
Anna M. 26, Elisabeth M. 28			
SIEGEL, Otto	24	Saxony	50-1317
SIEGEL, Therese	28	Gaab	52-0895
SIEGEL, Wolfgang	20	Steinach	53-0888
SIEGER, Louis	24	Halzganz	52-1321
SIEGESKRON, Samson	29	Bamberg	48-1184
SIEGEWALD, Heinr.	25	Weissendorf	54-1371
SIEGLER, Bertha	18	Winterbach	54-0987
SIEGMANN, Cath.	18	Rieneck	52-1625
SIEGMANN, Georg	45	Wende	54-1094
Christina 38, Friedrich 18, Heinrich 5			
SIEGMANN, Luise	41	Minden	50-0021
August 17, Wilhelmine 15, Pauline 14			
Ferdinand 12, Carl 5, Johannes 1			
SIEGMANN, Wilhelm	43	Reinsdorf	53-1086
SIEGRIST, Henry	24	Duisburg/Pr.	48-0447
Sivilla 23			
SIEHOFE, Henrietta	22	Cassel	54-1341
SIEKAR, Johann	40	Dresden	50-0379
Clara 9			
SIELER, Carl	30	Dresig/Pr.	52-0560
SIELING, Franz	30	Holtorf	52-0558
SIELING, Heinrich	22	Amt Nienburg	48-1179
SIELSCHOTT, Adolph	19	Hunteburg	54-1371
SIEMANN, Lehmann	16	Langenschwanz	54-0830
SIEMANN, Wilhelm	18	Loeningen	53-1062
SIEMER, Diedrich	33	Wollings	52-1625
SIEMER, W.	19	Wilbende	51-0517
SIEMERS, Anna	20	Hohenmoor	53-1016
SIEMERS, Carl	31	Erichshagen	54-1443
Dorothea 33, Heinrich 15			
SIEMON, Dor.	38	Neuendorf	47-0868
Josh. 14, Els. 7, W. 3			

NAME	AGE	RESIDENCE	YR-LIST
SIEMON, Joh.	59	Suhl	54-0930
Johanna Barb 44, Christian 17, Emilie 14			
Gottlieb 8, Ernst 5			
SIEMON, Otto	19	Frischenhause	52-1200
SIEMONSMEYER, Fr.	27	Varenholz	51-1160
Wm. 22			
SIEMS, Claus	24	Labstaedt	50-1236
SIEMS, Friedrich	18	Bremervorde	47-0828
SIEN, Gesche	21	Lilienthal/Ha	52-1620
SIENON, Christoph	24	Oberellen	52-1410
SIERP, Ann Barbara	32	Venne/Hann.	49-0365
SIETZFELDER, Hess.	43	Burgkundstadt	54-1371
SIEVERS, August	51	Dielmissen	50-1132
Wilhelmine 52, Wilhelmine 24, Johanne 22			
Louise 17, Caroline 9, Wilhelm 14			
Heinrich 4			
SIEVERS, Bohle (m)	17	Dingen	48-0951
SIEVERS, Felix		Breslau	54-1443
SIEVERS, Ludw.	35	Amelgaetzen	54-0987
Friederike 27, Georg by			
SIEVERS, Wilhelm	34	Seelde	52-1625
Cath. 28, Carl 8			
SIEVERT, August	35	Neubrandenbur	53-0905
Marie 28, Caroline 13, Wilhelm 4			
SIEVERT, Elise	17	Hohenauffenbe	53-0838
SIEVERT, Elise	17	Hohenaverberg	53-0838
SIEVERT, Friedrich	27	Butzen	53-0838
SIEVERT, Heinr.	31	Burgwedel	54-1297
SIEVERT, Jochen	38	Grossfiden	53-0905
Johanne 27, Carl 4			
SIEVERT, Wilhelm	4	Neuenkirchen	53-0905
SIG, Ch. (m)	19	Darmstadt	48-0453
SIGEL, Margaretha	20	Weilheim/Wuer	52-0351
Eva Maria 18			
SIGGELKOW, Friedr.	32	Zuelow	54-1297
Marie 25, Sophie 1			
SIGGELKOW, William	58	Schwerin	53-0991
Charlotte 48, Rudolph 12			
SIGGELKOW, William	32	Schwerin	53-0991
Louisa 28, Ernest 4, John 2, Mary 6m			
SIGLHUBER, Anna M.	42	Niederummersd	54-1443
SIGNER, Eckard	33	Luteckwig	48-0269
SIK, Georg	26	Langenau	54-1717
SIKA, Joseph	26	Saaz	49-1106
SILBER, Bertha	15	Erfurt	51-0460
Johanne 13, (f) 12			
SILBER, Georg	49	Erfurt	51-0460
Maria 49, Auguste 12, Emma 11, Clara 2			
Louise 9, Julius 5, Otto 4			
SILBERBERG, Salom.	23	Krotoschin	53-1023
SILBERER, Nanette	28	Ellwangen	53-0991
SILBERHORN, G.M.	35	Schwabach	50-1071
Dorothea 30, Maria Doro. 8, Anna Doro. 6			
Joh. Daniel 4, Babid 2, Rosina 3m			
SILBERMANN, Carl	40	Bamberg	50-0021
Therese 33, Sabina 15, Babette 14			
SILBERMANN, Carol.	51	Baiern	48-0887
Rosalie 23, Amalie 20			
SILBERMANN, Samuel	21	Walsdorf	48-0269
SILER, C. (m)	22	Nordheim	50-0746
SILJAK, Johann	16	Bremerhafen	51-0756
SILLER, Philip	21	Neukirchen	53-0991
SILTER, Heinrich	25	Sielhorst	53-0905
SIMMERT, Franz	23	Altheinrichau	54-1443
SIMON, Adam	24	Etmershausen	53-1000
SIMON, Albert	23	Koennberg	54-1168
SIMON, August	2-	Zisar	49-1358
SIMON, Cath.	30	Jacobsmuehl	53-0914
SIMON, Ernst		New York	48-0269
SIMON, Eva	26	Seebach	50-0472
SIMON, F. Ferd.	22	Bansa	51-1640
SIMON, Friedrich	28	Eisenach/Sax.	52-1620
SIMON, Friedrich	19	Rehtenbach	54-0830
SIMON, Heinr.	18	Letell	52-1321
SIMON, Johann		Hesse-Cassel	52-1620
SIMON, Louis	40	Bonnhaller	52-1148
SIMON, Marie	28	Sontra	52-0699
SIMON, Martin	19	Salzwedel	54-1591

NAME	AGE	RESIDENCE	YR-LIST
SIMON, Sigmund	30	Hannover	50-0311
SIMON, Xaver	17	Lippe-Detmold	54-1452
SIMPSON, Anna	22	Bremen	51-1245
SIMPSON, Sanford	30	Atkintown	51-1245
Anna 22			
SIMSON, Erich	42	Ganheim/Bav.	47-0987
Catharina 41, Catharina 12, Andreas 11			
Louis 9, Kilian 6			
SINGER, Anton	24	Mittelruessel	49-0737
SINGER, Barbara	21	Daberg	53-0905
SINGER, Caspar	39	Esslingen	51-0460
Catharina 38, Hermann 11, Wilhelm 9			
Eduard 5, Adolph 3			
SINGER, Joh.	50	Ermreuth	52-0693
Anna 36, Margareth 13, Thomas 9			
Joh. Mart. 7, Kunig. 5, Thomas 20			
SINGER, Julie	17	Trosau	54-1078
SINGSTACK, Anna		Padingbuettel	54-1647
SINKERS, Amalia	22	Bremen	48-1114
SINN, Ernestine	21	Lobenstein	54-0987
SINN, Friedrich	23	Cassel	50-1236
SINNE, Eng. Maria	60	Nordbruch	47-0672
SINNE, H. Heinr.	72	Mesmerrode	47-0672
Eng. Maria 60, Eng. Maria 25			
SINSHAUER, Friedr.	17	Cultz	54-1724
SIPPE, Heinrich	17	Sonndra	52-1148
Maria 20			
SIPPEL, Christine	25	Raunsbach	54-1371
SIPPEL, Christoph	30	Lindewerra	51-1438
Margaret 24, Georg Wilh. 5, Johannes 3			
Georg 2, Juliane 6m			
SIPPEL, Elisabeth		Hutzdorf	54-1575
SIPPLE, Eth. (f)	25	Wuertt.	54-1724
SIR, Johann	52	Treptow	54-0872
Otto 23, Ferdinand 22, Minna 24			
SITTIG, Cath.	24	Batschel	53-0914
SITTLING, Ludwig	34	Berka	54-1554
Sophie 25			
SITUS, Martha	29	Oberhauptstag	54-1419
SIVERS, Joh. H.	44	Bederkesa/Han	51-1796
Marg. 36, Doris 18, Arents H. 15			
Kath. 12, Joh. H. 9, Marg. 8, Karl 6			
Hein. Dit. 9m			
SKALLA, Joseph	32	Boehmen	53-1000
Anna 29, Anna 3, Rosalie 2			
SKARIWIDA, Lorenz	46	Boehmen	52-1362
Maria 47, Maria 20, Barbara 18			
Franziska 16, Anton 14, Carl 12, Anna 10			
Theresia 5, Johann 2			
SKIWA, Joseph	22	Wien	54-1168
SKOEPPEL, J.G.	27	Heinsdorf	53-1016
SKONETZKI, F.A.	21	Frohburg	54-1566
SKOROSZEWSKY, Jul.	24	Ravende	54-1168
SKRAINKA, Wilhelm	32	Prag	48-1184
SLACHOTE, Anna	26	Saaz	49-1106
SLAMA, Anton	37	Sedlitz	54-1647
Maria 42, Martin 16, Joseph 10, Maria 8			
Johann 5			
SLAPPEL, Conrad	26	Porkholz	52-0515
Anna Cath. 28, Henry 3			
SLEGE, John P.	48	Ostenholze	50-0944
Catherine 45, Mary 20, Henry 17			
Cort Henry 15			
SLOHLFELDER, Joh.	29	Bamberg	52-0515
Margaretha 30			
SLOTMANN, Joh. B.	23	Luesche	52-0563
SLURM, Johanne	24	Gruenenplan	51-1438
SMAUS, Conrad	32	Allenrothe	54-0882
SMELACZEK, Victor	34	Strakowitz	54-1566
SMIDT, Anton	30	Roettenbach	53-1062
Louise 24			
SMIDT, El. (f)	20	Wuertt.	54-1724
SMIDT, Hugo	15	Dahl	54-1724
SMIDT, John	30	Baiern	54-1724
SMIDT, Ludwig	16	Meiningen	51-1588
John 16, Carloline 21			
SMITH, George L.	28	Mittelrueselb	49-0737
Margaretha 22			

NAME	AGE	RESIDENCE	YR-LIST
SNELL, Cath.	15	Osnabrueck	52-1512
SNELLE, G. H. (m)	27	Osnabrueck	52-1512
SNETLAGE, Wilhelm	17	Lienen	52-1362
SNOBADA, Louise	19	Lobenstein	54-0987
SNORSCH, Heinrich	22	Lilienthal/Ha	52-1620
SOBBE, Engel	20	Peppinghausen	51-1588
SOBBE, Ernst	50	Meinsen	52-1321
SOBBE, Sophia	24	Meinsen	52-1321
Wilhelm 14, Carl 10, Ernst 8			
SOBBE, v. Carl	21	Minden	51-0384
SODER, Gustav	19	Garsau	51-1796
SODOZ, Ed.	22	France	48-1015
SOEDER, Franz	13	Steinach/Bav.	53-0475
SOEDER, Mich. Jos.	17	Steinach	52-1304
SOEDER, Wilhelm	20	Hundelshausen	52-0563
SOEFFING, Adolph	24	Neustadt	53-0590
SOEFFLING, J.C.F.	40	Eichfeldt	49-0324
SOEHL, Wilhelm	17	Lenstedt/Hann	53-0475
SOEHLEIN, Johann	24	Bauner/Bav.	52-0351
Elise 17			
SOEHLER, Carl	26	Braunschweig	54-0872
SOEHNLEIN, Anna	11	Vilseck	54-1078
SOELCH, Georg	17	Hoehstaedt	53-0557
SOELCH, Maria	19	Bayern	53-0557
SOELDNER, Joh Geo.		Rethenweiler	53-1000
Charlotte 45, Cath. 23, Georg 20			
Andr. 17, Leonhardt 15, Margar. 11			
Simon 9, Matth. 5			
SOELL, H.	20	Urlhendorf	54-1419
SOELLICH, Minna	18	Koenigslutter	53-0492
SOELLTNER, Kilian	48	Bayern	53-0590
Margret 38, Johann 16, Caspar 13			
Ottilia 22, Alexander 9			
SOERENSEN, Theodor	29	Swendberg	48-1355
SOERGEL, Martin	22	Lauf	54-0872
SOERGEL, Wolfgang	60	Dehlau	52-1129
Albertine 32, Elisab. 34, Nicol. 6			
Peter 3, baby			
SOERGES, Joseph	33	Koenigshelf	54-1297
Peter 23			
SOERNAU, Ludwig	40	Landsberg	52-1661
Franziska 33, Maria 9, Emma 6			
SOETEBIER, J.C.	28	Cuxhafen	51-1160
SOFF, Francis	19	Treysa	53-0991
SOHERING, Margaret	25		47-0987
SOHL, Heinrich	30	Mittelberg/KH	53-0628
SOHL, J. (m)	28	Oberaula	50-0746
SOHL, Jacob	22	Redinghausen	50-0323
SOHLEINGING, H.J.	18	Alsfeld	54-1341
SOHN, Carl S.	50	Merseburg	50-1317
Marie 31, Carl S. 9			
SOHN, Wilhelm	30	N. Preussen	51-1084
SOLDAU, G. (m)	27	Hosenlowitz	54-1566
SOLDNER, Joh Georg	26	Weidelbach	53-1000
SOLEDER, Franziska	26	Hofdorf	52-1452
SOLEZKY, Heinrich	20	Braunschweig	52-1410
SOLLEDER, Johann	55	Haidhausen	54-1168
Gertrud 58			
SOLLER, Sebastian	24	Schoeltgruppe	53-0825
SOLLMANN, Fr.	48	Venne	53-1016
Anna 38, Johann 9, Friedrich 7, Wilhelm 5			
Anna 3			
SOLTAN, Kunigunde	30	Bremen	53-1070
SOLTER, Christ.	20	Hannover	50-0311
SOMMER, Adolph	15	Braunschweig	54-1649
SOMMER, Andreas	36	Haidhausen	54-1168
Magdalene 36			
SOMMER, Anna Barb.	20	Faddigau/Bav.	52-0351
SOMMER, Augustus	24	Ottensos	53-0991
SOMMER, Caroline	18	Wehrheim	53-1023
SOMMER, Cath. W.	20	Weitroth	52-0652
SOMMER, Friedrich	38	Almerode	54-1452
Anna Maria 35, Reinhard 6, Caroline 3			
Wilhelm by			
SOMMER, Georg	23	Wildeshausen	54-0053
SOMMER, Gottw.	17	Grosspuerschu	54-1297
SOMMER, Heinr.	37	Altenberge	53-0585
Maria 22			

NAME	AGE	RESIDENCE	YR-LIST
SOMMER, Jane	23	Driesbach	54-1470
SOMMER, Johann	24	Doeringstadt	54-0930
Margarethe 18			
SOMMER, Marg.	17	Baiern	54-1724
SOMMER, Xaver	34	Lauternhofen	50-0840
SOMMER. Carl Gottl	48	---tendorf	54-0987
Joh. Julie 42, Ottilde 20, Agnes 18			
Selma 15, Ernestine 7			
SOMMERE, Sebastian	32	Saeusen	50-1236
SOMMERKAMP, H. (m)	27	Dessen	52-0652
SOMMERKAMP, Mary	52	Seggen	54-1470
SOMMERMANN, Johann	45	Fuerstenhagen	51-1639
Anna 45, Elise 23, Maria 17, Eduard 12			
Heinrich 14, Johannes 9, Wilhelm 6			
Margretha 5, August 3			
SOMMERMANN, Monika	16	Fuerstenhagen	51-1639
SOMMERNIG, Louis	20	Schlossheltru	49-0781
SONDERGELT, Heinr.	16	Fulda/Hess.	51-1532
SONDERHAUS, Marg.	26	Becka	52-0370
SONDERMANN, Georg	21	Falkenhagen	51-0405
SONDERMEIR, Christ	37	Fillengen	51-1035
SONN, Rozo	19	Bilshausen	54-0830
SONNEKALLE, Carl	23	Rohrbach	49-0574
SONNENBERG, Isaac	19	Foehrsheim	52-1410
SONNENBERG, Mich.	33	Wimislaw	49-0742
A. (f) 22, B. (m) 10, A. (m) 8, J. (m) 5			
F. (m) 4			
SONNENFELD, Nanny	22	Breslau	54-1092
SONNET, Johann	24	Dachsveiler	51-1084
SONNTAG, F.S.	23	Merane	53-0435
SONNTAG, Jos.	50	Boehmen	54-1724
Barbara 40, Franz 5, Mary 5			
SONNTAG, Wilhelm	18	Eisenberg	52-1512
SONNTAG, Wilhelm	22	Meerane	54-1168
SONTAG, Wilhelm	18	Eisenberg	52-1512
SONTHEIM, Johann	29	Fexen	53-0492
SORBER, Rudolph	30	Zuerich	54-1283
SORGER, Joh. G.	32	Pruideritz/Bv	52-0960
SOSALL, Joh. Gust.	34	Plauen	54-1647
Christine 48, Gustav 16, Julius 6			
SOSSEN, v. Trina	23	Lintig	51-1084
SOTT, Heinrich	23	Guetinburg	54-1282
SOTTEN, F. (m)	19	Coeln	48-0453
SOWOTKA, Marie	60	Polna	54-1297
SOYFERT, P.	19	Gohrmitz	54-0987
SPAAR, Samuel	34	Bersrod	52-1105
Marg. 26, Philipp 5, Elisabeth 2			
SPACK, Christine	32	Michenad	48-1131
SPAEHLER, Carl Rob	20	Bieberach	52-1200
SPALL, August	19	Langenleube	53-0914
SPANGENBERG, Carl	29	Eschwege/Hann	53-0475
Theodor Ludw 19			
SPANIER, Lewis	28	Hamburg	53-1164
Jane 30, Maurice by			
SPANIER, Tine	16	Rothenberg	49-1358
SPANMUTH, Carl	28	Frankenhausen	53-0492
Caroline 30			
SPANNER, Johann	23	Buch	54-1419
Kunig. 22, Magdalene 27			
SPATH, Andr.	34	Stettfeld	54-1575
SPATH, Georg	23	Hohenstadt	49-0574
SPAU, August	19	Langenleube	53-0914
SPAUNG, Joseph	43	Herthen	52-1625
Johanne 33, Joseph 13, Richard 10			
Wilhelmine 5, Martin 3			
SPECHT, August	26	Braunschweig	53-0267
Elisabeth 55			
SPECHT, Ernst	23	Barliburt	52-0370
SPECHT, Joh. Fr.	25	Dissen	48-1179
Henriette 22, Joh. Heinr. by			
SPECHT, Johannes	32	Kleinensee	48-0284
Christoph 7, Margareth 19			
SPECHT, Wilhelm	25	Duderstadt	51-0500
SPECK, Ludwig	24	Strasseversba	52-1410
SPECKELS, Anton	47	Varel	47-0828
SPECKERT, Josepha	41	Wagenschwendt	51-0384
Josepha 23			
SPECKETZER, Claus	22	Kassebruch	54-1716

NAME	AGE	RESIDENCE	YR-LIST
SPECKNER, Sebast.	28	Rauzenthal	54-1078
SPEGG, Franz Jos.	37	Hassfurt	52-1200
SPEIBER, Georg	19	Sellmuth	52-0515
SPEIBER, Johann	41	Heimersdorf	52-1321
SPEICHER, Rosine	36	Wieblingen	51-1455
SPEIDEL, Otto	17	Friedenthal	49-0345
SPEIDEL, Wilhelm	23	Oberschmitten	48-0269
SPEIER, Eleonore	16	Londorff	47-0840
SPEIER, Jacob	22	Waldeck	50-0311
Benjamin 16			
SPELLARBERG, Anton	20	Erker	51-1245
SPELLENBERG, Georg	21	Heidenheim	49-0352
SPELLENBERG, Heinr	18	Uslar	52-1304
Dorothea 26			
SPELLERBERG, Wilh.	18	Uslar	51-0500
SPELTMANN, L.B.(m)	28	Elberfeld	48-0453
SPELZHAUS, Derrick	28	Eistrup	48-1209
SPENDER, Cath.	23	Kaltern	54-1282
SPENDLER, Philipp	26	Preussen	53-0590
SPENGER, Xaver	25	Oberndorf	53-0492
SPENGLER, Friedr.	19	Eisnen	52-1512
SPENGLER, George	20	Braunschweig	50-0323
Theodor 18			
SPENGLER, Theodor	18	Eisnen	52-1512
SPENGLES, Cath.	20	Gartenroth	54-0930
SPENK, H. (m)	20	Dorein	48-0453
SPERBER, Johann	41	Heimersdorf	52-1321
SPERBER, W.	25	Leimberg	53-0582
SPERFECHTER, Fr.	19	Kupfersell	54-0918
SPERL, Christina	28	Bavaria	54-1554
SPERL, Friedrich	33	Baiern	54-1554
SPERL, Kunigunde	19	Nuernberg	50-1317
SPERMANN, Georg	36	Walburgkirche	54-1078
SPETH, Michel	60	Fla--ngen	50-0944
Bernhard 28			
SPEYER, Herz (m)	52	Volkershausen	52-0279
Fradel (f) 55			
SPICHER, Heinr.	27	Bleicheralte	52-1321
SPIEGEL, Maria	23	Osnabrueck	52-1512
SPIEGEL, Thielmann	33	Nesselroeden	47-0828
Heinrich 30			
SPIELBUSCH, Henry	24	Beckum	50-0840
SPIELMANN, Jacob	33	Ingolstadt	54-0053
Theresa 29, Victoria 15, Maria 10			
Joseph 9, Waldbuerger 3			
SPIELMANN, Johann	21	Steinheim	52-1512
SPIER, Friedrich	27	Wiedenbruck	48-0447
SPIER, Jette	21	Paderborn/Han	51-0048
SPIER, Meier	20	Mittelberg/KH	53-0628
SPIES, Wilhelm	28	Elberfeld	48-0565
SPIESS, Valentin	55	Ferdinandsdor	51-0384
Anton 29, Jacob 27, Franz Joseph 26			
SPIKER, Dorothea	29	Liegnitz	54-1371
Max 4, Hulda 4m			
SPILKE, John	40	Schomburg	54-1591
Anna 40, Joseph 12, Mary 11			
SPILKER, Charles	38	Baltimore, Md	48-1015
(f) 35, Charles Jr. 5, Mary 3			
Clementine 1			
SPILL, Margaretha	30	Bayern	53-1013
Conrad 9, Margaretha 5			
SPILLERBERG, Franz	42	Paderborn/Pr.	51-1532
Joseph 9			
SPILLERBERG, Heinr	26	Hannover	54-1078
SPILLING, Fr.	29	Cassel	54-1078
SPILLNER, Peter	18	Rotenburg	54-1575
SPILMANN, Wm.	37	Germany	51-1588
Margaret 17			
SPINDLER, Amalie	21	Gumbelshausen	53-0320
SPINDLER, Aug.	31	Talhausen	51-1796
Caroline B. 31			
SPINDLER, Cathrina	22	Wolfersgruen	52-1580
SPINDLER, Gottl. H	44	Syrau/Sax	48-0053
Ann Christ. 43, Carl August 11			
SPINDLER, Sophie	57	Landringhause	53-1000
SPINNER, John	18	Goettingen	52-0370
SPITTAELLER, C.	30	Wien	53-0888
SPITZBART, Johann	25	Lagech	49-0742
SPIZELBERGER, Lor.	24	Frondenhausen	54-1717
SPOERRE, Conrad	58	Kleinensee	52-1148
Maria Elis. 42, Maria 12, Catharine 9			
George 7, Anna Maria 36			
SPOHR, Anna	17	Grossenglis	52-0775
SPOHR, Louis	16	Barfelde	53-0590
SPONSEL, J. Chr.	15	Steierhof	53-0905
Marie 25			
SPREINER, August	30	Hameln/Hann.	54-1092
SPRENG, Sebastian	29	Gaisenhausen	54-1168
SPRENGE, Joseph	22	Gellmern	51-1245
Anton 13, Anton 8, Elise 4			
SPRENGER, Anton	28	Muenster	51-1084
SPRICK, Margarethe	20	Bremen	54-1371
SPRIEGEL, Regina	19	Ellwangen	48-1355
SPRINGER, Elis.	25	Sinnstadt	54-0600
SPRINGER, Johann	52	Niederklein	51-0460
Catharina 49, Heinrich 29, Elisabeth 21			
Maria 16, Georg 9, Catharina 5			
SPRINGER, Leonhard	24	Steinhart	48-0951
SPRINGER, Valentin	18	Schonstadt	54-1168
SPRINGER, Wentzel	24	Michelsdorf	54-0872
SPRINGMEYER, W'mne	22	Dessen	52-0652
SPRINGNISGUTH, Chr	27	Riepen	50-1132
SPROEDA, John	23	Nuisberg	49-1106
SPROEGEL, Clemens	18	Gera/Reuss	52-0960
SPROEGEL, Wm.	19	Gera	51-1160
SPRUDLER, Johann	18	Schonweisa	47-0672
SPUHR, Carl	16	Schuhzach	53-0267
STAAKE, Henry	58	Braunschweig	51-1725
Antoinette 18			
STAB, Jacob	31	Altdorf	52-0279
Anton 27			
STABLER, Goths.	23	Mittelruessel	49-0737
STADEL, Wilhelm	19	Aderweisag	52-1101
STADELMANN, Aug'ta	49	Ilsfeld/Hann	54-1092
STADELMANN, Kunig.	19	Oberlendenbac	53-0320
STADEN, D. (m)	16	Bederkesa	47-0104
STADEN, J.V.	15	Bremervoerde	50-1067
Maria 11			
STADEN, Marg.	21	Bremervoerde	51-1035
STADERMANN, Plaud.	18	Blankenau	51-0405
STADLER, Anna M.	27	Niederklein	52-1321
STADLER, Franz	19	Hanau	54-1371
STADLER, George L.	20	Mittelruessel	49-0737
STADLER, Joh. Conr	19	Buechelberg	54-1371
STADTLER, J.F.	28	Flohe	54-1716
STADTMAIER, Julius	24	Baiern	54-1724
STADTMUELLER, L(f)	24	Carlsruhe	54-1371
STAEBER, Friedr.	30	Eichzow	54-0987
Elisa 28			
STAEBLEIN, Rudolph	29	Roth	51-0500
STAEDINZ, Chr.	45	Welsede	48-0445
S. (f) 47			
STAEHL, Albert	31	Roeblingen	54-1168
STAEHLIN, Ottilie	22	Memmingen	50-0439
STAEMBKE, Cath.	47	Osterhage	49-0352
Wilhelmine 11			
STAEMBKE, Heinrich	37	Osterhage	49-0352
STAENDER, Johann	30	Geismar/Pr.	52-1423
STAENDNER, Andreas	37	Gleick	52-0279
Elise 31			
STAFFLER, Th. (f)	28	Aallen	50-0746
STAHL, Albert	31	Rudolphsdorf	54-1168
STAHL, Georg	29	Cronach	53-0825
STAHL, Johann	25	Weiler	49-0352
STAHL, John George	19	Erlangen	53-0991
STAHL, Salomon	21	Gilsenberg	51-0352
STAHLE, Benedict	23	Boxdorf/Bav.	48-0053
STAHLHERT, Friedr.	31	Roeke	51-1588
STAHLMANN, Wilh.	27	Nuernberg	50-1071
STAHMANN, Johann	18	Brinkum	51-1101
STAIK, Franz Jos.	42	Schnaitlaetz	54-0903
STAINHUSEN, Jas. G	37	Mittelruessel	49-0737
Hannah 28, Helena 16			
STALHUT, Carl	17	Papinghausen	49-0329
STALLING, Diedrich	26	Varel	48-0887
STALLMANN, Chr.	30	Hannover	51-1160

NAME	AGE	RESIDENCE	YR-LIST
STALLMANN, Gottl.	27	Bundle	51-1639
STALLMANN, L. (m)	43	Germany	48-1015
Caroline 30, Lena 10, Johanna 7, Louisa 5			
Louis 2			
STAMANN, Heinrich	28	Kakelbeck	52-1580
STAMBERGER, Sabine	20	Bavaria	50-0311
STAMM, Allex	23	Hammerstadt	54-1283
STAMM, Catharine	19	Hofgarten	51-0460
STAMM, Heinr.	17	Wielinghausen	51-1160
STAMM, Johanette	20	Giesen	53-1000
STAMM, Zacharias	29	Bruck	53-0320
STAMMEN, Johann	30	Mittelruessel	49-0737
Gerhard 32			
STAMMER, Andreas	43	Mittelruessel	49-0737
Anna 39			
STAND, Mathilde	25	Meinertzhagen	53-0557
STANDEN, Ed. Alex.	27	Potsdam	54-1647
Mathilde 24, Maximilian 1			
STANDINGER, A. (m)	28	Weisenberg	50-0746
STANER, Wilhelm	31	Mittelruessel	49-0737
STANG, Catharina	22	Solms	53-0942
STANG, Christine	27	Hattenbach	54-1575
STANG, Marie	23	Erdmansrode	52-0652
STANG, Valentin	29	Asbach	53-1070
STANGE, August	51	Breslau	54-1724
STANGE, Christine	23	Wissen/Pr.	51-0048
STANGE, Heinrich	36	Erdmannsroth	52-1661
STANGE, Joh Heinr.	20	Gehrde	51-0352
STANGE, Joseph	25	Hochwartel	53-0914
Marie 25, Marg. 2, George 56, Marie 54			
Joseph 17			
STANGE, Valentin	18	Kirchheim	53-0267
STANGE, Wilhelm	16	Mitterrude/He	54-1092
STANGER, Wilh.	22	Urach	54-0600
Christ. 23			
STANZE, Heinrich	28	Braunschweig	53-1062
Henriette 28			
STAPF, Wilhelm	23	Ostheim	49-0574
STARK, August		Lilienthal	48-1131
STARK, Carl	20	Weimar	50-0439
STARK, Gottlieb	32	Bakenau	49-0345
STARK, Leonhard	21	Burk	49-1106
STARK, Marie	25	Baiern	52-0895
STARK, Rudolph	29	Ravensberg	54-1371
STARK, Theresia	28	Kehlbach	49-0352
STARKE, Chr.	18	Kohlenfeldt	53-0492
STARKLEFF, Carl	30	Gotha	52-1362
STARKLOFF, Ernst	32	Gotha	52-1410
Marie 35			
STARKLOFF, Marie	35	Wiesbaden	52-1410
STARTZ, Johann	19	Dorum	49-0329
STASSENAUER, Dam.	27	Hessen	51-0405
STATGE, Conrad	54	Niedershausen	53-0928
Luise 53			
STAU, M. Dorothea	18	Ebersbach	47-0672
STAUB, Catherine	50	Hannover	54-1168
STAUBACH, Christ.	28	Herpstein	51-1101
STAUBER, Friedrich	30	Eichzow	54-0987
Elisa 28			
STAUBER, Joseph	18	Prag	53-0435
Dom. 54			
STAUBES, William	24	Solingen	53-1164
STAUBNER, Conr.	29	Ohrenbach	54-1078
Susanna 23			
STAUCH, Christoph	26	Saalfeld	52-0699
STAUCH, Eduard	24	Gotha	52-1410
STAUCH, Ernst	24	Prussia	54-1724
Georg 29			
STAUCH, G.	31	Sattelgrund	53-0582
Cath. 31, Augusta 7, Paulina 5, E. 3			
STAUCH, Georg	22	Rodach/Coburg	53-0590
STAUDEMEYER, Jos.	29	Wuertenberg	53-0557
Theresia 26			
STAUDT, Erasmus	18	Kommershausen	54-1566
Johann 16			
STAUSCH, Alfred	17	Kammersberg/G	53-0628
STEBELING, A.B.(f)	19	Salzungen/M.	52-0960
STEBIG, Chr.	25	Weberstadt	51-1160

NAME	AGE	RESIDENCE	YR-LIST
Joh. Elise 21, H. Wilh. 9m			
STECHEL, Friedrich	23	Linden/Hannov	53-0628
STECK, C. (m)	23	Berkheim	49-0329
STECK, Dor.	44	Leipzig	49-1358
Otto 4, P. (f) by			
STECKER, Paul	37	Ebersberg	54-0850
Walpurga 38, Petronilla 5			
STECKLE, Fr'derike	18	Leonberg/Wuer	52-0351
STEDE, Christian	34	Wernighaus/Wa	54-1092
STEDEL, Christ.	28	Halle	54-0987
STEDTKORNEN, Elnor	50	Meiningen	52-0699
STEDTLER, Theod.	31	Crimmitschau	53-1016
STEENBLOCK, Anna	27	Rhauderfeen	51-1532
Tinna 23, Ahlrich 19, Margretha 17			
Dirk Harms 14, Gesine 7			
STEFAN, Wm. Friedr		Seebuch/Pr.	51-1796
Maria Friedr 25			
STEFFEN, Heinr.	19	Herford	52-0895
STEFFENS, Christ.	21	Cuxhaven	54-1716
STEFFENS, Diedrich	22	Lamstedt	51-1639
STEFFENS, Fried. W	25	Oelder	50-0292
STEFFENS, Friedr.	29	Neuhausen	52-1512
STEFFENS, Friedr.	19	Bremervoerde	54-1371
Meta 19			
STEFFENS, Johann	28	Hannover	50-1317
STEFFENS, John	60	Oldenburg	53-0991
STEFFENS, Margr.	20	Felde	54-1647
STEFFINS, Carl	46	Morsum	52-0515
Joshena 47, Margareth 16, Henry 14			
Charles 3, Joice (m) 36			
STEFFLING, Christ.	53	Kaustein	48-0887
Sophie 28, Mary 4			
STEFTER, Max	18	Ansbach	53-0991
STEGE, Anna Sophie	18	Riepen	50-1132
STEGE, Conrad	21	Riepen	47-0672
Charlotte 25, Maria 3, Johann 18m			
STEGE, Fried.	20		54-1716
STEGE, John P.	48	Ostenholze	50-0944
Catherine 45, Mary 20, Henry 17			
Cort Henry 15			
STEGELMANN, Marie	26	Brodersdorf	54-1297
STEGEMAMN, Jos.	28	Osnabrueck	54-1371
STEGEMANN, Johann	22	Soelsingen/Ha	53-0475
Heinrich 16			
STEGER, Barbara	21	Schlossberg	52-1129
Georg 25			
STEGER, Franz	19	Hausen	53-0590
STEGER, George	25	Wadern	52-1129
STEGGER, Heinrich	40	Ostenholze	50-0944
Catherine 28, Catherine 10, William 5			
STEGMANN, Caroline	24	Moenchsroth	54-1168
STEGMANN, Heinrich	17	Sandstedt	50-0366
STEGMEIER, Doris	22	Heinsen	49-1358
Sophie 20			
STEGMUELLER, J Gus	35	Weils	54-1371
Theresia 40			
STEGMUELLER, Matt.	20	Illingen	53-1000
STEGNER, Wilhelmin	14	Coburg	53-1164
STEHFEST, Hermann	25	Schwoora	54-0872
STEHL, Carl	20	Soden	53-0838
STEHLING, Lorenz	42	Sachs.-Gotha	50-1236
Christiane 37, Dorothea 13, Johanne 15			
Friederike 11, Christiane 8, Maria 5			
Luise 3, August 9m			
STEHMANN, Friedr.	31	Luenen	48-1184
STEHR, Heinrich	28	Albertshausen	52-0563
STEIBEL, Herz	17	Langenschwanz	54-0830
STEIBEN, Joh Heinr	36	Hohnhorst	47-0672
Dorothea 39, Justina 11, Joh. Heinr. 3			
Joh. Conrad 3, Joh. Philip 13			
Carl Wilhelm 19			
STEIDLE, Carl Hein	20	Koechberg	49-0352
STEIFREGE, Friedr.	27	Hannover	51-1639
STEIGAUF, Geo Andr	27	Ohrenbach	51-1438
Margaret 28			
STEIGER, Joh. Bapt	38	Indersdorf	54-0872
Maria 25			
STEIGERWALD, Gertr	21	Rothenburg	54-0903

NAME	AGE	RESIDENCE	YR-LIST
STEIL, Paulus	18	Ostheim	49-0574
STEIN, Carl	23	Nossen	52-1148
STEIN, Catharine	32	Unterweiler	54-0872
Barbara 22			
STEIN, Christian	21	Solms	53-0942
STEIN, Christoph	57	Fernbreitenba	48-0284
Anna 54, Catharina 24, Adam 18, Conrad 14			
Christoph 11, Christ. Magd 8			
Anna Elise 2			
STEIN, Conrad			51-1455
STEIN, Ernst	29	Kamstaedt	53-0652
STEIN, Friedrich	23	Dorschen	53-1164
STEIN, Georg	23	Minden	53-0991
STEIN, George	19	Dankmarshause	48-0284
STEIN, Isaac	18	Dreissa	54-1717
STEIN, J.A.	27	Berlin	48-1243
STEIN, Joh. Gottl.	23	Nuernberg	52-0895
Joh. Georg 22			
STEIN, Marg.	22	Ermenreuth	51-1160
Nicol. 9m			
STEIN, Maria	23	Forth	50-0439
STEIN, Mathilde	23	Bavaria	53-0628
STEIN, Minna	24	Hallbach	53-1070
STEIN, Peter	30	Lingelbach	50-0840
Elisabeth 27			
STEIN, Philipp	22	Kleinensee	48-0284
Carl 18			
STEINACHEN, Rete	24	Ebersbach	47-0672
STEINACKER, Conrad	18	Fulda	53-1016
STEINAGEL, Marg.	23	Storndorf	52-0652
STEINAMM, Abraham	14	Heu-ngfeld	53-1000
STEINBACH, Anna	19	Wehdel	50-0366
STEINBACH, J. (m)	15	Schwarzenfeld	48-0445
STEINBAUER, Johann	42	Kl.Steinb./Bd	52-1332
Caroline 37, Caroline 9, Theodor 4			
Sophie 3			
STEINBERG, Heinr.	23	Doepel	50-0472
STEINBERG, Johann	19	Brilett/Hann.	53-0475
STEINBERGER, Carol	24	Calenberg	52-0895
STEINBERGER, Jos.	31	Donauwoerth	54-0903
STEINBERGER, Nicol	40	Feierenhausen	54-1168
STEINBERGER, Peter	34	Millewetsch	53-0905
Marie 25, Johann by			
STEINBERGER, Rich.	30	Oberod	53-0914
STEINBOCK, Jacob	20	Friedrichshau	47-0828
STEINBORN, Heinr.	26	Hannover	50-0021
STEINBORN, Ludwig	18	Oldendorf	52-1512
STEINBRECKER, Fr'd	22	Gross Cotter	48-0053
STEINBRIGGE, Fried	34	Essen	53-1086
Leonore 37, Louise 11, Heinrich 2			
STEINBRUECK, Fried	31	Salsdorf	52-1304
STEINBRUEGGE, E.	25	Boebber	53-1086
STEINBRUEGGE, Fr'd	22	Boebber	53-1086
STEINE, John	75	Kohlberg	48-0951
STEINECKE, Heinr.	35	Burgwedel	54-1078
Dorette 47			
STEINECKE, Heinr.	18	Wittlage	49-0413
STEINEKE, Wilhelm	20	Hannover	49-0383
STEINEL, Lorenz	28	Rothenbach	50-1236
STEINER, A. Marg.	20	Schorchnitz	51-1160
Wilhelm 6m			
STEINER, Dorothea	17	Roetha	53-0267
STEINER, Lorenz	38	Oberwackersta	52-1200
Anna Maria 38, Therese 7			
STEINER, Matthias	34	Eferding	53-0991
Mary 27, John 57, Catharina 59			
Michael 26			
STEINERT, Gottfr.	48	Sanimertz	54-1443
Christine 36, Michel 27, Heinrich 23			
Sophie 17, Ernestine 4, Emma 2			
Gottfried 2m			
STEINERT, Lorenz	47	Altenstein	54-1647
STEINFELDER, John	29	Bamberg	52-1304
Kunigunde 35, Margarethe 21			
STEINFELS, Anton	34	Nassau	54-1724
STEINFORT, C.	34	Langenberg	48-0565
L. 30, G. 3, J. 1			
STEINHAEUSER, Aug.	27	Leibingen	50-0840

NAME	AGE	RESIDENCE	YR-LIST
STEINHARD, Herm.	21	Rethem	51-0405
STEINHARDT, C. (m)	17	Buhlerthan	54-1341
STEINHARDT, Franz	50	Prag	54-1591
Mary 40, Franz 11, Vincenz 3, Anton 11m			
Anna 9			
STEINHAUER, August	21	Heidelberg	51-1035
STEINHAUER, Marie	12	Gabelow/Bav.	52-1332
STEINHAUER, Simon	30	Reiselberg	53-0914
STEINHEISEN, Heinr	27	Gehaus	53-0942
Gottfr. 36, baby			
STEINHOFF, Friedr.	27	Osterode	52-0895
Johanne 34, Minna 8, Louise 9m			
STEINHUEBLER, Balt	29	Wuertt.	54-1724
Elis. 39, Margaret 6m, Martin 10			
STEINKAESTER, Aug.	28	Barmen	48-0565
STEINKAMP, Ludw.	18	Wittlage	54-0987
STEINKOPF, Wilhelm	39	Neubrandenbur	52-0095
STEINLE, Johann		Steinkirchen	54-1575
Friederike 27, Louise 22, Barbara 20			
Wilhelm 6m			
STEINLEIN, Anna	37	Woehrd	54-1575
STEINLEIN, Anna	37	Woehro	54-1575
STEINLEIN, Chr.	41	Coburg	52-1661
STEINLEIN, Wilhelm	25	Pappenheym	53-0320
STEINMANN, H.C.	42	Hornburg	53-1164
STEINMEIER, Heinr.	21	Pyrmont	50-1071
STEINMETZ, Anna	27	Schoenau	54-1554
STEINMETZ, August	38	Eisenach	50-1067
STEINMETZ, Georg	25	Frensdorf	52-0370
STEINMETZ, Maria	19	Grossenglis	52-0775
STEINMETZ, Wilh.	28	Gerstungen	52-1304
STEINMEYER, David	27	Odershain	54-1297
Christiane 24			
STEINMEYER, Henry	30	Schledehausen	51-1588
STEINMIRTZ, P. (m)	16	Otterndorff	50-0746
STEINNIGERWEG, Fr.	47	Osnabrueck	52-1432
Christine 48, Heinrich 26, Wilhelmine 22			
Wilhelm 15			
STEINPFER, Jos.	45	Hamm	53-0914
STEINREICH, Josefa	48	Waldeck	50-0021
Friederike 12, Marie 10, Louis 8			
STEINREICH, Samuel	22	Muenchen/Bav.	54-1092
STEINREXEN, Aug'ta	23	Guenzerode	54-1554
STEINSICK, Conrad	54	Tullembeck	52-1661
STEINTEN, Louis	22	Stine	48-0269
STEIOFF, Henriette	64	Dillenburg	52-1129
Heinr. 21, Marie 24, Theodor 26			
STEIOFF, Theodor	26	Siegen	52-1129
STEIR, Henry	24	New York	53-0991
STEITEN, August	22	Wechselburg	53-0585
STELJES, Catharina	24	Sandstedt	52-0699
STELJES, Diedrich	21	Huettenbusch	50-0366
STELL, Anton	27	Almen	52-1580
STELLER, Adelheid	25	Salzwedel	54-1591
STELLFLUG, Hermann	21	Natzungen	53-0435
STELLMANN, John	41	Celle	54-1470
STELLPFLUG, Anton	20	Kamstein	48-0887
STELZAR, M.	61	Waldorf	54-1419
STELZFROW, Fritz	24	Woldegk	53-0905
STELZING, Christ.	37	Hessen	52-0895
STELZNER, Wilhelm	25	Braunschweig	54-1371
STEMM, Heinrich	44	Weidenhausen	53-0320
STEMMERMANN, Gerd	19	Gnarenburg/Ha	52-0807
STEMMERMANN, H.	16	Koehlen	51-0460
STEMMERMANN, J.(m)	20	Schiffdorf	48-0447
STEMMERMANN, Meta	26	Bockeln	51-1101
STEMPEL, C. (f)	23	Brunk	49-0742
STEMPFER, Nicolaus	32	Michingen	54-0903
STENDER, Friedrich	40	Wanfried	47-0872
Martha 42, Wilhelm 14, Malchen 9			
Caroline 7, Johanne 61			
STENDER, Heinrich	17	Rechtenfleth	50-0366
STENGEL, Ciprian	32	Kollingen	54-1371
STENGEL, D. (m)	32	Mannheim	48-0453
STENGEL, Joh.	33	Lauffen	52-0370
STENGEL, Leonhard	19	Nuernberg	52-0693
STENGEL, Maria	21	Sallach	54-1554
STENGER, Anna Wilh	20	Schoellkrippe	54-0903

NAME	AGE	RESIDENCE	YR-LIST
STENGER, Carl W.	39	Weimar	50-0439
STENILE, Johann		Steinkirchen	54-1575
Friedrike 27, Louise 22, Barbara 20			
Wilhelm 6m			
STENTEL, John	25	Foeisch	48-1209
STENZ, Caroline	29	Esslingen	53-0991
STEPF, Adolph	26	Leipzig	54-1168
STEPHAN, Conrad	19	Kerigshausen	54-0930
STEPHAN, Elis.	28	Kothen	52-0515
STEPHAN, Heinr Chr	37	Niederdorla	51-1455
Dorotha 30, Martha 11, Michael 9			
Johanna 3			
STEPHAN, Lewis	33	Wiesbaden/Nas	48-0447
K. (f) 27, Lewis 5, Ed. 1			
STEPHANI, Carl	21	Melle	54-0872
STEPHANI, Therese	57	Wien	53-0888
STEPHENS, Cornel.	20	New York	51-1035
STEPPAN, C.G.	39	Milren	49-1517
Mrs. 41, William 18, Pauline 16, Sarah 10			
Emilie 8			
STEPPARELL, Herman	18	Dinklage	53-0492
STERGENT, H.	28	Landenhausen	51-0517
G. (f) 30, F. 6, C. 8			
STERLMEIER, H. (m)	28	Emsdetten	49-0416
J. (f) 26			
STERN, Abraham	42	Mausbach	54-1554
Tretchen 9			
STERN, Eleonore	18	Windheim	53-1016
STERN, Emanuel	45	Buren	51-1455
Fridika 9, Hirtz 4			
STERN, Ertl. (f)	23	Robelshausen	52-0279
Wilhelm 16, Daniel 13			
STERN, Friedrich	21	Kurhessen	53-0590
Meyer 19			
STERN, Jacob	19	Werda	52-1625
Julchen 22			
STERN, Jasaias Ant	19	Steinbach	49-0345
STERN, Johanna	18	Warstein	48-0951
STERN, Johanne	25	Vocka	54-0872
STERN, Joseph	19	Meinstockheim	53-0991
STERN, Sebastian	20	Niederohmen	52-1452
STERN, Susmann	23	Raboldhausen	50-0323
STERN, Theodor	25	Hano. Muenden	53-0267
STERNAEKER, Georg	23	Geibach	51-0405
Christ. 28			
STERNBACH, Dorothe	20	Boerstel	54-1443
STERNBACH, Loew	24	Kairlindach	52-0693
STERNERS, Anna	28	Bordel	51-1588
STERZEL, H.	42	Breslau	54-1078
STETZEL, Engelbert	34	Deuz/Preussen	53-0475
Jacob 32, Thomas 30, Philipp 26			
STETZEL, Gertrud	45	Deuz/Preussen	53-0475
STETZEL, Thomas	58	Deuz/Pr.	53-0475
Johanne 36, Wilhelm 28			
STEUBE, Andreas	23	Issney	49-0352
STEUBE, John	41	Helda	54-1470
Ann 42, Catharina 15, Mary 23			
Margarethe 13, Henry 7			
STEUERNAGEL, Casp.	24	Oberseiberten	53-1023
STEUNER, Fr.	23	Melle	54-1470
STEWART, W.J.	43	New York	48-1015
Mrs. 39			
STEYERBERG, Carle	29	Meinsen	51-1588
STHULMANN, Adelh.	23	Harpstedt	48-0284
Catharine 22			
STICH, Georg	28	Hochstrass	54-1078
STICH, Josephina	19	Mittelruessel	49-0737
STICHELER, Friedr.	22	Rethslingen	54-1554
STICHT, Chr.	26	Celle	54-1724
STICKEL, Friedrich	23	Wuertenberg	53-0557
STIDDIG, Friedrich	26	Braunschweig	47-0868
STIEBERITZ, Hein C	33	Alten Jena	51-0352
STIEBRITZ, Wilhelm	21	Krautheim	50-0472
STIELER, Leopoldin	24	Neustadt	54-0053
STIER, Carl	31	Koenigslutter	51-1532
STIER, Friedrich	38	Blankenheim	53-0905
STIER, Hermann	30	Gera	53-0905
Emilie 26, Ern. Minna by			

NAME	AGE	RESIDENCE	YR-LIST
STIERENEN, Eduard	48	Erfurt	50-1067
Louis 18			
STIFFERLER, Wilh.	20	Wittingshause	54-1716
STIFTBERGER, Anna	25	Martinsbach	49-0574
STIGNOTTE, Ludwig	18	Sondershausen	54-0930
STILLE, Barbara	22	Neumuehle	54-1554
STILLE, Caspar	25	Schweinfurt	50-1317
Barbara 25, Friedrich 23			
STILLE, Heinrich	26	Brellingen	50-1067
STILLEKE, Wilh.	27	Erwede	53-0585
STILLING, Heinrich	25	Bagel/Hann.	53-0475
STILZER, Jacob	25	Medenbrechen	49-0912
STIMMER, Michael	20	Eichendorf	52-1452
STIMPFER, Jos.	45	Hamm	53-0914
STINKEL, Philipp	21	Obersinn	52-0563
STIPPE, Wilhelm	30	Nieheim	54-1168
STIPPICH, Justus	20	Thalhausen/He	50-0323
STIRNWEISS, Eberh.	19	Muehlhausen	49-0352
STOBAEUS, Albrecht	21	Regensburg	53-1062
STOBER, Johann	27	Ellingrode	51-1639
STOCAMP, Peter	25	Versmold	52-1512
STOCK, A. (m)	24	Sulza	49-1358
STOCK, Bernh.	19	Buckhold	52-1321
STOCK, Eva	16	Zindelhammer	54-0987
STOCK, Georg	40	Roth	51-0500
Margarethe 41, Regina 10, Franz 8			
Amanda 6, Gregor 5, Rosina 2			
STOCK, H. (m)	34	Lanoberg	48-0453
STOCK, Louise	42	Brake	48-1355
STOCK, Ludwig	23	Storndorf	49-0352
STOCKDER, Carl Ed.	19	Remscheid	54-1371
STOCKER, Conrad	50	Neubreslau	54-1716
Catharine 48, Marie 20			
STOCKER, Paul	37	Ebersberg	54-0850
Walpurga 38, Petronilla 5			
STOCKER, Victoria	21	Maihingen	52-1200
Ottilie 27			
STOCKHAUS, Ernst	60	Boebber	53-1086
Anna Elisab. 53, Marie 22, Ernst 21			
STOCKHOFF, J. Hein	58	Engter	47-0762
Anna Marie 60, Anna Marie 25			
Engel Marie 22, Heinrich Wm. 31, Louise 4			
Lisette 6m, Joh. Heinr. 22			
STOCKMEYER, Eduard	19	Bremen	53-0888
STOCKTON, Marie	34	Hannover	52-1410
STOECKEL, Friedr.	38	Hippolstein	52-1129
Marg. 42			
STOECKEL, Georg	55	Almos	52-1129
Anna 50, Barbara 27, Anna 20, Wolfgang 17			
Johann 12, Anna Marie 9			
STOECKEL, Joh. Chr	28	Pirk	54-1297
Joh. Martin 32, Joh. Friedr. 25			
Joh. Marie 19			
STOECKER, Heinr. W	23	Wolfhagen	51-0352
STOECKINGER, Melch	23	Geiselwind/Bv	52-0807
Balthasar 21			
STOEHHAN, H.	26	Dorstadt	54-1341
Sophia 23			
STOEHR, Barbara	54	Geiz/Baiern	53-0475
Eva 22			
STOEHR, Joseph	56	Weissenstedt	53-0475
STOEHR, Maria	64	Eilenburg	50-1071
STOEKLER, Isaak	37	Pilsen	54-1078
STOELTING, Friedr.	25	Blomberg	54-1168
Christian 30			
STOELTING, Wilhelm	16	Blomberg	54-1168
STOEPEL, Gustav	26	Querfurt	53-1164
STOERKER, Wilhelm	19	Gehrde	50-1236
STOERMER, Stephan	27	Wederath	51-1062
STOERMER, William	20	Andreasberg	54-1575
STOESSEL, Eduard	22	Ronneburg	54-0930
Richard 19			
STOESSER, Georg T.	28	Hall/Wrt.	54-1092
STOETTER, Maria	22	Riegertin	54-1371
STOEVER, Heinrich	20	Barwede	54-1452
STOEVER, Wilhelm	24	Lindewerra	51-1438
STOHARNNES, Herm.	33	Meiningen	48-1131
STOHER, Robert	37	Mittelruessel	49-0737

NAME	AGE	RESIDENCE	YR-LIST
STOHLMANN, August	22	Bremen	52-1410
STOHLMANN, Bernh.	27	Brake	48-1355
STOHLMANN, Gottfr.	22	Lilienthal	48-1131
Marie 25			
STOHN, Georg Nic.	22	Sonnenfeld	52-1304
STOHR, Joseph Rupp	36	Leingruben/A.	53-0628
STOHR, v. Helene	26	Hamburg	52-0515
STOKER, Lorenz	28	Schneckenlohe	51-1588
STOLE, Johann	26	Echsell	53-0838
Elisabeth 28, Elisabeth 43			
STOLE, Johann	26	Echzell	53-0838
Elisabeth 28, Elisabeth 43			
STOLL, Carl	23	Hannover	49-0574
STOLL, Conrad	30	Leigestern	53-1000
Elisabeth 26, Marie 2			
STOLL, Jacob	26	Fruchtelfinge	51-1640
Barbara 22			
STOLL, Joh.	47	Baden	51-1686
Catharine 47, Ferdinand 21, Leopold 17			
Conrad 11, Francisca 19, Theodor 13			
Pauline 7			
STOLL, John Adam	24	Wunsiedel	53-0888
STOLL, Matth.	31	Cinsmansdorf	53-0582
STOLL, Peter	26	Helborg	54-1282
STOLLBERG, John E.	30	Frankenhausen	53-0492
Christine 30, Aug. 3, Gustav 2			
STOLLMEYER, J Hein	15	Wittlage	49-0413
STOLMAKER, John	24	Berglebshause	50-0944
STOLTE, Friedrich	22	Hoya	52-1362
STOLZ, Anton	23	Wuertenberg	52-1620
STOLZ, Antonia	37	Blankenburg	54-1371
Auguste 9, Amalie 31, Franziska 29			
STOLZ, Bernhard	28	Disselhausen	49-0912
Christiane 26			
STOLZ, Friedrich	29	Bremen	53-0991
STOLZ, Jacob	21	Deckhausen	53-0435
STOLZ, Otto	23	Lingen	49-0345
STOLZALTER, W.	22	Babber	53-1086
STOLZE, Amalia	15	Sarnsig/Sax.	50-0323
STOLZE, Christ.	30	Fuhrbach	51-1084
Joh. 24			
STOLZHEISE, Adolph	24	Bindheim	54-1717
STOOL, Elisabeth	29	Reichelsheim	53-0838
STOPF, Heinrich	22	Lauterbach	51-1101
STORATH, Marie	22	Stockheim	54-1297
STORCH, E.A. (m)	17	Diepholz	50-0021
STORCH, Heinrich	24	Bernstadt	52-0095
STORCH, Herman	33	Armsen	53-0838
Catharine 3			
STORCH, J. (m)	25	Hohenaverberg	49-0383
H. (m) 19			
STORCH, Kunigunde	24	Kockenhof	51-0460
STORCHMEIER, Jos.	28	Hoexter/Pruss	53-0628
STORCKA, Franz	27	Dieben	53-1000
Louise 25			
STORCKAN, Joseph	30	Klattau	54-1575
STORG, Friedrich	28	Bruntrup	52-0775
Wilhelmine 29			
STORK, Margarethe	25	Oberbernharz	51-0500
STORKING, Johanna		Lorenzreuth	50-0323
STORM, Eduard	15	Ofenstedt	53-0888
Mathilda 19			
STORM, Gustav	28	Stuetzerbach	53-0888
STORM, Michael	21	Jellburg	54-1168
STOSSINGER, Lorenz	28	Untergroening	54-1282
STOTT, Wilhelm	27	N.Y.	52-1452
STOTTE, Friedr.	48	Erfurt	53-0914
STOTZ, Carl	45	Augsburg	54-0053
STRACHINUS, J Geo.	25	Lauterberg	48-1131
STRACK, Elisabeth	50	Wohra	52-0699
STRACK, Georg	21	Kleineglas	50-0292
STRACKE, Chr.	42	Waldeck	50-0021
STRACKE, Wilh. F.	35	Niederschelde	49-0781
Agnes 30, Catharine 8, Friedrich 4			
Catharine 40, Wilhelm 14			
STRACKY, Conrad	29	Halsdorf	52-0515
Cath. 29, Supinit 3			
STRACKY, Separt	56	Halsdorf	52-0515

NAME	AGE	RESIDENCE	YR-LIST
Friedrich 19			
STRADLER, Joh.	27	Aisch	54-1168
STRAEGLER, George	23	Bremen	53-0914
STRAETZ, Conrad	28	Schoenbach	48-0887
STRAHL, Kilian	30	Bischwind	47-0918
STRANDMANN, August	27	Stolzenau	50-1317
STRANG, Heinrich	32	Altenburg	49-1358
STRANKMANN, Sophie	31	Heemsen	54-1443
STRAS, Sophie	18	Schoenlind	54-1566
STRASS, Simon	18	Schonlindt/Bo	53-0628
STRASSBERGER, Fr.	37	Passau	54-1716
Johanna 48			
STRASSBURG, Wilh.	28	Schlossheltru	49-0781
Johanne 28, August 22			
STRASSBURGER, Alex	17	Sonneberg	53-0557
STRASSBURGER, Rika	15	Kleinheubach	54-1297
STRASSEN, Gust Ad.	41	Eisfeld/Sachs	52-0117
STRASSER, Anton	45	Hausen	53-0492
STRASSER, Franz'ka	30	Hausen	51-1160
STRASSER, John M.	30	Schnelldorf	52-0515
Eva Eliz. 44			
STRASSMANN, Egid.	36	Elbersroth	54-1566
Catharine 56			
STRASSMEIER, Casm.	35	Sonnenberg	48-0887
STRATE, Louis	24	Lippe	50-1071
STRATMANN, Carolin	33	Minden	53-1023
STRATMEYER, J Hein	27	Holzhausen	53-1062
STRAUB, Alex.	30	Brueggenau	52-0279
STRAUB, Em.	28	Blasbach	49-0574
STRAUB, Emil	26	Frankfurt	53-1164
STRAUB, Susanna	24	Pommern	49-0574
STRAUBE, Carl	27	Ober Arnsbach	53-1062
Eleanore 22			
STRAUBE, J.H. (m)	24	Erfurt	49-0416
STRAUBE, J.S. (m)	31	Obergruna	50-0379
Wilhelm 19			
STRAUBEL, Anna	33	Nuernberg	52-1512
STRAUCH, Joseph	39	Niedentreten	48-0951
Elisabeth 32, Henry 6, John 4, Louisa 9m			
STRAUS, Adelheid	22	Wennings	49-0912
STRAUS, Maria	24	Alt Luneburg	47-0828
STRAUSS, Andreas	22	Bayern	53-0590
STRAUSS, Calmann	31	Unterriedberg	54-0987
Hanne 31, Ephraim by			
STRAUSS, Carl Fr.	22	Stuttgart	53-0320
STRAUSS, Caroline	27	Kairlindach	51-1245
STRAUSS, Christian	24	Nordlingen	53-0888
STRAUSS, David	44	Germany	48-1243
STRAUSS, Geert	17	Amoeneburg/He	51-1796
STRAUSS, Georg Chr	18	Jacobsmuehl	53-0914
STRAUSS, H. (f)	25	Storndorf	47-0868
STRAUSS, Heinr Aug	24	Hornhausen	54-0987
STRAUSS, Heinrich	34	Obernkirchen	54-1282
Magdalene 23, Carl by			
STRAUSS, Heinrich	20	Goesee	50-0439
STRAUSS, Isaac	31	Pauter	54-1566
Rosa 26, Bertha 6, Marie 2, Therese 3m			
STRAUSS, Johann	32	Bergenzell	53-0825
STRAUSS, John Chr.	46	Fuerth	52-1304
STRAUSS, Leopold	15	Herzbach	54-0987
STRAUSS, Raf.	25	Brueckenau	54-1282
STRAUSS, Sam.	40	Wenings	51-1588
STRAUSS, Samuel	18		49-0912
STRAUSS, Sara	53	Pretzfeld	54-1554
Sophie 21, Caroline 17, Isaak 14			
Jacob 11, Benjamin 9			
STRAUSS, Sophie	26	Adelsdorf	48-1184
STRAUTMANN, Casper	39	Laer	53-0991
STREAKLE, Paul Fr.	40	Lauterberg	48-1131
STREBEL, Leonhard	38	Kuhlsheim	50-0840
Dorothea 30			
STREBLY, Johann	24	Wien	53-0652
STRECK, Friedrich	23	Frankenstein	47-0828
Florentine 28, Anna 5			
STRECKER, Naue (m)	26	Langenfeld	54-0872
STRECKEWAND, Heinr	22	Hohenhameln	48-1179
STRECKFUSS, Chr'ne	28	Neukibohm	54-1647
STREICHER, Andreas	22	Almen	52-1580

NAME	AGE	RESIDENCE	YR-LIST
STREICHER, Joseph	34	Hessia	50-1317
STREITEMEIER, Pet.	27	Hellern/Pr.	52-1432
Elise 30, Wilhelmine 9m			
STRELITZ, Marcus	32	Breslau	54-1092
Rosa 28			
STREMMEL, Matthias	33	Dillenburg	54-0830
STRENG, Marie	22	Taberschassen	51-1438
STRENG, Martin	17	Bavaria	50-0311
STRENG, Sabine	26	Feuchtwangen	52-0515
STRENGER, Albert	14	Stuttgart	53-1016
STRENGH, Mayer	20	Odensos	49-0574
STRETER, Gerhard	28	Emsdetten	54-0903
Antonia 10			
STRETZ, Andreas	29	Bamberg	51-1640
STRETZ, Georg	36	Weissbrunn	48-0101
Margarethe 48			
STRETZ, Margarethe	34	Tatschenbrunn	48-0101
Eve 8			
STREUFFAT, Carl	31	Treusin	54-1371
STREVE, And.	30	Michelbach	51-1686
Barbara 28, Johann 6			
STREVE, Wilhelm	23	Munsterbrock	53-0825
STREVELING, Marie	32	Michelbach	51-1686
Georg 7, Barbara 41			
STRICHEL, Johann	25	Burghetz	54-1676
Gottlieb 21			
STRICK, Ernst	20	Ostheim	49-0574
Joh. 22, Ras. 18			
STRICK, F. W.	24	Bremen	52-1148
STRICK, R. (m)	14	Zrainsche	48-1015
STRICKY, Ludwig	48	Radim	52-0699
Anna 45, Johann 14			
STRIDELMEIER, Mar.	18	Lienen/Pr.	52-1432
STRIEBE, Mag.	22	Geckenheim	51-1686
STRIEGEL, Georg	50	Baiern	51-1245
Anna 48, Margaretha 14, Anna 10, Georg 18			
Lorenz 16			
STRIEGEL, Michael	19	Dormitz	49-1358
STRIEP, Joseph		Schermede	54-1575
STRIEPEN, Charles	36	Augsburg	53-0582
STRIETHMEYE, Elisa		Schermede	54-1575
Auguste			
STRINGSMANN, Herm.	25	Halle	52-1512
STRIPPE, Gehr. H.	18	Osnabrueck/Ha	52-1332
STRIPPEL, Wil'mine	20	Wernborn	52-1321
STRITESKY, Joseph	37	Boehmen	52-0699
Anna 33, Anna 6, Sophie 9m			
STRITT, Charles	33	Wiesbaden/Nas	48-0447
STRITT, Crescencia	25	Grafenhausen	52-1105
STRITT, Lewis	35	Wiesbaden/Nas	48-0447
STROBEL, Barbara	23	Liritzhofen	52-1129
STROBEL, Christoph	28	Gottfriedsgru	47-0672
Elisabeth 25			
STROBEL, Franziska	22	Belzheim	54-0850
STROBEL, Hanna	6	Hof	50-1071
Elisabeth 3m			
STROBEL, Johann	23	Schwarzenbach	48-1184
Charlotte 22, Georg 1			
STROBEL, Josephine	20	Wuerzburg	53-0267
STROBELIER, Margr.	20	Emden	53-0324
STROBER, Heinrich	34	Pottigo	54-0987
David 60, Johanne 26, Eva 22			
STRODTHOF, Henry	20	Harpstedt	48-0284
STROEBEL, Auguste	29	Kirchberg	49-0352
STROEBLER, Cath.	24		49-0416
STROEHLA, Elisab.	19	Raunergrund	54-1371
STROEHLA, Johann	39	Meierhof	54-1371
STROELEIN, Friedr.		Markgroeninge	54-1575
STROEMER, Roelf	39	Wittmanns	53-1062
Roeshen 39, Theodor 12, Gesina 10			
Henrika 7			
STROEMSDOERFER, Ev	22	Ermenreuth	53-1164
STROEVER, Elis.	23	Spanflech	51-1084
STROH, Georg Peter	17	Murkefel	51-0352
STROHCOHL, D. (m)	24	Altenbruck	48-0453
STROHLEIN, John	28	Humendorf	51-1588
STROHM, Carl	26	Gera/Sachsen	51-1725
Rosalie 28			

NAME	AGE	RESIDENCE	YR-LIST
STROHM, Eliz.	27	Wiesenbach	52-0515
STROHM, Emilie	31	Gera	54-1297
Anna 11, Ida 8, Richard 3			
STROHM, Friedrich	19	Leonberg/Wuer	52-0351
STROHM, John	29	Wiesenbach	52-0515
STROHMEIER, Friedr	24	Seich	52-0370
STROHMEYER, Andr.	28	Allfeldt	50-0292
STROHMEYER, Fr.	24	Bremen	53-1000
STROHMEYER, Friedr	21	Herstelle/Pr.	51-0048
STROHMEYER, Johann	25	Sachs.-Weimar	53-0324
STROHMEYER, Louise	21	Hucksiel	53-0557
STROHN, Louise	39	Wilmars	51-1455
STROHRUEZEN, Conr.	26	Windheim	47-0762
STROHSAHL, Anton	20	Suederwisch	49-0345
STROHSAHL, Math.	24	Cuxhafen	51-1160
STROM, Regina	24	Tiefenorth	53-0320
STROMEYER, Cath.	38	Bonland	47-0872
STROPPEL, Conrad	25	Obervorschutz	52-0370
STROTBAUM, Theodor	27	Hatewinkel	50-0292
STROTH, H.	25	Waldsachsen	51-0405
STROTHENKE, Johann	48	Dornberg	54-1554
Maria 17, Wilhelm 3, Friedrich 19			
Wilhelm 38, Johann 6, Anna 40			
Friedrich 13			
STROTHMANN, Peter	28	Steinhagen	54-1371
STRROEVER, Elis.	23	Spanflech	51-1084
STRUBBE, Heinrich	50	Langerichen/P	52-1432
Wilh. 11			
STRUBBEN, Fr'drike	28	Lienen/Pr.	52-1432
STRUBE, Carl	58	Zwickau	54-0882
Wilhelm 19, Friederike 54			
STRUBE, Hermann	15	Zwickau	54-0882
STRUBE, Marie	25	Leimbach	48-0284
STRUBE, Mathias	48	Berka	50-0379
STRUBEL, Marie	21	Egloff-Steinh	49-0352
STRUCK, Conrad	26	Barfelde	53-0590
STRUCKMEYER, Carl	30	Schnathorst	54-0872
STRUCKMEYER, Chr.	19	Reinsdorf	53-1086
STRUEBEN, Magdalen		Hof	54-1283
STRUEBER, Aug.	29	Holzhausen	51-1160
STRUEVER, Juliane	25	Herzberg	53-1023
STRUEVER, O.	43	Goettingen	53-0492
W. 41, H. 15, H. 13, A. 10, O. 4			
STRUEVER, Wilh. T.	32	Bremerhaven	54-1092
Lina 26, T. Heinrich 2			
STRUMPFLER, Franz	23	Struemphelbru	51-0384
Carl 25, Valentin 58, Regina 28			
STRUNCK, (f)	30	Beckum	54-1297
STRUNCKEN, Peter	19	Wederwarden	54-1716
STRUNK, Peter	27	Terschen	52-0807
STRUPF, Andreas	37	Maria Culm	54-0987
Margareth 28, Anton 9, Franciska 8			
Margarethe 4, Elisabeth 2			
STRUPMAN, Friedr.	25	Rechern	47-0672
STRUSS, Friedrich	19	Hoya	52-1362
Friedr. 29			
STRUSS, Henry	18	Schweringen	48-1209
Friedrich 17			
STRUTH, Heinrich	19	Lauterbach	51-0352
STRUTH, Maria	40	Lauterbach	50-1067
STRUTZ, Ernst	25	Hasserode	54-1283
STRUTZ, K.	41	Mengshausen	47-0868
H. 13			
STRUVER, Friedrich	24	Fischbach/Nas	53-0628
STUBER, Johann	22	Eisenach	54-0882
STUBING, Catharina	16	Biederkopf	51-1725
STUBNAZE, Wolfgang	19	Fuerth	47-0828
STUCK, C.E. (f)	16	W. Ollendorf	52-0960
STUCK, Christian	22	Salzungen	49-0413
STUCK, H. (m)	16	Lengsfeld	54-1341
STUCK, Heinrich	33	Vitzerode	52-1452
Anna Cath. 29, Georg Heinr. 6m			
STUCK, Heinrich	19	Muehlhose	51-0756
STUCKE, Catharine	21	Herpersdorf	48-1179
STUCKE, Fritz	17	Lingen	51-1101
STUCKE, Heinrich	16	Funkerhofe	50-0366
STUCKEL, Stephen	18	Prussia	54-1724
STUCKELHOLD, Fried	56	Eikum	54-1554

NAME	AGE	RESIDENCE	YR-LIST
STUCKENBERG, Aug.	42	Merburg	53-1000
Louise 43, Dorothea 22, Justine 20			
Aug. 16, Heinr. 13			
STUCKWITSCH, M. E.	18	Ost. Cappeln	52-0960
STUDIER, Carl Fr.	34	Pasewalk	53-1023
STUEBER, Anna M.	59	Neumark	53-0905
STUEBER, Carl Fr.	17	Untersielming	54-1168
STUEBER, Henn.	34	Altenburg	52-1321
STUECK, Georg	27	Reichenachs	52-0370
STUECKEN, W'mne AS	20	Bremen	47-0987
STUEHLER, Andreas	35	Schweinshafen	52-1410
STUEHLER, Michael	25	Rueckshofen	52-1200
STUEMER, Joh.	27	Kohnendorf	51-1640
STUENECK, M.	30	Colleda	54-1283
STUERCKE, Joh.	21	Bavaria	50-1317
STUERKE, Emilie	12	Bremerhaven	54-1092
STUERKEN, Albert H	28	Spieka/Hann.	51-1796
STUERMANN, Joh.	19	Grimmen	49-0383
STUERMER, Carl	24	Niederwildon	49-0365
STUERSBERG, Ludwig	19	Lennep	54-1371
STUERZ, Amalia	20	Noerten	53-1164
STUETZER, Joh Mich	21	Hohenmuhl	53-0991
STUEVE, Bernard Th	25	Osnabrueck	54-1470
STUEVENBERG, Fr.	28	Roxal	49-1358
STUEVER, A.	19	Bueckeburg	53-0492
STUHLDREHER, Cathr	55	Voellinghause	50-1236
Wilhelm 32, Christian 28, Franz Ernst 25			
Anton 23, Theodor 19, Elisabeth 17			
Sophie 12, August 9			
STUHLMANN, Adelh.	23	Harpstedt	48-0284
Catharine 22			
STUHLMANN, Georg	55	Rachelhausen	52-1452
Carl 23, Johann 18, Heinrich 16			
Helene 27, Catharine 21, Jacob 3			
Jacob 35, Elisabeth 35, Johannes 9			
Georg 5, Carl 2, Georgine 3m			
STUHRS, Catharine	18	Meyenburg	51-0326
STUIK, Heinrich	19	Muehlhose	51-0756
STUKART, Anna	23	Ibra	52-1580
STUKE, Julie	19	Minden	54-1371
STUKE, Mathilde	17	Minden	54-1371
STULMANN, Joh Wilh	25	Merdebach	50-0292
STULPNAGEL, v. Wm.	26	Crossen	54-0882
STULTHOFER, Maria	22	Rahlbirken/Bv	53-0590
STUMPF, Andr.	34	Muehlbach	54-1575
STUMPF, Auguste	26	Darmstadt	54-1297
Louis 7, Fritz 11			
STUMPF, Carl	22	Oldenburg	48-0269
STUMPF, Heinrich	24	Bamberg	49-0345
STUMPF, Kunigunde	30	Wallenfels	54-0903
STUMPF, Maria	26	Steinberg/Bav	52-0807
STUMPFENHAUSEN, E.	24	Schweringen	48-1209
STUMPFER, Joseph	45	Hamm	53-0914
STUMPFF, Joh. Jost	22	Schrecksbach	51-1160
Anna Maria 23, Elisabeth 9m			
STUMPFIG, Barb.	29	Blaufelden	49-0574
Michael 25			
STUMPPF, Balthasar	34	Augsburg	54-1092
STUNZ, Carl	31	Gerstungen	51-0460
STURBEN, Joh. Wm.	16	Spieka/Hann.	51-1796
STURKE, Heinrich	19	Bremerhafen	50-1067
STURKEN, B.J. (m)	37	Pappenburg	48-0453
T. (f) 31, J. (m) 9, B. (f) 5			
STURM, Andreas	20	Igelheim	49-0912
STURM, Balthasar	49	Oberstreu	52-1580
Elise 28, Othilie 23, Barbara 16			
Aquilin 6			
STURM, Conrad	19	Schratsberg	51-1686
STURM, Friedrich	24	Daaden	53-1164
STURM, Gabriel	14	Furth	52-1105
STURM, Gottfried	27	Grossneuhause	54-0872
Marie 24			
STURM, Hermine	24	Schillbach	54-1283
STURM, Johann	21	Reichenberg	53-0267
STURM, Johann	32	Mecklenburg	54-0903
Betty 34, Heinrich 16			
STURM, Johanne	24	Gruenenplan	51-1438
STURM, John	37	Straubing	52-1304

NAME	AGE	RESIDENCE	YR-LIST
STURZER, Anna Mar.	24	Obernzell	54-0930
STURZNICKEL, Joh.	53	Kettwig/Pr.	51-1532
Ana M. 54, Alberta 20, Joh. Julius 18			
Aug. Ferd. 15, Ed. Ernst 12			
STUTER, Arnold	42	Lennep	49-0574
STUTER, Gerhard	28	Emsdetten	54-0903
Antonia 10			
STUTLER, Heinrich	16	Eichelsakern	49-0912
STUTZ, Joseph	50	Lengsfeld	49-0413
STUTZ, Wiegand	18	Ibra	52-1580
STUTZMANN, Jacob	33	Nentershausen	48-0269
Carl 32, Maria 33, Hanne 56, Franz 9			
Lorenz 7			
SUCHERT, Hermann	18	Iba	53-0324
SUDT, Ludwig	25	Wahlbach	53-0590
SUELING, Friedr. W	36	Dahle/Pr.	48-0053
SUELLENWALDE, Herm	26	Ost Friesland	54-0903
Reiner 23			
SUELLO, Sophia	28	Wegholz	53-1164
SUELSEBUSCH, Liset	23	Ascheberg	49-0324
SUELZER, Adolph	33	Wisconsin	52-1580
SUENDERMANN, Heinr	26	Verden	52-1580
SUERTH, Jean	19	Muehlheim/Rh.	54-1001
SUESS, Ad. (m)	18	Minden	50-1317
SUESS, Catharine	21	Lorenzrand	54-1282
SUESSDORF, August	24	Eisenach	48-1184
SUESSENGUT, Johann	21	Coburg	53-0267
SUESSMANN, A. (m)	28	Neuhaus	50-0311
SUESSMUTH, J Adolf	44	Oberwiddersha	53-0991
SUETTERLIN, Joh.	30	Dannenkirch	52-0960
SUHLING, August	32	Witzen	47-0828
Maria 25, Heinrich 6m			
SUHLING, Georg	28	Wietzen	54-1575
SUHR, Joh Diedrich	20	Holle	54-0987
Johann 17			
SULFLEISCH, Ad.	24	Coburg	54-1282
SULGER, Friedrich	58	Windheim	50-0944
Elisabeth 56, Maria 34, Wilhelmine 22			
SULMANN, Georg	30	Pommersfelden	48-0053
SULWAH, Herm.	24	Wittmund	51-1686
SULZBACHER, Isaak	19	Fuerth	53-0888
Jacob 23			
SULZER, Anton	21	Rothenburg	48-0887
Jacob 28			
SULZER, Carl	25	Meiningen	51-1245
SUMP, Metta	24	Hannover	53-0590
SUNDER, George	21	Barnstorff	49-1358
SUNDERMANN, J.H.	24	Quernheim	54-1341
SUNDHEIMER, Joseph	28	Birchenbach	52-1512
SUNDMACHER, Johann	39	Brokhusen	53-0825
Beeke Adelh. 43, Dorothea 13, Heinrich 8			
Metta 4			
SUNKEL, Barbara	22	Oberreuth	49-0781
SUNSER, Louise	16	Meinheim	54-1283
SUNTHEIMER, Joseph	23	Oberndorf	49-0742
SUPE, Wilhelm	51	Stroehen	50-1071
Conrad 17, Wilhelm 8, Maria 51, Maria 10			
SUPP, Casper	26	Untermausfeld	51-1588
SUPP, Friedr.	33	Friedberg	54-1297
SUPP, Friedrich	29	Wuertenberg	53-0557
SUPPIES, August	24	Holzhausen	49-0383
SUREN, Aug.	21	Holtfeld	54-1078
SUSCKER, J.G.	31	Gr. Zerbsdorf	54-1470
SUSENAP, August	24	Vallentrap	49-0574
SUSSMANN, Michael	25	Zeil	54-0053
SUSTE, Philipp	30	Butterich	51-1686
SUTBRO, Casp.	38	Grossenasch	51-1796
SUTENKOFF, W. (m)	19	Teigh	50-0746
SUTER, Bernhard	17	Cloppenburg	50-1067
SUTMAN, Carl Aug.	19	Zroelen	52-0515
SUTNER, Anna	28	Hamerganzler	48-0951
SUTTNER, Georg	32	Schuettelhof	54-1078
Marg. 34, Jacob 9m, Andr. 29			
SUTTNER, Johann	53	Hebersreuth	48-1355
Ursula 54			
SUTTOFF, Friedrich	24	Eimen	48-0951
SUUR, Heinrich	20	Hannover	50-0021
SWABADA, Anton	42	Andreyone/Boh	54-1676

NAME	AGE	RESIDENCE	YR-LIST
Maria 32			
SWAHN, Anton	20	Treisa	49-0345
SWARTZ, Meinhard	35	Leipzig	52-0807
Marie 30, Anna 7, Emil 3			
SWOBADA, Louise	19	Lobenstein	54-0987
SYDESCHUENER, Aug.	29	Sangerhausen	54-1649
Dorothea 49			
SYNIG, Wilhelm	57	Hehlen	48-1114
SYNKULE, Veronika	28	Bohy	54-1647
SYNKULE, Wenzel	37	Prodestad	54-1647
Maria 34, Johann 7, Anna 11, Josepha 9			
Maria 1			
SYVIRIN, Anna Mar.	18	Munster	49-0413
SZUHANY, Carl F.	34	Carlsruhe	51-0384
TAADJE, Heinrich	24	Riepen	47-0672
TAAKE, V. (f)	30	Rinteln	50-0476
TABEL, Michel	35	Mulns	50-0944
TABOR, Caroline	24	Pappenheim	54-0850
TACCHI, Dominico	23	Frankfurt/M.	54-1092
TACK, Franz	27	Beneshan	54-1676
TAEUBERT, Carl	48	Wien	48-1355
TAEUGET, Charlotte	28	Stolzenau	51-1035
TAFF, Eliz.	21	Farmbach	51-1455
TAGLAUER, Johann	36	Neustadt	53-0320
Theresia 32			
TAGLAUER, Theresia	32	Muenchen	53-0320
TAHGRACH, Heinrich	24	Sielen	54-1676
Karoline 26, Joseph 6m			
TAICK, Cath.	60	Weissenbrunn	51-1160
TAIMER, G. (m)	33	Schopfloch	50-0746
M. (f) 35, M. (f) 2			
TAJEKEN, John	21	Bremen	53-0888
TALLE, Johann	26	Niedertudorf	50-0379
TALLSTRICK, Ph'pne	34	Leipstadt	49-0781
TALMON, Wilh.	29	Frankenheim	51-1245
Elisabeth 24, Anna 2			
TAMMESDING, Bern.	25	Nordwalde	51-1455
TAMMINGER, S.	41	Emden	54-1647
Antje 44, Catharine 8, Diedrich 4			
TANKE, Johanne	24	Neuenkirchen	53-0905
TANKER, Engelbert	26	Gosfeld	50-1236
TANNBOHN, W. (m)	23	Erzien	48-0453
TANNENBAUM, Guetch	58	Hansbach	54-0930
Moses 28, Joseph 23			
TANNENBERG, Meyer	30	Hansbach	54-0930
TANNENBERG, Roesch	21	Falkenberg	54-0930
Moses 34, Tromet 27, Binchen 2			
TANNER, Johann	34	Breslau	54-0903
Anna Maria 33, Anna Maria 3			
TANZ, Carl	28	Gotha	53-0473
TAPNER, Maria	29	Weimar	52-1321
TAPP, Louise	21	Bormerborn	53-0825
TAPPE, Christian	37	Liebenburg	53-0905
TAPPE, Heinrich	55	Osterkappelln	47-0762
Dorothea 55, Carl 18, Georg 15, Louis 10			
TAPPELER, Friedr.	31	Deggerfelden	51-1035
TATJE, Heinrich	28	Riepen	50-1132
Engel Marie 31, Charlotte 15			
TAUBE, Aug.	22	Schlesien	53-0585
TAUBE, F.H. (m)	17	Engter	48-0445
TAUBE, Sophie	17	Altenburg	53-0942
TAUBER, Reinhart	49	Bergen/Hess.	52-0807
Catharina 47, Maria 26, Elisabetha 20			
Wilhelm 18, Philipp 12, Heinrich 9			
Christian 7, Jacob 5, Susanna 9m			
TAUBERT, Elisabeth	18	Martinrode	53-0942
TAUBMANN, Elisab.	55	Ladenburg	53-1000
Johs 25			
TAUCKE, Fr.	46	Eisleben	52-1661
TAUEL, Mariana	20	Mistelfeld/Bv	51-1532
TAUSSEG, J.L. (m)	51	Prague	48-1015
Carl 29, Moritz 25, Simon 26, Eva 47			
Elisabeth 16, Johanna 15, Wilhelmine 7			
Isidore 5			
TAUSSIG, Eduard	24	Bidschot	48-1184
TAUSSIG, Emanuel	24	Budin	53-0888
TAUSSIG, Ignaz	23	Rakonitz/Bohm	50-0323
TAUT, Louisa	24	Ortenberg	53-1164

NAME	AGE	RESIDENCE	YR-LIST
TAUTSCHECK, August	21	Weimar	50-0323
TEBBENHOF, Ernst	26	Fuerstenau	49-0324
TEBBENS, Annette	24	Lehe	54-1371
TEBBENS, Luepke	27	New York	50-1067
TEBUS, Wilhelm	26	Eberschuetz	54-1168
TECHER, Heinrich	25	Cassel	49-0413
TECK, Georg	26	Nassau	50-1236
TEDINGES, Anna	24	Breitenbach	54-1716
TEEMAN, Elise	20	Schwalenberg	51-1588
TEGELE, Sophie	33	Hannover	51-1438
TEGES, Erina	18	Knarenburg	53-0905
TEGTMEYER, Conrad	35	Grossenberkel	53-0914
Friedrich 53, Caroline 43, Minna 17			
TEGTMEYER, D.	32	Bueckeburg	53-0492
TEGTMEYER, Heinr.	43	Berkel	54-1443
Wilhelmine 58, Fritz 20, Christian 9			
TEIGHMANN, August	23	Bielefeld	53-0637
TEISINGER, Margret	21	Leimberg	53-0582
TEITZINGER, Anna	35	Wien	54-1297
Carl 8, Anna 2, Rosalie 12			
TEKUELVE, Johann	45	Suedlohn	54-1371
Catharina 43, Johann 19, Marie 17			
Joh. B. 15, Gerh. H. 9, J. Wilhelm 8			
Carl 5			
TELGER, Elise	27	Goesfeld	54-0600
TELLER, Caroline	20	Lichtenstadt	54-1371
TELLERT, Joseph	36	Oberreissfeld	53-0267
TELLING, F. (m)	30	Ehrenberg	49-0416
TELLMER, Adam		Schlehausen/H	50-0323
TEMBRUEGGE, Peter	27	Gosfeld	50-1236
TEMLER, Elisabeth	21	Sonnenberg/Sa	54-1092
TEMME, Heinrich	28	Boelhorst	49-0329
Ch. 24			
TEMPEL, Conrad	45	Meinberg	52-0775
Dorothe 35, August 10, Amalia 8			
Wilhelm 9m			
TENDICK, B. (m)	29	Vluyn/Pr.	48-0447
Peter 22			
TENGEL, Heinrich	25	Kappeln/Hann.	52-1332
Louise 21			
TENGEN, Gerh. Hein	29	Wesuwe	49-0324
Herm. Heinr. 22			
TENNE, Wilhelm	28	Barmen	48-0565
TENNER, Georg Hein	39	Salzungen	53-1000
Marie 38, Elise 2, Elisabeth 48			
TENNER, Heinrich	28	Hilders	52-0775
TENNINGER, Jacob	29	Zuerich	54-0053
TENTZELER, Rosalie	23	Ranneberg	48-1355
TENYES, Adolph	34	Appler	54-1716
TEPLE, John C.	25	----bach	50-0944
TEPPE, Anna Marie	58	Venne	53-1016
Elisabeth 28, Elise 18			
TEPPEL, Maria	20	Elmansdorf	53-1023
TEPPENS, Georg Chr	20	Leer	53-0324
TERHALLA, J. (m)	36	Hannover	50-1317
TERLINDE, Bernhard	29	Munster	51-1160
TERMATE, Joh Heinr	18	Suedlohn	54-1371
TERTELING, Theodor	43	Ochtrup	51-0352
Elisabeth 48, Theodor Alb. 17, Hedroth 15			
Catharine 12, Caroline 8, Bernh. Theod 26			
TERTIG, G. (m)	18	Reichenbach	49-0416
TESCH, (f)	26	Schwiettenber	53-0905
TESEKER, Sophia	15	Scheeren	54-1341
TETTENBACH, Marg.	29	Vilseck	54-1078
TETZING, Anna	22	Geilsdorf	54-1566
TEUBER, August	26	Mittelruessel	49-0737
Ernst 30			
TEUBNER, J. Fr.	45	Bremen	51-0048
TEUFEL, A. Marg.	24	Ebersbach	51-1160
TEUFEL, Adam	48	--tswind	47-0918
Anna 42			
TEUFEL, Anna	30	Glashuetten	54-1443
TEUFEL, Georg	31	Bueg	48-1179
TEURER, Jacob	18	Fruchtelfinge	51-1640
TEUSCHER, Anton	30	Tauschem	54-0850
Joh. Therese 29, Ros. Liberta 8			
Ernst Albert 6, Ros. Car. Em 4			
Ant. Gustav 3, Eduard Herm. by			

NAME	AGE	RESIDENCE	YR-LIST
TEWERS, Ludwig	31	Riesenbeck	51-0405
TEWES, Bernhard	16	Alson	54-0053
TEWES, Franz	43	Wergiesen	53-1070
TEWES, Friedrich	24	Wildam	50-0840
Christian 22			
TEWES, Wilhelmine	32	Lageloh	49-0742
A. (f) 21			
TEXLAR, Peter	26	Hadamshausen	52-1321
TEXTOR, Anton	34	Langens	54-0965
Maria 30, baby			
THACTER, Catharine	19	Obereuth	49-0781
THADEN, Joh. H.	29	Jever	54-0987
THAILE, Ludwig	30	Braunschweig	47-0868
THAKE, Theod.	26	Melsungen	54-1566
THAL, Friedrich	25	Potsdam	54-1282
THALER, Cath.	17	Kalkreuth	53-0320
THALER, Christine	26	Neundorf	52-0693
THALER, Kunig.	29	Kalchreuth	52-0515
THALES, Wilhelm	21	Muhlheim	54-1716
THALHEIMER, Jacob	29	Langenzen	49-0912
THALOWITZ, Valent.	18	Reichenberg	53-0267
THAMM, Susanne	31	Breslau	53-1086
Carl 3			
THANKE, Bernhard	18	Roennebeck/Ha	51-1532
THEILE, Wilhelm	20	Blomberg	54-1168
THEIM, Fr'k Adolph	21	Frankenberg	51-1101
THEINE, Heinr.	42	Storg	52-1321
THEIS, Friedr.	32	Cultz	54-1724
Cath. 46, John 6, Henry 3			
THEIS, Heinrich	30	Coeln	51-1101
THEISS, Chr.	48	Hannover	50-1317
Mathilde 18, Laura 17			
THEISS, Christine	17	Kerstenhausen	53-0942
THEISS, Johannes	28	Motzfeld	50-0292
THEISS, Valentin	20	Motzfeld	51-0352
THEKER, Wilhelm	17	Bohmte	52-1200
Louise 22			
THEMEL, Dorothea	28	Erfurt	51-0460
THEMEYER, Carl	20	Bunde	54-0882
Herman 29			
THEN, Johann	19	Geusfer	52-1362
THENIUS, Otto	23	Dresden/Sachs	51-1725
THEODOR, Gustav	42	Muensterland	51-0326
THEODOR, Nicolaus	22	Dresden	53-0914
THERLING, Wilhelm	19	Alsfelt	51-1455
THESENFELD, Diedr.	50	Achim	50-1071
THEUNERT, Carl	25	Chemnitz	53-1070
THIDEBEIN, Friedr.	32	Iowa	53-0267
Catharina 21			
THIEL, Andreas	29	Tiefenort	54-1647
THIEL, Catharine	18	Schenk-Langef	49-0742
THIEL, Conrad	48	Reckelsdorf	54-1282
Catharina 36, George 4			
THIEL, Heinrich	34	Hainbach	49-0352
Elisabeth 23, Heinrich 3			
THIEL, Otto Ph.	22	Cassel	47-0828
THIEL, Wilhelm	20	Alten Peatow	54-1282
Friederike 22			
THIELE, Auguste	23	Boebber	53-1086
THIELE, Fritz	19	Nordhausen	54-0987
THIELE, Henry	25	Altenlotheim	50-0323
THIELE, Louise	26	Helsen	53-0825
THIELE, Susanne	47	Herford	50-0439
Ludwig 8, Johannes 4, Heinrich 10			
THIELE, Wilhelm	27	Schwarzpuhe	54-1371
THIELEMANN, Joseph	24	Ikenhausen	50-0292
THIELEN, Franz	21	Cappel	50-1067
THIELEN, Franz	37	Muenster	54-1297
THIEMANN, Chr'tine	24	Oesselse	54-1371
THIEMANN, Heinrich	22	Obernkirchen	48-1355
THIEMANN, Joh Ger.	23	Alstette	48-0269
THIEMANN, Louisa	19	Laer	53-0991
THIEMANN, William	27	Vorhalle	53-0991
THIEME, Robert	18	Utersleben	54-1554
THIEN, Hermann	25	Herbron	51-0500
THIER, G.	18	Halzbremen	51-0517
THIERAUT, Georg			47-0840
THIERET, Chr.	29	Bayern	51-1245
THIERFELDER, Aug.	50	Stelzendorf	53-1070
Christiane W 50, Carl August 12			
Christiane W 7			
THIERFELDER, Fr.	24	Loessnitz	48-1179
THIERMANN, Henry	55	Baltimore	53-0888
THIERS, H.	32	Uenzen	51-1160
THIES, Carl Georg	31	Stolz--	48-0053
THIES, Joh. Adam	26	Schwarzenau	52-1200
Anna Maria 24, baby (m) bob			
THIESSENHUSEN, Hen	46	Gresloh	53-1164
Elisabeth 40, Dorothea 20, Eliza 18			
Sophia 16, Minna 14, Henry 9			
THIESSENHUSEN, Wm.	40	Draguhne	53-1164
Elisabeth 39, Mary 8, William 1			
THISLAND, Heinr.	28	Untersag	51-1455
THOELEN, Henry	30	Abbehausen	53-0888
THOELKE, Heinrich	24	Bockeln	52-1625
THOENE, Anton	50	Borgentreich	50-0292
Agnes 33, Maria 18, Helene 9m			
THOENE, Aug. C.	21	Loewen	51-0405
THOENE, Wilhelm	26	Loewen	51-0405
Joseph 24			
THOENE, Zerians	27	Cassel	49-0413
THOGODE, Wilh'mine	17	Beverstedt	54-0903
THOMA, Franz	40	Boehmen	53-1000
Franziska 26, Marie 14, Franz 12			
Victoria 10, John 9, Mathilde 6			
THOMA, Friedrich	66	Celle	51-1438
Marie Sophie 55, Elise 31, Dorothea 21			
Carl 16, Philipp 11			
THOMA, Georg	29	Wettmar	51-1438
Maria Anna 26, Elise 11m, Dorothea 2m			
THOMAS, Ad. (m)	26	Wohltmuthause	49-1358
THOMAS, Amalia	23	Dresden/Sachs	51-1725
THOMAS, Andreas	33	Berka	53-0928
Anna 33, Anna 9, Catharine 6			
THOMAS, Andreas	27	Pattzehne/Pr.	51-0048
THOMAS, Carl	27	Osnabrueck	50-0292
Johanne 27			
THOMAS, Conrad	18	Kirchheim	54-1716
Catharine 16			
THOMAS, David	20	Grochwitz	49-0574
THOMAS, Emilie	21	Seligenstadt	51-1084
THOMAS, Ferd.	27	Trunzig	53-1164
THOMAS, Georg Herm	28	Siegel/Pr.	51-1725
THOMAS, Heinr.	19	Pickelsheim	51-0405
THOMAS, Heinrich	34	Leipzig	50-0021
THOMAS, Hermann	23	Memmingen	50-1071
THOMAS, Johanne	21	Magdeburg	53-0267
THOMAS, Johannes	18	Wippersheim	53-0942
THOMAS, John	30	Muckefild	51-1455
THOMAS, Marg.	33	Leimburg	52-1321
Georg 14, Anna 6, Marg. 4			
THOMAS, Mart.	30	Leimbach	52-1321
THOMAS, Wilhelm	26	Hebenshausen	52-0807
THOMASIUS, Ernst	14	Coburg	53-1013
THOMASMEYER, Heinr	22	Essen	54-0600
THOMPSON, Lucas	30	United States	48-1015
THOMS, Leonore	35	Siedenburg	54-0987
THOMSON, Bernhard	19	Meiningen/Sax	51-1725
THON, Christian	31	Erfurt	51-0460
THONE, A. (m)	32	Loewen	52-0652
THORL, Marie	22	Wenzen	54-1371
THORMANN, Felix	36	Solothurn/Sw.	51-1725
THORMEHLE, Heinr.	21	Schierholz/Ha	52-1332
Marie 24			
THORN, Joh. Peter	27	Fischbach/Nas	53-0628
Johannette 24, Caroline by			
THORNE, W.	25	New York	48-1015
Mrs. 23, Eleanor 6m			
THORWAGEN, Georg	36	Oberhilperthe	51-1725
THRUE, Johann	21	Steinheim	52-1580
THUERGEN, August	26	Grossenheim	54-0053
THUERMER, Hedwig	35	Saida	53-1086
Hermann 7, Robert 5			
THUERMUELLER, J.	24	St. Gallen	49-0416
THUERNAU, Dorothea	34	Hannover	53-0585
Louis 13			

NAME	AGE	RESIDENCE	YR-LIST
THUERNAU, William	49	Winzlar	53-1164
Friederika 45, Eleonora 59, Henry 17			
Deric 17, August 9, Friedrich 4			
Carolina 13			
THUN, v. Claus	22	Otterdorf	52-0048
THURM, Jacob	19	Riedlingen/Bv	52-0960
THWELE, Fried.	34	Gruenenplan	51-1796
TIARKS, Johann	58	Neuensyhl	47-0868
To. (f) 57, S. (m) 29, A. (f) 65			
TIARKS, Theda Mar.		Wayens	54-1297
TICKER, Margareth	22	Mittelruessel	49-0737
TIEBEL, Anna	25	Rimpertshause	50-0323
TIEDEMANN, Hermann	38	Ebersdorf	49-0345
TIEDEMANN, Hermann	18	Ebersdorf	49-0345
TIEDEMANN, J Heinr	20	Wellen	53-1070
TIEDEMANN, Joh.	19	Pechshofen	53-0590
TIEDEMANN, Luise M	23	Bremen	50-1236
TIEDEMANN, Marg.	17	Alstaedt/Hann	53-0475
TIEDEMANN, Marg.	23	Hannover	53-0590
TIEDEMANN, Marg.	21	Lahmstedt	51-1035
TIEDLER, Heinrich	23	Konradsreuth	47-0868
TIEDMANN, Fanny	22	Altenmuhr	51-1160
TIEGEL, Adam	46	Weisenborn/He	51-1725
Catharina 32, Elisabeth 17, Catharina 3			
TIEGEL, Christine	27	Wangen	51-1639
TIEGLER, Wolfgang	26	Gross Waerthh	47-0868
TIEMANN, Friedr.	27	Hausberg	52-1661
TIEMANN, Margareth	30	Soegel	53-1016
Gretchen 24, Catharina 22			
TIENCKEN, Anna Ch.	27	Ottenburg	52-0351
TIENKEN, Catharina	20	Ringstedt	51-1101
TIENKEN, Claus	20	Beverstedt	51-1084
TIENTHAL, Minna	24	Buren	51-1455
TIETJEN, Adelheid	20	Meinertshagen	54-1575
TIETJEN, Diedrich	18	Hevenburg	54-0987
TIETJEN, Hedwig	15	Scharmbeck	52-1362
TIETJEN, Joh. Mart	28	Bremen	54-0987
TIETJEN, Marg.	20	Zwingenfeld	51-1035
TIETJEN, Metta	23	Osterholz	54-0987
TIETSMANN, Charles	28	Eisenach	48-0887
TIETYER, Martin	17	Eidkamp	54-1716
TIETZ, Eduard	38	Potsdam	51-1062
TIETZEN, Adelh.	20	Meinertshagen	54-1575
TIFFELT, Hermann	44	Seitendorf	49-1517
Mrs. 37, Ernstine 15, Pauline 14			
Robert 11			
TIGEL, Margarethe	20	Weilheim/Wuer	52-0351
Eva Maria 18			
TIGGERS, Jac. Hein	31	Lienen	52-1362
Anna Cath. 34, Friedrich 15, Dora 30			
TILL, Henrich	28	Boebber	53-1086
Friedr. 18			
TILLING, Eduard	33	Breslau	53-0942
TILLMANN, J. (m)	34	Loewen	52-0652
TILLMANN, Julius	20	Unnei	52-1410
TILO, Ferdinand	35	Eisenach/Weim	54-1092
TIMKEN, Marie	42	Mehringen	52-1452
TIMKENS, Maria	45	Freidorf	47-0872
TIMLER, Johannes	28	Sachsendorf/B	52-0351
TIMM, Christine	29	Frischborn	51-0352
TIMM, Nicolaus	28	Otterndorf	52-0699
Johann 22			
TIMME, Christian	23	Buende	48-1355
Heinrich 20, Elsche 56			
TIMME, Wilhelm	17	Burg	53-0585
TIMMER, Dorothea	22	Salmenhausen	53-0628
TIMMERDORFER, Jos.	22	Laubach	52-1580
Moritz 30			
TIMMERMANN, Cath.	25	Quackenbrueck	50-1132
TIMMS, Beta	16	Wersabe	52-0048
TIMRING, Georg	40	Bargen	49-0912
TINCK, John	40	Oelsnitz	53-0928
TINNEMANN, Franz	34	Sachsen/Gotha	53-0628
Carolina 29			
TIPP, Marie	18	Bederkesa	51-1084
TIPPEL, Johann	29	Elberfeld	48-0565
TIRSCHNER, W.	16	Leimberg	53-0582
TISCHENDORF, Fr A.	24	Zadelsdorf/Sa	52-1423

NAME	AGE	RESIDENCE	YR-LIST
TISCHER, Andreas	19	Hessen	53-0590
TISCHER, Friedr Wm	38	Zillbach/Weim	50-0323
Anna Rosine 36, Mary Magdal. 14			
Benjamin 13, Elisabeth 10, Magdalene 9			
Christ Theod 3, Elise Minna 1m			
TISCHER, G. Heinr.	23	Steindorf/Pr.	51-1796
TISCHER, Heinriett	28	Breslau	54-0987
TISCHNER, Joh.	43	Weissenoh	52-0693
Margaretha 42, Jacob 16, Barbara 14			
Elisabetha 10, Anna 8, Catharine 4			
Georg (died) 1			
TISCHNER, Martin	28	Kreiselbach	54-0930
Barbara 37			
TITSCHE, Nic.	49	Waldshut	51-1686
TITTEL, Herm.	31	Bauen	54-1283
Louise 23			
TITUS, Franz	23	Wachenroth	52-1321
TOBIAS, M. (m)	35	Leipzig	50-1317
TOBIASSEN, Conrad	29	Meienburg/Han	54-1092
TOBISCH, Michael	47	Battenhain	50-1071
TOBKE, Johann	16	Debstedt	52-0699
TOD, Famma Jansen	30	Nesslersil	53-1062
Maria 2			
TODICK, Dorothea	28	Schwarzbuch	49-0912
TODL, Carl	27	Bohemia	50-0311
Josepha 12, Ignaz 8, Anton 6, Marie 4			
TODT, Carl	36	Luttrum/Hann.	54-1092
TODT, Heinrich	21	Aalfeld	51-0405
TOECHEN, Christine	20	Bederkesa	47-0872
TOEDTEBURG, Wilh.	27	Afferode	54-1443
TOEHL, John	28	Boston	53-0914
TOELBERG, Chr.	19	Wetterfeld	54-1575
TOELKE, Heinrich	25	Lage	52-1410
TOENEMANN, Joseph	46	Drieburg	52-0370
Cathrine 40, Johann 5			
TOENJENS, Julius	15	Kedingen	51-1084
TOENJES, Anna	23	Quackenbrueck	52-0095
TOENJES, Friedrike	20	Quackenbrueck	50-1317
TOENJES, Geo Fr. W	19	Ritterhude	53-0838
TOENJES, Hermann	25	Tecklenburg	52-1432
TOENS, Kancher (f)	54	Lebe	48-0887
TOENSING, Johann	22	Essen	53-1086
TOEPEL, Gottlieb	56	Ottmansdorf	47-0828
Maria 49, Anna 24, Maria 20			
Wilhelmine 15, Caroline 11			
Carl Friedr. 19, Louis 6m			
TOEPFER, Carl	44	Rudolstadt	50-0021
TOEPFER, Johannes	32	Sachsen	53-0590
TOEPKEN, Victor	19	Bremen	53-1070
TOEPNER, Gottl.	44	Burgau	52-1321
TOEPPE, Franz	18	Osnabruck	49-1106
TOEPPEN, August	18	Loeningen	53-1062
Gerhard 23			
TOEPPEN, Michel	26	Kohlstadt	50-0944
Wilhelmina 28			
TOERINGER, Conrad	45	Wallrod	52-1105
Elisabeth 45			
TOERNAU, Ludwig	40	Landsberg	52-1661
Franziska 33, Maria 9, Emma 6			
TOESSLING, J Heinr	23	Minden	48-0565
TOEZEL, Chr.	55	Burghausen	54-0600
TOHM, Michael	44	Schotlow/Bav.	52-1332
Margrethe 46, Caroline 13, Christine 7			
Heinr. 9, Georg 4			
TOHR, Mathias	19	Evelter	50-1067
TOHRS, Anton	63	Arnshausen	49-0912
TOLL, Michel	38	Rudingen	53-0914
Margaretha 33, Elise 3			
TOLLE, Hermann	30	Hardegsen	54-1371
Heinrich 24			
TOLLE, Wilhelm	24	Lederfohers	51-1639
TOMBACH, Caspar	39	Knetzgau	52-1661
Elisabeth 38, Caspar 14, Margareth 12			
Johann 9, Nicolaus 7, Joseph 4			
Joh. Heinr. 31			
TOMFOHRDE, Ludwig	23	Bremervoerde	54-1371
TOMHAGEN, Heinrich	16	Kampe/Hann.	53-0475
TONES, David	56	Osterlinde	54-1371

NAME	AGE	RESIDENCE	YR-LIST
August 16			
TONJES, Jurgen	16	Beverstedt	51-1035
TONJES, Meta	18	Schiffdorf	54-1716
TONS, Helene	20	Cappeln	50-0366
TOOT, Franz	50	Arensberg	52-0699
John 30, Theresia 28, Franz 9m			
TOOT, Therese	24	Arensberg	52-0699
Marie 22			
TOPF, Friedrich	24	Schoenau	52-1200
TOPF, Helene	23	Redwitz	53-0267
TOPF, Nicolaus	22	Reusch	51-1686
TOPPE, Veit	24	Koboitz	53-1000
TORKEL, Wilhelm	54	Coburg	54-1297
Anna 18			
TORLIG, Friedrich	40	Krakewey	48-0406
Caroline 42, Julius , William 17			
Albert 14, Friedrich 11, Albertine 9			
Gustav 5			
TORNEY, Friedr.	16	Bevhoerde	54-0987
TORSTRICK, Heinr.	24	Bremen	50-1317
TOSTMANN, Christ.	23	Braunschweig	52-1423
Louis 20, Minna 28			
TRAB, Heinrich	28	Mellrichstadt	52-1620
TRABANT, Ed.	19	Cassel/Hesse	51-1796
TRABERT, W. (m)	34	Prussia	50-1317
TRAEGER, Carl	26	Freyburg	54-0872
TRAEUBLER, Eberh.	32	Gr. Eislingen	52-0351
Marianne 27, Anton 2, Marian(died) 7m			
TRAGER, Elisabeth	25	Walpenreuth	54-1341
TRAMM, Mandel	34	Sassenbach	51-1455
Soloman 8			
TRAPP, Georg	45	Nonnenroth	47-0868
Hell. 15, Dan. 12			
TRAPP, Joseph	30	Elters	51-0500
TRAPPE, Friedrich	23	Wolfenbuttel	49-0781
TRAUBE, Lazarus	20	Pforzheim	48-0269
TRAUBE, Wilhelmine	20	Wickerode	54-0930
TRAUBNER, J.G. (m)	59	Wendelstun	49-0416
TRAUBWEIN, Valent.	22	Ropdorf	49-0781
TRAUGOTT, Christne	25	Triptis/Weim.	52-1620
Emilie 1			
TRAUKETTREIM, Fr.	25	Triptis/Weim.	52-1620
TRAUM, Elisabeth	21	Bobenhausen	53-1023
TRAUMILLER, M. (m)	29	Upper Austria	49-1358
TRAUNDRETTER, Ern.	26	Berlin	49-0742
TRAUPMEIN, Valent.	22	Ropdorf	49-0781
TRAUTMANN, Caspar	25	Bettenhausen	54-0918
TRAUTNER, Therese		Wodmann	53-0942
TRAUTT, Wilhelm	28	Hanau	52-1512
TRAUTWEIN, Georg	31	Hornberg/Bade	52-0807
TRAUTWEIN, Gottl.	24	Kirchberg	49-0352
TRAUTWETTER, Henry	33	Martinrode	53-0942
TRAVERS, Juliane	21	Wiesbaden	54-0987
TREDLEIN, Kunig.	30	Nuernberg	50-1317
Bartolomaeus 7			
TREFFINGER, Johann	21	Weiler	50-0379
TREIK, George	72	Mittelruessel	49-0737
Maria 60, Peter M. 30, Jacob 24			
Allegunde 23, Gertruda 16			
TREIWER, Andreas	32	Kreissdorf	53-0267
TRELLE, Franz	27	Soest	48-0260
TREMBLAU, Peter	35	Minden	50-1317
TREMPEL, Math.	30	Oberbrunnreut	54-0600
TRENKLE, Emelius	28	Waldkirch	53-0991
TRENKLE, Josepha	47	Waldkirch	53-0991
TREPPER, Andreas	25	Cuelmbach	53-1023
TRESSELT, J Friedr	28	Dothen	52-1200
TRESZ, Friedrich	19	Grosshasslag	49-0352
TRETBAR, Ferdinand	21	Braunschweig	52-1625
TREUTLER, Alban	22	Dresden	52-1200
TREVES, Joseph	15	Triest	53-0838
TRIBER, Friedr.	47	Luetz/Sax	51-1796
TRIEBEL, Daniel	20	Suhl	53-1164
TRIEDEL, Catharina	26	Marberg	53-0905
TRIES, Rud.	29	Schlingen	54-1001
TRIESCHMANN, Elise	31	Hersfeld	52-1129
TRIEST, Isaak	16	Tiegersfeld	53-0888
TRIETJEN, Charles	19	Wellen/Hann.	50-0323

NAME	AGE	RESIDENCE	YR-LIST
TRIGGE, Heinr.	15	Osterholz	53-1086
Rebecca 20			
TRIMPER, Christian	23	Nesselreden	48-0284
TRINGEL, Cath.	27	Albershof	54-0930
TRINKAUS, Cath.	23	Giessen	53-1070
TRINKLE, David	25	Almen	52-1580
TRINKMAYER, A Hein	30	Osnabrueck	51-1796
TRIPPE, Joh. H.	23	Unzen	53-1016
TRIPS, Peter	32	Asperg	47-0872
TRISCHMANN, Adam	45	Ostheim	51-1062
Marie 47, Adam 8, Conrad 17			
TRISCHMANN, Anna	48	Zimmernoth	50-1132
Andreas 20, Elisa 15, Catharina 10			
Martha 4			
TRIVO, Heinrich	40		54-0987
Friederike 26, William 5, Marie 3			
TROCHE, Elisabeth	19	Oberluebbe/Bv	53-0628
TROEBA, Tom	19	Buchbach	52-0515
TROEGER, Georg	19	Wasserkurt/Bv	52-1332
TROEGER, Margareth	24	Weickenreuth	53-0628
TROLL, Franz	38	Wien	50-1132
Barbara 28			
TROLL, Marie	25	Untersihmeyer	54-1443
TROMPEL, Joh. G.	22	Mittelruessel	49-0737
TRONAPFEL, Alb. V.	31	Birkenhof	53-0320
TRONK, Joseph	40	Millewetsch	53-0905
Eva 34, Maria 14, Martin 8, Georg 4			
TROP, Gustav	30	Laubau	53-0888
TROST, Carl	19	Frankenberg	53-1016
TROST, Johann	18	Freyenstein	54-1168
TROUDMANN, Thomas	6	Hamburg	52-0515
TRUDEL, Catharina	26	Marberg	53-0905
TRUEGER, Marg Barb	20	Martinlamitz	52-0351
TRUEMNER, Andreas	22	Gilverberg	50-0366
TRUHNER, Joseph		Besau	54-1168
Anna 25			
TRUMMERT, Johann	20	Stickach	53-0320
TRUNK, Caroline		Sucha	53-0942
TRUPPEL, Christine	28	Eisenberg	54-1717
TRUPPENROTH, E.(f)	38	Maila	52-0558
TUCHARDT, Heinrich	20	Lauterbach	53-1000
TUCHARDT, Theresa	18	Laer	53-0991
TUECHTER, Eberhart	29	Lengerich/Pr.	52-1432
TUEMMEL, August	25	Hannover	50-1317
TUENKEN, Claus	20	Beverstedt	51-1084
TUERK, Ernestine	16	Obersitzke	53-0991
TUERK, Rudolph	28	Lienen/Prss.	52-1332
TUERK, Rudolph	28	Lienen/Pr.	52-1332
Jacob 26			
TUERMANN, Peter	30	Bamberg	53-0267
TUMMLER, Johanne	25	Langhessen/Sa	52-1332
Caroline 33			
TUNISEN, Friedr.	27	Galdern	50-0439
TUNNEL, Adolph	27	Bielefeld	51-1739
TURBA, John	27	Walddorf	53-0914
Elisabeth 21, Catharina 26			
TURBA, Kaspar	30	Walddorf	53-0914
TURBA, Wenzel	21	Susating	51-1035
TURCK, Serapf (m)	26	Neufra	52-0370
TURCK, Theodor	15	Coburg	50-0439
Louise 49			
TURNA, Christ.	20	Luedersfeld	53-1086
TURNAU, Christ.	20	Luedersfeld	53-1086
TURNEKER, Margaret	25	Arzberg	47-0672
TURNOW, Hieronimus	54	Thueringen	51-1438
Marie Sophie 52, Simon Theod. 26			
Louise Wilh. 21, Meta Emiline 13			
TUSCH, Johann	41	Dresden	52-1620
TWACHMANN, Linnia	16	Holtdorf	54-1443
TWECKLOF, Gertrude	19	Emsdetten	51-1455
Theodosia 24			
TWERDY, Wenzel	41	Raudnitz	47-0672
Luglia 31, Carl 4, Wenzel 3			
TWICKLER, Bernhard	25	Muenster	54-0903
Therese 16			
TWISTE, Florentine	26	Buehne	50-0379
TWISTE, Friedrich	25	Buehne/Prss.	50-0323
TZSCHUCK, Bruno	25	Koenigsberg	51-0652

NAME	AGE	RESIDENCE	YR-LIST
UBISHOFF, Ernst	56	Lienen	52-1362
UCHTMANN, Amalie	19	Siedenburg	54-0987
Doris 23			
UCHTMANN, Heinrich	21	Meienburg/Han	54-1092
UEBER, Jos.	58	Oberndorf	53-0492
A.Mar.(died) 54, Marianne 20			
UEBERHAGEN, Wm.	52	Uhrbach	52-0558
J. (f) 51, H. (m) 25			
UEBERWASSER, Heinr	20	Layer	51-0756
Louise 18			
UELTZ, August W.	28	Bodenfelde/Ha	54-1092
UELZEN, Wilhelm	19	Vorsfelde	54-1371
UERPMANN, Peter C.	24	Warburg	52-1200
Marie 26			
UHDE, Gustav	22	Mittelruessel	49-0737
Friedrich 32			
UHL, Michael	19	Rothensoul	52-0515
UHLAND, Joh. Fr.	24	Wimmer	53-1086
Marie 24, Marie Els. 22, M. Clara 19			
M. Ilsabein 11, Christine 50			
UHLE, Herrmann	25	Leipzig	48-0260
UHLENKAMP, Conrad	28	Leer	49-0574
Henriette V. 26, Johann 25			
UHLFELDER, Meier	30	Lenkersheim	54-1297
UHLIG, Gust.	16	Woelpe	54-0987
UHLIG, Joh. Aug.	31	Kentald	48-1131
UHLIG, Johann	43	Chemnitz	53-1023
UHLMANN, Bapt.	48	Constanz	52-1101
UHLMANN, Caroline	22	Keise	53-0914
UHLMANNSIEK, Heinr	22	Buehr	51-1686
UHRBACH, Friedrich	19	Bieber	54-1371
UHRMACHER, Johann	27	Burscheid	54-1371
ULF, Julius	27	Danzig	49-1106
Ida 23			
ULHOFF, Margaret	19	Teggin	51-1588
ULLER, Christian	26	Pittsburg	50-0840
ULLISCH, Hermann	30	Delitsch	48-1184
ULLMANN, W.	43	Schoenlind	54-1566
Rebecca 42, Charlotte 8, Moritz 5, W. 9m			
ULLRICH, Heinrich	27	Rochlitz	48-1114
ULM, Dorothea	26	Unterlindelba	49-0737
George 3, Johann G. 1			
ULMER, Cathrina	-5	Gehrde	50-1236
ULNBAU, Joseph	30	Salzungen	51-1739
ULRICH, A.F. (m)	24	Langenst	52-1512
ULRICH, A.F. (m)	24	Langenstein	52-1512
ULRICH, August	27	Schwarzberg	50-1067
ULRICH, Chr. Fried	55	Gotha	50-0323
ULRICH, Christian	43	Mansbach	53-0942
Catharina 45, Juliane 11, Christian 5			
ULRICH, Elisab.	19	Tringhausen	52-0563
ULRICH, Elise	59	Altenstedt	54-1282
ULRICH, G. A. (m)	48	Natz	52-1512
Anna 38, Friederika 14, Tusnelda 5			
ULRICH, Georg	36	Nentershausen	48-0269
Fr. 4, Marie 24			
ULRICH, J.C.	26	Sittensen	47-0828
ULRICH, Johann	41	Fraustadt	48-1184
Barbara 27			
ULRICH, Magdalene	51	Neuhaus/Bav.	53-0475
Johann 26, Michel 21, Lorenz 17, Anna 13			
ULRICH, Mathias	22	Muehlhausen	52-0351
ULRICH, Michael	33	Grosselfingen	52-1423
Margarethe 33, Catharina 3			
ULRICH, Valentin	43	Herges Vogtei	52-0370
Anna 46, Magarete 16, Friedrich 14			
Dorotea 9, Wilhelmine 6			
ULRICH, William	27	Zwickau	53-0991
ULRICHS, Eberd.	35	Emsdetten	51-1455
Marianna 70, Elizabeth 38			
ULRICI, Heinrich	20	Buer	53-0652
ULTENBUETTEL, Joh.	21	Esel/Hann.	51-1725
ULTSEN, Johann B.	19	Weissmain	53-1023
UMBACH, H.	34	Wolfershausen	49-1358
UMMINGER, Jacob	20	Mittelruessel	49-0737
UNBEWUSST, Valent.	32	Dankmarshause	48-0284
Catharina 28, Anna Marg. 3, Adolph 1			
Adam 29			

NAME	AGE	RESIDENCE	YR-LIST
UNGEMACH, Chr'tine	13	Wuertt.	54-1724
UNGER, Anna Barb	26	Furth	49-0352
UNGER, Barbara	23	Fuerth/Bav.	54-1092
UNGER, Bernhard	28	Baiern	52-1512
Marie 28, Ferd. 6m			
UNGER, Joseph	30	Meseritz	53-0991
Jane 25, Debora 58			
UNGER, William	21	Oberroth	53-0888
UNGEWITTER, Fr'zka	55	Bockhorst	49-0352
UNGLAUB, Christine	25	Pottigen	54-0987
UNGLAUB, Johann	20	Muenchberg	48-0565
UNGLAUB, Martin	26	Blankenstein	54-0053
UNGRUE, Gerhard	26	Hoerstel	48-0269
UNLAENDER, Wilhelm	30	Muenster	53-0473
UNRATH, Carl	27	Ibenhausen	51-0757
Louise 21, Marie 19			
UNSELD, Carl	21	Ulm	54-1575
UNSERSTAL, Heinr.	27	Melle	49-1358
UNSINN, Helene	30	Memmingen	50-0439
UNTERPINTNER, A.	23	Pfaffenberg	54-1283
UNTZ, Friedrich	42	Wuertenberg	53-0557
Eva Cath. 36, Christian 9, Friedericke 8			
Cathrine 11m, Elisabetha 10			
UNVERICHT, August	26	Vaiha	47-0868
UNVERZOGT, Heinr.	18	Dahle	52-0563
URBAN, J.C.H. (m)	35	Wandersleben	52-0960
URBAN, Joseph	33	Trojan	54-1647
URSPRUCH, Conrad	20	Wassmuthhause	54-0053
USINGER, Caspar	32	Wierheim	49-0912
Maria 32, August 6, Jacob 10			
USLAR, v. Ernst	28	Grossenscheen	53-1023
UTHE, August	36	Polle/Hann.	51-0048
Charlotte 34, Auguste 9			
UTHOFF, Theodor	26	Hildesheim	54-0930
UTRITZ, Hein.	48	Alengenrode	51-1796
VAAFTS, John	21	Neuhaus	52-0699
VAASS, Andrew	63	Hannover	53-0991
VAATS, John	21	Neuhaus	52-0699
VAGTS, Gerd	22	Armstorf/Hann	51-1725
VAHLERN, Robert	36	Breslau	54-1168
VAHLKAMP, Heinrich	21	Barthausen	49-0352
VALENTA, Joseph	27	Maleschau	51-1245
VALENTIN, Henriett	26	Leer	49-0574
VALENTIN, Louise	17	Glasbach	53-0590
VALK, Friedr.	23	Noerdlingen	54-1282
VALTER, Cath.	48	Kuebs	51-1084
VAN, Diedrich	32	Niederwald	54-1676
VANANER, Friedrich	52	Neu Ulm	49-0574
VANDERHEIDT, Phil.	32	Zwickershause	48-1131
VANDERPOOL, Oakley	33	Virginia	48-1015
VANHOF, Caroline	24	Hessen	54-1716
VANSIEDER, Johann	55	Oetdorf	51-1035
Elisabeth 53, Martin 24, Anton 19			
Conrad 16, Reinhard 9, Farnansina 25			
Franziska 21, Marie 14, Jacob 32			
Elisabeth 5, Bertha 2			
VASSE, H.	30	Kufenthal	53-0492
VATER, E.P.	23	Lambersdorf	51-1084
VATTER, Cath.	28	Zweibruecken	52-0699
VAUCHEL, Louise	25	Schildhorst	54-0987
VAUPEL, Christ.	32	Obermoellrich	50-0472
Anna 28, Johann 7, Conrad 3, Catharine 6m			
VAUPEL, Josepha	43	Wien	54-1297
VAUPEL, Wilhelm	30	Hengsberg	54-0930
VEBT, J. (m)	28	Aschenbach	50-0746
VEDDER, Rudolph	26	Cincinnati	53-0888
VEDT, Nicolas	30	Leiterode	54-0930
Martha Elis. 28, Eckhard by			
VEGES, Erina	18	Knarenburg	53-0905
VEHRKENS, H'ch Aug	25	Ottersdorf	51-1101
Friedr. Wilh 20			
VEHTMANN, Heinrich	26	Siedenburg	54-0987
VEIGT, Wilhelm Chr	32	Remmingsheim	52-0351
Rosina 25, Anna R. bob			
VEITENGRUBER, Mich	31	Altenhuedinge	54-1371
VEITUN, Louis	29	Hainau	54-1078
Fanny 25			
VELISCH, Cath Marg	18	Arzberg	51-1640

NAME	AGE	RESIDENCE	YR-LIST
VELK, Sophie	19	Hannover	49-1517
VELKESKAMP, Marie	19	Boebber	53-1086
VELLINGER, Heinr.	21	Gruenenplan	51-1438
VELRUP, J. Schulte	28	Emsdetten	49-0416
VELTER, Elias	28	Braunschweig	53-0652
Dorothea 29			
VENATOR, Emil	33	Mittelruessel	49-0737
VENNEMANN, Theodor	40	Cincinnati	48-0101
Elisabeth 40, Theodor 11, Louise 7			
Josephine 4, August 2			
VENNETISCH, Bernh.	26	Bautzen	49-0574
VENT, Fr.	38	Nuernberg	53-1000
VENTER, Augustus	24	Braunschweig	53-0991
VENZEL, Barb.	26	Hildburg	54-1282
VENZMER, Otto	31	Ribnitz/Meckl	52-0960
VEPER, Wilhelmine	23	Waldeck	54-1443
VEPP, Georg	25	Nenderoth	54-0930
VERMLHEIM, Leonh.	31	Erlangen/Bav.	52-0117
VETH, Georg	26	Fuerth	48-1355
Louise 32			
VETH, Mina	19	Cassel	54-0930
VETTE, William	25	Hannover	53-0888
VETTER, George	24	Heldburg	51-0352
VETTER, Gottlieb	28	Coburg	52-0895
VETTER, Jacob	37	Lankenau	52-1101
VETTER, Nicolaus	24	Hammelburg	49-1517
VETTER, Wilhelm	21	Dierdorf	51-1640
VETTERLEIN, Carl F	33	Crimmitschau	53-1023
Ernestine 33, Carl 12, Oscar 10			
Paulise 9, Herrmann 5, Maria 6m			
VETTERS, Friedrich	30	Hermsdorf	53-1164
VICTAR, Alfr.	22	Leipzig	52-1321
VIEBROCK, Henry	20	Osteranden/Ha	50-0323
VIEBROCK, Johann	21	Zeven	50-1132
VIEBROK, Heinrich	17	Rhadereissted	53-0475
VIEDENZ, Carl	27	Geseke	54-1297
VIEHERS, L. (f)	28	Erzien	48-0453
VIEHMEYER, Franz	18	Pyrmont	52-1661
VIEL, Adam	44	Mansbach	53-0942
Juliane 40, Anna 20, Catharina 18			
Peter 13, baby			
VIER, Heinrich	20	Rotenburg	54-1649
VIERECK, Fer.	51	Schlawe	54-1282
VIERECK, Friedrich	39	Arolsen	49-0324
VIERING, J.F.	21	Kuelte	51-1160
VIERNEUSEL, Marg.	43	Ebera	54-1078
VIERTEL, Joh.	32	Kaligroth	52-1362
Anna 29, Georg 9, Johann 6, Barbara 4			
Anna 2, Joseph 4w, Johann Simon 11m			
VIETH, Elisa Betha	28	Emsdetten	53-1062
VIETS, Joachim H.	20	Westerholz/Ha	52-0351
VIEWEG, Carl	46	Triplow	54-1566
Louise 38, Anna 15, Carl 3			
VILGRUEFER, Jakob	26	Abterode	51-1796
Elise 23			
VILLMER, Johann	30	Osterhofen	53-1000
Christine 24			
VINKEN, Herrmann	64	Kassebruch	51-0756
Hedwig 46, Heinrich 3			
VINTGEN, M. (f)	29	Bremerhafen	48-0453
VINZENS, Wilhelm	42	Salzungen	52-0370
Lisbet 42, Elias 17, Catrine 7, Anna 3			
VIRTUE, James	24	Gt. Britian	48-1015
VITT, Eberhardt	24	Wilnsdorf/Pr.	52-1620
VITT, Hermann	35	Willsdorf/Pr.	53-0475
Helene 32, Emilie 7, Helene 5, Alvine 3			
VOECKEL, Paulus	24	Lispenhausen	53-1023
VOEDISCH, An Marie	18	Bayern	53-0557
VOEDISCH, Barbara	20	Arzberg	50-1236
VOELCK, Georg	39	Sachsen	53-0590
VOELGER, Franz'ka	30	Fulda	53-1023
Catharine 34			
VOELK, J. (m)	18	Schwey	49-0416
VOELKEL, Joseph	44	Benifer	54-1717
Catharina 48, Caroline 12, Julianna 8			
VOELKER, Francis	19	Schweinheim	53-1164
VOELKER, Georg	18	Saxony	50-0311
VOELKER, Heinrich	42	Marburg	54-1717

NAME	AGE	RESIDENCE	YR-LIST
VOELKLE, Leopold	22	Stupferich/Bd	53-0475
VOELPERT, J.C. (m)	22	Merenburg	49-0416
VOEPEL, Wilh.	36	Bronskirchen	52-1512
Lisetta 36, Karl 3, Ludwig 6m			
VOGEL, Adam		Schleida	54-1575
VOGEL, Andreas	27	Poeppeln	54-0872
VOGEL, Andreas	25	Heiligersdorf	50-0439
VOGEL, Anna	28	Pommern	52-0693
VOGEL, Anton	22	Gellmern	51-1245
VOGEL, Charles	15	Kleinern	50-0840
VOGEL, Christian	31	Altmannsreuth	54-1297
Wolfgang 25			
VOGEL, Clara	20	Eiterfeld/Hes	51-1532
VOGEL, Edel	31	Brithenheim	48-0951
Ephrad (f) 10			
VOGEL, Eduard	23	Bairitz	53-0590
VOGEL, Elizabeth	32	Wenigendoft	48-1131
VOGEL, Franz	63	Koniz	51-0757
Johanne 53, Caroline 27, Franziska 22			
Bertha 18, Rosalie 15			
VOGEL, Friedrich	28	Mehnen	53-0942
VOGEL, Georg	17	Langenleube	54-1168
VOGEL, H. (m)	36	Lutzenreuth	52-0558
VOGEL, Heinrich	28	Homberg	51-0352
VOGEL, J.G.	22	Zwenkaw	51-1455
Friederike 25			
VOGEL, Jacob	13	Hermansdorf	53-1062
VOGEL, Joh.	23	Waldhau	54-1078
VOGEL, Joh.	15	Armsfeld	51-0405
VOGEL, Joh. Eduard	24	Kreuensorg	54-0930
VOGEL, Joh. Otto	39	Prussia	50-1236
Auguste Fr. 29, John Richard 5			
VOGEL, Johann	22	Erfurt	52-0095
VOGEL, Johanna	25	Kraftshof	52-0693
VOGEL, John	30	Weissreuth/Bv	52-0960
VOGEL, Joseph	17	Weilheim	52-1200
VOGEL, Joseph	20	Hunsfeld	51-1588
VOGEL, Marg. Cath.	17	Nordling	53-0590
VOGEL, Mary	36	Prag	48-1209
VOGEL, Moritz	27	Weissels	53-0905
VOGEL, Richard	19	Wittenberg	53-0435
VOGEL, Thomas	24	Marbach	51-0352
VOGEL, Wolfgang	46	Reichsbach	47-0918
Anna 37, Ignatz 12, George 10, Marie 6			
Erasmus 4, Neumilke 1			
VOGELER, Franz	27	Koppendorf	53-0582
VOGELER, Georg	45	Stotel	51-1160
Anna 29, Helwine 13, Anna 10, Carl 8			
Doris 2, Louise 29			
VOGELER, John	28	Altstarter	53-0492
VOGELER, Marg Barb	24	Wiedenberg	50-0292
VOGELER, Peter	27	Braunach	50-0379
VOGELL, Anna	19	Eichensell	51-1588
VOGELPOHL, Cath.	22	Luesche	52-0563
VOGELPOHL, H. (m)	27	Wimmern	52-0652
VOGELSANG, F.W.(m)	25	Duesseldorf	49-0416
VOGELSANG, Fr'drke	32	Bielefeld	52-1512
Lina 9, Doris 8, Bernhard 5, Hermann 9m			
VOGELSANG, Heinr.	25	Spenge	53-1062
Anna Margr. 23			
VOGELSANG, Heinr.	21	Hannover	51-1725
VOGELSANG, Marie	20	Schmehingen	54-1282
VOGELSBERG, August	11	Arnstadt	53-1304
VOGELSBERG, Johann	27	Koelleda	54-1649
Wilhelmine 23			
VOGES, Anton	18	Dattenhausen	54-0882
VOGES, Friedr.	40	Moensen	54-1554
Caroline 34, Auguste 4, Wilhelm 6			
Carl 12			
VOGES, Rike	17	Roringen	52-0563
VOGLER, Georg	18	Markseid	52-1661
VOGLER, Louis	34	Rahden	48-1355
VOGT, Carl	19	Guetersiohe	50-1236
VOGT, Elise	11	Gr. Almerode	54-0930
VOGT, Ernest	21	Sondershausen	48-0053
VOGT, Friedrich	19	Oberschuetz	54-0882
VOGT, Jacob	18	Kuellstedt	52-0563
VOGT, Joh.	34	Friedberg	54-1297

NAME	AGE	RESIDENCE	YR-LIST
VOGT, Johann	18	Schweisdorf	53-0637
VOGT, Johann	27	Foerden	54-0882
VOGT, Johann	28	Bremen	50-1067
Marianne 34, Anton 7			
VOGT, Louis	17	Giessen	53-1086
VOGT, Sholastica	18	Eiterfeld/Hes	51-1532
Friedrich 17			
VOGT, William	24	Boverden	53-0888
VOIGHT, Caspar	30	Loch	54-1419
Christine 27, Margarethe 7			
VOIGT, Anthony	29	Zwickau	53-0991
VOIGT, Aug. Adolph	40	Mucheln	47-0762
Joh. Christ. 35, Friedrich 11, August 9			
Carl 7, Franz 6, Gustav 3			
VOIGT, Carl	18	Salzungen	51-1245
VOIGT, Francis	1-	Grossenbach	49-0365
VOIGT, Herm.	24	Schmiedefeld	53-0585
VOIGT, Herm.	17	Zwickau	54-0600
VOIGT, Hermann	39	Weissenfels	49-0324
VOIGT, Joh. D.	22	Hannover	50-0311
VOIGT, Joh. Theoph	31	Crimmitschau	53-1164
VOIGT, Johann	43	Elberfeld	48-0565
Minna 40, Balthasar 20, Fritz 14, Otto 3			
VOIGT, John	44	Untertruebel	53-0928
VOIGT, Joseph	34	Schmechten	54-0965
VOIGT, Julius	22	Vogelsberg	54-0987
Friedrich 22			
VOIGT, Robert	22	Neustadt	53-1164
Rosalie 18			
VOIGTMANN, Andreas	16	Hilgershausen	51-1062
VOLCKER, Heinr.	23	Leer	51-0757
VOLCKLAND, Robert	26	Ronnsdorf	53-1013
VOLGSTAEDT, Theod.	21	Weimar	52-0895
VOLK, Andreas	34	Oetlingen	49-0574
VOLK, Friedrich	23	Noerdlingen	54-1282
VOLK, Gertr.	22	Bamberg	52-1321
VOLK, Henry	30	Lemmingen	50-0840
VOLKAR, Anna Mart.	26	Scheffelbach	52-0515
VOLKARDT, Carl	36	Salzungen	49-1106
Lisette 36, John 3, Margaretha 1			
VOLKEL, Joh. Jacob	48	Rueckersfeld	48-1131
VOLKER, Georg	27	Evelter	50-1067
Gertrud 22, Louis 9m			
VOLKER, H. (m)	21	Hofgeismar	54-1566
VOLKER, Joseph	36	Schrokenloh	53-0324
Kunigunde 32, Catrina 8, Agnes 5			
Barbara 2m			
VOLKERS, Antoinett	23	Jewer	53-0590
Hermann 19			
VOLKERS, Diederich	19	Brake	51-0500
VOLKERT, Barbara	22	Nuernberg	53-0914
VOLKERT, Nicolaus	25	Nuernberg	47-0828
VOLKHAMMER, Georg	39	Bavaria	51-0405
Henriette 39, Michael 11, Josepha 9			
Joseph 6, Georg 11m			
VOLKMANN, F. J.	19	Neuwirtschen	51-0517
VOLKMANN, Peter	26	Alsfeld	54-1341
Sabine 25			
VOLKMANN, Sophia	22	Wolf	52-1661
VOLKMAR, Ferdinand	20	Borsch	51-0500
VOLKMAR, Otto	15	Zelle	52-0895
VOLKMER, Heinrich	23	Wienhagen	47-0762
VOLKSDORF, Dorothe	22	Luebeck	47-0987
VOLL, Hermann	23	Meisselwitz	50-1071
VOLLBERT, Adam	23	Milchenbach	52-1423
VOLLBRINK, Wilh.	48	Rheydt---	48-0565
VOLLERS, Hanke	17	Spaden	50-0366
VOLLERT, Marg. F.	25	Waldsachsen	51-0405
VOLLHEIDE, H. (m)	38	Hillersee	52-1512
Dorothea 58, Friedr. 30			
VOLLMANN, Jetta	19	Erfurt	54-1001
VOLLMER, Adam	32	Forkendorff	51-0517
C. (f) 29, H. 8			
VOLLMER, Friedr. W	25	Osterode	53-1000
VOLLMER, Gottlieb	14	Aalen/Wuertt	54-1092
VOLLMER, Heinrich	27	Brelingen	50-1071
VOLLNERSHAUSEN, C.	50	Bracht	54-1341
Mary 50, Charles 14			

NAME	AGE	RESIDENCE	YR-LIST
VOLLRATH, Henriett	23	Eisenberg	54-1283
VOLMER, Franz	26	Soest	50-0366
VOLPELHEIM, Franz	26	Hallenberg	53-0585
VOLT, Margaret	22	Hittersroth	51-1588
VOLTZ, Johann	17	Hetteroth	52-1101
VOLZ, Maria	18	Hettensroth	51-1588
VOMHOF, Beate	21	Treffurt	54-1297
VORBRUEGGE, Leonh.	26	Sunzenhausen	52-1304
VORDRAM, Michael	29	Oberweissenbo	51-0460
VORGE, Fr.	22	Oberod	53-0914
VORNDRA, Nicolaus	30	Bischwind	50-0379
VORNHALS, Johannes	40	Londoff	47-0840
Elisabeth 36, Peter 10, Elisabeth 7			
Helena 2, Heinrich 5			
VOROLES, John	42	Virginia	48-1015
VORWERCK, Gustav	33	Eberfeld	48-0101
VOSS, Bernh.	21	Hannover	50-1317
Joh. 16, Gertrude 18			
VOSS, Carl	26	Hokesheim	52-1580
Julie 27			
VOSS, Conrad	34	Elberfeld	48-0565
VOSS, Franz	48	Schoeningen	52-0563
VOSS, Joh Heinrich	17	Stockhausen	53-1062
VOSS, Johann Georg	24	Seistring/Han	52-1332
Gerh. Heinr. 54			
VOSSKOHL, Elis.	28	Emsdetten	51-1455
Bernard 5			
VOSSMEYER, Christ.	17	Barkhausen	53-1023
Julie 18			
VOSSMEYER, Julie	18	Minden	53-1023
VOSTEEN, Joh. H.	26	Buerstel	51-1160
(f) 28			
VOTZ, Ludwig	18	Gellhausen	52-1101
VRIES, de B. (m)	-4	Groningen	49-0416
H. (f) 39, H. (m) 10, B. (m) 5			
VROBOESE, Fr'drike	21	Doerigsen	54-1168
VULMANN, Heinrich	28	Hoya	53-0324
WAAG, Conrad	27	Rostof	51-0352
WAAS, Benedict	29	Philadelphia	52-1661
WAAS, Jos. Mich.	42	Langenbrandt	54-1078
WAAS, Phil.	39	Neustadt	52-0370
WABER, Maria	22	Hoelcheersdor	53-0435
WACHE, Eduard	36	Berlin	54-1092
Minna 30, Albert 9			
WACHLER, Gustav	23		54-1716
WACHSMUTH, Christ.	20	Gultbach/Goth	52-0351
WACHTENDORF, Just.	17	Brockhausen	52-1512
Friedr. 24			
WACHTENDORF, Soph.	26	Affinghausen	52-1512
Heinrich 9m			
WACHTER, Christoph	28	Eisenach	52-0370
WACHTER, Ernst W.	25	Bielefeld	51-1245
WACKER, Gottfried	26	Sondershausen	53-0473
Ernestine 26, Caroline 22			
WADDENDORF, Chr'ne	27	Ladbergen	48-0260
Elisabeth 20, Herrmann 13			
WADEWITZ, J Friedr	19	Ostrieff/Sax.	50-0323
WAECHTER, Jonas	38	Hundelshausen	52-0563
Christine 34, Heinrich 15, Grethe 11			
Bernhard 8, Elise 6			
WAEGNER, Christ.	34	Dombuehl	54-1168
WAESCH, Henry	28	Bockenau	53-1164
WAETJEN, Charles	19	Walzerode/Han	48-0053
WAETZEN, Margr.	27	Leeste	54-0987
WAGEMANN, Heinrich	29	Heede	53-1062
WAGEMANN, Regina	27	Murberg	51-1455
WAGEMANN, Wilh'mne	24	Lenkemaine	49-0352
WAGENER, R. (m)	37	Wolfenhofen	54-1341
Therese 27			
WAGENSCHWANZ, Jos.	25	Brengberg	52-1101
WAGNER, A. Wilhelm	19	Zundorf	53-0905
WAGNER, Adam	27	Heeringen	48-0284
Elisabeth 20			
WAGNER, Adolph	28	Isny	54-0872
WAGNER, Anna	47	Gudensberg	52-0370
Elisabeth 24			
WAGNER, Anna Marg.	23	Bischberg	54-1554
WAGNER, Berthold	29	Oberzell	53-0435

NAME	AGE	RESIDENCE	YR-LIST
WAGNER, Carl	29	Wachternach	53-0652
Regine 22			
WAGNER, Carl Heinr	31	Loebau	48-1355
WAGNER, Catharina	18	Lauerbuch	48-1131
WAGNER, Chr.	20	Dudeldorf	50-0439
WAGNER, Christian	24	Erfurt	49-0324
Gottfried 29			
WAGNER, Christiane	21	Battenberg	53-1000
Louise 27			
WAGNER, Christine	27	Niefern	51-0352
WAGNER, Conr.	15	Hohenkirchen	51-0757
WAGNER, Crecentia	26	Reimlingen	54-0872
WAGNER, David	23	Erlangen	49-1106
WAGNER, Elise	22	Cassel	53-0557
Caroline 20			
WAGNER, Elise	24	Redinghausen	50-0323
WAGNER, Fr.	29	Rosenberg	51-0757
Rosine 27, Chr. 56, Wilhelmine 24			
Christine 20			
WAGNER, Fr.	20	Rhaden	50-1317
WAGNER, Friedrich	28	Nentershausen	53-1070
Anna Cath. 28, Joh. Martin 10m			
WAGNER, Friedrich	2-	Ressdorf/Mein	50-0323
WAGNER, G.	48	Sommerau	54-1566
Susanne 33, Christoph 7			
WAGNER, Georg	19	Fritzlar	52-1580
WAGNER, Georg	18	Bosserode	52-0558
E. (f) 22			
WAGNER, Georg	30	Hausen/Bav.	52-0960
Marg. 33			
WAGNER, Georg	25	Busendorf	51-1640
WAGNER, Gottl. Fr.	17	Schuetzingen	54-1168
WAGNER, Heinrich	21	Blankenbach	52-1148
Anna Elisa 19			
WAGNER, Heinrich	22	Braunau	54-0882
Daniel 23			
WAGNER, Heinrich	24	Marksuhl	49-0383
WAGNER, Heinrich G	28	Gross Almerod	54-1297
Marie 27			
WAGNER, Helene	42	Homberg	48-1184
WAGNER, Henry	14	Sievern	48-0951
WAGNER, Jacob	52	Giesen	53-1000
Marg. 49, Sophie 20, Caspar 25, Marie 24			
Georg 23			
WAGNER, Jacob	39	Wadern	52-1129
Marie 28, Peter 19, Marie 22, baby			
baby , Marg. 4			
WAGNER, Jacob	30	Baden	50-0021
WAGNER, Joh. Heinr	20	Ridmardhausen	49-0574
WAGNER, Joh. Jos.	51	Roth	48-0951
John 22, Cathrine 16, Anne 14			
WAGNER, Johann	26	Geppingen	52-0095
WAGNER, Johanne	25	Wisbaden/Nass	52-1423
WAGNER, Johannes	37	Naunheim	54-0965
Elise 33, Catharina 8, Elisabeth 6			
Elise 3			
WAGNER, Johannes	32	New York	50-0379
WAGNER, Johannes	50	Tiefenort	49-0413
Johann 28, Johannes 24			
WAGNER, Joseph	23	Hildburghause	52-0279
WAGNER, Justus	20	Osnabrueck	53-0838
WAGNER, Kunigunde	27	Birkenfeld	52-0370
WAGNER, Lorenz	23	Widersbach/Pr	52-1620
WAGNER, M.	22	Unterkujers	54-1566
WAGNER, Marg.	4	Lockweiler	52-1129
WAGNER, Marg.	20	Cronach	51-1160
WAGNER, Marg.	20	Vireth	51-1160
WAGNER, Margrethe		Riedwordhause	53-0942
WAGNER, Maria	12	Frieling	52-1105
WAGNER, Marie	28	Lockweiler	52-1129
WAGNER, Mary	19	Sievern	48-0951
WAGNER, Nicolaus	32	Wehlau	50-0439
WAGNER, Peter	40	Sachsen-Meini	53-1013
Elisabeth 42, Louis 16, Samuel 11, Joh. 7			
Mathilde 1			
WAGNER, R. (m)	23	Reutlingen	49-0329
WAGNER, Severin	38	Heilbronn	54-1371
WAGNER, Sophia	30	Epfingen	53-1164

NAME	AGE	RESIDENCE	YR-LIST
WAGNER, Wilhelm	28	Eisleben	51-0352
WAGNER, Wilhelm	26	Mengeringhaus	50-0323
WAGNER, Wilhelm	33	Halberstadt	54-1297
WAHL, Carl	33	Murchau/Wuert	52-0117
WAHL, Catharina		Telbershausen	54-1575
WAHL, Emil	30	Friedberg	54-0987
WAHL, Joseph	32	Hallenberg	51-1639
WAHL, Wilhelm	23	Neuhof	49-0352
WAHLE, Adelheid	45	Dresden	54-1371
Gustav 18, Hilma 16, Adelheid 15, Lina 14			
Oda 13			
WAHLE, August	31	Eb-i-sen	48-1131
WAHLMANN, Heinrich	18	Lueddsfeld	49-1106
WAHSTIN, Charles	18	Mingershausen	51-1455
WAIDER, Nicolaus	32	Petersberg	53-0320
WAITERER, Caspar	22	Mittelruessel	49-0737
WAITZ, Caroline	20	Lengsfeld	49-0413
WALCKER, Louis	23	Tuebingen	53-0888
WALD, Heinrich	26	Lengsfeld	53-0905
Catharine 19			
WALD, Ludwig	17	Redwitz	48-0269
WALD, Margaretha	27	Oberklein	51-0460
WALD, Mary	37	Kengsfeld	54-1341
WALDAU, Ernest Aug	25	Frankenberg	53-0888
WALDBAUM, Wilhelm	50	Oldendorf	54-1717
WALDBAUR, Barthol.	24	Len-ldt	50-0944
WALDBURG, Charles	27	Braunschweig	53-0991
WALDE, Stephen	36	Seibranz	53-1070
Anna Maria 25			
WALDECK, Sarah	25	Vacha	54-1371
WALDEI, Carl	20	Albaxen	48-0209
WALDEMADE, Georg	29	Limmer	51-1160
Doris 29			
WALDER, Carl	20	Bremerlehe	54-1591
WALDER, Carl	-9	Waldsachsen	49-1358
WALDERKOSTEN, Gerh	39	Schledhausen	51-1588
Henry 20, Louisa 16, Anna 9			
WALDHAEUSER, Marg.	23	Steinbach	54-0053
WALDLIEGER, Joseph	18	Warburg	54-1649
Eduard 16			
WALDMANN, A. (m)	37	Vluyn/Pr.	48-0447
WALDMANN, A.(m)	17	Gerabronn	54-1341
WALDMANN, Herm.	31	Osnabruck	51-1455
WALDMANN, Samuel	14	Kairlindach	48-1179
WALDMANN, Theresia	19	Knurbach	53-0324
WALDMEIER, Wilh.	24	Canton Aargau	51-1245
WALDNER, Christ.	24	Waldburg	49-0352
WALDNER, Johann	29	Sandhofer	53-1013
Franciska 27			
WALE, Dorothea	14	Bakenau	49-0345
WALE, Joh. Carl	24	Berlin	54-1078
Gust. Conr. 21			
WALK, David	15	Eggershausen	49-0912
WALK, Martin	48	Setzelbach	48-1184
Sophie 60			
WALKER, Anna	23	Kirch Telling	52-0351
Elise 27			
WALKERING, Joseph	20	Ahrhaus	54-0600
WALLACH, Dav.	19	Neukirchen	51-1160
WALLACH, Isaac	46	Oberaula	52-1105
Elise 28, Elise 3			
WALLACH, Isaak	19	Falkenberg/He	51-0048
WALLACH, Joh. Ludw	26	Cassel	48-1355
WALLACH, Julia	30	Oberaula	53-0991
WALLACH, Velene	23	Graefenstein	51-1035
Abraham 21			
WALLENFELS, Carl		Giesen	54-1443
WALLENHORST, G.(m)	17	Engter	48-0445
Elise 24			
WALLENREUTHER, Ann	22	Ohrenbach	54-1078
WALLER, Ant.	40	Pissighaim/Bd	51-1796
WALLIS, Friedrich	25	Herzberg	53-1023
WALLY, August	24	Goding/Holst.	53-0628
WALPEN, Simon	31	Vahlen/Hess.	50-0323
Catharine 25			
WALPER, Johann	57	Heinebach	54-0053
WALSCH, Barbara	28	Reutlingen	52-0095
WALSEMANN, Helene	22	Hannover	51-1725

NAME	AGE	RESIDENCE	YR-LIST
WALSEMANN, Wilhelm	28	Hannover	51-1725
WALSER, Math.	25	Mimchesch	51-1455
WALSHER, Adam	28	Spiltenstein	51-1588
WALT, Aug. Ferd.	18	Bitterfeld	53-1000
WALTE, Ferdinand	30	Chemnitz	52-1362
Auguste 32, Minna 6, Marie 3, Anna 9m			
Julius 23			
WALTEMATH, Friedr.	23	Niese	54-1575
WALTEMATHE, Chr. W	18	Petershagnerh	54-0930
WALTER, Anna	21	Klosterheilbr	52-0693
WALTER, August	27	Zella/Sachsen	54-0965
WALTER, Bertha	24	Oberbeinbach	53-1062
WALTER, Carl	20	Carlsruhe	52-1362
WALTER, Catharina	34	Wien	50-1132
WALTER, Conrad	22	Grafsazlach	53-0652
WALTER, David	10	Baiern	48-0887
WALTER, Georg	58	Stade	54-0830
Georg 21, Heinrich 30, Heinrich Chr 18m			
Anna Cath. 50, Marie 24, Margarethe 22			
WALTER, H. (m)	21	Beverstedt	48-0453
WALTER, Heinr.	52	Biskirchen	54-1078
Cath. 47, Louise 24, Magdalena 18			
Aug. 15			
WALTER, Heinrich	48	Nidda	52-1512
WALTER, Heinrich	20	Dorenhagen	54-0930
WALTER, J.	19	Naumburg	48-0565
WALTER, Joh Lorenz	18	Erfurt	54-0053
Therese 47, Therese 18			
WALTER, Johann	24	Bortfeld	48-1184
WALTER, Johann	10	Wohnbach	47-0868
M. 8, El. 4			
WALTER, Julia	25	Siegenhausen	52-1321
WALTER, K.	40	Wohnbach	47-0868
Rh. 42			
WALTER, Lorenz	20	Schwartzau	53-0585
WALTER, Mary	31	Heldrungen	53-1164
WALTER, Ther(died)	22	Mergdorf	52-1464
WALTER, Vital	30	Pfullendorf	50-1071
WALTER, Wilhelm	42	Wahlen/Darm.	50-0323
WALTERS, A.G.C.(m)	18	Braunschweig	49-0383
WALTERS, Joh Jacob	24	Imschen/Hann.	52-0117
WALTERS, Nicolaus	28	Wickers	47-0918
WALTHAUSEN, v. Wm.	17	Neuhaus	54-1371
WALTHER, Adam	40	Herford/Pr.	51-1725
WALTHER, Fr.	54	Wickenreuth	54-1283
WALTHER, Georg	29	Coburg	52-0895
WALTHER, Heinrich	60	Oberwiddershe	52-1105
Elisabeth 57, Catharina 23, Friedrich 16			
WALTHER, Moses	31	Boich	54-1371
WALTHER, Otto	33	Meiningen	49-0574
WALTHES, Caetchen	17	Auerbach	54-1371
WALTIN, Heinrich	21	Breitenbach	52-1580
WALTJEN, Doris	15	Baden	48-0951
WALTKE, Carl	30	Heimsen/Pr.	51-1725
Friedrike 25, Fried. Luise 11m			
WALTMANN, Heinrich	19	Beningbuettel	51-1532
Trina 19			
WALTMANN, Trina	19	Bargten/Hann.	51-1532
WALZ, Jacob	20	Wuertt.	54-1724
WALZ, Joh.	27	Bofsheim	52-0558
Rosine 25, Caroline 21, J. (f) 16			
WALZ, John	30	Wuertt.	54-1724
Dorothea 33, Auguste 26			
WALZ, Regina	23	Oberjesingen	53-1164
WAMBACH, Elisabeth	27	Pruessburg	48-0260
WAMBACH, Joh.	36	Knetzgau	54-0053
WAMBOLD, Abraham	18	Cronheim	52-0895
WAMSLER, John	22	Strassdorf	53-0914
WAND, Ludwig	40	Hargenhausen	52-1101
WANGE, Auguste	21	Blumenthal	49-0324
WANGEMANN, Theresa	17	Jena	54-1168
WANGENBACH, J. (m)	24	Limburg	49-0416
WANGENHEIM, Salmon	17	Marisfeld	48-1131
WANKE, Carl	31	Manslau/Pruss	53-0628
WANNER, Ludwig	38	Isnich	53-0435
WAPLON, Ignatz	28	Pudenz	52-1464
WAPPLER, Carl Wilh	23	Leissneg	48-1179
WAPPLER, Veronica	15	Almen	52-1580

NAME	AGE	RESIDENCE	YR-LIST
WARD, W. (m)	39	United States	48-1015
WARKER, Anna	18	Almos	52-1129
WARKER, Marg.	16	Eichenstrut	52-1129
WARMIRSCH, Maria		Zell	53-0942
WARMSBOLD, Conr.	22	Lehnstedt	52-1625
WARNCKEN, John	37	New York	53-1164
WARNECKE, Hermann		Braunschweig	54-0987
WARNEKE, Friedrich	27	Hannover	48-1184
WARNEKE, Juerg	40	Farven	54-0918
Sophie 32, Margarethe 6, Jacob 4, John by			
Friedrich 59, Frees (f) 14			
WARNER, Eira	21	Haus	49-0737
WARNICKE, Henriett	14	Braunschweig	54-1168
WARNKE, F.S. (m)	26	Engter	48-0445
WARNKE, Louise	25	Celle	54-1647
WARNKEN, Auguste	20	Roennebeck	49-0329
WARNKEN, Hermann	21	Kirchweih/Han	54-1092
WARNS, Meinke	24	Oldenburg	50-0292
WARSTNIS, M.E. (f)	51	Alsfeld	54-1341
WARTENBURG, Doris	46	Potsdam	51-1160
Carl 12			
WARTENSLEBEN, H.	25	Hannover	50-1317
WARTH, Emanuel	36	Untersucklian	54-1443
Elisabeth 36, Rosalie 2m			
WARTHLING, Ernst	27	Roesingfeld	48-0260
WARTZ, Georg	19	Prussia	54-1724
WARWEG, Ch. (m)	31	Heitzunder	49-0329
WASCH, Andreas	34	Jessen	53-0905
WASMAR, W. (m)	30	Boehmen	49-1358
WASMUTH, Justus	14	Grossenritt	54-0965
Cathrine 25			
WASS, Johann	19	Baiern	53-0324
Maria 18			
WASSENBERG, J. (m)	26	Emsdetten	49-0416
WASSERMANN, Carol.	21	Adelsdorf	52-0693
WASSERMANN, Caspar	30	Gerstungen	52-1148
Johann 24			
WASSERMANN, Heinr.	25	Roth	48-1184
Fanny 24			
WASSERMANN, Henr't	50	Lengsfeld	52-1321
Magd. 9			
WASSERMANN, Johs.	50	Lengsfeld	52-1321
WASSERMANN, Rachel	24	Kunreuth	53-0991
WASSERTRAGER, Abr.		Germany	48-1131
WASSMANN, August	19	Heldrungen	53-0825
WASSMER, Joseph	31	Prussia	53-0628
Therese 24			
WATENSTEIN, David	21	Volkershausen	54-1341
WATERMAN, C. (m)	35	Savannah, Geo	48-1015
K. (m) 29			
WATGE, Johann	20	Emden	54-0882
WATIER, Hermann	19	Leipzig	49-0345
WATSON, William	39	Great Britian	48-1015
Mrs. 35			
WATTENBERG, Fr. C.	16	Rotenberg/Han	51-0048
WATZEL, Fr. (m)	23	Prussia	54-1724
WATZNAUER, Joseph	28	Reichenberg	53-1070
WAWRA, Joh.	35	Muichowitz	54-1575
Barbara 23			
WAYMANN, Joseph		Amendingen	54-0903
WEBBER, Edward	33	Baltimore, Md	48-1015
Caroline 24			
WEBEL, Caroline	30	Radeln	52-1129
Charlotte 18			
WEBEL, Charlotte	18	Luebbecke	52-1129
WEBENSHUT, Christ.	41	Grossweitscha	53-0914
Christiane 41, G. William 15, John 13			
Friedrich 9, John 8, August 4			
WEBER, A.E. (f)	25	Elberfeld	48-0453
WEBER, Adam	24	Creuzlichtes	52-1101
WEBER, Ana	20	Leimbeck/Hess	51-1532
WEBER, Andreas	23	Almen	52-1580
WEBER, Anna	18	Neuenschmied	51-1588
WEBER, August	26	Nuernberg	51-0326
WEBER, Baltas	19	Wuestenbuchau	53-0320
WEBER, Barth.	28	Elchingen	52-0515
Walberga 28			
WEBER, Bernhard	25	Emsdetten	54-0903

NAME	AGE	RESIDENCE	YR-LIST
WEBER, Carl	46	Istrup/Pr.	54-0965
Josephine 21, Rika 14, Ferdinand 13			
Johannes 10, baby			
WEBER, Carl	38	Wernigerode	48-1179
Christiane 37, Hermann 7, Bruno 2			
WEBER, Carl Theod.	19	Leipzig	48-1209
WEBER, Cath. Elis.	25	Flieden/Hesse	49-0365
WEBER, Charles	43	Fischbach/Pr.	51-0048
Wilhelmine 33, Louis 10, William 9			
Peter 8, Charles 6			
WEBER, Christ	17	Arnsberg	51-1686
WEBER, Christian	46	Dillenburg	53-1023
Charlotte 46, Catharine 24			
WEBER, Christian	19	Sablenhausen	53-0825
WEBER, Christian	32	Fischbach/Nas	53-0628
Catharina 31, Johanette 10, Anton 5			
Elisabeth 2			
WEBER, Claus	42	Alterode	54-0600
Anna Marg. 36, Andreas 9, Joh. Jost 9m			
Joh. 5			
WEBER, Daniel	28	Coetlitz	53-1016
WEBER, Eduard	36	Berlin	53-0628
WEBER, Elisabetha	17	Schwarzenbach	54-1371
Joh. Erhard 26			
WEBER, Elise	16	Elsoff	52-0563
WEBER, Eliza	60	Celle	53-0991
Augusta 23			
WEBER, Eva	24	Baunn	54-0903
WEBER, Eva	18	Ilsensdorf	49-0737
WEBER, Franz Jos.	60	Waldmichelsba	51-1532
Margretha 57, Franz 25, Peter 20			
Maria 11			
WEBER, G.C.	32	Darnstaedt	50-0379
Wilhelmine 29, Ida 6, Carl 4, Emil 3			
WEBER, Genofeva	29	Michelsdorf	54-0987
WEBER, Georg	20	Neuenheim	53-1000
Christine 25			
WEBER, Georg	27	Esplingerode	53-1023
Friederike 26			
WEBER, Georg	20	Freirittenbac	48-1179
WEBER, Gottlieb	15	Lobenstein	48-1184
WEBER, Grete	20	Konigsbronn	51-1796
WEBER, H. (m)	48	Hagen	48-0453
WEBER, J. (m)	18	Schwarzenbach	47-0762
WEBER, Jacob	23	Bicken	54-1443
WEBER, Jacobine	21	Storndorf	52-0652
WEBER, Joh.	20	Ziegenhain	54-0600
Margrethe 18			
WEBER, Joh.	28	Eschenrode	52-1321
WEBER, Joh. August	44	Herrnhut	53-0888
Eugenia 39, Laura 17, Katinka 13			
Armaut 7, Theodor 2			
WEBER, Joh. Christ	27	Ellertshausen	51-1062
WEBER, Joh. Fried.	18	Konigsbronn	51-1796
WEBER, Johann	29	Fuerth/Bav.	54-1092
WEBER, Johann	18	Eichelsachsen	52-1321
WEBER, Johann	18	Hessen	53-0590
WEBER, Johann	25	Freirittenbac	48-1179
WEBER, Johann	58	Neuschonefeld	48-1184
WEBER, Johann	22	Storndorf	49-0352
Maria 24, Heinrich 6m			
WEBER, Johann	24	Dreisbach	51-0352
WEBER, Johann Jost	20	Burge	54-0930
WEBER, Johanna	25	Flettau	54-1716
WEBER, Joseph	24	Elsoff	52-0563
WEBER, Joseph	29	Bregrenz	54-1371
WEBER, Keh. (m)		Bremen	52-0515
WEBER, Leopold	34	Veitsteinbach	52-1661
WEBER, Ludwig	28	Lispenhausen	52-1661
WEBER, Margarethe		Neuershausen	53-0942
Constantin			
WEBER, Maria	29	Wetter	54-0930
WEBER, Maria	19	Langenhausen	53-0905
WEBER, Maria	22	Budingen	49-1106
WEBER, Marie	17	Bremen	52-1362
WEBER, Mathaus	23	Heinebach	54-0930
WEBER, Michael	16	Aschbach	53-0825
WEBER, Michel	24	Itzing/Bav.	54-1092

NAME	AGE	RESIDENCE	YR-LIST
WEBER, Nicol.	25	Staffelstein	52-1129
WEBER, Philipp	17	Altenkirchen	53-0267
WEBER, Reinhard	33	Wetter	54-0053
WEBER, T.	34		52-1101
WEBER, Therese	22	Kollerbach/Pr	53-0628
WEBER, Therese	25	Hing/Bavaria	54-1452
WEBER, V.H.	29	Herdingen	54-1470
WEBER, Vinzenz	38	Immerkingen/W	54-1092
Creszenz 39, Joseph 10, Eduard 9			
Barbara 7, Josepha 6, Sepha 3, V. Zw. bob			
WEBER, Wilhelm	59	Fischbach/Nas	53-0628
Elisabeth 50, Elisabeth 23, Heinrich 20			
Peter 17, Catharina 8			
WEBER, Wilhelmine	32	Wirtenbach	53-1070
Dorothea 6			
WEBER, v. Carl	25	Augsburg	54-1297
WEBERLING, Friedr.	42	Salzgitter	53-1164
Carolina 37, Henry 9, Theodor 5			
Friedrich 2			
WEBERT, Chr. W.	34	Kirchbergen	54-1470
WEBSTERS, Cath. M.	19	Osnabrueck	52-1512
WECHEL, Cathrine	23	Wuertenberg	53-0557
WECHELN, v. J.H.	20	Mulsum	49-0329
WECHSELBERG, Alwin	19	Barmen	48-0565
Johanna 21			
WECHTERSCHEUSSER,C	20	Kirchgoens	54-0965
WECK, Andreas	31	Obertheers	54-1554
Dorothea 30			
WECK, Carl	23	Vaihingen	52-1625
WECK, Ottoweg	58	Hungen	54-1282
Tina 22, Philip 15, Charlotte 16			
WECKE, Herm	31	Lippedetmold	53-0324
WEDDERMANN, Marie	27	Hannover	50-0021
Lene 2			
WEDDIG, Theresia	28	Emsdetten	48-0260
WEDE, Christian	30	Buehne	50-0379
WEDEBUSCH, C.	17	Herstadt	54-1716
WEDECKE, Franz	29	Braunschweig	54-1554
WEDEKIND, August	24	Konigshofen	52-1580
WEDEKIND, Georg	21	Hannover	48-0406
WEDEKIND, Heinr.	28	Einbeck	52-1105
WEDEKIND, Heinrich	44	Gilten	50-1132
Marie 45, Heinrich 17, Louise 14			
Sophie 12, Friedrich 6, Marie 8			
Wilhelm 3			
WEDEKIND, Joseph	28	Burg	52-1580
Amalie 31			
WEDEKIND, Marie	56	Gilten	50-1132
Heinrich 22, Louis 16, Ernst 13			
WEDEL, Marg.	21	Ermreuth	53-0320
WEDEL, Moritz	21	Frauenbreitun	51-1588
WEDEMEIER, August	22	Osnabrueck	48-0053
WEDEMEIER, Charlot	26	Wolfhagen	52-1512
WEDEMEIER, Hellene	20	Hannover	53-0628
WEDEMEYER, Charlot	19	Udeborn	52-1625
WEDEMEYER, Friedr.	26	Bremen	53-1086
WEDEMEYER, George	20	Bueckeburg	53-1164
WEDEMEYER, J.C.	20	Bremen	53-0161
WEDEMEYER, Mad.	38	Ein--m	50-0439
Gottl. 14, H.(m) 11, T.(m) 9			
WEDEMEYER, Wilh.	31	Midlum	53-1000
Anna 24			
WEDER, Joseph	28	Burg	52-1580
Amalie 31			
WEDKER, Elisabeth	18	Rinbath	51-1588
WEDY, Joseph	33	Berergern	51-1455
Josephine 40, Joseph 6			
WEEBER, Wilhelm	24	Baaden	52-1620
WEECK, Carl	23	Vaihingen	52-1625
WEFEL, G.H. (m)	23	Osnabrueck	52-1512
WEFER, Wilhelm	28	Strickhausen	52-1423
Christiane 28			
WEGEHENKEL, Elis.	21	Quentil	54-1554
WEGELE, Regina	21	Oberkingen	49-0912
WEGEMANN, Joh. Fr.	46	Langenberg	49-0352
Elisabeth 38, Anna 20, Auguste 15			
Lisette 12, Carl 8, Johanne 4, Auguste 6m			
WEGEMANN, Wilhelm	27	Langenberg	49-0352

NAME	AGE	RESIDENCE	YR-LIST
Amalie 23, Wilhelm 6m			
WEGENER, Henry	36	Nordheim	48-1209
WEGENER, L.	34	Greibau	54-1575
Ulrike F.			
WEGENER, Ludwig	34	Basse	53-1086
Anna 37			
WEGENHUESER, Andr.	22	Wanfurt	50-0379
WEGESINN, Bals. C.	18	Kruckum	54-1443
WEGLEHNER, Marie	32	Regensburg	53-0492
WEGLEIN, Carolin	21	Neuhaus	53-1062
WEGMAN, Eleanor	31	Linne	51-1588
Wilhelmina 24, Ann 3			
WEGMANN, Friedrich	21	Linne	51-1588
Catherine 18			
WEGMAYR, John	29	Linz	53-0991
WEGNER, August	35	Solbeck	54-0882
Heinrich 6			
WEGWARTH, Cath.	17	Waechtersbach	52-1625
WEGWERTH, Ernst	19	Bueckeburg	50-1236
WEHA, J. (m)	55	Unterkremmach	48-0447
WEHAGEN, Gerhard	40	Wildeshausen	52-1620
Anna 43, Marie 10, Carl 9, Johann 3			
WEHE, Henriette	36	Dresden	52-1620
Oscar 7, Gustav 8			
WEHL, Friedrich	56	Illingen	53-1000
WEHLE, Caroline	20	Ungarn	53-0557
WEHLER, Carl	27	Alterndorf	53-0324
Wilhelm 23			
WEHLER, Carl	22	Neuenkirch	49-0345
WEHLING, L. (m)	32	Essen/Ruhr	48-0447
WEHMAYR, Christoph	29	Buchel	54-0053
WEHMEYER, Herm.	26	Herford	51-1245
WEHMUTH, H.	26	Lamstedt	54-1470
WEHNER, Carl Gottf	30	Essingen	48-1184
WEHNER, Cath.	36	Schopback	51-1639
WEHNS, F. (m)	23	Bebra	52-0652
WEHR, Joh. G.	37	Dettendorf	52-0693
Catharine 27, Kunigunde 5, Margar(died) 3			
Conrad 44, Michael 11, Andreas 8			
WEHRFRITZ, Hugo	18	Schweppenhaus	54-0987
Carl 19			
WEHRING, Anna	17	Essen	53-1086
WEHRING, Franz	35	Kleinwaldstad	54-0987
Elise 32			
WEHRING, Gertrude	40	Kleinwaldstad	54-0987
Gertrude 3, Christine by			
WEHRKAMP, Wilhelm	24	Polstenkamp	48-1015
WEHRMANN, C.	64	Tefenhausen	50-0746
M. (f) 60, D. (f) 26, F. (f) 23			
C. (f) 20, H. (f) 18, S. (m) 15			
WEHRSDOERFER, P.	23	Schwey	49-0416
WEHRT, Wilhelm	21	Braunschweig	54-1452
WEHRURSIN, Georg	46	Schoeneiche	54-1371
Margarethe 41, Margarethe 16, Johann 14			
Anna 9			
WEIBEL, Berh.	16	Wuertt.	54-1724
WEIBEL, Catharine	23	Wuertt	53-0557
WEIBEZAHN, Th.	36	Hannover	51-1160
Louise 26, Wilhelm 7, Louise 5, Friedr. 3			
Ed. 38, Elise 32			
WEICHE, Wilhelm	24	Luechow	54-1297
WEICHHARDT, Peter	24	Oldenburg	54-1470
WEICHSCHNEIDER, J.	43	Hindelang	53-0492
Victoria 50, Crescencia 16, Josepha 15			
Marie 12, Balbine 7			
WEID, Joseph	21	Seisheim	49-1106
WEIDE, Gottfried	37	Immenrode	54-0903
Charlotte 34, Minna , Carl 6			
WEIDEBOERNER, Jos.	47	Muckenhausen	47-0872
Therese 40, Catharina 16, Walpurga 12			
Johann 10, Barbara 8, Theresa 6			
WEIDEMANN, Heinr.	24	Weimar	50-1236
WEIDEMANN, Heinr.	33	Erkshausen	47-0672
WEIDENMUELLER, F.E	22	St. Lengsfeld	54-1371
WEIDENMUELLER, Ric	21	Lengenfeld	54-0987
WEIDHAIM, Ch. Gott	30	Konigswalde/S	51-1796
WEIDINGER, Heinr.	19	Koepern	53-1023
WEIDLER, Aloys	56	Igelsbach	53-0825

NAME	AGE	RESIDENCE	YR-LIST
WEIDMANN, Christ.	34	Bayern	53-0557
Eva 30, Margretha 9			
WEIDMANN, Magdalen	56	Bayern	53-0557
Johann 27, Christoph 34, Eva 30			
Margaretha 9			
WEIDMANN, Nicolaus	28	Wasserlosen	48-0887
WEIDMUELLER, Joh.	41	Chimmeritz	49-1358
Rosalie 32, Matilde 13, Willibald 11			
WEIDNER, Andreas	35	Mittelsinn	52-0563
WEIDNER, Carl Ern.	21	-eibendorf	54-0987
WEIDNER, Charles	47	Hannover	50-0292
WEIDNER, E. (m)	31	Un. Glogau	50-0746
WEIDNER, Friedrich	40	Baiern	52-0370
WEIDNER, Joh Gottl	48	Neuenkirchen	48-1355
WEIDNER, Joh.	26	Rineck	52-1625
WEIDT, Georg	20	Darmstadt	50-0021
WEIERSHAUSEN, Cath	55	Eppsdorf/Kurh	53-0628
Christine 17			
WEIERSHAUSEN, Fr'z	32	Eppsdorf/Kurh	53-0628
Elisabeth 37, Sebastian 5, Johannes 3			
Heinrich 2, Caspar by			
WEIERSHAUSEN, Gert	21	Mittelberg/KH	53-0628
WEIFFENBACH, Heinr	31	Alsfeld	51-1455
WEIGAND, Elisabeth	25	Auerbach	54-1371
WEIGAND, Eva	29	Sulzbach	54-1443
WEIGAND, Georg	58	Knetzgau	54-0053
Elisabeth 53, Kunigunde 25, Johann 24			
Caspar 20, Elisabeth 18, Georg 15			
Franz 13, Adam 10			
WEIGAND, Johann	20	Ammnau	52-1321
WEIGEL, Friederike	21	Bayreuth	50-0379
WEIGEL, Samuel	21	Wiseck	54-1554
WEIGEMAN, Gerhard	31	Lingen/Hann.	51-1532
WEIGERT, Anton	24	Hohenfels	53-0825
Joseph 16			
WEIGMAN, Friedrich	26	Hvese	51-1588
Freed 20			
WEIHE, C.L. (m)	14	Stadthagen	52-1321
WEIHE, Carl	26	Westphalen	51-1035
WEIHEL, Cathrine	23	Wuertenberg	53-0557
WEIHMANN, Heinr.	24	Kloster	52-1512
WEIKE, Charles Aug	43	Bansdorf/Hess	50-0323
Caroline 38			
WEIL, Ernst	28	Wiesbaden/Nas	48-0447
WEIL, Jacob	26	Gross Schares	48-1179
WEIL, Jette	20	Pelchau	48-1179
WEILACHER, Friedr.	30	Friedrichsdor	51-0384
WEILAND, Auguste	37	Lippaene	53-1000
Carl 15			
WEILAND, Christ.	25	Meinsen	52-1321
WEILAND, Gerson	44	Rabboldshause	54-1647
Gittel 45, Bertha 20, Jonas 15, Sara 7			
WEILAND, Wilhelm	31	Meinsen	51-1588
WEILBACH, Max Aug.	34	Noerdlingen	54-0850
WEILEPP, Auguste	37	Querfurt	53-1164
WEIMANN, Carolina	32	Untochen	54-0930
Rosine 59, Johanna Ros. 24			
WEIMANS, Marianne	58	Horsdorf	51-1062
Margaretha 18, Andreas 17, Lorenz 14			
WEIMAR, C. (f)	24	Orle/Nassau	48-0447
WEIMAR, Jacob	33	Wuertenberg	53-0557
Cathrine 27			
WEIMECK, Joh. Carl	37	Mittelruessel	49-0737
Therese 24			
WEINAND, Johann	21	Bodensberg	50-1067
WEINBEER, Marg.	28	Bischwind	47-0918
Elisabeth 5			
WEINBERG, Benedict	24	Werther	52-1625
WEINBERG, Friedr.	22	Rappe	53-1086
WEINBERG, Isaac	28	Steuerberg	53-1016
WEINBERG, Jos.	21	Langenschwanz	51-1796
Judn. (m) 17			
WEINBERG, Marianne	18	Rehburg	54-1371
WEINBERG, Marie		Wien	53-0914
WEINBERG, Samuel	20	Hoeringhausen	54-0987
WEINBERGER, Magd.	57	Maas	54-1283
WEINBINDER, Adam	29	Wetzlar	54-0830
WEINBOERNER, Ignaz	20	Fulda	54-1554

NAME	AGE	RESIDENCE	YR-LIST
WEINBURGER, Johann	40	America	47-0762
Catharina 43, Catharina 14, Caroline 10			
Hermann 9, Louise 7, Wilhelmine 2			
Heinrich 1			
WEINER, Clara	27	Mittelruessel	49-0737
Rosina 28			
WEINER, Philipp	39	Stein Grundau	47-0840
Maria 27, Friedrich 5			
WEINGAERTNER, Bern	33	Wuertzburg/Bv	51-0326
WEINGART, Margaret	28	Wasserlosen	48-0887
WEINGELS, Henry	31	Prussia	54-1724
WEINGUTH, Charles	27	Meiningen	48-1131
R. (f) 23			
WEINHARD, Wilh.	29	Hall	51-0326
WEINHAUER, Elisabe	48	Walzerode/Han	48-0053
WEINHAUER, Mary	14	Fulle	48-0053
WEINMEISTER, Soph.	27	Moellenfelde	54-1168
WEINREICH, Carl	17	Netze	54-1575
WEIRTH, Christ.	40	Waldweinmersb	52-0117
WEIS, Carl	32	Sachsen	53-0590
WEIS, He.	36	Telbershausen	54-1575
Margarethe 40, Lisabeth 6			
WEIS, Joseph	26	Hannau	52-0699
WEIS, Marie	26	Burghaid	53-0320
WEIS, Peter	20	Walhen	51-1084
WEISACH, Lazarus	15	Altenstein	48-1179
WEISBRIG, Carl	29	Mannsdorf	54-1443
WEISBROD, Christ F	32	Fulda	53-0628
WEISE, Carl	56	Leipzig	53-1016
WEISE, Charl.		Bergern	52-1321
WEISER, Andreas	27	Beschwind	53-1016
WEISER, Carloline	40	Marburg	51-1588
Christine 38			
WEISHUT, Marie	21	Mehlis	48-1131
WEISKOTTEN, Robert	28	Viersen	48-0565
Anna Cath. 26, Fr. Wilh. 8, Otto 3			
Ernst 18m			
WEISS, Amalie	22	Duerwangen	53-0590
WEISS, Elise	22	Ilzingen	53-0267
WEISS, Elise	23	Bayern	53-0557
WEISS, Elise	23	Arzberg/Bav.	53-0557
WEISS, Elise	30	Gruenberg	54-1443
WEISS, Ernst	26	Brunswig	51-1796
WEISS, Ferd.	19	Wien	54-1078
WEISS, Heinr.	19	Hebbach	48-0269
WEISS, Heinrich	23	Oberfranken	53-0557
WEISS, Isaac	35	Neustadt	51-1640
WEISS, Jacob	44	Friedrichsdor	51-0384
Maria 40, Carolina 13, Johann 10			
Gustav 4, Jacobina 2			
WEISS, Johann	42	Maehren	53-1000
Marianne 41			
WEISS, Joseph	24	Baunach/Bav.	52-1620
Margarethe 21, Anna 4			
WEISS, Joseph	24	Duerrmaul	54-1566
WEISS, Lorenz	18	Nuernberg	48-1179
WEISS, Michael	40	Coburg	53-0267
Christiane 37, Bernhard 7, Adolph 5			
WEISS, Michel	54	Wiesbaden/Nas	48-0447
WEISS, Paul	21	Gotha	52-0895
WEISS, Philip	50	Wiesbaden/Nas	48-0447
D. (f) 42, Eliza 20, Emil 19, Reinhard 17			
Luisa 16, Pauline 9, Bertha 7			
WEISS, Rudolph	18	Hessen	53-0590
WEISS, Victoria	23	Bayern	53-0557
WEISSBROD, Adam	24	Fritzlar	50-1236
WEISSENBACH, Carl	24	Langenthal	50-0472
WEISSENBACH, Heinr	31	Alsfeld	51-1455
WEISSENBORN, Ed'rd	26	Regensburg	54-0987
Elise 29, Carl by			
WEISSENSEE, Johann	36	Altenmuenster	52-1200
WEISSENSTEIN, Pine	21	Rothenberg	49-1358
WEISSFICH, O.	27	Bueckeburg	53-0492
WEISSGERBER, Andr.	31	Hannover	53-0991
WEISSGERBER, H.J.	25	Weberstadt	51-1160
Georg F. 34, M. Wilh (f) 31, Friedrike 4			
Ernestine 3m			
WEISSGERBER, Hen't	32	Hannover	53-0991

NAME	AGE	RESIDENCE	YR-LIST
WEISSKOPF, Edward	30	Roeschelau	54-1282
Benj. 32, Bened. 36, Jos. 18			
WEISSKOPF, Heinr.	18	Rzeschlau	54-1078
WEISSKOPF, Salomon	28	Boehmen	48-1179
WEISSSCHAEDEL, J R	26	Cannstadt	48-1355
WEIT, Lib. (f)	24	Wunsiedel	54-1282
WEIT, Margareth	26	Damstadt	54-1282
WEITENPFANER, Ant.	37	Hermansdorf	53-1062
Anna 41			
WEITER, Philipp	21	Eiterfeld/Hes	51-1532
WEITH, Adam	29	Bamberg	48-1114
WEITHAS, Louisa	34	Dresden	53-0991
Carl Heinr. 14, Georg Ernst 7			
Mary Theresa 9, Ann Louisa 6			
WEITTENBACH, Tilm.	30	Niederschelde	49-0781
Elizabeth 25, Caroline 4, baby			
WEITZE, Johann	52	Wiedelah	54-0872
Sophie 42, Caroline 18, Louis by			
WEITZEL,	32	Barmen	48-0565
WEITZEL, Adam	51	New York	54-0053
WEITZEL, H.	16	Ahus	51-0517
C.(f) 23			
WEIVERT, Gerhard	37	Petterweil	53-1000
WEIZ, Carl	33	Siegen	48-0269
WEIZEBACH, Helene	25	Hofgeismar	54-1566
WEIZEL, Elisabeth	20	Oberingelheim	49-0912
WEIZEL, Emil	30	Obereisenhaus	52-1452
WEIZEL, Georg	27	Trebersdorf	51-1438
Conrad 17			
WELCK, Anna Cath.	21	Rothenburg	52-0515
WELFRUM, Friedrike	29	Mord-gen	50-0944
WELGE, Theodor	27	Braunschweig	51-1725
WELKE, Gottlieb	44	Floth/Pr.	53-0475
Anna 42, Samuel 17, Theodor 15, Gustav 11			
Robert 10, Bertha 6, Julie 4			
WELKNING, Sophia	3	Stuttgart	54-1341
WELLBROCK, Claus	28	Kollheim	48-1355
Diedr. 18, Meta 20			
WELLBROCK, Meta	20	Heidorf	48-1355
WELLE, August	18	Dissen	54-1371
WELLEMEYER, J.H.	19	Ibbenbuehren	48-0445
WELLENDORF, August	21	Arnstadt	54-0850
WELLENWOCK, Adelh.	19	Salzwedel	54-1591
WELLER, Caroline	23	Preussen	53-0590
WELLER, Joh. Georg	22	Eutendorf	48-1355
WELLER, John	34	Ulrichshausen	52-0515
WELLHAUSEN, F. (m)	37	Krueckeberg	52-0652
A. (f) 31, C. (f) 16, M. (f) 14, J. (m) 4			
WELLIGE, Joseph		Schermede	54-1575
Anton			
WELLIN, Franz	32	Andresone	54-1676
Maria 34, Agnes 10, Franz 7, Andrea 9m			
WELLINGHAUS, Heinr	24	Dissen	47-0918
WELLMANN, Justine	23	Meyenburg	53-1070
WELLMEIER, Henriet	8	Lengerich/Pr	52-1432
WELLNER, Margareth	21	Donau	53-0905
WELLNER, Th.	46	Bavaria	50-0311
WELLS, Clarence	23	France	48-1015
WELPHAUSEN, Meyer	26	Archshofen	54-0053
WELSCH, Barbara	28	Traeuan	54-1566
WELSCH, Joh.	28	Vaibach	54-1078
WELSCH, Johann	44	Koppelsdorf	53-0825
Barbara 45, Elisabeth 15, Anna Barbara 13			
Margaretha 11, Augusta 7			
WELSCHER, John	19	Cronach	53-0914
WELSU, G.	16	Scheiden	51-0517
WELZEL, Johann	18	Weissenstedt	53-0475
WEMSCHE, Friedrike	27	Bochlitz	48-1131
WENCKE, Louise	36	Middelhausen	51-1438
WENCKE, Ludwig	34	Bayerneusbruc	51-1438
Louise 36, Auguste 5, Gottlieb Rob 3			
WENDAUER, Heinrich	10	Wangen	50-1067
WENDE, Gottfried	29	Goerlitz	53-0888
WENDEHACK, August	23	Braunschweig	53-0320
Doris 28			
WENDEHACK, Julius	26	Braunschweig	54-0872
WENDEL, Heinrich	19	Achim	52-1512
WENDEL, Rosine	20	Wuertemberg	52-0895

NAME	AGE	RESIDENCE	YR-LIST
Friedrich 24			
WENDELKEN, Gesche	22	Meinertshagen	54-1575
WENDELKEN, Henry	18	Hagen	53-0991
WENDELKER, Georg	16	Worpswede	51-0460
WENDELKIN, Gesche	22	Meinertshagen	54-1575
WENDELKIN, Johann	31	Charleston NC	54-1716
WENDELMUTH, Ch. W.	34	Dittleben/Got	52-0960
WENDEMEYER, Georg	29	Warburg	50-0292
WENDISCH, Wilhelm	23	Kirchheim	53-1070
WENDLER, Kunigunde	18	Weisdorf	53-0637
WENDROTH, Georg	42	Dagobertshaus	51-1062
Elisabeth 52, George 20, Johann 10			
Martha 12, Conrad 27			
WENDT, David	22	Langenzlau	48-0951
WENEN, van Antony	45	Dordrecht	49-0912
Johanna 48, Maria 20, Bastian 17			
Antonia Joh. 12, Herbert 11, Johannes 10			
Antony 5			
WENER, Michael	3	-jenhausen	48-0260
WENG, Mich.	19	Schwabach	52-1129
WENGER, Joseph	27	Salzmos/Bav.	54-1092
WENGERT, Marie	19	Grossassbach	49-0352
WENHAUSEN, Sophie	14	Wremen	47-0828
WENIG, Johann	26	Ettenhausen	53-0928
WENISCH, Georg	17	Aibach	52-1304
WENK, Marie		Buedingen	54-1371
WENNEKING, Anna	22	Hannover	49-0329
WENNER, Christine	29	Darmstadt	48-1355
Justus 8, Joh. Georg 6, Wilh. 4			
Christiane 6m			
WENTE, Heinrich	16	Mehringen	52-1452
WENTE, Heinrich	20	Hannover	50-1317
WENTEL, William	27	Mittelruessel	49-0737
WENTERNITZ, Heinr.	22	Prag	48-1131
Hen. 20			
WENTEROTH, Anna El	21	Remsfeld	51-0352
WENTHE, Friedrich	30	Poggenhagen	52-0563
Sophie 30			
WENTINGER, Marg.	31	Kornhoechstad	52-0563
WENTSEL, Johanne C	39	Untergreistau	49-0324
WENTTE, Johanne	32	Boston	52-1410
Charles 8, William 6			
WENTZEL, Wilh'mine	22	Angelhausen	52-1304
WENTZELMANN, H. N.	19	Magdeburg	53-1016
WENZEL, A. (f)	17	Eutendorf	54-1341
WENZEL, Andr.	27	Kaltenbrun/Sa	52-0960
WENZEL, Joh Philip	53	Zeitloss	51-1101
Joh Philipp 12, Dorothea 9			
WENZEL, Louise	45	Feuerbach	54-1554
Elise 20, Sophie 13			
WENZLER, Ana Marie	21	Neukirch/Cbrg	52-1332
WERB, Magd.	27	Humrechtshaus	54-1283
WERB, Michael	48	Humrechtshaus	54-1283
Margarethe 44, Maria 22, Margarethe 20			
Bernhard 11, Michael 9, Marianne 4			
Ferdinand by			
WERBACH, Louis	20	Meiningen	52-0895
WERBE, J.F. (m)	20	Gestendorf	49-0574
WERCHAN, Adolph		Herseburg	54-1168
WERDENBERG, Henry	49	Oldenburg	54-1724
WERGHOLD, John	25	Verden	54-1341
WERHE, Georg	23	New York	52-0563
WERKER, Carl	25	Altenburg	49-0413
WERKMEISTER, Soph.	26	Scharmbekstot	50-1067
WERMANN, Christoph	25	Neuenwalde	53-0991
WERMEIER, Arnold	27	Lengerich/Pr.	52-1432
Elisabeth 27, Friedrich 10m			
WERMEIR, Franz	21	Emsdetten	48-0260
WERMERR, Franz	21	Emsdetten	48-0260
WERNEBURG, Georg	25	Hessia	50-0311
WERNECKE, Andrew	57	Herringen	48-0951
Charl. A. 21, Ernst 18			
WERNECKE, F.F.	25	Natzugen	53-0435
WERNECKE, Henry	39	Lipprechtrode	48-0053
WERNER, Abraham	39	Offenbach/Bav	54-1452
Friederike 30, Hedwig 10, Rosa 8, Ernst 6			
Ida 4			
WERNER, Andrew	54	Nebonitz	53-0991
WERNER, Anna	22	Arolsen	54-1554
WERNER, Aug.	30	Dresden	54-1168
WERNER, Carl	24	Dreba	52-1625
WERNER, Carl	18	Cur Hessen	53-0557
WERNER, Carl	18	Kur-hessen	53-0557
WERNER, Ernest	45	Metzgels	53-0582
Eva Maria 32, Wilhelmine 11			
Cath. Maria 10, August 7, Ferdinand 11m			
WERNER, F. (m)	29	Gotha	48-0445
WERNER, Friedrich	32	Zella/Sachsen	54-0965
Emilie 26, Laura 2			
WERNER, Georg	22	Marburg	53-0590
Henriette 20			
WERNER, Georg	22	Goettingen	50-1317
WERNER, Heinr.	39	Langelsheim	49-0324
WERNER, Heinrich	25	Koenigslutter	54-1282
Caroline 53, Wilhelm 14, Theodor 11			
Carl 29, Julie 36, Carl 12, Louis 10			
Hermann 7, Fritz 18			
WERNER, Joh.	70	Harterode	51-1796
WERNER, Joh. G.	18	Hannover	50-1317
WERNER, Johann	70	Harterrode	51-1796
WERNER, Joseph	34	Coburg	54-1094
WERNER, Joseph	24	Amoeneburg	51-0352
WERNER, Joseph	27	Knetzgau	50-0379
Daniel 19			
WERNER, Kunigunde	13	Langelsheim	49-0324
WERNER, Ludwig	27	Weimar	54-0872
WERNER, Maria	25	Pohlen	48-1184
WERNER, Valentin	42	Wachtdorf	52-1362
WERNER, Wilhelm	15	Wetzlar	53-0590
WERNER, Wilhelm	25	Zabboden	48-1184
Maria 25			
WERNING, Christina	29	Emsdetten	53-1062
WERNLEIN, Anna	22	Ehlmannsfurth	49-1106
WERSTERLING, Marg.	24	Mittelhauser	53-0825
WERTH, Johann	26	Wasmuethhause	53-0320
WERTH, John	36	Prussia	54-1724
WERTHEIM, Israel	33	Mettwitz/Bav.	53-0628
WERTHEIM, Meyer	24	Rothenburg	53-0991
WERTHEIM, Roessche	17	Angenrod	53-1062
WERTHEIMER, Jacob	68	Medwitz	48-0887
Helene 32, Mathilde 18, Moritz 33			
WERTHEIMER, Simon	25	Roth	51-0352
WERTHELEIN, Gottl.	16	Weiler	50-0379
WERTHMANN, Hugo	27	Eilenburg	51-1160
WERWINGEL, Heinr.	30	Wetschen	53-1062
Stinau 22, August 1			
WESELOH, Anna	22	Leeste	53-1164
WESEMANN, C.H.	23	Genhorst/Hann	48-0053
WESEMANN, Heinr.	22	Pyrmont	49-1358
Mad. (f) 21			
WESEMANN, Heinrich	24	Loecum	50-1067
WESER, Eva	54	Huntsbach	53-0928
WESER, Joseph	51	Lauf	53-0928
Os. 45, Mar. 18			
WESP, Joh. Heinr.	37	Bremen	53-1000
WESSEL, Cath.	19	Alfhausen	51-1160
WESSEL, Clemens		Osnabrueck/Pr	50-0323
WESSEL, Henry	20	New York	51-0326
WESSELMAN, Herman	24	Rorup	48-0951
WESSELS, Cathrine	22	Bremen	49-0329
WESSELS, Friedrich	36	Pannerhausen	52-1304
WESSELS, G. (m)	20	Habenhausen	49-0383
WESSELS, Heinr.	28	Hannover	51-0405
Hans. 15, Marie 21, Ilse 18			
WESSELS, John	18	Lesumstotel/H	51-0048
WESSELS, John Hell	19	Bremen	51-1725
WESSELS, Wilhelm	23	Maven	51-0352
WESSELS, Wilhlmine	23	Prussia	52-1432
WESSER, Wilhelm	26	Oesenberg	53-0590
WESSING, Joh. Died	26	Brunninghorst	48-1184
Caroline 30, Sophie 6m			
WESSMANN, Regine	19	Konigsbronn	51-1796
WESTDORFER, Cather	18	Bavaria	50-0311
WESTEN, Auguste		Neuwied	49-0912
WESTERCAMP, Marie	54	Essen	52-1410
Johanne 18			

NAME	AGE	RESIDENCE	YR-LIST
WESTERDORF, Bernh.	35	Voerden	54-0872
wife 22, baby 5			
WESTERFELD, Wilh.	42	Gramberg	53-1086
Katharine 33, Elisabeth 60, Maria 5			
Engel 3			
WESTERMEIER, Marie	21	Leutkirch	53-0435
WESTHOLD, W. (m)	40	Dessen	52-0652
Cath. 37, J. (m) 12, M. (f) 6m			
WESTKAMP, Bd. Gd.	26	Alstaette	48-0269
WESTMANN, Louise		Pyrmont	53-1016
WESTMEYER, Cath.	21	Hessen	52-0699
WESTPHAL, Heinrich	32	Liegnitz	52-1105
WESTPHAL, Theodor	29	Gerzi	54-1297
WETKEN, J.G. (m)	16	Werschen	49-0324
WETTE, Crescense	18	Empfingen	52-0279
WETTE, Sophie	25	Munster	49-0413
WETTERICH, Georg	33	Rosswalden	48-1131
A. (m) 25, D. (f) 20, F. (m) 16			
M. (f) 35, N. (m) 40, V. (m) 30			
WETTERLEFSKY, Carl	31	Gravens	54-1371
WETTERMANN, Mich.	25	Mittelruessel	49-0737
WETTERN, v. der C.	24	Braunschweig	51-0352
WETTERNN, Friedr.	17	Blankenbach	48-0284
Martha 19			
WETTFELD, Gustav	25	Moers	48-0260
WETTSTEIN, Heinr.	32	Barmen	48-0565
WETTSTEIN, Theodor	36	Barmen	48-0565
Lisette 40, Theodor 12, Otto 10, Lina 10			
Hermann 8, Pauline 6, Adolph 3, Laura 9m			
WETZEL, Henry	18	Thalhausen/He	50-0323
WETZEL, Nic.	22	Svet	53-1016
WETZEL, W.	23	Dumburg	51-0517
WETZEN, Anna		Leerte	51-0756
WETZLAR, Julius	33	Leipzig	48-1243
WEUB, Valet	24	Nauheim	54-0830
WEUDLER, Carl H.J.	40	Uhlstedt	47-0918
WEUHE, Wilhelm	24	Luechow	54-1297
WEYFAHRT, Johann	28	Rothenkirchen	52-1464
WEYHLEB, Friedmann	31	Tauhart	52-1148
Christiane 30, Maria 6, Carl 4, Eduard 2			
WEYL, Fanny	36	Fuerth	52-1410
WEYL, Maria	20	Farmbach	51-1455
WEYMANN, Adam	24	Cronberg	52-1101
Elisabeth 29			
WEYMASTER, Joh.	30	Hannover	54-1168
Catharine 30			
WEZEN, Friedr.	28	Obberhibbe	47-0762
WHEI, Michel	49	Ahldorf	52-1101
WHELM, Therese	21	Dermbath	51-1588
WHERMANN, Charlott	18	Destel	52-1200
Anna Maria 16			
WHILLMER, Peter	36	Neuenschmied	51-1588
WIBBELSMANN, Elis.	30	Glane	52-1105
WICH, Barbara	32	Drossdorf/Bav	52-1620
WICH, M. (f)	28	Hoefliss	47-0868
WICH, Nicolaus	18	Mettwitz	53-0324
WICHEN, Johann	25	Westerholz/Ha	52-0351
WICHERING, Wilhelm	23	Bohmte	50-1236
WICHHAGEN, Casper	27	Berge	54-0882
WICHHARDT, H. (m)	21	Wolfhagen	52-1512
WICHMANN, A. (m)	23	Donhelbe	54-0918
WICHUM, Ehregott	25	Schalkan	49-0574
WICHURN, Heinr.	30	Meinsen	52-1321
WICK, Anne B.	25	Mittelruessel	49-0737
WICKE, Friedrich	17	Bremen/Bremen	53-0475
WICKELAND, Heinr.	20	Bremen	51-1686
WICKER, Anna	22	Maden/K.-Hess	52-1332
WICKLAGE, Wilh.	24	Polle	51-0460
WICKLEIN, Conr.	28	Doerfles	51-1160
WIDDELKUMP, J. Her	51	Badbergen	50-1132
Cath. Marie 56, Johann 20, Cath. Marie 16			
WIDEMEYER, Anna	21	Luesche	52-0563
WIDMANN, Christian	23	Schrohenhause	54-0850
WIDMANN, Fr.	28	Schnurrfeld	54-1283
WIDMANN, Sabine	38	Wien	54-1283
Pauline 14			
WIEBE, Fr.	20	Bremen	52-1625
WIEBE, Lewis	29	Manausloh	53-0914

NAME	AGE	RESIDENCE	YR-LIST
Dorothee 23, Caroline 9m			
WIEBER, Franziska	27	Kappel	52-0370
WIEBER, Mar. Cath.	25	Dasigacker	49-1358
WIEBERS, J. (f)	23	Voerde	52-0652
WIECHEL, Friedrich	34	Mecklenburg	51-1725
WIECHING, Anton	25	Emsdetten/Pr.	50-0323
WIECHMANN, Carsten	23	Buettel	54-0987
WIECHMANN, Heinr.		Hannover	54-0987
WIECK, Ch.	20	Heilbronn	49-0329
WIEDAU, Heinrich	18	Bassum	50-0366
WIEDEBURG, Carl	28	Lobenstein	49-0574
WIEDEHOLD, M.	25	Frankfurt	51-1084
WIEDEMANN, Amanda	25	Sachsen	53-0590
WIEDEMANN, Anton	21	Dalkingen	53-0435
WIEDEMANN, Carl	25	Forst	52-1625
Maria 23			
WIEDEMANN, Joh.	22	Topfheim	54-1168
WIEDEMANN, Johann	33	Wehringen	54-1371
Walburga 33			
WIEDEMANN, Joseph	28	Forst/Baden	48-0053
WIEDEMANN, Marg.	23	Nordling	53-0590
WIEDEMAYER, August	37	Eltingen	51-1639
Cathrina 43			
WIEDEMEYER, Friedr	40	Hannover	54-0987
WIEDENFELD, Wlhmne	37	Lennep	49-0574
Julia 18, Alwina 12, Charlotte 8			
Albert 4			
WIEDENHOFF, Julius	32	Lippstadt	54-1092
WIEDER, Joseph	28	Burg	52-1580
Amalie 31			
WIEDERSPATRER, Fr.	26	Salmuenster	53-0825
Elisabeth 26			
WIEDITZ, Bernhard	23	Abterode	54-1282
WIEDMANN, Fr'drike	26	Leonberg	52-0351
WIEDMANN, Joh Gott	25	Stuttgart/Wrt	52-0351
Friederike 26			
WIEDMANN, Paul	27	Katzwangen	52-1580
WIEGAERTNER, Ursel	51	Dormitz	53-1023
WIEGAND, Anna	22	Salzungen	52-0370
WIEGAND, Carl Th.	36	Basdorf	48-1184
Clara 35, Theodor 11, Amalia 8			
Catharine 6, Michael 3			
WIEGAND, David	38	Hersfeld	51-0405
WIEGAND, J.G.	30	Mosheim	53-1016
Minna 28, Maria 5, Philipp 4			
WIEGAND, Joh. Adam	21	Eiterfeld/Hes	51-1532
WIEGAND, Joseph	18	Borgentreich	54-0882
WIEGAND, Louise	47	Goettingen/Ha	52-1620
Rosa 17			
WIEGAND, Marg.	21	Eiterfeld	52-0515
Rened (f) 30			
WIEGERING, Rosine	24	Bremen	51-0352
WIEGMANN, Diedr.	31	Gehlbergen	53-1016
Margarethe 26, Kosmus 8, Diedrich 4			
Heinrich 1			
WIEGMANN, H.	38	Uhrbach	52-0558
WIEGMANN, Heinrich	17	Heimsen/Pr.	51-1725
WIEGMANN, Marie	28	Nienburg	50-0021
WIEGNER, Amalie	18	Leipzig	53-1062
WIEGREFE, Johann	29	Luchbo	48-1131
WIEHE, Christian	59	Lippe	54-0882
Christoph 21, Friederich 15			
Wilhelmine 18			
WIEHE, Henry	28	Hoja	48-1209
WIEKE, August	17	Prussia	49-0329
WIELAND, Adolph F.	36	Kentald	48-1131
WIELAND, Louise C.	21	Reichenberg	49-0352
WIELAND, Marie	32	Hereldinge	52-1101
WIELENBERG, Heinr.	20	Damme	48-0101
WIELMANN, Fresiene	48	Albruek	53-0905
Fritz 18, Philippina 23, Albertina 16			
Barbara 13			
WIEMANN, Friedrike	17	Frankenhausen	54-0918
WIEMANN, Rosalie	22	Burgkunstadt	51-1035
WIEMAS, Jos.	16	Rombeck	52-0515
WIEMER, Anna	33	Drisau	52-1304
Theresia 8, Caspar 6			
WIEMER, Jacob	28	Wien	48-0260

NAME	AGE	RESIDENCE	YR-LIST
Louise 24			
WIENANDT, William	34	Gr. Wasseiwit	50-0323
WIENECK, Johann	26	Humbressen	52-1464
WIENECKE, Georg	14	Schoningen	54-1297
WIENECKE, Heinrich	45	Albertshausen	54-1297
Georgine 34, Heinrich 13, Georg 11			
Friederich 4			
WIENECKE, Johannes	29	Humbressen/He	51-1532
Ana Louise 22			
WIENER, Adolph	34	Koeln	53-1000
WIENER, Heymann	18	Schwerzenz	53-1164
WIENER, Julius W.	28	Schneeberg	53-0435
WIENER, Ludwig	23	Breslau	53-1000
Adolph 34			
WIENERS, Friedr. W	30	Roschitz	48-1131
WIENERS, Friedrich	40	Warburg	50-0021
WIENFELDER, David	27	Merschenbach	51-1640
WIENHOLT, Joseph	20	Muenster	50-0021
WIENHUSER, Anton	22	Lichtenau/Pr.	51-1532
WIENITZKY, Carl	48	Wittingen/Boe	54-1092
Anna 32, Carl 14, Johanna 12, Emanuel 8			
Johann 6, C. 6m			
WIENTGE, Hermann	21	Osnabrueck	53-1016
WIERHAKE, Anna	11	Babber	53-1086
WIERTH, Doroth.	16	Allswerd/Pr.	52-0960
WIESE, August	30	Greene	54-1371
WIESE, Carl	28	Bremen	54-0872
WIESE, Christian	38	Lehmershagen	50-0323
Johanne Wilh 32, John Henry 7			
Henriette 10m			
WIESE, Friedr.	32	Doernthen/Han	52-1332
WIESE, Heinrich	42	Schoffstadt	49-1106
WIESENBURG, Heinr.	59	Hopfgarten	54-0987
Sibille 56, Nicolaus 31			
WIESENPFAD, Magdal	23	Borndorf	49-0574
WIESENTHAL, Georg	27	Wanfried	52-1661
WIESER, Elcopha		Wolmedingen	54-1443
Irene			
WIESER, P. (m)	33	Hoeckersried	53-0435
A.M. (f) 30, Anna 1			
WIESER, Therese	33	Walzhude	51-1245
WIESING, Heinr.	29	Benningsen	49-0574
WIESMANN, C. (m)	24	Elte	49-0416
G. (f) 26			
WIESMEIYER, Marcus	25	Regensburg	54-0903
WIESNER, Gustav	26	Schlesien	54-0918
WIESSNER, Georg	25	Berlin	52-0895
WIESSNER, Moritz	28	Dresden	52-1129
WIETING, Betty	24	Delmenhorst	50-1067
WIETING, Ludwig	27	Bremervoerde	51-1035
Charlotte 32			
WIETRARD, Heinrich	30	Lachfezhagen	48-1131
WIETZKE, Friedr.	25	Gumtow	54-1078
WIGAND, John Georg	19	Eiderfeld	53-0628
John Georg 18			
WIGAND, Margarethe	25	Frankenhein	47-0672
WIGAND, Valentin	25	Schafhausen	47-0672
WIGANT, Elisabeth	27	Salzingen	53-0324
WIGANT, Johannes	25	Eisenach/Pr.	52-1432
WIGEROLZ, Carl	45	Dresden	50-0379
Amalie 40, Adelheid 9			
WIGT, Meta	15	Misselwarden	54-0987
WILCKE, H. (m)	22	Sondershausen	48-0445
WILCKE, Wm.	27	Heltrungen	53-0492
WILCKENS, Meta	23	Bremen	53-1013
WILD, Carl	24	Ensingen	54-1717
WILD, Elisabeth	45	Lichtenfels	54-0872
Eva 6			
WILDERER, Cath.	24	Waldenbuck	53-1023
WILDERHUSEN, H.(m)	22	Lintig	49-0329
WILDERSEN, Jos.	22	Bindersdorf	51-1796
WILDHAGEN, Christ.	28	Pikeburg/Hann	51-1796
WILDHAUER, Carl	26	Dorhau/Bav.	53-0628
WILDMAN, Joh. M.	18	Mittelruessel	49-0737
WILDSCHUETZ, Karl	27	Wetterberg	54-1554
WILHARM, Chr. (m)	28	Schirneichen	52-1321
WILHAUER, Jacob	25	Berwangen/Bad	52-0117
WILHELM, Adam	21	Breitenbach	51-1686
WILHELM, Anton	37	Andressen/Boh	54-1676
Johanna 30, Carl 8, Anton 6, Franz 9m			
WILHELM, Aug.	15	Batsche	54-0987
WILHELM, Carl	32	Holzappel	54-1371
Sophie 18			
WILHELM, Charles	25	Solingen	48-0406
WILHELM, Johannes	23	Elingrode	52-1362
WILHELM, Joseph	43	Andreson	54-1676
Anna 32, Maria 54, Franz 4, Joseph 6m			
WILHELM, Louis	18	Zwickau/Sax.	50-0323
WILHELM, Nicol.	50	Ziegenhagen	52-0563
Cath. E. 49, Wilhelm 21, Johannes 15			
Ludwig 9, Heinrich 8			
WILHELMI, Julius	21	Baden	48-1355
Franz 26			
WILHELMS, Caroline	22	Hohenauffenbe	53-0838
WILHELMY, C. (m)	25	Wunstorf	50-0439
WILKE, Aug.	20	Dreta	49-0574
WILKE, Carl	30	Colberg/Pr.	52-0960
WILKE, Carol.	41	Guelitz	54-1282
Rud. 21, Adolph 19, Minna 17, Eduard 15			
Ferdinand 9, Emma 7, Heinrich 5			
WILKE, Caroline	29	Druette/Braun	52-1332
WILKE, Friedr.	28	Mengeringhaus	49-0383
Ida 21			
WILKE, Friedrich H	22	Wetschen	53-1062
WILKE, Heinrich	27	Braunschweig	54-0830
Emilie 24			
WILKE, Johann	26	Artern	50-0379
WILKE, Wilhelmine	38	Renig	49-0781
WILKENING, Conrad	28	Sohldorf	50-1132
WILKENING, Heinr.	27	Soldorf	51-1101
WILKENING, Soph.	57	Grosshegsdorf	53-1086
WILKENS, Eide (m)	18	Midlum	53-1000
WILKENS, Heinr.	19	Scharmbek	51-0326
WILKENS, Rebecka	19	Bremen	51-0500
WILKER, Francisca	30	Emsdetten	48-0260
WILKIE, Albert	29	Mittelruessel	49-0737
WILKONING, W. (m)	30	Schneeren	54-1341
Charlotte 26, child 6m, H. (m) 45			
Mary 55, Henry 16			
WILL, Cath. Marg.	17	Schwarzenbach	54-1371
WILL, Christina	22	Porkholz	52-0515
WILL, Diedrich	17	Bruettendorf	54-1371
WILL, Elisabetha	25	Kulmbach	53-1062
WILL, Emil	26	Hersfeld	54-1168
Johannes 17, Eduard 20			
WILL, Georg	37	Schoenbrun	48-0269
WILL, Johann	33	Stadelhofen	53-1023
WILL, Tillmann	30	Niederschelde	49-0781
WILLE, Amalie	19	Bremen	51-0500
WILLE, Anna	31	Coburg	50-0439
Marie 18, Heinrich 14, Ludwig 12			
S. Dorothea 27			
WILLE, Gottlieb	40	Querfurt	53-1000
Pauline 3			
WILLE, Heinrich	25	Willershausen	54-0053
WILLE, Martin	20	Seilberg	51-1686
WILLE, Philipp	29	Riepen	47-0672
Dorothea 27			
WILLE, S. Dorothea	27	Hosten	47-0672
WILLENDORF, August	21	Arnstadt	54-0850
WILLENSDORF, Conr.	27	New York	50-0379
WILLENTROP, Maria	30	Bremen	49-1106
WILLERS, Heinr.	36	Oldenburg	50-1236
WILLGEROTH, Heinr.	32	Minden	53-1023
WILLHARM, Cath.	43	Kreutzrehn	47-0672
WILLHARM, Philipp	35	Osten	47-0672
Catharina 43, Philipp 4			
WILLHAUSEN, Hen'tt	24	Hoeffingen	51-0405
WILLIG, Johann	17	Gotha	53-0473
Johanna 19			
WILLITZER, Andreas	24	Mittelruessel	49-0737
WILLKER, Herm.	24	Osnabrueck	52-1512
WILLKER, Mary	17	Endorf/Hes.-D	50-0323
WILLMANN, Henry	18	Huntlosen	53-0888
WILLMEIER, Friedr.	40	Lengerich/Pr.	52-1432
Marie 42, Friedrich 12, Wilhelmine 10			

NAME	AGE	RESIDENCE	YR-LIST
Henriette 8, Marie 6			
WILLMER, Auguste	23	Herzberg	51-0460
WILLMER, Friedr.	29	New York	54-1078
WILLMERS, Franz	26	Warburg	50-0292
Nette 20			
WILMER, Heinr. Chr	28	Brackwedde	48-1355
WILMS, Friedr.	34	Berlin	54-1168
WILMS, Gustav	30	Bremen	53-1164
WILSON, Gustaf	25	Philadelphia	52-1452
WILTS, Doris	47	Hessen	50-1067
WILZTHUM, Georg	28	Bayern	53-0590
WIMMEL, Martha	19	Cassel	52-1321
WIMMEL, William	24	Mittelruessel	49-0737
WIMMER, Anna Cath.	21	Edersfeld	54-1371
WIMMER, August	42	Warburg	48-0269
Eduard 14, Maria 53, Sophia 10			
WIMMER, Franz	29	Neuttenkam	54-1371
Therese 29, Therese 2, Anna 57			
Crescentia 34, Johanna 33, Franziska 32			
Caroline 8			
WIMMER, Martin	49	Schoellnstein	54-1371
Theresia 53			
WIMMER, Mathias	36	Bachham	52-1200
WIMMER, Michael	35	Alkhofen	54-1371
Marie 32, Therese 9, Catharine 6			
Andreas 55			
WIMMER, Peter	33	Linz	54-1371
Maria 33, Maria 14, Elise 9, Johann 9			
Franz 11m, Johann 30			
WINCKER, Joseph	26	Emsdetten	48-0260
WINCZEK, Andreas	28	Reichenhall/B	52-1620
WIND, de N. (f)	34	St.Thomas	49-0413
WINDELS, Wilh'mine	20	Bassum	52-0699
WINDENBURG, Ludwig	25	Giersleben	54-0930
WINDHAM, H. (m)	30	Nienburg	54-1341
Caroline 30, Sophie 6, William 3, son 6m			
WINDHOFER, Claus	42	Wien	49-0324
WINDHORST, Ferd.	24	Tarmstedt	54-1371
WINDISCH, Margaret	26	Muehlberg	54-1283
WINDISCH, Valentin	18	Pommersfeld	47-0918
WINDLER, Carl	22	Heiligersdorf	50-0439
WINDLER, Gesche	30	Binkel	49-0574
WINDLER, Klem. Aug	20	Berching	49-1358
WINDLER, Rebecca	21	Alten Buellst	49-0574
WINDMEYER, J. Gerd	26	Alstaette	48-0269
WINDSCH, James G.	27	Mittelruessel	49-0737
WINDSHEIMER, M.(m)	33	Rodenburg	49-0416
WINDUS, Caspar	35	Hofgeismar	54-1566
Marie 40			
WINGENAKEL, Aug'te	30	Leipzig	48-1131
WINGENBURG, H.	43	Wienhagen	47-0762
Marie 31, Heinrich 4, Wilhelm 1			
WINHEIM, Otto	23	Homberg	52-0699
WINHERT, Cha. (f)	26	Bunech	53-0435
WINIGEN, Johann	43	Maehren	53-1000
Monika 42, Franziska 15			
WINK, Eva	29	Kurhessen	53-0557
WINK, Johannes	34	Andershausen	51-0460
Elisabeth 35			
WINKEL, August	26	Grossen--	50-0439
Therese 26, Tobias by			
WINKELHAUSEN, Alw.	23	Leichlingen	53-0991
WINKELMANN, Cath.	23	Hohenaverberg	50-0323
Herman Fried 15			
WINKELMANN, Friedr	25	Mittelruessel	49-0737
WINKELMANN, H.F.	40	Osnabrueck	54-1168
WINKELMANN, J.F.	17	Hohenaverberg	49-0383
WINKELMANN, Marie	48	Armsen	53-0838
WINKELMANN, Theres	24	Laer	53-0991
WINKELS, Heinrich	46	Staphorst	49-0912
Johann 20, Lucas 18			
WINKELS, Jantje		Arnshausen	49-0912
WINKELSITH, Chr'ne	23	Delmenhorst	49-0574
WINKELVOSS, Aug.	20	Ruettgerode	48-0269
WINKERS, Martha	58	Holstein	51-1588
George 20, Elies 18, Henry 16			
WINKLER, Alois	36		54-1716
WINKLER, Ann Mary	54	Ibbenbueren/P	48-0053

NAME	AGE	RESIDENCE	YR-LIST
Auguste 3, Friedrich 23			
WINKLER, Anne	27	Baiern	54-1724
WINKLER, Auguste	3	Albany	48-0053
WINKLER, Barbara	24	Killmuenz	51-1640
WINKLER, Carl Gott	19	Siebenen	51-1101
WINKLER, Charlotte	19	Schwerin	53-0991
WINKLER, Charlotte	14	Rotenburg	54-1282
WINKLER, Elise	32	Bossum/Hann.	50-0323
WINKLER, Franz	34	Sonnenberg	54-1371
WINKLER, Friedrich	23	Rochterbecken	48-0053
WINKLER, Joh Gotth	44	Siebenlehn	54-0987
Christiane 42, Pauline 18, Marie 17			
Anna 11, Aurora 7, Emilie 2			
WINKLER, Johann	28	Hasenbach	51-1588
WINKLER, Kunigunde	34	Schwabach	50-0439
Louise 9, Franz 15			
WINKLER, Kunigunde	43	Eilersbach	47-0918
Cathrina 19, Conrad 13			
WINKLER, L.	35	Erfurt	53-0914
WINKLER, Max	21	Breslau	52-1625
WINKLER, S.	35	Erfurt	53-0914
WINKLER, v. Mrs.	34	Cassel	48-1243
Marianna 10			
WINNE, Wilh.	20	Grabensdorf	54-1724
Char. 54			
WINNER, Johann	23	Gehede	54-0987
WINNIEK, Jos.	39	Muichowitz	54-1575
Maria 33, Anna 14			
WINNIG, August	35	Blankenburg	54-1371
Sophie 33, Caroline 9, Bertha 4, Otto 2			
WINNIG, Joseph	32	Maehren	53-1000
Magdal. 32, Joseph 6, Augustin 4, Aloys 3			
Joh. 2			
WINTER, Anna	15	Witzebricht	54-0965
WINTER, Balsar	23	Obersheim	48-1184
WINTER, Bernhard	17	Emsdetten	54-0903
Franciska 28			
WINTER, C. (f)	23	Limbach	50-0746
Ch. (f) 3			
WINTER, Christian	26	Frahausen	50-0379
WINTER, Conr.	30	Hoefling	52-1129
WINTER, Dorothea	19	Niedermoln	53-1023
WINTER, Elisabeth	24	Emsdetten	48-0260
WINTER, Friedrich	23	Friedrichschw	54-1717
August 21			
WINTER, Friedrich	30	Henne	54-1168
WINTER, H.V. (m)	38	Alsfeld	49-0324
WINTER, Heinrich	19	Northen	53-0585
WINTER, Heinrich	22	Quetzen	54-1554
WINTER, Henriette	35	Einbeck	54-0053
WINTER, Ignaz	17	Klein Auheim	52-1512
WINTER, Joh.	26	Bug	52-0693
WINTER, Magdalene	21	Weinberg	52-1661
Caecilie 26			
WINTER, Marie	37	Frankenhausen	50-1236
Mine 10, Luise 7			
WINTER, Meta	20	Hannover	50-0311
WINTER, Philipp	28	Homberg	52-0279
Anna Loise 28, Johann 4, Anna Christ. 3			
WINTER, Renade	21	Rodach	53-0267
WINTER, W. (m)	23	Altenbruch	51-1640
WINTER, Wilhelm	23	Schwarzach	53-0838
WINTERLE, Maria	34	Muenchen	52-1321
Johanna 9m			
WINTERLE, Moses	29	Muenchen	52-1321
WINTERNITZ, Salmon	19	Muenchengraet	54-1078
WINTERS, Anthony	21	Marssel	53-1164
Claus 63			
WINTERSTELLER, Rup	24	Reichenhall	52-1423
Anton 19			
WINTJER, Carl	24	Lengerich	48-1015
WINTZENBURG, Aug.	16	Greinhausen	54-1443
WINTZER, Heinr.	23	Herford	53-1000
WINTZLER, Chr'tine	27	Noerten	53-1164
WINZCEK, G.	26	Schlawentzis	51-0757
Philippine 22			
WINZEK, Andreas	28	Reichenhall/B	52-1620
WINZELMEYER, Fr'ka	34	Heiligenberg	51-1245

NAME	AGE	RESIDENCE	YR-LIST
WINZER, Moriz	56	Dresden	50-1317
Wilhelmine 56, Anna 21, Eugen 20, Emma 18 Guido 16			
WIPKEN, Margareth	20	Bederkesa	50-1317
WIPPERMANN, Heinr.	23	Melle	54-1297
WIPPERN, Joh.	24	Niedersred/Br	52-1332
WIPPICH, Johann	26	Wartenburg	54-1452
WIREFELD, S. (m)	33	Aan	50-0746
WIRSCHING, Martin	55	Eisfeld	53-0914
Friederike 46, Albert 22, Eduard 20 Sigmund 17, Christine 15, Hermann 13 Rosalie 11, Ernest 7			
WIRSCHINK, Joseph	23	Heilbronn	52-1580
Margretha 20, Cathrina 6m			
WIRSING, Peter	16	Rossfeld	53-0267
WIRSTEIN, Marie	29	Empfingen	52-0279
WIRTH, Lorenz	27	Langendorf	54-1554
WIRTH, Margaretha	22	Wuestenselbit	53-0637
WIRTH, Margarethe	19	Buechelberg	54-1371
WIRTH, Math.	29	Neustadt	52-1512
WIRTH, Nicolaus	23	Stambach	53-0492
WIRTH, Robert	26	Breslau	50-0840
WIRTHENSOHN, Clem.	19	Muenster	50-0021
WIRTHMANN, Barb.	17	Scheubach	52-1625
WISBACH, Phillip	20	Cassel	52-1620
WISCH, Ludwig	44	Magdeburg	54-1371
WISCHERT, Andreas	24	Rineck	52-1625
WISCHHAUSEN, J.B.	22	Bloklande	51-0326
WISCHHOEFER, Aug.	21	Rehburg	53-1070
Sophie 27			
WISCHMEYER, Caspar	34	Osnabrueck	52-1362
Clara 30, Catharina 1			
WISCHMEYER, Chr(f)	24	Wellingen	54-1470
Christine 24			
WISCHMEYER, Fr.	38	Wellingen	54-1470
Margarethe 37, Catharine 9, Catharine 7			
WISCHMYER, Else	26	Ostercappeln	51-1455
WISKER, Valentin	28	Hessen	52-0699
WISPLAR, Martin	27	Ottenburg	52-0351
WISSENBACH, Wil'ne	46	Dillenburg	52-0807
WISSINGEN, Andr.	24	Utzwingen	54-1297
WISSMANN, Ch.	29	Ludwigslust	53-1164
Marianne 28			
WISSMANN, G.H.	28	Venne	53-1016
Maria 30, Juliane 8			
WISSMANN, M.E. (f)	24	W. Ollendorf	52-0960
WISSMER, Philipp	30	Winburg/Bav.	54-0965
WISSMETH, Barbara	27	Schneitenbach	54-0965
WISSMUTH, Joseph	33	Schneitenbach	54-0965
Barbara 6, Anna 45, Margretha 3			
WISSNER, Heinr.	39	Nordeck	53-1013
Elisabeth 29, Johannes 9, Adam 6 Elisabeth 3			
WISSNER, Natalie	18	Oelze	53-0585
WIST, Wilhelm	20	Detmold	54-1371
WITICHEN, Rebecca	15	Frischluneber	51-1160
WITJEN, Charl.	22	Dingen	48-0951
WITNER, Lisette	3-	Jena	49-1358
WITSCHEN, Anna	17	Sellstedt	51-0756
WITSCHEN, Claus	25	Beverstedt	51-1084
WITSCHEN, Heinr.	20	Hannover	50-1317
WITSCHENSKA, W.	19	Inowraclaw/Po	54-1283
Troma 50			
WITT, Adolphus	18	Koenigsberg	50-0840
WITTBURG, Wilhelm	30	Soest	48-0260
WITTE, Carl	21	Eichholz	49-0352
WITTE, Carl	23	Stolzenau	51-1035
Heinrich 8, Minna 3			
WITTE, Georg	32	Haidt	48-0887
WITTE, H. Heinrich	26	Luesche	52-0563
WITTE, Johann	18	Ebersdorf	49-0345
Diedrich 30			
WITTE, Lucie	22	Hannover	51-1725
WITTE, Sophie	24	Fresdorf/Hann	52-1332
WITTEKIND, Isaac	28	Kissen	54-1297
WITTEL, Adam	19	Hinterweiler	53-0320
WITTELSBERGER, Fr.	48	Sachsen	53-0590
WITTELSBERGER, Geo	28	Sachsen	53-0590

NAME	AGE	RESIDENCE	YR-LIST
WITTEMEYER, Heinr.	20	Hille	51-1455
WITTEMEYER, J Hein	19	Hille	51-1101
WITTENBERG, Betty	17	Willmers/Bav.	53-0628
WITTENBERG, Carl	24	Nordheim	51-1101
WITTENBERG, Fran'a	29	Braunschweig	54-1371
WITTHAHN, Heinrich	16	Ottersdorf	51-1101
WITTHAUER, Caspar	23	Ostheim	51-0405
WITTHUHN, Henry	27	Lodingsen	51-1588
WITTIBSCHLAEGER, A	52	Hornrieth	54-1717
Catharina 50			
WITTICH, Johannes	22	Herschlitt	48-0284
Martin 21, George 29, Anna Magd. 28 Valentin 3, Anna Marg. 3m			
WITTICH, Wilhelm	24	Dresden	53-0652
WITTIG, Adam	38	Bebra	47-0840
Anna Martha 34, Conrad 15, Sabine 12 Anna Cath. 9, Martha Elis. 7, Heinrich 4			
WITTIG, Charles	12	Alteschitz/Sa	50-0323
WITTIG, Herrmann	24	Coburg	53-0267
WITTISCH, Maria	21	Lispenhausen	53-1023
WITTKOPF, Anna	3	New York	54-1647
WITTKOWSKA, Minna	25	Berlin	48-1114
WITTKOWSKY, August	19	Minden	50-0366
WITTLEIN, Johann	30	Cronach	48-1355
WITTMAIR, Franz	32	Oetdorf	51-1035
Johannes 2			
WITTMANN, Adam	22	Oberhinbach	53-0652
WITTMANN, Andreas	19	Kreissdorf	53-0267
WITTMANN, Anna	21	Bavaria	53-0628
WITTMANN, C. (m)	23	Kingsheim	50-0746
WITTMANN, Carl	18	Bockenheim	51-1725
WITTMANN, Cath.	31	Walkersbrunn	52-0693
WITTMANN, Fanny	19	Fromberg	53-0582
WITTMANN, Joseph	38	Niederheking	52-1452
Anna Maria 35, Anna Maria 10, Anton 9 Elisabeth 7, Joseph 1, Hanne 3m			
WITTMANN, Mich.	48	Salzburg	53-0435
WITTMANN, Wolfgang	28	Nuernberg	51-0352
WITTNER, B. (f)	21	Bubenreuth	51-1160
WITTNEY, Heinrich	25	Savannah	52-1452
WITTORF, Wilhelm	30	Otterndorf	53-1016
WITTROCK, Heinrich	43	Grafengaldern	47-0672
Wilhelmine 44, Wilhelmine 11, Charlotte 9 Caroline 8			
WITTROCK, Wil'mine	44	Arensdorf	47-0652
WITTROCK, Wil'mine	11	Galdern	47-0672
WITTSCHEN, Fr.	32	Charleston	50-0366
Helene 30			
WITTSITIEN, Metta	17	Ottenburg	52-0351
WITTSTEIN, Fr.	21	Gotha	54-1470
Mary 26, daughter 9m			
WITTVER, Ernst	24	Greditzberg	50-1071
WITTVOGEL, Anna	24	Bremerhaven	50-0366
WITZELHOFER, T.(f)	35	Regensburg	53-0888
WITZER, Cath.	21	Laufen	51-1640
WITZHOLD, Johann	30	Magdeburg	50-1132
WITZIGMANN, Louise	22	Unterfulbach	50-0439
WITZSCHE, Carl	33	Meuchen	50-1071
WIX, Heinrich	18	Prussia	51-1725
WLECKE, Friedrich	18	Oldendorf	54-1554
WLEKEN, Maria Aug.	25	Osnabrueck	52-1512
WLENSHAGEN, Helene	36	Quackenbrueck	52-1512
WOBY, H. (m)	21	Rothhelmersha	54-1575
WOCHENHAUSER, Marg	19	Kleinsteinach	54-1283
WOCHER, Joh.	23	Langenargen	54-0987
Regine 25, Anton by			
WOCHER, Leopold	20	Baden	52-0699
WODWACKER, Joseph	20	Zamrsk/Bohm.	52-1304
WOEHLTJEN, Henry	18	Uphusen	53-0991
WOEHMER, Georg	39	Burgrupp	51-1438
Margret 27, Georg 2			
WOEHNER, Elisabeth	20	Untereldorf	50-0379
WOEHNER, Georg	23	Untereldorf	50-0379
WOEHNER, J. Valent	16	Rothenhof	54-1168
WOEHRER, Joseph		Churfasthmut?	54-1078
Rosine , child 9m			
WOELFEL, Adam	30	Boxdorf	52-0693
WOELFERTS, Wilh.		Freudenberg	53-0585

NAME	AGE	RESIDENCE	YR-LIST
Johanne , Emma , Olga			
WOELFL, Joh.	28	Wohleinsdorf	52-1129
Magd. 18, baby			
WOELFL, Magd.	18	Herzogswind	52-1129
WOELKER, Ann	24	Hattenbach	52-0652
WOELLE, Philipp	55	Boeckendorf	49-1106
Sophia 50, Engel 28, Sophia 24			
Charlotte 22, Heinrich 26, Engel 6m			
WOELTER, Carl	25	Hameln	52-1129
WOELTZEN, Heinrich	22	Uphausen	54-1297
WOEMPNER, Christ.	27	Hameln	54-0930
WOENER, Joh Friedr	18	Moehringen/Wu	52-0351
WOEPKING, Hein.	28	Evessen	52-1321
WOERDEHOFF, Schult	35	Wordehoff	54-1371
Julie 25			
WOERLEN, Christian	26	Noerdlingen	54-1297
WOERMANN, H.H. (m)	34	Enger	49-0329
WOERMERSBY, Louisa	67	New Jersey	48-1209
WOETZEN, Friedrike	29	Plauen	54-1647
WOEWARTH, Anna	16	Meiningen	51-1588
WOGLEHNER, Marie	32	Regensburg	53-0492
WOHFRUNN, Mary	16	Lauterberg	48-1131
WOHLER, Magdalene	65	Ottersberg	49-1358
WOHLERS, Heinrich	20	Ottersberg	49-1358
Magdalene 65			
WOHLERS, Joh Fried	35	Cuxhaven	51-1101
WOHLERS, Johann	16	Hasseln	50-0366
WOHLFAHRT, Adam	32	Aidhausen	47-0872
Margaretha 30, Dorothea 22			
WOHLFAHRT, Emilie	18	Bremen	48-0078
WOHLFAHRT, Johann	34	Neuburg	54-1716
WOHLFAHRT, Johann	48	Bayern	53-0590
Wilhelm 14, Elisabeth 9			
WOHLFAHRT, Peter	28	Kaufbimen	50-0379
WOHLFRAM, Mary	16	Lauterberg	48-1131
WOHLKEN, Theodor	16	Hannover	49-0329
WOHLLEBEN, Adolph	37	Waldenburg	54-1566
WOHLLEBEN, Friedr.	30	Lippstadt	53-1000
Carol. 26			
WOHLRATH, Karl	22	Sangerhausen	49-1106
WOHLTMANN, Hedwig	21	Aastedt	51-1101
WOHNHAS, Magdalena	17	Ebingen	53-1164
WOHNKE, Julius	30	Lippaene	53-1000
Johanne 29			
WOKEK, Friedrich	24	Koenigsberg	54-1452
Louise Amal. 20, August 3, Robert by			
WOLEY, H.	21	Rothhelmersha	54-1575
WOLF, (m)	25	Immelborn	53-0320
WOLF, Andr.	18	Gundliz	51-1455
WOLF, Andreas	30	Ottenreuth	53-1023
WOLF, Anna Marg.	21	Helldrit	53-0267
WOLF, Carl	29	Giessen	53-1086
Minna 27			
WOLF, Carl	18	Mittelruessel	49-0737
WOLF, Catharine	27	Heidelberg	51-0352
WOLF, Charles	28	Niederrosch	50-0840
WOLF, D. (m)	24	Waldenbron	49-0329
WOLF, Ernst Jul.		Katschenbroda	54-1575
WOLF, Friedrich	31	Tennessee	52-1620
Dorothea 28, Emilie 7, Eduard 6			
Emilie 16			
WOLF, G. (m)	26	Schoenbrun	49-0383
Johanna S. 22			
WOLF, Georg	36	Martelshausen	49-0574
Friederike 30, Friederike 5			
WOLF, Heinrich	23	Borstel	51-1101
WOLF, Heinrich	40	Rotenburg	51-0756
WOLF, Heinrich	20	Pottigo	54-0987
WOLF, Joh.	17	Dehlau	52-1129
WOLF, Johann	28	Mitteldorf	52-0693
WOLF, Johann	32	Liebenstein	50-1236
WOLF, Johann	25	Kaufbeuren	51-0352
WOLF, Johanna	32	Nuisberg	49-1106
WOLF, John	22	Rumstedt	52-0515
WOLF, Ludwig	21	Pfaffenstedt	52-0279
Friedr. Wm. 31			
WOLF, Philipp	30	Albstadt/Bav.	52-1423
WOLFEL, Georg	24	Letten	52-0693

NAME	AGE	RESIDENCE	YR-LIST
WOLFF, Amalie	27	Neustadt	54-1297
WOLFF, Andreas	18	Lauhend	54-0053
WOLFF, Anton	20	Wilderstadt	54-0053
WOLFF, Barbara	16	Lauf	53-1016
WOLFF, Caroline	48	Brackenheim	54-1371
WOLFF, Catharine	22	Wintersberg	47-0672
WOLFF, Catharine	69	Pruessburg	48-0260
Valentin 40, Kunigunde 37, Magaretha 27			
WOLFF, Cathrine	33	Bayern	53-0557
Magdalene 17			
WOLFF, Christian	36	Brunswick	50-0311
WOLFF, Elisabeth	24	Immelborn	54-0987
WOLFF, Gabriel	22	Velde	48-0260
WOLFF, George	32	Alstadt	51-1588
WOLFF, Gustav	26	Wolfenbuettel	50-1071
WOLFF, Heinrich	48	Nidda	54-1717
Barbara 36, Johannes 14, Heinrich 11			
Elisabetha 7, Wilhelm 4			
WOLFF, Hermann	32	Brake	53-0557
Wilhelm 34			
WOLFF, Johanna	20	Holtschberg	50-0439
WOLFF, John	32	Innsbrueck	53-0991
WOLFF, Julius	34	Wackerbartsru	53-0928
WOLFF, Ludwig	22	Waldenbronn	49-0329
WOLFF, Paul	28	Ziebnzig	53-0991
WOLFF, Paulus	30	Gundelsheim	54-1297
WOLFF, Rudolph	26	Hannover	51-1245
Aug. 25			
WOLFGRAMM, Cath.	24	Gehrde	50-1236
Adelheid 17			
WOLFNERSHAUSEN, C.	50	Bracht	54-1341
Mary 50, Charles 14			
WOLFRAM, Carl	22	Zella	49-0383
Christine 25, Friedrich 11m			
WOLFRAM, Chr. Lew.	30	Schleusingen	53-0991
WOLFRAM, Elisabeth	26	Pottigen	54-0987
WOLFRAM, Elise	45	Selbitz	49-1106
Johann 26			
WOLFRAM, Fr.	30	Erfurt	54-1647
Wilhelmine 36			
WOLFRAM, Johann	21	Naila	54-0930
WOLFRAM, Lor.	24	Quentel	54-1554
WOLFSCHMIDT, Kunig	21	Prettbraun	54-1283
WOLFSTEIN, Isaak	20	Korbach	51-1160
WOLFSTEIN, Samuel	27	Borgentreich	51-1160
Isaak 20			
WOLFSTICH, Theodor	21	Braunschweig	50-0323
WOLK, Jacob	41	Fulda	51-0405
WOLK, Lukas	26	Neustadt	49-1106
WOLKE, Friedrich	22	Holzhausen	52-1410
WOLKE, Wilhelm	55	Kohlgrund/Wal	53-0628
Wilhelmine 26			
WOLLENWEBER, Gottf	28	Neustadt	50-0840
Caroline 20, Hubert 1			
WOLLF, Sophia	23	Lemfoerde	54-0882
WOLLFROM, Heinrich	31	Naila	48-0565
Caroline 3			
WOLLIN, Therese	24	Geestendorf	50-0366
Antonia 3, Albert 11m			
WOLLINGS, Diedrich	64	Holzen	51-0756
WOLLMACHER, Theres	25	Bayern	53-0590
WOLLMANN, Joseph	25	Graetz	52-1580
WOLLRATH, Conr.	26	Wildenberg	51-1160
Conr. 6			
WOLLSTAEDTER, Bern	29	Hanau	53-0991
WOLTER, August	27	Ringelheim	52-1625
Friedrich 25			
WOLTER, Friedrich	30	Sulingen	53-1000
Sophie 31, Sophie 6, Anna 3, Dorothea 53			
WOLTERS, Carl Wilh	43	Weferling	54-0872
Wilhelmine 43, Georg 16, Johann 12			
Friedrich 6, Johanne 9, Anna 8, Marie 5			
WOLTERS, Elise	23	Hossel	53-0914
WOLTERS, Georg	51	Fescherhode/H	53-0475
Anna 44, Johann 19, Catharine 15			
Johann 9, Gesche 9, Hermann 7, Metta 7			
WOLTERS, J.H.	28	Bremen	53-0991
WOLTHER, Heinrich	36	Bayern	53-0590

NAME	AGE	RESIDENCE	YR-LIST
WOLTJEN, Anna	24	Delmenhorst	53-0590
WOMPNER, Ernst	29	Jetenburg	52-1321
WORCH, Hermann	33	Quedlinburg	49-0352
WORDMANN, Chr'tine	23	Bohnhorst	52-1661
WORNLEIN, Leonhard	28	Baiern	53-0585
WORTMANN, Franz H.	32	Osnabrueck	53-1016
WORTMANS, Rosette	24	Severns	53-0942
WOTJEN, Friederike	20	Scharmbeck	50-0366
WRAMPELMEIER, Fr'k	33	Cincinatti	52-0117
Auguste 23			
WRANNA, Louise	24	Bremen	54-0830
WRECK, Heinrich	16	Boestel	48-0269
WREDEN, Christoph	33	Stenstedt	52-0048
WRIGHT, Henry	13	Berlepech	48-1015
WRUSMANN, Thor.	21	Mittelruessel	49-0737
WUEBBERN, H.	17	Frischluneber	51-1160
WUEKENBERG, Carl	28	Wuekenberg	48-0406
WUELBERN, Johann	15	Appeln	50-0366
WUERFEL, Anton	58	Kratzau	54-0872
Marie 16, Marianne 18			
WUERFEL, Anton	30	Kratzau	54-0872
Barbara 25, Franz 4, Marie 3, Anton by			
WUERFEL, Friedrich	38	Bayreuth	53-1023
WUERTENBERGER, Jos	59	Steiermark	51-1035
Anna 40, Franz 11, August 8, Joseph 6			
Mathias 4			
WUERTTENBERGER, G.	23	Tuebingen	50-1317
WUERZEBACH, Maria	15	Hofgeismar	53-1062
Elisabeth 26			
WUERZLER, Friedr.	19	Kronichfeld	51-1438
WUEST, Adam	17	Heroldsbach	52-0960
WUESTEFELD, Benina	24	Hannover	54-1554
Katharina 30			
WUESTEFELD, Madame	29	Girboldehause	54-1566
Lorenz 6, Fritz 4, Ottilie 2			
WUESTHOFF, Heinr.	55	Barnstorf	54-0903
Charlotta 23			
WUESTHOFF, Heinr.	55	Barmstorf	54-0903
Johann 19, Charlotta 23			
WUESTLING, Anton	23	Kahla	54-1283
WUHELIUS, Carl	28	Hanau	54-0882
WUHLE, Gottlob	54	Cotaniz	54-1717
Eleonore 41, Ernst 19, Caroline 9			
Ernestine 2			
WUHRMANN, Joh Died	17	Bensen	47-0872
WUKIERKEN, Ludwiga	23	Prag	54-1716
Anton 10m			
WULAND, Louise	22	Bakenau	49-0345
WULBEN, Aug.	21	Rothenburg	51-0757
WULF, Anna	17	Rockeln	50-0366
WULF, Friedrich	22	Boden/Hann.	53-0475
WULF, Friedrich	24	Teplinghausen	50-0323
Henry 22			
WULF, Mary	2-	Stegenburg/Ha	50-0323
Friedrich 24, Henry 22			
WULFF, Carl	26	Silmen	54-1371
WULFF, Jette	22	Buchfeld	53-0942
WULFHOP, Hermann	18	Seckenhausen	51-1101
Gesche 16			
WULFHORST, Heinr.	19	Leste	49-0324
WULKOPF, Bernhard	58	Altendorf/Hes	52-0351
WULLERT, Johann	13	Wuerttemberg	49-0324
WULLNER, Carl	27	Eisenberg	53-0942
WULS, M. (f)	53	Schopfloch	50-0746
WULSCH, Carl	29	Altplato	54-1168
WUMMELSDORF, Heinr	22	Albertshausen	52-0563
WUNDER, Joh. Chr.	49	Plauen	49-1358
Ad. (m) 16			
WUNDERLICH, Carl	24	Remetsen	54-1282
WUNDERLICH, Erhard	25	Langenau	52-1362
Margaretha 27			
WUNDERLICH, Erhard	17	Wunsiedel	53-0888
WUNDERLICH, J Chr.	22	Unterhartsmnr	52-0351
WUNDERLICH, Johana	23	Siegen/Pr.	53-0475
WUNDERLICH, Magd.	53	Neustadt	52-1105
WUNDERLICH, Marie	22	Lobenstein	49-0383
WUNSCHER, Johann C	62	Pfiffelbach	52-1148
WUPPE, J.P. (m)	22	Hannover	50-0311

NAME	AGE	RESIDENCE	YR-LIST
WURM, Magaretha	23	Siegen	52-1101
WURM, Marie	24	Unterbergstet	52-0652
WURST, Catharine	25	Sulzbach	54-1575
WURST, Ekart	28	Armetise	52-0804
Elisabeth 26, Henry 2m			
WURST, Friedrich	27	Oberstein	54-1554
Gertrud 26			
WURST, Gerhard	19	Sittling	54-1078
WURST, Johannes	16	Bayreuth	51-1739
WURST, John	39	Calw/Wuertt.	48-0447
WURSTE, Louis	40	Endebruek	51-1686
WURSTER, Alois	29	Tremding	51-1245
Elise 24			
WURSTER, Elise	24	Aufkirchen	51-1245
Alois 29			
WURSTER, Gottlieb	19	Backnang	49-0352
WURTMANN, Diedr.	20	Prussia	50-1317
WURZEL, Carl	40	Ruehrchen	54-1168
Wilhelmine 36, Friederich 19, Wilhelm 14			
Auguste 11, Caroline 9			
WUSSLER, G. (m)	21	Geugenbach	52-1512
WUSSLER, W. Magd.	50	Ohlsbach	51-1640
Theresia 20			
WUSTEWALD, Friedr.	25	Ndr. Berndorf	52-0370
WUTCHTEL, Moses	19	Gehaus	54-1341
WUTH, Bernhard	20	Blehla	53-0492
WUTTKE, Rosina	31	Kronersdorf	53-0991
WUTZ, Cath.	41	Wien	54-0872
Carl 9			
WUTZ, J. (m)	32	Hirschbach	52-0652
WUTZBACHER, Chr'ne	22	Lobenstein	49-0383
WYNMERT, Carl Gust	49	Breslau/Pr.	52-0117
YOLL, Justin	25	Ornshausen	53-0585
YOUNG, Hermann	38	Gera	54-0987
YOUNG, Mathias	16	Buchdorf	54-0903
ZABEL, Helene	66	Fahrwald	54-1297
Wilhelmine 24, Carl 21			
ZACH, Paul	28	Krisczin	54-1282
ZACHER, Christoph	33	Erfurt	51-0460
Johanne 30, Henriette 16, Andreas 4			
Ludwig 2, Christian 30			
ZACHER, Friedrich	56	Gotha	51-1438
Wilhelmina 58, Emilie 26, Ernestine 20			
Robert 16			
ZACHRICH, Friedr.	25	Weperstedt	52-0699
ZAENKER, Louise	23	Chemnitz	54-1554
ZAETSCH, August	15	Bremerlehe	51-0500
ZAGELMEIER, F.E.	25	Potsdam/Pr.	52-0960
ZAGENBERG, Joh. W.	32	Schledehausen	52-1148
Caroline 32, Georg 7			
ZAHN, Adam	21	Cassel	54-0930
ZAHN, August	42	Eissberg/Sax.	48-0053
ZAHN, Magretha	18	Reinerschredt	52-1101
ZAHNER, Anton	28	Hratz	53-1000
Franziska 30, Franziska 7			
ZAHNWETZER, Anna	24	Lichtenau	54-1554
ZAININGER, Cathr.	32	Goettersdorf	54-1647
Joseph 13, Anna 9, Cathr. 6			
ZAMBACH, Anna	25	Doll/Boehmen	52-0807
ZANDER, Ludwig	34	Bamberg	52-1304
ZANG, Joh. Marie	19	Eisfeld	53-0914
ZANGERHAUSEN, Luis	50	Muehlhausen	52-1304
ZANKL, Johann	28	See/Baiern	54-0965
Margretha 23			
ZANNECK, C.D.	20	Thalheim	54-1078
ZAPF, Friedr.	54	Rossbach	52-0370
ZAPPERT, Leopold	34	Prague	48-1243
Caroline 28			
ZARNACK, H.	18	Berlin	53-0492
ZAUNER, Math.	17	Schaumberg	53-0435
ZECH, Johann	27	Karm	54-1554
ZECHEL, Emanuel	20	Boehmen	53-1000
ZECHER, Otto	58	Marburg	53-1000
Anna 58, Catharine 24, Otto 16			
ZECKRZWESKY, Peter	38	Watenberg/Pol	52-1620
ZEDEL, Mariana	24	Mistelfeld/Bv	51-1532
ZEEWOGEL, Auguste	17	Naumburg	54-1297
ZEH, Joh. Heinr.	23	Frossen	54-1297

NAME	AGE	RESIDENCE	YR-LIST
ZEH, Johanna	19	Baiern	54-1724
ZEHNDER, Sophie	20	Heilbronn	54-1575
ZEIDLE, Barbara	17	Culmbach	54-1717
ZEIDLER, Rich.	24	Asch	53-0914
ZEIFANG, Georg	27	Sonderbach	53-0838
ZEIFANG, Joh Georg	20	Suestheim	53-0838
ZEIGER, Rosina	23	Wuertt.	54-1724
ZEIGLER, John	24	Ganheim/Bav.	47-0987
ZEILER, Charles	45	Eightersheim	51-0048
ZEILMANN, Anna	20	Pottenreuth	48-1355
Janna 7			
ZEILNER, Friedr.	34	Redwitz	54-1554
Julia 38, Friederike 4			
ZEINER, Engelbert	41	Rudelsdorf	54-0987
Anna 31, Engelbert 8, Ferdinand 5			
Franz 4			
ZEINERT, Wilh.	17	Rossweil	53-1016
ZEIPF, Wilhelm	26	Wiesenbrun	53-1023
ZEISS, Margaretha	23	Seckbach/Hess	52-0807
ZEISS, N. (m)	25	Marksuhl	52-0558
A. (f) 21, E. (f) 6			
ZEITELHACK, August	31	Longstein	53-1013
Sophie 33, Selma 3m			
ZEITLER, Maria	23	Lindau	54-1554
ZEITTER, Maria	23	Lindau	54-1554
ZEITZ, Andreas	33	Almerode	54-1452
ZEITZ, Barbara	30	Oeschenbach	48-1355
Franz 19, Louis 15			
ZEITZ, Caroline	44	Hellenthal	47-0872
ZEITZ, Gottfried	28	Birkenfeld	49-1358
ZELL, E. (f)	21	Maila	52-0558
ZELLER, Aug. Fr.	16	Marbach	53-0838
ZELLER, August	31	Tuebingen	50-0439
ZELLER, Barbara	22	Lauchheim	53-0991
ZELLER, Ch. (f)	39	Trienz	50-0746
Ch. (m) 39, V. (m) 16, L. (m) 14			
Ch. (m) 8, A. (f) 2, R. (f) 18, Ch. (f) 5			
ZELLER, Joseph	27	Almen	52-1580
ZELLER, Marie	19	Neustadt	52-1512
ZELLER, Pauline	21	Gross Eisling	52-0351
ZELLER, Wilh. Gott	29	Goppingen	53-0838
ZELLING, Elise	27	Rannebek	51-0326
ZELLINGHAUS, Ferd.	46	Aschersleben	54-1724
ZELLMANN, Carl	49	Ilsfeld/Hann	54-1092
ZELTNER, Elis. Bar	19	Fischbrunn	53-0888
ZENG, Anna	30	Schweisdorf	54-1575
ZENGLE, Chr.	30	Hof	53-0914
ZENKE, Margret	24	Herolzbach	53-0590
ZENTER, Franz	24	Wittenberg	54-0987
ZENTGRAF, Adam	27	Erlau	53-0928
Emilie 24, Henriette 4, Alberth 5m			
ZENTGRAF, Emilie	24	Suhl	53-0928
ZENTGRAF, Johann	23	Schleusingen	54-0903
ZENTGRAPF, Valent.	33	Hotzberg	52-0370
Lorenz 30			
ZERAHN, Mathilda	30	Sommerfeld	54-0987
ZERGMANN, Ernst	25	Prussia	49-0329
ZERIN, Herrmann	33	Chemnitz	53-1023
Caroline 34, Ludwig 7, Theodor 6			
Linna 3m			
ZERPEL, Rike	19	Minden	50-0366
ZERTEL, Elisabeth	33	Hofgeismar	54-1566
ZESTERFLETH, Fried	21	Elsfleth	53-1070
ZETKA, Franz	26	Londsel	54-1676
Joseph 14			
ZETNICK, Vincenz	39	Costelitz/Boe	52-1332
Catharine 38, Marie 12			
ZETSCH, Albert	41	Sachsen-Mein.	53-0628
ZETTLER, Georg	21	Leutkirch/Wrt	54-1092
ZEUG, Elisabeth	14	Bullach	48-1179
ZEUG, Georg	27	St.Martin	52-1200
ZEUG, Mathilde	45	Bielefeld	54-0965
Emma 20, Hedwig 17, Minna 15, Meta 12			
ZEUNER, Axel	29	Wiesbaden/Nas	48-0053
Christiana 27			
ZEUNER, Charl.	20	Bokenem	50-1132
ZEUNER, Christiana	27	Bieberich	48-0053
ZEUNER, Jos. Leop.	20	Neustadt	51-1640

NAME	AGE	RESIDENCE	YR-LIST
ZICKLER, Fritz	30	Wetzlar	53-0652
ZIDING, Carl	19	Dottendorf	53-0652
ZIEG, Joh.	49	Altershausen	54-1168
ZIEGELER, Conrad	42	Fuerstenwald	54-0930
Julia 34, Heinr. Wilh. 31			
ZIEGELER, David	25	Wuertenberg	53-0557
ZIEGELER, Gottlieb	18	Oberfranken	53-0557
ZIEGELER, Johann	25	Werendorf	51-0500
ZIEGELHOEFER, Joh.	41	Merkendorf	54-1575
ZIEGELHOEFER, Jos.	27	Moersbach	54-1078
ZIEGELMUELLER, Jos	34	Hansen	51-1160
ZIEGENBEIN, Johann	20	Bonshausen	53-1023
ZIEGENBEIN, Johann	16	Osterholz	50-1067
ZIEGER, Franz	25	Sachsen	53-0590
ZIEGERMULLER, Jos.	43	Dinkelsbuehl	50-0840
Franziska 39, Ulrich 3, Marianne 2			
Joseph 1			
ZIEGLER, Alb.	18	Waiblingen	54-1078
ZIEGLER, Anna	16	Ermreuth	53-0320
ZIEGLER, Cath.	18	Ermreuth	52-0693
ZIEGLER, Conrad	29	Brand	54-1282
ZIEGLER, Conrad	23	Nat--op	50-0944
Catherine 26			
ZIEGLER, Elisabeth		Besse	50-0840
ZIEGLER, Henry	20	Duermenz	53-1164
ZIEGLER, Joh.	28	Hildenburghau	52-1512
Therese 23			
ZIEGLER, John	31	Cassel	48-1209
ZIEGLER, John	55	Bischofsheim	50-0840
Elisabeth			
ZIEGLER, Joseph	50	Wien	54-1297
ZIEGLER, Justus	28	Berge	51-1062
ZIEGLER, Marie	24	Sossau	52-0515
ZIEGLER, Marie	22	Ilbenstedt	49-0383
ZIEGLER, Marth.	24	Rotenburg	54-1575
ZIEGLER, Martin	26	Waldenburg	53-0585
ZIEGLER, Philipp	26	Dattensoll	54-0053
ZIEGLER, Rosine	40	Beckartswedle	54-1283
ZIEGLER, Valentin	22	Gauaschach	54-0053
ZIEGLOCH, Joh.	26	Meinsheim	52-0370
ZIEGNER, Jos.	29	Rieneck	52-1625
ZIEHER, Heinr.	31	Feuchtwangen	52-0515
ZIEHR, Georg	43	Gerston	54-1282
Anna 42			
ZIEKE, Christ.	43	Burg	53-0585
Dorothea 50			
ZIEMA, Jos.	41	Rokitzau	54-1575
Josephine 38, Florentin 5, Johanne 3			
Joseph 1			
ZIEMANN, Johanne	6	Philadelphia	52-1661
Gertrude 20			
ZIERENBERG, Carl	21	Adelebsen	53-0991
ZIERMEYER, Joseph	42	Andling	52-1452
Therese 38, Joseph 11, Naepermuck 7			
Johann 2			
ZIEROLD, Gottlieb	29	Milzen/Sax.	52-1332
Johanne Soph 26, Wilhelmine 3, Franz 8			
ZIESE, Adam	42	Rockensoes	52-1129
ZIESENITZ, Carl Fr	34	Luechow	54-1297
ZIESSE, Wilh.	24	Hezewye	51-1455
ZIETYER, Martin	17	Eidkamp	54-1716
ZIGLER, Gottlieb	29	Sontheim/Sax.	51-1796
ZILCH, Heinrich	24	Burgham	50-0472
ZILCH, Helene	17	Gutensberg	50-0472
ZILING, Mathias	38	Esingen	51-1686
Margarethe 41, Barbara 7, Margarethe 5			
ZILLER, Johann	40	Salzungen	49-0413
ZILLIS, Elisabeth	44	Neustaedtles	52-1620
ZILOH, Heinrich	55	Iba	54-0930
Cath. Elise 22, Heinrich by			
ZIMAN, Anton	22	Peppinghausen	51-1588
ZIMMER, A.	37	Schoeppensted	51-0517
St. 20			
ZIMMER, Henry	48	Dannenberg	53-0991
Dorothea 36, Jane 9			
ZIMMER, Lucas	18	Preussen	52-0370
ZIMMERER, Ferdin.	14	Wellingdingen	54-0053
ZIMMERMANN, (f)	24	Magdeburg	49-0324

NAME	AGE	RESIDENCE	YR-LIST
Ottilie 2			
ZIMMERMANN, Adolph	20	Henfstedt	48-0887
ZIMMERMANN, Anna	28	Eimelrode	53-1164
ZIMMERMANN, Aug.	27	Grochwitz	49-0574
ZIMMERMANN, Blas.	46	Weil	51-1686
ZIMMERMANN, C. (f)	16	Trienz	50-0746
ZIMMERMANN, Carl	34	Hamburg	48-1243
Pauline 27, Emma 2, Dortha 5			
ZIMMERMANN, Christ	52	Tauschem	54-0850
Anna Christ. 54			
ZIMMERMANN, Friedr	26	Berlin	48-1243
ZIMMERMANN, Joh G.	26	Obern--bach	53-0825
Johannes 18			
ZIMMERMANN, Joh Wm	25	Haus Stade	54-1371
ZIMMERMANN, Johann	20	Reifenberg	52-1321
ZIMMERMANN, Johann	29	Mureionburg	48-1015
Jacob 30, Helene 25			
ZIMMERMANN, Josefa	25	Obwingen/Wrt.	54-1092
ZIMMERMANN, Joseph	29	Halbendorf	52-1321
ZIMMERMANN, Louise	29	Iserlohn	52-0895
ZIMMERMANN, Ludwig	15	Weilheim/Wuer	52-0351
Elisabeth 23			
ZIMMERMANN, Martin	26	Schonau	52-0370
ZIMMERMANN, Matth.	19	Benzingen	50-0292
August 22			
ZIMMERMANN, Philip	22	Rugheim	49-1358
ZIMMERMANN, Phl'pa	21	Marburg	53-0991
ZIMMERMANN, Wilh.	34	Artern	50-0379
ZINDEL, Andreas	29	Hundelshausen	52-0563
Caroline 30, Elise 5, Christian 3			
Elise 2			
ZINDEL, Peter	40	Hundelshausen	52-0563
Elisabeth 25, Peter 9, Bernhard 5			
Cath. 3, An.Cath. 58, Georg 20			
ZINGER, Josepha	23	Wagenschwendt	51-0384
ZINK, Johann	20	Hanau	49-1358
Barbara 20			
ZINK, W. (m)	18	Heilbronn	49-0329
ZINKER, Philip	19	Schweisdorf	53-0637
ZINN, Anna	20	Ebersdorf	54-0987
ZINN, Heinrich	57	Storndorf	49-0352
Elise Carol. 24			
ZINN, Heinrich	6m	Storndorf	49-0352
ZINSGA, Friedrich	39	Giessen	54-1676
ZINTGRAFF, George	25	Mittelruessel	49-0737
ZINZER, Ludwig	25	Danzig/Pr	53-0475
ZINZTORD, William	27	Greifswald	53-0905
ZIP, Heinrich	4	Niedershausen	53-0928
Henr. 9m			
ZIPF, Georg	33	Forst	52-1464
ZIPFEL, Friedrich	30	Schmiedhausen	54-1092
ZIPP, Johann	40	Gr. Altenstad	49-0574
Anna Marie 37, Peter 13, Philipp 11			
Marie Christ 9, Heinrich 3			
ZIPP, Philipp	68	Kl. Altenstad	49-0574
Anna Elis. 64, Philipp 4, Lisetta 2			
Catharina 26			
ZIPPERER, Joseph	30	Friedrichstha	53-0905
ZIRB, Wilhelm	20	Volbertshause	54-1443
ZISCHKAU, Georg	27	Waldorf/Mein.	52-0960
ZITTLER, David	28	Waldangelo	50-0292
ZITZMANN, Margaret	51	Hinternach	54-0987
Joh. 24, Eva 28, Ludwig 2, Egidius 4			
ZITZNER, Elisabeth	19	Schwarzenbach	53-0475
Friedrich 16			
ZIZNER, Joh Heinr.	51	Moschendorf	53-1062
ZOEBELEIN, Franz	24	Pilgersdorf	54-0850
ZOECHFELTH, Julius	20	New York	54-0987
Elisabeth 25, Ida by			
ZOEFFKER, Heinrich	25	Ostendorff	49-0413
ZOEGER, Werner	21	Alsfeld	51-0352
Wilhelm 22, Elisabeth 25			
ZOEN, Albertine	32	Driesen	53-1023
ZOLLNER, Franz	28	Scholgripen	52-1101
ZOLLNER, Joh.	28	Schlueselfeld	54-0930
ZOPPLER, Joseph	44	Hofdorf	52-1452
Barbara 44, Johanna 20, Anna 14			
Helenna 9, Franziska 8			
ZORN, Ad.	35	Landsberg	54-0600
ZORN, Philipp	26	Fischbach/Nas	53-0628
ZOTH, G.M.	17	Schoenbrunn	54-1078
Marie 21			
ZOTHE, Fr. W.	30	Breslau	54-1078
Dorothea 23, Emil 3, Anna 9m			
ZOTSCH, Fr. August	23	Egeln/Prussia	53-0628
ZOTZL, Joh.	35	Thirschenreut	54-1283
Cath. 34			
ZSCHANDERLEIN, J G	40	Blankenheim/S	52-1332
ZUCKER, Martin	53	Stockach	47-0828
Walburga 50, Anna 26, Christine 22			
Ehrhard 20, Barbara 18, Johann 13			
Michael 10, Christine 6			
ZUELLICH, J. (m)	24	Remscheid	49-0416
ZUGSCHWAL, Ch. (m)	25	Waldenbron	49-0329
ZULAUF, Carl	22	Hessen	50-1236
ZULAUF, Christian	28	Frankenheim	52-0095
ZULAUF, Johann	43	Roth	54-1566
Anna 32, Susanne 6, Joh. 6m			
ZUMBROCK, H.F.	54	Sudende	54-1470
Bette 52, Ann 21, Auguste 15, Herm. F. 18			
H.F. 13			
ZUNDER, Bertha	58	Fuerth	54-1297
Bette 22, Sara 16			
ZUR HOLLEN, August	28	Duesseldorf	52-1512
Agnes 26, Wilhelm 9m			
ZURBERG, August	20	Osnabrueck	52-1101
ZURL, Anna Maria	9	Oberwackersta	52-1200
ZUTMAN, Andr.	24	Memelsdorf	52-0515
ZWANG, Maria	27	Baiern	54-1724
ZWEITINGER, Ignatz	24	Aschhausen	53-1062
Jacob 19			
ZWICK, Wilhelm	18	Graefenhainic	52-1148
Heinrich 15			
ZWICKEL, Steph.	28	Mittelruessel	49-0737
Marcus 19			
ZWICKER, Ernst	42	Luetzenau	50-1132
ZWICKER, Johann	32	Kunitz	54-1575
Barbara 25, Barbara 2			
ZWINGE, Bernhard	23	Grosseneder	50-0292
ZWOLLE, Joh. Ricke	32	Leer	50-0292
Sophie Henr. 24